CYBERPSYCHOLOGY AND THE BRAIN

Cyberpsychology is a relatively new discipline that is growing at an alarming rate. While a number of cyberpsychology-related journals and books have emerged, none directly address the neuroscience behind it. This book proposes a framework for integrating neuroscience and cyberpsychology for the study of social, cognitive, and affective processes and the neural systems that support them. A brain-based cyberpsychology can be understood as a branch of psychology that studies the neurocognitive, affective, and social aspects of humans interacting with technology, as well as the affective computing aspects of humans interacting with computational devices or systems. As such, a cyberpsychologist working from a brain-based cyberpsychological framework studies both the ways in which persons make use of devices and the neurocognitive processes, motivations, intentions, behavioral outcomes, and effects of online and offline use of technology. *Cyberpsychology and the Brain* brings researchers into the vanguard of cyberpsychology and brain research.

THOMAS D. PARSONS, PhD, is Associate Professor of Psychology at the University of North Texas. He has also served as Assistant Professor and Research Scientist at the University of Southern California's Institute for Creative Technologies. He is a leading scientist in the integration of neuropsychology and simulation technologies. He has directed 17 funded projects and been an investigator on an additional 13 funded projects. In addition to his patents for eHarmony.com's Matching System, he has invented and validated virtual reality–based neuropsychological assessments. He has more than 200 publications and has been awarded the National Academy of Neuropsychology's Early Career Achievement award.

CYBERPSYCHOLOGY AND THE BRAIN

The Interaction of Neuroscience and Affective Computing

THOMAS D. PARSONS

University of North Texas

CAMBRIDGE
UNIVERSITY PRESS

CAMBRIDGE
UNIVERSITY PRESS

University Printing House, Cambridge CB2 8BS, United Kingdom

One Liberty Plaza, 20th Floor, New York, NY 10006, USA

477 Williamstown Road, Port Melbourne, VIC 3207, Australia

4843/24, 2nd Floor, Ansari Road, Daryaganj, Delhi – 110002, India

79 Anson Road, #06–04/06, Singapore 079906

Cambridge University Press is part of the University of Cambridge.

It furthers the University's mission by disseminating knowledge in the pursuit of education, learning, and research at the highest international levels of excellence.

www.cambridge.org
Information on this title: www.cambridge.org/9781107094871
DOI: 10.1017/9781316151204

First published 2017

Printed in the United States of America by Sheridan Books, Inc.

A catalogue record for this publication is available from the British Library.

ISBN 978-1-107-09487-1 Hardback
ISBN 978-1-107-47757-5 Paperback

I dedicate this book to a monkey, a bearcat, a bugaboo, and a beagle. Together we make a family.

Contents

Figures

Tables

Preface

While cyberpsychology is a relatively new discipline, it is one that is growing at an alarming rate. Perhaps this is due to the fact that humans are witnessing a time of rapid progress in an increasingly connected world. As a result, we have seen the emergence of a number of cyberpsychology-related societies, conferences, journals, and academic-level texts. Interestingly, none of these academic journals or books on cyberpsychology directly addresses the rapid progress in neuroscience. There are now dozens of laboratories around the world that have converged to investigate neurocognitive, affective, and social questions. While there is a great deal of work in cyberpsychology that deals with neural correlates of persons interacting with technology and neuroscientific investigations of cyberpsychology issues, there is no text that pulls together this material for cyberpsychologists. This book is a first attempt at bringing together this information for researchers and students in cyberpsychology.

To encourage the inclusion of brain science research in the cyberpsychology domain, this book proposes a framework for integrating neuroscience and cyberpsychology for the study of social, cognitive, and affective processes and the neural systems that support them. Given these emphases, a brain-based cyberpsychology can be understood as a branch of psychology that studies (1) the neurocognitive, affective, and social aspects of humans interacting with technology and (2) affective computing aspects of humans interacting with devices/systems that incorporate computation. As such, a cyberpsychologist working from a brain-based cyberpsychological framework studies both the ways in which persons make use of devices and the neurocognitive processes, motivations, intentions, behavioral outcomes, and effects of online and offline use of technology. Research in a brain-based cyberpsychology framework ranges from studies with offline platforms (using desktop computers, word processors, virtual/augmented reality, gaming consoles, and statistics packages), to online Internet use (how we engage in online banking, shopping, dating, and

xi

gaming), to mobile phones. These studies emphasize the study of neuro-cognitive, affective, and social processing behaviors in relation to the ways in which persons use and communicate via technological devices. Cyberpsychologists view these devices as tools that either facilitate or impede human interaction and communication.

Cyberpsychology has a lot to offer human neuroscience research. Specifically, there is increasing acknowledgment among social, cognitive, and affective neuroscientists that there is a need to move beyond the static stimulus presentations found in their investigations of human neurocognition. While many of the pioneering paradigms in the human neurosciences reflected a noteworthy emphasis on laboratory control and experiments that involve participants observing static stimuli that are devoid of inter-actions, there are increasing questions about whether knowledge gained using these static stimuli will generalize to the social, cognitive, and affective processes found in everyday activities. Cyberpsychologists can aid these neuroscientists by introducing them to the more ecologically valid scenarios found in cyberpsychology simulations (e.g., virtual and augmented reality).

In addition to the positive impact that cyberpsychology stimuli and platforms can have on the human neurosciences, there is a great deal that cyberpsychology can gain from the cognitive, affective, and social neuro-sciences. While neuroscientific research is highlighted throughout this book, many of the examples provided reflect assessments of behavioral performance. Although it can be challenging to operationalize the extent to which a stimulus approximates activities of daily living, this book gives examples of stimuli and virtual environment–based contexts that span the implied continuum. The studies reviewed in this book are not meant to be exhaustive. Instead this review focuses on cyberpsychology research that highlights the ways in which persons respond to clinical, affective, and social stimuli in simulations that approximate real-world activities and interactions.

The cognitive, affective, and social neurosciences can support cyberpsy-chology by offering supplementary assessments of the assumptions that cyberpsychologists make regarding neurocognitive and affective aspects of interacting with technologies. In turn, lessons learned from cyberpsychol-ogy can aide efforts to formulate and specify neuroscientific models of humans interacting with technology. Increasingly, brain researchers have become interested in identifying neuronal networks involved in Internet use, neuropsychological aspects of virtual environments, ethical decision-making, and social interactions using virtual humans. Cyberpsychology approaches can be of use to these efforts by offering reliable and empirically valid approaches to human–computer interactions that affective and social neuroscientists are beginning to use.

Organization of This Book

To provide a framework for a brain-based approach to cyberpsychology, this book is divided into five parts.

Part I provides an introduction to the framework for a brain-based cyberpsychology. Following the opening chapter that introduces components of this framework, Chapter 2 provides the reader with a primer on brain anatomy and terminology. While some areas are briefly discussed for the sake of completeness and continuity, other areas, such as large-scale brain networks and frontal-subcortical circuits, receive greater attention. Instead of presenting a comprehensive account of these structures and functions, Chapter 2 aims to present a foundation for the conceptualization of the material covered in the chapters that follow. Chapter 3 offers a synopsis of psychophysiological metrics and quantification parameters describing the assessment of particular physiological structures and systems.

Part II contains a discussion of the impact of various media on the brain. In Chapter 4, there is a discussion of the impact of the Internet on the user's brain. In addition to the impact of the Internet on brain anatomy and function, this chapter introduces an "extended mind" theory, in which cognitive processes are understood as going beyond wetware (i.e., brain) to software and hardware used by the brain. This perspective allows for an understanding of human cognition as processed in a system coupled with technology. Chapter 5 looks specifically at the relations between Facebook and the socially networked brain. It attempts to answer questions related to why we are so motivated to connect with others online. The brain's reward network is likely activated when using Facebook (e.g., user receives a "like" to their posted content on a Facebook page). This chapter also explores Robin Dunbar's social brain hypothesis in the age of the Internet. According to Dunbar, human intelligence evolved as a means of surviving and reproducing in complex social groups. In the 1990s Dunbar proposed a neurocognitive limit to the number of people a person can have in their social network. Recent studies of humans afford evidence of quantitative relations between social group size and brain regions that perform an important part in social cognition. These findings reflect work done in offline social networks. This chapter explores whether the seemingly ubiquitous and perpetual use of social media challenges the continued relevance of Dunbar's number. In Chapter 6 there is a discussion of media multitasking and its impact on the brain. With the ubiquity of media technologies, people increasingly add greater amounts of media content into the same amount of time. This is accomplished through the use of numerous media types concurrently, in this manner taking part in "media multitasking." There are some who have hypothesized that the increased prevalence of media multitasking is problematic, because frequent engagement in media multitasking may have negative impact on cognitive control processes. Others have argued that media multitaskers do not attend to the information that is relevant to one task at a time. Instead, heavy media multitaskers have a cognitive style that includes a greater breadth of attention. This chapter discusses these issues. Finally, Chapter 7 delves into issues of cyber addictions. There is a growing body of cyberpsychology research into the relations between online media use and compulsive behaviors, self-regulation, impulse control, and substance abuse. This chapter explores the impact of excessive Internet on brain anatomy and functioning.

In Part III, the book turns a spotlight on the ways in which cyberpsychology can enhance research done in human neuroscience. This part starts with Chapter 8, wherein the reader is presented with a discussion of the ways in which simulation technologies found in cyberpsychology can offer ecologically valid alternatives to the static stimuli found in the affective (Chapter 9), social (Chapter 10), and clinical (Chapter 11) neurosciences. In Chapter 9 the aim is to provide a framework for ecologically valid cyberpsychology investigations into the cognitive and affective aspects of everyday lived experience. Herein, affective computing is introduced as a cyberpsychology approach that can aid and benefit from affective neuroscience. That said, there is a realization that much of our everyday lives involves interactions with others. As such, Chapter 10 presents a social neuroscience–informed approach to ecological validity. Finally, in Chapter 11, there is the issue of moving beyond cyberpsychology paradigms with healthy controls into the realm of clinical neuroscience. Advances in the clinical neurosciences have greatly enhanced our understanding of the brain's cognitive and affective processing in neurologic and psychiatric disorders. The noteworthy developments made at the end of the twentieth century in understanding the genetic and neural correlates of many diseases affecting the brain are important for a brain-based cyberpsychology. Cyberpsychologists interested in clinical neuroscience research and practice should be aware of both the contributions of clinical neuroscience to cyberpsychology and the potential that cyberpsychology research and practices have for the clinical neurosciences.

Part IV presents an introduction to psychophysiological computing in cyberpsychology (Chapter 12), the cyberpsychology of videogames (Chapter 13), and NeuroIS (Chapter 14). In Chapter 12, psychophysiological assessment is presented as a way to enhance experimental control in virtual environments that are being used for cyberpsychology applications. Psychophysiological metrics provide an excellent measure of presence and autonomic arousal. Hence, they provide a profile of the user state and a validation of the impact of the virtual environment on the user. In Chapter 13, there is a review of the growing body of literature that focuses on assessment of action videogame player cognition. Furthermore, there is a discussion of the neural correlates underpinning the enhanced cognitive processing favoring videogamers. Chapter 14 closes this section with a review of the development of NeuroIS and its relation to cyber-security. Information systems research is a recent area to incorporate the behavioral neuroscience literature. In the same way that other areas of cyberpsychology are drawing from recent advances in brain and behavioral neurosciences, information systems researchers are looking at the complex interplay between information technology and neuroeconomics, information processing, and social neuroscience. Information systems researchers have started to investigate the potential of the human neurosciences (e.g., social, cognitive, and affective neurosciences) for information sciences research.

Finally, Part V concludes the book with a discussion of scientific and pragmatic challenges for bridging cyberpsychology and neuroscience. A brain-based cyberpsychology represents an emerging effort to integrate neuroscience methods (e.g., neuroimaging) with cyberpsychological methods to address issues of assessment and training. This chapter presents potential concerns about connecting neuroscience to cyberpsychology. The chapter first articulates some potential concerns and then reinterprets them as potential opportunities. Throughout the book there has been a presentation of instances in which neuroscience findings and methods have been found to be relevant for cyberpsychology. The goal of this book is to offer cyberpsychologists a window into contemporary neuroscience to prepare them to think more specifically about the prospects of a brain-based cyberpsychology.

Acknowledgments

I wish to acknowledge the significant people who inspired the writing of this book.

Collaborations with my colleagues at the University of Southern California and the University of North Texas have inspired a number of ideas found in this book. I spent a number of years as a research scientist and faculty member at the University of Southern California's Institute for Creative Technologies. During that time I had the great fortune of working with scholars who were passionate about cyberpsychology. In particular, Patrick Kenny and I spent countless hours in Venice Beach discussing the potential impacts of integrating neuroscience into cyberpsychology theory and research praxes. At the University of North Texas, I have benefited from collaborative work and conversations with Ian Parberry in Computer Science and Lin Lin in Learning Technologies.

I should also mention that much of my interest in cyberpsychology was aided by studying the works of Umberto Eco, Jorge Luis Borges, Ludwig Wittgenstein, David Chalmers, and Andy Clark. First, Eco's work on semiotics (e.g., semiological guerrilla) has taught me how to travel with a salmon in my pocket, to consider the platypus using Kantian categories, and to appreciate the aesthetics of chaosmos. My first artificially intelligent cognitive architecture was named Abulafia in tribute to the computer system in Eco's *Foucault's Pendulum*. I am also indebted to Jorge Luis Borges for his discussions of libraries, labyrinths, time, and infinity. Next, there is Ludwig Wittgenstein's brilliant early work in the *Tractatus Logico-Philosophicus*, and his later work in the *Philosophical Investigations*, wherein he discarded much of what he argued in the *Tractatus*! Finally, the work of Andy Clark and David Chalmers on extended cognition has provided a framework for extending cognitive processes via an active externalism that has helped me conceptualize technology and neurobiology in terms of a "coupled system."

There are also a number of students and postdoctoral fellows who both inspired me and diligently assisted with research for the manuscript. Two graduate students stand out as exemplars of why I "do what I do" each day: Christopher Courtney from the University of Southern California and Timothy McMahan from the University of North Texas.

Finally, I am most indebted to my best friend Valerie Parsons. After a couple of decades with her I still find her smile infectious and her encouragement invaluable. She is my favorite monkey. Also, our children, Tommy and Sophie, give me an opportunity to experience the adventures of a bearcat and a bugaboo. Oh, and I cannot forget the world's best beagle! Together, they make up the best partners a cyberpsychologist could have on walks through simulated woods.

PART I

Introduction

CHAPTER I

Cyberpsychology: Changing Roles and Tools

1.1 Cyberpsychology: Defining the Discipline

What is cyberpsychology? The answer is often more in line with a definition of human computer interaction than the emerging psychology of social media and simulation technologies. That said, there are some definitions that tap into cyberpsychology as a subdiscipline of psychology. For example, Norman's (2008) definition breaks the term "cyberpsychology" down into the prefix "cyber" and "psychology." The prefix "cyber" comes from the term "cybernetics," which represents a study of the operation of control and communication systems. The "psychology" part of cyberpsychology refers to the study of behavior and cognitive processing. For Norman, cyberpsychology is best understood as research into the impact of computers, technology, and virtual environments on the psychology of individuals and groups. Alison Attrill (2015) expands the discussion of cyberpsychology to include research into the psychological processes (e.g., motivations, intentions, impacts) and behavioral outcomes that occur relative to an individual's online and offline association with any form of technology. Perhaps one of the most progressive definitions of cyberpsychology (as it relates to contemporary developments in affective computing) is Giuseppe Riva's (2014) definition of cyberpsychology.

> Cyberpsychology is a recent branch of psychology whose main research objects are the processes of change induced by new technologies. Some of these processes are related to and involve a variety of affective processes. The discipline's overlaps with affective computing and human-computer interaction in general are significant, yet its psychological origins suggest that the research communities have somewhat different focuses. (p. 547)

While cyberpsychology is a relatively new discipline, it is one that is growing at an alarming rate. Perhaps this is because humans are witnessing a time of rapid progress in an increasingly connected world. Needless to say, technology is seemingly ubiquitous in the everyday lives of most readers of this text. Users may connect or disconnect from others via multiple telecommunication options: Internet, smartphones, tablets, gaming consoles, and wearables.

The growth of cyberpsychology as a discipline is apparent in the development of dedicated societies, journals, and book series. For example, 2016 marked the 21st Annual Conference on CyberPsychology, CyberTherapy and Social Networking. For over two decades this conference has been a premier cyberpsychology conference and has regularly showcased presentations on studies using virtual-reality, social networking, online behavior, serious games, augmented/mixed reality, virtual humans, virtual worlds, mobile health, and other emerging applications. This conference is the destination of many members of the International Association of CyberPsychology, Training, & Rehabilitation (iACToR). Furthermore, there are currently a number of peer-reviewed academic journals dedicated to cyberpsychology (see Table 1.1).

Table 1.1 *Peer-reviewed academic journals dedicated to cyberpsychology*

Title	Editor-in-Chief	Issues Per Year	Current Volume	Impact Factor
Computers in Human Behavior	Robert Tennyson	1	56	2.694
Cyberpsychology, Behavior, and Social Networking	Brenda Wiederhold	12	18	2.182
Cyberpsychology: Journal of Psychosocial Research on Cyberspace	David Smahel	4	9	N/A
Journal of Computer-Mediated Communication	S. Shyam Sundar	4	20	3.117
Journal of Media Psychology	Nicole Krämer	4	27	0.882
Media Psychology	Silvia Knobloch-Westerwick	4	19	2.457
New Media & Society	Steve Jones	8	17	2.007
Presence: Teleoperators and Virtual Environments	Janet Weisenberger Roy Ruddle	4	24	0.731

Note: The listed journals are examples of established journals that cover cyberpsychology topics. This is not an exhaustive list.

In addition to societies, conferences, and journals dedicated to cyberpsychology, a number of academic-level texts have emerged. Early texts by Riva and Galimberti (2001) "Towards cyberpsychology: Mind, cognition, and society in the internet age" and Norman (2008) "Cyberpsychology: An introduction to human-computer interaction" paved the way for recent publications. New cyberpsychology book series are emerging from publishers such as Cambridge University Press and Palgrave (Palgrave Studies in Cyberpsychology). Examples of recent texts in cyberpsychology include:

- Attrill, A. (Ed.). (2015). *Cyberpsychology.*
- Attrill, A. and Fullwood, C. (Eds.). (2016). *Applied cyberpsychology: Practical applications of cyberpsychological theory and research.*
- Connolly, I., Palmer, M., Barton, H., and Kirwan, G. (Eds.). (2016). *An introduction to cyberpsychology.*
- Power, A., and Kirwan, G. (2013). *Cyberpsychology and new media: A thematic reader.*

The material discussed in these cyberpsychology texts ranges from studies with offline platforms (using desktop computers, word processors, virtual/augmented reality, gaming consoles, and statistics packages) to online Internet use (how we engage in online banking, shopping, dating, and gaming), to mobile phones. Cyberpsychologists view these devices as tools that either facilitate or impede human interaction and communication.

Interestingly, these academic journals and books have offered very limited direct coverage of the rapid progress in brain sciences. This is surprising given the advances in the human neurosciences over the past couple of decades. Specifically, clinical, social, and affective neurosciences have seen extraordinary increases in their theory and praxis (Parsons, 2015). There are now dozens of laboratories around the world that have converged to investigate neurocognitive, affective, and social questions. While there is a great deal of work in cyberpsychology that deals with neural correlates of persons interacting with technology and neuroscientific investigations of cyberpsychology issues, there is no text that pulls together this material for cyberpsychologists. This book is a first attempt at bringing together this information for researchers and students in cyberpsychology.

Why has it taken so long for cyberpsychology to embrace neuroscientific approaches to studying human neurocognitive and affective processes? Potential reasons include the apparent resistance to the notion of neurological reductionism and a belief that an understanding of brain mechanisms is not needed for developing theories and praxes in cyberpsychology. While there are good reasons to question an eliminative materialism that wants to replace words like "mental states" with a vocabulary of "brain states," there are also good reasons to embrace advances in the human neurosciences to inform the theory and praxes of cyberpsychology.

1.1.1   Cartesian Dualism and Folk Psychology

Reticence to embrace neuroscientific advances may reflect a received folk psychology that has not kept pace with neuroscientific progress. Folk psychology represents the way most people understand how thinking occurs. A common folk psychological assumption follows a dualism, formulated by Rene Descartes, in which persons are understood as consisting of an immaterial mind that is both ontologically distinct and interactive with a material body. Within Cartesian dualism, the immaterial mind somehow causes actions of the physical body. Furthermore, perceptions are delivered to the immaterial mind from the material body. According to Descartes, this interaction takes place in the brain's pineal gland. Unfortunately, he never clarified how a completely immaterial mind could have a causal effect on the material brain, or vice versa.

If the cyberpsychologists want to maintain a Cartesian dualist perspective (though I would wager that many do not), then the differences in the vocabularies of cyberpsychology and neuroscience might limit interdisciplinary theorizing. From a Cartesian dualist perspective, the vocabulary of cyberpsychology belongs to the social sciences and includes mental terms such as understanding and identity. It is tailored for the description of behavioral phenomena – both psychological and social. Contrariwise, for the Cartesian dualist the vocabulary of neuroscience belongs to the biological sciences. This vocabulary includes material terms such as hemodynamic response and white matter tracts. This vocabulary is tailored to describe physical occurrences. Hence, a Cartesian dualism seems to preclude any reconciliation between the mental terms of cyberpsychology and the material terms of neuroscience.

1.1.2   Behaviorism and the Cognitive Revolution

In the early twentieth century, behaviorism arose out of developments in psychology and philosophy, which came together and challenged Cartesian Dualism. For the behaviorists, mental events can be reduced to stimulus-response pairs. Moreover, descriptions of observable behavior are the only scientific way to describe mental behavior. Hence, for the behaviorists, utterances about mental events (e.g., images, feelings, desires) are better understood using a vocabulary of behavioral dispositions. This behavioral revolution transformed experimental psychology and established a new vocabulary. Words like "perception" became "discrimination," "language" became "verbal behavior," and "memory" became "learning." In response to the behaviorist revolution, a cognitive counter-revolution occurred. George Miller (2003) of Princeton University was part of the cognitive revolution, in which psychology freed itself from behaviorism and restored cognition to scientific respectability. Following the cognitive revolution, words like "cognition" were defined as processing of information incoming to the brain from the external environment through sensory entrances. Within the pervasive Computational Theory of Mind found in cognitive science "cognition" is often used as a mark of brain functions used to facilitate behavioral adaptations and survival.

1.1.3   Rethinking the Cognitive Revolution from an Affective Neuroscience Perspective

Since the ushering in of the cognitive revolution in psychological science, the term "cognitive" has been one of the most widely used conceptual terms in behavioral neuroscience. That said, there are some that argue that the resulting choice of conceptual terms used to describe mental functions may actually limit research by constraining study results to ostensibly expedient "conceptual" categories that actually are not reflective of neurobiological processes. Howard Cromwell and Jaak Panksepp (2011) argue that the term "cognition" has been both overused and misused. Moreover, they contend that top-down perspectives found in cognitive approaches miss the affective and motivational "state-control" perspectives. Specifically, they call for a greater inclusion of a bottom-up affective neuroscience approach, in which lower-level (i.e., subcortical) brain networks are foundational for the construction of higher-level (cortical) "information-processing" aspects of mind.

1.1.4   Social Cognitive Affective Neuroscience

A recent development in the understanding of mental events is the acceptance of the fact that not all cognitive and/or affective processes occur in isolation of other people. This is important because a good deal of cognitive neuroscience research has focused on the cognitions and/or affects of persons in isolation from others. Today, we find social neuroscientists endeavoring to answer central questions about the nature of human social cognition by adding neuroscience techniques to methods used by social scientists (Adolphs, 2009; Cacioppo, 1994; Ochsner & Lieberman, 2001). Social neuroscience is a discipline that endeavors to identify the genetic, cellular, neural, and hormonal mechanisms that underlie social behavior (Cacioppo et al., 2010). Through these investigations, social neuroscientists seek a greater understanding of the reciprocal associations and influences among social and neurobiological levels of organization. Much of this work has resulted from our growing interest in the human brain's ability to facilitate, make use of, and be molded by social interactions (Cozolino, 2014; Gazzaniga, 2008; Lieberman, 2013). While research into the neural correlates of social processes has been discussed in the literature for decades (Cacioppo & Bernston, 1992), the advent of functional neuroimaging has resulted in a period of rapid expansion (Adolphs, 2003; Ochsner & Lieberman, 2001).

1.1.5   Extended Cognition via Technology

An additional component for our understanding of cognitive, affective, and social processes for cyberpsychology is the notion that technology is an extension of our cognitive processes. It is becoming increasingly apparent that the social media technologies (e.g., Internet, Twitter, texting, smartphones) have the potential to extend our cognitive processes beyond the embodied cognition of our forebears. Theorizing in this area by Andy Clark and David Chalmers (1998) has resulted in an "extended mind" theory, in which cognitive processes are understood as going beyond wetware (i.e., brain) to software and hardware used by the brain. This perspective allows for an understanding of human cognition as processed in a system coupled with the environment (Clark, 2008; Clark & Chalmers, 1998). In their work, they describe the "extended mind" in terms of an extended cognitive system that includes both brain-based cognitive processes and external objects (e.g., technologies like the Internet) that serve to accomplish functions that would otherwise be attained via the action of brain-based cognitive processes acting internally to the human. The potential for the extended cognitive processing perspective seems even more apparent with the advent of mobile technologies. Whilst early iterations of the Internet were bounded by wires, later iterations only had to be in close proximity to a router. Today, with the arrival and augmentation of tablets and smartphones, the enormous knowledgebase of the Internet is available in one's pocket. The number of tablets and smartphones in use is rapidly approaching the point where billions will have access. Furthermore, the technological properties of smartphones proffer a number of enhancements to discussions of externalization. While early metaphors focused on external memory storage, smartphones connected to the Internet extend beyond memory assistants to powerful mobile computation devices. In fact, mobile technologies connected to the Internet allow for novel investigations into the interactions of persons as they engage with a global workspace and connected knowledgebases. Moreover, mobile access to the Internet may allow for interactive possibilities: a paradigm shift in how we see ourselves and the ways in which we understand the nature of our cognitive and epistemic capabilities.

1.2 Neuroscience and Cyberpsychology

To encourage the inclusion of brain science research in the cyberpsychology domain, this book emphasizes the potential of neuroscience for the study of cognitive, affective, and social processes found in cyberpsychological research and the neural systems that support them. Given these emphases, cyberpsychology will be understood as a branch of psychology that studies (1) the neurocognitive, affective, and social aspects of humans interacting with technology; and (2) affective computing aspects of humans interacting with devices/systems that incorporate computation. As such, the cyberpsychologist studies both the ways in which persons make use of devices and the neurocognitive processes, motivations, intentions, behavioral outcomes, and effects of online and offline use of technology. This expanded definition and framework emphasizes a network approach to brain function that provides a principled approach to predicting cyberpsychological processes associated with specific brain systems. In this framework, a systems neuroscience view is adopted that considers cyberpsychological processes (cognitive and affective functions during media use) to arise from the interactions of brain areas in large-scale distributed networks (Bressler & Menon, 2010; Mesulam, 2000). Findings from systems neuroscience have characterized specific large-scale brain networks that are identifiable in the brain both while it is active and when it is at rest (Seeley et al., 2007). The three most prominent networks are the executive control network, the default mode network, and the saliency network. The first two networks can be recognized straightforwardly by observing the profile of activation and deactivation typically found during cognitive tasks. The executive control network typically shows increases in activation during cognitively demanding tasks, whereas the default mode network has decreased activation. The third network is a salience network that processes affective stimuli and allows for switching between the competitive interactions of two other major networks.

While some of these processes are controlled processes in which nodes are activated through the controlled attention of the person, other processes are activated automatically without the necessity for conscious control or attention by the person (Schneider & Shiffrin, 1977; Shiffrin & Schneider, 1977). This dual-process perspective that human cognition may be made up of automatic and controlled processes was introduced by William James (1890) over a century ago. Dual-process models of automatic and controlled processes have been proposed in nearly every domain of executive functioning. Specifically, controlled processes (e.g., inhibiting a prepotent response during the Stroop task) are associated with conscious awareness, effort, intention, and the capacity for inhibition. Contrariwise, automatic processes (e.g., overlearned responses like reading) are not necessarily in conscious awareness and occur spontaneously (see Table 1.2).

Examples of automatic and controlled processing in cyberpsychology literature are plentiful: automatic and controlled assessments of social status on social media sites (Slagter van Tryon & Bishop, 2012); automatic and controlled social browsing and social searching on Facebook (Wise, Alhabash, & Park, 2010); relationships between individual differences in

Table 1.2 *Dual processes theories: Automatic and controlled processes*

Automatic	Controlled
Fast processing	Slow processing
Spontaneous (heuristics and biases)	Effortful and deliberate
Parallel processing	Serial processing
Non-reflective consciousness	Reflective consciousness
Phylogenetically older	Phylogenetically older
Similar across species	Unique in humans
Independent of general intelligence	Correlated with general intelligence
Brain Regions: Ventromedial prefrontal cortex, dorsal anterior cingulate cortex, lateral temporal cortex, ventral striatum, amygdala	Brain Regions: lateral prefrontal cortex, medial prefrontal cortex, lateral and medial posterior parietal cortex, rostral anterior cingulate cortex, hippocampus and surrounding medial temporal lobe

Note: Descriptions of the brain areas can be found in Chapter 2 of this book.

automatic and controlled aspects of self-regulation and problematic Internet use (Billieux & Van der Linden, 2012); effects of distracting ads on automatic responses and controlled processing of online news stories (Kononova, 2013); automaticity and executive control in videogames (Boyle et al., 2013); and the use of virtual-reality environments for assessment of the supervisory attention system in lieu of automatic and controlled processes (Armstrong et al., 2013; Parsons et al., 2011; Parsons, Courtney, & Dawson, 2013).

This chapter provides an introduction to large-scale brain networks, the automatic and controlled processes involved in each, and their applications to a framework for cyberpsychology and the brain. This framework aims to emphasize the study of neurocognitive processing and behavior in relation to the ways in which persons use and communicate via technological devices.

1.3 Large-Scale Brain Networks

From the neurosciences, we have learned of the collaborative function of brain areas working together as large-scale networks (Bressler, 1995; Mesulam, 1990; Sporns et al., 2004). The neuroanatomical structures of large-scale brain networks offer a network of linked brain areas that expedites signaling along particular pathways to support specific neurocognitive functions (see Chapter 2; Figure 2.9). Over the course of evolutionary development, the primate brain has evolved to increase survival via behaviors that are adaptive to multifarious environmental contingencies. The result is a brain with large-scale brain networks that can be used to analyze environmental conditions, compare perceptual information with learned concepts, and ultimately generate solutions to the immediate environmental contingencies. There is a growing acceptance of the idea that the brain is a collection of interconnected large-scale brain networks acting together to generate solutions and corresponding behaviors (Bressler & Menon, 2010). Hence, large-scale functional networks can be understood as networks of interconnected brain areas that interact to cause circumscribed functions (Mannino & Bressler, 2015).

1.3.1 Executive-Control Network

The brain's large-scale functional networks apply organized effects on cortical areas, subcortical brain structures, and effector organs during a variety of neurocognitive functions. Large-scale functional networks carry out diverse activities; some processes are automatic and others are controlled. The executive-control network has been identified for controlled attention to pertinent stimuli as behavioral choices are weighed against shifting conditions. The executive-control network exerts control over posterior sensorimotor representations and maintains relevant information so that actions may be selected. This network appears to include brain areas that are known to have capacity for sustained attention (e.g., dorsolateral prefrontal cortex, lateral parietal cortex; see Chapter 2 in this book). For example, coordinated prefrontal and posterior parietal control areas have been found to direct and coordinate sensory and motor areas during (and in preparation for) perceptuomotor processing (Bressler et al., 2008).

For cyberpsychologists, these executive functions are of interest because they have been linked to media multitasking. Ophir, Nass, and Wagner (2009) found that young adults that engaged frequently in media multitasking had poorer performance on a number of executive control tasks (e.g., filtering distractions and task switching) than participants who were low in media multitasking. Contrariwise, when Baumgartner and colleagues (2014) explored the relationship between media multitasking and executive control they did not find the executive control deficits. In fact, adolescents who engaged more frequently in media multitasking actually showed a tendency to be better at ignoring irrelevant distractions. This may reflect a positive impact of media multitasking on the ability to willingly ignore distractions. Hence, heavy media multitaskers may have learned to ignore distractions when desired. These topics will be explored in Chapter 5 of this book.

1.3.2   Default-Mode Network and Mentalizing Network

Neuroimaging of the human brain while persons are in a state of quiet repose (e.g., with eyes closed) has revealed a default mode network that activates when external demands are low (Raichle, 2015). These findings have resulted in a suggested role of the default mode network in self-generated cognition that is decoupled from the external world (Andrews-Hanna, 2012; 2014). An independent body of work in the social neurosciences has revealed an overlapping "mentalizing network" that reveals the neural correlates of a person's ability to mentalize (i.e., infer) the cognitions and feelings of others. The similarity between the default and mentalizing networks has generated questions in social neuroscience about whether the core function of the default network is to mediate internal aspects of social cognition (Li, Mai, & Liu, 2014). The concepts of automatic and controlled processing within the social neurosciences have been reformulated to reflect a controlled "reflective" system and an automatic "reflexive" system (Lieberman, 2007). The reflective system for social neuroscience corresponds with a controlled social cognition system. The reflexive system corresponds with an automatic social cognition system. When persons engage in goal-directed behavior of a nonself-referential nature, certain areas of the brain decrease their activity. During quiet resting states a default mode network activates (Raichle & Snyder, 2007), which consists of areas in dorsal and ventral medial prefrontal and parietal cortices (see Chapter 2 in this book). Results from recent studies have revealed that the default mode network is involved in perspective taking of the desires, beliefs, and intentions of others (see for example Buckner et al., 2008). These functions are all self-referential in nature. The reduction of activity in the default mode network during effortful cognitive processing reflects an attenuation of the brain's self-referential activity as a means of more effectively focusing on a task.

For social cognitive neuroscience there has been an increasing emphasis upon answering central questions about the nature of human neurocognition by adding neuroscience techniques to methods used by social scientists (Adolphs, 2009; Ochsner & Lieberman, 2001). Recently, social neuroscientists have started incorporating the sorts of platforms and approaches that were historically used by cyberpsychologists into their experiments. Furthermore, they are increasingly using virtual-reality stimuli in social neuroscience research (Adolphs, 2003, Schilbach et al., 2013; Wilms et al., 2010).

1.3.3   Salience Network

In addition to the executive-control and default mode networks, a salience network has emerged that reflects affective processing. The salience network is an intrinsically connected large-scale network anchored in the anterior insula and dorsal anterior cingulate cortex (see Chapter 2 of this book). The characterization of the salience network has enhanced our understanding of brain areas that take part in the processing of neurocognitively and affectively relevant events to direct flexible responding (Menon & Uddin, 2010; Seeley et al., 2007). The executive-control network and the saliency network may interactively support attentional processing. For example, the saliency network receives and affords selective amplification of salient information that prompts the executive control network to respond to salient information for attentional shift and control execution (Menon & Uddin, 2010).

For cyberpsychology researchers interested in action videogames, the interactive working of these networks is of particular interest. The experience of an action videogame involves a high level of attention and executive control for both working memory and salience processing. In a recent study, Gong and colleagues (2015) used functional magnetic resonance imaging (see Chapter 3 in this book for more information on neuroimaging) to examine the relation between action videogame experience and the integration of the executive-control network with the saliency network by comparing action videogame experts with amateurs. Study findings revealed enhanced intra- and inter-network functional integrations in action videogame experts compared to amateurs. The authors argue that these findings support the possible relation between action videogame experience and neural network plasticity.

1.4   Affective Neuroscience and Cyberpsychology

Historically, much of psychology has been understood as comprising three related fields: cognition, affect, and motivation. Until recently, cognitive psychology has been the most extensively studied of the three, with affect and motivation being comparatively neglected (Baddeley, 1981). Likewise, cyberpsychology research has had a strong emphasis on the cognitive processes involved in human and computer interaction. Part of the disproportionate emphasis is due to the fact that while cognition can be studied relatively easily in the laboratory, affect and motivation call for assessment of real-world activities (Masmoudi, Dai, & Naceur, 2012). In recent years, this emphasis upon cognition alone in psychology (including human and behavioral neuroscience) research has been challenged by a growing body of research into emotions (Kohler, Walker, Martin, Healey, & Moberg, 2010; Stuss & Levine, 2002). Results from studies have revealed that although affective processing can in principle be separated from executive control, in praxes neurocognitive and affective processes are highly intertwined and mutually dependent (Inzlicht, Bartholow, & Hirsh, 2015; Pessoa, 2013; Phelps, Lempert, & Sokol-Hessner, 2014).

1.4.1   Evolutionary Coupling of Neurocognitive and Affective Processes

From an evolutionary perspective, the coupling of neurocognitive and affective processes seems important for survival. Emotions and affective processes have deep evolutionary roots, and increase survival potential via homeostatic processes (Damasio & Carvalho, 2013). Both cortical (e.g., insula; see Chapter 2 of this book) and subcortical nuclei (e.g., amygdala, hypothalamus, hippocampus, brainstem; see Chapter 2 of this book) play important roles in the formation of emotions and affective decision-making (Koziol & Budding, 2009; Parvizi, 2009). In his recent comprehensive review of the interconnected processes of neurocognitive and affective processes, Pessoa (2013) points out that during the course of evolution the older subcortical brain regions (e.g., amygdala and hypothalamus; see Chapter 2 in this book) have been integrated with newer cortical regions and neuronal networks. This has allowed for the development of novel functions that support enhanced capacities for interacting with the environment. Furthermore, the interaction of neurocognitive and affective processes promote survival by facilitating learning and memory (Immordino-Yang & Damasio, 2007). A person's past experiences result in somatic markers that bias future behaviors and decision-making (Bechara & Damasio, 2005).

1.4.2   Importance of Bottom-Up Affective and Motivational State-Control Perspectives

Cromwell and Panksepp (2011) describe the historically cognitive emphasis as a top-down (cortical → subcortical) perspective that could hinder progress in understanding neurological and psychiatric disorders. As an alternative, they emphasize inclusion of bottom-up (subcortical → cortical) affective and motivational state-control perspectives. This approach accentuates the importance of human affect and emotional experience for human learning and decision-making. In normally functioning persons, the automatic processing (i.e., covert biases) of stimuli (including environmental and contextual factors) related to previous emotional experience of analogous conditions influences decision-making (Bechara & Damasio, 2005). Furthermore, positive affect has been found to increase intrinsic motivation and cognitive control (Yang, Yang, & Isen, 2013). Dopamine is the neurotransmitter argued to serve as motivational reward and the dopamine circuit plays an essential role in the brain's affective functioning and basic impulse to seek, explore, inspect, and make sense of the environment (Alcaro & Panksepp, 2011).

The affective neuroscientist Jaak Panksepp identified the "seeking" circuitry that compels persons to seek their environments for information that will help them survive (location of food; or a link to a new social networking site). The seeking system is a dopamine-energized, mesolimbic system that arises from the ventral tegmental area. Dopamine is released each time one explores his or her environment. The dopaminergic-induced sense of euphoria one experiences is typically not a product of a reward, but of seeking itself. For example, a person could decide to do a quick Google search to find out what movie Steve McQueen starred in as the incarcerated safecracker Henri Charrière (i.e., *Papillon*) only to find an hour later that one's quick search has led to an hour of Googling. This dopaminergic response can also be seen in the experience of being "liked" on Facebook. This is a significant social event and essential to motivating human behavior (see Chapter 4 of this book).

1.4.3   Non-Salient "Cold" and Affectively "Hot" Cognitions

Progress in affective neuroscience has resulted in an understanding that brain areas are involved in both non-salient "Cold" and affectively "Hot" cognitions. Goel and Dolan (2003) examined the neural basis of emotionally neutral ("Cold") and affectively salient ("Hot") reasoning using event-related functional magnetic resonance imaging (see Chapter 3 in this book for more on neuroimaging). Findings revealed that a reciprocal engagement of the dorsolateral prefrontal cortex for "Cold" and the ventromedial prefrontal cortex for "Hot" processing provides evidence for a dynamic neural system for information processing. The pattern of which is robustly influenced by affective saliency. This approach emphasizes distinction between executive inhibition and reactive inhibition (Nigg, 2003). Executive inhibition involves top-down (cortical → subcortical) effortful neurocognitive processing aimed at inhibitory control (Nigg, 2000, 2003); and reactive disinhibition reflects bottom-up (subcortical → cortical) processes, in which the individual attempts to regulate behavior in affect-laden situations (Nigg, 2003, 2006). This affective neuroscience approach represents a more embodied view, which accepts that cognitions are essentially related to both the participant's neurology and the environments in which study participants operate (Panksepp, 2009, 2010).

The idea of Hot decision-making has been described as being consistent with the somatic marker hypothesis (Bechara & Damasio, 2005), in which the experience of an emotion (e.g., gut feeling; hunch) results in a somatic marker that guides choice of action. The somatic marker is hypothesized to play a role in hot decision-making in that it biases the available response selections found in decision-making tasks. When persons are faced with decisions, they experience somatic sensations in advance of real consequences of possible different alternatives. The Iowa Gambling Task (IGT; Bechara, 2007) is a computerized assessment of reward-related decision-making that measures temporal foresight and risky decision-making (Bechara et al., 1994). Neuroimaging studies of persons performing the IGT have revealed activation in the orbitofrontal cortex (Ernst et al., 2002; Windmann et al., 2006), which appears to be significant for signaling the anticipated rewards/punishments of an action and for adaptive learning. Evidence for the somatic marker hypothesis's role in hot decision-making over IGT trials can be found in the demonstration of an anticipatory electrodermal response in healthy controls to card selection (Bechara et al., 1996). For example, prior to selecting a card from a risky deck, a healthy control will show a physiological reaction indicating that the participant is experiencing bodily the anticipated risk. Further, studies have shown that damage to the ventromedial prefrontal cortex and the amygdala prevents the use of somatic (affective) signals for advantageous decision-making (Bechara et al., 1996). It is noteworthy that there are different roles played by the ventromedial prefrontal cortex and amygdala in decision-making. While ventromedial prefrontal cortex patients were able to generate electrodermal responses when they received a reward or a punishment, amygdala patients failed to do so (Bechara et al., 1999).

1.5   Affective Computing

The discipline of cyberpsychology has also experienced increased interest in the importance of affect, as is apparent in the proposal and development of affective computing (Picard, 1997, 2014). The phrase "affective computing" was originated by MIT Professor Rosalind Picard in her (1997) book *Affective Computing*. Picard is a pioneer of affective computing endeavors to remove the affective barrier between humans and machines. Picard (1997) has described affective computing as a discipline that pulls from computer science, engineering, psychology, and education to investigate how affect impacts interactions between humans and technology. As a discipline, affective computing has been gaining popularity rapidly in the last decade because it has apparent potential in the next generation of human-computer interfaces (Calvo et al., 2014).

1.5.1   Affective Computing Systems That Can Recognize Human Emotions

Researchers in affective computing aim to design machines that can recognize human emotions and respond accordingly. Affective computing researchers aim to model affective communication found in human interactions and apply these models to interactions between humans and computers. An important finding for linking affective computing to cyberpsychology and recent work in social cognitive neuroscience are results that suggest humans interact socially with computer and machines in a manner that is similar to the way humans interact with other humans (McEneaney, 2013). Given these findings it is likely that affective computing and cyberpsychological studies of human-computer interactions can be enhanced using the same principles that govern human–human interactions found in social neuroscience. It is important to note that there is a distinction in affective computing between feeling and expressing emotions. Affective computing researchers do not need to build computers that actually feel emotions in the same way that humans do. Instead, it is enough that affective computers express emotions (Picard, 2003). Artificial communication of emotions can be accomplished by enabling virtual human avatars (or simpler agents) to have facial expressions, diverse tones of voice, and perform empathic behaviors (Brave, Nass, & Hutchinson, 2005).

1.5.2   Affective Computers That Respond to Real-Time Changes

One goal of affective computing is to design a computer system that responds in a rational and strategic fashion to real-time changes in user affect (happiness, sadness, etc.), cognition (e.g., frustration, boredom), and motivation (Serbedzija & Fairclough, 2009), as represented by speech (Dai et al., 2015; Wu, Parsons, & Narayanan, 2010), facial expressions (McDuff et al., 2013), physiological signals (Fairclough, 2009), neurocognitive performance (Parsons et al., 2009; Parsons, 2016; Wu, Lance, & Parsons, 2013), and multimodal combination (Wu et al., 2010). Of specific interest to the focus of this book is the use of psychophysiological measures. Research studies in social and affective neuroscience have shown that emotions can elicit different physiological changes that can be measured directly using psychophysiological measures (Cacioppo, Tassinary, & Berntson, 2007).

A significant factor involved in social interaction is the capacity for dealing with the affective dimension appropriately. Therefore, researchers in affective computing develop ways to derive human affective states from various intrusive and non-intrusive sensors. A number of approaches have been used to estimate emotional states, including behavioral response, startle response, autonomic assessment, and neurophysiologic measurement. For example, dopamine levels act on voluntary movement and affective arousal that produce increased heart rate and blood pressure. Considerable attention has been given to the use of electroencephalography (EEG) for inferring emotional states, as EEG can reveal emotional states with relatively low costs and simplicity (Kim et al., 2013).

1.6   Social Cognitive Neuroscience of Social Media

The rise of social media technologies is an interesting development that reflects social and affective neuroscience principles. Over the last decade, social cognitive and affective neuroscientists have uncovered a good deal of support for the notion that the human brain facilitates, makes use of, and is partially molded by a broad array of social interactions (Cacioppo & Decety, 2011; Lieberman, 2007). This perspective is compatible with the social brain hypothesis, which is the leading elucidation of the expansion of the human brain during the course of evolution. According to Oxford University's Robin Dunbar (1998, 2011) the size of the neocortex (as compared to the whole brain) among primates correlates with a number of indices of social complexity: prevalence of social play, frequency of social learning, frequency of coalitions, male mating strategies, rate of tactical deception, grooming clique size, and social group size. Social neuroscientists argue that the human brain developed beyond brains of other species to allow humans to connect with each other (Lieberman, 2013). Social media technologies offer cyberpsychologists a fertile area for investigating social networks. Online social networking and the increasing use of digital media might allow cyberpsychologists opportunities to assess the social brain and related hypotheses about relations among social networks and various brain areas. With the rise of social networking sites cyberpsychologists have the opportunity to study the results of broadcasting one's information to many members of one's network at once. Furthermore, social networking sites offer cyberpsychologists opportunities to study the impact of continuously updating our understanding of network members' behavior and thoughts.

While the social brain hypothesis helps us to understand that there is a relation between the size of the neocortex and social relations, we are still left with the question of what part of the brain is social. One way to understand this issue is something called the brain's default mode network, which is constantly running in the background. As mentioned above, when not engaged in some other activity, the default mode network is activated as the brain ruminates about self and others. This automated processing is turned down when doing an active control process (e.g., doing difficult math problems; Schilbach et al., 2008). Recent evidence suggests considerable overlap between the default mode network and regions involved in social, affective, and introspective processes (Forbes & Grafman, 2010; Mars et al., 2012). Moreover, self-referential processing, autobiographical memory, and social cognition have been tied to the default mode network (Amodio & Frith, 2006; Qin & Northoff, 2011; Raichle, 2015; Spreng, Mar, & Kim, 2009).

An independent body of work in the social neurosciences has revealed an overlapping "mentalizing network" that reveals the neural correlates of a person's ability to mentalize (i.e., infer) the cognitions and feelings of others. The similarity between the default and mentalizing networks has generated questions in social neuroscience about whether the core function of the default network is to mediate internal aspects of social cognition (Li, Mai, & Liu, 2014). Amft and colleagues (2015) considered the overlapping brain regions thought to be involved in the social-affective part of the default mode network. Language and social cognition were related to a cluster formed by the temporo-parietal junction and anterior middle temporal sulcus/gyrus. Their findings highlight a strongly interconnected network that may be central to social-affective processing.

In a recent review of the emerging neuroscience of social media, Meshi, Tamir, and Heekeren (2015) discuss the growing global phenomenon of online social media (almost two billion users worldwide regularly using these social networking sites) and the potential for neuroscientists to make use of these pervasive social media sites to gain new understanding of social cognitive processes and the neural systems that support them. Cyberpsychologists can leverage these studies and the proposed social media examples to enhance understanding of brain processes involved when humans interact with social media. Studies have already been performed that examined the relation between online social network size and gray matter density (Kanai et al., 2012; Von Der Heide et al., 2014). Results revealed that social media users with larger online social networks had larger amygdalae than users with lesser social networks. These results are important because they replicate previous research with real-world social networks (Bickart et al., 2011). These findings support the viability of using social media metrics for investigating social neurocognitive processes.

1.7 Brain-Based Cyberpsychology

To encourage the inclusion of the brain science research in the cyberpsychology domain, this book proposes a framework for integrating neuroscience and cyberpsychology for the study of social, cognitive, and affective processes and the neural systems that support them. Given these emphases, cyberpsychology will be understood as a branch of psychology that studies (1) the neurocognitive, affective, and social aspects of humans interacting with technology; and (2) affective computing aspects of humans interacting with devices/systems that incorporate computation. As such, a cyberpsychologist working from a brain-based cyberpsychological framework studies both the ways in which persons make use of devices and the neurocognitive processes, motivations, intentions, behavioral outcomes, and effects of online and offline use of technology. Research in a brain-based cyberpsychology framework ranges from studies with offline platforms (using desktop computers, word processors, virtual/augmented reality, gaming consoles, and statistics packages) to online Internet use (how we engage in online banking, shopping, dating, and gaming), to mobile phones. These studies emphasize the study of neurocognitive, affective, and social processing behaviors in relation to the ways in which persons use and communicate via technological devices. Cyberpsychologists view these devices as tools that either facilitate or impede human interaction and communication.

This expanded definition and framework has emerged from clinical, affective, and social neuroscience research. In the last decade, human neuroscience research and particularly studies including neuroimaging methods have undergone substantial changes in the stimulus modalities employed to explore human neurocognition. This has involved a movement toward the use of more ecologically valid stimuli, as compared to highly laboratory-controlled, simplified stimuli (Parsons, 2015). While many of the pioneering paradigms in the human neurosciences reflected a noteworthy emphasis upon laboratory control and experiments that involve participants observing static stimuli (e.g., simple, static representations of stimuli; static photographs of emotionally valenced facial expressions) that are devoid of interactions (Blair et al., 1999), there are increasing questions about whether knowledge gained using these static stimuli will generalize to the social, cognitive, and affective processes found in everyday activities (Chakrabarti, 2013: Ochsner, 2004; Schilbach et al., 2006, 2013). This has led to confusion about the neural bases of interpersonal understanding because studies of shared representations between self and others usually ask the perceiver to observe and imitate target movements or have participants directly rate their own sensory states and observe those states in others. This is done without requiring participants to make any judgments about target states. Further, researchers examining the shared representations and mental state attributions of perceivers often make use of static stimuli that fail to represent the types of information that participants must process when they experience dynamic stimuli in real-life social interactions (Risko et al., 2012; Schilbach, 2015; Zaki & Ochsner, 2009).

The use of more ecologically valid stimuli allows for novel approaches to assessing brain activity arising from complex stimulus material such as virtual environments (Parsons, 2015; Parsons et al., 2015), virtual humans (de Borst & Gelder, 2015; Schilbach, 2015), videogames (Bavelier et al., 2012), and social media (Meshi et al., 2015). These advances have significantly influenced the fields of cognitive, affective, and social neuroscience in particular, as these areas may benefit significantly from the use of ecologically valid stimuli. Furthermore, these more dynamic and ecologically valid stimuli are attractive because they have the advantage of being multi-modal, engaging, temporally coherent, and allow for enhanced understanding of the ways in which the brain processes information in complex everyday situations. Additionally, the use of virtual environments provides a means of experimentally controlling the events and interactions to which the participant is exposed (Tikka et al., 2012).

In addition to the positive impact that cyberpsychology stimuli and platforms can have on the human neurosciences, there is a great deal that cyberpsychology can gain from the cognitive, affective, and social neurosciences. While neuroscientific research is highlighted throughout this book, many of the examples provided reflect assessments of behavioral performance. Although it can be challenging to operationalize the extent to which a stimulus approximates activities of daily living, this book gives examples of stimuli and virtual environment–based contexts that span the implied continuum. The studies reviewed in this book are not meant to be exhaustive. Instead this review focuses upon cyberpsychology research that highlights the ways in which persons respond to clinical, affective, and social stimuli in simulations that approximate real-world activities and interactions.

The cognitive, affective, and social neurosciences can support cyberpsychology by offering supplementary assessments of the assumptions that cyberpsychologists make regarding neurocognitive and affective aspects of interacting with technologies. In turn, lessons learned from cyberpsychology can aide efforts to formulate and specify neuroscientific models of humans interacting with technology. Increasingly, brain researchers have become interested in identifying neuronal networks involved in Internet use (Meshi, Tamir, and Heekeren, 2015); neuropsychological aspects of virtual environments (Campbell et al., 2009), ethical decision-making (Skulmowski et al., 2014), and social interactions using virtual humans (Schilbach et al., 2006). Cyberpsychology approaches can be of use to these efforts by offering reliable and empirically valid approaches to human–computer interactions that affective and social neuroscientists are beginning to use.

CHAPTER 2

The Brain and Cyberpsychology: A Primer

2.1 Introduction

Cyberpsychologists interested in brain functioning should realize that, contrary to common assumptions, the brain is not a general-purpose computer with a unified central processor. Instead, brain functional activity is better conceptualized in terms of large-scale neural networks that represent distinctive subsystems and relationships among them: language, face-and-object recognition, spatial attention, memory-emotion, and executive function-comportment (Mesulam, 2000). Whether at rest (default-mode network), in the course of performing cognitive control tasks (executive-control network), or responding to salient information (salience network), the brain continuously generates and reshapes multifaceted patterns of correlated dynamics. Consciousness, neurocognition, and behavior are understood as emergent properties of these large-scale neural networks (Bartolomeo, 2011; Ross, 2010). These networks have nodes that can be separated into critical and participating epicenters. Lesions to a critical network epicenter conclusively impair performance in a neurocognitive domain. Functional imaging activations (see Chapter 3 of this book) of participating areas occur when persons are performing tasks related to the same neurocognitive domain (Catani & Mesulam, 2008). A great deal of our understanding of brain structure and functioning has resulted from a combination of focal brain disease studies and functional imaging experiments.

This chapter investigates the significance of these neural networks and related brain structures for neurocognition, affective regulation, and behavior. While some areas are briefly discussed for the sake of completeness and continuity, other areas, such as large-scale networks and frontal-subcortical circuits, receive greater attention. It is important to note that almost all recent textbooks of neuropsychology (Kolb & Whishaw, 2015), neuroscience (Kandel et al., 2012), or psychophysiology (Cacioppo et al.,

2007) proffer up-to-date, well-illustrated, and comprehensive accounts of the structures and functions of the mammalian nervous system. Again, instead of presenting a comprehensive account of these structures and functions, this chapter aims to present a foundation for the conceptualization of the material covered in the chapters that follow. This chapter is presented at the level of cyberpsychologists who are not yet conversant with nervous system structure and function. While an encyclopedic knowledge of the nervous system is not a prerequisite for the cyberpsychologist, there is a need for a basic understanding of neural networks and related brain structures for investigating the neural correlates of various media (e.g., social media, videogames, virtual-reality).

2.2 Human Nervous Systems

The human nervous system is composed of three parts: the central nervous system (CNS), the peripheral nervous system (PNS), and the autonomic nervous system (ANS). The CNS is mainly composed of the brain and the spinal cord and is contained within the skull and the spinal column. Within the skull, the brain is supported and protected by successions of membranes, or meninges: dura mater (i.e., hard mother), the arachnoid layer (looks like spider's web), and the pia mater (i.e., soft mother). The brain is also fueled by a very rich blood supply (about a fifth of the blood pumped by the heart) system. The brain is supported by cerebrospinal fluid (CSF) that affords mechanical protection (absorbs shocks to the CNS) and supplies nutrition to the brain. The CSF is generated within the brain's lateral ventricles (large chambers within the brain) and circulates through tapered passages into midline third and fourth ventricles, and then out into the spaces surrounding the brain and the spinal cord.

As for the spinal cord, while some cyberpsychologists may underrate its importance, various aspects of behavior are in fact organized and integrated within it. The spinal cord is made up of a series of layers, and each layer is related to a spinal vertebra. Further, each of these layers has a ventral and dorsal pair of spinal nerve roots that links the PNS to the CNS. Fibers that enter the dorsal aspect of the spinal cord transport data from the body's sensory receptors (dorsal root). Fibers that leave the ventral part of the spinal cord transport data from the spinal cord to the muscles (ventral root). The spinal cord allows for motor information to be transmitted from the brain to the body, and it receives sensory information in return. Reflexes are behaviors that are organized entirely within the spinal cord and then the sensory information links directly (via a reflex arc) to a motor nerve, which then exits back out to the PNS.

The CNS is connected to the rest of the body through nerve fibers that carry information to and away from the CNS. These fibers constitute the peripheral nervous system, or PNS. The PNS conveys information (temperature, pain, light touch, pressure, position sensation) from receptors distributed around the body into the CNS, and also transmits information back out to effectors. An additional aspect of the human nervous system is the ANS, which is a specialized system formed from components of both the CNS and the PNS.

The ANS is particularly involved in the study of the affective and psychophysiological computing.

The ANS is involved in general activation of emotion and emergency response. While the parasympathetic division supports resting-level increases in the body's supply of stored energy, the sympathetic division of the ANS is primarily involved in activities requiring energy expenditure. For example, while playing an action videogame, a user may become excited, and the sympathetic nervous system will cause an increase in blood flow to skeletal muscles that stimulate the secretion of epinephrine, which results in increased heart rate and a rise in blood sugar levels.

2.3   Neurons and Communication

The discussion of the nervous system leads to an important note: The totality of the nervous system is comprised of neurons and neuroglia. The neurons convey minute electrical impulses throughout the nervous system that communicate (via synaptic transmission) with other neurons or muscles (in the periphery). Although glia play an array of vital supportive roles, it is doubtful that they are directly involved in conveying either nerve impulses or synaptic transmission. While most physiological or neuropsychology textbooks (see, for example, Cacioppo et al., 2007; Kandel et al., 2012; Kolb & Whishaw, 2015) include sophisticated explanations of these processes, the following summary may help provide a clearer idea of the basics of neuronal communication.

Although neurons vary in size and shape, they have four common features (Figure 2.1):

1. A *cell body* (including a nucleus), which controls and maintains the neuronal structure

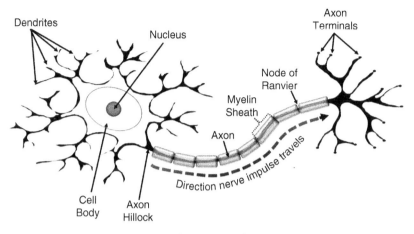

Figure 2.1 The structure of a neuron.

2. *Dendrites*, which are extensions that branch from the neuron into the immediate neighborhood of the cell body and send chemical transmissions from one neuron to another

3. An *axon*, which extends away from the cell body and transmits electrochemical data from the cell body to the synapse through microtubules. *Note*: Several axons are enclosed in a myelin sheath, which accelerates the speed of axonal transmission.

4. *Terminal synaptic buttons*, which are close to the end of the axon, and act as the site of interneuronal contact. The terminal buttons are where neurochemical data is transmitted from one neuron to another. *Note*: The terminal button is the presynaptic area of the synapse, where electrical nerve impulses cause the release of a neurotransmitter.

Neurons exchange information via reception, conduction, and transmission of electrochemical signals. While the data that travel along the axon from the cell body to the terminal buttons are electrical, the neuron does not transmit the data down the axon in the same way that electricity is conducted down an electrical wire. Instead, chemical alterations in the axonal membrane result in exchanges of various ions between the axon and its surrounding fluid to produce an electrical current.

Neurons have a resting potential (i.e., membrane potential, usually between -40 and -55 mV) when they are inactive. This resting potential is a small electrical imbalance between the outer and inner membrane surfaces due to the separation of electrically charged ions. For neural communication to occur, ions (electrically charged sodium, potassium, calcium, and chloride) must pass through small channels in the axon wall. On the inside of the axon the charge is electrically negative with respect to the outside. When the neuron is at rest (i.e., not firing), the sodium (Na+) ions are kept outside of the neuron. The sodium-potassium pump is a biological transport system that exchanges three sodium ions for every two potassium (K+) ions across the axonal membrane.

The generation of a nerve impulse requires that a cell membrane depolarize. This depolarization occurs when a Na+ channel across the membrane temporarily opens and Na+ ions pass through it into the cell and its voltage decreases to at least 35 mV reduction of polarization toward zero. At this point the membrane opens its Na+ gates and the neuron fires with an action potential. It is important to emphasize that nerve impulses conform to the "all or none" law, in which they either occur completely or not at all. Hence partial action potentials do not result in action. When a nerve impulse is at a specific location along an axon, it "excites" the region of axon just in front of it. This causes the neural impulse to continue on to the next region of axon. While there are a variety of factors that may influence a neuron and cause (or hinder) the production of nerve impulses, they are most likely influenced by other neurons via synaptic transmission.

Nerve impulses may be conceptualized as minute electrical signals that travel along the surface of a long, slender projection of a neuron called the axon. The axon conducts electrical impulses away from the neuron's cell body. Most nerve impulses are formed at an area known as the axon hillock – where the cell body "becomes" the axon. It is important to note that this type of conduction is considered as "active" in comparison with the "passive" conduction of data along dendrites and over a neuron's cell body. When stimulated, a neuron generates its own nerve impulses that, once formed, travel at a fixed speed and amplitude. These nerve impulses tend to occur in bursts (volleys) rather than unaccompanied. Hence, a small number of nerve impulses may specify a weak stimulus. A larger number of nerve impulses will convey a robust stimulus.

A presynaptic neuron transports an action potential down its axon until it loses its myelin sheath and separates into multiple branches (also known as buttons, or synaptic knobs). These synaptic buttons expand at the end to intensify the contact region with the postsynaptic neuron. The synaptic buttons themselves do not come in physical contact with the postsynaptic cell (enclosed with myelin and surrounded by neuroglia). Between the two neurons lies a minute space known as the synaptic gap (or synaptic cleft).

2.4   Neurotransmitters

Synaptic vesicles containing neurotransmitters are found in the terminal buttons. These synaptic vesicles are distinctive cellular assemblies that characteristically gather close to the presynaptic membrane. The neurotransmitters are synthesized until they are transported to the receptor sites on the postsynaptic neuron. While numerous neurotransmitter molecules exist, the primary ones mentioned in this text are acetylcholine (ACh), norepinephrine (NE), serotonin (5HT), dopamine (DA), gamma-aminobutyric acid (GABA), and glutamate (GLU; see Table 2.1 for more on these neurotransmitters). Each neurotransmitter is shaped differently and has its own "key" fit to a specific receptor that determines how the synaptic endings evoke responses (excitation or inhibition) in the postsynaptic neuron. The synapse itself includes the following: a presynaptic membrane, synaptic gap (or cleft), and the postsynaptic membrane. On occasions when a neural impulse from the presynaptic

Table 2.1   *Select neurotransmitters*

Neurotransmitter	Functions
Acetylcholine (ACh)	ACh is released by motor neurons controlling skeletal muscles. ACh contributes to the regulation of attention, arousal, and memory.
Dopamine (DA)	DA contributes to the control of voluntary movement, reward, pleasurable emotions, and cognition.
Serotonin (5HT)	5HT is involved in the regulation of sleep, wakefulness, mood regulation, appetite, and muscle control.
Norepinephrine (NE)	NE contributes to the modulation of mood, arousal, and fight-or-flight response (increased heart rate, increased glucose in bloodstream, increased oxygen to brain and muscles).
Glutamate (GLU)	GLU is the most important *excitatory* neurotransmitter in the brain. Also involved in long-term potentiation, memory.
Gamma-Aminobutyric Acid (GABA)	GABA has direct *inhibitory* effects on CNS.

neuron reaches the button, the vesicles release a specific amount of a neurotransmitter into the synaptic cleft.

2.5   Brain Architecture and Function

The brain is conventionally divided into a number of regions. While these divisions have some benefit from a phylogenetic perspective, they fall short of providing a model that is helpful for cyberpsychologists. From a phylogenetic perspective of brain development there is some importance in appreciating brain structure for enhancing understanding of the functional interrelationship of brain areas. Brain evolution reveals a succession of layers enfolded around a fundamental core including the spinal cord and the brainstem. Moving forward, each layer represents an "advanced" level of functional development that progressively stretches the functional capacity of the brain as a system.

2.5.1   *Planes and Orientations*

It is important to note that throughout this chapter there will be some references to various planes and orientations. For example, cross-sections of the brain include axial (sliced along the horizontal plane), coronal (sliced vertically, viewing the brain from the front or back), and sagittal (sliced vertically, viewing the brain from the side) (see Figure 2.2).

While these cross-sectional slices of the brain are helpful, the neuroscience literature often references the dorsal (i.e., the back) and ventral (i.e., the belly) surfaces. From the perspective of the dorsal surface, one can see the approximate bilateral symmetry of the cerebral hemispheres (see Figure 2.3).

On the dorsal surface, the chief landmarks on each hemisphere are the central sulci and parieto-occipital sulci. Turning the brain over to expose the ventral view reveals the olfactory tracts, which extend along the inferior surface of the frontal lobe (close to the midline).

These dorsal and ventral aspects are important because there are a number of dorsal and ventral distinctions for various neurocognitive and affective processes. These dorsal/ventral distinctions are often referred to as dual pathway models. Examples of these dual pathway models include: (1) *visual "where" and "what"*: Data leaving the occipital lobe follows a dorsal path for processing an object's spatial location (i.e., "where") and a ventral path involved in object identification and recognition (i.e., "what"; Goodale & Milner, 1992); (2) *dual stream model for*

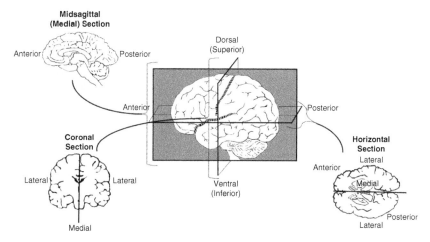

Figure 2.2　Typical cross-sections with directions labeled. Axial: sliced along the horizontal plane; Coronal: sliced vertically, looking at the brain from the front or back; Sagittal: sliced vertically, looking at the brain from the side.

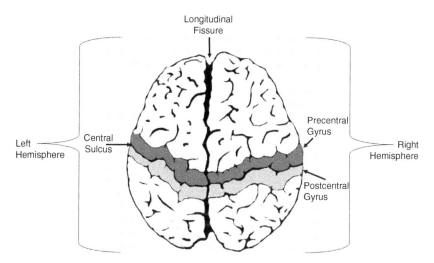

Figure 2.3　Dorsal view of the human brain.

language processing: Auditory data follows a dorsal stream involved in mapping sound to articulation and a ventral stream involved in mapping sound to meaning (Saur et al., 2008); and (3) *dual stream frontoparietal model of attention*: The dorsal system mediates top-down guided voluntary allocation of attention and the ventral frontoparietal system detects unattended or unexpected stimuli (Corbetta & Shulman, 2002). It is important to note that there is often overlap in the dual streams and that the flexible interaction between both streams enables the dynamic control of brain processes (Vossel, Geng, & Fink, 2014). Furthermore, it is important to note that these brain areas are best thought of as systems – not dichotomies of dorsal and ventral pathways.

2.5.2   *The Brainstem*

Starting with the brainstem, one finds an area subserving sensation via olfactory nerves (i.e., smell), auditory nerves (i.e., hearing and equilibrium), facial, optic nerves (i.e., vision), glossopharyngeal, and vagus nerves (i.e., taste). The brainstem can be subdivided into three areas: (1) hindbrain, (2) midbrain, and (3) diencephalon.

2.5.2.1   *The Hindbrain*

The dorsal aspect of the hindbrain (above the fourth ventricle) includes the sensory nuclei of the vestibular system that governs balance and orientation. The ventral aspect of the hindbrain (below the ventricle) includes more motor nuclei of the cranial nerves. The brainstem plays an important role in vital processes, as well as other visceral and somatic functions. All of these processes may be altered by impulses incoming via cranial nerves from the cerebellum or the forebrain. The cerebellum (i.e., "little brain") is a structure adjoined to the brainstem and has significant direct connections with both the spinal cord and the forebrain. It underlies the occipital and temporal lobes of the cerebral cortex with a primary role in coordination of muscular activity (e.g., postural and locomotor mechanisms). The automatic control processes of the cerebellum operate via reception of information from the skin, muscles, tendons, joints, organs of positional sense, and auditory and visual systems. Further, the cerebellum sends messages to the cerebral cortex and spinal cord to coordinate the timing and execution of motor events. The nuclei and fibers found in the brainstem make up a network known as the reticular formation, which plays a role in waking and sleeping.

2.5.2.2   *The Midbrain: Mesencephalon*

In this brain region one also finds the midbrain and its two main subdivisions: 1) the tectum (i.e., "roof"), which is the roof of the third ventricle, and 2) the tegmentum (i.e., "floor"), which is its floor. Primarily, two sets of bilaterally symmetrical nuclei make up the tectum. There is the anterior pair that is made up of the superior colliculi (i.e., "upper hills"), which receive projections from the retina and facilitate several visually associated behaviors. There is also a posterior pair called the inferior colliculi (i.e., "lower hills") that receive projections from the ear and mediate various auditory-related behaviors. The midbrain also includes the tegmentum, which contains nuclei for some of the cranial nerves, including a number of motor nuclei. Hence, in the midbrain (as is the case in the spinal cord) the dorsal aspect is sensory and the ventral part is motor.

2.5.2.3   Diencephalon (Between Brain)
The neurocognitive and affective processes at the level of the diencephalon begin to show greater import for the cyberpsychology researcher because the structures in this region involve awareness, affect, motivation, and the ANS. In general, the diencephalon is made up of three thalamic structures: thalamus (i.e., "inner room"); epithalamus (i.e., "upper room"); and hypothalamus (i.e., "lower room"). The thalamus is the primary control center governing movement and sensation. It is composed of nuclei that project to specific areas of the neocortex. Thalamic nuclei send data from three sources to the cortex:

1) **Sensory system data to targets:** Some thalamic nuclei relay data from sensory systems to their appropriate targets. An example of this can be seen in the lateral geniculate body that receives visual projections; the medial geniculate body that receives auditory projections; and the ventral-posterior lateral nuclei that receive sensations of touch, pressure, pain, and temperature projections from the body. In turn, these areas project to the visual, auditory, and somatosensory regions of the cortex.

2) **Data between cortical areas:** Other thalamic nuclei relay data between cortical areas. An example of this can be seen when the posterior cortex transmits projections to and receives projections back from the pulvinar nuclei (lesions of the pulvinar can result in attentional deficits and neglect syndromes).

3) **Data from forebrain and brainstem regions:** Some of the thalamic nuclei relay information from other forebrain and brainstem regions.

In summary, just about all the information that the cortex receives is first relayed through the thalamus.

Below the thalamus one finds the hypothalamus, which is composed of around twenty-two small nuclei, fiber systems that pass through it, and the pituitary gland. The pituitary gland is a pea-sized body that acts as the brain's primary endocrine gland. The pituitary is significant for its control of the growth, development, and functioning of other endocrine glands. The hypothalamus contains pairs of nerve centers that influence (turn on or off) fight or flight, rage reaction (along with the ANS), reward/punishment response, eating/drinking, sleeping/waking, and sexual behavior. Further, the part of the hypothalamus known as the mammillary bodies receives signals from the hippocampus via the fornix and projects them to the thalamus. In turn, the anterior nuclei of the thalamus receive input from the mammillary bodies that are involved in memory processing.

Another thalamic structure making up the diencephalon is the epithalamus. While its function is not well understood, it does include the pineal body, which seems to regulate seasonal body rhythms. An interesting note is that the philosopher Rene Descartes was so impressed by the unitary character of the pineal body (in comparison with other brain structures) that he contended that it is the seat of the soul. Descartes felt that the pineal gland was the location that mind and matter met and that it was also the source of the cerebral spinal fluid that he conjectured to initiate movements. From the diencephalon upward, the brain is made up of pairs of structures (two hypothalami, two thalami, and so on).

2.5.3   *Telencephalon (End Brain): Neocortex*

The neocortex (Latin for "new bark") is the largest and most recently evolved part (covers the two cerebral hemispheres) of the cerebral cortex in the human brain. It is involved in higher cortical functions such as conscious thought, language, initiation of motor movement, spatial reasoning, sensation, and perception. A number of folds are found in the cortex, which allows a larger cortex to fit into an appropriate dimension for the human head. At times the cortex is referred to as "gray matter" because of the gray that comes from the cell bodies of the neurons. The brain also includes "white matter" that comes from the myelin covering the fiber bundles making up brain tracts.

At this point, it is important to note that, like the diencephalon, the telencephalon is made of pairs of structures. It includes two cerebral hemispheres that are divided by the longitudinal fissure and a considerable divider called the falx that extends down from the meninges. The primary connection between the two cerebral hemispheres is made up of a series of cerebral commissures: corpus callosum, anterior commissure, and posterior commissure.

The cortex has a number of furrows on the surface called sulci (singular: sulcus) or fissures. The cortex also has rises or islands that are called the gyri (singular: gyrus). An obvious feature of the cortex is the horizontal line called the Sylvian fissure (also known as the lateral fissure) or sulcus. The sulcus that travels from the top of the brain down to meet the Sylvian fissure is called the Rolandic fissure (also known as the central fissure) or sulcus. Using these landmarks, cyberpsychologists can, more or less completely, map out the four lobes that divide the cortex: the frontal, temporal, parietal, and occipital lobes. First, the cortex includes two practically symmetrical hemispheres (a left and a right hemisphere) that are separated by the longitudinal fissure. The frontal lobes have stable boundaries that include a posterior limit at the central sulcus, an inferior boundary at the lateral fissure, and a medial boundary at the cingulate sulcus. For the temporal lobes there is a dorsal boundary at the lateral fissure. For the parietal lobes there is an anterior boundary at the central sulcus and an inferior boundary at the lateral fissure. It is interesting to note that there are no definite boundaries among the occipital and parietal and temporal lobes on the lateral surface of the brain.

2.6   Lobes of the Brain

As is evident from the description, the cerebral cortex is often divided into four lobes: frontal lobe, parietal lobe, occipital lobe, and temporal lobe. Each of these lobes is attendant to various functions that range from reasoning to sensory perceptions (see Figure 2.4).

2.6.1   Frontal Lobes

The frontal lobe is found at the front of the brain and is known for its involvement in executive-control: the ability to regulate one's behaviors, plan ahead, develop and maintain goals, maintain flexibility, and problem solve (Shallice & Burgess, 1996; Burgess & Simons, 2005; Chan, Shum, Toulopoulou, & Chen, 2008; see Diamond, 2013, for review). Traveling to the back of the frontal lobe to an area near the central sulcus one finds the motor cortex, which receives data from various areas of the brain and utilizes that data to direct body movements. Most of the dopamine-sensitive neurons of the cerebral cortex are found in the frontal lobes and are associated with reward, attention, short-term memory, planning, and motivation. Three distinct areas are found in the frontal lobe: 1) dorsolateral prefrontal cortex (dlPFC); 2) anterior cingulate cortex; and 3)

Introduction

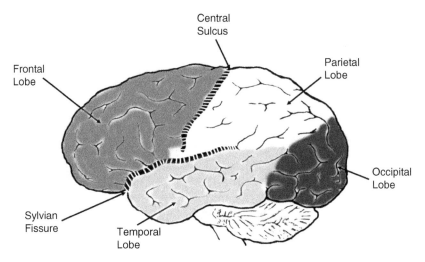

Figure 2.4 Lobes of the brain.

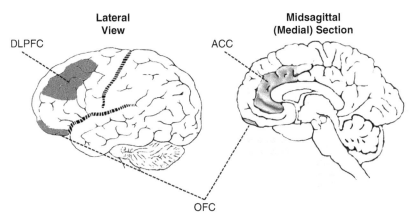

Figure 2.5 Lateral (left) and mid-sagittal (right) sections of the brain illustrating dorsolateral prefrontal cortex (DLPFC); orbitofrontal cortex (OFC); and anterior cingulate cortex (ACC).

orbitofrontal cortex (see Figure 2.5). The dlPFC is responsible for executive functions, working memory, cognitive flexibility, planning, inhibition, and abstract reasoning. The dlPFC has been implicated in online gaming disorders and tends to be activated in response to game cues (Ko et al., 2009). The ACC plays a role in a broad array of autonomic functions (e.g., regulating blood pressure and heart rate) and rationality (e.g., reward anticipation, decision-making, empathy, impulse control, and emotion). The anterior cingulate has been shown to have increased activation among excessive Internet game players following exposure to Internet video game cues (Han et al., 2010). The OFC (anatomically synonymous with the ventromedial prefrontal cortex) receives projections from the medial nucleus of the thalamus, and is thought to represent emotion and reward in decision-making. Reduced orbitofrontal cortical thickness has been found in individuals with Internet addiction (Hong et al., 2013). Furthermore, the frontal lobes include the piriform cortex (i.e., pyriform cortex), which is part of the rhinencephalon (situated in the telencephalon) and is associated with olfaction.

The frontal lobes are particularly vulnerable to damage due to their large size, location at the front of the cranium, and proximity to the sphenoid wing. It is important to note that the prefrontal cortex (i.e., frontal lobe) is connected to parts of the basal ganglia to form fronto-striatal connections (Hoshi, 2013; see section below on frontal subcortical circuits).

2.6.2 Parietal Lobe

As one continues to travel past the edge of the frontal lobe (i.e., past the central sulcus), one finds the parietal lobe that is associated with processing tactile sensory data (e.g., pain, touch, pressure). Within the parietal lobe is the somatosensory cortex, which is an essential processor of bodily senses. The parietal lobe integrates data from various senses in order to construct a coherent representation of the surrounding world. Some researchers have developed neurogaming applications that use the high alpha activity measured over the parietal lobe (related to relaxed alertness) for controlling characters in "World of Warcraft." For "Alpha-World," Alpha activity (EEG: 8–12 Hertz) recorded over the parietal lobe is used to control aspects of the game character (Bos et al., 2010). This work builds on the idea that a P300-based brain computer interface relies on stimuli that flash in succession (e.g., letters or symbols) that represent goals (e.g., controlling a cursor). Selective attention to such specific stimuli (e.g., a specific flashing symbol/letter) elicits a brain pattern called P300, which develops in centro-parietal brain areas about 300 milliseconds after the presentation of the stimulus (Citi et al., 2008).

For cyberpsychology research it is interesting to note that the brain categorizes objects via a ventral stream that arises from early visual areas and projects to regions in the occipito-temporal cortex to allow the person

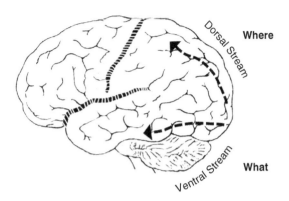

Figure 2.6 Schematic representation of the two visual processing pathways in the
human cerebral cortex.

to know "what" something is; and a dorsal stream that projects instead to
the posterior parietal cortex to identify "where" something is located (see
Figure 2.6).

2.6.3   Temporal Lobe

Traveling down from the lateral fissure one finds the temporal lobe.
Within the temporal lobe resides the primary auditory cortex, which is
important for interpreting sounds and language. In the medial aspect of the
temporal lobe (underneath the cortical surface) one finds the hippocampus
(named for its resemblance to a seahorse), which is associated with the
consolidation of information from short-term memory to long-term
memory and spatial navigation. In the parahippocampal gyrus, one finds
the entorhinal cortex, which is considered to be part of the hippocampal
region because of its anatomical connections. Additionally, one finds the
mammillary bodies and septal nuclei. The entorhinal cortex functions as
a hub in an extensive network for memory and navigation. It is the primary
interface between the hippocampus and neocortex. As such, the entorhinal
cortex-hippocampus system plays an important role in declarative (autobiographical, episodic, semantic) memories and, in particular, spatial
memories (memory formation, consolidation, and optimization in sleep).
Furthermore, the entorhinal cortex takes part in pre-processing of input
signals and impulse association. While the hippocampus is believed to be
involved in spatial learning and declarative learning, another part of the
medial temporal lobe called the amygdala (almond-shaped groups of

nuclei) is thought to be involved in emotional memory. Furthermore, the amygdala takes part in the modulation of memory consolidation. It is important to note that after a learning event the long-term memory for the event is not molded immediately. Instead, data about the event is gradually integrated into long-term storage in the temporal lobe over time (e.g., fear conditioning via long-term potentiation).

A function important for cyberpsychology and affective computing is the temporal lobe's capacity for processing faces. The fusiform face area is located on the ventral surface (part of the ventral pathway) of the temporal lobe on the lateral (lateral to the parahippocampal area – usually larger in the right hemisphere) side of the fusiform gyrus. While the fusiform face area and hippocampus are involved in encoding and recognizing a face, the amygdala tells one whether they like recognizing another's face. It is important to note that the central and medial nuclei of the amygdalae are considered to be part of the basal ganglia and limbic area.

2.6.4 Occipital Lobe

In the back portion of the brain one finds the occipital lobe, which is associated with the interpretation of visual stimuli and data. Located in the occipital lobe is the primary visual cortex, which receives and interprets information from the eyes. The occipital lobe is an important region for extracting data associated with visually evoked potentials used for brain–computer interactions (Allison et al., 2008).

2.6.5 Insula

Hiding in the depths of the Sylvian fissure is an additional cortical area called the insular cortex that not so long ago was only marginally of interest to the scientific community. In fact, the insular cortex did not receive a number on Brodmann's map (Craig, 2010a, 2010b). As a result, until recently little attention has been given to the examination of its role in neurocognitive and affective processes. That said, science has emerged that emphasizes the importance of the secret lobe that was concealed in the depths of the Sylvian fissure all along. Interestingly, new understandings of the insula are emerging and it has come to be understood as an epicenter of interoception, emotion, and awareness (Craig, 2009a, 2009b, 2010a, 2010b). Recent studies have revealed its role in attention processing and executive functioning (Droutman et al., 2015). Furthermore, across multiple studies, the insular cortex is increasingly viewed as a neural component that is regularly activated

(Duncan & Owen, 2000; Nelson et al., 2010; Yarkoni et al., 2011; Chang et al., 2012). It is important to note that many of these studies identify the importance of the insular cortex's involvement in various facets of decision-making (Garavan, 2010).

2.6.6   *Limbic Lobe and Basal Ganglia*

In addition to the neocortex, there are two other primary forebrain structures: the limbic lobe and the basal ganglia. The limbic lobe represents a course in the evolution of the human brain that covers the periphery of the brainstem. With the successive development of the neocortex, the limbic structures were positioned between the neocortex and the earlier brain structures. Given the evolutionary origin of these structures, some discuss this area as the reptilian brain. Furthermore, some argued for a "limbic system" that acts as the emotional center of the brain, with cognition being the business of the neocortex. That said, LeDoux (2003) has argued that the term "limbic system" is obsolete and should be abandoned. By this he means that neurocognition depends on acquisition and retention of memories via a primary limbic structure called the hippocampus. Specifically, LeDoux points to the fact that the "boundaries" of the "limbic system" have been redefined multiple times following advances in neuroscience. Hence, while it is the case that limbic structures are more closely related to affect, the brain is best thought of as an integrated whole. As a result, Broca's description of this area as a limbic lobe in 1878 is currently the most commonly accepted phraseology. The limbic lobe includes a complex set of brain structures that are located on both sides of the thalamus (right under the cerebrum). It is important to note that this is not a distinct system. Instead the limbic set represents a collection of brain structures from the mesencephalon, diencephalon, and telencephalon. This set of brain areas making up the limbic set include:

- **Cortical areas** such as the orbitofrontal cortex, piriform cortex (part of the olfactory system), hippocampus (consolidation of new memories), entorhinal cortex (related with memory and associative components), fornix (connects hippocampus with mammillary bodies and septal nuclei), and limbic lobe.
- **Subcortical areas:** Septal nuclei (pleasure zone), amygdala (emotional processes), and nucleus accumbens (reward, pleasure, and addiction).

- **Diencephalon:** Hypothalamus (regulates multiple autonomic processes), mammillary bodies (recollective memory), and anterior nuclei of thalamus (memory processing).

Each individual's affect is largely understood as an extension of her or his limbic set, and these areas have a great deal to do with the formation of memories. Furthermore, the limbic lobe structures are the areas in which the subcortical structures meet the cerebral cortex.

The basal ganglia ("lower knots" below the cortex) are an important part of the limbic system. This set of subcortical structures (including striatum) directs intentional movements. The basal ganglia perform functions largely associated with those described for the thalamus and hypothalamus. The basal ganglia include a number of structures: caudate, putamen, nucleus accumbens, olfactory tubercle, globus pallidus, ventral pallidum, substantia nigra, and subthalamic nucleus.. These brain structures are connected to the cortex. The area known as the caudate nucleus accepts projections from all areas of the cortex and transmits projections through the putamen and globus pallidus to the thalamus. From there data travels to the motor areas of the cortex. The basal ganglia also have reciprocal connections with the substantia nigra ("black area" in the midbrain). From a functional perspective, the main components of the basal ganglia can be understood in terms of the following:

- **Dorsal striatum:** caudate nucleus and putamen – mediates cognition involving motor function, certain executive functions, and stimulus-response learning.
- **Ventral striatum:** nucleus accumbens and olfactory tubercle – mediates reward, reinforcement, and motivational salience.
- **Globus pallidus:** regulation of voluntary movement.
- **Ventral pallidum:** inhibits motor-related areas; also involved in drug addiction.
- **Substantia nigra:** striatal input for dopamine; role in reward, addiction, and movement.
- **Subthalamic nucleus:** uncertain functionality; may perform action selection.

Note that this list primarily reflects a functional and not structural organization, as the dorsal striatum and globus pallidus can be conceptualized as anatomically distinct from the substantia nigra, nucleus accumbens, and subthalamic nuclei. The striatum (i.e., neostriatum or striate nucleus) is an

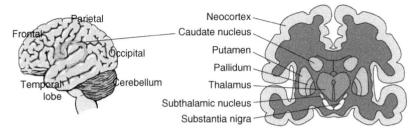

Figure 2.7 Basal ganglia. (A.M. Graybiel, *Current Biology*, 2000. Reprinted by permission of the publisher).

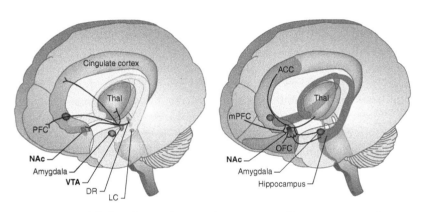

Figure 2.8 The brain's reward system. Dopaminergic afferents originate in the ventral tegmental area (VTA) and release dopamine in the nucleus accumbens (NAc), as well as other limbic areas. LC = locus coeruleus and DR = dorsal raphe (serotonergic) modulate reward. mPFC = medial prefrontal cortex, OFC = orbito-frontal cortex, ACC = anterior cingulate cortex, Thal = thalamus – these along with the amygdala and hippocampus send excitatory projections to the nucleus accumbens. (A.J. Robison and E.J. Nestler, *Nature Reviews Neuroscience*, 2011. Reprinted by permission of the publisher).

important component of the reward system that receives dopaminergic and glutamatergic contributions from various brain areas. Given that the striatum acts as the main input to the basal ganglia system, the basal ganglia are also believed to play an important role in stimulus-response learning (i.e., habit learning; see Figure 2.7).

Human neuroimaging studies have implicated a dopaminergic circuit (midbrain, striatum, amygdala, and prefrontal cortical regions) that is involved in processing rewards and supporting motivated behavior (see Figure 2.8).

The dorsal aspect of the striatum (caudate nucleus and putamen) is an important part of the reward system. Along with the nucleus accumbens, the dorsal striatum moderates the encoding of new motor programs that are associated with future reward acquisition. The ventral aspect of the striatum contains the nucleus accumbens, which tends to be active when an individual receives positive social feedback concerning their reputation (Izuma et al., 2008). The nucleus accumbens has a well-established association with processing of various types of reward (Haber & Knutson, 2010). Furthermore, a recent meta-analysis of 1351 studies revealed that when reward tasks are performed, the nucleus accumbens is active during the task 90 percent of the time (Ariely & Berns, 2010). Meshi and colleagues (2013) found that the nucleus accumbens responds significantly to gains in reputation and is predictive of social media use. The nucleus accumbens maintains close relations with the ventral tegmental area (in the midbrain at the top of the brainstem), which synthesizes dopamine. For cyberpsychologists, this dopaminergic circuit is notable for its engagement during video game play (Koepp et al., 1998; Hoeft et al., 2008).

2.7 Cortical Organization in Relation to Inputs and Outputs

Various regions of the cortex have different functions. While some regions receive information from sensory systems, others direct movements, and others are connecting sites between sensory and motor areas. As mentioned earlier, the most sensory inputs are relayed through the thalamic nuclei. The sites of these different inputs and outputs can be represented via a projection map that traces axons from the sensory areas into the brain and tracing axons from the neocortex to the motor systems (i.e., brainstem and spinal cord). Primary projection areas receive projections from structures outside the neocortex and/or conduct projections to the neocortex. For example, there are projections from the eye that can be traced to the occipital lobe; projections from the somatosensory system to the parietal lobe; projections from the ear to the temporal lobe; projections from the olfactory system to the ventral frontal lobe; and motor projections from the frontal lobe to the spinal cord. The primary sensory areas send projections to secondary adjacent areas and the motor areas receive fibers from secondary adjacent areas. These secondary areas can be understood as being more engaged in interpreting perceptions and/or organizing movements than are the primary areas. Finally, there are areas that lie between the various secondary areas that are referred to as tertiary or association areas that serve to connect and coordinate the functions of the secondary areas. These areas mediate more complex activities such as planning, memory, language, and attention. Again, it is important to note that these brain areas are best thought of as systems – not dichotomies or islands of brain areas for cognitive and affective processing. Hence, these brain areas can be viewed as a system of inputs, outputs, and sets of constituent components that work collaboratively to produce apposite outputs for particular inputs.

2.8 Large-Scale Networks and Frontal-Subcortical Circuits

As can be seen from the brief review in this chapter, the brain can be approximately separated into two main portions: the cortical and subcortical regions. As was mentioned earlier, the subcortical regions are phylogenetically older. These subcortical areas are associated with control of vital functions (e.g., heart rate, respiration, and temperature regulation), affective and instinctive responses (e.g., reflexes, fear, and reward), and basic neurocognitive processes (e.g., learning and memory). Cyberpsychologists interested in affective computing often use psychophysiological measures for physiological computing. For example, cyberpsychologists may monitor arousal via respiration rate, pupil constriction, muscle tonicity, salivary cortisol, electrodermal activity, and electrocardiogram sensors. The evolutionarily newer cerebral cortex supports most sensory and motor processing as well as "higher"-level functions (e.g., reasoning, strategizing, planning, pattern recognizing, and language processing). Given its accessibility for electroencephalography, this region is commonly used in cyberpsychology for brain–computer interface research.

2.8.1 *Early Conceptualizations of Large-Scale Brain Networks: Mesalaum's Five Principal Networks*

According to Mesalaum (2000), there are at least five principal networks that can be identified in the human brain: 1) right hemisphere-dominant spatial attention network with epicenters in the frontal eye fields, cingulate gyrus, and dorsal posterior parietal cortex (Doricchi et al., 2008); 2) a left hemisphere-dominant language network with epicenters in Wernicke's area and Broca's area (Catani & Mesulam, 2008); 3) a memory-emotion network with epicenters in hippocampo-entorhinal regions and the amygdaloid complex (Park et al., 2010); 4) an executive function-comportment network with epicenters in lateral prefrontal cortcx, orbito-frontal cortex, and posterior parietal cortex (Zappala et al., 2012); and 5) a face-and-object identification network with epicenters in lateral temporal and temporopolar cortices (Fox et al., 2008). While support for Mesalum's large-scale brain networks continues to emerge, it is important to note that the nodes of these large-scale networks were inferred from functional magnetic resonance imagery activations during tasks that manipulate one or more of these neurocognitive functions. As such, a full characterization of these large-scale functional brain networks will require a great deal of additional studies to validate the nodes of these networks by additional measures, assessment of their edges, and for the determination of whether other core networks exist (Bressler & Menon, 2010).

2.8.2   Executive-Control, Default-Mode, and Salience Networks

As mentioned in Chapter 1, large-scale brain networks are identifiable in the brain both while it is active and when it is at rest (Seeley et al., 2007). Currently, the three most prominent networks are the executive-control network, the default-mode network, and the saliency network. The first two networks can be recognized straightforwardly by observing the profile of activation and deactivation typically found during cognitive tasks. The executive-control network typically shows increases in activation during cognitively demanding tasks, whereas the default-mode network has decreased activation. The third network is a salience network that processes affective stimuli and allows for switching between the competitive interactions of two other major networks. This triple network model is useful for both functional (Bressler & Menon, 2010) and aberrant (Menon, 2011) neurocognitive processing. (see Figure 2.9).

The executive-control network appears to include brain areas that are known to have capacity for sustained attention (e.g., dorsolateral prefrontal cortex, lateral parietal cortex). Furthermore, the executive-control network has been identified for controlled attention to pertinent stimuli as behavioral choices are weighed against shifting conditions. The executive-control network exerts control over posterior sensorimotor representations and maintains relevant information so that actions may be selected. For example, coordinated prefrontal and posterior parietal control areas have been found to direct and coordinate sensory and motor areas during (and in preparation for) perceptuomotor processing (Bressler et al., 2008).

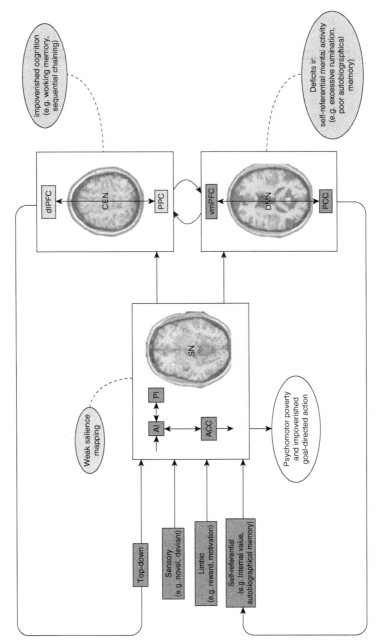

Figure 2.9 Large-scale brain networks. This figure illustrates key nodes for the three large-scale brain networks: Salience Network (SN): anterior insula (AI) and anterior cingulate cortex (ACC); Central Executive Network (CEN): dorsolateral prefrontal cortex (dlPFC) and the posterior parietal cortex (PPC); Default-Mode Network (DMN): ventromedial prefrontal cortex (vmPFC) and posterior cingulate cortex (PCC). This figure is notable for its depiction of both normal and aberrant functioning of the SN, CEN, and DMN. As depicted in the ovals, the figure presents situations in which weak salience processing plays a role in dysfunctional cognitive and affective behavior (V. Menon, *Trends in Cognitive Sciences*, 2011. Reprinted by permission of the publisher).

The default-mode network (dorsal and ventral medial prefrontal and parietal cortices) has been found (via neuroimaging) to be active while persons are in a state of quiet repose (e.g., with eyes closed; Raichle, 2015). Andrews-Hanna (2012, 2014) has suggested that these findings suggest a role for the default-mode network in self-generated cognition that is decoupled from the external world. Later in this book (Chapter 10), there will be a discussion on independent research in the social neurosciences that has revealed a "mentalizing network" that overlaps the default-mode network and includes neural correlates of a person's ability to mentalize (i.e., infer) the cognitions and feelings of others. Given the similarity between the default and mentalizing networks, questions have been generated in social neuroscience about whether the mentalizing network has mediation of internal aspects of social cognition as a core function (Li, Mai, & Liu, 2014).

In addition to the executive-control and default-mode networks, a salience network has emerged that reflects affective processing. The salience network is an intrinsically connected large-scale network anchored in the anterior insula and dorsal anterior cingulate cortex. The characterization of the salience network has enhanced our understanding of brain areas that take part in the processing of neurocognitively and affectively relevant events to direct flexible responding (Seeley et al., 2007).

2.8.3   Frontal-Subcortical Circuits

Frontal-subcortical circuits offer an additional way to understand neurocognitive and affective processes that involve composite inputs from the central nervous system to moderate the manifestation of neurocognition and affect through behavior and movement. Early conceptions by Alexander and colleagues (1986) emphasized the motor thalamocortical circuit as an architectural template to build the conception of other frontal-subcortical circuits. They described five cortically anchored circuits that offer a source for succeeding explication of the ways in which these five circuits influence movement and behavior. These cortically anchored circuits include behaviorally significant circuits that originate in the dorsolateral prefrontal, orbitofrontal, and superior medial frontal cortices. Furthermore, there are significant roles for posterior parietal and inferotemporal cortical areas via open connections to these circuits. Each frontal-subcortical circuit (FSC) shares a similar template of topography and physiology. The FSCs involve the same fellow structures, which are arranged in parallel (generally separated from each other) with anatomical positions that are preserved as they pass through the striatum (i.e., caudate and putamen), globus pallidus, substantia nigra, and thalamus (Mega & Cummings, 1994). Although each FSC also involves the same neurotransmitters and neuropeptides, the dissemination of neuroreceptor subtypes may mediate different activations for each FSC (see Figure 2.10).

Each FSC has a direct pathway and indirect pathway. The direct pathway results in sustained activation of the cortical component and releases glutamate to the corresponding areas of the striatum, which typically involves the caudate nucleus. Furthermore, some FSCs include the putamen or ventral striatum, which involves the nucleus accumbens. The binding of glutamate at receptors (i.e., N-methyl-Daspartate) in the striatum causes a release of GABA in the globus pallidus interna and substantia nigra. This results in diminished GABA release from the globus pallidus interna to the thalamic element of the circuit. When the thalamus is disinhibited it increases glutamatergic excitation of cortical regions.

In addition to the direct pathway, there is an indirect pathway for each FSC that balances the direct pathway. This indirect pathway deviates from the direct pathway when striatal efferents project to the globus pallidus externa. For the indirect pathway, there are GABA-ergic pallidal fibers that spread to the subthalamic nucleus and stimulate the direct pathway's globus pallidus interna with glutamate. A result of the glutamatergic influence on the globus pallidus interna is a counterbalancing of the direct pathway's GABA-ergic input at the globus pallidus interna (this would otherwise lead to inhibition of cortical activation via the thalamus). Hence, the direct pathway of the FSCs disinhibits the thalamus, whereas the indirect pathway inhibits it. The influences of direct and indirect pathways govern the control of thalamocortical connections and the cognitive, motoric, or behavioral outputs of the FSCs. Each of the pathways start with excitatory (glutamatergic) projections from the frontal cortex to particular areas within the striatum and then striatal output neurons project to either the direct (globus pallidus interna) or indirect (globus pallidus externa) pathway. While the direct pathway involves dopamine type 1 receptors, the indirect pathway has dopamine type 2 receptors. Furthermore, a number of neurotransmitters (and neuropeptides) influence the cortex, striatum, and globus pallidus within the FSCs. It is important to note that no single neurotransmitter has one role in activating or inhibiting a given FSC.

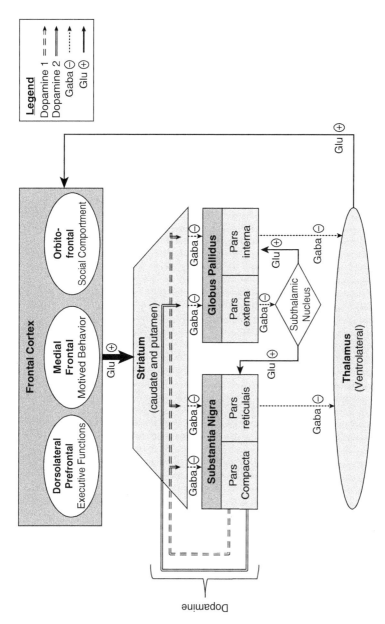

Figure 2.10 Frontal-subcortical circuits.

The FSCs have been found (from lesion and functional neuroimaging studies) to play roles in executive functions, motivation, affect, and motor control. To a large extent, there are three FSCs of interest to the current text: dorsolateral prefrontal (dlPFC) that controls executive functions, superior medial frontal (i.e., anterior cingulate) that regulates motivated behavior, and medial orbitofrontal (OFC) circuits involved in social comportment. Furthermore, there is a contributing role for the lateral OFC.

2.8.3.1 Executive-Control
Stuss (2007) described the importance of FSCs for executive-control, which includes 1) task setting (left dlPFC; Stuss et al., 2002), 2) task initiation (left and right superior medial frontal FSCs; Stuss et al., 2001), 3) error detection (right dlPFC; Stuss et al., 2002), and 4) behavioral-emotional self-regulation (medial OFC circuit; Stuss, 2007).

2.8.3.2 Motivation
The FSCs have also been found to be involved in motivation. Specifically, the anterior cingulate (Damasio & Damasio, 1989) and other areas of the superior medial frontal cortex (e.g., the supplementary motor area) and its subcortical circuit can be involved in motivation (Bechara & Van der Kooy, 1989). It is important to note that the superior medial circuit has open connections with limbic and hippocampal areas. Furthermore, the amygdala contributes (as a minor open afferent) to the superior medial circuit. The medial OFC circuit relays its prioritization of internal drives (aversive, appetitive) to the superior medial FSC (Mega & Cummings, 1994).

2.8.3.3 Affect
The OFC (medial and lateral) plays a role in affect and social behavior. Both the medial and lateral aspects of the OFC mediate a person's affect, impulse control, and recognition of reinforcing stimuli. In addition to the prototypical FSC connections to the ventral striatum, the medial OFC has open connections with limbic and paralimbic regions. Furthermore, the medial OFC has the most robust reciprocal associations with the amygdala (Zald & Kim, 1996). Given that the amygdala is also the major source of efferents to the brainstem and hypothalamus, affective processing by the medial OFC impacts a spectrum of endocrine, autonomic, and involuntary behavioral responses (Mesulam, 1985; Amaral, Price, Pitkaenen, & Carmichael, 1992; Critchley, Elliott, Mathias, & Dolan, 2000).

The ventromedial prefrontal cortex (vmPFC) has been found to be associated with emotion regulation.

Another important aspect of the limbic circuit is the amygdala. The amygdala includes a number of strong connections such as the vmPFC (emotion regulation) and superior temporal sulcus (multisensory processing capabilities for social cognition). These areas are consistently implicated within a broad neural workspace for social cognition. The amygdala is anatomically connected with almost every other brain region implicated in the social brain. Given the broadly circulated topography of the amygdala's anatomical connections (Freese & Amaral, 2009), Bickart and colleagues (2014) have argued that the amygdala can be understood as a hub within the social brain. Kanai and colleagues (2012) examined the relation between the number of friends a person has on an online social networking site and grey matter density in these areas. Findings revealed that the right superior temporal sulcus, left middle temporal gyrus entorhinal cortex, and the amygdala were related to online social network sizes. Hence, their findings suggest that the size of a person's online social network is related to focal brain structures that have been implicated for social cognition.

2.9 Dorsal (Cold) and Ventral (Hot) Pathways

At this point it is important to add a final structural and functional dichotomy to understandings of decision-making and executive-control. A relatively recent distinction has been made between executive inhibition and reactive inhibition (Nigg, 2003). Executive inhibition involves top-down (cortical → subcortical) effortful neurocognitive processing aimed at inhibitory control (Nigg, 2000, 2003); and reactive disinhibition reflects bottom-up (subcortical → cortical) processes, in which the individual attempts to regulate behavior in affect-laden situations (Nigg, 2003, 2006). This dual-process approach of "Hot" and "Cold" processing is increasingly prevalent among human neuroscientists (Goel & Dolan, 2003; Kerr & Zelazo, 2004; Bechara & Damasio, 2005; Seguin et al., 2007; Chan et al., 2008; Brock et al., 2009; Potenza & De Wit, 2010; Rubia, 2011).

The Cold cognitive control found in top-down executive functioning is contrasted with Hot affective aspects of cognitive control found in bottom-up processing (Zelazo et al., 2003). While Cold cognitive processing tends to be relatively logic-based and free from much affective arousal, Hot affective processing occurs with reward and punishment, self-regulation, and decision-making involving personal interpretation (Seguin et al., 2007; Chan et al., 2008; Brock et al., 2009). A number of studies have found that impairments in either the Cold or Hot cognitive functions may be related to deficits in everyday decision-making and functioning (e.g., independence at home, ability to work, school attendance, and social relations; see Chan et al., 2008, for review). For example, a notable source of ADHD-related deficits has been executive dysfunctions. While most traditional neuropsychological measures of executive functioning assess "cold" cognitive processes, little assessment of "hot" affective processing is included (Chan, Shum, Toulopoulou, & Chen, 2008). Research from studies using measures of cold executive functioning has revealed inconsistent results that make ADHD subtype differentiation unreliable (Willcutt et al., 2005).

Given the large overlap in the cyberpsychology literature between ADHD and social media use (e.g., Internet gaming, videogames, Facebook, media multitasking), it is important to understand the potential for a dual-pathway approach to understanding executive functioning. According to the dual-pathway model, executive functioning deficits are most apparent in complex activities of daily living where hot affective and motivational processes interact with cold decision-making processes (Rubia, 2011). Cold executive functions are the ones that are assessed by classic neuropsychological tests (e.g., attentional processing, working memory, planning, and inhibition) that are known to be mediated by lateral inferior and dorsolateral frontostriatal and frontoparietal networks (Castellanos et al., 2006; Rubia et al., 2006, 2007). Hot executive-control occurs in situations that involve robust affective significance. These hot executive-control tasks activate areas of the brain that are involved in emotional regulation and the brain's reward systems: orbito-frontal cortex, ventral striatum, and the limbic system (Kerr & Zelazo, 2004; Northoff et al., 2006).

One approach to differentiate hot and cold decision-making processes is to assess a user's ability to make advantageous choices. Here one finds support from the work of Damasio and colleagues in the development of the somatic marker hypothesis (Bechara & Damasio, 2005). According to the somatic marker hypothesis the affective component of experiences (e.g., "gut feelings" or "hunches" measured by heart rate and skin conductance) guide decision-making. The somatic marker is hypothesized to play a role in hot decision-making in that it biases the available response selections found in decision-making tasks. When persons are faced with decisions, they experience somatic sensations in advance of real consequences of possible different alternatives. Studies have shown that damage to vmPFC and the amygdala prevents the use of somatic (affective) signals for advantageous decision-making (Bechara et al., 1996, 1998; Bechara, Tranel, & Damasio, 2000).

2.10   Conclusions

In summary, this chapter has attempted to present a foundation for the conceptualization of the material covered in the chapters that follow. It is important to reiterate that this chapter is presented at the level of cyberpsychologists who are not already conversant with nervous system structure and function. The idea being that the material that follows may require the reader to return to this chapter for reminders related to basic understandings of neural networks and related brain structures for investigating the neural correlates of various media (e.g., social media, video games, virtual-reality).

An important aim of this chapter was to emphasize that the brain is not a general-purpose computer with a unified central processor. Instead, brain functional activity is better conceptualized in terms of large-scale neural networks that represent distinctive subsystems and relationships among them: language, face-and-object recognition, spatial attention, memory-emotion, and executive function-comportment. In the following chapters, examples will be given related to the way in which, both at rest and in the course of performing cognitive tasks, the brain is continuously generating and reshaping multifaceted patterns of correlated dynamics. The consciousness, neurocognition, and behavior of social media users, virtual environment participants, and video game players are understood as emergent properties of these large-scale neural networks. That said, these networks have nodes that can be separated into critical and participating epicenters. Throughout the rest of this book, emphasis will be placed on both large-scale networks and epicenters for understanding results gleaned from cyberpsychology research studies.

CHAPTER 3

Measurement in Cyberpsychology

3.1 Introduction

Affective computing platforms and cyberpsychology simulations offer the potential to stimulate and measure changes in the users' emotion, neuro-cognition, and motivation processes. The value in using simulation technology to produce virtual environments and videogames targeting such processes has been acknowledged by an encouraging body of research. Specific areas merging human neuroscience and simulated environments (e.g., virtual environments; virtual humans) include: clinical neuroscience, affective neuroscience (including affective computing), social neuroscience (including social media), and applied areas (videogame analytics, NeuroIS, and neuroergonomics). The use of psychophysiological measures in affective and neurocognitive studies of persons immersed in simulations and interacting with computers offers the potential to develop current physiological computing approaches (Allanson & Fairclough, 2004) into affective computing (Picard, 1997) scenarios.

The incorporation of psychophysiology into research with simulation and videogaming technologies is advancing at a steady rate. New discoveries and techniques are demanding a more rapid and advanced paradigm. In response to the demands, a wide variety of simulations and methods for affect detection have been developed. The range and depth of these approaches cover a large domain, from psychophysiological assessments of user experience in simple low fidelity task environments, to measures of users immersed in complex high-fidelity full-immersion simulators. All of these approaches rely on some type of representation of the real world.

This chapter offers a synopsis of psychophysiological metrics and quantification parameters that describes the assessment of particular physiological structures and systems. While this is not a comprehensive overview, it does offer a snapshot of the commonly used measurement process in psychophysiology. Given that much of affective computing,

psychophysiological computing, and cyberpsychological research is interested in examining the effects of varying levels of stimulus salience (e.g.,
intensity, arousal, automatic processing) and executive-control (cognitive
workload, controlled processing), these two indices will be discussed
throughout this chapter.

3.2 What is Psychophysiology?

The field of psychophysiology is interested in observing the interactions
between physiological and psychological phenomena. Psychophysiology
can be said to involve both the investigation of behavioral responses of the
user's psychophysiology at a biochemical and anatomical level, and the
impact of behavior on these same physiological properties. It is interesting
to note that the history of psychophysiological research has resulted in two
large bodies of scientific literature on psychological states and physiological
events that have only recently become effectively related to one another: (1)
central nervous system mechanisms of various psychological processes; and
(2) psychological factors and peripheral biological activities including
physical health.

Cacioppo and colleagues (2007) point out that although these two
bodies of literature have leaned toward an emphasis upon different psychological processes, there is cumulating evidence that these two areas of
study have much in common. For example, investigating the brain during
exposure to stressful stimuli can be a significant means for studying
biological stress and evaluating its impact in various systems. In fact,
psychophysiological investigation is increasingly interested in interdisciplinary approaches to affect, behavior, cognition, and personality.
The literature is coming together, and the potential for a brain-based
cyberpsychology is evident in a number of areas.

3.2.1 Affective Neurosciences

Affective neuroscience approaches that use psychophysiological metrics are
increasingly applied to affective computing (Calvo & D'Mello, 2010;
Picard, 1997), psychophysiological computing (Fairclough, 2009), and
assessments methods for neurocognitive and psychophysiological assessment (Courtney et al., 2010; Parsons, Courtney, & Dawson, 2013).
Historically, studies using affective psychophysiological approaches were
concerned with the relations between information processing and physiology (Jennings & Coles, 1991). Over the years, applied psychophysiology

approaches have been applied to investigate the relations between top-down cognitive task performance and bottom-up physiological events (see Chapter 6 for more on affective neuroscience). To illustrate this idea, one may consider an affective psychophysiology experiment in which the researcher aims to assess the ways in which perception, movement, attention, language, and memory in a virtual environment may be associated with particular autonomic and brain electrical activity (Parsons et al., 2009a; Wiederhold & Rizzo, 2005).

3.2.2   Clinical Neurosciences

In the clinical neurosciences, psychophysiological metrics are used for the study of psychological disorders and their relationship with physiological functioning and malfunctioning (Halliday, Butler, & Paul, 1987; Magina, 1997). At times, these psychophysiological measures are applied as part of a cognitive assessment. For example, the Iowa Gambling Task (IGT; Bechara, 2007) is a computerized assessment of reward-related decision-making that measures temporal foresight and risky decision-making. Studies have shown that damage to vmPFC (part of the orbitofrontal cortex) and the amygdala prevents the use of somatic (affective) psychophysiological signals for advantageous decision-making (Bechara, Tranel, & Damasio, 2000). While vmPFC patients were able to generate electrodermal responses when they received a reward or a punishment, amygdala patients failed to do so (Bechara et al., 1999). Furthermore, the clinical neurosciences are concerned with the examination of treatment outcomes and the impacts of drugs on psychological behavior and affective responses. For example, outcomes of virtual-reality exposure therapy are assessed in terms of behavioral outcomes and changes to physiological parameters (Costanzo et al., 2014; Côté & Bouchard, 2005; Diemer et al., 2014).

3.2.3   Social Neuroscience

Social neuroscientists use psychophysiology to study the interactions between physiology and behavioral responses during social processes (Cacioppo, 1994, Cacioppo, Berntson, & Crites, 1996). For example, interpersonal phenomena and group dynamics may be examined via observation of the interplay among various behaviors and each participant's psychophysiological responses (e.g., electrodermal response, pupil diameter, heart rate variability). Psychophysiological metrics are increasingly being used for assessment of social cognition using dynamic simulations (Macedonio et al., 2007; Schilbach, 2015). In a recent review of the emerging neuroscience of social media, Meshi, Tamir, and Heekeren (2015) discuss the growing global phenomenon of online social media (almost two billion users worldwide regularly using these social networking sites) and the potential for neuroscientists to make use of these pervasive social media sites to gain new understanding of social cognitive processes and the neural systems that support them.

3.2.4 Applied Psychophysiology

Applied psychophysiology can be found in psychophysiological metrics for videogame analytics, psychophysiological computing, and NeuroIS. This area is involved in the application of psychophysiological techniques and findings to recreational, occupational, and other areas of interest. For example, cyberpsychologists may be interested in monitoring particular physiological activities within an individual, and providing instant and appropriate feedback about this activity. This is known as biofeedback and has been used as an aid for relaxation therapy and a variety of other practical problems whose treatment may be amenable to self-control therapeutic techniques (Schwartz & Andrasik, 2003). Also under the applied psychophysiology umbrella is neuroergonomics, which combines information gleaned from the fields of psychophysiology, human neuroscience, and human factors (for a review see, Parasuraman & Rizzo, 2006). Psychophysiological metrics provide information regarding the participant's functional state to make real-time adaptations to a system designed to improve efficiency or vigilance, or reduce stress (Parasuraman & Wilson, 2008). In terms of videogame analytics, Nacke and colleagues (2008a, 2008b, 2010) have applied psychophysiological metrics to action games, which produce a visceral experience. Nacke's (2013) manuscript offers a thorough discussion for cyberpsychologists interested in psycho-physiological metrics for videogame research.

In summary, psychophysiological measures have a number of distinct advantages relative to behavioral measures for use in adaptive systems, and for improving human–computer interaction (HCI) in general. Psychophysiology involves covert signals that do not require added tasks from the participant; the data trace is continuously available for monitoring, whereas behavioral data tends to be available intermittently. Psychophysiological signals can still be monitored even if the system becomes completely automated, leaving no overt behavior from the participant (Alanson & Fairclough, 2004).

3.3   Principal Areas of Psychophysiological Data Acquisition

A person's arousal levels can be measured via self-reports, behaviors, and psychophysiological assessments (Cacioppo et al., 2007). Self-reports ask the participant to introspect and/or rate their perceptions of their internal psychological states or physiological sensations. While self-reports provide access to the participant's subjective experience, they may reflect the participant's misunderstanding of a scale or inaccurate recall of events. For example, the item's wording, context, and format are all factors that may influence self-report responses. Moreover, users will invariably have different reactions to a given application/environment, and without an assessment tool that can be employed online the cyberpsychology researcher will experience difficulties in identifying the causes of these differences, which may lead to a loss of experimental control of the research paradigm.

Another important limitation of self-reports is that certain affective responses are automatic neurocognitive processes. Unfortunately, self-reports miss this automatic processing because they are administered as questions and tap into controlled decision-making. According to dual-process models of automatic and controlled cognitive processing, controlled processes (e.g., performing a difficult calculus problem) are slow and accurate; and automatic processes (e.g., automatic response to a negative picture) reflect heuristics and biases that are fast and lower in accuracy. Additionally, self-reported measures require controlled (i.e., conscious) decision-making. This is a limitation because studies have revealed that self-report measures are uncertainly related to measures in which participants may or may not be unaware (in control) of the impact of their attitude and cognition. Such automatic responses are inherently difficult to self-report.

Another limitation of self-report measures is the temporal ordering of the questioning related to behaviors that were performed in the past. If a researcher wants to record risk perceptions as they occur (automatically and "in the moment"), then it is important to ask while the behavior is occurring instead of after the fact. Hence, a limitation of questionnaires is that they are given after the actual processing of the information occurred and represent post hoc appraisals of information that may have been processed automatically and unconsciously.

In the cyberpsychology literature, there is growing acceptance that although self-report measures have been found to be useful in some studies, these subjective questionnaires are susceptible to certain biases that can undercut the validity of study findings. An alternative is the use of psychophysiological metrics that record physiological events such as heart rate variability, electrodermal activity, muscle tension, brain waves and patterns, and changes in pupil diameter. In the following sub-sections, there will be a synopsis of psychophysiological metrics and quantification parameters. It is important to note that this is not a comprehensive over-view. That said, this review does offer a snapshot of the commonly used measurement process in psychophysiology. As mentioned earlier, there is an emphasis upon the effects of varying levels of stimulus salience (e.g., intensity, arousal, automatic processing) and executive-control (cognitive workload, controlled processing) throughout this chapter (see Table 3.1).

3.3.1 Electrodermal Activity

Electrodermal activity relates to how aroused a user is when they are exposed to a stimulus (e.g., gaming events while playing a game). Galvanic skin response involves the measurement of the direct response to an event. The measurement of skin conductance levels over time involves measuring the electrodermal activity of the skin. Assessing the activity of the sweat glands involves assessment of electrical activity on the surface of the skin. This activity is responsive to changes in affective and neurocognitive activity in general, and is often used as a general assessment of arousal.

Changes in the activity of the eccrine sweat glands are responsible for fluctuations in electrodermal activity. The eccrine sweat glands provide an atypical and useful index of autonomic functioning in that they are innervated exclusively by the sympathetic nervous system, as opposed to cardiovascular measures, which are influenced by parasympathetic vagal tone as well. Thus, skin conductance response can be utilized as a direct measure of sympathetic activation. Of particular interest in the current study is the way skin conductance responses are affected by fear-inducing or stressful stimuli. Öhman & Soares (1994) found that subjects high in fear for a certain biologically prepared stimulus (i.e., pictures of snakes or spiders) will exhibit potentiated electrodermal responses when presented with pictures of their specifically feared stimulus. Likewise, Globisch et al. (1999) found that fearful subjects showed increased skin conductance responses to feared stimuli relative to neutral and positive stimuli. Amygdala activation has also been demonstrated to co-occur with skin conductance responses when subjects view fearful faces (Williams et al., 2001). Additionally, individuals with a fear of flying showed a greater

Table 3.1 *Commonly used psychophysiological measures*

Psychophysiological Measure	Description	Strengths	Weaknesses
Electrodermal activity (EDA)	EDA detects electrical conductance of the skin relative to the level of sweat in the eccrine sweat glands. EDA occurs as a result of activations of the autonomic nervous system.	EDA is widely available, inexpensive, and commonly used. It has good temporal resolution.	EDA does not measure neural activity directly. The signal is noisy and degrades over time.
Electrooculography (EOG)	EOG and eye-tracking measures pupil dilation (index of arousal and valence) and eye movement. It allows for tracking of visual attention.	EOG is noninvasive and relatively easy to use. It has good temporal resolution and is sensitive to multiple factors.	EOG does not measure neural activity directly.
Electromyography (EMG)	EMG detects muscle activity, in which the electrical potentials that are associated with contractions of muscle fibers are measured.	EMG is widely available and noninvasive. It has good temporal resolution.	EMG does not measure neural activity directly. Electrode placement on the face can be disruptive for some participants.
Electrocardiography (ECG)	ECG detects heart rate responding. During highly arousing situations ECG reveals increased heart rate, as opposed to orienting responses which reduce heart rate.	ECG is widely available, inexpensive, and noninvasive. It has good temporal resolution.	ECG does not measure neural activity directly. Heart rate variability can be complicated to analyze.
Respiration	Respiration rate detects breathing changes in response to levels of arousal.	Respiration is widely available and noninvasive. It has good temporal resolution.	Respiration does not measure neural activity directly.

number of skin conductance fluctuations and higher skin conductance levels during flight than did controls (Willhelm & Roth, 1998). These findings indicate that greater levels of fear response result in greater skin conductance response potentiation and increased skin conductance levels. Skin conductance will generally increase as executive-control demands increase. For example, larger skin conductance responses are elicited during assessments of automatic and controlled processing. During the Stroop task, greater skin conductance responses are found when executive-control is needed (incongruent stimuli) (Kobayashi et al., 2007). Likewise, increased task difficulty using an *n*-back task results in increased skin conductance levels (Mehler et al., 2009).

An example from cyberpsychology can be seen in a study by Courtney and colleagues (2010), in which computer-generated stimuli were compared to standardized images of "real" phobic objects (e.g., the International Affective Picture System). In their study, they investigated skin conductance measures of negative affect when viewing static International Affective Picture System images, static computer-generated images, and moving videos of computer-generated images of feared stimuli and other negative stimuli which were not specifically feared. For example, a picture of a spider would be a "feared" stimulus for a spider-fearful participant, whereas a picture of a snake would be categorized as a "negative" stimulus for that participant. Findings revealed that the computer-generated videos elicited greater skin conductance arousal responses than the International Affective Picture System images and the computer-generated static images. In fact, computer-generated stills and International Affective Picture System images did not differ in eliciting skin conductance responses. Additionally, high-fear participants showed larger skin conductance responses to their feared stimulus than to the negative stimulus, especially when viewing computer-generated moving videos.

Another well-known use of skin conductance responses is for providing empirical support for the somatic marker hypothesis (see Chapter 9 of this book for more on the somatic marker hypothesis). Specifically, skin conductance is measured using an affective decision-making paradigm aimed at mimicking real-life decision-making in the way it factors uncertainty, reward, and punishment: the Iowa Gambling Task (IGT; Bechara et al., 1994; Bechara, 2007). According to Bechara and colleagues (1997), there is a correlation between successful performance and heightened skin conductance responses when healthy participants anticipate unconsciously disadvantageous decisions on the IGT (Bechara et al., 1997; Crone et al.,

2004; Suzuki, Hirota, Takasawa, & Shigemasu, 2003). These anticipative skin conductance responses have been interpreted as an index of somatic marker signals.

3.3.2 Electrocardiography: Cardiac Response, Blood Pressure, and Blood Volume

Heart rate response during highly arousing and fearful situations is generally associated with defensive responding, which results in increased heart rate, as opposed to orienting responses, which reduce heart rate (Berntson et al., 1992; Fredrickson, 1981). Van Oyen, Witvliet, and Vrana (1995) found the greatest increase in heart rate acceleration when startle probes were presented during a high arousal mental imagery task compared to low-arousal imagery. Fearful subjects exposed to prolonged fear-inducing situations have also been evidenced to maintain a sustained heightened heart rate compared to controls during the exposure period (Willhelm & Roth, 1998). In general, increased arousal caused by fearful situations tends to result in heart rate increases.

ECGs of participants taking part in paced auditory serial addition tasks (PASAT) have shown increased heart rate at onset of the task, and elevated rates throughout compared to baseline (Ring et al., 1999). Additionally, numerous studies using various cognitive tasks have evidenced increased heart rate associated with increased cognitive workload (e.g., Carroll et al., 1986; Kennedy & Scholey, 2000; Mehler et al., 2009; Sloan et al., 1991).

An example from cyberpsychology research can be found in a study by Parsons and colleagues (2013), in which the authors attempted to assess the potential of a three-dimensional virtual-reality Stroop task for investigation of supervisory attentional processing. The virtual-reality Stroop task was completed during exposure to the high- and low-threat zones. The virtual-reality Stroop task consisted of four conditions: (1) word reading, (2) color naming, (3) simple interference (stimuli presented in the middle of windshield), and (4) complex interference (stimuli presented in variable locations on windshield). Heart rate metrics were collected to assess varying levels of user arousal. A psychophysiological difference (i.e., heart rate) in arousal was found between low- and high-threat zones.

3.3.3 Respiration

Respiration rate has consistently been shown to increase in response to heightened levels of arousal associated with fear (for review, see Boiten,

Frijda, & Wientjes, 1994). Etzel et al. (2006) found that music clips that subjects rated as fearful led to significantly increased rates of respiration compared to sad music clips. Likewise, responses to fear-inducing film clips have been demonstrated to significantly increase respiration rates compared to sad and neutral film clips (Kriebig et al., 2007). Mental imagery of fearful events has also been shown to increase rates of respiration (Rainville et al., 2006).

An increase in respiratory rate has been consistently associated with increased cognitive demand (e.g., Backs & Selijos, 1994; Brookings, Wilson, & Swain, 1996; Mehler et al., 2009). Backs and Selijos (1994) found that rates of respiration increased as task difficulty increased in a working memory task. During an air traffic control simulation with three levels of task difficulty, air traffic controllers exhibited increased rates of respiration as task difficulty increased (Brookings, Wilson, & Swain, 1996).

An example from cyberpsychology is a study by Owens and Beidel (2014), in which they investigated the potential of a virtual environment to elicit the physiological and subjective arousal typically associated with public speaking. This study aimed to (1) determine whether speaking to a virtual audience elicited significant increases in physiological response (e.g., respiratory sinus arrhythmia) and subjective distress over baseline resting conditions; (2) assess whether participants with social anxiety disorder had a greater increase in physiological arousal and subjective distress when speaking in front of a live audience vs. the virtual environment; and (3) investigate if participants with social anxiety disorder had greater changes in physiological and self-reported arousal during each speech task compared to controls. All participants gave an impromptu speech in front of an in vivo and virtual audience while measures of physiological arousal and self-reported distress were obtained. Findings suggested that the virtual-reality task elicited significant increases in respiratory sinus arrhythmia and self-reported distress over baseline conditions.

3.3.4   Electrooculography: Eye Movements and Pupillary Response

Pupil dilation tends to operate in a similar fashion to electrodermal activity in relation to fear-induced arousal. Negative sounds have been associated with increased pupil dilation, and subjective ratings of arousal were also positively correlated with pupil dilation (Partala & Surakka, 2003). Indeed, electrical stimulation of the central nucleus of the amygdala, resulting in a fear response, leads to pupil dilation.

Pupil dilation is often utilized as an index of executive-control (e.g., cognitive workload and task difficulty). The Index of Cognitive Activity (ICA) was created to measure the dilation reflex, which is a response caused by the presence of a cognitive stimulus, as opposed to the light reflex, which is caused by changes in the light source (Boehm-Davis et al., 2003). The two reflexes are controlled by different muscle groups. The dilation reflex results in activation of the radial muscles and inhibition of the circular muscles, creating a burst of dilation larger than either muscle group could produce alone. Numerous studies have reported increased pupil dilation in response to increased cognitive demand (Beatty & Wagoner, 1978; Pomplun & Sunkara, 2003; Porter, Troscianko, & Gilchrist, 2002; Schaefer et al., 1968).

Examples of some cyberpsychology applications of electrooculography (EOG) include:

- Usakli and Gurkan (2010) used EOG for using a virtual keyboard;
- Deng et al. (2010) used EOG for operating a TV remote control and for a game;
- Gandhi et al. (2010) used EOG for controlling a multitask gadget.

3.3.5   Electromyography: Measurement of Muscle Activity

Electromyography (EMG) is a technique used by cyberpsychologists to measure muscle activity. During a typical EMG assessment, electrical potentials that are associated with contractions of muscle fibers are measured. The potentials from these contracting muscles are transitory impulses that last between 1 and 5 milliseconds (ms). These EMG potentials are detected using devices known as transducers. Amplitudes of recorded signals may fluctuate between about 1 and 1000 microvolts (μV). Note that recordings of less than 20μV are difficult to obtain. Frequencies of electrical impulses can occur someplace between 20 and 1000 hertz (Hz). The available EMG quantitative measures vary depending upon the focus of investigation. If a cyberpsychology researcher is looking at the behavior of a single nerve fiber (or a homogeneous group of fibers), the single (or compound fibers) action potential may be measured in response to a specific stimulus (e.g., small electric shock). For situations in which the cyberpsychologist is interested in looking at the long-term activity of muscle fibers, the integrated amplitude, frequency of nerve firing (impulses) and gradients of frequency responses may be examined. One use of EMG (i.e., startle eyeblink) has been for the assessment of automatic and controlled attentional processes in orienting responses. The orienting response is often understood as a controlled attentional processing of an orienting stimulus (e.g., salient stimulus) in the environment (Dawson et al., 1982; Kahneman, 1973; Öhman, 1992). According to this view, habituation of the orienting response results in greater automatic processing and reduced controlled attentional processing of the stimulus. For example, Dawson, Filion, and Schell (1989) have shown that habituation of the orienting response is associated with reduced allocation of controlled resources as indicated by secondary reaction time.

In a cyberpsychology study using EMG and other indices, Ravaja and colleagues (2008) investigated emotional valence- and arousal-related phasic psychophysiological responses to different violent events in a first-person shooter videogame called "James Bond 007: NightFire." They recorded event-related changes in zygomaticus major, corrugator supercilii, and orbicularis oculi EMG activity and skin conductance level (SCL). The participants recorded their emotions. During gameplay, wounding and killing an opponent elicited increased SCLs and decreased zygomatic and orbicularis oculi EMG activity. Another result from gameplay was that wounding and death of the player's own character (i.e., James Bond) resulted in increased SCL and zygomatic and orbicularis oculi EMG activity. Further, there was a decrease in corrugator activity.

3.4   Neuroimaging Used in Cyberpsychology Research

In addition to psychophysiological measures of autonomic responding, there are a number of studies incorporating neuroimaging measures. The incorporation of neuroimaging into research with simulation and videogaming technologies is advancing at a steady rate. New discoveries and techniques are demanding a more rapid and advanced paradigm. In response to the demands, a wide variety of simulations and methods for affect detection have been developed (see Table 3.2).

3.4.1   *Electroencephalography: Electrical Potentials of the Brain*

Cyberpsychologists may use an electroencephalogram (EEG) to measure neural activity in the cerebral cortex. A number of electrodes are

Table 3.2 *Neuroimaging techniques used in cyberpsychology research*

Psychophysiological measure	Description	Strengths	Weaknesses
Electroencephalography (EEG)	EEG detects (at the surface of the scalp) electrical potential differences that are derived from neural activity	EEG is widely available and noninvasive. Its long history of use has resulted in a well-established theoretical basis for neural processing. It has excellent temporal resolution	EEG does not measure neural activity directly. The signal must travel through tissue and skull. EEG has poor spatial resolution
Magnetoencephalography (MEG)	MEG is a functional neuroimaging technique for mapping brain activity by recording magnetic fields produced by natural occurring electrical currents	MEG is noninvasive. It has independence of head geometry compared to EEG. MEG has high temporal resolution as opposed to fMRI	MEG is expensive. While EEG is sensitive to both tangential and radial components of a current source in a spherical volume conductor, MEG detects only its tangential components
Structural Magnetic Resonance Imaging (sMRI)	sMRI uses a variety of techniques to image brain morphology	VBM allows for comparison of the volume of brain areas and the density of gray and white matter. DTI helps to identify interconnected brain structures	sMRI is expensive. MEG has better temporal resolution
Functional Magnetic Resonance Imaging (fMRI)	fMRI measures the changes in the levels of blood oxygen in the brain that are indicative of neuronal activity	fMRI allows for finer and more detailed imaging of the brain relative to structural MRI. Further, fMRI is fast,	fMRI is expensive. Further, PET is preferred in situations where research questions

Technique	Measures		
Positron Emission Tomography (PET)	PET measures the brain's metabolic activity via photons from positron emissions (i.e., positively charged electrons)	has enhanced spatial resolution, and it does not have health risks (e.g., PET) PET allows for the mapping of neuronal activity during the performance of a particular task. Further, neurotransmitters can be distinguished with PET, which makes it advantageous over MRI techniques	require neurotransmitters be distinguished PET is invasive (inject a radioactive 2-DG. PET has low spatial resolution, time needed to obtain a scan, as well as potential radiation risk
Single Photon Emission Computed Tomography (SPECT)	SPECT, like PET, measures the brain's metabolic activity. Increased metabolic activity in specific brain regions equals enrichment of gamma rays	SPECT, unlike PET, allows for counting individual photons	SPECT resolution is poorer because resolution depends on proximity of gamma camera
Functional Near-infrared Spectroscopy (fNIRS)	fNIRS allows researchers to localize and measure cerebral blood flow and oxygenation	fNIRS has the potential to allow more ecologically valid investigations that can translate laboratory work into more realistic everyday settings	fNIRS is a relatively non-invasive, safe, portable, and low-cost method

positioned in precise areas (i.e., anterior, posterior, left and right) of the participant's head. Once positioned, these electrodes can be used to measure voltage fluctuations between pairs of electrodes. The voltage fluctuations result from excitation of neuronal synapses (Schomer & Da Silva, 2012). These electrical signals are very small and are measured at the order of microvolts. Spontaneous EEG is a continuous stream of neural activity that is constantly extant within the brain. This neural activity can be understood as oscillatory waveform patterns that have traditionally been subdivided into four main bands relative to their frequency:

- delta (low frequency, 0.5–4 Hz; amplitude 20–200µV)
- theta (low frequency, 4–7 Hz; amplitude 20–100µV)
- alpha (dominant frequency, 8–13 Hz; amplitude 20–60µV)
- beta (high frequency, 13–40 Hz; amplitude 2–20µV)

Frequently, researchers have used EEG to measure levels of arousal that range from delta for deep sleep through beta for alert attentiveness.

In other situations, cyberpsychologists are interested in recording spontaneous brain activity, in which a response of the brain to quantifiable stimuli results in a change in electrical activity. In such situations, cyberpsychologists use event-related potentials (ERPs) to measure the brain and behavior relationships, These ERPs occur as a result of electrophysiological neuronal responses to stimuli (Luck & Kappenman, 2011). While some ERPs last less than 10 ms (e.g., brainstem auditory evoked potential generated by subcortical areas), others last up to a second or longer (e.g., Bereitschafts potential or readiness potential). Given the low level of brain response over (and above) normal background EEG activity, several evoked responses are collected, summed, and averaged to produce an average evoked response (AER). The basis for this summation is that activity in the waveform that is not generated in response to the stimulus will be almost random and hence sum to near zero over occasions, while activity that is related to the stimulus will be enhanced by adding these stimulus-generated signals together. Fourier analysis is a mathematical technique used for analyses of spontaneous EEG data. Using Fourier analysis, the cyberpsychologist decomposes the EEG waveform into separate oscillating components, with each including a particular frequency of oscillation and magnitude. After this transformation, the cyberpsychologist has an index of signal power at certain frequencies.

3.4.2 Magnetoencephalography

Magnetoencephalography (MEG) measures the tiny magnetic fields in the brain that emerge when neurons talk to each other via electrical messages. A primary component of MEG is the small wire coils that are called super-conducting quantum interference devices (SQUIDs). These SQUIDs register the brain's magnetic field. A SQUID is very sensitive, but only works in settings wherein the temperature is extremely low (i.e., about 270°C below zero). In an effort to keep them cool, the SQUIDs are covered in liquid helium. In the MEG, hundreds of SQUIDs are arranged outside a helmet. MEGs are used by cyberpsychologists for measuring time courses of activity. Using MEG, cyberpsychologists can resolve events with a precision of 10 milliseconds or faster. This is a significant increase over fMRI, which depends on changes in blood flow and can at best resolve events with a precision of several hundred milliseconds. Furthermore, MEG can accurately pinpoint sources in primary auditory, somatosensory, and motor areas and create functional maps of the human cortex during more complex cognitive tasks. The use of MEG responses in the brain before, during, and after the introduction of such stimuli can then be mapped with greater spatial resolution than it can with EEG.

3.4.3 Positron Emission Tomography

Positron Emission Tomography (PET) is a neuroimaging technique that allows the cyberpsychologist to study brain function at the molecular level. The brain's metabolic activity is measured through the use of photons from positron emissions (i.e., positively charged electrons). A radioactive 2-deoxyglucose (2-DG) solution is injected into a participant. The 2-DG is taken up by active neurons in the brain. The 2-DG amounts in neurons and positron emissions are incorporated for the quantification of metabolic activity in the brain. Hence, PET can be used for mapping of neuronal activity while the participant takes part in a particular task. A particular benefit of PET is that individual neurotransmitters can be distinguished. In certain situations, this makes PET advantageous over MRI techniques. PET can measure activity distribution in detail. While there are some advantages to PET, there are also some limitations. For example, PET has relatively low spatial resolution; it takes a good deal of time to obtain a scan. Historically, one of the greatest concerns for PET has been the potential radiation risk (Townsend, Valk, & Maisey, 2005).

A recent cyberpsychology study by Kim and colleagues (2011) used PET to investigate striatal dopamine D2 receptors (see Chapter 2 for more on dopamine) in individuals with Internet addiction. This study reflects the growing interest in associating Internet addiction with abnormalities in the brain's dopaminergic brain. To assess whether Internet addiction is related to reduced levels of dopaminergic receptor availability in the striatum, a radiolabeled ligand [C]raclopride and PET were used to assess dopamine D2 receptor binding potential in men with and without Internet addiction. Results revealed that participants with Internet addiction had decreased levels of dopamine D2 receptor availability in subdivisions of the striatum including the bilateral dorsal caudate and right putamen.

3.4.4   Single Photon Emission Computed Tomography

Single Photon Emission Computed Tomography (SPECT) is a subform of PET. It is similar to PET in that radioactive tracer is injected into the participant's blood stream that speedily travels to the brain. The greater the metabolic activity in specific brain regions, the greater the enrichment of gamma rays. Computerized techniques measure the radiation emission in accordance with brain layers and metabolic activity. A difference between PET and SPECT is that SPECT allows for counting of individual photons. This additional functionality comes at a price because the resolution from SPECT depends on the proximity of the gamma camera that measures neuronal radioactivity (Meikle, Beekman, & Rose, 2006).

An example of SPECT in cyberpsychology research is Hou et al.'s (2012) examination of reward circuitry dopamine transporter levels in Internet addicts compared to a control group. The research team performed 99mTc-TRODAT-1 SPECT scans using Siemens Diacam/ e.cam/icon double detector SPECT. Results revealed reduced dopamine transporters in the group of Internet addicts. These results are similar to neurobiological abnormalities found in other behavioral addictions. Furthermore, they found that striatal dopamine transporter (DAT; necessary for regulation of striatal dopamine) levels were decreased in the group of Internet addicts and that volume, weight, and uptake ratio of the corpus striatum were reduced relative to controls. Interestingly, the reported dopamine levels were similar to those found in persons with substance addictions.

3.4.5   Structural Magnetic Resonance Imaging

Structural Magnetic Resonance Imaging (sMRI) makes use of various techniques to image brain morphology (Huettel, Song, & McCarthy, 2004). For example, Voxel-Based Morphometry (VBM) can be used to compare the volume of brain areas and the density of gray and white matter (Ashburner & Friston, 2000). Voxel-based morphometry (VBM) is a neuroimaging technique that allows the cyberpsychologist to investigate focal differences in brain anatomy. It uses a statistical approach called statistical parametric mapping. While traditional morphometry allows for assessment of the volume of the whole brain (or its subparts) through the identification of regions of interest on brain scanned images, VBM is faster and each voxel represents the average of itself and its neighbors. Another technique used for sMRI is Diffusion-Tensor Imaging (DTI), which is an approach utilized when the cyberpsychologist is interested in imaging white matter. Specifically, DTI measures the diffusion of water molecules in the brain, which aids the cyberpsychologist in identifying interconnected brain structures by using fractional anisotropy. The results from DTI offer an index of fiber density, axonal diameter, and myelination in white matter (Le Bihan et al., 2001).

For the cyberpsychologist interested in the impact of heavy media multitasking on the brain, an example of VBM can be found in a neuroimaging study by Loh and Kanai (2014). They used voxel-based morphometry to investigate the brain structures of 75 adults. Findings revealed that, independent of individual personality traits, participants who were heavy media multitaskers had smaller grey matter density in the anterior cingulate cortex (see Chapter 2). The anterior cingulate cortex is important for sensorimotor, nociceptive, neurocognitive, affective, and motivational processes. The authors argue that the findings of a smaller anterior cingulate cortex in heavy media multitaskers most likely reflects higher cognitive processes since media multitasking has been consistently associated with cognitive control.

3.4.6   Functional Magnetic Resonance Imaging

Functional magnetic resonance imaging (fMRI) is a rapidly growing technique for relating brain activity to behavior. Using fMRI, cyberpsychologists can measure changes in the levels of the brain's blood oxygen that are indicative of neuronal activity. Specifically, using fMRI cyberpsychologists can measure the ratio of oxyhemoglobin (i.e., hemoglobin containing oxygen) to deoxyhemoglobin (i.e., hemoglobin that has released oxygen) in the brain. Blood flow in "active" brain areas increases to transport more glucose and brings in more oxygenated hemoglobin molecules. The fMRI measures changes in blood oxygen level dependent (BOLD) response, which are associated with changes in underlying neural activity in a given brain area. For the cyberpsychologist, measurement of this brain-based metabolic activity allows for finer and more detailed imaging of the brain than can be obtained from sMRI. Furthermore, fMRI has the following advantages: speed of brain imaging, spatial resolution, and it does not have the potential health risk found in PET scans (Sexton, 2013).

An example of fMRI and virtual-reality for cyberpsychology research can be found in Hung and colleagues' (2014) manuscript that used fMRI and virtual-reality technology to predict driving ability after brain damage. Results revealed that cerebellar functioning is associated with motor-speed coordination and complex temporal-motor integration necessary to execute driving behaviors. While the speed control during basic driving conditions of drivers with cerebellar damage was significantly compromised, their ability to perform during interactive driving situations was preserved.

3.4.7   *Functional Near-Infrared Spectroscopy*

Functional Near-infrared Spectroscopy (fNIRS) is a neuroimaging tool that allows the cyberpsychology researcher to localize and measure cerebral blood flow and oxygenation. The fNIRS tool offers real-time diagnostic and non-invasive measures that are capable of measuring tissue oxygenation StO_2, using relatively inexpensive and portable tools. The fNIRS uses optical radiation (i.e., photons with wavelengths near the infrared range of 700–950nm). The fNIRS probes have light sources that breach tissues, and optical fibers (detectors) that detect light radiation leaked from the biological tissue after completing a depth and bended variable path.

An example from cyberpsychology can be found in Seraglia et al.'s (2011) presentation of a methodology that involves the use of NIRS while participants experienced immersive VR. For their study, they wanted to insure a proper fNIRS probe application. They developed a custom-made VR helmet. In their efforts to test the adapted helmet, they used a virtual version of the line bisection task. In the task, participants could bisect the lines in a virtual peripersonal or extrapersonal space through the manipulation of a Nintendo Wiimote controller that allowed for the participants to move a virtual laser pointer.

To summarize, psychophysiological metrics provide a means of obtaining objective and ongoing measures of user-state through noninvasive and non-conscious methods to improve experimental control. Arousal responses to salient stimuli and executive-control are two aspects of participant-state that provide vital information for the successful implementation of affective computing and (psychophysiological computing) systems that can be applied to improve real-world performance. However, testing such systems in real-world environments can be dangerous and costly (e.g., development of a psychophysiologically based system to assist airplane pilots during flight). Virtual-reality (VR) scenarios offer the potential for simulated environments to provide cogent and calculated response approaches to real-time changes in user emotion, cognitive state, and motivation processes. The value in using simulation technology to produce virtual environments targeting such processes has been acknowledged by an encouraging body of research.

3.5　Quantifying of Biosignal Data

3.5.1　Level of Measurement

Psychophysiological metrics have a high level of precision and are almost always at true ratio level, which means that these metrics act like interval level measurements and possess a true zero. Nevertheless, cyberpsychologists using these measures have to determine the psychological meaningfulness of biosignal changes. For example, a statistically significant change in heart rate variability may not necessarily signify a psychologically meaningful change in executive-control. Therefore, the interpretation of psychophysiological data is often more qualitative than our quantitative metrics seem to imply. As a result, when interpreting physiological metrics, cyberpsychologists endeavor to balance associations between brain activations, autonomic responses, behaviors, and interpretations about what the aforementioned mean. According to Cacioppo and colleagues (2007) there are five common associations between cognitions and body responses:

- **One-to-one relationship:** A cognitive process is directly associated with a bodily response (and vice versa). Such a relationship would allow the cyberpsychologist to identify cognitive process based on a bodily response. Note, such a relation is rarely possible.

- **One-to-many relationship:** A cognitive process is associated with many bodily responses. Note that for this relation the cyberpsychologists cannot draw a conclusion regarding cognitive processes.
- **Many-to-one relationship:** Multiple cognitive processes are associated with one bodily response. Note that even though this scenario is less effective than a one-to-one relation, it is often used in psychophysiological evaluations. Furthermore, it allows the cyberpsychologist to make assumptions about cognitive processes based on a bodily response.
- **Many-to-many relationship:** Multiple cognitive processes are associated with a number of bodily responses. Note that like the others (mentioned above) this association does not allow for conclusions regarding cognitive processes based on bodily responses.
- **Null relationship:** No relation exists between cognitive processes and bodily responses.

Of the above relational possibilities, the most common is the many-to-one relationship. For the many-to-one relation, one bodily response may be related to multiple cognitive effects or processes. As a result, cyberpsychologists need to maintain that there is not a direct mapping of a discrete emotional state to bodily responses. Hence, when cyberpsychologists measures bodily signals, they are measuring basically the activities of nerves, muscles, and glands.

It is important to note that the scale of psychophysiological measurement is superior to that of nearly all other psychological data (e.g., surveys and self-reports). That said, while the electrically based psychophysiological measures are exact to a predetermined level of accuracy, they are also susceptible to noise that can utterly distort any parameter or signal. In order to measure any psychophysiological parameter, it is important that the cyberpsychologists have fairly detailed knowledge of the underlying physiology (see Chapter 2), the physical properties of the transducers or sensors, the properties of the signals generated, and the superfluity of potential approaches to analyses.

3.6   Conclusion

This chapter describes the psychophysiological and neuroimaging measures that have been (and continue to be) used for affective computing platforms and cyberpsychology simulations. The incorporation of psychophysiology into research with simulation and videogaming technologies is advancing at a steady rate. New discoveries and techniques are demanding a more rapid and advanced paradigm. In response to the demands, a wide variety of simulations and methods for affect detection have been developed. The range and depth of these approaches cover a large domain, from psychophysiological assessments of user experience in simple low-fidelity task environments to measures of users immersed on complex high-fidelity full immersion simulators. All of these approaches rely on some type of representation of the real world.

The field of psychophysiology was discussed in terms of both the investigation of behavioral responses of the user's psychophysiology at a biochemical and anatomical level, and the impact of behavior on these same physiological properties. Psychophysiological investigation is increasingly interested in interdisciplinary approaches to affect, behavior, cognition, and personality. While these literatures are coming together, their application to the human neurosciences is evident in a number of areas: affective neurosciences; clinical neurosciences; social neuroscience; and applied psychophysiology.

In summary, psychophysiological and neuroimaging measures have been discussed in terms of their distinct advantages relative to behavioral measures for use in adaptive systems, and for improving human–computer interaction in general. Psychophysiology involves covert signals that do not require added tasks from the participant; the data trace is continuously available for monitoring, whereas behavioral data tends to be available intermittently, and psychophysiological signals can still be monitored even if the system becomes completely automated, leaving no overt behavior from the participant.

PART II

The Medium Is the Message that Changes the Brain

CHAPTER 4

This Is Your Brain on the Internet

4.1 Introduction

An abundant medium for cyberpsychology research is available as a result of the Internet. Tim Berners-Lee developed the Internet and it first functioned as an information exchange network that was used by academics and scientists all over the globe. The Internet was officially released for public use in April 1993 and has since evolved into an integral part of users' lives. Recent surveys have revealed that over 3.1 billion people now have access to the Internet. The distribution of this number by country reveals the following: China = 642 million; United States = 280 million; India = 243 million; Japan = 109 million; Brazil =108 million; Russia = 84 million, among others (Internet Live Stats, 2015). In the United States 86.75 percent of residents have access to the Internet. Although now seemingly ubiquitous, the Internet is actually a recent medium that has allowed for extraordinary access to multifarious information.

Once logged in to the hyperconnected global information network, users can easily search for any information they desire. Furthermore, online social networking sites allow the exchange of thoughts, feelings, and experiences. In the 1960s Marshall McLuhan (1964) famously turned the world's attention to technology's impact by proclaiming "the medium is the message." Today, that clarion call is prominently evident in the now ubiquitous social media of the Internet. The effortlessly available online knowledgebase found in the Internet has essentially succeeded other media in terms of acquiring knowledge for daily life. According to Prensky (2001), this has resulted in at least two cohorts that relate very differently to technology, each with differing cognitive styles. "Digital Natives" are users that had Internet technologies as part of their development; and "Digital Immigrants" are users who adopted these technologies later in life. Digital Natives are "native speakers" of the digital language of computers, video games, and the Internet. While Digital Immigrants learn and adapt to the digital environment, they always retain, to some degree, their "accent." For example, the "digital immigrant accent" is apparent in how they gather their information. The Internet does not tend to be their first choice for information. Another example would be printing out an email or a digitized document in order to edit it. On the other hand, if one is a digital native, the use of the Internet and consumption of digitized information is second nature. However, this facility with technology may come at a price. For Digital Natives there tends to be an increased engagement in multitasking behaviors, which may lead to increased distractibility (Ophir et al., 2009).

4.2   Slouching toward Google: Is the Internet Bad for Our Brains?

Access to the Internet has certainly transformed the way that we gather and store information. The use of search engines like Google has become an integral part of the daily lives of the majority of the world's population. A number of people expend more time online and in their online social networks than with any offline persons on any particular day. Furthermore, the development of the Internet and related technology (e.g., tablets, smartphones) has resulted in both an explosion of available information and a revolution in increased access. From a theoretical and qualitative review perspective, Nicholas Carr (2008; 2010) has explored the potential effects of the Internet explosion in a *The Atlantic* magazine article "Is Google Making Us Stupid?" and in his 250-page book, *The Shallows: What the Internet Is Doing to Our Brains*, which has been published in both the United States and the United Kingdom. In *The Shallows*, Carr reviews human innovations such as the map, the clock, and the typewriter. The focus of this review is to illustrate the extent to which these innovations influenced the essential modes of human thought. He also argues that while the "age of the book" ushered in intelligent, contemplative, and imaginative information processing, the Internet is a "cacophony of stimuli" that offers a "crazy quilt" of data that have resulted in "cursory reading, hurried and distracted thinking, and superficial learning."

According to Carr, the Internet offers search engines (e.g., Google) with continuous accessibility of both immediate information and distractions that may impact the way we process information. Carr contrasts the sort of deep concentration involved in scholarly reading with the mere surface skimming involved in online Internet viewing of material. Some support for this idea can be found in David Nicholas and colleague's (2008) study on the "Google generation's" (people that are born after 1993) Internet habits. They found that 60 percent of e-journal users viewed a maximum of three pages of an article. Furthermore, 65 percent of readers never returned to finish the articles. Additionally, average viewers typically only expended four minutes on e-books and eight minutes on e-journal sites.

Carr also theorizes that the Internet may in fact alter the cerebral cortices of its users. Carr draws from research on the malleability of human neural circuitry: "Over the past few years I've had an uncomfortable sense that someone, or something, has been tinkering with my brain, remapping the neural circuitry, reprogramming the memory. My mind isn't going – so far as I can tell – but it's changing. I'm not thinking the way I used to think. I can feel it most strongly when I'm reading" (Carr, 2008). Carr's statements reflect his understanding of the ways in which a person's experience rewires their brain's circuits throughout their lives. By this he is referring to neuro plasticity: "If, knowing what we know today about the brain's plasticity, you were to set out to invent a medium that would rewire our mental circuits as quickly and thoroughly as possible, you would probably end up designing something that looks and works a lot like the Internet." Hence, Carr believes that the Internet is changing the way people read; and it may also be changing the way Internet users think. The negative conclusion for Carr is that Internet users are rescinding their ability to concentrate. Although much of Carr's presentation reflects theorizing on the potential impacts of Internet use on the brain, researchers have recently begun to investigate the neurocognitive and affective impact of being online (Brand et al., 2014; Loh & Kanai, 2014; Small et al., 2009; Sparrow, Liu, & Wegner, 2011; Sparrow & Chatman, 2013).

4.3 Heavy Internet Use and the Media Multitasking Brain

Heavy Internet use (coupled with simultaneous use of other forms of media) can also impact memory performance in negative ways. Heavy media multitasking has been found to negatively impact working memory tasks (Cain & Mitroff, 2011; Ophir et al., 2009; Sanbonmatsu et al., 2013; Uncapher et al., 2015), and long-term memory tasks (Uncapher et al., 2015). For example, Uncapher and colleagues (2015) used a signal detection framework and argued that the poorer memory performance of heavy media multitaskers was due to a reduced ability to discriminate between information in working memory and long-term memory – instead of a difference in decision bias (e.g., requiring less confirmation to make a decision).

Chronic media multi-taskers have been found to be more attentive to irrelevant stimuli in the external environment and irrelevant representations in memory. Ophir, Nass, and Wagner (2009) examined cognitive control dimensions that they theorized could indicate cognitive control in media multitaskers: attention allocation to environmental stimuli; holding and manipulating task stimuli and task set representations in working memory; and the control of responses to stimuli and tasks. While it would seem that the regular performance of multiple tasks at the same time and the frequent switching between tasks (or media) would allow HMMs to outperform LMMs in measures assessing multitasking, Ophir and colleagues (2009) found that HMMs performed worse than LMMs in a task-switching experiment. Furthermore, HMMs also performed worse on other measures: AX-continuous performance task; filter task; and N-back task. It is important to note that the performance deficits observed when comparing HMMs and LMMs were not global in nature. Instead they appeared to be specific to situations that involved distractors. This distinction was evident on the AX-continuous performance task. While participants in the HMM group and LMM group performed equally well in the condition that did not include distractors, performance in the HMM group had slower response times in a condition that included distractors. The authors concluded that media multitasking might have negative effects on executive-control. This led to a lowered resistance to distractors.

For Lin Lin of the University of North Texas (2009) the findings of Ophir and others may have limited ecological validity. Lin argued that media multitaskers do not attend to the information that is relevant to one task at a time. Instead HMMs have a cognitive style that includes a "greater breadth of attention." This breadth-biased approach to cognitive processing is an intriguing suggestion that suggests performance will be enhanced in situations where a task involves some unexpected information that is important to the task at hand. For example, when a media multitasker reads, he or she may more readily detect a ringtone from a mobile phone, even though the ringtone does not carry information useful for the primary task of reading. In fact, such situations seem to actually be more representative of what happens in activities of daily living (Lin, 2009).

The brains of heavy media multitaskers are different. Loh and Kanai (2014) used voxel-based morphometry to investigate the brain structures of 75 adults. Voxel-based morphometry is a commonly used neuroimaging approach that enables voxel-wise statistical analyses of pre-processed images from magnetic resonance imagery. Participants also completed a Big Five Personality Inventory and a Media Multitasking Questionnaire. Findings revealed that, independent of individual personality traits, participants who were HMMs concurrently also had lower grey matter density in the anterior cingulate cortex (ACC). The ACC is important for sensorimotor, nociceptive, neurocognitive, affective, and motivational processes (Bush, Luu, & Posner, 2000). The authors argue that the findings of a smaller ACC in HMMs most likely reflects higher cognitive processes since media multitasking has been consistently associated with cognitive control performance (Lui & Wong, 2012; Ophir, Nass, & Wagner, 2009).

4.4 Internet Search and Reward

What happens when an individual searches the Internet and finds some elusive piece of information? Typically, this represents a rewarding experience for the person and promotes further searches. What impact does Internet searching have on the brain and the ways in which persons approach Internet usage? The answer may involve the nucleus accumbens – part of the ventral striatum that lies in a region in the basal forebrain rostral to the preoptic area of the hypothalamus. Specifically, the reinforcing effect that occurs when a person seeks and finds resources on the Internet reflects activity in the cortico-striato-thalamo-cortical loop. The nucleus accumbens and ventral tegmental area (VTA) have important roles in the neurocognitive processing of reward, pleasure, reinforcement learning, aversion, and motivation. Dopamine acts in the nucleus accumbens to attach motivational significance to stimuli associated with reward. Dopaminergic neurons found in the VTA connect via the mesolimbic pathway and modulate the activity of neurons within the nucleus accumbens that are activated directly or indirectly by drugs like opiates and amphetamines. Internet searches tap into the reward areas of the brain, and this impacts the searcher's ability to focus on other things.

In fact, Internet searches reflect the "seeking" circuitry described by the affective neuroscientist Jaak Panksepp. Our brains have evolved to seek out our environments for information that will help us survive (location of food; or a link to a new social networking site). The seeking system is a dopamine-energized, mesolimbic system that arises from the ventral tegmental area. Dopamine is released each time one explores his or her environment. Interestingly, the dopaminergic-induced sense of euphoria we experience is typically not just a product of a reward, but of seeking itself. For example, a person could decide to do a quick Google search to find out what the Japanese word "otaku" means only to find an hour later that one's quick search has led to an hour of Googling. While it only took us a minute to find out that "otaku" is a Japanese term for persons with obsessive interests – regularly anime and manga fandom – it leads to an hour of dopamine-charged searching for information about its contemporary usage, its origination with Akio Nakamori's essay in Manga Burikko, then to Haruki Murakami's *Norwegian Wood*, next to the Beatles, then to Thomas Mann's *Magic Mountain*, and so on.

Moreover, our internal sense of time is moderated by emotional and interoceptive states that are hypothesized to rely on a dopamine-modulated "internal clock" in the basal ganglia. Tomasi and colleagues (2015) used functional magnetic resonance imaging to assess sense of time in the striato-cortical pathways. Findings revealed the involvement of the nucleus accumbens and anterior insula in the temporal precision of the responses. Furthermore, the ventral tegmental area was involved in error processing. The authors conclude that to the extent that activation of the nucleus accumbens is associated with addictive behaviors, its activation could aid understanding of why videogames that rely on time prediction can trigger compulsive behaviors.

To some extent the Internet can be seen as a massive web of personalized Skinner boxes, where the behavior of each Internet user may be reinforced through classic and operant conditioning mechanisms. For example, positive intermittent reinforcement of searching behavior is progressively shaped over time as the user becomes more and more practiced at seeking and finding the reading information on the Internet. This behavior resembles short-odds continuous gambling practices. The rate of online reinforcement represents a variable-ratio schedule that produces the sort of high steady rate of responding found in gambling and lottery games. In fact, the Internet has multiple variable-ratio reinforcement schedules built into it – a search of Google could result in some unexpected and pleasing information; a coveted sale for shoes, a lost friend's location, a flattering review of one's work. Any of these situations (among the many other possible) might place the user in a state of anticipation. This variable-ratio pattern of reinforcement can be more addicting than receiving the exact same information every time because (at least in part) the user's brain endeavors to predict rewards. In variable-ratio reward schedules the brain cannot find the pattern and it will promote a behavior until it finds one. In situations where the rewards are random, the brain's attempt at pattern recognition may continue compulsively. As might be expected, there is a higher pre-valence of Internet-related addictive behaviors that may reflect altered reward-processing (Greenfield, 2011).

While the extent to which these Internet-based personalized Skinner boxes will result in positive or negative shaping of behaviors is unclear, there is some emerging evidence from neuroimaging studies that suggests relations between Internet use and structural changes in the brain (Brand et al., 2014; Loh & Kanai, 2014; Small et al., 2009). That said, there is still some debate about the impact of Internet and gaming technologies. While some have pointed to the promises of technological progress on cognitive processes (Bavelier et al., 2010; Choudhury & McKinney, 2013; Mills 2014), others have emphasized the potential for negative outcomes (Carr 2010; Montag & Reuter, 2015).

4.5 Google Brain: Impact on the Brain's Encoding and Recall of Information

The relative newness of the Internet has resulted in a great deal of spec-ulation about its potential impact on our brain and cognitive processing (Carr, 2008; 2010). The Internet has refined algorithmic search engines that allow users to access information with ease. People are no longer hindered by costly efforts to find desired information. With the Internet, we can search the world's libraries, repositories, and archives to find articles online. We can shop, play games, watch videos, Google old friends, look up the author who was on the tip of our tongue, learn how to assemble a computer, and find out the world's news.

This widespread Internet use represents a new opportunity to con-sider McLuhan's (1964) famous proclamation that "the medium is the message," which called attention to the impact of technological change on the world. While not everyone has agreed with the import of McLuhan's proclamation, technological interventions like the Internet can have enduring alterations to user's neurocognitive and affective processing. Dehaene and Cohen (2007) discussed the ways in which the acquisition of a new tool could influence user cognitions over time in a way that restructured preexisting brain systems that performed analogous functions. For example, specialized brain regions for arith-metic operations and orthographic processing were part of primitive neural networks involved in visual recognition and numerical func-tions. Dehaene and Cohen (2007) referred to this as "neuronal recy-cling" of preexisting brain systems for novel functions (e.g., literacy and arithmetic). The Internet has now been around for three decades and represents not only a new medium but a new tool that has the potential for impacting the neural networks of users.

Dr. Gary Small is a professor at the Semel Institute for Neuroscience and Human Behavior at the University of California Los Angeles (UCLA). He holds UCLA's Parlow-Solomon Chair on Aging. In a study at UCLA, Small and colleagues (2009) investigated the brains of computer-savvy middle-aged and older adults. In their study, they focused on measuring brain activation patterns related to cognitive tasks that involved searching the Internet. Given that practice of cognitive tasks has been found to alter neural activation patterns, they wanted to see whether prior experience of using Internet search engines would impact brain activation patterns. Specifically, they investigated differences in brain activity on a task that reflected normal reading processes to advance understanding of specific participants versus an Internet search task that required the user to actively search for and identify the most relevant information. They wanted to find out whether the active search condition would preferentially engage neural circuits (specifically in dorsal and ventral prefrontal cortex) involved in integrating semantic information, working memory, and decision-making.

The primary tool for investigating these issues was functional magnetic resonance imaging (fMRI; see Chapter 2 in this book) of the brains of older persons during Internet searches. They also aimed to assess whether prior search engine experience influenced the degree and extent of activations. The study sample was made up of 12 experienced Internet users and 12 digital newcomers. All participants used Google while their brains were scanned. Results revealed that there is a key initial difference between the two groups in an area of the brain called the dorsolateral prefrontal cortex (see Chapter 2 in this book), which deals with working memory and decision-making.

Reading

– For both groups, simply reading text evoked brain regions that are commonly involved in reading
– Inferior and middle frontal gyri, medial temporal gyrus, angular gyrus, hippocampus, posterior cingulate, visual cortex

Internet Search

– The nonexperienced participants showed activation patterns that were similar to those found in the reading condition
– Internet-experienced participants showed additional brain activations

- Frontal pole, right anterior temporal cortex, cingulate cortex, and hippocampus

Comparisons between Internet Search and Reading
- Revealed increased extents of activation in Internet-experienced participants in frontal and occipital regions

In summary, while the Internet-naive group showed very little activity, the Internet-savvy group showed large activations. These findings illustrate that searching the Internet may help kindle and potentially enhance brain functioning.

In an extension of this study, Small and Vorgan (2008) found that the Internet novices spent an hour a day online for six days. Small and colleagues rescanned the two groups' brains. Interestingly, this time, in neuroimages of both sets of brains the patterns of activations representing mental activity were nearly identical. Hence, after only a few days of practice, the identical neural circuitry in the dlPFC of the brain became active in the Internet-naive participants.

4.6   Internet as Transactive Memory Partner

While a number of theories and hypotheses have emerged, there is need for empirical investigations into the impact of cybertechnologies on the brain. One approach has been to look at the cognitive processes involved. Betsy Sparrow from Columbia University and her colleagues decided to focus on memory processes of Internet users. Sparrow and colleagues (2011) conducted a series of four studies that investigated the ways in which the Internet is changing the way we remember basic information.

For the first experiment, Sparrow and colleagues administered trivia questions of variable levels of difficulty, and participants responded "yes" or "no" to each question. After completing a set of trivia questions, participants took part in a modified Stroop task that included computer-related base-words (e.g., Internet; Yahoo; Google) and noncomputer words that were brands (e.g., Nike; Target). Stroop results revealed that after participants were presented with a set of questions that they could not answer, the Stroop computer words resulted in longer reaction times than noncomputer words. The Internet search engine words were more accessible following the unanswerable trivia questions, which produced an interference effect (participants were only to name the font's color). Computer terms showed increased interference with color naming even when easy trivia questions were presented. Sparrow and colleagues suggest that when users come across demanding trivia questions (i.e., ones to which they do not know the answer), they are primed for computer-related words, which makes the computer words more challenging to ignore (increased interference for color naming).

For the second experiment, Sparrow and colleagues investigated whether participants would remember information to which the participants believed they would have later access. The idea was that this scenario would mimic information and availability that a user might normally search for online. The participants were directed to read 40 memorable trivia statements that were meant to replicate a common (and random) Google search. An example of a trivia statement is: "The Atlantic Ocean is saltier than the Pacific Ocean" (Sparrow et al., 2011). Next, participants were asked to use the keyboard and type the statements into a computer. After this, it was communicated to the participants that their answer would be either (1) saved for later access; or (2) deleted after the participant was finished with their typing. Half of the participants in each condition were explicitly directed to attempt to remember the trivia statements. Next, the participants were given a piece of paper and instructed to freely recall as many of the trivia statements as possible. Then participants were administered a recognition test that included the presentation (again) of the 40 trivia statements. Note that 20 of the trivia statements were duplicates (exactly as previously presented) of the first presentation and 20 were slightly altered (e.g., changed name or date). The participants were instructed to make judgments on each trivia statement as either "exactly as previously presented" or "altered."

Results of this second experiment revealed deficient recall of the trivia statements. Participants who believed that their statements had been deleted (no longer accessible) had the best recall. There was no main effect for the instruction to explicitly remember/not remember. According to Sparrow et al. this finding is supported by research on intentional vs. incidental studying of material (there is generally no effect of explicit instruction). For the recognition test results, there was an interaction between memory instructions and the participant's belief that the information will be saved or deleted. For the explicit memory instruction there was an interaction effect, with the delete and remember condition having the best memory. Explicit instruction resulted in improved memory (though not significantly), but only for the participants that did not expect to have access to the information later. Participants who had been explicitly instructed to remember, believed that they had saved the trivia statements, and believed that they would have access to them later, had the most deficient recognition scores.

In the third experiment, Sparrow et al. more closely assessed memory and where participants go to find the desired information. Participants were presented with 30 trivia statements and typed the statements into a computer (Medialab was used for the experiment). Following one third of the statements, participants were informed that "Your entry has been erased." For the second third, participants were informed that "Your entry has been saved." For the final third, participants were informed that "Your entry has been saved into the folder X," which was one of six folders: FACTS, DATA, INFO, NAMES, ITEMS, or POINTS. The folders were randomly generated. The participants were informed that they would have access to the "saved" trivia later in the experiment. Following the typing task, participants were administered a recognition test, in which they were required to identify whether statements were identical to their previous presentation or slightly altered (e.g., by name or date). Furthermore, they were queried about whether the statement had been saved or erased. Additionally, they were asked whether the statement had been saved to a folder. In situations where the statement had been saved to a folder, the participant was instructed to identify to which of the six folders the information had been saved.

Results revealed that participants had the best recall for statements they believed had been deleted, and the worst memory for statements that they believed had been saved in specific folders. It is interesting to note that when the question was changed from "Was this statement exactly what you read?" to "Was this statement saved or erased?" the opposite pattern emerged. The results for the "Was this statement saved or erased?" question showed significantly better memory for saved information, in a specific folder. The worst memory performance was found for deleted statements. According to Sparrow and colleagues, these findings can be interpreted in terms of the participant's belief about whether s/he will have further access to the information. If the participant believed that s/he will not have further access to information, their recall was better. If the participant believed that the information was saved externally then they had enhanced memory for the fact that the information could be accessed.

Finally, for their fourth experiment, Sparrow and colleagues endeavored to find out whether their participants would recall the actual information, or if they would instead recall where to find that information. The participants read and typed 30 trivia statements into the computer (i.e., Medialab). For the trivia portion of the experiment, the participants typed a statement and then they were informed "Your entry has been saved into the folder X" (Folder "X" was again one of six folders). The experimenters informed the participants that they would have access to saved information. Two memory tests were administered: (1) free recall for the trivia statements; and (2) cued recall of the folder to which the trivia facts were saved. Results revealed increased memory performance for where (i.e., which folder) the statements were kept. Participant performance was much lower for the recall of actual statements. According to Sparrow and colleagues, these findings were surprising because the trivia statements were specific and the folder names more general.

For Sparrow et al. the results of these experiments revealed the following:

(1)   Participants turned to computers for information when they did not know trivia information.

(2)   Participants remembered information better if they thought they would not have later access to that information.

(3)   Participants prioritized "where" information is saved over the information itself.

(4)   Transactive memory can be used to explain the main effect of accessing and storing the trivia information on computers.

By referring to transactive memory, they were drawing from the work of their co-author Daniel Wegner. Wegner (1985) defines transactive memory as a set of distinct memory systems that combine with the communication that occurs between individuals (Wegner, Giuliano, & Hertel, 1985). In particular, this theoretical formulation asserts that people are less concerned with remembering information than they are with remembering who knows what information. Sparrow et al. build on the idea of transactive memory and move from another person as partner in transactive memory to a computer as partner in our transactive memory system. Hence, we make an effort to learn and recall the information accessible via the computer so that we do not have to encode and recall all of the information ourselves.

In summary, Sparrow and colleagues conducted a series of four studies that investigated the ways in which the Internet is changing the way we remember basic information. Results revealed that when users are faced with difficult questions, they are primed to think about computers. When users have the expectation that they will have future access to information, their recall rates are lower for the information itself. On the other hand, they also have enhanced recall for where to access the desired information.

Hence, the Internet has become a chief form of external or transactive memory, in which information is stored collectively outside the users.

4.7 Internet May Be More than Just another Memory Partner

According to Adrian Ward (2013), the Internet may be more than just another memory partner. It may in fact be understood as an informational repository that can be used to reduce the amount of information stored in both (1) other external sources like our current human transactive memory partners; and (2) internally stored information that resides on the user's own brain. Ward discusses the Internet in terms of a supernormal stimulus that excels according to three criteria.

(1) **Availability of Information:** The Internet is effectively omnipresent and access points are virtually ubiquitous in homes, offices, and on smartphones. This allows numerous people to carry a portal to the Internet with them wherever they go. Information retrieval from the Internet is as simple as entering the correct search terms. Moreover, the user does not need to worry that his or her transactive memory partner is available (e.g., the Internet does not go out of town on vacation or a business trip).

(2) **Depth of Information:** Information retrieved from the Internet tends to have a relatively higher level of expertise in a given area than any one individual. Furthermore, the data tends to be regularly updated, and some sources are peer-reviewed (Arbesman, 2012).

(3) **Breadth of Information:** Information retrieved from the Internet has a remarkable level of breadth. Transactive memory with human partners is often incomplete because not all information can be gathered and stored within a network of friends and family.

Ward points to the beneficial reductions in cognitive demands that may result from offloading information demands to the Internet. Such offloading may allow for enhanced capacity for information processing because there will be increased availability of cognitive resources. Perhaps users will become more efficient and creative in their problem solving (Sparrow & Chatman, 2013). That said, there are some potential concerns about too great a reliance upon the Internet for memory. Given that the Internet outperforms the human brain as an information storage and retrieval device, users may begin to replace their biological memory banks with digital storage. A further consequence may be interference with the user's motivation and ability to process information and formulate new memories.

4.8   The Internet, Mobile Technologies and Extended Cognitive Systems

As can be seen from the above review of work in the labs of Sparrow and colleagues (2011) as well as Ward (2013), the Internet is increasingly being viewed as an extension of our cognitive processes. It is becoming increasingly apparent that the Internet has the potential to extend our cognitive processes beyond the embodied cognition of our forebears. Theorizing in this area by Andy Clark and David Chalmers (1998) has resulted in an "extended mind" theory, in which cognitive processes are understood as going beyond wetware (i.e., brain) to software and hardware used by the brain. This perspective allows for an understanding of human cognition as processed in a system coupled with the environment (Clark, 2008; Clark & Chalmers, 1998). In their work, they describe the "extended mind" in terms of an extended cognitive system that includes both brain-based cognitive processes and external objects (e.g., technologies like the Internet) that serve to accomplish functions that would otherwise be attained via the action of brain-based cognitive processes acting internally to the human. Moreover, they employ a "parity principle," which states:

> If, as we confront some task, a part of the world functions as a process which, were it to go on in the head, we would have no hesitation in recognizing as part of the cognitive process, then that part of the world is (so we claim) part of the cognitive process. (Clark & Chalmers, 1998, p. 8)

Clark and Chalmers employ a thought experiment using fictional characters Inga and Otto to illustrate the parity principle. In the thought experiment, both characters are traveling to a museum. While Inga is able to recall the directions from her internal brain-based memory processes, Otto's Alzheimer's disease requires him to rely on directions found in a notebook, which serve as an external aide to his internal brain-based memory processes. Hence, the extended mind can be understood as information-processing loops that extend beyond the neural realm to include elements of our social and technological environments (Gallagher, 2011; Gallagher & Crisafi, 2009). Paul Smart (2012) at the University of Southampton has applied the idea of extended cognitive processes to the specific sociotechnical context of the Web. The result is a notion of the "Web-extended mind," in which the Internet can serve as a mechanistic substrate that realizes human mental states and processes. A number of examples can also be found in the ways in which we regularly enhance our cognitive performance with various technologies (e.g., smartphones, global positioning systems, Google, etc.). It appears that we are able to store our memories using technologies. While I cannot remember what the Japanese word "otaku" means, I, plus my technology, can recall that it is a Japanese term for persons with obsessive interests – regularly associated with anime and manga fandom.

The potential for the extended cognitive processing perspective seems even more apparent with the advent of mobile technologies. Whilst early iterations of the Internet were bounded by wires, later iterations only had to be in close proximity to a router. Today, with the arrival and augmentation of tablets and smartphones, the enormous knowledgebase of the Internet is available in one's pocket. The number of tablets and smartphones in use is rapidly approaching the point where billions will have access. Furthermore, the technological properties of smartphones proffer a number of enhancements to discussions of externalization. While early metaphors focused on external memory storage, smartphones connected to the Internet extend beyond memory assistants to powerful mobile computation devices. In fact, mobile technologies connected to the Internet allow for novel investigations into the interactions of persons as they engage with a global workspace and connected knowledgebases. Moreover, mobile access to the Internet may allow for interactive possibilities: a paradigm shift in how we see ourselves and the ways in which we understand the nature of our cognitive and epistemic capabilities.

Barr and colleagues (2015) at the University of Waterloo have studied the extended cognitive systems perspective as it relates to smartphone technologies. They were interested in the impact of having access to the Internet and its associated knowledgebases at one's fingertips. They framed smartphone use in terms of the extended cognitive processes approach, as well as automatic and controlled processing. Specifically, they investigated whether the availability of easy access to information via smartphones would cause users to forego controlled processing (e.g., effortful analytic thinking) in lieu of automatic (i.e., fast and easy intuition) access to information (i.e., via smartphones). Results from three studies revealed that users who emphasize an automatic processing approach (e.g., think more intuitively) were more likely to rely on their smartphones (i.e., extended mind) for information in their everyday lives. The researchers argue that these findings suggest that users may offload cognitive processes to technology. Given these results, cyberpsychologists may want to do further research into the integration of brain-based cognitive processes and media.

As can be seen in the foregoing discussion, the Internet offers its users immediate access to an extraordinarily large amount of information. Such access can impact the ways in which persons process cognitive data (Fisher, Goddu, & Keil, 2015; Sparrow, Liu, & Wegner, 2011; Ward, 2013). While Carr (2010) theorizes that continuous access to the Internet results in negative consequences, others argue that Internet use alone does not necessarily impede one's ability to use the information found online (Clowes, 2013). In a recent investigation, Ferguson and colleagues (2015) examined whether having access to the Internet's wealth of information impacted participants' controlled cognitive processes. They tested the hypothesis that Internet access adjusts participants' willingness to volunteer answers to general knowledge questions. Findings from their study revealed that Internet access inclined participants toward willingness to volunteer answers. While this led to a decrease in correct answers overall, greater accuracy existed when an answer was offered. Moreover, Internet access influenced "feeling-of-knowing," which the authors asserted accounted for some of the impact on willingness to volunteer answers. Ferguson and colleagues argue that these findings demonstrate that Internet access can influence controlled cognitive processes, and contribute novel insights into the operation of the transactive memory system formed.

4.9   Internet for Collective Knowledge Building

In addition to cyberpsychology research into the impact of Internet use on the user, there are a number of other notable aspects of the emergence of the Internet. Technological developments in the use of the Internet for collective knowledge building are apparent in Web 2.0 practices that involve specialized Web tools (O'Reilly, 2007). Web 2.0 represents a trend in open platform Internet use that incorporates user-driven online networks and knowledgebases. While there are no large Internet-based repositories for cyberpsychological data, the Cognitive Atlas (www.cognitiveatlas.org/) was developed to address the need for a collaborative knowledgebase that captures the comprehensive collection of conceptual structures (Miller et al., 2010). To do this, the Cognitive Atlas project describes the "parts" and processes of cognitive functioning in a manner similar to descriptions of the cell's component parts and functions in gene ontology. While this project does offer promise, it is still in its infancy and requires development if it is to provide a solid basis for annotation of behavioral neuroscience (e.g., neuroimaging of cognitive processes) data. Further, like other collaborative knowledgebases (e.g., Wikipedia), its realization will depend on the involvement of a large number of interested neuropsychologists (Poldrack, 2010).

Some psychologists are calling for greater inclusion of Web-based neurocognitive assessments (Jagaroo, 2009). The exponential increase in access to computers and the Internet across the lifespan allows for interactive Web-based cyberpsychological assessments (Bart, Raz, & Dan, 2014; Brandt et al., 2013; Raz et al., 2014; Troyer et al., 2014; Wagner et al., 2010; Zakzanis & Azarbehi, 2014). Web-based cyberpsychological assessments offer tools for enhanced presentation and logging of stimuli. When properly used, Web-based assessments can greatly enhance the assessment in terms of precision and rapid implementation of adaptive algorithms. Online assessment may enhance dissemination of testing because tests could be administered in a variety of settings (e.g., office, home, school), at different times of the day, and by multiple persons at the same time.

4.10   Internet Research and Mechanical Turk

The growth of the Internet has transformed it from a simple academic resource to a global tool that can be accessed by an exceedingly large and diverse population. As a result, the Internet is quickly becoming an essential tool for cyberpsychological research. In a recent review, Gossling and Mason (2015) discussed the ways in which traditional psychological research methods have been adapted to the online setting. For example, Internet technology is increasingly being used to deliver surveys, questionnaires, and experiments. Delivery of standard measures via the Internet offers a number of advantages including automated data entry, automatic checks for item completion, adaptive testing, and provision of immediate feedback to participants. Relatedly, new methodological opportunities, such as data mining big data, have emerged.

Furthermore, they reviewed novel research paradigms that have been developed using the new capabilities of the Internet. Part of this comes from the ways in which online behavior is different from offline behavior. Hence, novel research programs have developed for cyberpsychology research into the flow of information from person to person. Furthermore, the ways in which people are connected through social media and social networking sites offers cyberpsychologists an important set of research questions. Interpersonal communication represents a primary aspect of multiple aspects of social behavior. While spoken language-based communication leaves no trace of the interaction, written language-based communication on the Internet does leave a trace. This offers enterprising cyberpsychologists a host of possibilities.

Additionally, there is the issue of what happens when so many real-world interactions are now mediated by the Internet? Questions that were formerly asked about impression formation in offline contexts (e.g., based on physical appearance) have been redirected to online contexts. This, of course, leads to the question of how does the cyberpsychology researcher know the characteristics of our study participants? This reflects the reality of current Internet-based research. In addition to the benefits, Internet-related research comes with new challenges.

One of the greatest strengths and limitations can be found in the use of crowdsourcing Websites like Amazon's Mechanical Turk (MTurk), CrowdFlower, and Clickworker. These crowdsourcing Websites are online marketplaces designed to match human intelligence tasks with individuals willing to complete those tasks. For cyberpsychological researchers, the tasks are questionnaires and experiments. The cyberpsychologists uses the crowdsourcing system to create the tasks, match requesters with workers, compensate workers, and rate the quality of the requests and worker performance. The cyberpsychologists can develop and post just about any task that can be done using a computer (e.g., questionnaires, experiments). While these sources have the potential for rapidly and inexpensively gathering data from diverse populations, problems have arisen as a result of their popularity. For example, because of the increased number of cyberpsychologists using MTurk, it is becoming increasingly difficult to find naive participants. In fact, there are such large numbers of MTurk workers participating in multiple studies that they have been named superturkers. These superturkers account for a disproportionately high number of the participants that take part in MTurk studies. For example, Chandler and colleagues (2014) investigated the participants in 132 studies and found that the top 1 percent of the most prolific workers completed 11 percent of all the MTurk studies. For cyberpsychologists, these very prolific workers cause major problems when there is some selection criterion (e.g., being a gamer, or a smoker, or any other specific characteristics). Moreover, MTurk participants can share information about selection criteria, manipulation checks, frequently used designs, and measures on community message boards. There are some methodological approaches that have emerged to counteract these issues. It will be important for cyberpsychology researchers to develop and implement specific pre-screening techniques (see Chandler et al., 2014).

While there are some significant challenges for research using the Internet, the widespread adoption of Internet methods in cyberpsychology (not to mention psychology as a whole) suggests that the opportunities outweigh the costs. The Internet's ability to facilitate psychology research via its reach to large and diverse samples is unprecedented. Further, its ability to automatically collect and store data on actual behaviors offers cyberpsychologists an opportunity to extend their research samples/populations beyond college samples and contrived lab studies. That said, the lack of control and limited ability to confirm demographics of users means that small-scale laboratory research will continue to be a necessary approach to answer some questions.

4.11 Research Using the Internet-Based Second Life and Other Multiverse Platforms

A further development of the Web 2.0 paradigm for cyberpsychologists may be found in the expanding metaverse of networked virtual worlds found on the Internet. Networked virtual worlds are made up of online communities in which persons interrelate in simulated environments (Singhal & Zyda, 1999). In the 1980s, networked virtual environments were primarily used for military simulations (e.g., SIMNET: Simulator networking; see Miller & Thorpe, 1995). Since then, networked virtual worlds have been applied to massively multiplayer online games and interactive virtual communities. In 2003, Second Life was launched by Linden Labs (Linden Labs, San Francisco, CA). Second Life is an online virtual world that allows users to build their own worlds. Once immersed in Second Life, the user is provided with a vast array of opportunities in which to engage (e.g., role play, sky-diving, gaming, dancing, and shopping). Evidence suggests that online virtual worlds provide a venue for need fulfillment, self-expression, and liberation (Barnes & Pressey, 2011; Partala, 2011). Furthermore, online virtual worlds provide opportunities for gender-swapping (Hussain & Griffith, 2008) and the exploration of different self-representations, which may represent the user's "ideal self" (Bessiere, Fleming, & Kiesler, 2007).

Given the nature of online virtual worlds, there is opportunity to study Clark and Chalmers's (1998) extended mind theory in terms of an "embodied cognition" hypothesis, in which cognitive processes involve interactions between perceptions, actions, the person's body, and the environment (Barsalou, 2008; Clark, 1997, 1999). Research into embodied cognition investigating the differing roles of actions in cognitive processes has suggested that cognitive processes are closely related to sensorimotor experiences. Within an embodied cognition framework, cognitive processes develop when a closely coupled system supervenes upon interactions between individuals and their environments, with the interactions being real-time and goal-directed (Barsalou, 2008; Clark, 1997, 1999; Glenberg, 1999). Online virtual worlds have potential to enhance physical embodiment through avatar generation.

When a user is immersed in Second Life, they can interact via their digital representations, called avatars. Avatars are created by the user via registration at the Second Life Website. Immersion into Second Life requires the user to perform a login procedure. Following authentication, the user's avatar enters the virtual world. Once in the virtual world, the user's avatar can navigate (walk, run, and sometimes fly – depending on the regions settings) within a region and also directly move to adjacent regions (provided they have access). The user's avatar has a limited visibility area (called the area of interest) that corresponds approximately to a sphere with a radius of 35 meters. Via an avatar, the user can take part in numerous interactions as they engage in individual and group activities. Avatars allow users to explore virtual surroundings, engage in conversations, and interact socially. Second Life includes chat options (e.g., text and audio) that are coupled with animated gestures (for nonverbal virtual expression) that mimic real-world social interactions. Moreover, Second Life allows users opportunities to create, join, and/or moderate groups that connect them with other users.

Second Life is made up of virtual lands that are divided into fixed-size regions, which are independent lands of size 256 x 256 meters. Each of these regions can have up to four adjacent regions that are either private (owned by individuals or companies) or public (owned by Linden Labs). When users own private regions, they have total control of their virtual land. For example, they can limit access to a selected set of other users. Users are able to participate in the development of the Internet-based virtual world by (1) creating objects (e.g., vehicles, buildings, foliage, and terrains); (2) buying and selling objects and services (virtual economies); and (3) taking part in interactive simulations (e.g., role playing games, fantasy, and social networking). An innovative feature of Second Life is that users can take part in its virtual economy by buying and selling objects, services, and lands. Since the introduction of Second Life a full-blown economy has emerged. Second Life offers tools (i.e. scripting and graphics) and environments that facilitate the creation of virtual environments that can be made available to potentially thousands of research subjects in an economical manner (Bainbridge, 2007; Boulous, 2007).

4.11.3   Research Using Online Virtual Worlds

Technological advances in computing and the World Wide Web in the last couple of decades (Abbate, 1999) have allowed Internet-based virtual worlds testing with potentially more diverse samples in respect to socioeconomic status, sex, and age than traditional samples that are often drawn from undergraduate university students (Gosling et al., 2004). The continued progress in the development of robust technologies has led to more rapid and secure Internet connections. As a result, the cyberpsychology literature has seen an ever-increasing interest in virtual worlds (Boulos & Wheeler, 2007; Boulous, Hetherington, & Wheeler, 2007). In a recent article in *Science*, Bainbridge (2007) discussed the robust potential of virtual worlds for research in the social and behavioral sciences. For cyberpsychology researchers, virtual worlds reflect developing cultures, each with an emerging ethos and supervenient social institutions (for a discussion of supervenience see Hare, 1984). In addition to the general social phenomena emerging from virtual world communities, virtual worlds provide novel opportunities for studying them. According to Bainbridge (2007), virtual worlds proffer environments that facilitate the creation of online laboratories that can recruit potentially thousands of research subjects in an automated and economically feasible fashion. Virtual worlds like Second Life offer scripting and graphics tools that allow even a novice computer user the means necessary for building a virtual laboratory. Perhaps even more important is the fact that social interactions in online virtual worlds (e.g., Second Life) appear to reflect social norms and interactions found in the physical world (Yee et al., 2007).

4.11.4   Virtual Worlds for Medical and Health Educational Projects

Online virtual worlds also offer multiple medical and health educational projects (Boulos, Hetherington, & Wheeler, 2007). Although these programs focus primarily on the dissemination of medical information and the training of clinicians, a handful of private islands in Second Life (e.g., Brigadoon for Asperger's syndrome; Live2give for cerebral palsy) have been created for therapeutic purposes. Moreover, there is the potential of virtual worlds to improve access to medical rehabilitation. Klinger and Weiss (2009) describe the evolution of virtual worlds along two dimensions: the number of users and the distance between the users. According to Klinger and Weiss, single-user and locally used virtual worlds have developed into three additional venues: (1) multiple users located in the same setting; (2) single users remotely located; and (3) multiple users remotely located. According to Klinger and Weiss, single-user, locally operated virtual worlds will continue to be important for rehabilitation within a clinical or educational setting. However, the literature, to date, has been limited to descriptions of system development and reports of small pilot studies (Brennan, Mawson, & Brownsell, 2009). It is anticipated that this trend is changing and future years will see evidence of the effectiveness of such virtual worlds for therapy. In a recent article by Gorini et al. (2008), the authors describe such sites and the development and implementation of a form of tailored immersive e-therapy in which current technologies (e.g., virtual worlds; bio and activity sensors; and personal digital assistants) facilitate the interaction between real and 3-D virtual worlds and may increase treatment efficacy. Parsons (2012) described a number of advantages of Internet-delivered online virtual worlds:

- Systematic presentation of cognitive tasks targeting both construct-driven and function-led neuropsychological performance beyond what is currently available using traditional computerized neuropsychological assessment devices.
- Enhanced reliability of function-led neuropsychological assessment and treatment of affective and cognitive disorders in online virtual worlds by better control of the perceptual environment, consistent stimulus presentation, and more precise and accurate scoring.
- Improved validity of neurocognitive measurements via the increased quantification of discrete behavioral responses, allowing for the identification of more specific cognitive domains.
- Assessment and treatment of cognition and affect in situations that are more ecologically valid. Participants can be evaluated in an online

virtual world that simulates the real world, not a contrived testing environment.

• The option to produce and distribute identical "standard" simulation environments to large samples in which performance can be measured and treated.

Within such digital scenarios, normative data can be accumulated for performance comparisons needed for assessment/diagnosis and for treatment/rehabilitation purposes. In this manner, reusable archetypical online virtual worlds constructed for one purpose can also be applied for applications addressing other clinical targets.

4.11.5   Important Caveats about Research Using Virtual Worlds

While the increasing number of social interactions using digital media may blur distinctions between virtual environments and "real-world" environments, there are still significant differences (Gilbert et al., 2011). Many digitally mediated experiences are different from the sorts of interactions that take place in real-world environments that are face-to-face with a researcher and in a particular geographic space and time. Furthermore, users can adjust their avatars to have characteristics they may not possess in real life. For example, a user may create an avatar that is of a different age, sex, race, or adjust it to have above average height. A potential result may be that their responses to questions would change, as may their social interactions and health behaviors. That said, findings from studies have revealed that many real-world characteristics can be reliably simulated in virtual worlds: personal space (Lomanowska & Guitton, 2012); non-verbal communication (Amaoka et al., 2011; Friedman et al., 2007); and a sense of self (Behm-Morawitz, 2013). Given these findings, there is reason to be optimistic about the potential of virtual worlds for research into a broad range of cognitive performance, affective responding, social interactions, and therapeutic interventions.

4.12   Conclusions: The Internet as an Extended Cognitive System

In conclusion, the Internet has had a substantial impact on almost every aspect of human cognitive processing. In addition to online shopping, social networking sites have transformed the ways in which we interact with our significant others. Furthermore, real-time news feeds have altered the ways in which persons stay well-informed about current affairs. While there are both detractors and proponents of the Internet, it appears that the Internet stands ready to influence significantly the ways in which persons live their lives, and perhaps ultimately the Internet will influence the social, political, and economic forces that determine the ways in which our lives are lived.

That said, for the cyberpsychologist, there are a number of unanswered research questions related to the rapid growth and infiltration of the Internet. Important questions have emerged about the Internet's effects. These questions are not limited to our social activities, but also involve questions about the nature of our cognitive and epistemic profiles. While it appears obvious that the Internet is a transformative technology, this transformative impression does not necessarily discontinue at the social processes that govern everyday interactions. Examples of technological innovations that have transformed society include systems of writing, maps, and measures of time (e.g., clocks). These innovations have also exerted subtle (and sometimes not so subtle) transformations of our cognitive and intellectual capabilities. The Internet offers novel prospects for collaboration and engagement with global knowledgebases of information and interactive opportunities that may result in a paradigm shift in both the ways in which we see ourselves and in the nature of our cognitive processes.

A number of interesting questions emerge: What is the nature of this transformative influence? By what mechanisms does the Internet transform our cognitive and epistemic capabilities? A potential answer raised in this chapter comes in the form of the extended mind hypothesis (Clark & Chalmers, 1998). As described, the extended mind approach argues that human cognition is at times constituted by information-processing loops that extend beyond the neurobiological processes found in the internal workings of the human brain. As such, the machinery of human neuro-cognition is understood as extending beyond the neurocognitive realm to include elements of our social and technological environments. The application of this idea to the specific sociotechnical context of the Internet has resulted in a "Web-extended mind" approach, or the idea that the technological and informational elements of the Internet can serve as part of the mechanistic substrate that realizes human mental states and processes.

CHAPTER 5

Facebook and the Socially Networked Brain

5.1 Introduction

Each day, one billion posts are sent to Facebook by its more than 1.5 billion active users (http://newsroom.fb.com/company-info/). Online social network sites such as Facebook consist primarily of a representation of each user and their social links. These online social networking sites allow users to articulate and make visible their friendship networks (Anderson et al., 2012; Boyd & Ellison, 2007). According to a survey by the Pew Research Center (2014), in a sample of 1597 Facebook users, 70 percent reported using this platform daily. Hampton and colleagues (2011) surveyed over 2000 American adults and found that 92 percent of all social networks are on Facebook. Furthermore, slightly over half of Facebook users access Facebook daily. With so many people using Facebook and other social media sites there is an accompanying change in questions asked by cyberpsychologists. Will social media change the fundamental ways in which humans relate to one another and share information? The answer appears to be yes. Ralph Adolphs, the Director of the Emotion and Social Cognition Laboratory at the California Institute of Technology, has suggested that the emergence of social media has resulted in a profound shift in the type and quality of our social interactions. Our online interactions (e.g., email, texting, social networking) have supplemented (and even supplanted) face-to-face interactions. There is now an open question of how social cognitive development will be impacted by this drastic change in how we interact (Stanley and Adolphs, 2013).

What is it about having a network of Facebook friends that is so appealing? Are there aspects of being part of a Facebook network that has value to users? Do Facebook-related behaviors like "friending" of others, being liked, and having a social network fulfill various survival or well-being needs that are comparable to other biologically relevant goals or rewards (e.g., feeding, sex). The answers to these questions are increasingly being pursued by cyberpsychologists. The large number of Facebook users robustly suggests the significance placed on social networks in the general public. The importance of establishing social groups and maintaining close relations makes sense given that these activities reflect evolutionarily conserved phenomena (Dunbar, 2012; Rand et al., 2011). Robin Dunbar's social brain hypothesis argues that human intelligence evolved as a means of surviving and reproducing in complex social groups (Dunbar, 1992, 2011). According to the social brain hypothesis, increased neocortex size evolved so that primates could sustain more complex social interactions (Dunbar, 1993, 1998).

A number of studies with humans have found correlations between social group size and brain regions that perform an important part in social cognition (Kanai et al., 2012; Lewis et al., 2011; Powell et al., 2012). Individual differences in human amygdala volume are predictive of variations in social network size and complexity (Bickart et al., 2011; Kanai et al., 2012; Sallet et al., 2011; Von Der Heide, Vyas, & Olson, 2014). The amygdala works in aggregate with an array of other brain regions that make up the "social brain." For example, the amygdala is connected to the ventromedial prefrontal cortex (vmPFC) and superior temporal sulcus. Moreover, the amygdala has a broadly distributed topography of anatomical connections that makes it a hub within the social brain.

The brain's reward network is likely activated when a Facebook user receives a "like" to their posted content on a Facebook page. The nucleus accumbens and ventral striatum are key areas that may be involved in the reinforcing effect that happens when a "like" occurs on a user's Facebook page. The nucleus accumbens is often described as being part of a corticostriato-thalamo-cortical loop and it receives major inputs from specific brain areas (prefrontal cortex, amygdala, and the ventral tegmental area). The reward network has an important role in the neurocognitive processing of reward, pleasure, reinforcement learning, aversion, and motivation. *Dopamine acts in the reward network to attach motivational significance to stimuli associated with reward.*

Given the growing interest of social neuroscientists in online social media sites, there is an opportunity for cyberpsychologists to bring novel neuroscience approaches to traditional questions about: "What impact is social media having on us?" and "Why do we even use these online social networks?" With the considerable efforts already put into social network analysis more generally (e.g., from Google, media psychology, social neuroscience), cyberpsychologists are uniquely positioned to develop tools and metrics for the analysis of electronically available social data (e.g., online social interactions). This chapter presents examples of research from affective science and social neuroscience to provide cyber-psychologists with a platform for discussing the current state of research on the use of online social media.

5.2   Online Social Networking and the Desire to Connect

The rise of Facebook is an interesting development that reflects social and affective neuroscience principles. Over the last decade, social cognitive and affective neuroscientists have uncovered a good deal of support for the notion that the human brain facilitates, makes use of, and is partially molded by a broad array of social interactions (Cacioppo & Decety, 2011; Lieberman, 2007). This perspective is compatible with the social brain hypothesis, which is the leading elucidation of the expansion of the human brain during the course of evolution. According to Oxford University's Robin Dunbar (1998, 2011) the size of the neocortex (as compared to the whole brain) among primates correlates with a number of indices of social complexity: prevalence of social play, frequency of social learning, frequency of coalitions, male mating strategies, rate of tactical deception, grooming clique size, and social group size. To survive, humans have had to work collaboratively to deal with the many threats to our species. Throughout our evolutionary history, coping with threats has necessitated the combined efforts of many individuals. Social neuroscientists argue that the human brain developed beyond brains of other species to allow humans to connect with each other (Lieberman, 2013). As will be discussed in this chapter, humans have large-scale brain networks that are activated during social cognition (Meshi, Tamir, & Heekeren, 2015). Hence, individuals in our species may have evolved to interact with each other in a way that allows individuals to work collectively and thrive in our everyday environments. This capacity was developed for social interactions that would increase the probability of surviving and defending against threats, procuring essential resources, and managing the environment (Fitzsimons, Finkel, & vanDellen, 2015).

5.3   Social Network Size and the Brain

5.3.1   Dunbar's Social Brain Hypothesis

Comparison of primate brains to other vertebrates reveals an increased neocortex size in primates that results in a disproportionately large brain-to-body ratio that is related (monotonically) to the size of their social groups (Finlay & Darlington, 1995). These findings have led to the social brain hypothesis, which is the leading elucidation of the enlargement of the human brain during the course of evolution. Oxford University's Robin Dunbar proposed the social brain hypothesis and suggested that human intelligence did not evolve mainly as a way to resolve ecological difficulties. Instead, human intelligence is argued to have evolved as a means of surviving and reproducing in complex social groups. The typical size of social groups in primates correlates closely with neocortex size in general (Dunbar, 1992), and with the more frontal units of the neocortex in particular (Dunbar, 2011; Joffe and Dunbar, 1997). According to Dunbar and Shultz (2007) this hypothesis suggests that among primates the size of the neocortex (when compared to the whole brain) correlates with many indices of social complexity: clique size, social group size, coalition frequency, male mating strategies, social play, grooming, tactical deception rate, and social learning frequency. According to the social brain hypothesis, increased neocortex size evolved so that primates could sustain more complex social interactions (Dunbar, 1993, 1998). Recent studies of humans afford evidence of quantitative relations between social group size and brain regions that perform an important part in social cognition (Kanai et al., 2012; Lewis et al., 2011; Powell et al., 2012).

5.3.2   Dunbar's Number

In the 1990s Dunbar proposed a neurocognitive limit to the number of people a person can have in their social network. For Dunbar, these relationships are ones in which a person knows who each person is in their social network and the ways in which each person in the network relates to every other person in the network (Dunbar, 1992, 1993). Dunbar's number was developed to explain the correlation between primate brain size and average social group size. Dunbar argues that natural social networks are regulated into a distinct succession of hierarchically inclusive layers that reflect both interaction frequencies and emotional closeness. In humans, these layers have values that approximate 5, 15, 50, and 150 (Dunbar, 2014). The resulting number of a 150 stable relationship limit was extrapolated from studies of primates and the average human brain size. It is important to emphasize that Dunbar's number is meant to reflect the number of stable relations a person knows and with whom they maintain social contact. As such, it does not include people just generally known. According to Dunbar, this limit is relative to neocortical size, which in turn limits group size. Neocortical processing capacity limits the number of people that a person can have in their social network.

Dunbar's number comes primarily from work done before the advent of online social networks like Facebook. Does the seemingly ubiquitous and perpetual use of social media challenge the continued relevance of Dunbar's number? Perhaps it is possible to maintain more stable relations with Facebook, Twitter, and Instagram. Preliminary research into this question has revealed that even in virtual networks the Dunbar number holds. For example, Nicole Ellison and colleagues (2011) at the Michigan State University surveyed a random sample of undergraduates about their Facebook use and found that although their median number of Facebook friends was 300, the actual ones that they considered friends were around 75. Dunbar (2016) further explored this question using two surveys randomly stratified by age, gender, and regional population size. Results reveal that the number of online friends in a Facebook network that are actual friends is similar to that of offline face-to-face networks. In one of the samples, participants also indicated the number of friends in their network that could be considered part of a support clique and sympathy group. The number of these friends was similar in size to those observed in offline networks. For Dunbar, this suggests that there is a neurocognitive limit on the number of friends that a person can have in either offline or online social networks.

5.3.3　*Online Social Network Size and the Social Brain*

The Internet offers cyberpsychologists a fertile area for investigating social networks. Online social networking and the increasing use of digital media might allow cyberpsychologists opportunities to assess the social brain and related hypotheses about relations among social networks and various brain areas. With the rise of social networking sites cyberpsychologists have the opportunity to study the results of broadcasting one's information to many members of one's network at once. Furthermore, social networking sites offer cyberpsychologists opportunities to study the impact of continuously updating our understanding of network members' behavior and thoughts.

A critical survival ability for primates is the capability of forging and maintaining various social relationships. Interestingly, there is a great deal of variability in the size of social networks from one individual to the next. Research has revealed that individual differences in human amygdala volume predicted variations in social network size and complexity

(Bickart et al., 2011; Kanai et al., 2012; Sallet et al., 2011; Von Der Heide, Vyas, & Olson, 2014). From these studies it is apparent that the amygdala works in aggregate with an array of other brain regions that make up the "social brain." The amygdala is strongly connected with the vmPFC and superior temporal sulcus and has a broadly distributed topography of anatomical connections, which allows it to be considered a hub within the social brain. The connectional organization of the amygdala places it in an essential locus to influence a range of brain networks that are significant for social cognition (Bickart, Dickerson, and Barrett, 2014).

Studies of offline social networking have found that the size and complexity of social networks correlated significantly with amygdala volume (Bickart et al., 2011). Recently Kanai and colleagues (2012) investigated the relation between users' involvement in online social networks and the anatomical structure of human brain regions implicated in sociocognitive behaviors. For the study, they made use of voxel-based morphometry in a large sample of adult humans. Specifically, they aimed to explore the relations between sociability indices (number of Facebook friends and sociability) and amygdala volume as well as volume of several cortical regions. Specific brain regions were chosen (left middle temporal gyrus, right superior temporal sulcus, right entorhinal cortex) because they have been previously identified as being associated with theory of mind competences. Results revealed that the number of social contacts on a major online social networking site was strongly associated with the structure of focal brain regions. Specifically, they found that variation in the number of Facebook friends significantly predicted grey matter volume in left middle temporal gyrus, right superior temporal sulcus, and right entorhinal cortex. Furthermore, they found that the grey matter density of the amygdala that was earlier shown to be linked with offline social network size was also significantly related to online social network size.

While Kanai and colleagues' (2012) findings that the density of gray matter in the amygdala, right superior temporal sulcus, left middle temporal gyrus, and entorhinal cortex correlated with differences in social network size, other studies have also found that portions of the frontal lobe (including orbitofrontal cortex) have significant correlation with social network measures (Lewis et al., 2011). An issue that may be responsible for the discrepancies is the different social network measures used by different research groups. In a study by Von der Heide and colleagues (2014) efforts were taken to examine the importance of one online measure of social network size (e.g., number of Facebook friends) and two real-world measures (Dunbar's number and Norbeck Social Support Group).

They found that volumetric differences predict social network size across a range of measures. Furthermore, findings provide support for left and right amygdal involvement. Support was also provided for the orbital frontal cortex and entorhinal/ventromedial anterior temporal lobe in processes required for the maintenance of robust social networks.

5.4 Large-Scale Brain Networks and Social Media

While the social brain hypothesis helps us to understand that there is a relation between the size of the neocortex and social relations, we are still left with the question of what part of the brain is social. One way to understand this issue is something called the brain's "default-mode network" (DMN). The DMN is constantly running in the background and is involved in thinking about one's self and others. When not engaged in some other activity, the DMN is activated as the brain ruminates about self and others. This automated processing is turned down when doing an active control process (e.g., doing difficult math problems; Schilbach et al., 2008). The DMN is made up of anterior and posterior medial cortices and lateral parietal lobes. Recent evidence suggests considerable overlap between the default-mode network (DMN) and regions involved in social, affective, and introspective processes (Forbes & Grafman, 2010; Mars et al., 2012). Moreover, self-referential processing, autobiographical memory, and social cognition have been tied to the DMN (Amodio & Frith, 2006; Qin & Northoff, 2011; Raichle, 2015; Spreng, Mar, & Kim, 2009).

An independent body of work in the social neurosciences has revealed an overlapping "mentalizing network" that reveals the neural correlates of a person's ability to mentalize (i.e., infer) the cognitions and feelings of others. The similarity between the default and mentalizing networks has generated questions in social neuroscience about whether the core function of the default network is to mediate internal aspects of social cognition (Li, Mai, & Liu, 2014). Amft and colleagues (2015) considered the overlapping brain regions thought to be involved in the social-affective part of the DMN. Among the identified regions of this, the extended social-affective default network, the amygdala, and hippocampus formed a cluster associated with emotional processes and memory functions. Areas involved in motivation, reward, and cognitive modulation of affect included ventral striatum, anterior cingulum, subgenual cingulum, and ventromedial prefrontal cortex. The identified areas for mentalizing, self-reference, and autobiographic information included the posterior cingulum/precuneus

Table 5.1 *Three proposed brain networks that may be involved in the use of social media*

Network	Brain areas	Example(s)
Mentalizing Network	• Dorsomedial prefrontal cortex (dmPFC) • Temporoparietal junction (TPJ) • Anterior temporal lobe (ATL) • Inferior frontal gyrus (IFG) • Posterior cingulate cortex (PCC)	• A social media user may think about how persons in her network will respond to a post. • A social media user may think about how a specific user may react upon reading feedback related to a post. • A social media user may think about the other user's motivations for posting information.
Self-referential Cognition Network	• Medial prefrontal cortex (mPFC) • PCC	• A social media user may think about herself and then broadcast those thoughts, which may provoke further self-referential thought. • A user may receive feedback that results in reflected self-appraisals. • Social comparison requires users to think about their own behavior in relation to other users.
Reward Network	• Ventromedial prefrontal cortex (vmPFC) • Ventral striatum (VS) • Ventral tegmental area (VTA)	• A Facebook user may receive positive feedback in the form of a "like," or "friend" request. • Reading others' posts may elicit reward activity, because receiving information elicits curiosity. • These rewards activate the user's brain reward system and compel the user to return to Facebook for more.

Note: This table represents an aggregate of information drawn from Meshi, Tamir, and Heekeren (2015).

and dorsomedial prefrontal cortex. Language and social cognition were related to a cluster formed by the temporo-parietal junction and anterior middle temporal sulcus/gyrus. In summary, their findings highlight a strongly interconnected network that may be central to social-affective processing.

In a recent review of the emerging neuroscience of social media, Meshi, Tamir, and Heekeren (2015) discuss the growing global phenomenon of online social media (almost two billion users worldwide regularly using these social networking sites) and the potential for neuroscientists to make use of these pervasive social media sites to gain new understanding of social cognitive processes and the neural systems that support them. They also outline social motives that drive people to use social media and propose neural systems supporting social media use (see Table 5.1).

Cyberpsychologists can leverage these studies and the proposed social media examples to enhance understanding of brain processes involved when humans interact with social media. Studies have already been performed that examined the relation between online social network size and gray matter density (Kanai et al., 2012; Von Der Heide et al., 2014). Results revealed that social media users with larger online social networks had larger amygdalae than users with lesser social networks. These results are important because they replicate previous research with real-world social networks (Bickart et al., 2011). These findings support the viability of using social media metrics for investigating social neurocognitive processes.

5.5 Facebook and the Reward Network

What happens when an individual receives a "like" to their posted content on a Facebook page? Typically, this represents a rewarding experience for the person and promotes further social networking. However, what happens in the person's brain when he or she sees someone "like" their Facebook post? The answer may involve a part of the ventral striatum that lies in a region in the basal forebrain rostral to the preoptic area of the hypothalamus. Specifically, that reinforcing effect that occurs when a person experiences a "like" on Facebook reflects activity in the nucleus accumbens.

There are a number of major inputs to the nucleus accumbens from specific brain areas (prefrontal cortex, amygdala (basolateral), and the ventral tegmental area (VTA)) and the nucleus accumbens is often described as being part of a cortico-striato-thalamo-cortical loop. The nucleus accumbens has an important role in the neurocognitive processing of reward, pleasure, reinforcement learning, aversion, and motivation. *Dopamine acts in the nucleus accumbens to attach motivational significance to stimuli associated with reward.* Dopaminergic neurons found in the VTA connect via the mesolimbic pathway and modulate the activity of neurons within the nucleus accumbens that are activated directly or indirectly by drugs like opiates and amphetamines. Dopamine offers a powerfully rewarding experience and has been linked to romantic love. In fact, the VTA and dopamine were important aspects of Helen Fisher (2006) of Match.com's model of the brain systems involved in mating and reproduction. She aimed to distinguish between romantic love and attachment. The brain activations associated with romantic love scores (e.g., VTA) have been found to be distinct from brain area activations associated with attachment (e.g., GP, SN).

This leads to the issue at hand. Social media and online dating sites tap into the reward areas of the brain and that impacts the user's ability to focus on other things. Our default-mode network is inclined toward social processes and it takes the overriding control process of the executive-control network to inhibit automatic impulses, especially impulses to which we are strongly drawn. In the same way that the brain resists doing complex calculations in our heads, it requires extra effort to control impulses.

5.5.1   Nucleus Accumbens and Facebook

What does the nucleus accumbens and being liked have to do with Facebook? The answer is in the experience of being liked itself. This is a significant social event and essential to motivating human behavior. In a study by Davey and colleagues (2010) there was an investigation of the neural correlates of the "being liked" experience in a group of 15- to 24-year-olds. This cohort was chosen because for participants in this cohort the formation of friendships has a great degree of salience. Furthermore, for participants in this cohort the explicit representation of relationships is apparent in their frequent use of social networking technologies. Participants were told that other participants had judged their likability based on their appearance in a photograph. During functional magnetic resonance imaging they viewed the photographs of people who had ostensibly responded favorably to them. Findings suggest that being liked activated primary reward- and self-related regions: nucleus accumbens, midbrain (corresponding to the ventral tegmentum), ventromedial prefrontal cortex, posterior cingulate cortex, amygdala, and insula. Furthermore, greater activation was found in the ventromedial prefrontal cortex and amygdala in response to being liked. In a related way, it may be the case that dopaminergic neurons can also be activated by taking part in rewarding experiences like someone liking one's posts on Facebook (Davey et al., 2010; Meshi, Morawetz, and Heekeren, 2013). Additionally, the rewarding "like" can promote increased time and energy the user expends on a given social media site.

When someone makes a post to their Facebook page, they are typically doing so to get others from their social network to read and value it. In situations where someone from that user's social network actually read it and "like" the posts there is a rewarding feeling that results. In a recent study, Meshi, Morawetz, and Heekeren (2013) used functional magnetic resonance imaging (fMRI) to examine the brains of 31 Facebook users as they read positive captions that accompanied pictures of either themselves or others. The researchers were interested in both the intensity of Facebook use and social comparison (via "Likes") using Facebook. For the experiment, participants were in one of the following conditions: (1) informed that they have a good reputation; (2) informed that another person has a good reputation; or (3) informed that they received money.

The fMRI technology allowed Meshi and colleagues to measure each participant's brain activity via detection of blood flow to activated areas of the brain. Specifically, they used fMRI to examine the extent to which the participant's brain activity was related to the participant's use of Facebook. Results revealed that it is possible to predict the intensity of participants' Facebook use outside the fMRI scanner by looking at their brain's response to positive Facebook responses inside the fMRI. Specifically, there was greater activation in the nucleus accumbens for praise for oneself when compared to praise for others. Furthermore, this increased nucleus accumbens activation was related to greater time on the social media site. Interestingly, the amount of nucleus accumbens response to monetary reward was not predictive of Facebook use.

Given the fact that social affirmation tends to be a rewarding experience for the vast majority of users it is not surprising that Facebook affirmations would result in activation of the nucleus accumbens. Dopamine neurons located in the ventral tegmental area and projecting to the nucleus accumbens play a key role in the processing of reward-related stimuli, including those associated with drugs of abuse (Wise, 2008). Furthermore, the prefrontal cortex and amygdala share interconnections with the ventral tegmental area and nucleus accumbens and can modulate dopamine transmission and neuronal activity. However, just because these areas have been found to be associated with Facebook likes, activation alone is not sufficient for the establishment of an addiction. Nevertheless, brain activations in these areas do raise an interesting possibility that Facebook "likes" and other affirmations (chime for an incoming text or email) might be the first step toward an addiction in some users (Turel & Serenko, 2012).

5.5.2   Online Self-Disclosure and the Reward Network

Why do people self-disclose so readily on Facebook? Part of the answer is that Facebook was designed in a way that encourages self-disclosure. For example, the Facebook status update box asks "what's on your mind," which may prompt users to self-disclose. Furthermore, Facebook has gone to great lengths to offer a user-friendly platform that facilitates the posting of pictures, thoughts, likes, status updates, and sharing of other Web content with Facebook friends. In addition to Facebook's design, users have been designed via evolution to self-disclose. From as early as nine months of age, human infants attempt to draw the attention of others to features of the environment they think are important (Woodward et al., 2009). This proclivity continues across the lifespan as adults attempt to convey their knowledge to others. Likewise, Diana Tamir and Jason Mitchell (2012) found that 80 percent of posts to social media sites were self-disclosures about the user's own immediate experiences. In their investigation of why so many social media users self-disclose (e.g., share their everyday thoughts, locations, activities, and opinions), they found that self-disclosing activates the brain's reward network. Specifically, self-disclosure was found to be robustly related to increased activation in brain regions that make up the mesolimbic dopamine system: nucleus accumbens and ventral tegmental area. As a consequence, the user experiences rewards like the ones we experience when eating or having sex.

5.5.3   Variable-Ratio Schedules

An additional component influencing Facebook's strong impact on users is that affirmations from social media (e.g., likes, text chimes, ringtones) from other users occur only sporadically. From a cyberpsychology and behavioral perspective, this rate of online reinforcement represents a variable-ratio schedule that produces the sort of high steady rate of responding found in gambling and lottery games. How does this reward system become activated for Facebook users? The answer is that Facebook has multiple variable-ratio reinforcement schedules built into it – a user could receive a "like", friend request, comment on the user's status update, or be tagged in a photo. Any of these situations (among the many other possible ones) might place the user in a state of anticipation. This variable-ratio pattern of reinforcement can be more addicting than receiving affirmation every time because (at least in part) the user's brain endeavors to predict rewards. In variable-ratio reward schedules the brain cannot find the pattern and it will promote a behavior until it finds one. In situations where the rewards (e.g., affirmations, chimes) are random, the brain's attempt at pattern recognition may continue compulsively.

5.6 Dark Side of Social Networking

The activation of the reward network via variable-ratio schedules may help to explain the increasing usage trend that is apparent in recent years. Moreover, they may help to explain the increased instances of social media use resulting in cyber addiction (Kuss & Griffiths, 2012). Excessive social media use can become a serious problem. It may be the case that self-disclosing and subsequent activation of the reward pathways in the brain is linked to the development of cyber addiction.

5.6.1 Neural Correlates of Facebook "Addiction"

Given that addictive behaviors typically result from imbalances of two brain systems, the prefrontal cortex (reflective system of executive-control) and the amygdala-striatal (reflexive system of automatic and impulsive response) brain systems, there is need for cyberpsychological studies that examine whether these brain systems underpin a specific case of technology-related addiction. Lieberman (2007) describes these two systems in terms of a reflective (controlled) system and a reflexive (automatic) system. The reflective system represents a controlled cognitive processing system made up of the prefrontal cortex (lateral and medial), parietal cortex (lateral and medial), medial temporal lobe, and rostral anterior cingulate cortex. Lieberman also describes a reflexive system that represents automatic cognitive processing in the amygdala, basal ganglia, ventromedial prefrontal cortex, lateral temporal cortex, and dorsal anterior cingulate cortex.

5.6.2   Online Social Interactions and Executive Functions

Given findings that portions of the frontal lobe including the orbitofrontal cortex have been found to be related to social network size (Lewis et al., 2011; Von der Heide et al., 2014), it may behoove cyberpsychologists to look at the relationships between online social interactions and executive functioning. The frontal lobes are involved directly and indirectly across a wide spectrum of human thought, behavior, and emotions. A specific capacity of the frontal lobes is collectively referred to as executive functioning: selective attention, inhibitory control, planning, problem solving, and some aspects of short-term memory (see Diamond, 2013, for review).

Results from earlier studies have implicated the orbitofrontal cortex in social networking. The orbitofrontal cortex (medial orbitofrontal cortex; and lateral orbitofrontal cortex) and adjacent ventromedial prefrontal cortex transmit reward representations and mediate flexible behavior in the face of changing circumstances (Noonan et al., 2012). These abilities sound a lot like the sorts of abilities needed for an effective social interaction, which frequently involves online and dynamic production of a mental-model of another user's beliefs, expectations, affect, and motivations. Furthermore, online social interactions require the executive functioning capacities for maintaining attention, problem-solving, and pursuing goals in the face of distractions (Ybarra and Winkielman, 2012).

It is important to note that there is growing evidence that Internet addiction is related to brain structural changes and decreased executive-control processes. A study using the Stroop color-word test, a widely used measure for assessing inhibitory control, found that adolescents with Internet gaming disorder had impaired cognitive control (Yuan et al., 2013). Further evidence from neuroimaging has shown that brain regions associated with executive function (e.g., orbitofrontal cortex) had decreased cortical thickness in Internet-addicted adolescents (Hong et al., 2013). Consistent results were found from neuroimaging that also revealed brain regions associated with executive function (e.g., left lateral orbitofrontal cortex, insula cortex, and entorhinal cortex) had decreased cortical thickness in Internet gambling disordered participants. Further, reduced cortical thickness of the left lateral orbitofrontal cortex was associated with impaired cognitive control.

Hence, an aspect of executive functioning that has received increasing interest is self-control (i.e., inhibitory control). Self-control has been defined as "the self's capacity to override or change one's inner responses, as well as to interrupt undesired behavioral tendencies and to refrain from acting on them" (Tangney et al., 2004, p. 274). This definition emphasizes self-control as an inhibitory mechanism. Self-control has been shown to be very important and beneficial to the human experience and is associated with a pleasant and healthy life. High levels of self-control have also been positively related to self-esteem and good interpersonal skills (Tangney et al., 2004). The robustness of a person's self-control is predictive of whether they can attain goals that require self-control. There is now evidence that persons with low levels of self-control may have greater propensity for Internet addiction (Muusses et al., 2013).

A further executive functioning component that may be related to extensive Facebook use is action-state orientation, which is an individual difference variable associated with volitional processes that are used by individuals to engage in goal-directed behaviors (Kuhl, 1981). From the perspective of executive functioning, action orientation can be understood as the ability to regulate one's cognitions, affects, and behaviors in accordance with intentions. Deficits are related to the difficulty in dedicating neurocognitive resources to task fulfillment and include difficulties in initiating or maintaining action. In a study by Błachnio and Przepiorka (2015) researchers aimed to look at whether insufficient self-control in Facebook users was associated with addiction to Facebook. Their findings revealed that self-control and action control are related to Facebook addiction. Furthermore, lower levels of self-control and failure-related action orientation were related to Facebook addiction. These findings comport well with findings from the general literature that suggest good self-control results in better life coping. (Tangney et al., 2004). Additionally, findings from the literature reveal that high levels of self-control are associated with healthy Internet use (Muusses et al., 2013). Results from the study by Błachnio and Przepiorka suggest that participants who are low in self-control have difficulties with dysfunctional Facebook use. Furthermore, their findings revealed that low levels of failure-related action orientation are related to Facebook addiction.

5.6.3   *Shallow Information Processing: Rapid Attention Shifting and Reduced Deliberations*

An issue for avid users of current and emerging social media technologies is that they gravitate toward "shallow" information processing that is characterized by rapid attention shifting and reduced deliberations. Their approach to information processing and proclivity for multitasking has been associated with increased distractibility and poor executive-control (Ophir, Nass, and Wagner, 2009). These "Digital natives" also tend to have a higher prevalence of Internet addiction, altered reward-processing, and decreased self-control. According to Nicholas Carr (2010), intensive Internet use is associated with increases in this shallow information processing because the users are continually shifting attention, examining the text at a shallow level, cogitating less about the content, and have decreased ability to retain information. Carr's argument has found support in the work of Sparrow, Liu, and Wegner (2011) who noted that having information at one's fingertips (i.e., Google or other search engines) is associated with lowered information retention. As a result, there is a tendency to become overly reliant on one's computers and the information stored on the Internet. Furthermore, Loh and Kanai (2014) have cited a great deal of empirical research that has shown increased browsing is related with decreased sustained attention.

In a recent study of Facebook addiction, Turel and colleagues (2014) examined neural activities in the prefrontal (reflective-controlled) and amygdala-striatal (reflexive-automatic) systems when Facebook users are exposed to Facebook cues. The study presented participants with a Go/No-Go paradigm while they were in a functional magnetic resonance imaging setting. The researchers examined these two brain systems in 20 Facebook users as they responded to Facebook and less potent (traffic sign) stimuli. Before entering the scanner, participants completed an online version of the Facebook "addiction" scale (adapted from van Rooij et al., 2011) that asked participants to report the frequency of typical Facebook "addiction" symptoms (e.g., withdrawal, salience, relapse, loss of control, and conflict).

While in the scanner, participants performed two Facebook-specific Go/No-Go tasks: (1) Sign Go/Facebook no-go task: Participants were asked to initiate a button press when they viewed a traffic sign image, and resist button pressing when they viewed a Facebook-related image; and (2) Facebook Go/Sign no-go task: Participants were asked to initiate a button press when they viewed a Facebook-related image, and resist button pressing when they viewed a traffic sign image. The authors argued that this Go/No-Go paradigm allows for assessment of both the brain responses to Facebook stimuli and the inhibition of pre-potent responses to Facebook stimuli. Results revealed that although technology-related "addictions" share some neural features with substance and gambling addictions, they differ from such addictions in their brain etiology. Specifically, amygdala-striatal (reflexive) brain system activation was positively related with Facebook "addiction" scores. However, there was not a significant link between activation of the prefrontal cortex (reflective) brain system and Facebook "addiction" scores.

What does this all mean? The authors argue that these findings suggested that participants with low to medium levels of addiction-like symptoms have a hyperactive amygdala-striatal (reflexive) system that makes Facebook "addiction" similar to many other addictions. However, these participants do not have a hypoactive prefrontal lobe (reflective) system and this makes Facebook "addiction" different from many other addictions (e.g., addiction to illicit substances). Consequently, Facebook "addiction" appears to not present with the exact brain etiology found in substance and gambling addictions.

5.6.4　Facebook and Depression

That said, links have been made between Facebook and depression. While a number of studies have found that depression was increasing with increased use of social media, the understanding of why this is the case is a more recent development. According to Steers and colleagues (2014) at the University of Houston the explanation comes from social comparison theory. Humans are constantly prompted to take part in "social comparison," and they become habituated to it as "upward comparisons" (e.g., a recent divorcée might experience depressive symptoms related to being single after observing recent engagement photos posted on Facebook) result in negative affect and "downward comparisons" (e.g., a student that received an A on a test may experience increased confidence after reading a status update about a friend's failing grade on an exam) result in positive affect.

In a study by Steers and colleagues (2014) participants were asked about their Facebook usage and how likely it would be for them to make social comparisons (e.g., "I always pay a lot of attention to how I do things compared with how others do things"). Participants were also queried about the frequency with which they experienced negative affects (e.g., depressive symptoms). Results revealed that participants that reported greater Facebook use tended to have more depressive symptoms.

In a second part of the study the researchers aimed to go a bit deeper and develop a protocol that follows previous face-to-face research on social comparisons that found upward social comparisons (e.g., participant looking at someone more popular or attractive than s/he) tended to make people experience negative affect. This research had also found that downward comparisons (e.g., participant compares self to someone with lower grades) tended to make participants experience positive feelings. For the second part of the study the researchers aimed to investigate this difference by asking participants to report their exact feelings when they viewed other people's posts (e.g., "Today, when I was on Facebook, I felt less confident about what I have achieved compared to other people"). Results revealed that participants who spent greater amounts of time on Facebook had more depressive symptoms. These results suggest that it was irrelevant whether a participant was making upward or downward social comparison because both resulted in a greater likelihood for depressive symptoms.

Given the power of social media, it is not surprising that social media use has been linked to reductions in mental health (Hugues & Lewis, 2015; Sampasa-Kanyinga & Lewis, 2015). A recent study by Sampasa-Kanyinga and Lewis (2015) investigated the relation between time spent on social networking sites and mental health support, self-rated mental health, and reports of psychological distress and suicidal ideation in a representative sample of middle and high school children in Ottawa, Canada. Findings from this study suggest frequent social media use may also affect the psychological well-being of young adolescents. In fact, adolescents and teens (i.e., grades 7–12) using social media sites for two or more hours a day were significantly more likely to suffer from poor mental health, psychological distress, and suicidal thoughts.

Related findings were found in a study by researchers at Ohio State University that examined the impact of media multitasking on university students' social and psychological well-being (i.e., normalcy, social success, and self-control). To address inconsistent findings in recent literature, Xu, Wang, and David (2016) characterized media multitasking behaviors by motivations, characteristics, and contexts. Specifically, they examined the motivation of the main task and the synchronicity of the task in the presence of social interactions. Findings revealed that synchronous social interactions were significantly and positively related to normalcy, social success, and self-control.

5.7   Social Brain Networking

Cyberpsychologists are increasingly using Facebook and other online social media to collect information and disseminate opinion. For example, with a Facebook page, cyberpsychologists can discuss topics and link to primary articles and data. As a result, Facebook offers an opportunity for more rapid scientific discussion, wider access to specialist debates, and increased cross-disciplinary interaction. Cyberpsychologists are increasingly using the Internet as a platform to collaborate with their colleagues and others. Furthermore, Facebook can offer a forum for instant broadcasting of thoughts and comments. Hence, cyberpsychology posts on Facebook can expedite communication with colleagues and to the interested public. For the cyberpsychologist, this permits discussion of cyberpsychology research in the psychologist's own words and it affords the cyberpsychologist with a greater prospective audience than when cyberpsychology research is reported in a newspaper or magazine. Moreover, Facebook readers can offer rapid and automatic reply postings. Another bonus of the Facebook platform is that cyberpsychologists can post a topic of interest and offer links directly to primary sources in the scientific literature.

A further benefit of Facebook is that it offers cyberpsychologists a fertile research backdrop. While there are an increasing number of studies into Facebook's influence on users and societies (Wilson, Gosling, & Graham, 2012), the potential of this powerful research tool for both online and offline research in cyberpsychology is often overlooked. That said, cyberpsychologists are increasingly making use of Facebook multiple tools for inexpensive recruitment of large and diverse samples. As a result, cyberpsychologists can go beyond the overreliance on relatively small and disproportionately Western, educated, industrialized, rich, and democratic samples (Henrich, Heine, & Norenzayan, 2010). Facebook can also be used as a potent data-recording tool because it stores detailed demographic profiles and records of a massive amount of actual behavior expressed in a naturalistic context. With Facebook users' consent, cyberpsychologists can record participant data retrospectively, which greatly reduces the limitations found in self-report and laboratory-controlled studies (Paulhus & Vazire, 2007).

Michal Kosinski and colleagues (2015) point to the growing proportion of human activities that are now mediated by digital devices and services such as Facebook: social interactions, entertainment, shopping, and information gathering. These digitally mediated behaviors can be straightforwardly logged and analyzed. Moreover, research using Facebook can facilitate the change from small-scale experiments to large-scale projects based on thousands or millions of individuals. Experimenting with large samples permits cyberpsychologists to curtail concerns due to sampling error and enhance detection of patterns that might not be observable in smaller samples. Facebook also provides the opportunity for significant insights into the dynamics and organization of Facebook users' behaviors and social systems (Lazer et al., 2009).

5.8   Conclusions

Online social network sites such as Facebook consist primarily of a representation of each user and their social links. These online social networking sites allow users to articulate and make visible their friendship networks. Our online interactions (e.g., email, texting, social networking) have supplemented (and even supplanted) face-to-face interactions. There is now an open question of how social cognitive development will be impacted by this drastic change in how we interact.

Given the enthusiasm for applying social neuroscience to online social media sites, there is an opportunity for cyberpsychologists to bring novel neuroscience approaches to traditional questions. With the considerable efforts already put into social network analysis more generally, cyberpsychologists are uniquely positioned to develop tools and metrics for the analysis of electronically available social data. This chapter presented examples of research from affective science and social neuroscience to provide cyberpsychologists with a platform for discussing the current state of research on the use of online social media.

Following the growing global phenomenon of online social media and the potential for neuroscientists to make use of the pervasiveness of social media sites, researchers have started to theorize about the social motives that drive people to use social media and propose neural systems supporting social media use. The result has been an increasing interest in the neural correlates of online social networking and the desire of users to connect. Some research has drawn from Robin Dunbar's social brain hypothesis, which has been used by cyberpsychology researchers to understand that there is a relation between the size of the neocortex and online social networks.

In addition to this work, this chapter summarized some of the work being done that links Facebook "Likes" and reward in the nucleus accumbens. In fact, there are a number of major inputs to the nucleus accumbens from specific brain areas (prefrontal cortex, amygdala (basolateral), and the ventral tegmental area (VTA)) and the nucleus accumbens is often described as being part of a cortico-striato-thalamo-cortical loop. Social media and online dating sites tap into the reward areas of the brain and that impacts the user's ability to focus on other things.

The activation of the reward network via variable-ratio schedules may help to explain the increasing usage trend that is apparent in recent years. Moreover, they may help to explain the increased instances of social media use resulting in cyber addiction. Excessive social media use can become a serious problem. It may be the case that self-disclosing and subsequent activation of the reward pathways in the brain are linked to the development of cyber addiction.

Finally, Cyberpsychologists are increasingly using Facebook and other online social media to collect information and disseminate opinion. With a Facebook page, cyberpsychologists can discuss topics and link to primary articles and data. As a result, Facebook offers an opportunity for more rapid scientific discussion, wider access to specialist debates, and increased cross-disciplinary interaction. A further benefit of research with Facebook is that it offers a powerful research tool for both online and offline research in cyberpsychology.

CHAPTER 6

The Media Multitasked Brain

6.1 Introduction

Today people are increasingly exposed to a multiplicity of diverse media types. Given the accessibility of these media technologies, the ways in which people use media have changed dramatically. With the ubiquity of media technologies, people increasingly add greater amounts of media content into the same amount of time. This is accomplished through the use of numerous media types concurrently, in this manner taking part in "media multitasking." Examples of media multitasking (MMT) include multitasking in situations where the person is using media and taking part in a non-media activity (e.g., sending instant messages while doing work); and multitasking with two or more types of media (e.g., surfing on the Internet while watching television). For each of these media multitasking examples there is a requirement that users frequently shift between two or more tasks (e.g., set-shifting); and that attention to one task (e.g., doing one's work) is disrupted by switching to another task (e.g., answering a text). Hence, media multitasking involves the simultaneous use of multiple media streams. It is important to note that there is a difference between a person using a lot of media and extensive multitasking while using media. A media multitasker is one that not only consumes a lot of media, but one that does so concurrently.

In an early account on the phenomenon of MMT the Kaiser Family Foundation reported that American youth spend more time with media than in any other activity (Rideout et al., 2010). Specifically, they spend an average of 7.5 hours per day, every day of the week. When considering the 29 percent of time spent managing several media streams simultaneously, American youth averaged almost 11 hours of MMT every day. Interestingly, even younger children have been found to expend approximately two hours per day with screen media (Rideout, 2011). Furthermore, half of 5- to 8-year-olds take part in MMT at least occasionally (Rideout,

2011). It is important to note that media multitasking is not only an American phenomenon. In a study of media multitasking behaviors across three countries (i.e., United States, Russia, and Kuwait) Kononova (2013) found a number of parallels to the findings of Rideout and colleagues. The wide availability of media use and attendant MMT has resulted in a great deal of scientific and societal interest. In addition to interest in determining whether and how MMT impacts cognition, affect, and behavior, there has been increasing interest in its impact on brain structure and function.

Research into MMT has generally revealed negative impacts of MMT on cognitive processing and well-being. As a result, this research has resulted in concerns among parents, educators, and employers regarding the impact of MMT during certain types of activities (e.g., completing work, classroom learning in technology-rich environments). For example, Rideout (2015) found that many teenagers report at least sometimes doing homework while using another medium:

- Watching television (51 percent)
- Social-networking (50 percent)
- Text-messaging (60 percent)
- Listening to music (76 percent)

It is important to note that media multitasking inhibits concurrent learning, and heavy media multitasking is associated with cognitive differences even when people are performing single tasks. A number of researchers are increasingly interested in the ways in which the use of modern technology may alter how individuals process information. Studies have revealed that distraction while new information is learned leads to decreased retention and may even alter the neural systems involved (Foerde, Knowlton, & Poldrack, 2006). This may result in an increasing prevalence of media multitasking that may influence everyday activities and cognitions beyond the classroom.

6.2   Media Multitasking and Learning in College Students

Research with college students has revealed that students frequently engage with media (that is not relevant to the material) while they are attempting to learn. In one study of college students, 91 percent reported that they had texted in their classes. Furthermore, 62 percent believed that in-class texting is acceptable as long as it does not disturb other students (Tindell & Bohlander, 2012). In another study, two-thirds of students in a college-aged sample endorsed using electronic media while in class and when studying (Jacobsen & Forste, 2011; Junco & Cotton, 2011). Similar findings have been found with Israeli students (Hammer et al., 2010). For cyber-psychologists, the next logical question is what effect does media multitasking have on the student? Research into the impact of media multitasking while college students are attempting to learn has revealed mixed results. While a number of studies have shown limited (Rosen et al., 2013) to null (Kolek & Saunders, 2008; Pasek, More, & Hargittai, 2009) relations between media multitasking and grade point average, other studies have found that text-messaging and Facebook use had a negative relationship to grade point average (Burak, 2012; Clayson & Haley, 2013; Junco & Cotten, 2012; Lee, 2012).

In addition to research findings related to grade point average, results with respect to reading while a television was playing in the background revealed declines in students' ability to comprehend narrative (Lin, Robertson, & Lee, 2009) and recall prose (Armstrong, Boiarsky, & Mares, 1991). These deficits increased when students were actively watching the television program (Lin, Robertson, & Lee, 2009). Moreover, a study looking at reading efficiency while replying to instant messages found that the time needed to read a passage increased from 29 minutes (when not text messaging) to 49 minutes while text messaging (Bowman et al., 2010).

Another area revealing the impact of media multitasking on college students is that they tend to learn less when dividing attention between using handheld devices and listening to lectures. This has been found in situations where the students were sending or receiving text messages (Rosen et al., 2013), taking part in a direct chatting task (Kinzie et al., 2005), and social networking and instant messaging (Wood et al., 2012).

6.3   Media Multitasking and Learning in Children and Adolescents

What about future college students? What are the impacts of media multitasking on children and adolescents? Rideout (2011) reported that parents of young children (starting around 5–8 years of age) endorsed that their children multitasked during homework. Moreover, even at earlier ages parents have reported that their infants often played while the television was playing in the background (Masur & Flynn, 2008). Studies by Pool and colleagues in the Netherlands found that eighth graders that watched a Dutch-language soap opera while working had reduced accuracy (Pool et al., 2000; Pool et al., 2003a) and speed (Pool et al., 2000; Pool et al.,

2003b) on both a memorization task and a paper-and-pencil task. Further support can be found in a study that found decreased accuracy on problem-solving homework tasks as students switch more frequently to other computer-based tasks (Adler & Benbunan-Fich, 2013). Furthermore, completing homework while sending text messages may do more than just reduce speed and accuracy. Studies have also found a negative impact on the learner's perceived ability to perform homework (Junco & Cotten, 2011).

What are the neural correlates of these media multitasking–related learning deficits? One thought is that these learning deficits reflect distractions. In a functional magnetic resonance imaging (fMRI) study, Poldrack and Foerde (2007) found that participants had greater difficulty in learning new material when their brains were distracted by another task. Specifically, neuroimaging results revealed that the hippocampus was activated when participants learned material and there were no distractions. However, when participants learned material while multitasking, the striatum was activated and the hippocampus was not engaged. The striatum is involved in skill learning and habitual task performance (see Chapter 2 in this book). Interestingly, these brain differences may not necessarily be negative. Research studies have revealed that practice and training may in fact enhance brain processing speed, working memory, and improve a user's ability to multitask (Dux et al., 2009; Jaeggi et al., 2008; Ruthruff et al., 2006). Lin (2009) points out that being continuously immersed in multitasking settings may result in the development of different brain processing and situational awareness in heavy media multi-taskers. For Lin, this means that it is imperative that cyberpsychologists delineate the context, measurement, and valued outcomes of learning when investigating the effects of media multitasking on learning.

6.4   Psychological Profiles of Media Multitaskers

Heavy and prolonged levels of media multitasking have been associated with a number of psychological profiles. For example, media multitasking behavior has been found to positively correlate with trait impulsivity (Minear et al., 2013; Uncapher et al., 2015). Specifically, ratings on the attentional subscale have been found to be related to cognitive differences. When persons received higher ratings of media multitasking and attentional impulsivity they typically also had worse discrimination abilities on working memory tasks (Uncapher et al., 2015). In addition to impulsivity, media multitasking has also been found to be related to social anxiety and depression (Becker et al., 2013), neuroticism (Becker et al., 2013; Wang & Tchernev, 2012), sensation-seeking (Sanbonmatsu et al., 2013), and lower perceived social success (Pea et al., 2012). It is important to note that these findings are drawn from a rather small number of studies. Hence, a great deal of work needs to be done before making too strong associations regarding these psychosocial variables as representing media multitaskers.

6.5   The Memory of Multitaskers

In addition to attentional differences between heavy media multitaskers and light media multitaskers, differences in memory performance have been observed in heavy media multitaskers. In addition to deficits in working memory tasks (Cain & Mitroff, 2011; Ophir et al., 2009; Sanbonmatsu et al., 2013; Uncapher et al., 2015), deficits in long-term memory tasks have also been found (Uncapher et al., 2015). For example, Uncapher and colleagues (2015) used a signal detection framework and argued that the poorer memory performance of heavy media multitaskers was due to a reduced ability to discriminate between information in working memory and long-term memory – instead of a difference in decision bias (e.g., requiring less confirmation to make a decision).

6.6   Comparing the Executive-Control Processing of Heavy and Light Media Multitaskers

A group from Stanford University was interested in the question of whether persons who report engaging in heavy media multitasking are systematically different from those who do not. Specifically, Ophir, Nass, and Wagner (2009) asked, "Are chronic multi-taskers more attentive to irrelevant stimuli in the external environment and irrelevant representations in memory?" (Ophir et al., 2009, p. 15583). To answer this question, they developed a Media Use Survey that asks participants about their use of 12 forms of media. For each form, they were asked how often they simultaneously engage in any of the other eleven forms. From these data, a media multitasking index (MMI) was developed and used to distinguish between heavy media multitaskers (HMMs) and light media multitaskers (LMMs) on the basis of the top and bottom quartiles of the MMI distribution. The MMI represents the extent to which a person self-reports media multitasking (Ophir, Nass, & Wagner, 2009). When a person scores one standard deviation above the population average that person is categorized as a heavy media multitasker (HMM), whereas a person scoring at one standard deviation below the mean is categorized as a light media multitasker (LMM).

They examined cognitive control dimensions that they theorized could indicate cognitive control in media multitaskers: attention allocation to environmental stimuli; holding and manipulating task stimuli and task set representations in working memory; and the control of responses to stimuli and tasks. The following measures were used:

- Filter task was used to assess filtering of environmental distractions. For this test of filtering ability participants observed two consecutive exposures of an array of rectangles. They were instructed to ignore distractor (blue) rectangles and indicate whether or not a target (red) rectangle had changed orientation from the first presentation to the second. They assessed performance for arrays with two targets and 0, 2, 4, or 6 distractors.
- AX-Continuous Performance Task required participants to observe cue-probe pairs of letters, and then to respond "yes" when they observed the target cue-probe pair, "AX," that is, an "A" (cue) followed by an "X" (probe).
- Two- and three-back tasks were used to examine the monitoring and updating of multiple representations in working memory. The participant was presented with a sequence of stimuli and instructed to indicate when a current stimulus matches the one from two (or three) steps earlier in the sequence.
- Task-cued stimulus-classification was used to assess task-set switching abilities. Participants were presented a number and a letter, and performed either a letter (vowel or consonant) or a number (even or odd) classification task depending on a cue presented before the stimulus. Switch cost was calculated as the difference in mean response time between trials preceded by a trial of the other type (switch trials) vs. trials preceded by a trial of the same type (nonswitch trials).

While it would seem that the regular performance of multiple tasks at the same time and the frequent switching between tasks (or media) would allow HMMs to outperform LMMs in measures assessing multitasking, Ophir and colleagues (2009) found that HMMs performed worse than LMMs in a task-switching experiment. Furthermore, HMMs also performed worse on other measures: AX-continuous performance task; filter task; and N-back task. It is important to note that the performance deficits observed when comparing HMMs and LMMs were not global in nature. Instead they appeared to be specific to situations that involved distractors.

This distinction was evident on the AX-continuous performance task. While participants in the HMM group and LMM group performed equally well in the condition that did not include distractors, performance in the HMM group had slower response times in a condition that included distractors. The authors concluded that media multitasking might have negative effects on executive-control. This led to a lowered resistance to distractors.

However, in a later study by researchers at the University of Wyoming, Meredith Minear and colleagues (2013) were not able to replicate the findings of Ophir and colleagues. Minear's group used the same media multitasking index (MMI) developed by Ophir et al. to identify HMMs and LMMs. Next, they assessed participant performance in each group on measures of attention, working memory, task switching, and fluid intelligence. They also assessed participants' self-reported impulsivity and self-control. Results revealed no evidence to support the proposition that HMMs are worse than LMMs on multitasking or that they show any deficits in dealing with irrelevant or distracting information. Interestingly, they did find that even though there was no difference in actual performance, the HMM participants self-reported greater levels of impulsivity.

It is important to note that this was a cross-sectional study; it may be the case that participants who were less resistant to distractors or who focused on breadth more than depth with regard to executive-control might also engage more frequently in media multitasking. Furthermore, participants who were lower in attentional control might be more attracted to multitasking as a work strategy.

In another study, researchers at the University of Waterloo found a negative impact of media multitasking in some measures (e.g., metronome response task). However, no significant impact was found for other measures of sustained attention (e.g., sustained-attention-to-response task). Furthermore, participants in the HMM group were less resistant to distractors (Ralph et al., 2015).

As can be seen, the findings are inconsistent. There are some who have hypothesized that the increased prevalence of media multitasking is problematic because frequent engagement in media multitasking may have negative impact upon cognitive control processes (e.g., executive function). As discussed above Ophir, Nass, and Wagner (2009) of Stanford University found that young adults that engaged frequently in media multitasking had poorer performance on a number of cognitive control tasks (e.g., filtering distractions and task switching) than participants with low engagement in media multitasking. Although these findings are interesting there is need for replication; it remains unknown how media multitasking is related to key components of executive functioning (e.g., inhibition, working memory, and set-shifting).

In a study performed by researchers at the University of Amsterdam, Susanne Baumgartner and colleagues (2014) explored the relationship between media multitasking and executive functions in 523 early adolescents. Specifically, they investigated three central components of executive functions (i.e., working memory, shifting, and inhibition) using self-reports and standardized performance-based tasks (Digit Span, Dots–Triangles Task, Eriksen Flankers task). Results revealed that frequent media multitasking was related to self-reported deficits in everyday activities. In fact, adolescents who multitask reported a variety of executive functioning deficits in their everyday lives: focus deficits, decreased inhibition, and ineffective switching between tasks. In addition to self-reports, standardized performance-based tasks (Digit Span, Dots–Triangles Task, Eriksen Flankers task) were given. Interestingly, media multitasking was not related to performance on the Digit Span and Dots–Triangles task. Perhaps even more interesting is the finding that media multitasking was found to be related to performance-based assessment of inhibition using the Eriksen Flankers task. However, instead of revealing executive functioning deficits, adolescents who engaged more frequently in media multitasking actually showed a tendency to be better at ignoring irrelevant distractions. This may reflect a positive impact of media multitasking on the ability to willingly ignore distractions. Hence, heavy media multitaskers may have learned to ignore distractions when desired.

Given the executive functioning demands of multitasking, it is not unexpected that the involvement of the prefrontal cortex and basal ganglia are thought to be critical in its execution (Dreher, Koechlin, Tierney, & Grafman, 2008). Evidence for the involvement in these brain areas comes from studies of participants with prefrontal lobe lesions that evidenced both everyday functioning and substantial deficits on multitasking measures (Gouveia et al., 2007; Shallice & Burgess, 1991).

6.7 Multitaskers May Have a Greater Breadth of Attention

For Lin Lin of the University of North Texas (2009) the findings of Ophir and others may have limited ecological validity. Lin argued that media multitaskers do not attend to the information that is relevant to one task at a time. Instead HMMs have a cognitive style that includes a "greater breadth of attention." This breadth-biased approach to cognitive processing is an intriguing suggestion that suggests performance will be enhanced in situations where a task involves some unexpected information that is important to the task at hand. For example, when a media multi-tasker reads, he or she may more readily detect a ringtone from a mobile phone, even though the ringtone does not carry information useful for the primary task of reading. In fact, such situations seem to actually be more representative of what happens in activities of daily living (Lin, 2009).

Support for this idea can be seen in a study by Cain and Mitroff (2011) at Duke University that used a singleton task to assess breadth-biased attention. During this task, participants were presented with an array of shapes (e.g., squares and circles) and instructed to state which shape was presented in the target shape (e.g., circle) while ignoring the nontarget shapes (squares). For half of the trials the shapes are green and in the other half of the trials one of the shapes is red (additional singleton). The participants were informed of two experimental conditions: (1) *Sometimes Condition*: color could be the target; and (2) *Never Condition*: color was never the target. Comparison of performance across conditions in persons from the HMM group revealed that they did not modulate their responses between these two tasks. The authors conclude that this suggests persons in the HMM maintained a broader attentional scope despite the explicit task instructions.

In a study by researchers at the Chinese University of Hong Kong, Lui and Wong (2012) extended earlier studies to look at potential advantages of a broader attentional scope. Participants were instructed to search for a vertical or horizontal line among an array of red and green distractor lines of multiple orientations. Within a trial the line colors changed intermittently. The target and distractor lines changed colors at different frequencies. The orientations of the lines were kept constant within each trial. In some conditions, a tone and flickering target line were presented in synchrony. It is important to note that participants were not explicitly informed about the meaning of the tones. Findings revealed increased target detection in the presence of the tones, with a positive correlation to scores on the MMI. According to Lui and Wong, this suggests that the breadth-biased attentional processes of HMMs allow them to better integrate multisensory information.

In summary, heavy media multitaskers appear less likely to use top-down attention to constrain task goals than light media multitaskers (Cain & Mitroff, 2011), and are more likely to adopt a split focus (vs. unitary focus) of visuospatial attention, in that they allocate attention to multiple (vs. single) locations (Lin, 2009; Yap & Lim, 2013).

6.8   Brains of Media Multitaskers

In a neuroimaging study at the University of Sussex's Sackler Centre for Consciousness Science, Loh and Kanai (2014) used voxel-based morphometry to investigate the brain structures of 75 adults. Voxel-based morphometry is a commonly used neuroimaging approach that enables voxel-wise statistical analyses of pre-processed images from magnetic resonance imagery (see Figure 6.1). Participants also completed a Big Five Personality Inventory and a Media Multitasking Questionnaire.

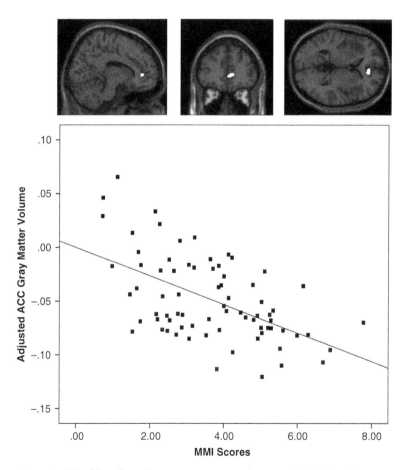

Figure 6.1 Voxel-based morphometry regression analyses revealed that MMT scores were significantly associated with gray matter density in the Anterior Cingulate Cortex. K.K. Loh and R. Kanai, *PLOS One*, 2014.
Reprinted by permission of the publisher.

Findings revealed that, independent of individual personality traits, participants who were HMMs concurrently also had smaller grey matter density in the anterior cingulate cortex (ACC). The ACC is important for sensorimotor, nociceptive, neurocognitive, affective, and motivational processes (Bush, Luu, & Posner, 2000). The authors argue that the findings of a smaller ACC in HMMs most likely reflects higher cognitive processes since media multitasking has been consistently associated with cognitive control performance (Lui & Wong, 2012; Ophir, Nass, & Wagner, 2009).

In summary, Loh and Kanai's work revealed that heavy media multitaskers exhibited less gray matter volume in the ACC relative to light media multitaskers. Although this finding suggests that there are potential anatomical differences in individuals who frequently media multitask compared to those who do not, a more well-developed investigation of the ways in which structural and functional brain networks manifest differently in high media multitaskers versus light media multitaskers is needed. Furthermore, there is need for studies that investigate task-based regional differences in brain functioning.

6.9   Media Multitasking Performance on Single Task Paradigms

It is important to note that previous studies have also assessed cognitive performance using single tasks paradigms. Typically, findings suggest that heavy media multitaskers performed worse than light media multitaskers. When compared to investigations of cognition during multitasking conditions (although within a single medium) the findings are less clear. For example, some studies found that heavy media multitaskers performed worse when switching between multiple tasks (Ophir et al., 2009; Sanbonmatsu et al., 2013). Contrariwise, other studies revealed no differences in task-switching (Minear et al., 2013). In fact, some studies actually found better task-switching in heavy media multitaskers than light media multitaskers (Alzahabi & Becker, 2013). Furthermore, it has been found that heavy media multitaskers may have an advantage during tasks that require the integration of multiple incoming information streams, such as when auditory information informs visual target detection (Lui & Wong, 2012).

6.10   Need for New Tests and Approaches to Assessing Multitasking

While there is a growing body of research regarding the neurocognitive and neuroanatomical architecture of multitasking, findings have been hampered by divergent (at times overlapping) operationalization of the construct. For example, a number of studies have used the term multitasking to designate simultaneously performing multiple tasks (e.g., dual-task paradigms; Meyer & Kieras, 1997). In other studies, multitasking is used to describe the allocation of attention to multiple streams of sensory input (e.g., media multitasking; Ophir, Nass, & Wagner, 2009). In another study, Scott and colleagues (2011) approached multitasking in a more ecologically valid way. They used a novel approach to multitasking, in which participants balanced the demands of four interconnected performance-based functional tasks (i.e., cooking, financial management, medication management, and telephone communication). They operationalized multitasking as the user's ability to plan and carry out multiple, distinct tasks within a specific timeframe where the user switches between tasks as required. In this context, the concurrent performance of tasks can ensue and may be advantageous in some circumstances. However, participants are not required to simultaneously perform tasks.

When comparing this definition of multitasking to others in the literature, it is important to note that it includes a number of cognitive processes that the participant must perform for successful execution. This approach to multitasking requires that the participant (1) organizes and strategizes from temporal and conditional relations between actions; and (2) sustains these relations in working memory, along with information about instantaneously presenting environmental stimuli, goals, and sub-goals (Burgess et al., 2000). These activities reflect findings that planning, set-shifting, and output monitoring can support multitasking activities (Burgess, 2000; Schwartz, 2006). Interestingly, decreased multitasking following brain injuries is often found even though the patients performed normally on traditional executive functioning measures (Alderman, Burgess, Knight, & Henman, 2003). Hence, the cognitive demands of multitasking may be different from the sorts of cognitive processes measured by traditional neuropsychological tests of executive functioning.

How might cyberpsychologists interested in the relation between online social interactions and brain functioning design their studies? While a handful of studies are beginning to report positive causal effects of social processes on executive functioning (Ybarra et al., 2008), Internet-related executive functioning and multitasking have been regularly concomitant with decreases in classroom learning, academic performance (Carrier et al., 2015), and negative impacts on executive functioning (Ophir et al., 2009). That said, it is important to note that research into heavy media multitaskers has revealed that the switching between media types that these users do results in a habituation toward a breadth-biased style of attention control with parallel processing of multiple information sources (Lin, 2009). A broader attention scope was also found by Lui and Wong (2012) when they found that the increased capacity for processing irrelevant stimuli in heavy media multitaskers resulted in improved performance on a multisensory integration task. Likewise, Yap and Lim (2013) found that heavy media multitaskers had increased abilities for dividing their visual focal attention.

Given the fact that these studies revealed decreased abilities on traditional tasks, but increased abilities on novel assessments of multitasking, cyberpsychologists may want to look into developing both novel designs and innovative assessments. One area that needs further consideration is the development and use of ecologically valid assessments of media multitasking that better reflect real-world activities (Lin, 2009). A recent development in the ecological validity discussion was introduced by Burgess and colleagues (2006) when they presented an analysis of neuropsychology's adaptation of outmoded conceptual and experimental frameworks. Burgess et al. proffer current construct-driven tests as examples of measures that fail to represent the actual functional capacities inherent in cognitive (e.g., executive) functions. They point out that while cognitive construct measures like the Stroop and Tower of London have been found to be useful tools for constrained assessment of specific cognitive constructs, they fail to replicate the diverse activities found in everyday living. An example found in media multitasking is to take a participant's performance on the Stroop that revealed difficulty inhibiting an automatic, overlearned response, and concluding that this will result in poor grades.

Goldstein (1996) questioned this approach because it is difficult to ascertain the extent to which performance on measures of basic constructs translates to functional capacities within the varying environments found in the real world. A decade later, Burgess et al. (2006) agree and argue that a further issue is that we need assessments that further our understanding about the ways in which the brain enables persons to interact with their environment and organize everyday activities. Instead of using the terms "verisimilitude" and "veridicality" when discussing "ecological validity," they use the term "representativeness" to discuss the extent to which a neuropsychological assessment corresponds in form and context to a real-world (encountered outside the laboratory) situation. They use the term "generalizability" to discuss the degree to which poor performance on a neuropsychological assessment will be predictive of poor performance on tasks outside the laboratory.

Following Burgess et al. (2006), it seems apparent that future development of cognitive assessments of media multitasking should result in tests that are "representative" of real-world "functions" and proffer results that are "generalizable" for prediction of functional performance across a range of situations. According to Burgess et al. (2006) a "function-led approach" to creating neuropsychological assessments will include neuropsychological models that proceed from directly observable everyday behaviors backward to examine the ways in which a sequence of actions leads to a given behavior in normal functioning; and the ways in which that behavior might become disrupted. As such, they call for a new generation of neuropsychological tests that are "function led" rather than purely "construct driven."

An example of an ecologically valid assessment of multitasking can be found in recent developments in virtual-reality. Advances in virtual environment technology offer platforms in which three-dimensional objects are presented in a dynamic, consistent, and precise manner. A virtual environment provides the researcher with an ecologically valid platform for presenting dynamic stimuli in a manner that allows for both the veridical control of laboratory measures and the verisimilitude of naturalistic observation of real-life situations (Jovanovski et al., 2012a, 2012b; Matheis et al., 2007). Virtual environment–based assessments can provide a balance between naturalistic observation and the need for exacting control over key variables (Campbell et al., 2009).

In a study by researchers at the University of Edinburgh, Logie and colleagues (2011) assessed multitasking using an Edinburgh Virtual Errands Task (EVET). They conceptualized "everyday multitasking" as comprising multiple distinct tasks with sub-goals. Participants completed tasks in a specific order and switched as each task was completed. It is important to note that their conceptualization of everyday multitasking differs from task-switching paradigms in that several tasks with obvious end points are involved and time scales are much longer (Logie et al., 2010). Furthermore, their approach differs from dual-task paradigms in that tasks are completed via interweaving instead of in parallel (Logie et al., 2010).

The virtual environment for the Edinburgh Virtual Errands Task was developed using the Hammer environment editor, which is part of the Half Life 2 software development kit. The researchers developed a 3-D model of a building that has four stories. Five of the rooms are found along the left and right ends of each floor near a central stairwell that has two sets of stairs (one left and one right). There is also a central elevator. In the study, the participants explored the virtual environment using the

Table 6.1 *Errand list A of the Edinburgh Virtual Errands Task.*

Errand 1	Pick up Brown Package in T4 and take to G6
Errand 2	Pick up Newspaper in G3 and take to Desk in S4
Errand 3	Get Key Card in F9 and unlock G6 (via G5)
Errand 4	Meet person S10 before 3:00 min
Errand 5	Get Stair Code from notice board in G8 and unlock Stairwell
Errand 6	Turn on Cinema S7 at 5:30 min
Errand 7	Turn off Lift G Floor
Errand 8	Sort red and blue Binders in room S2. Sort as many binders as you can.

standard keyboard – the keys "w" (forward), "s" (backward), "a" (left lateral movement), and "d" (right lateral movement). The "e" key was used for specific actions (e.g., picking up objects; opening doors). A mouse was used to look in any direction. Participant movement (represented as a series of x, y, z coordinates) within the virtual environment was automatically recorded at 10 Hz. Furthermore, actions were logged with corresponding time stamps.

For the Edinburgh Virtual Errands Task, participants had eight minutes to complete eight errands. Three of the errands involved two stages, in which participants were required to collect and deliver objects. Five of the errands required only one action. Two of these tasks had time limits (e.g., at 5:30 turn off the cinema). There was one open-ended task and it involved sorting of folders at any time during the eight-minute test period. Half of the sample was given Errand List A and started on the ground floor between the stairwells (see Table 6.1). The other half were given Errand List B and started in the equivalent position on the top floor (see Table 6.2). It is important to note that the errands were given in a nonoptimal order for completion, and participants were asked to plan the optimal order before they started the Edinburgh Virtual Errands Task.

A chief aim of this study was to investigate the cognitive factors that contribute to everyday multitasking using a virtual environment. The significance of this approach is that it moves beyond multitasking approaches that focus on each function in isolation to an approach that investigates complex cognition in which multiple cognitive functions are employed to operate in a coordinated fashion. This approach draws upon an existing statistical model of everyday multitasking that was developed by

Table 6.2 *Errand list B of the Edinburgh Virtual Errands Task.*

Errand 1	Pick up Computer in G4 and take to T7
Errand 2	Pick up Milk Carton in T3 and take to Desk in F4
Errand 3	Get Key Card in S9 and unlock T7 (via T6)
Errand 4	Meet person F10 before 3:00 min
Errand 5	Get Stair Code from notice board in T10 and unlock Stairwell
Errand 6	Turn on Cinema F7 at 5:30 min
Errand 7	Turn off Lift T Floor
Errand 8	Sort red and blue Binders in room F2. Sort as many binders as you can.

Burgess and colleagues (2000), in which investigation of the relationships between the cognitive constructs underpinning multitasking revealed three primary constructs: retrospective memory, prospective memory, and planning. The second two were found to draw upon the products of the first. They suggested that while the left anterior and posterior cingulates together play some part in the retrospective memory demands, the prospective memory and planning components make demands on processes supported by the rostral dlPFC. Interestingly, Logie and colleagues also identified separate constructs for memory, preplanning, and plan implementation, which suggests that memory and preplanning may involve different cognitive functions that are required for this form of multitasking. Moreover, their results are consistent with Burgess and colleagues' (2000) theorizing that planning is not a unitary construct. Further, Logie and colleagues found separate constructs for preplanning and for online planning during task performance.

Findings revealed significant independent contributions from measures of retrospective memory, visuospatial working memory, and online planning. However, there was not a significant contribution from independent measures of prospective memory or verbal working memory. The final model included a relationship between preplanning and plan following, as well as a relationship among three constructs (Memory, Planning, and Intent) in multitasking by healthy young adults. Although the Memory and Planning constructs had a weak link, both had a strong directional association with an Intent construct that reflected implementation of intentions. Higher scores were found for participants who followed their prepared plans (regardless of being efficient or poor). Interestingly, these results support the Burgess and colleagues (2000) model and yield new understanding of everyday multitasking. Moreover, the findings suggest the potential utility of using a virtual environment for investigating this form of complex human cognition.

6.11 Conclusions

The relation between self-regulation and media multitasking has been the principal focus of the literature reviewed in this chapter. Media multitasking has been found to impact learning of new material. Specifically, media multitasking inhibits concurrent learning, and heavy media multitasking is associated with cognitive differences even when people are performing single tasks. A number of researchers are increasingly interested in the ways in which the use of modern technology may alter how individuals process information. Studies have revealed that distraction while new information is learned leads to decreased retention and may even alter the neural systems involved. This may result in an increasing prevalence of media multitasking that may influence everyday activities and cognitions beyond the classroom.

The neural correlates of media multitasking and learning appear to reflect differing brain-based learning processes for distracting and non-distracting conditions. Specifically, neuroimaging results revealed that the hippocampus was activated when participants learned material and there were no distractions. However, when participants learned material while multitasking, the striatum was activated and the hippocampus was not engaged. The striatum is involved in skill learning and habitual task performance (see Chapter 2 in this book). Interestingly, these brain differences may not necessarily be negative. Research studies have revealed that practice and training may in fact enhance the brain processing speed, working memory, and improve a user's ability to multitask. Lin (2009) points out that being continuously immersed in multitasking settings may result in the development of different brain processing and situational awareness in heavy media multitaskers. For Lin, this means that it is imperative that cyberpsychologists delineate the context, measurement, and valued outcomes of learning when investigating the effects of media multitasking on learning.

In this chapter, there was also the suggestion that new approaches are needed for assessing the impacts of media multitasking. While there is a growing body of research regarding the neurocognitive and neuroanatomical architecture of multitasking, findings have been hampered by divergent (at times overlapping) operationalizations of the construct.

In one of the most cited media multitasking studies, by Ophir, Nass, and Wagner (2009), multitasking is understood in terms of the allocation of attention to multiple streams of sensory input. Their findings were different than those found in a study that approached multitasking in a more ecologically valid way. When comparing this definition of multitasking to others in the literature, it is important to note that it includes a number of cognitive processes that the participant must perform for successful execution. This approach to multitasking requires that the participant (1) organizes and strategizes from temporal and conditional relations between actions; and (2) sustains these relations in working memory, along with information about instantaneously presenting environmental stimuli, goals, and sub-goals. These activities reflect findings that planning, set-shifting, and output monitoring can support multitasking activities.

For Lin Lin of the University of North Texas (2009) the findings of Ophir and others may have limited ecological validity. Lin argued that media multitaskers do not attend to the information that is relevant to one task at a time. Instead HMMs have a cognitive style that includes a "greater breadth of attention." This breadth-biased approach to cognitive processing is an intriguing suggestion that suggests performance will be enhanced in situations where a task involves some unexpected information that is important to the task at hand. For example, when a media multitasker reads, he or she may more readily detect a ringtone from a mobile phone, even though the ringtone does not carry information useful for the primary task of reading. In fact, such situations seem to actually be more representative of what happens in activities of daily living (Lin, 2009).

An example of an ecologically valid assessment of multitasking can be found in recent developments in virtual-reality. Advances in virtual environment technology offer platforms in which three-dimensional objects are presented in a dynamic, consistent, and precise manner. A virtual environment provides the researcher with an ecologically valid platform for presenting dynamic stimuli in a manner that allows for both the veridical control of laboratory measures and the verisimilitude of naturalistic observation of real-life situations. Virtual environment–based assessments can provide a balance between naturalistic observation and the need for exacting control over key variables.

The chapter concludes with a study by researchers at the University of Edinburgh that assessed multitasking using an Edinburgh Virtual Errands Task (EVET). They conceptualized "everyday multitasking" as comprising multiple distinct tasks with sub-goals. Findings support the Burgess and colleagues (2000) model and yield new understanding of everyday multi-tasking. Moreover, the findings suggest the potential utility of using a virtual environment for investigating this form of complex human cognition.

CHAPTER 7

Cyber Addictions

7.1 Introduction

There is a growing body of cyberpsychology research into the relations between online media (e.g., social networking, online gaming, shopping, gambling, and Internet pornography) use and compulsive behaviors, self-regulation, impulse control, and substance abuse. Often excessive Internet use is associated with symptoms frequently linked to addiction, such as tolerance (increased Internet use over time), withdrawal (irritability when unable to access Internet material), and cravings (for Internet-mediated content).

7.1.1 Evolution of Cyber Addiction Disorder

Historically, there has been some consensus that reliance on Internet use can be understood as a behavioral addiction that operates on an adapted principle of classic addiction models. Studies of excessive Internet use have found that participants share a number of core symptoms with substance addiction such as tolerance, withdrawal symptoms, and relapse (Young, 1998a). Furthermore, people that excessively use the Internet often have psychiatric co-morbidity, including anxiety disorders, sleep disorders, attention deficit/hyperactivity disorder, and obsessive-compulsiveness (Ko et al., 2012; Yen et al., 2007). The roots of Internet addiction research involved the pioneering work of Kimberly Young at St. Bonaventure University in the United States and Mark Griffiths, Professor of Gambling Studies at Nottingham Trent University in England.

7.1.2 Kimberly Young: Internet Addiction

In the 1990s, Kimberly Young began a research program into the risk factors for problematic Internet use. In a recent article in the Journal

Table 7.1 *Questions from the Internet Addiction Diagnostic Questionnaire (IADQ)*

---

1. Do you feel preoccupied with the Internet (think about previous on-line activity or anticipate next on-line session)?
2. Do you feel the need to use the Internet with increasing amounts of time in order to achieve satisfaction?
3. Have you repeatedly made unsuccessful efforts to control, cut back, or stop Internet use?
4. Do you feel restless, moody, depressed, or irritable when attempting to cut down or stop Internet use?
5. Do you stay on-line longer than originally intended?
6. Have you jeopardized or risked the loss of a significant relationship, job, educational, or career opportunity because of the Internet?
7. Have you lied to family members, a therapist, or others to conceal the extent of involvement with the Internet?
8. Do you use the Internet as a way of escaping from problems or of relieving a dysphoric mood (e.g., feelings of helplessness, guilt, anxiety, depression)?

Note: These questions are from page 238 of Young (1998b).

Addictive Behaviors, Young (2015) recalls her first foray into Internet addiction research in 1995 when her friend's husband was seemingly addicted to America Online (AOL) chat rooms. He was spending 40 to 60 hours online at a time when it was still $2.95 per hour to dial into the Internet. In addition to the financial burdens, their marriage ended in divorce. During that time, she published an influential paper (Young, 1998a) and book (Young, 1998b) on Internet addition. In her influential paper on Internet addiction, Young (1998) compared and classified case studies of 396 dependent Internet users (problematic Internet users) and 100 nondependent Internet users by means of an eight-item questionnaire referred to as an Internet Addiction Diagnostic Questionnaire (IADQ). Given that pathological gambling was the closest diagnosis found in the *Diagnostic and Statistical Manual of Mental Disorders,* Young used modified criteria for pathological gambling to afford a screening instrument for classification of participants. Results suggested that significant behavioral and functional usage differences existed between the two groups. For example, persons with problematic Internet use were found to have greater difficulty controlling weekly usage and endorsed having more problems. Questions found in the Internet Addiction Diagnostic questionnaire can be found in Table 7.1.

For Young's Internet Addiction Diagnostic Questionnaire, participants who endorsed (answered "yes") five or more of the criteria (over a six-month period not associated with manic or hypomanic episodes) were classified as dependent Internet users (Dependents). Those who endorsed less than five were classified as nondependent Internet users (Nondependents). Evaluation of answers was done in terms of Internet usage that was non-essential (e.g., non-business or academically related use). Young contended that the cutoff score of five or more endorsements is consistent with the number used to diagnose pathological gambling.

Young (1999) has described what she calls "Internet addiction" as a broad phrase that encompasses a variety of impulse control problems with five specific subtypes:

(1) **Cybersexual addiction:** Compulsive use of adult Websites for cybersex and cyberporn.
(2) **Cyber-relationship addiction:** Over-involvement in online relationships.
(3) **Net compulsions:** Obsessive online gambling, shopping or daytrading.
(4) **Information overload:** Compulsive Web surfing or database searches.
(5) **Computer addiction:** Obsessive computer game playing.

Young's work in Internet addiction (IA) was pioneering and her writings on the topic have undoubtedly served as inspiration to other researchers interested in the area. In addition to a growing body of research, inpatient hospital programs for Internet addiction recovery have opened that offer several forms of intervention for Internet addiction.

7.1.3 Mark Griffiths: Excessive Users Are Not "Internet Addicts"

In Europe, Griffiths (1999a; 1999b; 2000) responded to Young's (1999) paper, contending that several of the excessive users identified by Young were not "Internet addicts." Instead, they were users that used the Internet excessively as a medium to fuel their other addictions. This perspective is now shared by leading scholars in the field (Billieux, 2015; Starcevic, 2013). In fact, his early formulations described such behavior as "technological addiction" (Griffiths, 1995). For Griffiths (2015), there is an important and theoretical dissimilarity between addictions on the Internet and addictions to the Internet. Griffiths has identified six criteria of technological addictions:

(1) **Salience:** Occurs when Internet use becomes the primary activity in a user's life and dominates thinking (i.e., pre-occupations and cognitive distortions), feelings (e.g., cravings), and behavior (i.e., deterioration of socialized behavior). For example, even when the person is "off line," they are thinking about the next time they will be on line.

(2) **Mood modification:** The positive subjective experiences that people report as a consequence of engaging in Internet use and which can be seen as a coping strategy for them (i.e., they experience an arousing "buzz" or a "high," or they experience a tranquilizing feeling of "escape" or "numbing").

(3) **Tolerance:** The process by which users increase the level of Internet use they partake in, to achieve its mood-modification effects. There is a tendency to gradually increase the amount of time spent online, in order to expand or extend those effects.

(4) **Withdrawal symptoms:** The unpleasant feeling-states and/or physical effects that occur when Internet use is discontinued or suddenly reduced. Withdrawal symptoms might include shakiness, moodiness, or irritability.

(5) **Conflict:** The various conflicts emerging as a result of the person's excessive Internet use: interpersonal conflict; conflicts with other activities (e.g., job, social life, other interests); or conflicts within the individual (intrapsychic conflict and/or feelings of loss of control).

(6) **Relapse:** The tendency for repeated reversals to, or recurrence of, prior behavioral patterns. Even the most extreme patterns of excessive Internet use or addiction can be rapidly restored by the user – even after periods of abstinence or control.

While there is some disagreement on whether persons that excessively use the Internet are addicted or just use the Internet excessively as a medium to fuel their other addictions, Internet gaming disorder has been categorized in the revised *Diagnostic and Statistical Manual of Mental Disorders* as a condition for further study (American Psychiatric Association, 2013). While there are parallels to other addictions, the American Psychiatric Association prefers the term "Internet Gaming Disorder" over "Internet addiction" because a gaming addict is not necessarily addicted to the Internet, but simply uses it as a medium to engage in the chosen behavior. According to Billieux (2012) Internet-related disorders are best conceptualized within a spectrum of related and yet independent disorders. For the purposes of this chapter, cyber addiction will be used for all discussions of various forms of Internet addiction and gaming disorders.

7.1.4   *Internet Addiction Test*

The Internet Addiction Test is a 20-item scale that cyberpsychologists can use for assessing the presence and severity of Internet dependency among adults. It was developed by Kimberly Young to assess symptoms of Internet addiction and compulsivity in a variety of test settings. The Internet Addiction Test is a self-report measure of compulsive Internet use for adults and adolescents. Interpretation of results from the Internet Addiction Test should be done with caution when the participant is from a clinical population that suffers from psychiatric conditions concurrent with compulsive syndromes. The Internet Addiction Test is an adaptation of the earlier eight-item scale. The Test views Internet addiction as an impulse-control disorder and uses the term "Internet" to refer to all types of online activity. The Internet Addiction Test is the first validated instrument to assess Internet addiction (Widyanto & McMurren, 2004) and is the most widely used Internet addiction scale. It has been translated into several languages including French, Chinese, Italian, Turkish, and Korean.

7.1.5   *Beyond the DSM: Cyber Addictions in the Age of RDoc*

In a recent review of the evolution of Internet addiction disorder, Young (2016) described the current state of research on cyber addictions. She emphasized the emergence of new statistical models that have identified moderating factors (e.g., coping styles and Internet expectancies) that determined functional and dysfunctional Internet use among adult populations. She also points to the growing body of neurological and neuroimaging studies revealing that the prefrontal cortex plays a significant role in the development of Internet addition (Brand, Young, & Laier, 2014). She described the potential of neural correlates for Internet disorders that are similar to other addictive syndromes. The emphasis upon Internet addiction in terms of neural correlates seems to comport well with the National Institute of Mental Health's (NIMH) Research Domain Criteria (RDoC), which emphasizes the need for a future diagnostic system that more directly reflects modern brain science (Insel et al., 2010). According to the NIMH RDoC, it is increasingly evident that mental illness (e.g., cyber addictions) will be best understood as disorders of brain structure and function that implicate specific domains of cognition, emotion, and behavior (Cuthbert, 2014). Moreover, NIMH's RDoC is an attempt to create a new kind of taxonomy for mental disorders by bringing the power of modern research approaches in genetics, neuroscience, and behavioral science to the problem of mental illness (Cuthbert & Insel, 2013). Hence, this chapter views the RDoc approach as superseding DSM classifications and uses the term cyber addiction throughout.

7.2   Large-Scale Brain Networks and Addiction

As discussed previously in the book (see Chapter 1) a notable advance in the neuroimaging literature over the last two decades is the demonstration that brain regions organize their activity into coherent functional networks (Bressler & Menon, 2010; Sporns, 2011). Researchers use functional magnetic resonance imaging (see Chapter 3) of these networks to reveal correlations of the low-frequency fluctuations in blood oxygenation level–dependent signal between brain regions. Although the precise number of functional networks and their functional roles are still being studied, there is an emerging consensus that there are between 7 and 20 distinct functional networks. The default-mode network is the most well known and the most studied of these functional networks. The default-mode network includes brain areas in dorsal and ventral medial prefrontal and parietal cortices. This network was discovered from neuroimaging of the human brain while persons were in a state of quiet repose (e.g., with eyes closed; Raichle, 2015). These findings have resulted in a suggested role of the default-mode network in self-generated cognition that is decoupled from the external world. As discussed in Chapter 10, an independent body of work in the social neurosciences has revealed an overlapping "mentalizing network" that reveals the neural correlates of a person's ability to mentalize (i.e., infer) the cognitions and feelings of others. In Chapter 10, there is a discussion of the social neuroscience questions that have been generated from the recognized similarity between the default and mentalizing networks (Li, Mai, & Liu, 2014).

The executive-control network appears to include brain areas that are known to have capacity for sustained attention (e.g., dorsolateral prefrontal cortex, lateral parietal cortex). Furthermore, the executive-control network has been identified for controlled attention to pertinent stimuli as behavioral choices are weighed against shifting conditions. The executive-control network exerts control over posterior sensorimotor representations and maintains relevant information so that actions may be selected. For example, coordinated prefrontal and posterior parietal control areas have been found to direct and coordinate sensory and motor areas during (and in preparation for) perceptuomotor processing (Bressler et al., 2008).

Maladaptive interactions between the default-mode network and the executive-control network partly underlie suboptimal performance (Prado & Weissman, 2011), in that decreased negative coupling between the default-mode network and the executive-control network predicts increased variability in trial-to-trial response times across individuals (Kelly et al., 2008). Compromised ability to suppress default-mode network activity has been posited to explain attentional-control maladjustments in conditions such as ADHD (Fassbender et al., 2009; Sonuga-Barke & Castellanos, 2007), autism (Uddin & Menon, 2009), and dementia (Menon, 2011). Altered connectivity between the default-mode network and the executive-control network has been reported in smokers following nicotine abstinence and linked with withdrawal-related cognitive deficits (Cole et al., 2010). Furthermore, examination of resting-state functional connectivity in current cocaine users has revealed that persons likely to be experiencing acute withdrawal have enhanced positive connectivity between the default-mode network and the executive-control network, which may reflect state changes associated with withdrawal.

The salience network also plays a role in addiction. The salience network is an intrinsically connected large-scale network anchored in the anterior insula and dorsal anterior cingulate cortex. The characterization of the salience network has enhanced our understanding of brain areas that take part in the processing of neurocognitively and affectively relevant events to direct flexible responding (Seeley et al., 2007). The salience network activates for salient sensory events, transitions from introspection to task performance, and during task initiation and switching (Sridharan, Levitin, & Menon, 2008.). Moreover, the salience network is believed to influence moment-to-moment information processing by identifying the most relevant stimuli (Seeley et al., 2007) and switching activity between the default-mode network and the executive-control network accordingly (Sridharan et al., 2008). A meta-analysis of the salience network found that it is a common neural substrate across psychiatric illness categories (Goodkind et al., 2015). The meta-analysis reviewed structural abnormalities across six psychiatric disorder categories (including addiction). Findings revealed that all of the psychiatric disorders revealed gray matter volume reductions in the salience network.

Excessive Internet use has been associated with a variety of negative psychosocial consequences. In a recent study Wei-na Ding and colleagues (2013) at the Shanghai Jiao Tong University used resting-state functional magnetic resonance imaging to investigate whether functional connectivity is altered in adolescents with Internet gaming addiction. Specifically, they investigated the default-mode network in adolescents with Internet gaming disorder. Findings suggest that adolescents with Internet gaming disorder exhibit different resting-state patterns of brain activity. Given that these alterations are to some extent consistent with those found in substance addiction, they support the hypothesis that Internet gaming disorder may be a behavioral addiction with neurobiological abnormalities similar to those found in other addictive disorders.

In another study, Yuan and colleagues (2015) at Xidian University investigated the role of large-scale brain networks in Internet gaming disorder. In their study, they investigated abnormal brain network interactions using multimodal imaging between adolescents with Internet gaming disorder and healthy controls. They combined functional connectivity, effective connectivity of intrinsic functional magnetic resonance imaging, and diffusion tensor imaging tractography. Furthermore, they used a Stroop task to assess for cognitive control deficits (Yuan et al., 2013). Results revealed abnormal functional connectivity within the central executive network and effective connectivity within the salience network in Internet gaming disorder. Furthermore, inefficient interactions between the central executive network and the salience network were observed. Reduced fractional anisotropy was found in salience network, the central executive network, and between-network pathways in participants with Internet gaming disorder. A significant correlation was observed in connections between the salience network and the central executive network. These results suggest that impaired cognitive control in adolescents with Internet gaming disorder is likely to be mediated by abnormal interactions and structural connections between intrinsic large-scale brain networks.

7.3   Neural Correlates of Executive-Control in Cyber Addictions

The neural correlates of cyber addiction behaviors have been extensively studied over the past decade and we now have a number of reviews that cover this growing body of literature (Brand et al., 2014; Kuss & Griffiths, 2012). These studies consistently find alterations in neural mechanisms involved in self-control mechanisms. Persons with cyber addictions have been found to have decreased gray matter densities in frontal-parietal structures, which are commonly involved in cognitive control (Hong et al., 2013; Weng et al., 2013; Zhou et al., 2011). Moreover, Yuan and colleagues (2011) found that participants with cyber addiction had smaller volumes in the dlPFC, OFC, ACC, and SMA. All of which were correlated with disorder duration. Brand and colleagues (2014) identify a number of

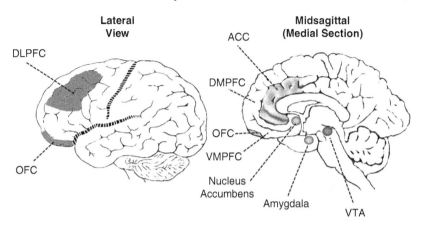

Figure 7.1 Brain regions associated with altered self-control and reward-processing in cyber addiction. Note, this figure is adapted from Brand and others, 2014. dlPFC = dorsolateral prefrontal cortex; ACC = anterior cingulate cortex; OFC = orbitofrontal cortex; dmPFC = dorsomedial prefrontal cortex; vmPFC = ventromedial prefrontal cortex; Nc.acc = nucleus accumbens; and VTA = ventral tegmental area.

brain regions that have been found to be associated with altered self-control and reward processing in cyber addiction. Brain areas associated with top-down response inhibition, error monitoring, and goal maintenance include: the dorsolateral prefrontal cortex (dlPFC) and the anterior cingulate cortex (ACC). Furthermore, they identified brain areas that are activated during reward processing during decision-making: the orbito-frontal cortex (OFC), the dorsomedial prefrontal cortex (dmPFC), and the ventromedial prefrontal cortex (vmPFC). Additionally, limbic structures were identified that are important in motivating and driving reward-pursuing behaviors: the amygdala, the nucleus accumbens (Nc.acc); and the ventral tegmental area (VTA). Figure 7.1 presents a summary of these brain regions.

The frontal lobes are involved directly and indirectly across a wide spectrum of human thought, behavior, and emotions. A specific capacity of the frontal lobes is collectively referred to as executive functioning: selective attention, inhibitory control, planning, problem-solving, and some aspects of short-term memory (see Diamond, 2013, for review). Results from studies have implicated the orbitofrontal cortex in social networking. The orbitofrontal cortex (medial orbitofrontal cortex and lateral orbitofrontal cortex) and adjacent ventromedial prefrontal cortex transmit reward representations and mediate flexible behavior in the face of changing circumstances (Noonan et al., 2012). These abilities sound a lot like the sorts of abilities needed for an effective social interaction, which frequently involves online and dynamic production of a mental model of another user's beliefs, expectations, affect, and motivations. Furthermore, online social interactions require the executive functioning capacities for maintaining attention, problem-solving, and pursuing goals in the face of distractions (Ybarra & Winkielman, 2012).

It is important to note that there is growing evidence that Internet addiction is related to brain structural changes and decreased executive-control processes. Evidence from neuroimaging has shown that brain regions associated with executive function (e.g., orbitofrontal cortex) had decreased cortical thickness in Internet-addicted adolescents (Hong et al., 2013). Consistent results were found from neuroimaging that also revealed brain regions associated with executive function (e.g., left lateral orbito-frontal cortex, insula cortex, and entorhinal cortex) had decreased cortical thickness in Internet gambling disordered participants. Further, reduced cortical thickness of the left lateral orbitofrontal cortex was associated with impaired cognitive control.

Hence, an aspect of executive functioning that has received increasing interest is self-control (i.e., inhibitory control). Self-control has been defined as "the self's capacity to override or change one's inner responses, as well as to interrupt undesired behavioral tendencies and to refrain from acting on them" (Tangney et al., 2004, p. 274). This definition emphasizes self-control as an inhibitory mechanism. Self-control has been shown to be very important and beneficial to the human experience and is associated with a pleasant and healthy life. High levels of self-control have also been positively related to self-esteem and good interpersonal skills (Tangney et al., 2004). The robustness of a person's self-control is predictive of whether they can attain goals that require self-control. There is now evidence that persons with low levels of self-control may have greater propensity for Internet addiction (Muusses et al., 2013).

7.3.1   Conflict Monitoring, Brain Circuits, and Internet Addiction

Findings from systems neuroscience have characterized specific large-scale brain networks that are identifiable in the brain both while it is active and when it is at rest (Seeley et al., 2007). The three most prominent networks are the executive-control network, the default-mode network, and the saliency network. The first two networks can be recognized straightforwardly by observing the profile of activation and deactivation typically found during cognitive tasks. The executive-control network typically shows increases in activation during cognitively demanding tasks, whereas the default-mode network has decreased activation. The third network is a salience network that processes affective stimuli and allows for switching between the competitive interactions of two other major networks.

While some of these processes are controlled processes in which nodes are activated through the controlled attention of the person, other processes are activated automatically without the necessity for conscious control or attention by the person (Schneider & Shiffrin, 1977; Shiffrin & Schneider, 1977). This dual-process perspective that human cognition may be made up of automatic and controlled processes was introduced by William James (1890) over a century ago. Dual-process models of automatic and controlled processes have been proposed in nearly every domain of executive functioning. Specifically, controlled processes (e.g., inhibiting a prepotent response during the Stroop task) are associated with conscious awareness, effort, intention, and the capacity for inhibition. Contrariwise, automatic processes (e.g., overlearned responses like reading) are not necessarily in conscious awareness and occur spontaneously.

A key brain region for conflict monitoring in automatic and controlled processing is the anterior cingulate cortex. The anterior cingulate cortex is also a key region in addiction research. Conflict monitoring plays an important role in addiction research because addicts are often confronted with the enticement of immediate drug consumption (i.e., reward) that must be weighed against long-term negative consequences. Studies have shown that addicts show an attenuated error-related activity of the rostral anterior cingulate cortex when performing a Go/No-Go task (Forman et al., 2004). In a Go/No-Go task the participant is instructed to suppress an overlearned behavior, such as pushing a button, when not appropriate.

Cocaine addicts have been found to have lower gray matter volume in the anterior cingulate cortex (Franklin et al., 2002). These findings can be applied in part to Internet addiction research, because Internet addicts have been found to have lower gray matter density of the anterior cingulate cortex (Zhou et al., 2011). Furthermore, Dong and colleagues (2010) found that Internet addicts had decreased activation in the conflict detection stage than the normal group on Go/No-Go tasks.

7.3.2   Stroop Performance in Cyber Addictions

In a follow-up study by Dong and colleagues (2011), they extended their findings in the same direction using a Stroop task. Participants in their group of Internet addicts had reduced medial frontal negativity on their EEG signals that went along with a greater number of errors made in the incongruent condition of the experiment. These EEG findings were also associated with longer reaction times. A number of other studies have looked at relations between executive-control and cyber addictions using neuropsychological assessments tapping into automatic and controlled processing. Like Dong and colleagues, these studies often use the Stroop task to evaluate the executive aspects of attention control. The Stroop task is increasingly used in cyberpsychology research (Armstrong et al., 2013; Henry et al., 2012; Lalonde, Parsons et al., 2011; Parsons, Courtney, & Dawson, 2013; Parsons & Carlew, 2016), and a number of researchers have used the Stroop with neuroimaging evaluation of cyber addictions.

Although there are variations in Stroop stimuli across these studies (e.g., number of items), they all measure freedom from distractibility, selective attention, response conflict, and response inhibition. Typically, the computerized Stroop task requires the user to press a computer key labeled red, green, or blue to identify each color stimulus presented. The participant uses a keypad to take the Stroop test. There are three possible blocks of trials for this test. In the first block, the words RED, GREEN, and BLUE are presented individually in black type on the display. The user is instructed to read each word aloud and to press a corresponding key for each word ("red" = 1; "green" = 2; and "blue" = 3). In the second block, a series of XXXXs is presented on the display in one of three colors (red XXXXs, green XXXXs, or blue XXXXs). The user is instructed to say the color of the XXXXs aloud and to press the corresponding key based on color. In the third block, a series of individual words ("RED," "GREEN," or "BLUE") are presented in a color that does not match the name of the color depicted by the word. The user is instructed to say the color of the word aloud rather than reading the actual word and to press the response key assigned to that color. The participants are asked to respond to each individual color stimulus as quickly as possible without making mistakes. Speed and duration of single-item stimulus presentations are often user-defined – meaning that a new stimulus appears only after the user has correctly identified the previous stimulus.

Individuals with cyber addiction typically show decreased abilities in controlling or inhibiting their responses. For the Stroop, poorer performance is indicated by increased error rates and increased reaction times between congruent and incongruent trials (Stroop interference effect). Participants with cyber addictions tend to commit more errors than controls on incongruent trials (Dong, Zhou, & Zhao, 2011; van Holst et al, 2012; Wang et al., 2015; Xing et al., 2014; Yuan et al., 2013). In terms of reaction times on the Stroop incongruent trials, findings comparing participants with cyber addiction to normal controls have been inconsistent. In some studies, participants with cyber addiction were slower (Dong, Zhou, & Zhao, 2011; Li et al., 2015; Xing et al., 2014). In other studies, they were faster (Wang et al., 2015). Furthermore, in some studies participants with cyber addiction were not different than controls (van Holst et al., 2012; Yuan et al., 2013). Further inconsistency in these studies is apparent in the lack of difference in Stroop performance for either errors or reaction times when comparing participants with cyber addictions to normal controls (Dong et al., 2012; Dong, Hu, Lin, & Lu, 2013; Dong, Lin, Zhou, & Lu, 2014). It is important to note, however, that these null findings may be due to the low statistical power of these studies. Support for this argument can be seen in the larger sample sizes found in the studies (mentioned above) that did find significant differences between participants with cyber addiction and normal controls.

In a recent study, Wang and others (2015) investigated the associations between alteration of gray matter volume and cognitive control in adolescents with Internet gaming disorder. Using the Stroop and an optimized voxel-based morphometry technique they found reduced gray matter volume in the anterior cingulate cortex, precuneus, supplementary motor area, superior parietal cortex, and dorsolateral prefrontal cortex. It is important to note that the decrease in anterior cingulate cortex volumes was correlated with decreased performance on the Stroop task. In another study using the Stroop, Yuan and colleagues (2013) found that participants with cyber addiction had decreased orbitofrontal cortex thickness, which was correlated with decreased performance on the Stroop.

In another study, Li and colleagues (2015) combined structural (regional gray matter volume, rGMV) and functional (resting-state functional connectivity, rsFC) metrics to investigate the neural mechanisms underlying increased tendencies toward Internet addiction in a large sample of 260 healthy young adults. Findings revealed that participants with increased tendencies toward Internet addiction also had rGMV in the right dlPFC. Given the dlPFC's role in executive-control, this may reflect decreased inhibitory control. Further, participants with tendencies toward Internet addiction also showed decreased anticorrelations between the right dlPFC and the medial prefrontal cortex (rostral anterior cingulate cortex). This is further support for decreased executive-control, with specific potential deficits in executive-control and self-monitoring. The Stroop interference effect was positively related to dlPFC volume and with the Internet addiction scores. In addition to the dlPFC, Stroop interference was related to connectivity between dlPFC and mPFC. The rGMV variations in the dlPFC and decreased anticonnections between the dlPFC and mPFC may reflect reduced inhibitory control and cognitive efficiency.

In a series of studies using functional imaging and event-related potential studies, Guangheng Dong of Zhejiang Normal University has also found altered neural activations in prefrontal regions as participants with cyber addiction took part in the Stroop and other response inhibition tasks (Dong et al., 2010; Dong, Zhou, & Zhao, 2011; Dong, DeVito, Du, & Cui, 2012; Dong, Hu, Lin, & Lu, 2013; Dong, Shen, Huang, & Du, 2013; Dong, Lin, Zhou, & Lu, 2014; Dong, Lina, & Potenza, 2015). In these studies, Dong and colleagues consistently found that cyber addiction was related to changes in both structural and functional imaging of brain regions involved in response inhibition. In a recent study, Dong and colleagues examined executive-control networks (links between dorsolateral frontal and parietal neocortices) during resting states and their associations with executive-control during Stroop task performance. Findings revealed that participants with cyber addiction had lower functional connectivity in the executive-control networks during resting state. Furthermore, functional-connectivity measures in executive-control networks were negatively related to Stroop interference and positively related to brain activations in executive-control networks. Dong and colleagues concluded that higher levels of functional connectivity in executive-control networks may underlie healthier executive-control and may provide resilience with respect to cyber addictions. Moreover, lower levels of functional connectivity in executive-control networks may be helpful in aiding our understanding and treatment of cyber addiction.

7.3.3 Go/No-Go Task Performance in Cyber Addictions

Another task that is often implemented in cyberpsychology research into cyber addiction is the Go/No-Go task, in which a participant's capacity for sustained attention and response control is measured. For example, a participant is instructed to press a button on a keypad (Go action) when certain stimuli are presented and refrain (inhibit) from pressing the keypad button when presented with a different set of stimuli (No-Go). As mentioned above, Dong and colleagues (2010) found that Internet addicts had decreased activation in the conflict detection stage than the normal group on Go/No-Go tasks. Likewise, Li and colleagues (2014) used a Go/No-Go task and found a decreased percentage of successful no-go trials in participants with cyber addiction. In a similar study using the Go/No-Go task, Littel and colleagues (2012) found that participants with cyber addictions reacted faster than normal controls and had similar error rates in "go" trials but had more errors in "no-go" trials. It is important to note, however, that other studies have actually found better performance from participants with cyber addictions (Sun et al., 2009) or no difference in performance between participants with cyber addictions and normal controls (Ding et al., 2014; Dong, Lu, Zhou, & Zhao, 2010). Given these inconsistent findings, there are a number of other studies using a modified approach to the Go/No-Go task that deserve mentioning. Specifically, Internet or gaming-related cues have been used with the Go/No-Go task. Results from these studies have been more consistent and have found repeatedly that participants with cyber addictions had faster reaction times and increased accuracy when the "go" stimulus was an Internet or gaming-related cue. They had decreased inhibition performance when the "no-go" stimulus was an Internet or gaming cue. Hence, participants with cyber addictions showed poorer response inhibition and this was further impacted negatively when Internet-related cues were presented (Decker & Gay, 2011; van Holst et al., 2012; Zhou, Z., Yuan, G., & Yao, J., 2012).

7.3.4   Risky Decision-Making and Cyber Addictions

Another test that is used for differentiating participants with cyber addictions from normal controls is the Iowa gambling task (IGT; Bechara & Damasio, 2005), which is used to assess probabilistic decision-making (see also Chapter 8 for research using this task). The IGT is a commonly used measure of somatic markers and decision-making (Bechara & Damasio, 2005; see Chapter 9 of this book for more on the somatic marker hypothesis). According to the somatic marker hypothesis, decisional processes are biased toward long-term prospects by emotional marker signals produced by a neuronal architecture comprising both cortical and subcortical circuits. Furthermore, the IGT measures the user's ability to forego larger immediate rewards that led to net losses, for smaller rewards that led to net gains. There is growing evidence that addiction is characterized by diminished ability to establish somatic markers that normally support the selection of adaptive behavior. In addictions, this results in deficient self-regulation, in which users have difficulty anticipating negative consequences of future action (Brevers & Noël, 2013; Verdejo-García & Bechara, 2009).

During IGT assessment, the patient is instructed to choose cards from four decks (A–D). Selection of each card results in on-screen feedback regarding either a "gain" or "loss" of currency. In the four decks there are two advantageous (C and D) decks that result in money gained ($250 every 10 cards) and low monetary loss during the trial. The other two decks (A and B) are disadvantageous and involve greater wins (around $100 each card) than C and D (around $50) but also incur greater losses, meaning that one loses $250 every 10 cards in Decks A and B. The primary dependent variables derived from the IGT are total score and net score ([C + D] – [A + B]) and block score ([C + D] – [A + B]) for each segment or block of 20 cards, frequency of deck choices, and spared or impaired performance according to a cut-off point of –10 (Bechara, Damasio, & Damasio, 2000) especially in brain-damaged subjects.

The IGT is an affective decision-making paradigm aimed at mimicking real-life decision-making in the way it factors uncertainty, reward, and punishment. According to Bechara and colleagues (1997), there is a correlation between successful performance and heightened skin conductance responses when healthy participants anticipate unconsciously disadvantageous decisions on the IGT (Bechara et al., 1997; Crone et al., 2004; Suzuki, Hirota, Takasawa, & Shigemasu, 2003). These anticipative skin conductance responses have been interpreted as an index of somatic marker signals. In studies on cyber addiction, researchers have used the IGT because individuals with cyber addictions have been found to have differences in the way they process rewards during decision-making tasks. Specifically, participants with cyber addictions less frequently select advantageous decks (smaller immediate rewards but leading to net gains) and are slower in learning the optimal strategy than normal control (Sun et al., 2009; Xu, 2012). For example, when normal controls received a big gain (i.e., disadvantageous decks), they would switch decks to evade possible greater losses that were expected to follow. The behavior of participants with cyber addiction was quite different. They tended to persist on the same deck after large gains cards (Xu, 2012). This suggests that participants with cyber addiction were highly biased toward larger immediate rewards even when they could lead to net losses.

7.4 Altered Reward Processing in Cyber Addiction

What causes cyber addiction? One answer may be the rewards that come from the highly stimulating and rewarding experiences that can come from the Internet and related media. According to David Greenfield (2011), founder of The Center for Internet and Technology Addiction, there are five main properties of the Internet's appeal:

(1) **Content factors:** the content found on the Internet (e.g., social information, music, videos, and games) is inherently pleasurable in nature.

(2) **Process and access/availability factors:** The availability of opportunities for the user to experience a fantasy (e.g., enacting a sexual fantasy with relative ease, disinhibition, and anonymity), or to act out a persona, is highly attractive.

(3) **Reinforcement/reward factors:** The Internet operates on a variable-ratio reinforcement schedule. Users are rewarded at both unpredictable frequencies (e.g., receiving of Facebook "likes") and magnitudes (e.g., Google search matches).

(4) **Social factors:** The Internet is both socially connecting and socially isolating. It affords titrated social connection within a highly circumscribed social networking medium. Hence, users can tailor their degree of social interaction in a way that maximizes comfort and mediates connection.

(5) **Gen-D factors:** Generation-Digital users are persons who have been raised with this technology.

For Greenfield, the reinforcement/reward factor seems to be the most significant element in contributing to the addictive nature of the Internet and other digital media technologies. What happens when an individual receives a "like" to their posted content on a Facebook page? Typically, this represents a rewarding experience for the person and promotes further social networking. However, what is it that happens in the person's brain when he or she sees someone "like" their Facebook post? The answer may involve a part of the ventral striatum that lies in a region in the basal forebrain rostral to the preoptic area of the hypothalamus. Specifically, that reinforcing effect that occurs when a person experiences a "like" on Facebook reflects activity in the nucleus accumbens.

There are a number of major inputs to the nucleus accumbens from specific brain areas (prefrontal cortex, amygdala (basolateral), and the ventral tegmental area (VTA)) and the nucleus accumbens is often described as being part of a cortico-striato-thalamo-cortical loop. The nucleus accumbens has an important role in the neurocognitive processing of reward, pleasure, reinforcement learning, aversion, and motivation. *Dopamine acts in the nucleus accumbens to attach motivational significance to stimuli associated with reward.* Dopaminergic neurons found in the VTA connect via the mesolimbic pathway and modulate the activity of neurons within the nucleus accumbens that are activated directly or indirectly by drugs like opiates and amphetamines. Given the fact that social affirmation tends to be a rewarding experience for the vast majority of users it is not surprising that Facebook affirmations would result in activation of the nucleus accumbens. Dopamine neurons located in the ventral tegmental area and projecting to the nucleus accumbens play a key role in the processing of reward-related stimuli, including those associated with drugs of abuse (Wise, 2008). Furthermore, the prefrontal cortex and amygdala share interconnections with the ventral tegmental area and nucleus accumbens and can modulate dopamine transmission and neuronal activity. However, just because these areas have been found to be associated with Facebook likes, activation alone is not sufficient for the establishment of an addiction. Nevertheless, brain activations in these areas do raise an interesting possibility that Facebook "likes" and other affirmations (chime for an incoming text or email) might be the first step toward an addiction in some users (Turel & Serenko, 2012).

Furthermore, affirmations from social media (e.g., likes, text chimes, ringtones) from other users occur only sporadically. From a cyberpsychology and behavioral perspective, this rate of online reinforcement represents a variable-ratio schedule that produces the sort of high steady rate of responding found in gambling and lottery games. How does this reward system become activated for Facebook users? The answer is that Facebook has multiple variable-ratio reinforcement schedules built into it – a user could receive a "like," friend request, comment on the user's status update, or be tagged in a photo. Any of these situations (among the many other possible) might place the user in a state of anticipation. This variable-ratio pattern of reinforcement can be more addicting than receiving affirmation every time because (at least in part) the user's brain endeavors to predict rewards. In variable-ratio reward schedules the brain cannot find the pattern and it will promote a behavior until it finds one. In situations where the rewards (e.g., affirmations, chimes) are random, the brain's attempt at pattern recognition may continue compulsively.

There is a growing body of research indicating that problematic Internet use is associated with abnormalities in the dopaminergic brain system (Kim et al., 2011; Park et al., 2010; Tian et al., 2014). Sang Hee Kim and colleagues (2011) at Korea University investigated whether problematic Internet use would be associated with reduced levels of dopaminergic receptor availability in the striatum. To test this hypothesis, they used a radiolabeled ligand [C]raclopride and positron emission tomography (PET) to measure dopamine D2 receptor binding potential in males with and without problematic Internet use. Findings revealed that individuals with problematic Internet use had lower levels of dopamine D2 receptor availability in subdivisions of the striatum, including the bilateral dorsal caudate and right putamen. These results contribute to the understanding of the neurobiological mechanism of problematic Internet use. Furthermore, these findings comport well with the findings from Han and colleagues' (2007) investigation of genetic polymorphisms of the dopaminergic system in a group of excessive Internet game players. Their findings revealed that individuals with increased genetic polymorphisms in genes coding for the dopamine D2 receptor and dopamine degradation enzyme had increased susceptibility to excessive Internet gaming.

Internet gaming disorder features diminished impulse control and poor reward processing. In order to enhance understanding of the neurobiological bases of Internet gaming, Hyun Soo Park and colleagues (2010) at Seoul National University College of Medicine investigated the differences in regional cerebral glucose metabolism at resting state between persons with Internet gaming disorder and those with normal use. They used 18F-fluoro-deoxyglucose (18F-FDG) PET imaging to investigate the differences of cerebral glucose metabolism at resting state between persons with Internet gaming disorder and healthy controls. Findings from assessment of impulsivity revealed that persons with Internet gaming disorder had greater impulsiveness than the normal users and there was a positive correlation between the severity of Internet gaming overuse and impulsiveness. Neuroimaging findings revealed that persons with Internet gaming disorder had increased glucose metabolism in the right middle orbitofrontal cortex, left caudate nucleus, and right insula. Furthermore, decreased metabolism was found in the bilateral postcentral gyrus, left precentral gyrus, and bilateral occipital regions compared with normal users. These findings suggest that persons with Internet gaming disorder may have neurobiological abnormality in the orbitofrontal cortex, striatum, and sensory regions, which are involved in impulse control, reward processing, and somatic representation experience.

7.5   Internet Gaming

Findings from these studies have consistently found that persons with cyber addiction behaviors show increased neural activations for Internet-related cues (Ko et al., 2009; Sun et al., 2012). This suggests an association between excessive Internet use and increased neural sensitivity to Internet-related cues. For example, Han and colleagues (2011) exposed healthy participants to a novel Internet game and found increased activation in response to game-related cues. When Kühn and colleagues (2011) looked at the regional gray matter density differences between frequent and infrequent Internet gamers, they found that the frequent gamers had higher gray matter density in the left ventral striatal region. From these findings they concluded that frequent gaming resulted in increased striatal volumes and enhanced dopaminergic release. Support for this perspective can be found in studies of persons with Internet addiction that have decreased dopamine regulation (decreased transporter expression and reduced D2 receptors) in the striatum (Hou et al., 2012; Kim et al., 2011). Furthermore, Kühn and colleagues (2011) investigated persons with Internet addiction and found increased activation in the same striatal region (increased dopamine release) when participants with Internet addiction experienced losses.

Internet gaming disorder has emerged recently from the umbrella term "Internet addiction." Users with Internet gaming disorder spend several hours each day playing videogames. For example, massively multiplayer online role-playing games (MMORPGs; e.g., World of Warcraft) are Internet games that have been related to negative consequences in terms of academic performance and social functioning (Gentile et al., 2011). The reward from videogames is apparent. In a classic raclopride–PET study, striatal dopamine release was detected in healthy participants as they played a primitive video game (Koepp et al., 1998). Today's videogames have much greater fidelity, interaction, and reinforcements. As a result, it is not surprising that reductions in striatal D2 binding have been found in participants with Internet addiction (Kim et al., 2011). Studies using fMRI have found cue reactivity from game screenshots impacting the medial prefrontal cortex (Ko et al., 2013; VanHolst et al., 2012). Moreover, today's MMORPGs contain some unique features that are not found in traditional computer games. For example, the MMORPGs have consistent characters (i.e., avatars) that gradually develop within the game environment across multiple game sessions. Further, MMORPGs have a multiplayer component, which means that the game continues while any individual player is offline. As a result, the user may feel compelled to be in-game to make sure that s/he is not missing any of the action or developments.

7.6   Conclusions

As can be seen from this review, there is a growing body of brain-based cyberpsychology research into the relations between online media use and compulsive behaviors, self-regulation, impulse control, and substance abuse. Often excessive Internet use is associated with symptoms frequently linked to addiction, such as tolerance (increased Internet use over time), withdrawal (irritability when unable to access Internet material), and cravings (for Internet-mediated content). While there is some disagreement on whether persons that excessively use the Internet are addicted or just use the Internet excessively as a medium to fuel their other addictions, Internet gaming disorder has been categorized in the revised *Diagnostic and Statistical Manual of Mental Disorders* as a condition for further study. While there are parallels to other addictions, the American Psychiatric Association prefers the term "Internet gaming disorder" over "Internet addiction" because a gaming addict is not necessarily addicted to the Internet, but simply uses it as a medium to engage in the chosen behavior. Internet-related disorders are best conceptualized within a spectrum of related and yet independent disorders. For the purposes of this chapter, cyber addiction will be used for all discussions of various forms of Internet addiction and gaming disorders.

Perhaps a DSM-based approach is less important now than it used to be as the growing body of neurological and neuroimaging studies reveal that the prefrontal cortex plays a significant role in the development of Internet addition. A better approach may be to emphasize the neural correlates of problematic Internet use that are similar to those underpinning other addictive syndromes. The emphasis upon Internet addiction in terms of neural correlates seems to comport well with the National Institute of Mental Health's Research Domain Criteria that emphasizes the need for a future diagnostic system that more directly reflects modern brain science. According to the NIMH RDoC, it is increasingly evident that mental illness (e.g., cyber addictions) will be best understood as disorders of brain structure and function that implicate specific domains of cognition, emotion, and behavior. Moreover, NIMH's RDoC is an attempt to create a new kind of taxonomy for mental disorders by bringing the power of modern research approaches in genetics, neuroscience, and behavioral science to the problem of mental illness. Hence, this chapter has described research that emphasizes the RDoc approach over DSM classifications.

Throughout this chapter the neural correlates of cyber addiction behaviors were discussed. As was apparent from the review, studies consistently find alterations in neural mechanisms involved in self-control mechanisms. Persons with cyber addictions have been found to have decreased gray matter densities in frontal-parietal structures, which are commonly involved in cognitive control. Furthermore, large-scale brain networks and a number of brain hub regions have been found to be associated with altered self-control and reward processing in cyber addiction. These brain networks and hubs are consistently associated with top-down response inhibition, error monitoring, and goal maintenance. Furthermore, the chapter reviewed brain areas that are activated during reward processing and during decision-making. Additionally, brain structures were identified that are important in motivating and driving reward-pursuing behaviors.

It is important to note that there is growing evidence that Internet addiction is related to brain structural changes and decreased executive-control processes. Evidence from neuroimaging has shown that brain regions associated with executive function have decreased cortical thickness in Internet-addicted adolescents. Consistent results were found from neuroimaging that also revealed brain regions associated with executive function had decreased cortical thickness in Internet gambling disordered participants. Further, reduced cortical thickness of the left lateral orbito-frontal cortex was associated with impaired cognitive control.

PART III

Cyberpsychology and the Neurosciences

CHAPTER 8

Cyberpsychology, Ecological Validity, and Neurosciences of Everyday Living

8.1 Introduction

A good deal of cyberpsychology is interested in the everyday functions that are regularly carried out by people as they interact with technologies. Many of us check our smartphone when we first wake up in the morning, use computers to help us navigate to work, actively use email and social media throughout the day, and then check our smartphones before heading off to bed in the evenings. These everyday interactions with technology involve a number of higher-order supervisory control processes to insure that we are able to flexibly regulate the complex goal-directed problem-solving thoughts and actions that confront us. Technologies bolster a multitude of everyday, "real-world" functions, including planning and sequencing complex task goals (e.g., from GPS navigation to desktop computers), reminders to initiate goal-directed behaviors (e.g., email and calendar alerts), and performing multiple tasks simultaneously (e.g., media multitasking). While laboratory-based tests provide important information about the ways in which our cognitive processes interact with technologies, they have been criticized for their failure to represent the social, cognitive, and affective facets of real-world activities. Furthermore, there are serious questions about the generalizability of sterile laboratory findings to the cognitively complex social and emotional activities of daily living (Neisser, 1982; Parsons, 2015). These issues are of even greater concern when the cyberpsychologist turns to studies with clinical populations. While standardized neuropsychological assessments provide important information related to patient's cognitive impairments, clinical scientists often question how predictive this information is of the patient's ability to deal with open-ended, loosely controlled environments that are regularly encountered in everyday activities (Manchester, Priestley, & Jackson, 2004; Wilson, 1993).

An area of interest to cyberpsychologists is the evolution of existing communication interfaces and social media toward an optimal immersion of human sensorimotor channels into simulation environments (Riva et al., 2015). A notable difference between virtual environments and other media or communication systems is the sense of presence, the "feeling of being there" (Waterworth & Riva, 2014). The use of presence in a brain-based cyberpsychology reflects the extent to which a user feels present in a simulated environment (Botella et al., 2009; Schubert et al., 2001; Slater & Wilbur, 1997). For cyberpsychologists issues of immersion and presence are specific ecological validity issues that need to be addressed. An important advance in this area is the development of virtual environments for neurocognitive and affective assessments in clinical, affective, and social neurosciences (Parsons, 2015). Seth and colleagues (2011) have proposed a presence model, in which presence is understood as an everyday phenomenon. According to their interoceptive predictive coding model, presence results from effective inhibition by executive cognitive control predictions of interoceptive (affective) signals evoked by automatic (e.g., autonomic and bodily) responses to afferent sensory signals. In everyday life, presence rests on continuous executive-control prediction of interoceptive (affective) states.

Here is where affective neuroscience and affective computing come into play for ecological validity. There is growing research interest in the ways in which users may be immersed in simulations that reflect the affective components of our everyday interactions with technology. As a result, there is a budding recognition of the need for assessment protocols that take seriously the interplay of cognition and emotion in our everyday decisions. For example, cyberpsychologists interested in the impact of videogames on adolescents may choose to investigate the interplay between cold cognitive processing (linked to dorsal and lateral regions of the prefrontal cortex) of relatively abstract, context-free information, and hot affective processing (linked to the functioning of the orbitofrontal cortex) involved when emotionally laden information is present. The development of affective computing and psychophysiological computing platforms offer examples of approaches to integrating affective neuroscience into cyber-psychology research.

A final issue of immersion and presence for an ecologically valid simulation is that of "being there with others." The idea here is that of social presence. In addition to cognitive assessments that can generalize beyond the narrow laboratory context, there is a developing desire for social neuroscience assessments that go beyond static stimuli (e.g., simple, static representations of socially relevant stimuli; static photographs of emotionally valenced facial expressions) that are devoid of social interactions to dynamic stimuli that will allow assessment of participants as they act upon stimuli.

In this chapter, the aim is to provide a framework for ecologically valid cyberpsychology investigations into the cognitive and affective aspects of everyday lived experience. That said, there is a realization that much of our everyday lives involve interactions with others. As such, there will also be discussions of a social neuroscience–informed approach to ecological validity. Finally, there is the issue of moving beyond cyberpsychology paradigms with healthy controls into the realm of clinical neuroscience.

The plan of this chapter will be as follows: Section 8.2 starts the ecological validity discussion from the perspective of cognitive neuroscience. First, there is a review of the historical discussion of the everyday versus laboratory research conflict. Specifically, there will be a review of Neisser and Banaji's debate about whether the laboratory imposes an artificial situation that does not represent the everyday world. Included in this section will be an introduction to the impact of perception and presence on ecological validity. In Section 8.3 the discussion is extended to include an enhancement of ecological validity via the inclusion of the interplay of cognitive processing and emotionally laden information. Next, in Section 8.4 the discussion is enhanced via the inclusion of others. Specifically, there is acknowledgment of the need for social neuroscience in our assessments of persons involved in everyday activities. Finally, in Section 8.5 the ecological validity discussion will revolve around the development of a definition that can be applied to clinical neuroscience (e.g., clinical neuropsychology). This section will include early attempts to offer a definition of ecological validity that was specific to neuropsychology. Furthermore, this section will include the theoretical model developed by Burgess and colleagues (2006), in which "function-led" approaches to neuropsychological assessment are presented.

8.2   Ecological Validity for the Cognitive Neurosciences

8.2.1   The Everyday/Laboratory Research Conflict

Cognitive neuroscience research has a strong emphasis upon internal validity and takes careful steps to (1) verify that every potentially confounding variable is foreseen and controlled; and (2) confirm that each feature of responding is cautiously and exactingly evaluated. However, the internal validity often comes at the cost of ecological validity in cognitive neuroscience research. There exists an essential tension between the internal validity and the ecological validity of any research initiative. Increased control means decreased naturalness, and vice versa. If one takes memory as an example, one finds that much of the early (e.g., first few decades) memory research fits a relatively customary pattern – word lists were prudently assembled to control for the effects of various extraneous variables. Moreover, the stimuli were presented under exactly controlled conditions, and participants' recall and/or recognition were tested. However, it can be argued that the number of words someone can recall from a list of concrete and abstract words presented for three seconds each does not give us much information about difficulties recalling autobiographical events from before age three.

The issue of ecological validity in cyberpsychological assessment has been expressed a number of times over the years via discussions of the limitations of generalizing sterile laboratory findings to the processes normally occurring in people's everyday lives. In 1978, Ulrich Neisser proffered an opening address at the first International Conference on Practical Aspects of Memory, in which he argued for an ecologically valid approach to memory research (published in Neisser, 1982). To a large extent, Neisser's critique was directed at the emphasis on internal validity in memory research. Neisser offered three main challenges to memory research:

(1)   The traditional approach has resulted in only a few new discoveries.
(2)   The preoccupation with broad theoretical issues (e.g., mechanisms of forgetting) has resulted in a neglect of questions relevant to everyday life (e.g., the forgetting of appointments).
(3)   Most of the experiments were conducted in artificial settings and employed measures that have few counterparts in everyday life (e.g., unrelated wordlists).

In Neisser's view such research lacks "ecological validity." Hence, Neisser was arguing that the findings from many traditional cognitive assessments have not been demonstrated to generalize beyond the narrow laboratory context. It is important to note that Neisser was not arguing for the abandonment of laboratory methods. In fact, he has argued that "the most typical characteristic of the ecological approach is not an aversion to the laboratory but an attempt to maintain the integrity of variables that matter in natural settings" (Neisser, 1985, p.25). That said, Neisser's work does emphasize the need for memory research to be representative of everyday activities. For example, laboratory studies using nonsense syllables would typically be considered lacking in straightforward reference to a meaningful object in everyday life. Likewise, the experimental setting is often an artificial and controlled situation (e.g., conventional psychological laboratory) that falls short of replicating the situations that one normally encounters in everyday life. Neisser also questioned whether laboratory findings were applicable to their real-world correlates.

It is important to note, however, that an essential tension exists between persons striving for ecological validity and persons interested in maintaining experimental control. In 1989, Banaji and Crowder denounced what they dubbed the "bankruptcy of everyday memory," challenging stalwartly most of Neisser's claims. They countered Neisser's arguments with the claim that the naturalistic study of cognition has not been productive. To illustrate their point, they drew an analogy between a psychologist who performs well-controlled laboratory research on memory and a chemist who conducts well-controlled studies on the properties of yeast so that she can establish why bread dough rises. From Banaji and Crowder's perspective, the exactingly controlled studies of the chemist have a greater probability of yielding significant results than "loitering in professional bakeries and taking careful notes" (p. 1187). Furthermore, Banaji and Crowder contend that everyday memory contexts (e.g., attempting to remember events from one's life) have so many uncontrolled factors that generalizability of findings is hindered instead of being increased. Hence, for Banaji and Crowder, the ecological approach to cognitive research is inconsequential and scientific progress necessitates greater emphasis on experimental control. Their challenge is that ecological validity is less detrimental than a lack of internal validity.

Following Banaji and Crowder's paper, a special issue of the *American Psychologist* (1991) was devoted to replies to the original article. A number of perspectives were presented related to the issue of whether memory capabilities that are called upon in the laboratory are similar to real-life tasks. From a neuropsychological perspective, these discussions would have been aided by then current discussions in the neuropsychological literature on prospective memory (Meacham, 1982) and the ways in which various environmental factors may define how memory deficits interact with other deficits (Schacter, 1983). In addition to memory, there were other domains being discussed at that time from an ecological perspective: problem-solving (Sinnott, 1989); intelligence (Rogoff & Lave, 1984; Sternberg & Wagner, 1986); and categorization (Neisser, 1987). While there was a great deal of controversy over whether cognitive assessment should emphasize standardized, laboratory-based methods or more observational and naturalistic assessment practices (e.g., Banaji & Crowder,

1989; Conway, 1991; Neisser, 1978), the debate has since subsided (deWall, Wilson, & Baddeley, 1994).

That said, there are important implications for cyberpsychology research from both the internal validity and ecological validity perspectives. What is needed is an approach that combines each of these validity issues into a research platform. In this book there are a number of examples of attempts to do just that. One area of particular promise is virtual-reality as it allows for precise control of environmental stimuli in simulations of real-world functioning.

8.2.2   *Impact of Perception, Immersion, and Presence on Ecological Validity*

For cyberpsychologists there is an additional aspect of ecological validity that is not always discussed in the psychological assessment literature. That issue is the sense of "presence" or "being there" for persons immersed in virtual environments that aim to provide cyberpsychology researchers with neurocognitive and affective assessments in clinical, affective, and social neurosciences (Parsons, 2015). A notable difference between virtual environments and other media or communication systems is the sense of presence, the "feeling of being there" (Waterworth & Riva, 2014). In cyberpsychology research, the concept of presence reflects an individual's phenomenological sense of reality of the world and of one's immersion within the environment (Sanchez-Vives & Slater, 2005).

8.2.2.1   *Perception and Immersion*

A wide variety of virtual-reality simulations have been developed. The range and depth of these simulations cover a large domain, from simple low-fidelity task environments to complex high-fidelity full immersion simulators. All of these simulators rely on some type of representation of the real world. An important issue for ecologically valid research into simulation for cyberpsychology is the determination of how advanced the simulator needs to be to adequately assess and/or train a particular individual or team. While high-end simulations can train a variety of user types, the cost associated with these devices can be difficult to justify (Langhan, 2008).

In the same way people experience physiological responses to stimuli in the real world, researchers seek to quantify participant experience by measuring responses evoked by stimuli in a virtual environment. On the one hand, low-fidelity virtual environment may be preferable in studies where a maximal amount of experimental control is desired because such environments may increase psychometric rigor through limiting the number of sensory variables available to the user. Contrariwise, high-fidelity environments are preferable for studies desiring increased ecological validity because they recreate more of the real-world environment – better capture the participant's performance as it would occur in a real-world setting.

Discussions of the level of fidelity and experimental control needed for a virtual environment often go beyond simple discussions of the "immersive" qualities of the environment to discussions of the impact upon the perceived feeling of "presence" of the individual while immersed in the virtual environment. Issues of fidelity tend to reflect levels of immersiveness found in the environment, while levels of presence reflect the user's experience relative to the level of fidelity/immersion. It is also important to differentiate between immersion and presence. Slater and Wilbur (1997) elucidate the discussion of immersion by framing immersion as an objective description of aspects of the system. The use of the term "immersion" herein reflects that which the overall virtual environment can deliver (e.g., the level of fidelity in representing the real world,' the field of view, the number of sensory systems it simulates, the frame-rate, and latency). Hence, the level of immersion is an objective property of a virtual environment that in principle can be measured independently of the human experience that it engenders. On the other hand, presence is understood as the "feeling of being there" that healthy users typically experience.

8.2.2.2 *Measuring Presence*

A number of presence studies have researched such issues using questionnaires (Lessiter, Freeman, Keogh, & Davidoff, 2001; Usoh et al., 2000; Witmer & Singer, 1998). While these subjective measures are widely used, this common approach is not without controversy. Critics argue that subjective measures tend to rely on post-test assessments of the user's feelings during the exposure to the VE, which is dependent on memory of the event. Moreover, self-report data, when used in isolation, are highly susceptible to influences outside the subject's own targeted attitudes (Freeman et al., 1999; Schwarz, 1999). The item's wording, context, and format are all factors that may affect self-report responses. A further limitation of questionnaire measures is that they can only be administered following a participant's immersion in a VE, but in order to assess participant experience during the actual immersion in a VE, researchers have sought a more objective measure. Online assessment of participant experience is difficult when using subjective measures, in that the very existence of subjective questions during immersion serves to break the continuity of the participant's conscious awareness currently being experienced. Direct inquiries about presence may also prompt or diminish experienced presence (Sanchez-Vives & Slater, 2005). Although particular behavioral measures can assess for correspondence between virtual and real-world environments, these measures are mainly applicable to behavioral interpretations of presence (Sanchez-Vives & Slater, 2005).

Given the limitations of subjective measures, a quite different view seems to be emerging, in which presence is treated as something rooted in physiological and behavioral activity (Meehan et al., 2005; Sanchez-Vives & Slater, 2005) and there is a growing emphasis upon physiological and behavioral assessment, as well as the relation between immersion and emotion (Baños et al., 2004; Baumgartner, Valko, Esslen, & Jäncke, 2006). Further, there has been increased use of neuroscience techniques for presence measurement, such as EEG (Baumgartner, Valko, Esslen, & Jäncke, 2006), transcranial Doppler (Alcañiz, Rey, Tembl, & Parkhutik, 2009), and fMRI (Baumgartner et al., 2008). Relatedly, there is a growing interest in experimentally manipulating the user's predictions and prediction errors to study presence. For example, prediction errors can be systematically manipulated by interjecting a mismatch between user behavior and sensory feedback using psychophysical methods and virtual environments (Nahab et al., 2011). According to Tamietto and de Gelder (2010) prediction errors can be manipulated by subliminal presentation of emotionally salient stimuli prior to target stimuli. Manipulations of executive control anticipations could be attained by adjusting the environment in which users are tested.

8.2.2.3   *Presence and Large-Scale Brain Networks*

Although theoretical models describing the neural correlates of presence and consciousness have been lacking (Sanchez-Vives & Slater, 2005), recent work by Seth and colleagues (2011) has formulated an interoceptive predictive coding model of conscious presence. Their theoretical model implicates a large-scale brain network for presence. Suggested brain areas contributing to interoceptive predictive coding include cortical (orbitofrontal cortex, insular cortex, and anterior cingulate cortex); subcortical (substantia innominata, nucleus accumbens, amygdala), and brainstem (nucleus of the solitary tract, periaqueductal gray, locus coeruleus) regions (Critchley et al., 2004; Tamietto & de Gelder, 2010). Among these areas, the insular cortex and anterior cingulate cortex are believed to have great import for the experience of presence. The insular cortex is posited as essential to the integration of interoceptive and exteroceptive signals, as well as the formation of subjective feeling states. Furthermore, anterior cingulate acts as a viceromotor cortex from which autonomic control signals originate. The anterior insula and the anterior cingulate are often coactivated (despite spatial separation) and form a large-scale brain network called the "salience network" (Seeley et al., 2007).

Within this theoretical neural network model, presence is understood as an everyday phenomenon. According to Seth et al.'s (2011) interoceptive predictive coding model, presence results from effective inhibition by executive-control predictions of informative interoceptive signals evoked by automatic (e.g., autonomic and bodily) responses to afferent sensory signals. In everyday life, presence rests on continuous executive-control prediction of interoceptive (affective) states. When an individual expects a negative encounter (e.g., with a person, place, or object), they make predictions about both their negative affective responses (e.g., fear, anxiety, frustration) and the biological change they will experience (e.g., autonomic responses like cardiovascular reactivity). When encountering the negative stimulus, the individual compares the predicted state with the actual interoceptive state that they experienced. Seth and colleagues point out that most of the time there will be a certain degree of mismatch between the predicted and the actual interoceptive state. For them, presence results from successful suppression of this mismatch.

8.2.2.4   *Neural Correlates of Presence and Virtual Environments*
Over a decade ago, Sanchez-Vives and Slater (2005) suggested the combined use of neuroimaging and virtual environments for direct manipulation of the degree of presence. Since that time, there have been an increasing number of studies using their suggested approach. For example, Baumgartner and colleagues (2008) used functional magnetic resonance imaging to assess presence while participants experienced a virtual-reality rollercoaster. Study findings revealed a distributed network of brain regions related to reported presence. In addition to the notable increased activation for the anterior insula, a number of brain areas had increased activation during strong presence states: superior parietal cortex, inferior parietal cortex, ventral visual stream, extrastriate and dorsal visual areas, premotor cortex, thalamic, brainstem, and hippocampal regions. In another study, Aardema and colleagues (2010) found that immersion in a virtual environment increased self-reports of dissociative symptoms on subsequent re-exposure to the real environment. This suggests that

immersion in virtual environments modulates the neural mechanisms underpinning presence. Other neuroimaging and virtual environment studies have found relations between presence and agency (Gutierrez-Martinez et al., 2011; Lallart et al., 2009).

8.3 Affective Neuroscience for Enhanced Ecological Validity

Affective computing is a relatively recent development in cyberpsychology that aims to design machines that can recognize, interpret, process, and simulate human affects (Schwark, 2015). The psychological discussions of affect can be traced back as far as William James (1884) and his nineteenth-century paper "What is emotion." James contended that emotions arise from an individual's perception of physiological changes in the body. While there have been challenges to this idea, it has continued to be developed over the last century. Recent frameworks for understanding emotion that have been influenced by James include Damasio's (2000) "somatic marker hypothesis," Craig's (2002, 2009) "sentient self" model; and the "interoceptive awareness" model by Critchley and colleagues (2004). Likewise, over the years there have been a number of different approaches to studying affect and computers. The affective computing literature is beginning to draw from affective and social neurosciences to move from idealized simulations toward real-world data that reflects the sorts of activities that humans perform in their activities of daily living.

Affective neuroscientists argue for the importance of salient emotional processes for everyday decision-making. Although cognitive-based understandings of brain-behavior relationships have grown in recent decades, the neuropsychological understandings of emotion remain poorly defined (Suchy, 2011). One reason for this deficit may be that the term "cognition" has been increasingly overused and misused since the cognitive revolution. An unfortunate limitation is the deficient development of a usable shared definition for the term "cognition." This deficiency raises concerns about a possible misdirection of research within behavioral neuroscience (Cromwell & Panksepp, 2011).

As is apparent above, theoretical models in cyberpsychology are increasingly interested in the neural correlates of presence and agency (Aardema et al., 2010; Baumgartner et al., 2008; Gutierrez-Martinez et al., 2011; Lallart et al., 2009; Sanchez-Vives & Slater, 2005). For the interoceptive predictive coding model of Seth and colleagues (2011), presence results from inhibition by executive cognitive control predictions of interoceptive (affective) signals evoked by automatic (e.g., autonomic and bodily) responses to afferent sensory signals. In fact, presence is apparent in the continuous executive-control prediction of interoceptive (affective) states found in our everyday lives.

Here is where affective neuroscience and affective computing come into play for ecological validity. There is growing research interest in the ways in which users may be immersed in simulations that reflect the affective components of our everyday interactions with technology. As a result, there is a budding recognition of the need for assessment protocols that take seriously the interplay of cognition and emotion in our everyday decisions. The coupling of presence and affective neuroscience is apparent each time an individual effectively inhibits executive-control predictions in the presence of interoceptive affective signals evoked by automatic (e.g., autonomic and bodily) responses to afferent sensory signals. In everyday life, presence rests on continuous executive control prediction of interoceptive (affective) states.

8.4 Social Neuroscience

In addition to what it feels like to be immersed in a virtual environment, there is the issue of one's sense of being with another in a virtual environment. In an early attempt to define social presence, Short and colleagues (1976) emphasized the degree of salience between people interacting and the resulting salience of the interpersonal relations. Biocca and colleagues (2003) expanded upon this sense of being together with another, by including basic responses to social cues, simulations of other minds, and the automatic generation of intentionality models of others. With the advent of social neuroscience, these ideas of being together with another can be developed into theoretical models reflecting the neural mechanisms of mentalizing (i.e., ability to represent other people's mental states) (Frith & Frith, 2003, 2008). Support for a neuroscience of social presence can be found in the results from functional neuroimaging studies that suggest the involvement of two large-scale brain networks. First there is the so-called mirror neuron system that is composed of the parietal and premotor cortices. The second one is the titular "social brain," that is composed of the medial prefrontal, temporopolar, temporoparietal cortices, and the amygdala (Keysers & Gazzola, 2007; Lieberman, 2007). Quantitative reviews have found that studies of person perception reveal activation in the "mentalizing" and "mirroring" networks (Denny et al., 2012; Van Overwalle & Baetens, 2009). In the quantitative review by Denny and colleagues (2012) results revealed that a number of brain areas in the "mentalizing" network have been found to be engaged when people make judgments about themselves and others. Moreover, the meta-analysis revealed evidence for a gradient from the ventromedial prefrontal cortex to the dorsomedial prefrontal cortex relative to whether people were making judgments about themselves or about others.

8.4.1   The Mentalizing Network

During social and emotional processing, activity is increased reliably within the ventromedial, dorsomedial prefrontal cortex, and posterior cingulate cortex (precuneus regions). These brain areas are known to be nodes within the brain's "default-mode" network (Andrews-Hanna et al., 2010), which has also been referred to as the "mentalizing" network (Amodio & Frith, 2006). Neuroimaging of the human brain while persons are in a state of quiet repose (e.g., with eyes closed) has revealed a default-mode network that activates when external demands are low (Raichle, 2015). These findings have resulted in a suggested role of the default-mode network in self-generated cognition that is decoupled from the external world (Andrews-Hanna, 2012, 2014). As mentioned earlier, an independent body of work in the social neurosciences has revealed an overlapping "mentalizing network" that reveals the neural correlates of a person's ability to mentalize (i.e., infer) the cognitions and feelings of others. The similarity between the default and mentalizing networks has generated questions in social neuroscience about whether the core function of the default network is to mediate internal aspects of social cognition (Li, Mai, & Liu, 2014).

Automatic and controlled processing within the social neurosciences have been reformulated to reflect a controlled "reflective" system and an automatic "reflexive" system (Lieberman, 2007). The reflective system for social neuroscience corresponds with a controlled social cognition system. The reflexive system corresponds with an automatic social cognition system. When persons engage in goal-directed behavior of a nonself-referential nature, certain areas of the brain decrease their activity. During quiet resting states a default-mode network activates (Raichle & Snyder, 2007), which consists of areas in dorsal and ventral medial prefrontal and parietal cortices (see Chapter 2 in this book). Results from recent studies have revealed that the mentalizing network is involved in perspective taking of the desires, beliefs, and intentions of others (see, for example, Buckner et al., 2008). These functions are all self-referential in nature. The reduction of activity in the default-mode network during effortful cognitive processing reflects an attenuation of the brain's self-referential activity as a means of more effectively focusing on a task. This network is engaged regularly during autobiographical memory (remembering personal events), prospection (imagining the future), moral reasoning, semantic memory (recall of word meanings), scene construction, context-based object perception, and social affiliation (Andrews-Hanna et al., 2010; Bar, 2007; Bickart et al., 2012; Buckner, Andrews-Hanna, & Schacter, 2008; Schilbach et al., 2012).

8.4.2   The Mirroring Network

The mentalizing and mirroring networks are believed to serve complementary roles in person perception. Although a number of studies have shown that regions associated with both the "mirroring" network and the "mentalizing" network are frequently engaged while making inferences about actions, they are rarely co-active (see meta-analysis by Van Overwalle & Baetens, 2009). The mirroring network is made up of the premotor cortex, superior temporal sulcus, and inferior parietal lobule (Iacoboni, 2009). The mirroring network shows an increase in activation when a person is detecting the goal-directed, voluntary movement of body parts. There may be potential for studying the mirror network using online virtual worlds. In cyberpsychology, there is a great deal of research on social presence and mirrored selves (Behm-Morawitz, 2013; Yee et al., 2007). Ideas of virtual selves in virtual worlds (e.g., Second Life) reveal potential for investigating the social dynamics found in cyberspace and real space. Sanchez (2009) referred to virtual worlds as "mirrored worlds," in which virtual life mirrors real life.

For social cognitive neuroscience there has been an increasing emphasis upon answering central questions about the nature of human neurocognition by adding neuroscience techniques to methods used by social scientists (Adolphs, 2009; Ochsner & Lieberman, 2001). Recently, social neuroscientists have started incorporating the sorts of platforms and approaches that were historically used by cyberpsychologists into their experiments. Furthermore, they are increasingly using virtual-reality stimuli in social neuroscience research (Adolphs, 2003; Schilbach et al., 2013; Wilms et al., 2010).

8.5   Clinical Neuroscience-Specific Definitions of Ecological Validity

The clinical neurosciences have seen a great deal of discussion about ecological validity issues for clinical neuropsychological assessment. This discussion followed the evolving roles of neuropsychologists from aiding in the diagnoses of brain lesions and/or uncovering the behavioral consequences of those lesions (Lezak, 1983) to questions of whether the patient could return to everyday activities. Much of this change was due to the advanced technologies adopted by clinical neurosciences. Specifically, neuroimaging applications resulted in a decreased need for neuropsychological assessments to localize lesions. Instead, neuropsychologists were increasingly asked to describe behavioral manifestations of neurologic disorders (Chelune & Moehle, 1986; Long, 1996; Sbordone & Long, 1996). A result of this new role for neuropsychologists was an increased emphasis upon the ecological validity of neuropsychological instruments (Franzen & Wilhelm, 1996; Rourke, 1982).

Given this new role, there was a growing need for neuropsychological measures that could provide sufficient information concerning their effects on a functional level (Costa, 1983; Mapou, 1988). An unfortunate limitation of this period is that efforts to operationalize assessment models tended to focus on laboratory or clinical performance tests (Welsh & Pennington, 1988; Welsh, Pennington, & Grossier, 1991), with their inherent construct and measurement problems (Pennington et al., 1996; Rabbit, 1997). In 1993, Barbara Wilson (1993) suggested the need for neuropsychologists to develop a comprehensive range of tests that could be used for evaluating both a patient's neuropsychological condition and their potential for returning to everyday life. An issue for cognitive assessment of everyday functioning was the specificity of many of the skills needed for activities of daily living. Given the great variability among the skills needed for various daily activities, there may not be enough similarity available to allow for an adequate study of the skills (Marcotte & Grant, 2009; Tupper & Cicerone, 1990, 1991). Williams (1988) emphasized the need to define clusters of skills needed for a given task relative to whether the skill is used in many tasks across environments (i.e., generic) or used in new tasks in a limited number of environments (i.e., specific). This would allow for the use of traditional testing procedures for assessing skills that are used in many tasks across environments. However, functionally based test measures would need to be developed for skills used in new tasks in a limited number of environments. The work of Williams and others prompted a need for a more refined definition of ecological validity for the theory and praxes of clinical neuropsychology.

8.5.1   *Defining Ecological Validity*

The terms "ecological validity" and "everyday functions" can be found increasingly in the neuropsychology literature during the 1990s (Tupper &

Cicerone, 1990, 1991). Neuropsychologists were increasingly aware of the significance of their findings for real-world activities (Sbordone & Long, 1996). A limitation was inherent in the lack of definitional specificity for the term "ecological validity" (Franzen & Wilhelm, 1996). Early attempts to define ecological validity in the clinical neurosciences underscored the functional and predictive relation between performance on neuropsychological tests and everyday functioning (Sbordone, 1996). Franzen and Wilhelm (1996) refined the definition of ecological validity for neuropsychological assessment via an emphasis upon verisimilitude (theoretical relation between the cognitive test and everyday activities) and veridicality (empirical relation between a test and everyday functioning).

8.5.1.1   Verisimilitude

According to Franzen and Wilhelm (1996), a neuropsychological test with verisimilitude is one with task demands and testing conditions that resemble the demands found in a person's everyday activities. Verisimilitude is similar to face validity in that it describes the "topographical similarity" (i.e., theoretical relation) between the neuropsychological test and the skills required for successful praxes in the natural environment. While the task demands of learning and recalling word lists has "theoretical" similarity to the sorts of tasks that people perform in their everyday lives, the actual activities found in neuropsychological testing may be more representative of laboratory experiments than everyday activities. Moreover, most neuropsychological assessments present stimuli (e.g., words, numbers, and colors) at a controlled rate in a setting that is typically free from distractions. Also, patients often have repeated opportunities to learn the target stimuli (e.g., learning word lists on the CVLT). While this results in reliability and internal validity, this level of administrative control may underestimate the impact of a patient's cognitive difficulties in everyday life and may overestimate functional difficulties (e.g., patient may use compensatory strategies in their everyday world). Verisimilitude means that the measure resembles a task the patient performs in everyday life and the test is developed while maintaining the relationship between task demands and the prediction of real-world behavior (Spooner & Pachana, 2006). Early discussions of verisimilitude in neuropsychology emphasized that the technologies current to the time could not replicate the environment in which the behavior of interest would ultimately take place (Goldstein, 1996).

Most neuropsychological assessments in use today are yet to be validated with respect to real-world functioning (Rabin, Burton, & Barr, 2007).

There are a few examples of neuropsychological assessments that emphasize verisimilitude in approximating cognitive constructs:

(1) **Attention**, the Test of Everyday Attention (Robertson, Ward, Ridgeway, & Nimmo-Smith, 1994)
(2) **Executive function**, the Behavioral Assessment of the Dysexecutive Syndrome (Wilson, Alderman, Burgess, Emslie, & Evans, 1996)
(3) **Memory**: the Rivermead Behavioral Memory Test (Wilson, Cockburn, & Baddeley, 1985)
(4) **Prospective Memory**, Cambridge Test of Prospective Memory (CAMPROMPT; Wilson et al., 2004)

While these tests were developed with ecological validity in mind, they are somewhat conflicted in that they are still cognitive construct-driven tests used for identifying "functional" abilities (Chaytor & Schmitter-Edgecombe, 2003).

8.5.1.2 Veridicality
Franzen and Wilhelm also emphasized veridicality, which is the need to develop and administer tests in such a way that the person's performance predicts some aspect of everyday functioning. Unfortunately, little is known about how well neuropsychological tests predict everyday behaviors. Moreover, difficulties are inherent in logging a person's everyday functioning in a psychometrically reliable and valid manner. That said, there have been studies that are more correlational in nature (Dunn et al., 1990). These studies have found weak to moderate relations between neuropsychological test data and self-report information. According to Guilmette and Kastner (1996), underperformance on neuropsychological assessments is a modest predictor of vocational functioning in clinical groups. Moreover, performance deficits may in fact be better at predicting failure than success. Examples of the moderate relations between performance on neuropsychological assessments and everyday functioning include:

(1) **Academic achievement in children** (Naglieri & Das, 1987)
(2) **Self-reported criminal behavior** (Pontius & Yudowitz, 1980)
(3) **Vocational status** (Bayless, Varney, & Roberts, 1989; Henninger, 2006; Kalechstein, Newton, & van Gorp, 2003)
(4) **Vocational capacity** (Guilmette & Kastner, 1996; Kibby, Schmitter-Edgecombe, & Long, 1998; Lysaker, Bell, & Beam-Goulet, 1995)
(5) **Vocational integration** (McGurk & Mueser, 2006)
(6) **Return to work** (Van Gorp et al., 2007)

While these correlational approaches offer some insight into everyday functioning, direct parallels between the demands found on neuropsychological tests and functional performance are often not evident (Makatura, Lam, Leahy, Castillo, & Kalpakjian, 1999; Wilson, 1993; Wilson, Cockburn, Baddeley, & Hiorns, 1989).

8.5.2   Coming Out of the Office

Paul Burgess at University College London's Institute of Cognitive Neuroscience has led an effort to better understand ecological validity issues in neuropsychological assessment. He has argued that performance on neuropsychological tests in constrained laboratory settings may be so unrelated to real-world situations that there is little correlation between the performance on the test and activities for daily living (Burgess, 1997; Burgess et al., 1998; Shallice & Burgess, 1991). Furthermore, many neuropsychological tests are limited in that they use tests designed for non-clinical populations to test abstract cognitive constructs (e.g., working memory). Furthermore, it is difficult to ascertain the extent to which performance on measures (e.g., WCST, Stroop, and Tower of London) of basic cognitive constructs translates to functional capacities within the varying environments found in the real world (Burgess et al., 1998).

Burgess and colleagues (2006) prefer the terms "representativeness" and "generalizability" over "verisimilitude" and "veridicality" when discussing "ecological validity." By representativeness they mean the extent to which a test corresponds in form and context to a real-world (experienced outside controlled laboratory) situation. The term "generalizability" is used to describe the extent to which reduced performance on a neuropsychological test is predictive of reduced performance on tasks in everyday life. An example of this can be found in the commonly used Wisconsin Card Sort Test (WCST; Heaton et al., 1993), in which participants are presented with stimulus cards and instructed to match these stimulus cards to target cards. Although the WCST was not originally developed as a clinical neuropsychology measure, Brenda Milner (1963) borrowed it from cognitive scientists for a study with patients that had dorsolateral prefrontal lesions. Results revealed that these patients had greater difficulty on the WCST than patients with orbitofrontal or nonfrontal lesions. That said, there has been a good deal of controversy over whether the WCST is in fact assessing frontal lobe functioning. The majority of neuroimaging studies have found activation across frontal and nonfrontal brain regions and clinical studies have revealed that the WCST does not discriminate between frontal and nonfrontal lesions (Nyhus & Barcelo, 2009; Stuss et al., 1983). While the WCST does look as if it provides some information relevant to the constructs of "set-shifting" and "working memory," the data do not necessarily offer information that would allow a neuropsychologist to predict what situations in everyday life require the abilities that the WCST measures (Burgess et al., 1998; Burgess et al., 2006).

8.5.3 Function-led Tests that Are Representative of Real-World Functions

As a result, Burgess and colleagues (2006) have called for the development and validation of neuropsychological tests that are "representative" of real-world "functions" and "generalize" in a way that allows for prediction of functional performance. A "function-led approach" to developing neuropsychological tests involves models that progress from directly observable everyday behaviors backward to examine how a sequence of actions leads to a given behavior in normal functioning. Moreover, there is need for an emphasis on the ways in which that behavior might become disrupted. A number of investigators have argued that performance on traditional neuropsychological construct-driven tests (e.g., Wisconsin Card Sorting Test, Stroop) has little correspondence to activities of daily living (Bottari et al., 2009; Manchester, Priestly, & Howard, 2004; Sbordone, 2008). Most traditional construct-driven measures assess at the veridicality level and do not capture the complexity of response required in the many multistep tasks found in everyday activities (Chan et al., 2008).

8.5.4 Real-World Assessments Using the Multiple Errands Tasks

The development of function-led tests that assess cognitive functioning in real-world settings is increasing. Shallice and Burgess (1991) developed the Multiple Errands Test (MET) as a function-led assessment of multitasking in a hospital or community setting. During the MET, patients perform rather simple but open-ended tasks (e.g., traveling to a specific location; buying particular items) without breaking a series of rules. The patient is observed and the neuropsychologist logs the number and type of errors (e.g., rule breaks, omissions). The MET has been shown to have increased sensitivity (over construct-driven neuropsychological tests) to elicit and detect failures in attentional focus and task implementation. It has also been shown to be better at predicting behavioral difficulties in everyday life (Alderman, Burgess, Knight, & Henman, 2003). It is important to note that there are a number of limitations for the MET that are apparent in the obvious drawbacks to experiments conducted in real-life settings. The MET (and other naturalistic observations in the real world) can be time-consuming, require transportation, involve consent from local businesses, be costly, and be difficult to replicate or standardize across settings (Logie, Trawley, & Law, 2011; Rand, Rukan, Weiss, & Katz, 2009). Further, there are times when function-led assessments in real-world settings are not feasible for participants with significant behavioral, psychiatric, or mobility difficulties (Knight, Alderman, & Burgess, 2002).

8.5.5   Virtual-Reality for Enhanced Ecological Validity

Virtual environments (VE) are increasingly considered as potential aids in enhancing the ecological validity of neuropsychological assessments (Campbell et al., 2009; Parsons, 2011; Renison et al., 2012; Schultheis et al., 2007). Virtual-reality (VR) has now emerged as a promising tool in many domains of assessment (Jovanovski et al., 2012a; Parsons, 2015), therapy (Opris et al., 2012; Parsons et al., 2008a; Powers & Emmelkamp, 2008), training (Coyle, Traynor, & Solowij, 2015; Ke & Im, 2013), and rehabilitation (Parsons et al., 2009b; Penn, Rose, & Johnson, 2009; Shin & Kim, 2015). Within this context VR technology represents a simulation of real-world training environments based on computer graphics. These can be useful as they allow instructors, therapists, and service providers to offer a safe, repeatable, and diversifiable environmental platform during treatment, which can benefit the learning of individuals, especially disabled users. Research has also pointed to VR's capacity to reduce patients' experience of aversive stimuli (Maskey et al., 2014) and reduce anxiety levels. The unique match between VR technology assets and the needs of various clinical application areas has been recognized by a number of authors (Cobb, 2007; Gorini & Riva, 2008; Trost & Parsons, 2014), and an encouraging body of research has emerged (Ke & Im, 2013; Parsons & Carlew, 2015; Riva, 2011, 2014).

In terms of ecological validity and presence in clinical psychology, findings have revealed a relation between presence and emotional experience in virtual-reality exposure therapy (Alsina-Jurnet et al., 2010; Bouchard et al., 2008; Price and Anderson, 2007; Price et al., 2011; Riva et al., 2007; Robillard et al., 2003). Typically, cyberpsychologists conclude that in virtual-reality exposure therapy, presence and fear can be understood to be dependent (Robillard et al., 2003; Price and Anderson, 2007). In a study by Price and colleagues (2011), scores on the presence subscale "involvement" predicted treatment outcome in a sample of patients undergoing virtual-reality exposure therapy.

8.6   Conclusions

In summary, this chapter has aimed at describing a number of areas that are important for advancing the ecological validity discussion. In the past 20 years in neuropsychology we have seen a shift in assessment from lesion localization to assessment of everyday functioning. Clinical neuropsychologists are increasingly being asked to make prescriptive statements about everyday functioning. This new role for neuropsychologists has resulted in increased emphasis upon the ecological validity of neuropsychological instruments. As a result, neuropsychologists have been experiencing a need to move beyond the limited generalizability of results found in many earlier developed neuropsychology batteries to measures that more closely approximate real-world function. However, neuropsychologists have been slow to establish tests that will address assessment of everyday functioning. Part of the delay has resulted from a lack of clear consensus on what constitutes an ecologically valid assessment.

In addition to these historical issues and emerging definitions for ecological validity in neuropsychological assessments, there is a growing desire for "ecological validity" to represent real-life situations rather than just involving simple cosmetic changes. Instead, there is a more fundamental issue that the most neuropsychological assessments focus upon various aspects of veridical constructs and neglect the reality that real-life veridical decision-making is merely a tool subordinate to adaptive decision-making.

A recent focus of the discussion by Burgess and colleagues (2006) emphasizes the need for "function-led approaches" to neuropsychological models and assessments. While these approaches have been gaining in popularity, there are a number of unfortunate limitations that are apparent in the obvious drawbacks to experiments conducted in real-life settings. Functional-led neuropsychological assessments can be time-consuming, require transportation, involve consent from local businesses, be costly, and be difficult to replicate or standardize across settings. Further, there are times when function-led assessments in real-world settings are not feasible for participants with significant behavioral, psychiatric, or mobility difficulties.

There is also a growing interest in the interplay of cognitive processing (linked to dorsal and lateral regions of the prefrontal cortex) of relatively abstract, context-free information, and emotionally laden information. Unfortunately, very little has been done to include affective components into the neuropsychological assessment. The work that has been done is largely represented by Damasio's somatic marker hypothesis and the computerized Iowa Gambling task that has been developed for assessment of reward-related decision-making that measures temporal foresight and risky decision-making. While the IGT represents some progress in that it adds an affective component to neuropsychological assessment, there is some controversy related to its efficacy. For example, alternative explanations of Bechara's findings have been presented. A further critique has pointed to failures to replicate the initial studies. Perhaps the most important issue is that IGT was created to assess the construct of decision-making in a laboratory setting, but it remains to be seen whether a relation between performance on the IGT and real-world decision-making exists.

Finally, this chapter discussed the importance of the sense of "presence" or "being there" for persons immersed in virtual environments. Presence can be viewed as a subjective phenomenon (e.g., sensation of being in a VE). While a number of presence studies have researched such issues using questionnaires, critics argue that subjective measures tend to rely on post-test assessments of the user's feelings during the exposure to the VE, which is dependent on memory of the event. Given the limitations of subjective measures, a quite different view seems to be emerging, in which presence is treated as something rooted in physiological and behavioral activity. In the chapters that follow, there will be a review of these issues for cyberpsychology.

CHAPTER 9

Affective Neuroscience for Affective Computing

9.1 Affective Computing

Affective computing is a field of study that aims to design machines that can recognize, interpret, process, and simulate human affects (Schwark, 2015). While psychological discussions of affect can be traced back as far as William James (1884) and his nineteenth-century paper "What is emotion," there are a number of different approaches to studying affect and computers over the years. Sloman and Croucher (1981) and Pfeifer (1988) represent early studies in artificial intelligence. Furthermore, support for what is now called affective computing came from findings that persons interact with computers and machines in a manner that is similar to the ways in which humans interact socially with other humans (Muir, 1988; Reeves & Nass, 1996). These studies offer the foundations upon which Picard (1997) and others have built the current discipline of "affective computing." That said, it is important to give credit to Rosalind Picard for coining the phrase "affective computing" in her (1997) book, *Affective Computing*. Furthermore, Picard is a pioneer of affective computing and director of the Affective Computing Research Group at the Massachusetts Institute of Technology (MIT) Media Lab. Picard (1997) has described affective computing as a discipline that pulls from computer science, engineering, psychology, and education to investigate how affect impacts interactions between humans and technology.

As a discipline, affective computing has been gaining popularity rapidly in the last decade because it has apparent potential in the next generation of human–computer interfaces (Calvo et al., 2014). In Picard's work, she endeavors to remove the affective barrier between humans and machines. A natural critique from the cyberpsychologist might be that it seems unlikely that a computer would actually experience affect and emotions in the same way that humans do. For Picard (2003), this is not a problem because she believes that success in affective computing does not require computers to experience emotions. Instead, Pickard argues, all that is needed for success in affective computing is that computers be able to express affects and emotions, not feel them. Artificial communication of emotions can be accomplished by enabling virtual human avatars (or simpler agents) to have facial expressions, diverse tones of voice, and perform empathic behaviors (Brave, Nass, & Hutchinson, 2005).

While the early focus of affective computing was on the recognition of prototypical affective states using single sensorial modalities, the emphasis evolved into replications of natural human–human interaction that are multimodal. In the late 1990s computer scientists began developing multi-modal platforms and studies for recognition of affective states (e.g., facial expressions and acoustic signals). During this time Pickard's work introduced approaches to detecting emotions that used psychophysiological metrics. Development since the 1990s has revealed an affective computing that combines multiple cues and modalities for affect sensing and recognition.

Today, researchers in affective computing aim to design machines that can recognize (not experience) human emotions and respond accordingly. Affective computing researchers aim to model affective communication found in human interactions and apply these models to interactions between humans and computers. An important finding for linking affective computing to cyberpsychology and recent work in social cognitive neuroscience are findings that reveal a similarity between the ways in which humans interact socially with computers and the ways they interact with other humans (McEneaney, 2013). Given these findings it is likely that affective computing and cyberpsychological studies of human–computer interactions can be enhanced using the same principles that govern human–human interactions found in social and affective neuroscience.

9.1.1   *Potential Roles for Affective States in Artificial Agents*

A limitation in the development of affective computing has been defining what research areas, emphases, and goals are needed for its progress. Some have looked at the functional roles of emotions for natural systems and considered whether affective states could provide similar functional roles in artificial systems. Scheutz (2004) aimed to specify 12 potential roles for affective states in artificial agents (see Table 9.1).

From Scheutz's (2004) list and the work that has been accomplished since that time, it is evident that there are a number of potential applications of affective computing: entertainment computing, training and

Table 9.1 *Twelve potential roles for affective states in artificial agents*

Potential role	Example(s)	Affective computing studies
1. Alarm mechanisms	Rapid reflex-like reactions in critical situations that interrupt other processes	Sloman, Chrisley, & Scheutz (2005) use an "alarm" subsystem that can rapidly interrupt or modulate a wide range of processes
2. Action selection	Select actions based on the current emotional state	Gadanho (2003) = simulated agents Murphy, Lisetti, Tardif, Irish, & Gage, 2002)
3. Adaptation	Short- or long-term behavior changes relative to affective states	Scheutz & Schermerhorn (2004) stopping games embedded in the larger context of an artificial life simulation – agents compete for food in order to survive and have offspring
4. Learning	Affective evaluations for reinforcement learning	Grossberg & Schmajuk (1987) *CogEM* models of learning cognitive, affective, and motor properties can account for several effects in Pavlovian fear conditioning
5. Motivation	Developing motives as part of emotional coping	Aylett, Dias, & Paiva (2006) used an affectively driven planner for synthetic characters – motives in intelligent virtual agents
6. Social regulation	Emotional signals used to achieve social effects	Parkinson (2014) discusses how computer mediation might affect emotional communication and coordination, and the challenges that socially situated emotions present for computer simulation and modeling
7. Goal management	Development of new goals or reprioritization of existing goals	da Rocha Costa & Computação (2014) – drives increase the degree of autonomy of agents, by creating self-referential internal processes, that separate the agents' concerns of achieving useful external goals from the concern of keeping themselves functioning well in the system

8. Strategic processing	Selection of different search strategies based on affective state	Flavián-Blanco, Gurrea-Sarasa, & Orús-Sanclemente (2011) analyzed the emotional outcomes of online search behavior with search engines
9. Memory control	Affective bias related to memory access and retrieval as well as decay rate of memory items	Lim, Aylett, Ho, Enz, & Vargas (2009). A socially aware memory for companion agents.
10. Information integration	Affective filtering of data from various information channels (or blocking of such integration)	Lim (2012) Memory models for intelligent social companions Scheutz & Schermerhorn (2004) used stopping games embedded in the larger context of an artificial life simulation, where agents compete for food in order to survive and have offspring
11. Attentional focus	Data selection to be processed based on affective evaluations	Iengo, Origlia, Staffa, & Finzi (2012). Attentional and emotional regulation in human–robot interaction.
12. Self-model	Affect as representations of "what" a situation is like for an agent	Marsella, Gratch, & Petta's (2010) computational models of emotion Maria & Zitar (2007). Emotional agents: A modeling and an application.

tutoring systems, affective natural language processing, and the design of user interfaces.

9.1.2   Areas of Development in Affective Computing

In an attempt to narrow the focus, Carberry and de Rosis (2008) described four areas of development. The first area involves the analysis and characterization of affective states: This includes studies that aim to identify affective states that are exhibited in natural interactions. Further, this would include analyses of the relationships between cognitive and affective processes (e.g., learning). The second is automatic recognition of affective states. Studies have found methods and systems for extracting affective state cues (e.g., analyzing facial expressions, linguistic expression, acoustic signals, and physiological responses). A third issue is adapting system response to affective states. Finally, there is the area of designing affective avatars. The goal is to design virtual humans that exhibit appropriate affective states and appear as lifelike characters for enhanced human–computer interactions. To a large extent, Carberry and de Rosis were aiming to proffer an affective computing paradigm in which successful progress requires lifelike avatars that are able to accurately recognize the affective state of the user. Hence, they placed strong emphasis upon the analysis and modeling of user affect.

In another formulation, Tao and Tan (2005) discussed three slightly broader areas: (1) computer's affective understanding of a user's affective state; (2) computer's affective generation of an affective response that can give the impression that it is actual and has a positive impact on the human user; and (3) research into application areas available for affective computing that could be employed and which aspects of activities could be improved with affective computing. While these categorizations and examples are helpful, Schwark (2015) has argued that the creation of concrete categorization of applications is limited because the potential influence of affective computing is unknown. Furthermore, much of this influence will be mediated by the realization and complexity of future possible affective computing systems. Schwark gives the example of small and large systems. In the situations where systems are small, inflexible, and have very narrow scopes, affective computing will probably be developed for a limited number of domains and purposes. On the other hand, if technological progress results in affective computing systems that are large and adaptive, cyberpsychologists would find affective computing applications for almost every aspect of life. Given that the potential for affective computing is likely large, Schwark argues for an affective computing taxonomy instead of predetermined, artificial, and constrained categories. At each level of Schwark's affective computing taxonomy a categorical decision is made regarding the development of the affective computing system. The reasoning is that the number of possible categories is undefined to make sure that cyberpsychologists and researchers in affective computing can make room for the large number of potential designs and applications of affective computing. Schwark's taxonomy contains five levels at which decisions take place for all affective computing systems that would be implemented in society.

- **System purpose or goal**: At the lowest level, the system's purpose (or goal) needs to be defined. Example purposes include education, service, or entertainment. The determination of purpose is an important start to system design because all subsequent decisions about the system must take into account the system's goal.
- **Integration**: The next level is integration, in which one must determine how integrated into society the affective computing system should be. For example, if the system purpose is education, the developer of the affective computing system must decide whether the system is going to replace or simply assist human educators. These sorts of questions must be answered at the integration level to further determine the characteristics of the system.
- **Affective understanding**: Given information from the first two levels, affective understanding addresses the degree to which the affective computing system needs to understand affect.
- **Affective generation**: Given information from the first two levels, affective generation addresses the degree to which the affective computing system needs to express affect.
- **Platform**: The system platform is devised from the decisions made at the previous four levels. For example, a service system that does not need a great deal of affective generation can get by with a standard computer program that speaks to the user. On the other hand, a program that requires a large amount of affective generation would likely need facial and body movements understood and generated from an avatar.

In summary, Schwark's affective computing taxonomy offers cyberpsychologists and researchers in affective computing a more straightforward approach to identifying commonalities between efforts. This allows for a simple and flexible approach to classifying systems that should help move efforts toward a more unified theory of affective computing.

Regardless of the taxonomy and/or categorization, affective computing has as its goal the design of computer systems that respond in a rational and strategic fashion to real-time changes in user affect (e.g., happiness, sadness, etc.), cognition (e.g., frustration, boredom), and motivation (Serbedzija & Fairclough, 2009), as represented by speech (Dai et al., 2015; Wu, Parsons, & Narayanan, 2010), facial expressions (McDuff et al., 2013), physiological signals (Fairclough, 2009), neurocognitive performance (Parsons et al., 2013; Parsons 2015; Parsons et al., 2015; Parsons et al., 2015; Parsons & Carlew, 2016), and multimodal combination (Wu et al., 2010; Wu, Lance, & Parsons, 2013). Of specific interest to the focus of this book are the neural correlates of user experience. Research studies in social and affective neuroscience have shown that emotions can elicit different physiological changes that can be measured directly using psychophysiological measures (Cacioppo, Tassinary, & Berntson, 2007).

A significant factor involved in social interaction is the capacity for dealing with the affective dimension appropriately. Therefore, researchers in affective computing develop ways to derive human affective states from various intrusive and non-intrusive sensors. A number of approaches have been used to estimate emotional states, including behavioral response, startle response, autonomic assessment, and neurophysiologic measurement. For example, dopamine levels act on voluntary movement and affective arousal that produce increased heart rate and blood pressure. Considerable attention has been given to the use of electroencephalography (EEG) for inferring emotional states, as EEG can reveal emotional states with relatively low costs and simplicity (Kim et al., 2013).

Further, the affective computing literature is beginning to draw from affective and social neurosciences to move from idealized simulations toward real-world data that reflects the sorts of activities that humans perform in their activities of daily living. Interestingly, this emphasis is important for persons like Ray Kurzweil (2005, 2012) who predicts that by 2030 humans will be able to affordably purchase information processing capacity equivalent to one human brain, and by 2060 digital computing will parallel the processing capacity of all the human brains on the Earth. Assuming that Kurzweil is correct, this increase in computing capacity will allow for affective computing systems that can move from simply developing more efficient and effective automated sensing, recognition, and expressive techniques to a more social, cognitive, and affective understanding of human–computer interaction. In this transitional process, affective computing research will need to find ways to comport technology and humans in a manner that moves from natural human–computer interaction to improved human–computer interfaces that reflect the sorts of progress found in studies of human–human interaction. Research from the affective and social neurosciences can inform affective computing on the ways in which real-life conditions, practices, and relationships impact humans.

Hence, the development of affective computing will require it to embrace the work developed in affective neuroscience. In the next section, affective processes (i.e., emotions) and affective neuroscience will be described and emphasis will be placed upon the ways in which affective neuroscience and cyberpsychology can be integrated.

9.2   What Are Affective Processes?

An obviously important aspect of affective computing is the participant's affective processing of emotional content. In Rosalind Picard's (1997) *Affective Computing* she specifies two aspects of emotional processing: (1) expressive information that directly originates from a participant; and (2) non-expressive information from the participant's context and environment. According to Picard, the participant's expectations will impact their affective perceptions, which means that the participant's psychophysiological responses are fashioned by their cognitive and affective processing and vice versa. Hence, a participant's affects will influence their cognitive processes. This idea can be found in a number of focus areas: affective neuroscience (Cromwell & Panksepp, 2011); human neuroscience (Pessoa, 2013); affective computing (Calvo & D'Mello, 2010); virtual-reality (Parsons, 2015); and videogames (Nacke, 2013). For each of these focus areas, there is an understanding that sophisticated cognitive–emotional behaviors have their base in the brain's dynamic neural networks. It is important to note that none of these dynamic coalitions of networks of brain areas should be understood as explicitly cognitive or affective. Pessoa (2008) describes the brain areas involved in these cognitive–emotional interactions as highly connected by hubs that are significant for regulating the flow and integration of information among regions.

9.2.1   James-Lange Theory

One of the earliest attempts at classifying emotions was the James-Lange theory, in which a person's emotion follows the experience of a physiological change (James, 1884; Lange, 1885/1912). In William James's (1884) seminal paper "What is an emotion?" he presented the perspective that physiological and behavioral responses come before the person's subjective experience of emotions, which are marked by "distinct bodily expression." In that same era (1885/1912), the Danish physiologist Carl Lange independently proposed a similar (though more limited) model of emotion. While both theories share the proposition that physiological responses are causal in the emotional experience (i.e., feelings), Lange focused on physiology (specifically vasomotor function) over consciousness for the shaping of emotions. That said, James (1894) acknowledged the close similarities of the two models and the two are often collectively labeled the "James-Lange theory of emotion."

9.2.2   Cannon-Bard Theory

An early challenge to the James-Lange theory came from the Cannon-Bard theory of emotion, in which the feeling occurs first that triggers behaviors based on how the emotion is processed. The person's emotional perception of the stimuli influences the physiological reaction. While Cannon had been an undergraduate student of James at Harvard, Cannon's later career was marked by studies of animal physiology to investigate aspects of James's theory. Philip Bard was a doctoral student of Cannon. Cannon severed afferent nerves of the cat's sympathetic branch of the autonomic nervous system and observed that when provoked, the cats still displayed species-typical emotional behaviors (e.g., hissing and piloerection). From these experiments, Cannon concluded that instead of autonomic feedback as a necessary component for emotional feelings, feelings and physiological responses are independent components of emotion. By this he meant that emotional stimuli are processed in the brain, which then independently produces both bodily responses and feelings (Bard, 1929).

9.2.3   1950s Psychophysiology

In the 1950s, psychophysiology was a burgeoning field and the topic of autonomic specificity was embraced. During this time, a good deal of evidence emerged for distinct autonomic nervous system responses to situations involving various emotions (e.g., anger, anxiety, pain) (Funkenstein, 1956; Funkenstein et al., 1954). For example, contra Cannon, anger and fear did not appear to share identical physiological response patterns. During this time emotion-specific physiological responses can be understood in terms of the psychophysiological principle of stimulus-response specificity (Davis, 1957; Lacey, 1959), in which specific stimulus contexts tend to produce discrete, identifiable, and reproducible somatic response patterns.

9.2.4   Schachter and Singer's Theory of Affect

While a good deal of promise resulted from this approach, it was pushed somewhat to the side in the wake of the cognitive revolution starting in the 1960s. Moreover, this notion of autonomic nervous system specificity received a staggering blow from Stanley Schachter and Jerome Singer's (1962) theory of affect. This alternative model agreed with James that physiological responses play a causal role in producing feelings, but followed the evidence that there are not distinct autonomic nervous system patterns for emotions. For Schachter and Singer, the absence of such differences means that people rely on environmental cues in determining subjective emotional states. For Schachter and Singer, when an emotion is experienced, physiological arousal occurs and the participant uses her or his environment to find emotional cues that will allow them to label the physiological arousal. Four conditions are found in the study: (1) Informed condition, in which participants were informed (accurately) of the expected effects of the injection (Cannon's "fight-or-flight" with increased heart rate, sweating, agitation; (2) uninformed condition, in which participants were not informed of these expected reactions; (3) misinformed condition, in which participants were informed that they would probably feel their feet go numb, and have an itching sensation over parts of their body, and a slight headache; and (4) control condition, wherein participants were injected with a placebo and were given no side effects to expect. All participants were afterwards placed in a room with a collaborator who posed as another participant (acting either angry or euphoric). Here, Schachter and Singer wanted to place participants in a situation where attributions for "unexplained physiological arousal" in the "uninformed" group could be derived. Results revealed that uninformed participants reported feelings similar to those of the confederate with whom they were paired. Results also revealed that informed participants (that anticipated the effects of epinephrine) did not show this tendency. Schachter and Singer concluded that uninformed participants misattributed their unexplained feelings of physiological arousal to environmental cues (i.e., their assigned experimental condition). Apparently, a common physiological state induced by epinephrine led to distinct feelings as a function of environment. This conflicted with the notion of distinct autonomic nervous system patterns. Yet, the physiological changes did result in feelings in the uninformed group. This is in contrast to the informed participants, who ascribed these alterations to the injection.

In summary, the cognitive psychology view of Schachter–Singer held that participants experience physiological arousal that is categorized consistently with their cognitive circumstances. Moreover, that label produces the subjective emotional state. Unfortunately, multiple conceptual and methodological flaws in this study were found by psychophysiologists. Specifically, they were concerned by the naive physiological assumptions upon which it was based. For example, Plutchick and Ax (1967) systematically dismantled the study by cataloguing its errors:

(1) Different physiological arousal levels were evoked by the various conditions.

(2) The placebo groups were not consistently different from the informed or uninformed groups on various affective indices.

(3) Self-report measures were deficient.

(4) The study was not conducted as a double-blind study.

(5) Overgeneralization was apparent in that they based a global model of affective processing on a limited number of conditions, emotions, and types of subjects.

There were also problems related to the validity of using an epinephrine injection to induce emotion (Fehr & Stern, 1970). Furthermore, there have been several replication studies that have failed to replicate Schachter and Singer's findings.

9.2.5 Jaak Panksepp's Affective Neuroscience

Recently, a number of neuroscientists have begun to move beyond the cognitive approach of Schachter–Singer and increasingly include research into emotions (Kohler, Walker, Martin, Healey, & Moberg, 2010; Stuss & Levine, 2002). This new approach argues that current approaches may overestimate cognitive processes and underestimate important dynamic situational and affective components (Parsons, 2015). Although cognitive-based understandings of brain–behavior relationships have grown in recent decades, the neuropsychological understandings of emotion remain poorly defined (Suchy, 2011). One reason for this deficit may be that the term "cognition" has been increasingly overused and misused since the cognitive revolution. An unfortunate limitation is the deficient development of a usable shared definition for the term "cognition." This deficiency raises concerns about a possible misdirection of research within behavioral neuroscience (Cromwell & Panksepp, 2011).

Jaak Panksepp (1998, 2009, 2010) has argued many times over the years that the emphasis upon top-down perspectives tends to dominate the discussion in cognitive-guided research without concurrent non-cognitive modes of bottom-up developmental thinking. He believes that this could hinder progress in understanding neurological and psychiatric disorders. The alternative found in affective neuroscience is an emphasis upon bottom-up affective and motivational "state-control" perspectives. The affective neuroscience approach represents a more "embodied" organic view that accepts that cognitions are integrally linked to our neurology as well as the environments in which we operate (Panksepp, 2009, 2010; Smith & Gasser, 2005; see Table 9.2).

Why has psychology (and for that matter neuropsychology) emphasized cognitive processing, with affect and motivation being rather neglected. Part of this neglect has to do with the fact that cognition can be studied relatively easily in the laboratory, whereas affect and motivation require assessment of real-world activities (Baddeley, 1981). That said, there is increasing interest in going beyond the artificial situation of the laboratory to assessments that reflect the everyday world and bringing together studies of cognition, emotion, and conation (Masmoudi, Dai, & Naceur, 2012).

Cromwell and Panksepp (2011) describe the historically cognitive emphasis as a top-down (cortical → subcortical) perspective that could hinder progress in understanding neurological and psychiatric disorders. As an alternative, they emphasize inclusion of bottom-up (subcortical → cortical) affective and motivational state-control perspectives. According to Panksepp (2005, 2007), progress in human neuroscience has resulted in an understanding that brain areas are involved in both non-salient and affectively influenced cognitions. Panksepp has found support for this view in Goel and Dolan's (2003) examination of the neural basis of emotionally neutral and affectively salient reasoning using event-related fMRI. Findings revealed that a reciprocal engagement of dorsolateral prefrontal cortex (dlPFC) for traditional approaches to cognitive processing and a vmPFC circuit for affective processing provides evidence for a dynamic neural system for information processing, the pattern of which is robustly influenced by affective saliency.

Recent developments of this approach emphasize distinction between executive inhibition and reactive inhibition (Nigg, 2003). Executive inhibition involves top-down (cortical → subcortical) effortful neurocognitive

Table 9.2 *Neuroanatomical and neurochemical factors involved in the development of basic emotions in the mammalian brain*

Basic emotional systems	Motivation	Brain areas	Neuromodulators	Inhibitory	Excitatory
Seeking	Expectancy	Nucleus accumbens – VTA, Mesolimbic and mesocortical outputs, Lateral hypothalamus – PAG	Dopamine, glutamate, opioids, neurotensin, many other neuropeptides		(+)
Rage	Anger	Medial amygdala to BNST, medial and perifornical hypothalamic PAG	Substance P, Ach, glutamate		(+)
Fear	Anxiety	Central and lateral amygdala to medial hypothalamus and dorsal PAG	Glutamate, CRH, CCK, DBI, alpha-MSH, NPY		(+)
Lust	Sexuality	Cortico-medial amygdala, BNST, preoptic hypothalamus, VMH, PAG	Steroids, vasopressin, oxytocin, LH-RH, CCK		(+)
Care	Nurturance	Anterior cingulate, BNST, preoptic area, VTA, PAG	Oxytocin, prolactin, dopamine, opioids	(–)	(+)
Panic	Separation/ Distress	Anterior cingulate, BNST and preoptic area, Dorsomedial thalamus, PAG	Opioids, oxytocin, prolactin, CRF, Glutamate	(–)	(+)
Play	Joy	Dorso-medial diencephalon, parafascicular area, PAG	Opioids, glutamate, Ach, TRH?	(–)	(+)

Note: ACh = Acetylcholine; BNST = bed nucleus of the stria terminalis; CCK = cholecystokinin; CRH = corticotropin releasing hormone; DBI = diazepam-binding inhibitor; LH-RH = lutenizing hormone-releasing hormone; alpha-MSH = alpha melanocyte stimulating hormone; NPY = neuropeptide Y; PAG = periaqueductal grey; VMH = ventromedial hypothalamus; VTA = ventral tegmental area; Minus signs indicate inhibition of an emotional process, plus signs indicate activation. Table was adapted from Panksepp (1998a; 2006) and Watt (1999).

processing aimed at inhibitory control (Nigg, 2000, 2003); and reactive disinhibition reflects bottom-up (subcortical → cortical) processes, in which the individual attempts to regulate behavior in affect-laden situations (Nigg, 2003, 2006). This affective neuroscience approach represents a more embodied view that accepts that cognitions are essentially related to both the participant's neurology and the environments in which study participants operate (Panksepp, 2009, 2010).

9.3 Large-Scale Brain Networks in Affective Neuroscience

Prior to the advent of affective neuroscience, affective responses like anger, fear, sadness, happiness, and disgust were viewed as emotional faculties that arise from distinct, innate, and culturally universal neural modules in the brain (Lindquist & Barrett, 2012; Pessoa, 2008). Typical neuroimaging studies of emotion assessed the emotional experience of participants as they viewed images or movies (e.g., facial expressions; nonlinguistic vocalizations; or body postures). Unfortunately, large-scale meta-analyses have revealed that emotional processing of stimuli from these tasks cannot be localized to activity in specific topographical regions of the human brain (Lindquist et al., 2012; Vytal & Hamann, 2010). In fact, brain regions (e.g., amygdala, insula, anterior cingulate cortex, and orbitofrontal cortex) once thought to be specific brain locations for various emotions reveal notably steady increases in activation in the course of various emotional states. This suggests that these brain regions are not as specifically tied to emotions as was once believed.

Today, there are increasing efforts to move beyond topographical localization to conceptualizations that emphasize a brain network approach to emotions (Barrett & Satpute, 2013). In particular, there is interest in conceptualizing emotional processing in terms of a large-scale brain network for salience processing. The salience network is a large-scale intrinsic network that has strong temporally organized coupling of activity across distributed brain regions. The major nodes with the salience network are the anterior cingulate and the bilateral anterior insula. The functional representations of the salience network can be conceptualized in terms of dorsal and ventral subnetworks. The dorsal subnetwork uses representations of homeostatic and metabolic information from the user's body to guide attention and behavior. The ventral subnetwork represents homeostatic and metabolic information in terms of affective feelings that are basic features of conscious states. Recent research in Lisa Barrett's Interdisciplinary Affective Science Laboratory at Northeastern University utilized a "seed and discovery" process to explore intrinsic brain networks in task-independent (i.e., resting-state) functional magnetic resonance imaging data. They analyzed data from 389 participants and found that there were not anatomically constrained networks for each emotion. Instead, various emotions (anger, sadness, fear, and disgust) result in a discovery map whose spatial overlap revealed a ventral attention network (i.e., "salience" network; see Wilson-Mendenhall, Barrett, & Barsalou, 2013). It is important to note that the nodes within the salience network are not specific for discrete emotions and they are not specific to the broader domain of emotion. Instead, nodes within the salience network appear to play some role in the brain's switching (i.e., reorienting) between internal and external events (Menon & Uddin, 2010).

9.4   Dual-Process Approaches: Hot Affective and Cold Cognitive Processing

Within affective neuroscience, the dual-process approach of "Hot" and "Cold" processing is prevalent among human neuroscientists (Bechara & Damasio, 2005; Brock et al., 2009; Chan et al., 2008; Goel & Dolan, 2003; Greene, Nystrom, Engell, Darley, & Cohen, 2004; Greene, Sommerville, Nystrom, Darley, & Cohen, 2001; Kerr & Zelazo, 2004; Potenza & De Wit, 2010; Rubia, 2011; Seguin et al., 2007). With this prevalence in mind, this review focuses on studies that have explicitly measured and/or manipulated a factor commonly linked to "Cold" cognitive and/or "Hot" affective processing.

• **Cold executive functions** are the ones that are assessed by classic neuropsychological tests (e.g., attentional processing, working memory, planning, and inhibition) that are known to be mediated by lateral inferior and dorsolateral, frontostriatal, and frontoparietal networks (Castellanos et al., 2006; Rubia et al., 2006, 2007).

• **Hot executive-control** occurs in situations that involve robust affective significance. These hot executive-control tasks activate areas of the brain that are involved in emotional regulation and the brain's reward systems: orbito-frontal cortex, ventral striatum, and the limbic system (Kerr & Zelazo, 2004; Northoff et al, 2006). Hot affective processing occurs with reward and punishment, self-regulation, and decision-making involving personal interpretation (Brock et al., 2009; Chan et al., 2008; Seguin et al., 2007).

A number of studies have found that impairments in either the Cold or Hot cognitive functions may be related to deficits in everyday decision-making and functioning (e.g., independence at home, ability to work, school attendance, and social relations; see Chan et al., 2008, for review).

9.4.1   Somatic Marker Hypothesis and the Iowa Gambling Task

One example of a neuropsychological measure that takes affect into account is the Iowa Gambling Task (IGT; Bechara, Damasio, Damasio, & Anderson, 1994; Bechara, 2007). The IGT was developed to assess the somatic marker hypothesis, in which the experience of an emotion (e.g., gut feeling, hunch) results in a somatic marker that guides choice of action. The somatic marker is hypothesized to play a role in affective decision-making in that it biases the available response selections found in decision-making tasks. When persons are faced with decisions, they experience somatic sensations in advance of real consequences of possible different alternatives. The somatic marker hypothesis emerged in relation to a subgroup of patients with VMPFC (i.e., orbitofrontal) lesions who appeared to have intact cognitive processing but had lost the capacity to make appropriate life decisions. According to Damasio (1994), they had lost the ability to weigh the positive and negative features of decision-based outcomes.

The IGT is a computerized assessment of reward-related decision-making that measures temporal foresight and risky decision-making (Bechara et al., 1994; Bechara, 2007). During IGT assessment, the patient is instructed to choose cards from four decks (A–D). Selection of each card results in on-screen feedback regarding either a "gain" or "loss" of currency. In the four decks there are two advantageous (C and D) decks that result in money gained ($250 every 10 cards) and low monetary loss during the trial. The other two decks (A and B) are disadvantageous and involve greater wins (around $100 each card) than C and D (around $50) but also incur greater losses, meaning that one loses $250 every 10 cards in Decks A and B. The primary dependent variables derived from the IGT are total score and net score ([C + D] − [A + B]) and block score ([C + D] − [A + B]) for each segment or block of 20 cards, frequency of deck choices, and spared or impaired performance according to a cut-off point of −10 (Bechara, 2007) especially in brain-damaged subjects.

Results from neuroimaging studies of participants performing the IGT have revealed orbitofrontal cortex activation (Ernst et al., 2002; Grant et al. 1999; Windmann et al., 2006). These results are notable because the orbital frontal cortex has been implicated in signaling the anticipated rewards/ punishments of an action and for adaptive learning (Schoenbaum et al., 2011). In studies using healthy controls, evidence for the somatic marker hypothesis's role in affective decision-making over IGT trials can be found in the demonstration of an anticipatory electrodermal response to card selection (Bechara et al., 1996, 1997). For instance, before selecting a card from a risky deck, a normal participant will show a physiological reaction indicating that s/he is experiencing bodily the anticipated risk.

In clinical studies with patients having damage to vmPFC (part of the orbitofrontal cortex) and the amygdala, results have revealed deficits in the use of somatic (affective) signals for advantageous decision-making (Bechara et al., 1996, 1998; Bechara, Tranel, Damasio, 2000). It is important to note that there are different roles played by the ventromedial prefrontal cortex (vmPFC) and amygdala in decision-making. This is apparent in findings from studies with these patients. Ventromedial PFC patients were able to generate electrodermal responses when they received a reward or a punishment. However, amygdala patients failed to do so (Bechara et al., 1999). Support for these findings can be found in other studies that have found positive correlations between the development of anticipatory skin conductance responses and better performance on a similar gambling task (Carter & Pasqualini, 2004; Crone et al., 2004).

While the IGT represents some progress in that it adds an affective component to neuropsychological assessment, there is some controversy related to its efficacy. For example, alternative explanations of Bechara's findings have been presented. Tomb et al. (2004) contended that the anticipatory responses are related to the belief that the risky choice will probably produce a large reward – higher immediate short-term benefits of the risky decks ($100 versus $50). It is argued that the anticipatory SCR effect is unrelated to any long-term somatic marker mechanism. That said, Tomb et al.'s (2004) account does not readily explain deficient performance in ventromedial PFC patients. While these patients fail to develop an anticipatory response to the decks with immediate short-term benefits, they also prefer these decks throughout the task (Clark & Manes, 2004).

A further critique has pointed to failures to replicate the initial studies (Hinson, Jameson, & Whitney, 2002, 2003). While results from Bechara et al.'s (1998) early studies suggested normal performance of patients with dorsolateral prefrontal lesions, a number of later studies indicate significant effects of lesions that include either dorsolateral or dorsomedial prefrontal cortex regions (Manes et al., 2002). Further, researchers have argued that the IGT is deficient for understanding the affective impact of emotional stimuli upon cognitive processing because the observed effects on the IGT may simply be cognitive (not affective) demands that resulted from such a complex decision task (Hinson, Jameson, & Whitney, 2002, 2003).

Moreover, Baddeley (2011) has argued that the IGT is more of a learning task, whereas a true assessment of affective impact upon cognitive processing requires a measure of the capacity to evaluate existing valences (i.e., positive, negative, and neutral). In a similar manner, Fellows and Farah (2005) have argued that an elemental deficit in reversal learning (instead of a deficit in decision-making) may better explain the VMPFC lesion patients' selections of disadvantageous and risky cards on the IGT. Evidence for this perspective is suggested by the better performance when the initial bias favoring the disadvantageous decks is removed by reordering the cards. Therefore, while inattentiveness to risk is often used to explain poor performance on the IGT, the learning and explicit reversal components of the IGT may better explicate into what the IGT is actually tapping into. Moreover, like other cognitive measures, the IGT was created to assess the construct of decision-making in a laboratory setting, but it remains to be seen whether a relation between performance on the IGT and real-world decision-making exists (Buelow & Suhr, 2009).

9.4.2   Dual-Process Approach to Moral Decision-Making

Differentiating aspects of Cold cognitive processing and Hot affective processing are increasingly being found in moral decision-making (Greene, Nystrom, Engell, Darley, & Cohen, 2004). Similar to neuroimaging studies into the somatic marker hypothesis using the IGT, the orbitofrontal cortex has been implicated in moral decision-making. Lesions to the orbitofrontal cortex result in abnormal social behavior and deficits in moral decision-making (Berthoz et al., 2002; Takahashi et al., 2009). The affective neuroscience of ethical dilemmas is reflected in vignettes that challenge a participant to deliberate over intentionally harming an innocent character in order to promote the greater good of other characters in the vignette. This greater good reflects a utilitarian (i.e., consequentialist) decision to act in a way that will bring about the best overall consequences for a group of persons at the cost of a single individual's well-being.

Examples of moral decision-making assessment include the Trolley and Footbridge Dilemmas, in which the participant reads a text in which a runaway trolley is heading for five immobile people on its tracks (Greene et al., 2004; Thomson, 1985). If the trolley is allowed to continue unmoved from its course, it will kill the five people. In the text of the Footbridge Dilemma, the participant is standing next to a very large stranger on a footbridge spanning the tracks through which the trolley will travel (Greene et al., 2004; Thomson, 1985). The participant's only option for saving the five defenseless persons is to heave the large stranger off the footbridge. While this will kill the large person, it also has the value of blocking the trolley from killing the five helpless persons. Participants reading these vignettes often find it difficult to decide that one answer (kill the large person to save the five others) is preferable to the other (saving the large person, but let the five die).

A dual-process theory has been proposed to describe the processes involved in resolving these moral dilemmas. According to the dual-process perspective both controlled cognitive responses and automatic affective responses perform essential roles in moral decision-making (see also Greene et al., 2008): (1) Automatic and Hot affective processes drive non-utilitarian processes and reflect prohibition of harm, in which negative affective responses are generated in the medial prefrontal cortex and the amygdala (Greene et al., 2004); and (2) Controlled and Cold cognitive evaluations drive utilitarian judgments and weigh the costs and benefits associated with an action. Neuroimaging research has demonstrated that damage to the vmPFC results in moral decisions promoting harmful behavior when it will result in the promotion of a greater good (Ciaramelli et al., 2007; Koenigs et al., 2007). While judgments of correct actions when reading these hypothetical trolley dilemmas tend to involve controlled (e.g., Cold) cognitive processes, the decision to apply direct physical force triggers automatic (e.g., Hot) affective responses.

A limitation of these hypothetical moral dilemmas is that while they have been effective in enhancing our understanding of moral decision-making, they do little to expand our knowledge of how these vignettes translate into real-world behaviors. While the use of text-based scenario descriptions (at times accompanied by a picture illustrating the scenario) and/or graphic-based questionnaires offer the experimental control found in laboratory-based assessment, the static presentation limits the contextual features of the dilemmas (Patil et al., 2014). Consequently, results from both paper-and-pencil and fMRI investigations may overestimate cognitive processes and underestimate important dynamic situational and affective components of the moral dilemmas (Bzdok et al., 2012).

9.5   Virtual Environments for Affective Assessments

Virtual-reality has recently become an increasingly popular medium for assessment of various aspects of affective arousal and emotional dysregulation (Parsons & Rizzo, 2008a). It has been found to be an especially useful modality for intervening with a participant when real-world exposure would be too costly, time consuming, or hazardous. In the following, a number of application areas for affective arousal using virtual environments are discussed: general fear conditioning; affective responses in everyday contexts; affective responses in threatening contexts; and affective processing of moral dilemmas. These areas were chosen because they cover the range of contexts for affective responding from simple fear conditioning to real-world moral dilemmas.

9.5.1   Virtual Environments for Studies of Fear Conditioning

One application of interest for affective neuroscience is the use of virtual environments for studies of fear conditioning (Alvarez et al., 2007; Baas et al., 2008). Virtual environments offer an ecologically valid platform for examinations of context-dependent fear reactions in simulations of real-life activities (Glotzbach, 2012; Mühlberger et al., 2007). Neuroimaging studies utilizing virtual environments have been used to delineate brain circuits involved in sustained anxiety to unpredictable stressors in humans. In a study of contextual fear conditioning, Alvarez et al. (2008) used a Virtual Office and fMRI to investigate whether the same brain mechanisms that underlie contextual fear conditioning in animals are also found in humans. Results suggested that contextual fear conditioning in humans was consistent with preclinical findings in rodents. Specifically, findings support Hot affective processing in that the medial aspect of the amygdala had afferent and efferent connections that included input from the orbitofrontal cortex. In another study using a virtual office, Glotzbach-Schoon et al. (2013) assessed the modulation of contextual fear conditioning and extinction by 5HTTLPR (serotonin-transporter-linked polymorphic region) and NPSR1 (neuropeptide S receptor 1) polymorphisms. Results revealed that both the 5HTTLPR and the NPSR1 polymorphisms were related to Hot affective (implicit) processing via a fear-potentiated startle. There was no effect of the 5HTTLPR polymorphism on Cold cognitive (explicit) ratings of anxiety. Given the ability of virtual environments to place participants in experimentally controlled yet contextually relevant situations, there appears to be promise in applying this platform to future translational studies into contextual fear conditioning.

9.5.2 Virtual Environments to Elicit Affective Responses in Everyday Contexts

The use of virtual environments has also been used to elicit affective responses in everyday contexts. For example, Riva et al. (2007) manipulated virtual parks to elicit affective arousal. All participants experienced anxious, relaxing, and neutral parks. Although all the same structure was found in all three parks, the parks differed in the aural and visual experience that was presented to the participant. Findings suggested that the three affective park presentations (anxious and relaxing) have some efficacy for eliciting specific emotional states. In related studies, virtual environments have successfully elicited heightened affective arousal in a virtual train (Freeman et al., 2008) and a virtual office (Klinger et. al., 2005; Roy et al., 2003). These results suggest that virtual environments can be used as an affect induction medium. In another virtual office scenario, participants were immersed in a virtual office scenario designed to elicit anger (Macedonio et al., 2007). Within a few seconds of starting the virtual environment, a virtual boss approaches and verbally confronts the participant in a hostile and condescending fashion. The study found physiological correlates of anger arousal stimuli from a virtual environment. In a more fully developed study, Mühlberger et al. (2008) matched arousal events in a virtual tunnel driving experiment with startle reflex methodology to investigate whether the phylogenetically relevant aversive context of darkness elicited fear responses. Results revealed increased negative affect during darker areas of the virtual tunnel. The increased logging abilities of these virtual environments allow for matching psychophysiological responses to events as they occur in the simulations.

9.5.3 Virtual Environments to Elicit Affective Responses in Threatening Contexts

Recently, virtual environments have been applied to the assessment of both "Cold" and "Hot" processes using combat-related scenarios (Armstrong et al., 2013; Parsons, Courtney, & Dawson, 2013). The addition of virtual environments allows affective neuroscience researchers to move beyond the ethical concerns related to placing participants into real-world situations with hazardous contexts. The goal of these platforms is to assess the impact of Hot affective arousal upon Cold cognitive processes.

For example, Parsons et al. (2013) have developed a Virtual-Reality Stroop Task (VRST) in which the participant is immersed in a simulated high-mobility multipurpose wheeled vehicle (HMMWV) and passes through zones with alternating low threat (driving down a deserted desert road) and high threat (gunfire, explosions, and shouting amongst other stressors) while dual-task stimuli (e.g., Stroop stimuli) were presented on the windshield. They found that the high-threat zones created a greater level of psychophysiological arousal (heart rate, skin conductance, respiration) than did low threat zones. Findings from these studies also provided data regarding the potential of military-relevant virtual environments for measurement of supervisory attentional processing (Parsons, Courtney, & Dawson, 2013). Analyses of the effect of threat level on the color–word and interference scores resulted in a main effect of threat level and condition. Findings from the virtual environment paradigm support the perspective that (1) high information load tasks used for Cold cognitive processing may be relatively automatic in controlled circumstances – for example, in low threat zones with little activity; and (2) the total available processing capacities may be decreased by other Hot affective factors such as arousal (e.g., threat zones with a great deal of activity). In a replication study, Armstrong et al. (2013) established the preliminary convergent and discriminant validity of the VRST with an active duty military sample.

In addition to virtual environment–based neuropsychological assessments using driving simulators, a number of other military-relevant virtual environments have emerged for neurocognitive assessment of Cold and Hot processes. For example, Parsons et al. (2012, 2014) immersed participants into a Middle Eastern city and exposed participants to a Cold cognitive processing task (e.g., paced auditory serial addition test) as they followed a fire team on foot through safe and ambush (e.g., Hot affective – bombs, gunfire, screams, and other visual and auditory forms of threat) zones in a Middle Eastern city. In one measure of the battery, a route-learning task, each zone is preceded by a zone marker, which serves as a landmark to assist in remembering the route. The route-learning task is followed immediately by the navigation task, in which the participants were asked to return to the starting point of their tour through the city.

Courtney et al. (2013) found that the inclusion of Hot affective stimuli (e.g., high-threat zones) resulted in a greater level of psychophysiological arousal (heart rate, skin conductance, respiration) and decreased performance on Cold cognitive processes than did low-threat zones. Results from active duty military (Parsons et al., 2012) and civilian (Parsons & Courtney, 2014) populations offer preliminary support for the construct validity of the VR-PASAT as a measure of attentional processing. Further, results suggest that the VR-PASAT may provide some unique information related to Hot affective processing not tapped by traditional Cold attentional processing tasks.

9.5.4 Virtual Reality–Based Moral Dilemmas

Virtual environments are also being applied to the affective neuroscience of moral decision-making. Recently, studies have emerged that take the classic Trolley Dilemma and modify the text-based approach via a Virtual Trolley Dilemma (Navarrete et al., 2012; Pan & Slater, 2011; Patil et al., 2014; Skulmowski et al., 2014). Further, while text-based hypothetical moral dilemmas led to gaps in our understanding of how results translate into real-world behaviors, virtual environments allow for observations of morally relevant decision-making behaviors in realistic three-dimensional simulations. With virtual environments, researchers can perform real-time assessment of the cognitive and affective factors inherent in explicit moral behaviors.

Patil et al. (2014) compared traditional text-based approaches to a virtual environment version of the trolley dilemma. They found a modality-specific difference in that participant behavior in the virtual environment reflected a utilitarian approach, but in the text-based descriptions the same moral dilemmas resulted in nonutilitarian decisions. Further, autonomic arousal was greater in virtual environments. These differences suggest that text-based scenario presentation does not include dynamic visual information that is available to persons in real-world environments. With virtual environments there appears to be enhanced capacity for the context-dependent knowledge that is critical for moral decision-making.

Navarrete et al. (2012) used virtual environments to observe behaviors and record autonomic arousal of participants as they confronted moral dilemmas. Specifically, they immersed participants into a virtual-reality version of the trolley problem. Participants were given the choice of whether or not to pull a lever that would determine the fate (e.g., death or safety) of some number of people. The virtual environment included virtual human agents that were capable of movement and sound in real time. Validity of the virtual trolley paradigm was apparent in that results were consistent with the behavioral pattern observed in studies using text versions of the trolley dilemma. Results also revealed that affective arousal was (1) associated with a reduced likelihood that participants were acting to achieve a utilitarian outcome; and (2) greater when participants were attempting to behaviorally resolve a dilemma that required committing an act than when participants were omitting an action. An important aspect of these findings is that they provide support for a relation between Hot affective processing and moral action. These findings also suggest that similar neurophysiological processes may mediate Cold processing of moral judgments and actions. Virtual environment–based moral dilemmas appear to offer an empirical platform for investigating the contents and contexts in which Hot affective and Cold cognitive processing occur.

In a study that builds on Navarrete et al.'s (2012) paradigm, Skulmowski et al. (2014) developed a virtual reality–based trolley dilemma that utilized a first-person perspective of the forced-choice decision-making paradigm. A novel aspect of the Skulmowski design is that the participants were the drivers of the train. This approach was chosen because research on presence and immersion in virtual environments has found that first-person perspectives elicit a greater sense of presence and involvement (Kallinen et al., 2007; Slater et al., 2010). The study also included psychophysiological assessment metrics drawn from pupillometry that were integrated into the virtual environment paradigm. Like Navarrete et al.'s virtual trolley study, Skulmowski's experiment replicated the behavioral pattern found in studies using text-based versions of the trolley dilemma. This further validated the use of the virtual trolley platform for research on moral decision-making. Additional findings included a peak in the level of arousal related to the moment that the moral decision was made. Further, eye-tracking revealed context-dependent gaze durations during decisions to sacrifice. These findings comport well with dual-process theories. Since decision time frames were able to be held constant in the virtual environment paradigm, events could be logged and marked for comparison to pupillometric measurements. This approach offers promise for moving beyond paper-and-pencil (e.g., text-based) approaches in which participants read scenario descriptions at varying speeds.

In summary, mere judgments about moral dilemmas results in a limited understanding. The hypothetical and text-based vignettes attempt to stimulate the imagination of participants and then use questionnaires or experiments involving low-level manipulations of harm to enhance understanding. The addition of virtual environments allows researchers to assess the expression of decision-making processes via real-time logging of behaviors. Given that virtual environments are more dynamic than text-based scenarios and that they do not involve the potential for harmful outcomes, they may bridge the gap between judgment and behavior via explorations of the underlying mechanisms. While the virtual environment approach does not offer a definitive solution to the long-standing trade-off between laboratory control and real-world behaviors, it does allow researchers a methodology for presenting participants with auditory and visual representations of real-world activities.

9.5.5   Brain Activations and Prosocial Behavior in Simulated Threat Situation

In a recent study of the neuronal basis of altruistic behavior, Zanon and colleagues (2014) examined functional connectivity within participant brain networks as they exhibited either a self-benefit behavior or an altruistic behavior during the simulation of a life-threatening situation using virtual-reality. Participants were in a virtual building that needed to be evacuated and had to decide whether to risk their own lives by stopping to help a trapped virtual human. The researchers used group-independent component analysis to analyze blood-oxygen-level-dependent images from functional magnetic resonance imaging. Results revealed increased functional connectivity in the salience network (i.e., anterior insula and the anterior cingulate cortex) in participants exhibiting selfish behaviors compared to those with prosocial behaviors. The findings suggest that increased functional connectivity of the salience network enhances sensitivity to the threatening situation.

9.6   Conclusions

In this chapter, there has been a review of affective computing as a field of study that aims to design machines that can recognize, interpret, process, and simulate human affects. While psychological discussions of affect can be traced back as far as William James, this chapter reviewed a number of different approaches to studying affect and computers. Support for what is now called affective computing came from findings that persons interact with computers and machines in a manner that is similar to the ways in which humans interact socially with other humans. These studies offer the foundations upon which Picard (1997) and others have built the current discipline of "affective computing." As a discipline, affective computing has been gaining popularity rapidly in the last decade because it has apparent potential in the next generation of human–computer interfaces (Calvo et al., 2014).

In Picard's work, success in affective computing results from computers being able to express affects and emotions, not feel them. Artificial communication of emotions can be accomplished by enabling virtual human avatars (or simpler agents) to have facial expressions, diverse tones of voice, and perform empathic behaviors. Today, researchers in affective computing aim to design machines that can recognize (not experience) human emotions and respond accordingly. Affective computing researchers aim to model affective communication found in human interactions and apply these models to interactions between humans and computers. An important finding for linking affective computing to cyberpsychology and recent work in affective neuroscience are results that suggest humans interact with computers and machines in a manner that is similar to the way humans interact with other humans. Given these findings it is likely that affective computing and cyberpsychological studies of human–computer interactions can be enhanced using the same principles that govern human–human interactions found in social and affective neuroscience.

An obviously important aspect of affective computing is the participant's affective processing of emotional content. Recent work in affective neuroscience suggests that sophisticated cognitive–emotional behaviors have their base in the brain's dynamic neural networks. It is important to note that none of these dynamic coalitions of networks of brain areas should be understood as explicitly cognitive or affective. Pessoa (2008) describes the brain areas involved in these cognitive–emotional interactions as highly connected by hubs that are significant for regulating the flow and integration of information among regions. Today, there are increasing efforts to move beyond topographical localization to conceptualizations that emphasize a brain network approach to emotions (Barrett & Satpute, 2013). In particular, there is interest in conceptualizing emotional processing in terms of a large-scale brain network for salience processing. The salience network is a large-scale intrinsic network that has strong temporally organized coupling of activity across distributed brain regions. Future cyberpsychology studies can draw from work in dual-process theories, findings related to the salience network, and advances in affective computing to develop next-generation studies of persons interacting with computers.

CHAPTER 10

Social Neuroscience and the Need
for Dynamic Simulations

10.1 What is Social Neuroscience?

Social neuroscience is a subdiscipline of neuroscience that endeavors to answer central questions about the nature of human social cognition by adding neuroscience techniques to methods used by social scientists (Adolphs, 2009; Cacioppo, 1994; Ochsner & Lieberman, 2001). Social neuroscience is a discipline that endeavors to identify the genetic, cellular, neural, and hormonal mechanisms that underlie social behavior (Cacioppo et al., 2010). Through these investigations, social neuroscientists seek a greater understanding of the reciprocal associations and influences among social and neurobiological levels of organization. Much of this work has resulted from our growing interest in the human brain's ability to facilitate, make use of, and be molded by social interactions (Cozolino, 2014; Gazzaniga, 2008; Lieberman, 2013). While research into the neural correlates of social processes has been discussed in the literature for decades (Cacioppo & Berntson, 1992), the advent of functional neuroimaging has resulted in a period of rapid expansion (Adolphs, 2003; Ochsner & Lieberman, 2001).

10.1.1 Doctrine of Multilevel Analysis

Findings from studies using a social neuroscience framework provide crucial insights into our understandings of a wide range of affective, cognitive, and social outcomes. In 1992 John Cacioppo (University of Chicago) and Gary Berntson (Ohio State University) devised the term "social neuroscience" in their paper on the contribution of social psychology to the "decade of the brain." In their manuscript, they put forth their "Doctrine of Multilevel Analysis" that called for the integration of knowledge about the elements on each structural level of a discipline and on the relational aspects of these elements across the levels. The doctrine of

Table 10.1   *Cacioppo and Berntson's Doctrine of Multilevel Analysis*

Principles	Description	Example
Multiple Determinism	An event may have multiple antecedents on various levels.	*Drug abuse*: While endogenous brain opioid receptor systems (i.e., bases for opiate drugs of abuse) are common across individuals, only some abuse drugs. There are proximate determinants of drug abuse – social factors (economics, peer group influences, and family dynamics).
Nonadditive Determinism	The whole may not be predictable from the sum of its parts.	*Amphetamine and Social Hierarchy*: While administration of amphetamine initially appeared to have no reliable effect on primate behavior, consideration of the primate's position in the social hierarchy revealed increase in dominance behaviors (for primates high in the social hierarchy) and increase in submissive behaviors (in low social hierarchy primates).
Reciprocal Determinism	Mutual influences between microscopic and macroscopic factors in determining brain and behavioral processes.	*Evolutionary analyses of social species*: Evidence from behavior genetics research suggests an extensive variety of genetic influences are repressed unless (or until) specific environmental factors are introduced.
Proximity (corollary)	Mapping between elements across levels becomes more complex as the number of intervening levels increases.	*Schizophrenic behavior*: An event at one level of organization can have a multiplicity of determinants at an adjacent level (e.g., cognitive) that may also have a multiplicity of implementations at the next level (e.g., neurophysiological), and so forth.

multilevel analysis included three main tenets and a corollary (see Table 10.1).

In this early formulation of social neuroscience, Cacioppo and Berntson were calling for an assimilation of research from animal and human studies to construct an interdisciplinary approach to understanding the neurobiological correlates of social behavior. Moreover, they proposed the use of neurobiological theories and practices to cultivate and enhance theories in the social and behavioral sciences.

10.1.2   Social Cognitive Neuroscience

While the project of social neuroscience continues to be understood as a cooperative venture among researchers emerging from social psychology and neuroscience, the advent of functional neuroimaging has resulted in a period of rapid expansion. Kevin Ochsner and Matthew Lieberman (2001) revised Cacioppo and Berntson's multilevel analysis approach to include social, cognitive, and neural emphases. They called their approach "social cognitive neuroscience" and aimed to integrate data from social, cognitive, and neural levels of analyses: (1) *Social level*: Emphasizes the behavior and experience of motivated individuals in contexts that are personally significant; (2) *Cognitive level*: Information processing mechanisms underlying phenomena on the social level; and (3) *Neural level*: Brain systems analyzed that instantiate the processes on the cognitive level.

There is an interaction among four levels of analysis that make up social cognition. Social neuroscientists investigate a host of topics across a range of potential social interactions. It is important to note Ochsner and Lieberman's emphasis on the cognitive level because social psychology and cognitive neuroscience both describe psychological processes in terms of information processing. The emphasis regarding the neurobiological basis is on the neural level.

Like cyberpsychology, social cognitive and affective neuroscience now holds many attributes of a discipline: dedicated journals, academic societies, conference series, and labs/research groups. Furthermore, a myriad of research studies have aimed at identifying neural correlates of social phenomena: attitudinal evaluation (Wood et al., 2005); cooperation (Edmonds et al., 2012); emotional reappraisal (Shafir et al., 2015); empathy (Decety & Yoder, 2015); ethical behavior (Domínguez D., 2015); expectancy effects (Harris & Fiske, 2010); judgment and decision-making (Schilbach et al., 2013); person knowledge (Wagner, Haxby, & Heatherton, 2012); political choices (Schreiber et al., 2013); relational cognition (Waldzus, Schubert, & Paladino, 2012); self-awareness (Otto, Zijlstra, & Goebel, 2014); self-knowledge (Kelly et al., 2002; Pfeifer, Dapretto, & Lieberman, 2010); self-serving biases (Beer, 2014); social exclusion (Eisenberger, 2015); social interactions (Pfeiffer et al., 2013); stereotypes (Amodio, 2014); and theory of mind (Sebastian et al., 2012). All of these areas reflect a key emphasis within social neuroscience upon the ways in which one person's brain develops the perception of another person as having beliefs, cognitions, affects, intentions, traits, and morals.

10.2 Large-Scale Brain Networks for Social Cognitive Processing

As the list of example studies reveals, social neuroscience research taps into several aspects of social cognition found in our daily lives. We are constantly engaging in reciprocal interactions with others and represent ourselves in the context of our social environments. Social neuroscience can offer potential new insights into social interactions, the ways in which interpersonal emotions are processed, and the neural correlates supporting these processes. While much of the early research into social cognition attempted to locate social cognitive processes in specific brain regions like the dorsomedial prefrontal cortex and/or the temporoparietal junction, recent developments in systems neuroscience approaches have emerged as studies are increasingly revealing that the neural correlates of person perception are organized into neural networks. Support for the systems neuroscience approach can be found in findings from meta-analyses that reveal person perception results in increased activation of a "mentalizing" network and a "mirroring" network (Denny et al., 2012; Van Overwalle & Baetens, 2009).

10.2.1 Mentalizing Network

The large-scale brain network for mentalizing (i.e., mentalizing network) is typically involved when persons represent and make sense of others' states of mind. Specific brain hubs include the anterior insula and anterior cingulate cortex that processes a person's bodily arousal during interpersonal experiences. The mentalizing network includes the neural correlates of a person's ability to mentalize (i.e., infer) the cognitions and feelings of others. An independent body of work in the social neurosciences has revealed an overlapping "default-mode network" that activates while persons are in a state of quiet repose (e.g., with eyes closed) and when external demands are low (Raichle, 2015). These findings have resulted in a suggested role of the default-mode network in self-generated cognition that is decoupled from the external world (Andrews-Hanna, 2012, 2014). The similarity between the default and mentalizing networks has generated questions in social neuroscience about whether the core function of the default network is to mediate internal aspects of social cognition (Li, Mai, & Liu, 2014).

Automatic and controlled processing within the social neurosciences have been reformulated to reflect a controlled "reflective" system and an automatic "reflexive" system (Lieberman, 2007). The reflective system for social neuroscience corresponds with a controlled social cognition system. The reflexive system corresponds with an automatic social cognition system. When persons engage in goal-directed behavior of a nonself-referential nature, certain areas of the brain decrease their activity. During quiet resting states a default-mode network activates (Raichle & Snyder, 2007), which consists of areas in dorsal and ventral medial prefrontal and parietal cortices (see Chapter 2 in this book). Results from recent studies have revealed that the default-mode network is involved in perspective taking of the desires, beliefs, and intentions of others (see for example Buckner et al., 2008). These functions are all self-referential in nature. The reduction of activity in the default-mode network during effortful cognitive processing reflects an attenuation of the brain's self-referential activity as a means of more effectively focusing on a task.

10.2.2   Mirroring Network

In addition to the mentalizing brain network, studies suggest that a "mirroring" network is related to a person's representation of facial movements and bodily gestures while making inferences about their meanings (Spunt, Satpute, & Lieberman, 2011). The large-scale brain network for mirroring is made up of hubs in the premotor cortex, superior temporal sulcus, and inferior parietal lobule (Iacoboni, 2009). The mirroring network has been taken as evidence for a first-person or simulationist account of social cognition (Schilbach, 2014). The mirroring network is thought to proffer an implicit knowledge of another's behavior (Rizzolatti & Sinigaglia, 2010). The mirroring network reveals increased activation when a person is detecting goal-directed and voluntary movement of body parts. The greater activation of the mirroring network is typically associated with action identification, in which physical movements are perceived as discrete behaviors. This can be contrasted with the mentalizing network's activation when the person is making inferences (theorizing) about the goals of those actions. The mirroring network can also be contrasted with the mentalizing network in that the latter is more strongly related to representing the contextual information that allows inference of another's mental state inference to occur.

10.3 Need for Enhanced Stimulus Presentations for Social Neuroscience Research

For social cognitive neuroscience there has been an increasing emphasis upon answering central questions about the nature of human neurocognition by adding neuroscience techniques to methods used by social scientists (Adolphs, 2009; Ochsner & Lieberman, 2001). A potential limitation to progress in social neuroscience is that many of the pioneering paradigms in social neuroscience reflect an emphasis upon laboratory control and experiments that fail to reflect social cognitive processing in everyday life. Zaki and Ochsner (2009) have argued that there are three critical ways that real-life social information differs from the sorts of laboratory stimuli found in many social neuroscience experiments. Specifically, they discuss the ways in which cues about target states in the real world are (1) multimodal (include visual, semantic, and prosodic information); (2) dynamic in that stimuli are presented serially or concurrently to participants over time; and (3) contextually embedded so that participants are presented with stimuli and environmental information that can frame their interpretation of another's internal states.

10.3.1 Multimodal Stimuli for an Ecologically Valid Social Neuroscience

Multimodal stimuli are important for an ecologically valid social neuroscience because social mentalizing and interactions occur in situations that involve the convergence of multiple channels such as auditory perception of social cues (verbal utterances, intonation, prosody); visual perception of social cues (nonverbal communication, gestures, postures, facial expressions); and emotional perception (positive and negatively valenced representations of the other's internal states). Zaki and Ochsner (2009) emphasize the importance of emotional modality because early neuroimaging studies of emotion treated cognitive phenomena as qualities (shape, size, or color) of a stimulus. They give the example of showing participants negatively valenced stimuli (e.g., gruesome picture) and then infer that this caused the participant to experience negative affect without actually measuring the participant's subjective experience or other behavioral indices of emotional responding.

10.3.2 Static Stimulus Presentations

Neisser's (1982) call for cognitive assessments that can generalize beyond the narrow laboratory context has recently surfaced in the context of social neuroscience. Many of the pioneering paradigms in social neuroscience reflect an emphasis upon laboratory control and experiments that involve participants observing static stimuli (e.g., simple, static representations of socially relevant stimuli; static photographs of emotionally valenced facial expressions) that are devoid of interactions (Blair et al., 1999; Morris et al., 1996). Although social neuroscience researchers have assumed that knowledge gained using these static stimuli will generalize to the social cognition in everyday activities, a number of researchers are beginning to question this assumption (Chakrabarti, 2013; Ochsner, 2004; Schilbach et al., 2006, 2013). In fact, this assumption can lead to confusion about the neural bases of interpersonal understanding because studies of shared representations between self and others usually ask the perceiver to observe and imitate target movements or have participants directly rate their own sensory states and observe those states in others. This is done without requiring participants to make any judgments about target states. Further, researchers examining the shared representations and mental state attributions of perceivers often make use of static stimuli that fail to represent the types of social information that participants must process when they experience dynamic stimuli in real-life social interactions (Risko et al., 2012; Schilbach, 2015; Zaki & Ochsner, 2009).

There is a need for greater emphasis upon dynamic stimuli that will allow assessment of participants as they act upon stimuli interactively instead of a passive response to static stimuli. While limiting stimuli to static representations with constrained variance along tractable dimensions is important for maintaining experimental control over the social cognitive processes studied in an experiment, such experimental constrictions can result in artificially constrained understandings of the social cognitive processes involved. There is a need to emphasize dynamic stimuli that reflect real-life interactions in which participants react to dynamic stimuli in an interactive way that modifies subsequent dynamic stimuli. Moreover, many social neuroscience approaches present static and controlled stimuli that lead the participant to believe and act "as if" the participant could modify the course of a social interaction. As such, many current social neuroscience approaches do not include real-time dynamic and adaptive virtual agents with complex cognitive architectures (Faur et al., 2013).

10.3.3   Contextualized Succession of Events

In addition to multimodal and dynamic stimuli, ecologically valid social neuroscience paradigms also involve the contextualized succession of events that are intuitively clear when associated within a sequence. While many social neuroscience approaches use various stimulus approaches (comic-strips, video-based mental state inferences) to depict an agent performing actions following a specific schema, they often do not promote a context that will prompt the participant to have an invested interest in this agent. Without adequate social context, the participant may not experience an empathetic relationship with the agent.

Further, given the assumption that social interaction may be experienced as motivating and rewarding, social neuroscience approaches should implement a social context that allows for assessment of motivations to interact socially. Social neuroscience experiments place participants in a scanner and instruct them to fixate on stimuli presented on a monitor. Neuroimaging resulting from such studies appears to be significantly dissimilar to studies in which the participant is performing such tasks together with another agent. The addition of another agent results in a differential increase of neural activity in brain areas that have been related to grasping another's mental states (Schilbach et al., 2008).

10.3.4   *Social Interactions Shape the Brain*

In addition to contextual embedding of dynamic and multimodal stimuli into social neuroscience research scenarios, there are limits to studies that do not involve social interactions. Our brains and behaviors are shaped and typically take part in interaction with other humans. That said, the methodological difficulties related to the sorts of complex dynamics found in interaction situations have resulted in limited understanding of the neural mechanisms underlying interactive behavior. Some have argued that the social processes that enable humans to interact with each other are internalized by participants. Therefore, it has been argued, they can be known via the exploration of individual brains (Konvalinka & Roepstorff, 2012). Following this argument, a number of studies have examined social cognition from a perception perspective by presenting single participants with socially relevant pictures or videos (Lieberman, 2013). While this has resulted in the identification of a set of regions composing the "social brain" (e.g., amygdala, orbital frontal cortex, medial prefrontal cortex), there is still little that is understood about the ways in which these social brain regions function and transfer information between brains in dynamic, real-time interactions (Liu & Pelowski, 2014). This is especially true when one turns to recent conceptualizations that have proposed that social cognition may be fundamentally different when a person engages in an interaction, instead of just observing the situation itself (Schilbach, 2010). As a result, there has recently been a call to move from the third person mentalizing approach to a second person neuroscience that involves social interaction (Schilbach et al., 2013).

The social interactions found in everyday exchanges involve a broad array of contexts, including verbal and nonverbal interactions, interpretation of others, representations of self and other, and joint attention. In order to understand social interactions, social neurosciences should have the methods necessary for assessing self-understanding, self and other interactions, and relations between self and other in everyday environments (Schilbach et al., 2013; Sebanz et al., 2006). An unfortunate limitation for many social neuroscience approaches is that they study a single participant's brain in isolation instead of during real-world interactions (Tanabek et al., 2012). For example, participants are often isolated from their natural environments and placed into a sealed room where the participant is exposed to static images, auditory stimuli, and/or video clips. Social neuroscientists have designed a number of innovative paradigms to investigate the neural bases of various aspects of social interactions: (1) the participant views video clips and/or pre-recorded interactions (Iacoboni et al., 2004; Walter et al., 2004); (2) the participant takes part in an online game (e.g., Cyberball) with an avatar that is playing catch with two other avatars (Eisenberger, 2012; Lieberman & Eisenberger, 2009); and (3) the participant views a noninteractive virtual human that shifts gaze toward or away from the participant (Pelphrey et al., 2003, 2004). While these methodological approaches afford significant information related to the potential neural underpinnings of social interaction, they are missing essential mechanisms of everyday social interactions (Hari & Kujala, 2009). The difficulties in either developing laboratory-controlled experiments or naturalistic interactions between two participants are apparent in fMRI studies (Montague et al., 2002).

In summary, the social interactions found in everyday exchanges involve a broad array of contexts, including verbal and nonverbal interactions, interpretation of others, representations of self and other, and shared attention. An unfortunate limitation of social neuroscience assessments is that it is difficult to generate study findings that can generalize beyond the narrow laboratory context. Many of the pioneering paradigms in social neuroscience involve observing static stimuli (e.g., simple, static representations of socially relevant stimuli; static photographs of emotionally valenced facial expressions) that are devoid of interactions. While there are a number of innovative paradigms to investigate the neural bases of various aspects of social interactions, they are missing essential mechanisms of everyday social interactions.

10.4   Cyberpsychology for Dynamic Presentations of Social Stimuli

In recent years there has been an increased interest in the application of neuropsychological and neuroscientific methodologies to research in contemporary social psychology (Adolphs, 2009; Lieberman, 2007). Although cognitive neuroscience has made gains in the exploration of the brain systems engaged when an individual shares and makes inferences about the internal states of others, they have emphasized isolation paradigms that rely on participant observations of others' behaviors to make inferences about the mental states of others (Becchio et al., 2010). Furthermore, researchers from the cognitive neurosciences typically use divergent and highly simplified stimuli and methods. As a result, research drawn from cognitive neuroscience studies using a strictly laboratory-focused approach has produced largely non-overlapping results and artificially constrained social theories (Zaki & Ochsner, 2009).

While many of the pioneering paradigms in social neuroscience have used static stimuli to study social cognition in everyday activities, a number of researchers are beginning to question this approach (Chakrabarti, 2013; Risko et al., 2012; Schilbach et al., 2006). While video recordings, movies, and imagery techniques have been used by social neuroscientists to elicit emotions (Zaki & Ochsner, 2009), enhanced ecological approaches increase the capacity to manipulate the content of interactive media to induce specific emotional responses. As Neisser (1980) argued, participants observing video-recordings of others and then making judgments of what they saw miss an important interactive component that occurs in a social exchange. Recently, social neuroscientists have started incorporating the sorts of platforms and approaches that were historically used by cyberpsychologists into their experiments. Furthermore, they are increasingly using virtual-reality stimuli in social neuroscience research (Adolphs, 2003; Schilbach et al., 2013; Wilms et al., 2010).

10.4.1   *What Is the Relation of Cyberpsychology to Social Neuroscience?*

Much of the early social psychology work used virtual environments for research in communication studies (Biocca, 1992a, 1992b; Biocca & Delaney, 1995; Biocca & Levy, 1995; Lanier & Biocca, 1992; Riva, 1999), presence (Biocca et al., 2003; Loomis, 1992; Mantovani & Riva, 1999), and social influence (Blascovich, 2001; Blascovich et al., 2002). Since these early days, a number of study areas have emerged. According to Fox and Bailenson (2009), these studies can be categorized into three primary areas: (1) human experience within virtual environments compared to experience in the real world; (2) training in virtual environments to achieve real-world goals; and (3) virtual environments to study social scientific phenomena. Today, these cyberpsychology approaches are being adopted by social neuroscientists and there is growing literature on the use of virtual environments and virtual humans for social neuroscience studies:

- interpreting others (Kokal et al., 2009; Newman-Norlund et al., 2008; Pfeiffer et al., 2013; Schilbach et al., 2006, 2010)
- social exclusion (Kassner, Wesselmann, Law & Williams, 2012; Wirth et al., 2010)
- age relations (Banakou et al., 2013)
- body shape/size issues (Normand et al., 2011; Preston & Ehrsson, 2014; van der Hoort et al., 2011)
- gender groups (Slater et al., 2010)
- race (Maister et al., 2013; Peck et al., 2013).

Virtual environments offer the social neuroscientist the ability to induce a feeling of presence in participants as they experience emotionally engaging background narratives to enhance affective experience and social interactions (Diemer et al., 2015; Gorini et al., 2011). Recently, social neuroscientists have started incorporating virtual-reality into their experiments and are increasingly using virtual-reality stimuli in social neuroscience research (Adolphs, 2003; Schilbach et al., 2013; Wilms et al., 2010). In addition to advanced presentation of dynamic stimuli, virtual environments allow for moment-by-moment logging of interactive scenarios that comport well with the constraints of neuroimaging settings. As such, virtual environments offer promise for advancing the investigation of the neural underpinnings of joint actions (Kokal et al., 2009; Newman-Norlund et al., 2008; Pfeiffer et al., 2013; Schilbach et al., 2006, 2010). With advances in simulation technologies, the trade-off between the experimental control found in the laboratory and the ecological validity of naturalistic observation may be alleviated, as virtual technology can be modified and adapted without compromising measurement control (Bohil, Alicea, & Biocca, 2011).

    Recently de Gelder and Hortensius (2014) have discussed the ways in which social interactions promote affective loops that result from our corporeal bodies interacting with the environment. Affective computer systems that can both be impacted by and influence users corporeally display a use feature that Kristina Höök (2009) has entitled an affective loop experience, wherein emotions are understood as processes that are assembled during the social interactions that occur in everyday bodily, cognitive, or social experiences. The affective computing system responds in ways that pull the user into the social interaction, touching upon end users' physical experiences. Throughout the social interaction the user is an active, meaning-making participant that chooses the ways in which to express themselves – the interpretation obligation does not lie with the system. For de Gelder and Hortensius (2014), affective loops occur when users take part in social interactions with their bodies and robust affective involvements are experienced. According to de Gelder and Hortensius (2014), virtual-reality offers the field of social neuroscience (and for this book's purposes it offers cyberpsychologists) a powerful tool for these investigations. First, virtual-reality allows the investigation of affective loops under laboratory control conditions that involve simulations of real-life activities that are not possible (e.g., too costly and/or unethical) if performed in a real-world context. Furthermore, virtual-reality is well suited for the study of complex social situations and phenomena. For example, in a virtual-reality study that provoked participants with a violent incident involving another person, Mel Slater and colleagues (2013) at University College London investigated the likelihood of the participant giving aid to the victim. Finally, virtual-reality combined with new techniques (e.g., motion capture) not only gives scientists the possibility of using point-light stimuli in body perception and social interaction research but also provides a tool to systematically vary certain components of a body or social interaction and makes it possible to analyze how kinematics differentiate between emotional scenarios

Hence, the use of virtual-reality and new techniques offers the field of social neuroscience valuable and significant tools to study the full extent of the social world in a well-controlled manner. It has been pointed out by Georgescu and colleagues (2014), however, that in studies that incorporate neuroimaging the coupling of technical advancements in virtual-reality and motion capture technologies for studying non-verbal communication in social interaction are limited. To increase statistical power, it is important to develop social scripts that are systematically manipulated, reduced, and presented repeatedly. Experimenters must also ensure that the motion-tracking systems are compatible with the available neuroimaging techniques. Furthermore, participants must be restricted in their movements to prevent artifacts during neural data acquisition. That said, Georgescu and colleagues (2014) also point out several ways to overcome these limitations. First, researchers need to develop virtual environments that allow for social interactions with the virtual environment and virtual others in a controlled manner via some limited input data in the scanner environment. For example, Baumann et al. (2003) have developed a VR system of integrated software and hardware for neurobehavioral and clinical studies for fMRI studies. The VR system includes a joystick for navigation, a touchpad, and an optional data glove with an attached motion tracker. Moreover, the virtual-reality setup enables the measurement of physiological data (heart rate, respiration, blood volume pulsatility, and skin conductance). Finally, the virtual-reality system provides synchronization of the simulation with the physiological recordings and the functional MR images. Furthermore, researchers can constrain their investigations to situations with minimal social interaction. Although this would only involve minimal non-verbal input, it would allow for the investigation of social interactions based on gaze behavior in real time.

10.4.2 *Neural Underpinnings Involved in Interpreting Others*

A number of studies have emerged using virtual-reality, psychophysiology, and neuroimaging of brain activity during interactions with virtual characters. Computer-animated characters are seemingly ubiquitous in popular social media and have begun to be used in social neuroscience research. A known issue for cyberpsychology research with virtual characters is the "uncanny valley" hypothesis, in which the acceptability of a virtual character is not a linear function of its human likeness (Mori, 1970; Mori et al., 2012). This hypothesis was developed by Japanese roboticist Masahiro Mori while investigating the social competence of robots (Mori, 1970). According to the "uncanny valley" hypothesis, the progressive development of humanlike appearance and motion in a robot results in a linear increase in emotional response by the human observer. Instead, the increase falls into a local minimum when the robot closely but imperfectly approximates a human being (see Figure 10.1).

The "uncanny valley" hypothesis has been extended to virtual characters (MacDorman, Green, Ho, & Koch, 2009). The more a virtual character looks like a human person, the more acceptable it is until it reaches a certain degree (local minima) of likeness in the uncanny valley.

From a mirror network perspective, there may be an overlap between neural processes devoted to perception and execution of actions and self-

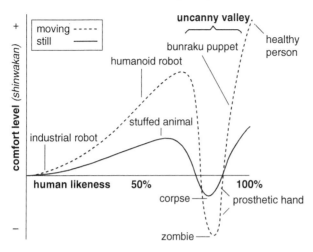

Figure 10.1 Uncanny Valley (K.F. MacDorman et al., *Computers in Human Behavior*, 2009. Reprinted by permission of the publisher).

identification with others. However, from a mirroring perspective, it is counterintuitive that increases in an artificial characters' anthropomorphism would decrease the perceived naturalness of their actions. In a recent study, Chaminade, Hodgins, and Kawato (2007) investigated how appearance of virtual characters influences human perception of their actions. Participants were presented with characters animated either with motion data captured from human actors or by interpolating between poses designed by an animator. The investigators asked the participants to categorize the virtual character's motion as "biological" or "artificial." They found that the response bias toward "biological" (derived from Signal Detection Theory) decreases with a virtual character's anthropomorphism. Moreover, sensitivity was only impacted by the simplest rendering style (i.e., point-light displays). Neuroimaging using functional magnetic resonance imaging revealed that the response biases correlated positively with activity in the mentalizing network (left temporoparietal junction and anterior cingulate cortex), and negatively with regions sustaining motor resonance. These results comport well with neuroimaging findings that the mentalizing network is recruited when participants reason about other people's minds (i.e., theory of mind). Specific brain regions involved in theory of mind include the medial prefrontal cortex, the bilateral temporo-parietal junction, the superior temporal sulcus, the precuneus, and the temporal poles (Kovács et al., 2014). Moreover, the medial prefrontal cortex and temporo-parietal junction have been claimed to be crucial for theorizing about minds (Frith & Frith, 2003; Saxe & Kanwisher, 2003).

Studies have also sought to identify brain regions involved in interpreting others' face and eye movements. When participants were approached by a virtual human exhibiting an angry expression, researchers found activation of the superior temporal sulcus, the lateral fusiform gyrus, and a region of the middle temporal gyrus (Carter & Pelphrey, 2008). In other eye-gaze paradigms, Schilbach et al. (2006, 2010) characterized the neural correlates of being involved in social interactions through the introduction of dynamic virtual humans in the scanner. The virtual humans were programmed to "gaze at" and "greet others." The "others" were lying passively in a scanner or a bystander. Findings revealed that the vmPFC underpins the perception of social communication and feeling of personal involvement (Schilbach et al., 2006). Further, when the participants initiated shared attention with the virtual humans, neural activity increased in the ventral striatum (Schilbach et al., 2010).

In a related study, Wilms et al. (2010) instructed participants in the scanner to "respond to" or "probe" the gaze of a virtual human that was being operated by another human. They were not told that the virtual human was in fact being operated by a computer. The goal of the participants was to establish eye contact with the virtual human and to attend jointly to one of three objects on a screen. The participants were instructed that the three objects represented the participant's eye-gaze. This approach allowed for the investigation of neural differences between successful initiation of joint attention and mere gaze following. A main effect was found for joint attention resulting in the activation of the medial prefrontal cortex, posterior cingulate cortex, and the anterior temporal poles.

10.4.3　Virtual Representations of Self and Other

Embodiment accounts of social cognition that emphasize shared bodily representations for self and other may be aided by the use of virtual-reality technology. Given that immersive virtual environments involve flexible computer platforms, the shape, form, size, or type of a virtual human body can be manipulated to represent something divergent from the participant's actual body. This flexibility of the virtual environment and the virtual human bodies can influence the participant's perceptions, attitudes, and behaviors (Slater & Sanchez-Vives, 2014). While there have been a number of studies looking at social behaviors of participants when they are exposed to virtual humans from other demographic groups (Dotsch & Wigboldus, 2008), there is increasing interest in the use of interactive virtual humans to examine the impact of virtual embodiment on implicit social cognitions related to the other's age (Banakou et al., 2013); body shape/size (Normand et al., 2011; Preston & Ehrsson, 2014; van der Hoort et al., 2011); gender groups (Slater et al., 2010); and race (Maister et al., 2013; Peck et al., 2013).

Taking part in social interactions involves automatic and controlled processes. During a social interaction, people automatically apply stereotypes to quickly categorize others. One of the most powerful cues that drive these categorizations is racial bias. These automatic heuristics and biases modulate our neurocognitive and affective reactivity to others. Sacheli and colleagues (2015) investigated whether implicit (automatic) racial bias shapes hand kinematics during the execution of realistic joint actions with virtual in- and out-group partners. They found that stronger visuo-motor interference occurred when participants were instructed to predict the partner's action goal for online adaptation of their own movements. These stronger visual motor inferences were also found during interactions with the in-group partner. They took this to indicate that the virtual partner's racial membership modulated interactive behaviors. The researchers interpreted their findings in terms of recent findings revealing that even basic forms of neurophysiological responses to interpersonal situations activate the mirror system, which is modulated by high-level cognitive and cultural influences. Specifically, they point to racial bias induced by the color of the skin as sensorimotor mirroring as well as the empathic sensorimotor and affective mapping. Furthermore, ethnic categorization has been found to modulate neural activations in the mirror network during intention understanding and imitation (Earls, Englander, & Morris, 2013).

The categorization of others by race may be a reversible by-product of human evolution used to detect coalitional alliances (Kurzban, Tooby, & Cosmides, 2001). A recent virtual-reality study demonstrated that when participants experienced being a dark-skinned virtual human there was a decrease in implicit racial bias (Peck et al., 2013). These findings suggest that racism may be curtailed using virtual environments. Related cyber-psychology research has found that the sensation of having a black rubber arm for White participants may be associated with changes in implicit racial bias (Farmer, Tajadura-Jimenez, & Tsakiris, 2012; Maister, Sebanz, Knoblich, & Tsakiris, 2013). As such, virtual-reality may offer the cyberpsychologist a tool that allows participants to experience embodiment in a race other than their own. This virtual embodiment involves wearing a wide field-of-view head-mounted display that tracks the user's movements. When users look down at themselves in the virtual environment they would see a programmed virtual body instead of their own real body. Moreover, in the study by Peck and colleagues, they were able to see the virtual body when looking at their (geometrically correct) reflection in a virtual mirror. Through the virtual embodiment of participants in bodies of different skin color Peck and colleagues were able to investigate the extent to which they could induce a body-ownership illusion in a differently raced avatar, and whether the body-ownership illusion could reduce negative implicit responses toward that other race. Results from their study revealed that when participants experienced being a dark-skinned virtual human there was a decrease in implicit racial bias.

Likewise, in an age-related study, Banakou et al. (2013) investigated the relationship between implicit attitudes and embodiment in adult participants that were immersed in virtual child bodies. Findings revealed that the adults inhabiting the virtual child's body overestimated the size of objects. The participants also demonstrated implicit attitude and behavioral changes that appeared more childlike. It is interesting to note that when the participants were in an adult body that was the size of a child's body they did not exhibit such changes. Maister et al. (2015) have suggested that changes in implicit attitudes occur via a process of self-association that occurs in the physical feeling (i.e., perceived increase in bodily similarity between self and other) domain and then extends to the cognitive (conceptual generalization of positive self-like associations to the other) domain.

10.4.4   Virtual Interactions Using Cyberball

Social neuroscientists have also started using the virtual gaming task called Cyberball to induce social exclusion in participants. A number of researchers have used the Cyberball game as an experimentally controlled social exclusion assessment that elicits affective (Wesselmann, Wirth, Mroczek, & Williams, 2012; Williams, 2007), neurobiological (Eisenberger et al., 2012), psychophysiological (Moor, Crone & Van der Molen, 2010; Sijtsema, Shoulberg, & Murray-Close, 2011), and hormonal (Geniole, Carré, & McCormick, 2011; Zwolinski, 2012) responses. Findings from neuroimaging studies have revealed that social exclusion activates a ventral affective salience network that involves a number of interconnected brain hub areas, including the medial prefrontal cortex, anterior cingulate cortex, amygdala, and anterior insula. Furthermore, being excluded during a Cyberball game has been found to be associated with ventrolateral areas of the prefrontal cortex involved in the regulation of social distress (Eisenberger et al., 2003; Guyer et al., 2008).

Throughout the Cyberball task, the participant is represented by an avatar that is playing catch with two other avatars. The two other avatars ostensibly represent two other human participants. Participants are either included or ostracized during the Cyberball tossing game by two or three other players who are, in fact, controlled by an experimenter. The virtual Cyberball game starts with each avatar catching and throwing a ball (each about a third of the time). During the "inclusion" condition, the participant continues to catch and throw the ball about a third of the time. However, during the "exclusion" condition, the other two avatars throw the ball back and forth and ignore (neither avatar looks at or throws the ball to) the participant.

It is interesting to note that telling participants that the avatars in the Cyberball game are controlled by a computer does not change the effects of ostracism. In fact, the ostracism delivered by computers was judged by participants to be just as unpleasant as ostracism by humans. Further, it did not matter to participants whether the human-controlled or computer-controlled players had a choice as to whom they threw the ball to (Zadro, Williams, & Richardson, 2004).

The use of the Cyberball game in ostracism research is expedient because it allows for flexibility modification for study of group interactions without the use of live confederates, to collect large samples over the Internet, and for neuroimaging studies. Recent results from neuroimaging studies have revealed that the experience of being excluded from ball-tossing reliably evokes increased activation of the dorsal anterior cingulate and anterior insula, which correlates with self-reports of physical pain (Eisenberger, 2012). A number of qualitative reviews of the fMRI and Cyberball social exclusion literature have emerged and all have concluded that nociceptive stimuli and social rejection both activate this physical pain matrix. Although the results from a recent meta-analysis suggest that the neural correlates of nociceptive stimuli and social rejection have some distinct patterns of activation, they still share commonalities (Cacioppo et al., 2013). In a more recent meta-analysis, Rotge et al. (2014) found that the Cyberball task activated the dorsal anterior cingulate circuit less than other experimental social pain tasks. These findings are consistent with the suggestion that the social pain that follows from Cyberball is less intense than the social pain that follows from more personal forms of social rejection (Eisenberg, 2013).

While the Cyberball paradigm has been widely used, some of the less robust findings may reflect the fact that early versions of the Cyberball task lacked the everyday realism and ecological validity that are now available in today's immersive virtual environments. A recent advance in the Cyberball paradigm is an immersive virtual environment version that places the participant into a virtual environment with interactive virtual humans (Kassner, Wesselmann, Law, & Williams, 2012). Results revealed that the more immersive virtual environments induced feelings of ostracism in participants. In addition to prompting feelings of ostracism that are consistent with negative effects found in minimalist environments, the immersive virtual environment effect sizes were medium to large in magnitude.

In addition to these robust effects, the immersive virtual environment Cyberball paradigm offers researchers the ability to control aspects (proxemics and non-verbal communication) of the social context that cannot be accomplished in minimalist ostracism paradigms. The inclusion of immersive virtual environments in Cyberball paradigms may allow for enhanced flexibility in manipulation of social information about the confederates' avatars, virtual humans, and/or their behaviors (Wirth et al., 2010). Further, the inclusion of virtual humans enhances the Cyberball paradigm because it allows for additional social information such as non-verbal (e.g., eye-gaze) information that has been found to convey ostracism (Wirth et al., 2010).

10.5 Conclusions

This chapter has reviewed the ways in which social neuroscience is moving from static to dynamic stimulus presentations in its endeavors to answer central questions about the neural correlates of human social interactions. While social neuroscience research has historically used static stimuli (e.g., simple, static representations of socially relevant stimuli; static photographs of emotionally valenced facial expressions) that are devoid of interactions, concerns have been raised that knowledge gained using these static stimuli will not generalize to the social cognition in everyday activities. In this chapter, there has been a discussion of the potential of virtual environments and virtual humans for presenting dynamic stimuli that will allow assessment of participants as they act upon stimuli interactively. We are constantly engaging in reciprocal interactions with others and represent ourselves in the context of our social environments. As the discussion of example studies reveals, the combination of cyberpsychology and social neuroscience research can be used to expand our understanding of everyday social cognition.

In addition to discussions of cyberpsychology tools for social neuroscience research, there has been an emphasis upon findings from neuroimaging for a brain-based cyberpsychology approach to social neuroscience. Neuroimaging studies are offering new insights into social interactions, the ways in which interpersonal emotions are processed, and the neural correlates supporting these processes. While much of the early research into social cognition attempted to locate social cognitive processes in specific brain regions like the dorsomedial prefrontal cortex and/or the temporoparietal junction, recent developments in systems neuroscience approaches have emerged as studies are increasingly revealing that the neural correlates of person perception are organized into neural networks.

Throughout, there was a discussion of large-scale brain networks for mentalizing (i.e., mentalizing network) and mirroring. We have seen that the mentalizing network is typically involved when persons represent and make sense of others' states of mind. Specific brain hubs include the anterior insula and anterior cingulate cortex that processes a person's bodily arousal during interpersonal experiences. The mentalizing network includes the neural correlates of a person's ability to mentalize (i.e., infer) the cognitions and feelings of others. In addition to the mentalizing brain network, studies suggest that a "mirroring" network is related to a person's representation of facial movements and bodily gestures while making inferences about their meanings. The large-scale brain network for mirroring is made up of hubs in the premotor cortex, superior temporal sulcus, and inferior parietal lobule. The mirroring network has been taken as evidence for a first-person or simulationist account of social cognition. This can be contrasted with the mentalizing network's activation when the person is making inferences (theorizing) about the goals of those actions. The mirroring network can also be contrasted with the mentalizing network in that the latter is more strongly related to representing the contextual information that allows inference of another's mental state to occur.

In this chapter we also explored the ways in which these large-scale brain networks are involved in both automatic and controlled processing. A brain-based cyberpsychology can be developed that studies both automatic reflexive and controlled reflective processes. Taking part in social media interactions involves both of these automatic and controlled processes. During a social media interaction, people automatically apply stereotypes to quickly categorize others. One of the most powerful cues that drive these categorizations is racial bias. These automatic heuristics and biases modulate our neurocognitive and affective reactivity to others. Using virtual embodiment, it is possible for the cyberpsychologist to explore shared bodily representations of the user's self and others. Given that immersive virtual environments involve flexible computer platforms, the shape, form, size, or type of a virtual human body can be manipulated to represent something divergent from the participant's actual body. The flexibility of virtual environments and virtual human bodies can influence the participant's automatic perceptions, attitudes, and behaviors. Furthermore, virtual environments can immerse users into a virtual body of someone from a different ethnicity and through controlled exposure racism may be curtailed. Hence, virtual-reality may offer the cyberpsychologist a tool that allows participants to experience embodiment in a race other than their own in a way that reduces negative implicit responses toward persons who are different from the user.

CHAPTER II

Clinical Neuroscience: Novel Technologies for Assessment and Treatment

11.1 Introduction

Individuals with neurocognitive, affective, and social impairments may experience decreased functioning in multiple domains, including attention, self-awareness, memory, reasoning, communication, and judgment. Such impairments represent significant obstacles to the patient's activities of daily living. Advances in the clinical neurosciences have greatly enhanced our understanding of the brain's cognitive and affective processing in neurologic and psychiatric disorders. The noteworthy developments made at the end of the twentieth century in understanding the genetic and neural correlates of many diseases affecting the brain are important for a brain-based cyberpsychology. Cyberpsychologists interested in clinical neuroscience research and practice should be aware of both the contributions of clinical neuroscience to cyberpsychology and the potential that cyberpsychology research and practices have for the clinical neurosciences.

11.1.1 Large-Scale Brain Networks Involved in Neurocognitive and Affective Dysfunctions

Cyberpsychologists that are interested in clinical neuroscience would do well to understand the large-scale brain networks involved in neurocognitive and affective dysfunctions found in psychiatric and neurological disorders. Recent work in this area has resulted in conceptual and methodological developments that are contributing to a paradigm shift in the study of psychopathology (Mennon, 2011). A brain-based cyberpsychology involves an understanding of the ways in which the human brain produces cognition via its large-scale organization (Bressler & Menon, 2010). Given the human brain's complex patchwork of interconnected regions, network approaches have become increasingly useful for understanding how functionally connected systems prompt and restrain neurocognitive functions (Menon & Uddin, 2010). Furthermore, large-scale brain network approaches provide new insights into aberrant brain organization in several psychiatric and neurological disorders. Clinical neuroscience studies into psychopathology are increasingly focusing upon understandings of the ways in which disturbances in large-scale networks contribute to neurocognitive and affective dysfunction.

Vinod Menon (2011) at Stanford University's Institute for Neuro-Innovation and Translational Neurosciences has proposed a triple network model of aberrant saliency mapping and cognitive dysfunction in psychopathology. Menon's triple network model focuses on three intrinsic connectivity networks that have turned out to be particularly important for understanding higher cognitive function and dysfunction: the central executive network, the default-mode network, and the salience network. First, there is the brain's (key nodes include the dorsolateral prefrontal cortex and posterior parietal cortex) central executive network that handles high-level neurocognitive functions such as planning, decision-making, and the control of attention and working memory (Sridharan, Levitin, & Menon, 2008). Next, we find the default-mode network that plays an important role in monitoring the person's internal mental landscape (Qin & Northoff, 2011). Finally, there is the salience network that is involved in detecting and orienting to salient external stimuli and internal events. The salience network plays a key role in both the attentional capture of neurobiologically relevant events and in the subsequent engagement of frontoparietal systems for working memory and higher-order cognitive control (Menon & Uddin, 2010; Seeley et al., 2007). Whereas the central executive network and salience network typically reveal increases in activation during stimulus-driven neurocognitive and affective information processing, the default-mode network reveals decreases in activation during tasks in which self-referential and stimulus-independent memory recall is not crucial (Raichle, 2015). The Menon model proposes that deficits in engagement and disengagement of these three core networks play a significant role in many psychiatric and neurological disorders. It is important to note that a key aspect of Menon's model is that inappropriate assignment of saliency to external stimuli or internal mental events can be found in dysfunctional processing.

11.1.2   *Cyberpsychology Research and Practices for Enhancing Clinical Neuroscience*

Psychological assessment and intervention have become important components of cyberpsychology research and practice. During an intervention, patients may perform systematically presented and functionally oriented activities that are based upon an assessment and understanding of the patient's functioning (Harley, 1992). Methodical interventions are intended to increase the patient's ability to perform activities of daily living (Wilson, 2000). Interventions often aim at functional enhancements through reestablishing previously learned behavior patterns or establishing new patterns of activity or compensatory mechanisms.

Some approaches found in the clinical neurosciences focus upon increasing activities of daily living by systematic evaluation of current performance and reducing deficits by furnishing the patient with success strategies from a range of settings (Ylvisaker et al., 2001). These approaches to treatment of the cognitive, affective, and motor sequelae of central nervous system dysfunction often rely upon assessment measures to inform diagnosis and track changes in clinical status. The cyberpsychologist has much to offer to clinical neuroscience. Specifically, cyberpsychologists are aware of, and practiced in, the application of advanced technologies. This is important given the fact that many clinicians employ outmoded technologies in their research and praxes. For example, they employ assessments and interventions that involve standardized paper-and-pencil technologies that are limited in their stimulus presentation and logging of patient responses, and lack ecological validity (Parsons, 2015; Parsons, 2016; Parsons, Carlew, Magtoto, & Stonecipher, 2015; Parsons & Phillips, 2016).

Instead of using advanced simulation technologies, many clinicians commonly use behavioral observation and ratings of the patient's performance in the real world or via physical mock-ups of functional environments. Mock-up environments (e.g., kitchens, bathrooms) and workspaces (e.g., classrooms, offices) are built, within which patients with motor and/or neurocognitive impairments are observed and their performance evaluated. The development of these environments for patients in a clinical setting can be problematic owing to practical constraints such as clinician time, budgetary limitations, safety concerns, and travel (Parsons et al., 2009a; Stichter et al., 2014). Aside from the economic costs to physically build these environments and to provide clinicians to conduct such evaluations and interventions, this approach is limited in the systematic control of real-world stimuli and in its capacity to capture detailed performance data.

11.2 Virtual Environment Platforms for Clinical Neuroscience

Within cyberpsychology there is a long history of using virtual-reality environments for clinical assessments and interventions. Early virtual

environments attempted to build upon the construct-driven neuropsychological assessments found in traditional paper-and-pencil assessments. For
example, a number of early virtual environments aimed to build upon the
Wisconsin Card Sorting Test (WCST) paradigm, in which participants
navigated to the exit of a virtual building through the matching of stimuli
to environmental cues (e.g., categories of shape, color, and number of
portholes) found on virtual doors (Pugnetti et al., 1995; Pugnetti et al.,
1998). A notable limitation of these early virtual environments was a heavy
reliance on navigating through a building, and this may have confounded
the results. In a novel and evolved iteration, the Virtual-Reality Look for
a Match (VRLFAM) test removed the navigational components and
immersed the participant in a virtual beach scene. Participants were
instructed to deliver Frisbees, sodas, popsicles, and beach balls to umbrellas
(Elkind et al., 2001). While these virtual environments were innovative
approaches, an unfortunate limitation of modeling virtual environment-
based neuropsychological assessments on the WCST is that the virtual
analogues, like the original WCST, may not be able to differentiate
between patients with frontal lobe pathology and control subjects (Stuss
et al., 1983). Further, while data from the virtual environment–based
assessments, like the WCST, do appear to provide information relevant
to the constructs of set-shifting and working memory, the virtual environment assessments seem to do little to extend ecological validity. As such,
neuropsychologists may be better served by traditional paper-and-pencil
measures than virtual adaptations of tests like the WCST.

While early virtual-reality platforms promised a number of advantages,
there were some drawbacks. Cost has long been a barrier to incorporating
advanced virtual environments. While a wide-field-of-view head-mounted
display (HMD) with tracking capabilities can cost thousands of dollars,
computer equipment setups are rapidly decreasing in size and price – with
a concomitant increase in computational power and ease of operation. For
example, the Oculus Rift is a new and lightweight (380g) head-mounted
display that only costs a few hundred dollars (i.e., $300) and it proffers an
extended field of view of 110 degrees, stereoscopic vision, and rapid head
tracking. Furthermore, these systems have historically been bulky HMD
helmets that engulfed the user's entire head and face, and weighed several
pounds. Given progress in the design of HMDs, these problems have
steadily diminished. Again, these problems are already diminishing dramatically with the Oculus Rift and its light weight (380g) and extended
field of view of 110 degrees, stereoscopic vision, and rapid head tracking.
The Oculus Rift has advanced data processing of stimuli that comes

through 3-axis gyroscope, accelerometer, and magnetometer, giving the user a fast image update with greatly limited delay.

It is important to note that the term "virtual-reality" does not limit the researcher to a particular configuration of hardware and software. Instead, VR may be understood as a development of simulations that make use of various combinations of interaction devices and sensory display systems. Typically, the design of these systems is developed with consideration of balancing level of immersiveness with level of invasiveness. Many historical users of VR have opted for highly immersive experiences using more invasive head-mounted displays. The invasiveness results from the user wearing an apparatus (i.e., an HMD) on her or his head, which often tethers the user to a computer. Given the desire for users to have a less invasive experience while exposed to a virtual environment, some researchers have turned to projection systems that use cameras for whole-body tracking and integration of body-state information into various simulations. These systems are noninvasive because the user is not encumbered by the need to wear accessories to enable the tracking of the user's movements. The increased availability of commercially available interaction devices (e.g., Microsoft Kinect, Nintendo Wii Sony Eyetoy, Konami Dance Dance Revolution) has allowed for less invasive VR applications that present three-dimensional (3D) graphic environments on flatscreen monitors. Whilst such noninvasive VR systems involve a lower level of immersion, the phenomenological experience of the user is one that involves a high potential for interaction with digital content using naturalistic body actions.

There is also the potential for unintended negative effects of exposure to virtual environments – stimulus intensity, if taken too far, may exacerbate rather than ameliorate a deficit. As we adopt newer and more immersive technologies (i.e. HMDs) it is important to consider the potential negative effects (i.e., dizziness, sickness, displacement) to ensure that wearable technologies (e.g., HMDs) can provide an acceptable space for participants to use, especially individuals with disabilities. Cybersickness continues to be a potential issue for some users. For some users, nausea results from immersion in virtual environments. This is typically understood as resulting from the incongruity between visual perception of motion and vestibular feedback that is not matched by vision. While this is of continued concern for virtual-reality researchers, the lag between the timing of tracked movements and updating of computer-generated imagery has alleviated the impact. With this said, there is some evidence that suggests children and young adults do not experience HMDs any more negatively than screen-based media (Parsons, 2007; Parsons & Carlew, 2016). Taken as a whole, the need to validate and confirm acceptance of evolving and very new technologies is evident and there is need for more research in this domain.

Another issue that is commonly raised is the need for technology skills for creation and maintaining, virtual environments. This issue is becoming less formidable as increasingly powerful tools are becoming available. In addition to the fact that many of these tools are free to users, large repositories of graphic assets are increasingly available for use in user-friendly visual programming and scripting languages (e.g., Virtools and Vizard). An important challenge in the design and development of VR technologies is the difficulty involved in putting together interdisciplinary research teams for developing appropriate interventions (Beardon, Parsons, & Neale, 2001). Furthermore, there is increasing recognition that representatives of intended user groups should also be included in order to achieve a better fit between identified needs and proposed solutions (Abascal & Nicolle, 2005). Though not without difficulties (Parsons & Cobb, 2014), such approaches also align with increasing awareness of the need to involve, for example, members from the clinical and educational communities in these research agendas more widely (Pellicano & Stears, 2011).

While early virtual environments had a number of limitations in their iterative development over the years, virtual-reality has now emerged as a promising tool in many domains of assessment (Jovanovski et al., 2012a; Parsons, 2015), therapy (Opris et al., 2012; Parsons & Rizzo, 2008a; Powers & Emmelkamp, 2008), training (Coyle, Traynor, & Solowij, 2015; Ke & Im, 2013), and rehabilitation (Parsons et al., 2009a; Penn, Rose, & Johnson, 2009; Shin & Kim, 2015). Within this context VR technology represents a simulation of real-world training environments based on computer graphics. These can be useful, as they allow instructors, therapists, and service providers to offer a safe, repeatable, and diversifiable environmental platform during treatment, which can benefit the learning of individuals, especially disabled users. Research has also pointed to VR's capacity to reduce patients' experience of aversive stimuli (Maskey et al., 2014) and reduce anxiety levels. The unique match between VR technology assets and the needs of various clinical application areas has been recognized by a number of authors (Cobb, 2007; Gorini & Riva, 2008; Trost & Parsons, 2014) and an encouraging body of research has emerged (Ke & Im, 2013; Parsons & Carlew, 2016; Riva, 2011, 2014).

Continuing advances in VR technology along with concomitant system cost reductions have supported the development of more usable, useful, and accessible VR systems that can uniquely be applied to a wide range of physical, psychological, and cognitive clinical targets and research questions (Bohil, Alicea, & Biocca, 2011). Virtual-reality makes use of virtual environments to present digitally recreated real-world activities to participants via immersive head-mounted displays (HMDs) and non-immersive (2D computer screens) media. Recent advances in VR technology allow for enhanced computational capacities for administration efficiency, stimulus presentation, automated logging of responses, and data analytic processing. Since virtual environments provide experimental control and dynamic presentation of stimuli in ecologically valid scenarios, they allow for controlled presentations of emotionally engaging background narratives to enhance affective experience and social interactions (Parsons, 2015). Moreover, the introduction of accessible and affordable HMDs has readied cyberpsychology to make the most of immersive and ecologically valid systems.

11.2.1   Adaptation of Brain Networks in Response to Stressors

In properly functioning affective systems, the responses to stressful stimuli are adaptive. LeDoux (2012a) posits survival circuits that enable humans to adapt to feared stimuli by organizing brain functions. The fear-induced arousal and activation of survival circuits allows for adaptive responses to take priority and other responses are inhibited. Further, attentional processing focuses on pertinent environmental stimuli and learning occurs (LeDoux, 2012b). Hence, adaptive survival circuits are optimized to detect threatening stimuli and relay the information as environmental challenges and opportunities. The adaptive survival circuits use this information to adjust behavioral and psychophysiological responses for appropriate adaptation and resolution. Excessive fear responses, however, can be restrictive and may be a sign of dysregulated anxiety. When exposure to stress occurs early in development and is repeated in persons with a particular genetic disposition, a decreased threshold for developing anxiety may result (Heim & Nemeroff, 1999). Further, over-excitation and deprivation can influence the affective system and may induce changes in the emotional circuitry of the brain that can contribute to stress-related psychopathology (Davidson, Jackson, & Kalin, 2000).

Within a virtual environment, cyberpsychologists can introduce stressful stimuli in a controlled fashion. The introduction of these stressful stimuli may initiate a complex response that impacts various neurocognitive and affective domains, with the objective of improving survival chances in the face of fluctuating environmental challenges. Erno Hermans and colleagues (2014) at Radboud University's Donders Institute for Brain, Cognition and Behavior in the Netherlands have bridged data from animals and humans at cellular and systems levels on large-scale brain networks to propose a framework that describes the ways in which stress-related neuromodulators trigger dynamic shifts in network balance to enable a person to reallocate neural resources according to environmental demands. They propose that exposure to stressful stimuli and events initiates a reallocation of resources to the salience network. This, in turn, promotes fear and vigilance, at the cost of the central executive network. Following the abatement of the stress response, resource allocation to the central executive network and the salience network reverses, which normalizes affective reactivity and enhances higher-order neurocognitive processes important for long-term survival.

This framework for dynamic adaptation of large-scale brain networks in response to stressors integrates data from the neuroendocrine, cellular, brain systems, and behavioral levels to describe global and dynamic shifts in brain network resource allocation in response to stressors. Herman's framework supports the ongoing paradigm shift within neuropsychiatry that follows Menon's proposed move from identifying abnormal brain areas toward the development of a global understanding of aberrations at the level of large-scale networks (Menon, 2011). Given that stress is a very important factor in development, maintenance, and re-emergence of psychiatric symptoms, this improved understanding of how stress changes brain function is significant for advancing our understanding of a wide range of psychiatric conditions.

11.2.2   Virtual-Reality Exposure Therapy for Anxiety and Specific Phobias

While dynamic adaptation of large-scale brain networks in response to stressors serves critical functions in organizing necessary survival responses in properly functioning affective systems, neuropsychiatric dysregulation found in anxiety disorders, specific phobias, as well as panic disorder and post-traumatic stress disorder, may lead to significant impairments in adaptive responses. Repeated and early exposure to stress in persons with a particular genetic disposition may result in a decreased threshold for developing anxiety (Heim & Nemeroff, 1999). Over-excitation and deprivation can influence the affective system and may induce changes in the emotional circuitry of the brain that can contribute to stress-related psychopathology (Davidson, Jackson, & Kalin, 2000).

Exposure therapy has been shown to be an effective intervention for reducing negative affective symptoms (Rothbaum & Schwartz, 2002). Exposure to emotional situations and prolonged rehearsal result in the regular activation of cerebral metabolism in brain areas associated with inhibition of maladaptive associative processes (Schwartz, 1998). Identical neural circuits have been found to be involved in affective regulation across affective disorders (De Raedt, 2006). Systematic and controlled therapeutic exposure to phobic stimuli may enhance emotional regulation through adjustments of inhibitory processes on the amygdala by the medial prefrontal cortex during exposure and structural changes in the hippocampus after successful therapy (Hariri, Bookheimer, & Mazziotta, 2000). A clinical neuroscientific approach to treatment interventions may include three large-scale brain networks that are intrinsically connected, including the central executive network, salience network, and default-mode network. Specific clinical symptoms observed in neuropsychiatric disorders may include cognitive dysfunction in the central executive network, hyper- and hypoarousal/interoception in the salience network, and an altered sense of self in the default-mode network (Lanius et al., 2015).

A novel tool for conducting exposure therapy is virtual-reality exposure therapy (VRET), in which users are immersed within a computer-generated simulation or virtual environment that updates in a natural way to the user's psychophysiological arousal, head and/or body motion (Bohil, Alicea, & Biocca, 2011). VRET comports well with the emotion-processing model, which holds that the fear network must be activated through confrontation with threatening stimuli and that new, incompatible information must be added into the emotional network (Wilhelm et al., 2005). When VRET is coupled with neurofeedback, it may have enhanced self-regulation in major brain networks such as the salience network and the default-mode network.

Although cyberpsychology researchers contend that VRET has been shown to be efficacious, a potential problem in interpreting and reconciling findings about the nature and extent of affective changes ensuing from VRET is that the vast majority of VRET studies have reported on small sample sizes and made use of inadequate null hypothesis significance testing. Until large-scale studies on the affective effects of VRET are published, statistical meta-analyses represent an interim remedy.

Regrettably, the majority of VRET trials to date have made use of a range of different outcome measures (see Opris et al., 2012; Parsons and Rizzo, 2008a; Powers & Emmelkamp, 2008).

While much of the initial VRET research has comprised case studies, open clinical trials, and uncontrolled designs, a number of quantitative reviews (Opris et al., 2012; Parsons and Rizzo, 2008a; Powers & Emmelkamp, 2008) of VRET have concluded that VRET has good potential as a treatment approach for anxiety and several specific phobias. A potential problem in interpreting and reconciling findings about the nature and extent of affective changes ensuing from VRET is that a number of factors other than virtual-reality exposure per se may be associated with such changes, including, for example, presence, immersion, anxiety and/or phobia duration, diagnostic groups, and demographics (e.g., age, gender, and ethnicity). Furthermore, the vast majority of VRET studies have reported on small sample sizes and made use of inadequate null hypothesis significance testing.

Powers and Emmelkamp (2008) completed a meta-analysis comparing in vivo exposure, VRET, and control conditions, aimed to collect well-controlled studies that had either random or matched assignment of VRET for anxiety disorders. Although the literature search produced 95 studies that had evaluated anxiety and/or phobia before and after VRET, only 13 articles met the eligibility criteria for inclusion in the meta-analysis. Results revealed that VRET had statistically large effects on all affective domains, as well as all anxiety/phobia groupings evaluated. An unfortunate limitation of these articles was that many of them did not adequately report moderator variables. Moderator variables are variables that impact the direction and/or strength of the relationship between an independent/predictor variable and a dependent/criterion variable (Baron & Kenny, 1986). Such variables are hypothesized to moderate or alter the magnitude of a relationship (e.g., gender, cybersickness, or immersability of the subject(s)). According to Hunter and Schmidt (1990, 1997), there are a number of problems with using a small number of studies to conduct a meta-analysis: (1) when sample size is viewed as the number of studies, the power to detect a given moderating variable relationship in the meta-analysis may be low; (2) with small numbers of studies, the moderators may be confounded with each other. For the Powers and Emmelkamp meta-analysis, this may be an even greater issue because they attempted to assess multiple hypotheses across groups (e.g., VRET, in vivo exposure, and control conditions) in a small number of studies (N=13) without adequate information related to potential moderators. Hence, the fact that the studies included in the meta-analysis did not provide adequate statistics severely limits the conclusions that can be drawn from the meta-analysis related to the differences between VRET and in vivo exposure.

Parsons and Rizzo (2008a) also completed a meta-analysis of VRET. For their quantitative review, they followed Hall, Tickle-Degnen Rosenthal, and Mosteller's (1994) guidelines for quality assessment, weighting, and reliability. As such, the parameters of their meta-analysis focused on magnitude of pre-/post-VRET-related changes in six domains and an overall effect size for affective functioning across studies (see Hall et al., 1994). Furthermore, they limited study selection to peer-reviewed journals that examined anxiety symptoms before and after VRET and were able to increase the available number of studies and limit confounds related to multiple groups. Similar to findings from Powers and Emmelkamp, results from this meta-analysis revealed that VRET had statistically large effects on all affective domains, as well as all anxiety/phobia groupings evaluated. While the Parsons and Rizzo meta-analysis limited the analyses to one group, it was less strict in its inclusion of case reports (see Meyerbroker and Emmelkamp, 2011).

Although the results for meta-analyses (Opris et al., 2012; Parsons and Rizzo, 2008a; Powers and Emmelkamp, 2008) revealed that VRET had statistically large effects on all affective domains, as well as all anxiety/phobia groupings evaluated, findings must be interpreted with caution given that many VRET studies do not include control groups, and many are not randomized clinical trials, limiting the confidence that affective enhancements were directly related to or caused by VRET. Even though VRET meta-analyses have attempted to identify possible moderators of affective improvements, this was not possible because necessary information was not reported or reported in insufficient detail. This lack of information related to affective improvements and presence, immersion, anxiety and/or phobia duration, demographics (e.g., age, gender, and ethnicity) may reflect a limited range of values given the selection criteria employed by most studies. Thus, the findings of these meta-analyses may not generalize to patients with anxiety disorders in general.

11.2.3 Virtual-Reality for Pain Distraction

Chronic pain can result in a somatoform disorder in which the predominant symptoms are bodily complaints of pain. Often patients with chronic pain disorder have difficulties recognizing and interpreting affective signals and perceive these signals as physical symptoms (Duddu, Isaac, &

Chaturvedi, 2006). Furthermore, the chronic pain disorder can result in significant neural alterations in the medial prefrontal cortex, anterior cingulate cortex, and the insula. These brain regions have been associated with affective awareness and bodily state monitoring (Craig, 2003). Sanna Malinen and colleagues (2010) at Aalto University School of Science and Technology in Finland investigated the spatial coherence of the salience network in 10 patients suffering from nociceptive chronic pain. Findings revealed that the salience network was altered in the resting state. Moreover, chronic pain was found to impact the temporal aspects of functional connectivity by changing the frequency of the rhythmic oscillations in the BOLD-signal within the salience network from lower levels (below 0.12 Hz) to a higher range (between 0.12 and 0.24 Hz). The researchers contend that these results suggest that persons with chronic pain have aberrant temporal and spatial activity in their affective pain-processing areas.

Immersive virtual-reality has been applied to persons in pain. One area of application has been virtual-reality for pain distraction during acutely painful experiences. Hunter Hoffman and colleagues (2000) at the University of Washington have found virtual-reality to be an effective distraction via immersion of the person using an HMD. Virtual reality–based tasks are understood as distractors that reduce the availability of neurocognitive resources for perceiving and elaborating upon nociceptive input. As a result, there are fewer executive-control resources available for conscious pain processing (McCaul & Malott, 1984). Immersive virtual environments have the potential to offer a level of distraction that goes beyond that found in simple forms of distraction (e.g., watching videos; Hoffman, Prothero, & Wells, 1998). Further, virtual reality–based distraction scenarios may improve analgesia through the reduction of visual cues associated with a painful procedure (Hoffman et al., 2000). Results from a recent systematic review of virtual environments designed for pain distraction suggest that the use of VR in adjunct with standard pharmacologic analgesics produces lower pain scores (during changes in wound dressing and physical therapy) than standard pharmacologic analgesics alone (Malloy & Milling, 2010).

It is important to note that there are limitations to interventions that rely exclusively on distraction. Although hypervigilance to pain sensations is an aspect of disability development/maintenance (Van Damme, Crombez, & Eccleston, 2004; Van Damme et al., 2010), results from experimental pain studies imply that persons endorsing high fear and catastrophizing levels may not benefit from distraction to the same extent as persons that endorse lower levels of fear (Campbell et al., 2010; Roelofs et al., 2004). Fearful individuals may engage in safety-seeking behavior during exposure to feared stimuli (e.g., guarding or bracing during movement), effectively diminishing the effect of exposure (McCraken & Eccleston, 2003; Vlaeyen et al., 2012; Vowles & Thomson, 2011). In this way, distraction from the emotional and cognitive content of fear comprises avoidance behavior.

The historical uses of virtual-reality interventions for pain distraction have primarily involved simulations of environments removed from those in which the patient must function. For example, Hoffman and colleagues have successfully employed SnowWorld for acute pain management (Hoffman et al., 2000). While in SnowWorld, the participant is transported to an icy canyon filled with snowmen that are hurling snowballs, flocks of squawking penguins, and woolly mammoths. While immersed in SnowWorld, patients throw snowballs as they fly through the softly falling snow. SnowWorld provides the patient with an environment in which they can experience a virtual world far removed from their current situation. While these virtual distraction environments often include an interactive component (e.g., shooting monsters; see Das et al., 2005), they typically do not include activities reflecting the patient's everyday activities. In contrast, exposure methodologies explicitly aim to situate the patient within contexts where treatment gains would be most useful.

11.2.4 *Virtual-Reality Exposure Therapy for Pain-Related Fear and Avoidance*

In a recent topical review, Keefe and colleagues (2012) looked at the use of virtual environments for both acute and persistent pain conditions. They conclude that the use of immersive virtual environments with HMDs holds considerable promise. In addition to immersive VR, recent developments in simulation technology have allowed researchers and clinicians enhanced flexibility in stimulus presentation. Cyberpsychologists now have the capacity to provide the patient with interactive digital content using more naturalistic body actions (e.g., Microsoft Kinect Microsoft, 2011; see also Obdržálek, Kurillo, Ofli, Bajcsy, Seto, Jimison, & Pavel, 2012). This trend appears to be increasingly focused upon full-body interaction for serious games. For the patient, this results in an interactive experience in a simulated environment that adapts in a natural manner with head and body motion (Parsons & Trost, 2014). In the context of interventions for chronic pain, such technological advances have resulted in new possibilities for combining VR exposure treatments, distraction paradigms, and visuomotor processing with validated treatments for chronic musculoskeletal disability. Thomas Parsons at the University of North Texas has developed an adaptive virtual environment for treatment of pain-related fear and avoidance behavior. This project combines current approaches to VRET with the innovative Xbox Kinect system by Microsoft (Parsons & Trost, 2014; Trost & Parsons, 2014). The Kinect is one of the most widely used whole-body trackers and has the ability to integrate body-state information into various simulations. The Kinect system uses image, audio, and depth sensors for movement detection, facial expression identification, and speech recognition. This interactive technology allows patients to interact with simulations using their own bodies as controls. An important advance is that, unlike previous attempts at gesture or movement-based controls, the patient is not encumbered by the need to wear accessories to enable the tracking of the user's movements. In this way, the VRET system for pain-related disorders represents a promising tool for the treatment of fear of specific physical exertions (e.g., vacuuming, picking up a child) as it inherently relies on (and captures) a patient's physical output.

The VRET protocol for pain-related disorders has been designed to offer an adaptive virtual environment that can be explored by patients under the supervision of a trained clinician. In this way, a VRET for pain-related disorders can offer an integration of a clinician's understanding of exposure therapy with advanced interactive multimedia technology that can be focused on delivering therapy optimized for each patient's individual differences. This would allow the clinician to manipulate idiosyncratic motivational factors that are believed to have an impact on the recovery of an individual patient (Maclean et al., 2002). Furthermore, a VRET for pain-related disorders protocol allows for enhanced patient autonomy during exposure and there is potential for automated monitoring and evaluation. Notably, the monitoring and data-gathering potential of VRET for pain-related disorders represents a major advance in detection of minor performance variations and affective changes that are not always sufficiently detectable by standard clinical scales that were constructed based on the human observer. VRET systems for pain-related disorders provide for increased standardization of administration; increased accuracy of timing presentation and response latencies; ease of administration and data collection; and reliable and randomized presentation of stimuli for repeat administrations. In short, as a hybrid of clinical intervention and VR technology, VRET for pain-related disorders offers the possibility for a new dimension of interactive exposure treatment.

11.3 Virtual Reality–Based Neurocognitive Assessments for Clinical Neuroscience

11.3.1 Paradigm Shift in Cognitive Neuroscience

A good deal of our current understanding of neurocognitive functioning has been received from the modular paradigm, in which brain areas are thought to act as independent processors for various cognitive functions. While this received view of modular processing has dominated the neuroscience literature, there is gathering evidence that questions this paradigm (Fuster, 2000). Steven Bressler and Vinod Menon (2010) have described a potential paradigm shift in cognitive neuroscience that favors conjoint function of brain areas working together as large-scale networks over the simplistic mapping of cognitive constructs onto individual brain areas found in the modular paradigm. Recent developments in the emerging paradigm of large-scale brain networks offer promising new understandings into the neural underpinnings of cognition. The large-scale brain networks paradigm reveals the ways in which cognitive functions arise from the interplay of distributed brain systems. Recent technological and methodological advances in the study of structural and functional brain connectivity offer opportunities for novel conceptualizations of large-scale brain networks.

Cyberpsychologists interested in brain functioning should take note of this shift from a modular view of the brain (general-purpose computer with a unified central processor) to an understanding of neurocognitive functioning in terms of large-scale neural networks that represent distinctive subsystems and relationships, among them: language, face-and-object recognition, spatial attention, memory-emotion, and executive function-comportment (Mesulam, 2000). Whether at rest (default-mode network), in the course of performing cognitive control tasks (executive-control network), or responding to salient information (salience network) the brain continuously generates and reshapes multifaceted patterns of correlated dynamics. Consciousness, neurocognition, and behavior are understood as emergent properties of these large-scale neural networks (Bartolomeo, 2011; Ross, 2010). These networks have nodes that can be separated into critical and participating epicenters. Lesions to a critical network epicenter conclusively impair performance in a neurocognitive domain. Functional imaging activations (see Chapter 3 of this book) of participating areas occur when persons are performing tasks related to the same neurocognitive domain (Catani & Mesulam, 2008). A great deal of our understanding of brain structure and functioning has resulted from a combination of focal brain disease studies and functional imaging experiments.

As mentioned in Chapter 1, large-scale brain networks are identifiable in the brain both while it is active and when it is at rest (Seeley et al., 2007). Currently, the three most prominent networks are the executive-control network, the default-mode network, and the saliency network. The first two networks can be recognized straightforwardly by observing the profile of activation and deactivation typically found during cognitive tasks. The executive-control network typically shows increases in activation during cognitively demanding tasks, whereas the default-mode network has decreased activation. The third network is a salience network that processes affective stimuli and allows for switching between the competitive interactions of the two other major networks.

The executive-control network appears to include brain areas that are known to have capacity for sustained attention (e.g., dorsolateral prefrontal cortex, lateral parietal cortex). Furthermore, the executive-control network has been identified for controlled attention to pertinent stimuli as behavioral choices are weighed against shifting conditions. The executive-control network exerts control over posterior sensorimotor representations and maintains relevant information so that actions may be selected. For example, coordinated prefrontal and posterior parietal control areas have been found to direct and coordinate sensory and motor areas during (and in preparation for) perceptuomotor processing (Bressler et al., 2008).

The default-mode network includes brain areas in dorsal and ventral medial prefrontal and parietal cortices (discussed as mentalizing network in Chapter 10). As discussed in Chapter 1, this network was discovered from neuroimaging of the human brain while persons were in a state of quiet repose (e.g., with eyes closed; Raichle, 2015). These findings have resulted in a suggested role of the default-mode network in self-generated cognition that is decoupled from the external world (Andrews-Hanna, 2012, 2014). As discussed in Chapter 10, an independent body of work in the social neurosciences has revealed an overlapping "mentalizing network" that reveals the neural correlates of a person's ability to mentalize (i.e., infer) the cognitions and feelings of others. The similarity between the default and mentalizing networks (see Chapter 10) has generated questions in social neuroscience about whether the core function of the default network is to mediate internal aspects of social cognition (Li, Mai, & Liu, 2014). In addition to the executive-control and default-mode networks, a salience network has emerged that reflects affective processing. As mentioned above, the salience network is an intrinsically connected large-scale network anchored in the anterior insula and dorsal anterior cingulate cortex. The characterization of the salience network has enhanced our understanding of brain areas that take part in the processing of neurocognitively and affectively relevant events to direct flexible responding (Seeley et al., 2007). These large-scale brain networks can be used by cyberpsychologists to understand neurocognitive and affective dysfunctions found in psychiatric and neurological disorders (Mennon, 2011).

11.3.2 *Virtual Environments for Research Emphasizing the Large-Scale Brain Network Paradigm*

Virtual environments may be particularly well suited for research emphasizing the large-scale brain network paradigm. Given that virtual environments represent a special case of computerized neuropsychological assessment devices (Bauer et al., 2012) they have enhanced computational capacities for administration efficiency, stimulus presentation, automated logging of responses, and data analytic processing. This greater computation power results in enhanced capacity for generating perceptual environments that systematically present and record neurobehavioral responses to dynamic stimuli. Advances in virtual environment technology offer platforms in which three-dimensional objects are presented in a dynamic, consistent, and precise manner.

Neuropsychologists are increasingly emphasizing the need for tasks that represent real-world functioning and tap into a number of cognitive domains (Chaytor & Schmitter-Edgecombe, 2003; Chaytor, Schmitter-Edgecombe, & Burr, 2006). Virtual environments are considered as potential aids in enhancing the ecological validity of neuropsychological assessments (Campbell et al., 2009; Renison et al., 2012). While early virtual-reality equipment suffered a number of limitations (large and unwieldy, difficulty to operate, and expensive to develop and maintain), today's virtual environment systems are more reliable, cost-effective, and acceptable in terms of size and appearance (Bohil, Alicea, & Biocca, 2011). A virtual environment provides the researcher with an ecologically valid platform for presenting dynamic stimuli in a manner that allows for both the veridical control of laboratory measures and the verisimilitude of naturalistic observation of real-life situations (Jovanovski et al., 2012a,

2012b; Matheis et al., 2007). Virtual environment–based assessments can provide a balance between naturalistic observation and the need for exacting control over key variables (Campbell et al., 2009).

Recently, virtual environments have been applied to the assessment of both executive-control processes found in the central executive network and affective processes found in the salience network using combat-related simulation (Armstrong et al., 2013; Parsons, Courtney, & Dawson, 2013). The addition of virtual environments allows cyberpsychologists to move beyond the ethical concerns related to placing participants into real-world situations with hazardous contexts. The goal of these platforms is to assess the impact of affective processes found in the salience network on executive-control processes found in the central executive network. For example, Thomas Parsons (2013) developed a Virtual-Reality Stroop Task (VRST) in which the participant is immersed in a simulated high-mobility multipurpose wheeled vehicle (HMMWV) and passes through zones with alternating low threat (driving down a deserted desert road) and high threat (gunfire, explosions, and shouting amongst other stressors) while dual-task stimuli (e.g., Stroop stimuli) were presented on the windshield. Parsons and colleagues (2013) found that the high-threat zones created a greater level of psychophysiological arousal (heart rate, skin conductance, respiration) than did low-threat zones. Findings from these studies also provided data regarding the potential of military-relevant virtual environments for measurement of supervisory attentional processing (Parsons, Courtney, & Dawson, 2013; Parsons et al., 2008b, 2008c).

Analyses of the effect of threat level on the color–word and interference scores resulted in a main effect of threat level and condition. Findings from the virtual environment paradigm support the perspective that (1) high information–load tasks used may be relatively automatic in controlled circumstances – for example, in low-threat zones with little activity; and (2) the total available processing capacities may be decreased by other salience processing factors such as arousal (e.g., threat zones with a great deal of activity). Hence, they found that salient threat levels impacted executive-control (i.e., Stroop interference effect), which resulted in a main effect of salient threat level and executive-control condition. A significant interaction resulted from a significant difference in performance only during the complex interference condition, such that the high-threat zones resulted in poorer performance than the low-threat zones. The authors interpret their findings in terms of the large-scale brain network paradigm. These findings reflect the perspective that high information–load tasks may be relatively automatic in controlled circumstances – for example, in low-threat zones with little activity. However, the total available processing capacities may be decreased by other factors such as arousal (e.g., threat zones with a great deal of activity). Maintenance of attention can be under voluntary control but not attentional intensity. These findings appear to reflect Seeley et al.'s (2007) differentiation of "executive-control" and "salience" networks. For the VRST, the executive network may be activated during low-threat conditions, and the salience network may activate in response to threats found in the high-threat zones. In a replication study, Armstrong et al. (2013) established the preliminary convergent and discriminant validity of the VRST with an active duty military sample.

These findings may also reflect Herman and colleagues (2014) large-scale brain network framework that describes the ways in which stress-related neuromodulators trigger dynamic shifts in network balance to enable a person to reallocate neural resources according to environmental demands. They propose that exposure to stressful stimuli and events initiates a reallocation of resources to the salience network. This, in turn, promotes fear and vigilance, at the cost of the central executive network. Following the abatement of the stress response, resource allocation to the central executive network and the salience network reverses, which normalizes affective reactivity and enhances higher-order neurocognitive processes important for long-term survival. This supports findings from Parsons and colleagues (2013) of learning effects on processing speed, as revealed when participants who experienced the low-threat zones first had slower reaction times in the low-threat zone than in the salient high-threat zone. Although this may seem counterintuitive given the fact that low-threat zones seem to be easier than high-threat zones, it actually comports well with the idea that automaticity develops relative to the degree of learned associations on respective tasks. Learned associations during the first half (low-threat zone) may result in faster reaction time in the second half even though it is a highly salient threat zone.

In addition to virtual environment–based neuropsychological assessments using driving simulators, a number of other military-relevant virtual environments have emerged for neurocognitive assessment of executive-control processes found in the central executive network and affective processes found in the salience network. For example, Parsons et al. (2012, 2014) immersed participants into a Middle Eastern city and exposed participants to an executive-control task (e.g., paced auditory serial addition test) as they followed a fire team on foot through safe and ambush (e.g., salient affective – bombs, gunfire, screams, and other visual and auditory forms of threat) zones in a Middle Eastern city. In one measure of the battery, a route-learning task, each zone is preceded by a zone marker, which serves as a landmark to assist in remembering the route. The route-learning task is followed immediately by the navigation task, in which the participants were asked to return to the starting point of their tour through the city.

Courtney and colleagues (2013) found that the inclusion of salient affective stimuli (e.g., high-threat zones) resulted in a greater level of psychophysiological arousal (heart rate, skin conductance, respiration) and decreased performance on executive-control processes than did low-threat zones. Results from active-duty military (Parsons et al., 2012) and civilian (Parsons and Courtney, 2014) populations offer preliminary support for the construct validity of the VR-PASAT as a measure of attentional processing. Further, results suggest that the VR-PASAT may provide some unique information related to salient affective processing not tapped by traditional executive-control tasks.

11.3.3 A Systems Neuroscience Approach to Neurodevelopmental Disorders

Functional connectivity studies reveal replicable large-scale brain networks that are believed to be relevant to understandings of brain–behavior relationships in neurodevelopmental disorders. Recent work in systems neuroscience has focused upon relating large-scale brain network profiles to neuropsychological and clinical measures (Castellanos & Proal, 2012). The central executive network underpins goal-directed executive-control processes and provides for adjustments to information processing in response to changing task demands. The central executive network guides decision-making by integrating exogenous information with endogenous representations. In neurodevelopmental disorders like attention-deficit/hyperactivity disorder (ADHD), the most-studied executive-control deficits have been for motor inhibition. It has been reported that the dorsal anterior cingulate is hypoactivated in ADHD during Go/No-Go, response inhibition, and attentional tasks (Bush, 2010). Furthermore, the involvement of the central executive network has been confirmed by resting-state studies in ADHD (Wang et al., 2009). Sonuga-Barke and Castellanos (2007) at New York University's Institute for Pediatric Neuroscience suggested that ADHD could be considered a default network disorder. They argued that the default network in ADHD may be noncompliant with regulation by other neural systems. As a result, the default-mode network would produce intrusions into or disruptions of ongoing cognition and behavior, which would manifest as periodic lapses in on-task performance. Support for this perspective can be found in findings revealing decreased default network coherence in ADHD (Castellanos et al., 2008), as well as decreased default network suppression and increased intra-individual variability in ADHD (Fassbender et al., 2009).

Virtual-reality environments may offer a novel approach to assessment of neurodevelopmental disorders. A recent approach to developing virtual environments has involved the addition of ecologically valid distractors (e.g., phone ringing, car driving by) to construct-driven stimuli (e.g., Stroop stimuli) presented in the virtual environment. For example, the virtual apartment presents Stroop stimuli on a large television set in the living room while the phone is ringing (Henry, Joyal, and Nolin, 2012). The addition of distractors into the virtual environment allows traditional cognitive constructs to be assessed with external interference and the distractors (auditory and/or visual elements). Virtual environment–based distractors pull for head movements that allow a better detection of subtle deficits (Henry, Joyal, and Nolin, 2012). As a result, a main advantage of these virtual environments is that they allow the researcher to introduce distractors into a task that is more similar to real-world functioning. A number of virtual classroom environments have emerged that include distractors (Climent & Bánterla, 2011; Diaz-Orueta et al., 2014; Iriarte et al, 2012; Lalonde et al., 2013). In these virtual classrooms the participant is seated at one of the desks and is surrounded by desks, children, a teacher, and a whiteboard much like they would be in a real-world classroom. Various construct-driven tasks can be presented on the whiteboard in the front of the room and the participant performs a task (e.g., Stroop or continuous performance tasks) with auditory (e.g., airplane passing overhead, a voice from the intercom, the bell ringing) and visual (e.g., children passing notes, a child raising his hand, the teacher answering the classroom door, principal entering the room) distractors in the background.

In a clinical trial of a virtual classroom with an embedded continuous performance task (CPT), Parsons et al. (2007) compared performance of children with attention deficit/hyperactivity disorder (ADHD; N=9) with typically developing children (N=10). In this study, children with ADHD performed differently from typically developing children in a number of ways: (1) children with ADHD made more commission and omission errors; (2) children with ADHD exhibited more overall body movement; and (3) children with ADHD were more impacted by distracting stimuli. Comparisons of children with ADHD and matched controls using the

Virtual Classroom CPT and the traditional CPT have revealed consistent findings (Adams et al., 2009; Bioulac, 2012; Pollak et al., 2010). A limitation of these studies is that the Virtual Classroom CPT simply replicated effects found in the traditional Conner's CPT. As a result, the Virtual Classroom did not add to our understanding of attentional processing. That said, the Parsons et al. (2007) study using the Virtual Classroom paradigm allowed for tracking of body movement and revealed that the addition of distractors increased body movement significantly more in the children with ADHD. The ability of the Virtual Classroom to quantify body movement represents a potential advance over subjective rating scales for identification of hyperactivity. Nevertheless, there is need for virtual environment measures that do more than correlate with traditional construct-driven measures.

11.3.4   Function-Led Virtual Environments for Neuropsychological Assessment

In the clinical neurosciences there is increasing interest in neuropsychological assessments that are representative of real-world functions. These function-led assessments are developed by proceeding from directly observable everyday behaviors backward to examine the ways in which a sequence of actions leads to a given behavior in normal functioning. While a number of function-led assessments in naturalistic environments have been developed, they face a number of limitations: time-consuming, require transportation to the location, involve consent from local businesses, costly, and difficult to replicate or standardize across settings (Logie, Trawley, & Law, 2011; Rand, Rukan, Weiss, & Katz, 2009). Further, there are times when function-led assessments in real-world settings are not feasible for participants with significant behavioral, psychiatric, or mobility difficulties (Knight & Alderman, 2002). To overcome some of these concerns, McGeorge et al. (2001) modeled a Virtual Errands Test (VET) on the original MET and found performance was similar for real-world and virtual environment tasks. In a larger study, the VET scenario successfully differentiated between participants with brain injuries and normal controls (Morris et al., 2002). An unfortunate limitation of these early virtual environments is that they included unrealistic graphics without event-based logging. Instead, assessment of performance involved the video recording of test sessions with subsequent manual scoring.

11.3.5 Virtual Environments that Reflect Real-World Tasks

A number of newer virtual environments with realistic graphics and event-based logging have been modeled on the MET. These function-led virtual environments have been created and validated in clinical samples. Given that these virtual environment protocols were developed by proceeding from directly observable everyday behaviors backward they examine the ways in which a sequence of actions leads to a given behavior in living and work settings: Virtual Office (Jansari et al., 2013; Lamberts, Evans, & Spikman, 2009; Montgomery, Ashmore, & Jansari, 2011); Virtual Apartment/Home tasks (Sweeney et al., 2010); Virtual Park (Buxbaum, Dawson, & Linsley, 2012); Virtual Library Task (Renison et al., 2012); Virtual Anticipating Consequences Task (Cook et al., 2013); Virtual Street Crossing (Clancy, Rucklidge, & Owen, 2006); and Virtual Kitchen (Cao, Douguet, Fuchs, & Klinger, 2010). Further, there are a number of virtual environment–based neuropsychological assessments that use driving simulators (Asimakopulos et al., 2012; Calhoun & Pearlson, 2012; Schultheis et al., 2007).

While there are a number of virtual environments available for function-led assessment, the Multitasking in the City Test (MCT) is especially useful because it involves an errand-running task implemented in a virtual city (Jovanovski et al., 2012a, 2012b). The MCT is made up of a virtual city that includes a post office, drug store, stationery store, coffee shop, grocery store, optometrist's office, doctor's office, restaurant/pub, bank, dry cleaners, pet store, and the participant's home. While immersed in the MCT, participants are assessed on their planning ability, self-monitoring, multitasking, prioritization of competing subtasks, and utilization of feedback to guide decision-making. The MCT errands consisted of everyday tasks such as meeting deadlines, making purchases, and staying within a budget. While the MCT is modelled on the real-world MET, it differs in that the MCT was intentionally developed as a less structured task without the explicit rules that may constrain behavior in the MET. Instead, the MCT tasks were developed to more closely resemble everyday behaviors. Further, unlike most versions of the MET that have no opportunity to plan tasks ahead of time, planning in the MET is assessed and compared to actual task performance. In a study with 30 healthy participants, Jovanovski et al. (2012a) found that the MCT may provide an ecologically valid method of objectively evaluating the integration of component executive functions into meaningful behavior. This represents a departure from traditional paper-and-pencil measures that aim to assess cognitive constructs (e.g., working memory) without reference to real-world settings. Further, using the MCT researchers were able to compare a sample of post-stroke and traumatic brain injury (TBI) patients to an earlier sample of normal controls. Jovanovski et al. (2012b) found that while participants in the clinical sample were able to develop adequate strategies for task execution, the actual completion of the tasks revealed a greater number of errors. The MCT's capacity for assessing subprocesses not tapped into by traditional measures is apparent in that most participants made errors during the MCT despite successfully completing all tasks. For example, participants often attempted to make a purchase before obtaining money from the bank, they entered a building but failed to perform the required task within the building, entered the same building on two separate occasions to perform two tasks that could have been performed in a single visit, and entered unnecessary buildings. Participants were also evaluated on their devising of which route they would take to complete errands around the city prior to task initiation. These findings move beyond paper-and-pencil measures and highlight the importance of prior planning for efficient and successful goal-directed behavior.

11.3.6 Comparison of Real-World Assessments to Virtual-World Assessments

A further example of function-led virtual environments is the Virtual Library Task (VLT). During the VLT, participants are required to perform numerous indicated tasks associated with the day-to-day running of the library, while observing predetermined rules: cool the library by navigating to the air conditioner and adjusting the controls; problem solve an alternative method to cool the room if the air conditioner is broken; check items that appear in the in-box; and move objects to desired locations. Renison et al. (2012) aimed to investigate whether performance on a Virtual Library Task was similar to performance of the same task in a real-world library. Findings revealed that scores on the Virtual Library Task and the real-world library task were highly positively correlated, suggesting that performance on the Virtual Library Task is similar to performance on the real-world library task. This finding is important because the virtual-reality environment allows for automated logging of participant behaviors and it has greater clinical utility than assessment in real-world settings. Comparisons of persons with traumatic brain injury and normal controls supported the construct validity of the Virtual Library Task as a measure of executive functioning. In fact, the Virtual Library Task was found to be superior to traditional (e.g., WCST) tasks in differentiating between participants with TBI and healthy controls. For example, the WCST failed to significantly differentiate between the two groups. This is consistent with studies that have reported no significant differences between control and brain-injured performances on the WCST (Alderman et al., 2003; Dawson et al., 2009; Ord et al., 2010). The authors contend that the disparity between the demands of functional assessments and traditional testing environments most likely accounts for the differences (Manchester et al., 2004).

In summary, a number of researchers have emphasized convergent validity between construct-driven virtual environments and paper-and-pencil assessments. That said, little is gained from the use of virtual environments when a paper-and-pencil measure can already answer the neuropsychologists questions. The inclusion of distractors in construct-driven virtual environments may enhance the ability to quantify body movement and perhaps diagnosis of "hyperactivity" in ADHD. However, this addition may not be enough to compel neuropsychologists to adopt new technologies. Greater enthusiasm is apparent for function-led virtual environments that were developed by proceeding from directly observable everyday behaviors backward to examine the ways in which a sequence of actions leads to a given behavior in normal functioning. While these virtual reality–based function-led assessments are at times correlated with traditional neuropsychological assessments, the most promising results have come from the increased understandings of the ways in which persons interact in everyday activities. They represent ecologically valid tasks that assess cognition and include the demands that participants face in the real world. It is important to note that the function-led assessments need not replace traditional neuropsychological batteries. Instead, function-led virtual environment–based tests may be seen as an addition to current batteries. These virtual environments may allow for increased knowledge of competence in everyday functioning.

11.4   Virtual-Reality for Neurocognitive Rehabilitation

Neuropsychological rehabilitation represents a multidisciplinary approach to address the range of cognitive, emotional, psychosocial, and behavioral factors that impact care. A further common method applied in the rehabilitation sciences employs behavioral observation and ratings of human performance in the real world or via physical mock-ups of functional environments. Activities of daily living within mock-up environments (i.e., kitchens, bathrooms, etc.) and workspaces (i.e., offices, factory settings, etc.) are typically built, within which persons with motor and/or neurocognitive impairments are observed while their performance is evaluated. Aside from the economic costs to physically build these environments and to provide human resources to conduct such evaluations, this approach is limited in the systematic control of real-world stimulus challenges and in its capacity to provide detailed performance data capture.

11.4.1 Virtual Environment–Based Rehabilitation Simulations

A perceived weakness is the limited ability to replicate the challenges that may occur outside a sterile office or hospital setting. With advances in technology, the possibility of simulating real-world situations while being able to control stimulus delivery and measurement is closer to fruition (Wilson, 2011, 2013). Virtual environment–based simulations include depictions of home settings, libraries, grocery stores, classrooms, and even combat environments. Virtual environments make use of symbols, stimuli, and concepts frequently experienced by the clinical population being assessed, and therefore consider the sociocultural milieu and not only injury or illness-related information (Imam & Jarus, 2014). Recording, measurement, and computational modeling of user behavioral responses while immersed in these simulations may help clinicians better understand and treat patient problems in their daily and complex routines (Wilson, 2011, 2013). Moreover, these ecologically valid virtual environments can be used for assessment (Parsey & Schmitter-Edgecombe, 2013) and rehabilitation (Koenig, Crucian, Dalrymple-Alford, & Dünser, 2009; Marusan, Kulistak, & Zara, 2006; Parsons et al., 2009a; Probosz et al, 2009).

Virtual environment–based assessments and rehabilitation programs have been explored in depth following brain injury. For example, virtual environments have been developed that assess way-finding skills and then provide training of spatial orientation skills via programming that allows increased complexity as participants progress though the program (Koenig, Crucian, Dalrymple-Alford, & Dünser, 2009). Virtual-reality research has been transitioning more recently to a focus upon clinical treatment of cognitive disorders (Imam & Jarus, 2014; Larson et al., 2014; Spreij, 2014). This includes innovative rehabilitation of stroke patients to reduce paresis and dyspraxias that impact expressive speech via multi-sensorial brain stimulation (Probosz et al., 2009). Various researchers have promoted the use of mental rotation paradigms – felt to be an essential skill in multiple cognitive functions – in the neurorehabilitation setting to enhance memory, reasoning, and problem-solving in everyday life (Marusan et al, 2006; Podzebenko, Ega, & Watson, 2005).

11.4.2 Brain–Computer Interfaces

In an attempt to widen the utility of computer assisted devices in rehabilitation, brain–computer interface (BCI) technology has generated a great deal of interest (Collinger et. al., 2013; Mak & Wolpaw, 2009; Shih et Al., 2012). From a rehabilitation psychology standpoint, BCI technology can be envisioned as a possible tool for cognitive assessment and intervention, pain management, stress management, and leisure activity exploration. BCI has been described as linking brain patterns to motor or mental intent in an effort to bypass the reliance upon peripheral nerves and muscles that may be compromised (Cincotti, 2008; Millian, 2010). To date, a primary focus of BCIs has revolved around motor-based activity and communication. Case examples and a few small studies have highlighted how BCI can be applied to neurorehabilitation populations such as stroke, amyotrophic lateral sclerosis, locked-in syndrome, and SCI (Enzinger et al., 2008; Kaufmann et al., 2013; Kiper et al., 2011; Salisbury et al., 2015; Schreuder et al., 2013). Still, much of the technology is not ready for mainstream implementation and the various challenges inherent with such interventions have been well detailed (see Danziger, 2014; Hill et al., 2014; Mak & Wolpaw, 2009; Millian et al., 2010; Shih et al., 2012).

The potential of BCI beyond motor and communication augmentation has received less attention, but is increasingly viewed as a fruitful area of application for assessment (Allanson & Fairclough, 2004; Nacke, Stellmach, & Lindley, 2011; Wu et al., 2010; Wu, Lance, & Parsons, 2013) and training (Berka et al., 2007; Parsons & Courtney, 2011; Parsons & Reinebold, 2012). This avenue of BCI research would be consistent with increasing support that psychological, social, and nonmotor-based factors are key aspects in perceived quality of life following injury (Tate, 2002). Studies have begun exploring the use of BCI in nonmedical populations to recognize emotions (Inventado et al., 2011; Jatupaiboon et al., 2013; McMahan, Parberry, & Parsons, 2015a, Pham & Tran, 2012), assess specific psychological symptoms (Dutta et al., 2013), mediate artistic expression (Fraga et al., 2013), and evaluate cognitive workload (Allison et al., 2010; Anderson et al., 2011; McMahan, Parberry, & Parsons, 2015b, 2015c; Treder & Blankertz, 2010).

Interest in BCI among individuals with SCI, particularly for augmentation of motor functioning, has been detailed in the literature (Collinger et al., 2013; Rupp, 2014; Tate, 2011). In a recent review of the use of BCI in persons with SCI, Rupp (2014) concluded that while BCIs seem to be a promising assistive technology for individuals with high SCI, systematic investigations are needed to obtain a realistic understanding of the feasibility of using BCIs in a clinical setting. Rupp identified three potentially limiting factors related to feasibility that should be considered: (1) availability of technology for signal acquisition and processing; (2) individual differences in user characteristics, and (3) infrastructure and healthcare-related constraints.

In summary, the potential for advanced technology appears far-reaching in the field of neuropsychological rehabilitation. Ultimately, more sophisticated programming may foster greater immersive experiences tailored to the patient's therapeutic goals. Thus, invaluable real-time clinician feedback could guide targeted therapeutic interventions that relate to daily situations. With repeat use, immersive training environments may capitalize on procedural memory that often remains relatively better preserved among patients with brain damage (Imam & Jarus, 2014; Larson et al., 2014; Spreij, 2014). Virtual environment paradigms could be systematically altered to meet changing patient care needs and goals based on the course of recovery. Furthermore, integration of patient-specific training prompts and cues may improve patient self-monitoring, guide problem-solving and promote less reliance on rehabilitation staff and caregivers (Christansen, Abreu, et al., 1996; Imam & Jarus, 2014; Larson et al., 2014; Spreij, 2014). The core challenges of bringing technology into a multidisciplinary rehabilitation milieu centers on initial cost, access to research laboratories with the technology, staff training, and establishing that such interventions have superior outcomes to traditional care.

11.5   Conclusions

While VR-based neuropsychological assessments are often referenced for their promise of enhanced ecological validity (Parsons, 2015), there are potential practical limitations that should be considered. Some VR-based assessments offer automated presentations that do not allow flexibility for clinical examiners to interrupt or "test the limits" during assessment. Future development of VEs should allow for flexible presentations, wherein clinicians may adjust graphics, stimuli, and task parameters via an interactive user interface (Parsons et al., 2015). Moreover, the dearth of established guidelines for the development, administration, and interpretation of these assessments could lead to important psychometric pitfalls. While these limitations are important to consider, advances in VR technology will allow for continued enhancements in approximations of real-world cognitive and affective processes.

A further concern for researchers wanting to incorporate virtual environments is that of psychometric validity. While a number of studies have attempted to establish the validity of these environments via comparisons with well-established paper-and-pencil as well as computer-automated platforms, results reveal the need for judicious use of these virtual platforms. Researchers must carefully judge the degree to which the virtual environments offer something beyond less expensive ones and modalities that are free from technological and cybersickness issues.

One challenge for this field of study is the lack of consensus on how to do trials. Although a review of VR interventions has revealed statistically large effects on a number of affective domains (Parsons & Rizzo, 2008a), findings must be interpreted with caution given that some VR studies do not include control groups, and many are not randomized clinical trials, limiting the confidence that the enhancements were caused by the VR intervention. A related issue is the need for establishing the psychometric properties of VR assessments and interventions. Prior to performing large-scale randomized clinical trials (RCTs) it will be important to look at validation studies using neurologically intact participants (Iriarte et al., 2012; Parsons & Carlew, 2016; Spooner & Pachana, 2006).

Following the establishment of psychometric properties of VR protocols, future work will be assisted by adopting procedures for standardized reporting of RCT outcomes. This is especially important in the context of new designs and relatively untested features of technology. A potential aide for future research can be found in the Consolidated Standards of Reporting Trials that ensure readers have the basic information necessary to evaluate the quality of a clinical trial.

With this in mind, there is a need, before we enter into VR RCTs, design, and intervention programs, to fully validate, understand users' perspectives, and ensure that ethical guidelines are established. This could be done in either lab-based or in situ settings; however, careful attention will need to be placed on developing protocols to ensure the voices of participants are always heard in any research endeavor involving VR technologies.

Investigations into these future research endeavors have potential to inform policy, theory, and praxes. Specifically, the addition of virtual-reality platforms to assessments and interventions offers an opportunity for advancing our understanding of the cognitive, affective, psychosocial, and neural aspects of persons as they take part in real-world activities.

PART IV

Applied Cyberpsychology

CHAPTER 12

Psychophysiological Computing in Cyberpsychology

12.1 Introduction

Human–computer interaction platforms typically involve a controlled cognitive process, wherein the user overtly interacts with the computer via peripheral devices (e.g., keyboard and mouse). For the brain-based cyberpsychologist this represents a limitation because we are interested in both controlled and automatic processes. As discussed in Chapter 1, controlled processes occur when brain network nodes are activated through the controlled attention of the person. Contrariwise, automatic processes occur without the necessity of conscious control or attention by the user. This dual-process perspective that human cognition may be made up of automatic and controlled processes is often overlooked in human–computer interaction. That said, there are straightforward approaches to executive control–based human–computer interaction using brain–computer interfaces (Allison et al., 2012; Tan & Nijholt, 2010). Furthermore, there are some novel approaches that include automatic processes that are done without volitional control. For example, psycho-physiological metrics offer indices of automatic and affective processing of information. Psychophysiological computing is a relatively new approach to human–computer interaction (HCI), in which system interaction is achieved by monitoring, analyzing, and responding to automatic (covert psychophysiological activity) and controlled (overt behavioral responses) cognitive processes from the user in real time (Allanson & Fairclough, 2004; Fairclough, 2014). Psychophysiological computing allows for the creation of a more empathic link between the computer and the user. As such, the computer has data about the user's cognitive and affective states and can adapt to better address the specific needs of the user (Fairclough, 2009). In the same way that human–human interaction is influenced by largely automatic (i.e., unconscious) processing of the other's behavior and arousal, psychophysiological and behavioral data from the user can provide the computer with knowledge to intelligently interact with the human user (Allanson, 2002).

In this chapter, psychophysiological assessment is presented as a way to enhance experimental control in virtual environments that are being used for cyberpsychology applications. Psychophysiological metrics provide an excellent measure of presence and autonomic arousal. Hence, they provide a profile of the user state and a validation of the impact of the virtual environment on the user. In Section 12.1, there will be a summary of subjective survey methods and objective psychophysiological metrics. A number of concerns with survey methods will be discussed. Further, quantitative measures will be presented as capable of enhancing cyberpsychological research. Next, in Section 12.2, there will be an introduction to psychophysiological computing and its potential for offering the next logical step in the evolution of the use of psychophysiological (affective) and neurocognitive profiling of users' responses while immersed in cyberpsychology simulations, videogames, and other human–computer interactions. Psychophysiological computing represents an innovative mode of HCI wherein system interaction is achieved by monitoring, analyzing, and responding to covert psychophysiological activity from the user in real time. In Section 12.3, adaptive environments will be presented with four interrelated objectives that are viewed as important for developing these adaptive environments. Next, in Section 12.4, an example is given of an adaptive environment that uses the principles of flow, presence, behavioral metrics (neuropsychological assessment), and psychophysiology to develop a novel application for adaptive applications. Finally, in conclusion, there will be a brief summary of the main ideas of this chapter. Adaptive virtual environments are presented as cyberpsychology applications that offer the potential for a broad empowerment process within the flow experience induced by a high sense of presence coupled with improved ecological validity

12.2 Subjective versus Objective Measures in Cyberpsychology

12.2.1 Subjective Survey Methods in Cyberpsychology

Assessment of the impact of a cyberpsychology application on the user is often difficult. Numerous studies exclusively employ subjective response questionnaires to draw conclusions about the user-state during virtual environment exposure (e.g., Carlin et al., 1997; Hodges et al., 1996; Renaud et al., 2002; Witmer & Singer, 1998). Self-report data, when used in isolation, are highly susceptible to influences outside the user's own targeted attitudes (Schwarz, 1999). The item's wording, context, and format are all factors that may affect self-report responses. Knowledge of the user-state during exposure to the computing environment is imperative for development and assessment of design in cyberpsychology. Individuals will invariably have different reactions to a given application/environment, and without an assessment tool that can be employed online, the cyberpsychology researcher will experience difficulties in identifying the causes of these differences, which may lead to a loss of experimental control of the research paradigm. A user may become increasingly frustrated with some aspect of the environment, but without proper measurement techniques to detect this frustration while it occurs, the user's sense of presence, or feeling of "being there," (Waterworth & Riva, 2014; see Chapter 8 in this book) may be diminished. While cyberpsychology platforms (e.g., social media, virtual environments, videogames) offer the capability of presenting a realistic simulation of the real world, online assessment of the user's reactions to that environment is vital to maintain an understanding of how the environment is affecting the user to preserve experimental control.

When one turns to brain processing in cyberpsychology, one finds another important limitation that is apparent for survey measures – certain affective responses are automatic neurocognitive processes. Unfortunately, self-reports miss this automatic processing because they are administered as questions and tap into controlled decision-making. According to dual-process models of automatic and controlled cognitive processing, controlled processes (e.g., performing a difficult calculus problem) are slow and accurate; and automatic processes (e.g., automatic response to a negative picture) reflect heuristics and biases that are fast and lower in accuracy (see Lieberman, 2007). Self-report measures require controlled (i.e., conscious) decision-making. This is a limitation because studies have revealed that self-report measures are uncertainly related to measures in which participants may or may not be unaware (in control) of the impact of their attitude and cognition. Such automatic responses are inherently difficult to self-report.

Another limitation of self-report measures is the temporal ordering of the questioning related to behaviors that were performed in the past. If a researcher wants to know risk perceptions as they occur (automatically and "in the moment"), then it is important to ask while the behavior is occurring instead of after the fact. Hence, a limitation of questionnaires is that they are given after the actual processing of the information occurred and represent post hoc appraisals of information that may have been processed automatically and unconsciously.

In addition to limitations, there are a number of biases that can result from survey methods. For example, "common methods bias" describes the variance that is attributable to artifacts of the survey instrumentation instead of the true variance between different constructs (Podsakoff, MacKenzie, Lee, & Podsakoff, 2003). Another example is "social desirability bias," which reflects the propensity of survey respondents to present themselves and their behaviors in a more socially acceptable manner (Paulhus, 1991). Subjectivity bias is another potential threat to the veracity of self-report study results. By subjectivity bias, psychometrists mean the difficulty of assessing the actual reality when asking participants for their subjective perceptions of reality (Theorell & Hasselhorn, 2005). Finally, there is the issue of demand bias, which relates to demand-induced behaviors when participants attempt to discern and intentionally confirm or disconfirm an experimenter's hypotheses (Orne & Whitehouse, 2000).

12.2.2   Objective Psychophysiological Metrics

Psychophysiological metrics provide a number of advantages over self-report for the enhancement of experimental control in cyberpsychology applications. The psychophysiological signal is continuously available, whereas behavioral or self-report data may be detached from the research environment (e.g., virtual environment, videogame) and presented intermittently (Allanson & Fairclough, 2004). Having continuously available signals is important for several reasons.

(1) It allows for greater understanding of how any stimulus in the cyberpsychology research environment impacted the user, not only those targeted to produce behavioral responses.

(2) It does not require a break in the user experience to ask the user about her experience of the simulated environment. A break in the user's sense of presence is not necessary, because the signal is measured continuously and noninvasively.

(3) It allows for assessment of times in which the user's sense of presence is broken. As Slater and colleagues (2003) report, it is even possible that psychophysiological measures can be used to uncover stimuli in the cyberpsychology environment that cause a break in presence.

(4) Assessment of automatic processes is possible with psychophysiological metrics. Psychophysiological responses can be made without the

user's conscious awareness, creating an objective measure of the user's state, which can include measures of cognitive workload (e.g., Berka et al., 2007; Brookings et al., 1996; Kobayashi et al., 2007), varying stress levels (Branco & Encarnacao, 2004; Fairclough & Venables, 2006), task engagement (Pope et al., 1995; Seery et al., 2009), and arousal (Bradley & Lang, 2000; Cuthbert et al., 1996; Cuthbert et al., 2000) among others.

(5) Multiple channels of psychophysiological data can be gleaned from various sensors continuously, which further increases experimental control by providing a combination of measures, so that one measure alone is not the sole basis for design decisions (Hancock & Szalma, 2003).

As can be seen, psychophysiological metrics offer a method for obtaining objective and ongoing (i.e., continuously available) measures of user-state through noninvasive and nonconscious (i.e., automatic processing) methods to improve experimental control. When psychophysiology is coupled with virtual and augmented reality scenarios, cyberpsychology researchers have tools for presenting simulated environments and for logging data. This may allow for the development of cogent and calculated response platforms that adapt to real-time changes in user emotion, neurocognition, and motivation processes.

12.2.3   Presence, Fidelity, and Immersion

The integration of simulation technology into neuroergonomic and psychophysiological research is advancing at a steady rate (see Parasuraman & Wilson, 2008). New discoveries and techniques call for increasingly advanced paradigms. A wide variety of simulations have been developed that range from simple low-fidelity task environments to complex high-fidelity full immersion simulators. All of these cyberpsychology applications rely on some type of representation of the real world. An important issue for research into simulation for cyberpsychology research is the determination of how advanced the simulator needs to be to adequately assess and/or train a particular individual or team. While high-end simulations can train a variety of user types, the cost associated with these devices can be difficult to justify (Langhan, 2008).

Although the determination of the level of scenario fidelity will be relative to the questions asked and the population studied, one significant factor for most investigations would be the extent to which the level of fidelity influences the user's experience of presence (Slater et al., 2009). In this chapter, "presence" is considered as the propensity of users to respond to virtually generated sensory data as if they were real (Sanchez-Vives & Slater, 2005). In the same way that people experience physiological responses to stimuli in the real world, researchers seek to quantify presence by measuring responses evoked by stimuli in an immersive virtual environment. A low-fidelity virtual environment may be preferable in studies where a maximal amount of control is desired because such environments may increase psychometric rigor through limiting the number of sensory variables available. Contrariwise, high-fidelity environments are preferable for studies desiring increased ecological validity because they recreate more of the real-world environment – better capture the subject's performance as it would occur in a real-world setting. It is important to note that the fidelity tradeoffs in the virtual environments may mimic the issues related to real-world assessments – psychological measures in controlled settings and behavioral ratings based upon naturalistic observations do not proffer consistently parallel findings. Further, dissimilar cognitive and affective components may be dissociated both by psychological measures in controlled settings and behavioral ratings based upon naturalistic observations (Gordon et al., 2006).

Discussions of the level of fidelity needed for a virtual environment should go beyond simple discussions of the "immersive" qualities of the environment to an understanding of the impact upon the perceived feeling of "presence" of the individual while immersed in the environment (Parsons et al., 2012; Slater, 2005). A number of discussions of the distinction between the terms "immersion" and "presence" can be found in the literature (Draper et al., 1998; Slater, 1999; Slater & Wilbur, 1997). This distinction is important because issues of fidelity tend to reflect levels of immersion, while levels of presence reflect the user's experience relative to the level of fidelity/immersion. The use of the term "immersion" herein reflects that which the overall virtual environment can deliver (e.g., the level of fidelity in representing the real world, the field of view, the number of sensory systems it simulates, the frame-rate, and latency). Hence, the level of immersion is an objective property of a virtual environment that in principle can be measured independently of the human experience that it engenders.

Presence can be viewed as the experience of being in an environment (e.g., virtual environment). While the vast majority of research on presence has represented the concept as a subjective state or feeling that is accessible and measurable by questionnaires (see Draper et al., 1998; Witmer &

Singer, 1998), a quite different view seems to be emerging, in which presence is treated as something rooted in activity (Sanchez-Vives & Slater, 2005). As such, researchers may study presence by looking at the psychophysiological responses of users to their surroundings and their ability to actively modify those surroundings (Flach & Holden, 1998; Meehan et al., 2002; Pugnetti et al., 2001). The recording of psychophysiological variables while participants operate within virtual environments has produced useful results in studies examining immersion and presence (Jerome & Jordan, 2007; Macedonio et al., 2007; Parsons et al., 2009b; Wiederhold & Rizzo, 2005). As such, the VR assets that allow for precise stimulus delivery within ecologically enhanced scenarios appear well matched for this research.

12.3 Psychophysiological Computing

Psychophysiological metrics make it possible for cyberpsychologists to develop symmetrical human-computer interactions, in which the computer system receives information about the user's controlled cognitive processing (e.g., overt inputs from the keyboard and mouse), as well as automatic processing (e.g., covert affective state of the user) of information. Using this overt and covert information, cyberpsychologists are able to develop adaptive systems that are capable of responding in real time to the cognitive, affective, and motivational information about the user. For example, adaptive systems can use psychophysiological feedback from the user to assess engagement and cognitive workload. Psychophysiological computing has been used to vary task difficulty to improve training scenarios (see Coyne et al., 2009, for review). Adaptive feedback can provide assistance to the user when attention is divided or cognitive overload occurs (Allanson & Fairclough, 2004; Byrne & Parasuraman, 1996; Middendorf et al., 2000). A common approach to automated feedback is found in brain–computer interfaces that rely primarily upon electroencephalographic user responses. Brain–computer interfaces have been employed to assist patients with motor disorders and provide a "mental prosthesis" (Donchin et al., 2000; Farwell & Donchin, 1988).

12.3.1 *Biocybernetic Loop between Human and Computer*

Psychophysiological computing adapts a computer system in real time based on the user's cognitive and affective states. A biocybernetic loop between the user and the computer system is a necessary component for an adaptive system (Fairclough, 2009). The formation of the biocybernetic loop requires that psychophysiological and behavioral data be gathered from the user using psychophysiological sensors (see Chapter 3 in this book), webcams, and eye tracking to record continuous signals and feed them into an interface. Next, the logged data are processed in real time to evaluate the user-specific cognitive and affective information (e.g., engaged, aroused). Algorithms designed to evaluate response patterns from the multiple data channels (e.g., skin conductance, heart rate, and respiration) are used to determine the user's cognitive and affective responding. Finally, command signals are sent to the computer system to allow adaptation of the presented environment (e.g., virtual environment, stimuli) to comport with the needs of the user. An example of this can be found in an action videogame, wherein a user's experiencing of an ambush results in large increases in arousal (e.g., stress response). The interface may be programmed to listen (e.g., using a message broker that translates signals from the user to a command module) for these psychophysiological signals and when the signals go above or below predefined thresholds there is a concomitant change in the intensity of the stimuli being presented to the user. The biocybernetic loop is completed when the user then responds to the changes that have been made in the environment and the process begins again (see Parsons & Reinebold, 2012).

The use of an adaptive system in a cyberpsychology application (e.g., virtual environment, videogame) allows for a psychophysiological computing system that can assess the user's automatic processing of information via psychophysiological data. This data can be used as a control signal (or an input to a control signal) without a requirement for any controlled cognitive response from the user. Findings from studies of motivations associated with approach/withdrawal behaviors have found that they are related to cognitive processing (Sutton & Davidson, 1997). Furthermore, studies have revealed relations between neurocognitive performance and affective style (Ackerman et al., 1995; Bell & Fox, 2003; Davidson, 1995; Schaie et al., 1991; Waggett & Lane, 1990). A psychophysiological computing addition to a virtual reality–based neuropsychological assessment would capture automatic (i.e., unconscious) facets of user state, which would open the bandwidth within the computer system by enabling an additional channel of communication from the user to the computer system. Such information exchange between a user and the computer system would be rendered symmetrical as the computer system develops, assesses, and responds to a dynamic representation of the user.

12.3.2   Affective Computing

Adaptive virtual environments are designed to adapt the virtual environment in a way that allows for optimal user experience. An adaptive virtual environment can utilize psychophysiological and behavioral measures to dynamically adjust the level of difficulty in the virtual environment so that it matches the user's ability level in real time. From an affective computing perspective this may include the alleviation of negative affective states (e.g., frustration during computer use). Within the field of affective computing (Picard, 1997) computers are developed to monitor the user's affective state and regulate undesirable states. As such the adaptive virtual environment reflects a biocybernetic loop designed for the personalization and optimization of user states.

Picard (1997) draws a parallel between psychophysiological responses and the ringing of a bell. If a bell were to represent a linear system, then a soft strike to the bell would cause a certain level of ringing, while a strike that is twice as forceful would cause exactly twice the level of ringing. However, if a bell is tapped too lightly, no sound will occur at all, and if it is struck too forcefully the bell may crack and not ring properly. Thus, the bell represents a non-linear system. A person's affective responses are similar, in that a given auditory stimulus may cause a skin conductance response, but playing that auditory stimulus twice as loud will probably not cause a skin conductance response that is exactly twice as large. If a system is time-invariant, it will respond the same way regardless of when the stimulus is presented. If the bell is rung with a given force at noon, it will respond at the same level of ringing at 1:00 if it is rung with the same force. That said, continuously ringing the bell without giving it time to stop ringing may result in an additive effect on the volume of the ring. The parallel can be found in humans. While, startling a person today may cause them to jump in the same way tomorrow if they are startled by the same stimulus, repeatedly startling the person will result in diminished response due to habituation. Affective response systems are thus non-linear, and are not time-invariant.

Picard describes two examples to explain how given inputs will result in varying outputs in human affective systems. First, a sygmoidal function curve is used to describe the output responses of an affective system. Stimulus intensity is mapped into an affective stimulus intensity by considering the nonlinearity when a subject perceives a stimulus. The model is a sigmoidal nonlinearity expressed by the equation:

$$y' = \frac{g}{1 + e^{-(x-x_0)/s}} + y_0,$$

where: x : is the input (i.e., the actual stimulus intensity to the subject). y' : is the affective stimulus intensity for the input x. It is the input to the Affective Systems Model. g : is a parameter determining the range of y'. x_0 : is a parameter to ensure that a tiny stimulus does not produce a noticeable effect. s: the steepness of the sigmoid, represents how fast y' changes with x. A smaller s gives a steeper sigmoid. y_0 : is a bias that moves the sigmoid up and down; it can be understood as the mood of the subject. A second model is used to show the decay of the response over time due to habituation. It is expressed mathematically by this equation: $y = y'e^{-bt}$, it describes the relationship between the physiological response y and the affective stimulus intensity y' over time. It is modeled by an exponential decay function, where the physiological response (e.g., heart rate), will decay over time depending on the stimulus intensity and a constant determining the speed of the response decay. Note that the above response decay model only considers the effect of one stimulus. If there is a sequence of stimuli, then the effects of stimuli before the current stimulus should also be taken into consideration.

Although Picard's models account for many of the properties of behavior in an emotion system (e.g., response decay, temperament and personality influences, nonlinearity, saturation, background mood, etc.), some modifications can be helpful for representation of the user and for adaptive control of the virtual environment. First, an increased consideration of all possible causes of saturation of a response system is desired. Although the sigmoidal nonlinearity considers the saturation when a single stimulus is very large, repeated large stimuli may still make the overall response curve increase without bound. Second, since affect tends to be time-variant, there are situations in which it may be desirable to have the capacity for adaptively updating the parameters of the models. The following revised models for affective signals and systems have been proposed to overcome these limitations.

Following Picard's model, Parsons and Courtney (2011) discussed an adaptation that converts an actual stimulus intensity to an affective response intensity, which is the input to their new "Affective Systems Model." Instead of considering each stimulus independently and then combining their corresponding response curves, as found in Picard's approach, they computed the affective response by incorporating the effects of all stimuli before and at the current time instant. Then, in the Affective Systems Model they no longer needed to combine the decaying response curves for previous stimuli. In this way they argued that they can handle more forms of saturation.

This new affective system model was proposed to enhance the description of the relationship between the physiological response and affective stimulus intensity. While Picard models this via an exponential decay function without delay, Parsons and Courtney prefer to incorporate the delay because physical systems need transition time. The response curves for different physiological signals (e.g., heart rate, EMG) may assume different shapes. They offer an intuitive method to identify, for example, the response curve for heart rate: they first generate some response curves starting from the relaxed state and then find a function to approximate these curves. The user is required to maintain a relaxed state before a response curve is generated to ensure that the response curve is not complicated by cumulative responses from previous stimuli. For example, if emotional pictures are used, then a long time interval may be needed before showing each new picture to the participant (i.e., user) so that the subject can "calm down," and return to a baseline level of responding. Once enough response curves are obtained, the cyberpsychologist can observe the obtained shapes and find a function to approximate them. Using emotional pictures with delays between them allows for an estimation of the range of responses that are typical of a given user. It is important to have an understanding of each individual's response patterns, as each user will respond somewhat differently to various stimuli. The range of responses determined by this baseline procedure would then be inputted into an algorithm that will allow for changes to the environment to be made based on the specific pattern of the individual's response systems.

Haarmann, Boucsein, and Schaefer (2009) carried out a procedure to establish response patterns of individuals before entering an adaptive flight simulator environment. The level of task difficulty imposed upon participants was relative to the participant's psychophysiological responses while performing the task. The participant's response range was established via a baseline scenario in which the plane would fly through a simulated environment with no turbulence. This baseline assessment was used to determine low response levels. Next the participants underwent a period of high turbulence to determine high levels of responding. From the responses generated, the researchers were able to assign response set points for each participant. If responses in the adaptive environment were to reach levels above the set point, the task would become more manageable, whereas, if response levels were to dip below the set point, the task would become more difficult.

12.4 Adaptive Virtual Environments

Advances in virtual environments (see Durlach and Mavor, 1994; Stanney, 2002) and psychophysiological models (Scerbo et al., 2001) have allowed cyberpsychology researchers to more adequately utilize adaptive environments. In these psychophysiological computing systems, the user's behavioral, biological, and/or psychophysiological information is collected. Additionally, information is collected about the situation in which the human is immersed and interacting with a virtual environment. The resulting information is processed in real time to draw reliable inferences about the then current state of the user's condition in order to dynamically alter and improve the nature of the information and control characteristics of the human–machine interface. These adaptive virtual environments can be used to construct an extensive communication channel between a participant and a virtual environment (e.g., Bennett et al., 2001; Scallen & Hancock, 2001). The development of adaptive interfaces is anchored on four interrelated objectives:

(1) Psychophysiological inference and the development of indices that represent the user's neurocognitive and psychophysiological profile through assessment of user affect (i.e., psychophysiological responses) and associated neurocognitive performance (i.e., performance on neuropsychological assessments).

(2) Development of signal processing algorithms for functional validation of psychophysiological indices.

(3) Translation of thresholds/signals into commands that may be instantiated in virtual environments.

(4) Validation of the enhanced adaptive virtual environment for neuropsychological assessment and training.

12.4.1 Psychophysiological Inference and Development of Neurocognitive and Psychophysiological Indices

An important concern for any biocybernetic system is that it accurately classifies the user state based upon the psychophysiological inference (Cacioppo & Tassinary, 1990). The interpretation of psychophysiological data using real-time analysis in an adaptive virtual environment paradigm is difficult because psychophysiological measures can be easily impacted by a range of confounds (e.g., movement). Furthermore, the biocybernetic system is unlikely to be operating with a perfect (one-to-one) representation of psychological state (see Chapter 3 for discussion). When a biocybernetic loop is instantiated to adapt the virtual environment there is no guarantee that the resulting change will be suitable and considered significant by the user.

One of the first issues is to ensure that the adaptive system processes psychophysiological data in terms of the individual differences of each user's neurocognitive and psychophysiological processing of environmental stimuli (e.g., virtual environment). The computer system's assessment of user behavioral and psychophysiological (or array of affective assessment measures) responses should provide an accurate representation of relevant neurocognitive and affective dimensions (e.g., mental effort, task engagement, arousal). That said, the linkage between neurocognitive performance in a virtual environment, assessments of affect, and physiological metrics may be contaminated by a response to other psychological elements (Picard, 1997, 2003). As a result, adaptation of the virtual environment may be hindered and cognitive, affective, and psychomotor learning may be frustrated. It is important to develop profiles that take into consideration the range of individual differences in various neurocognitive and affective reactivity parameters.

A number of examples of neurocognitive profiling models developed to address diverse neurocognitive function can be found in the literature: category learning (Berretty, Todd, & Martignon, 1999; Tenenbaum, 1999); stimulus representation (see, e.g., Shepard, 1980; Tversky, 1977); and memory (e.g., Anderson & Schooler, 1991; Laming, 1992). A typical neuroscience approach to assessment of neurocognitive functioning involves the administration of psychological tests to develop cognitive models that may be evaluated against data that have been averaged or aggregated across subjects. Individuals are typically modeled as invariants, not as individuals. An unfortunate result of averaging is that the resulting neurocognitive profile (i.e., model) assumes that there are no individual differences among users. As there are substantial individual differences in cognitive ability and affective responding in the general population, simply comparing a user's test performance with the relevant test norms (e.g., standardized test norms; see Lezak, 2004) alone will be of little value. A particular test score can represent an entirely average level of functioning for one individual and yet severe deficit for another. Therefore, it is necessary to compare current performance against an individualized comparison standard (Lezak, 2004). Hence, good neuropsychological tests are sensitive to a range of functioning, both at very low levels of cognitive functioning as well as in people with above-average cognitive abilities.

Extensive normative datasets are available for the widely used neuropsychological tests (Lezak, 2004; Mitrushina, 2005; Strauss et al., 2006). One method is to take three approaches to modeling the neurocognitive data for profiling of user abilities:

(1) stratified norms from validation studies
(2) regression-based norms
(3) model parameterization using stochastic approximation.

For the stratified normative sets, an individual test score is compared to the mean performance of a matched norm group in a current dataset, for example, people of comparable age and education level. Next, the raw score that a user obtains on a specific task is compared to a standard score that is corrected for factors such as age, education level, intelligence, and sex. This standard score can subsequently be interpreted using the normal distribution, which indicates the probability that a given performance is to occur in a normal population. For the regression-based norms, one can compute the individual's expected score based on a number of potentially confounding cohort variables (e.g., age, IQ, and gender) by means of a regression formula. The difference between the user's expected and actual score (the residue score) is then compared to a frequency table to determine the probability that this residue score is found in a normal population. Finally, we use parameterization, in which we attempt to accommodate individual differences assuming that each user behaves in accordance with a different parameterization of the same basic model, so the model is evaluated against the data from each subject separately (Ashby, Maddox, & Lee, 1994; Wixted & Ebbesen, 1997).

While common output device correlations are adequate for minimal understandings, they fall short of providing the representativeness and generalizability found in functionally defined psychophysiological indices. Following the work of Davidson (1998, 2000, 2003), the cyberpsychologist can develop psychophysiological profiles reflecting valence-specific features of emotional reactivity and affective responding. As such, specific parameters of neurocognitive and affective style can be objectively measured including:

(1) **Response threshold:** Individual differences are found in the response thresholds of users for eliciting components of arousal following a stimulus of a particular intensity. For example, high-threshold users may require a more intense stimulus to elicit the same response

as another user (with a less intense stimulus) with a lower threshold for responding.

(2) **Response magnitude:** Individual differences are found in the peak or amplitude of the response. For example, when presented with a series of graded stimuli that differ in intensity, the maximum amplitude (e.g., change in heart rate) is likely to differ systematically across users. Hence, some users will respond with a larger amplitude peak compared with others.

(3) **Rise time to response peak:** Signals from some users will rise rapidly in a particular response system, whereas others will rise more slowly. It may be the case that there is an association between the peak of the response and the rise time to the peak for some emotions (e.g., happiness versus anger).

(4) **Recovery time:** Following perturbation, some users recover quickly and others recover slowly. For example, following a fear-provoking stimulus, some users show a persisting heart rate elevation that might last for minutes, whereas other users show a comparable peak and rise time, but recover much more quickly.

The latter two are time-specific and have been described by Davidson as different aspects of affective chronometry. For the cyberpsychologist, this approach can be used to develop a psychophysiological interface through the collection of psychophysiological data from the user via psychophysiological assessment sensors and behavioral data. These data are then filtered and quantified to operationalize relevant psychological constructs (frustration, engagement). The psychophysiologically driven adaptive interface can be programmed to analyze these data to quantify the state of the user. Various possibilities can be considered for user state assessment with reference to absolute (e.g., heart rate exceeds 80 percent of baseline) or relative criteria (e.g., heart rate has risen 20 percent since the previous data collection epoch). Another approach is to have the assessment provided by a computer system be categorical in nature (Fairclough, 2009). For example, the pattern of heart rate activity and skin conductance level indicates that the user is in a negative emotional state.

12.4.2 *Signal Processing Algorithms*

Individual differences found in intensity of both tonic and phasic reactivity (in many autonomic response channels) are a potential problem for group comparisons. The aggregation of a participant's metrics is justified only if responses of a group of participants reveal similar distributions. Raw data needs to be transformed to ensure that responses of different participants will have approximately similar distributions (Parsons et al., 2009a, 2009b; Parsons & Courtney, 2011; Wu, Lance, & Parsons, 2013). Estimated range corrections have been suggested, but these estimates are limited by the requirement (in most cases) for longer rest periods than those needed for a real-time adaptive virtual environment (Ben-Shakhar, 1985). Signal processing often involves a constrained set of signal parameters developed for studies performed in highly controlled laboratory settings. The translation of psychophysiology procedures from "assessment" of persons' responses to an adaptive virtual environment presents the requirement of devising scoring protocols for situations to which the existing de facto standards may not be very suitable (Iyer et al., 2009). For example, in an experimental scenario where signal-to-noise ratio is a high priority, the designer can choose the highest filter width within the "plateau" region, thus representing a consensus of the requirements of traditional psychophysiology as well as engineering considerations. Furthermore, the sequence of values can be decomposed into components of different frequencies. This includes using various methods (e.g., Fast Fourier transform; FFT) to compute results quickly and efficiently (McMahan, Parberry, & Parsons, 2015a, 2015b; Parsons & Reinebold, 2012). Increased speed of processing with a FFT can be substantial, especially for long data sets. This process allows us to enhance the command signals from the psychophysiological interface to the virtual environment.

12.4.3   Thresholds/Signals into Commands

Given the need to move from a pure assessment approach in a low-fidelity environment to a high-fidelity virtual environment that has real-time adaptability, there is need for increased sophistication in data-scoring procedures – capable of dealing with a greater variety of metrics (Iyer et al., 2009; Wu & Parsons, 2012). A further issue is the need to program both negative and positive feedback controls. Control loops need to be developed in a manner that maximizes behavioral stability by reducing the discrepancy between the input signal (real-time psychophysiological measure of engagement) and a desired standard (the desired level of engagement). The misclassification of user arousal levels may evoke inappropriate changes in virtual environment.

In work by Thomas Parsons at the University of North Texas (and while at the University of Sothern California) virtual environment–based neurocognitive and psychophysiological feedback systems have been designed that are composed of three modules:

(1) **Profiling Module:** The Profiling Module is a system developed from multiple neurocognitive and psychophysiological assessment metrics from the user while immersed in the virtual environment. It has three functions: (1) extract and convert the analog psychophysiological signals into digital data; (2) assess neurocognitive functioning of the user while immersed in the virtual environment; and 3) transfer neurocognitive and psychophysiological data to the main controller.

(2) **Controller Module:** The second module is the Controller Module, which uses a message broker to listen for signals and then translates signals from the user to a command module. When the signals go above or below predefined thresholds there are "command" signals sent to the Command Module.

(3) **Command Module:** The "command" signal obtained from the main controller is fed to the third module, the Command Module, and becomes a parameter impacting the behaviors of the virtual environment. Values of the Command Module's "command" correspond to the changes in position, appearance, and size of objects in the virtual environment, the user's viewpoint of the virtual environment, and the instantiation or inhibition of immersive stimuli (e.g., scent machine, sounds, haptic feedback).

Finally, information, such as the timing of significant events in the virtual environment (e.g., presentation of stimuli), is then transferred from the virtual environment back to the psychophysiological interface program, and logged with the neurocognitive and psychophysical data.

12.4.4 *Interface Validation*

Validated measures are imperative for adequate establishment of neurocognitive and affective correlates of user experiences within virtual environments. Adequate validation involves a comparison of the inferred psychological states to a standardized reference measurement. The operationalization of an affective and/or neurocognitive process using a psychophysiological inference may not respond as anticipated by the user or the designer (Fairclough, 2009). Without validation, it is not possible to know how well the psychophysiological measure predicts a neurocognitive and/or outcome based upon another set of variables. As a result, both the assessment of the user and the resulting adaptations in the psychophysiological interface will be spurious.

Establishment of concurrent neuropsychological and psychophysiological validity represents a significant challenge for the development of psychophysiological computing. There are several possible routes by which the researcher can assess psychophysiological validity, which suffer from various flaws:

- Mood induction by media or standard task may be context-specific and may not generalize to other task contexts or different participant populations
- Specific techniques used to induce a particular individual's state may be incorrectly identified with generic user states.

The selection of robust neurocognitive and affective metrics for a psychophysiological computing system requires that these metrics have demonstrated a degree of validity. Hence, it is necessary that the results from the virtual environment be fully validated through tests of the quality of the psychophysiological inference. The accuracy of the psychophysiological inference can be calculated using the percentage of times that the psychological state inferred by the psychophysiological metrics was the same as the inferred state (Novak et al., 2012). For example, active brain-computer interface users have been found to expect and accept approximately 75 percent accuracy in recognition of desired movements (Ware et al., 2010). Confusion matrices are frequently used to describe accuracy through logging how often each psychological state is misclassified (Healey and Picard, 2005). Confidence values are also used at times in conjunction with accuracy (Picard et al., 2001). A final approach is to use estimation methods such as linear regression or fuzzy logic to output continuous values of a specific psychological dimension (Novak et al., 2012). While this is an intuitively helpful approach, it must be coupled with standardized validation metrics (e.g., norm-referenced findings from neuropsychology and psychophysiology).

12.5 Virtual-Reality for Cognitive Performance and Adaptive Training

In work by Thomas Parsons at the University of North Texas (and while at the University of Sothern California) adaptive virtual environments have been developed for assessment and training of neurocognitive and affective functioning (McMahan, Parberry, & Parsons, 2015a, 2015b; Parsons & Courtney, 2011; Parsons & Reinebold, 2012; Wu, Lance, & Parsons, 2013). An example adaptive virtual environment from Parsons's Computational Neuropsychology and Simulation (CNS) lab is a suite of interactive/adaptive virtual Iraqi/Afghani scenarios (virtual city, virtual checkpoint, virtual Humvee). Two primary goals define these virtual and adaptive environments: (1) a neuropsychological and psychophysiological assessment protocol that includes a battery of measures for assessment and development of a normative database; and (2) an adaptive environment, in which data gleaned from the assessment battery is used for refined analysis, management, and training of users.

While immersed in these adaptive environments, the user's neurocognitive and psychophysiological responses are recorded in an attempt to understand how the activation of particular brain areas is related to given tasks (Parsons, Courtney, & Dawson, 2013; Wu et al., 2010). Using this approach Parsons's lab aims to better uncover the relationship between the neural correlates of neurocognitive functioning in virtual environments for generalization to real-world functioning. Following the acquisition of this data, machine learning and artificial neural networks are used for nonlinear stochastic approximation and model-specific neurocognitive and affective processes of persons immersed in the virtual environments (Parsons, Rizzo, & Buckwalter, 2004; Wu et al., 2010; Wu & Parsons, 2011a, 2011b, 2012; Wu, Lance, & Parsons, 2013).

The virtual environments in Parsons's CNS lab make up a battery of neuropsychological measures to assess the ways in which the structure and function of the brain relate to specific psychological processes and overt behaviors: attention-vigilance (Parsons et al., 2007; Parsons et al., 2009a; Parsons & Rizzo, 2008c), effort, executive functioning (Parsons & Carlew, 2016; Parsons, Courtney, & Dawson, 2013; Parsons & Courtney, 2014; Parsons & Courtney, in press), navigation (Courtney et al., 2013; Parsons et al., 2013), visual-motor processing (Parsons et al., 2004a; Parsons et al., 2013), processing speed (Parsons, Rizzo, & Buckwalter, 2004), and memory (Parsons & Rizzo, 2008b). The virtual reality–based neuropsychological assessments used in the CNS lab are different from traditional paper-and-pencil neuropsychological tests in that they allow users to experience a greater "sense of presence" as they become immersed within the computer-created environment. Further, the virtual reality–based neuropsychological and psychophysiological assessments allow task stimuli and parameters (e.g., number, order, and speed) to be consistently manipulated and patient responses and behaviors to be closely monitored and automatically recorded. Hence, they allow the cyberpsychologist to measure complex sets of skills and behaviors that may relate closely to real-world, functional abilities. Again, this is different from standard instruments, in which components or isolated domains of cognitive function often are measured and clinicians combine data to predict real-world performance.

In Parsons's CNS lab they also make use of adaptive virtual environments that take the neurocognitive and psychophysiological profile information from the virtual reality–based neuropsychological assessments and use that information to drive adaptive virtual environments (McMahan, Parberry, & Parsons, 2015a, 2015b; Parsons & Courtney, 2011; Parsons & Reinebold, 2012). The goal is to have an adaptive virtual environment that develops neurocognitive and affective profiles from estimations of the user's cognitive abilities (e.g., from cognitive tasks embedded in a VR-based simulation of a Humvee) and affective state (from psychophysiological metrics) that may enhance existing training protocols. Such an adaptive virtual environment can adjust the presentation of both the difficulty (e.g., simple versus complex) and intensity (safe versus threatening) of stimuli delivered to the neurocognitive and physiological characteristics of each user.

Their approach follows findings from affective science research on affect that has shown that affect can be represented as points in a multidimensional space (Russell, 2003; Scherer, 2005). One of the most frequently used models of affective space consists of three dimensions (Lang et al., 1997):

- Valence: ranges from negative to positive
- Arousal: ranges from low to high
- Dominance: ranges from weak to strong

Among these dimensions, arousal is closely related to a user's performance on neuropsychological tasks. According to the well-known Yerkes-Dodson Law (1908), performance is a nonmonotonic function of arousal, as shown in Figure 12.1.

Performance increases with arousal when the arousal level is low, then reaches its peak at the optimal arousal level, and then decreases as arousal continues to increase. So, in an adaptive computing system that aims to improve the user's performance in mental tasks, such as learning and affective gaming, it is very important to be able to identify the user's optimal arousal level and to recognize whether or not the user's actual arousal level is close to that optimal level. For their work, Parsons and colleagues have made use of a neuropsychological assessment called the Virtual-Reality Stroop Task to find the user's optimal arousal level (Parsons et al., 2011; Parsons, Courtney, & Dawson, 2013). They chose the Stroop color interference task because it is among the most extensively

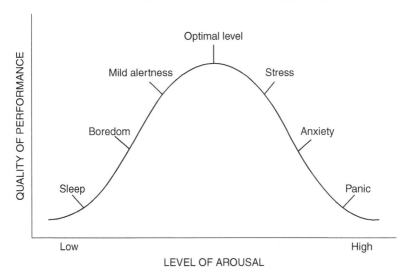

Figure 12.1 Yerkes-Dodson response curve (J.F. Hopstaken et al., *Psychophysiology*, 2014. Reprinted by permission of the publisher).

studied paradigms in neuropsychology and it has known relation to the anterior cingulate cortex (ACC). The Stroop color interference task produces a classic behavioral effect that consists of a lengthening in reaction time to color naming when the word meaning and the presentation do not match (i.e., they are "incongruent") relative to when they correspond (i.e., they are "congruent"). The ACC is known to be involved in a form of attention that serves to regulate both cognitive and emotional processing (Bush, Luu, & Posner, 2000). The ACC's involvement in the Stroop color interference task has been delineated by cognitive neuroimaging studies (Liotti et al., 2000; Pardo et al., 1990; Taylor et al., 1997). The extensive distributed network of activated regions suggests that the Stroop interference effect cannot be explained simply in terms of stimulus encoding or response interference. Further, the increased difficulty found in the Stroop interference task has been shown to directly evoke autonomic changes in cardiovascular arousal (Hoshikawa & Yamamoto, 1997).

In an initial study from Parsons's group, they aimed to: (1) assess whether or not it is possible to identify a user's optimal level of arousal using three stimuli presentations from Virtual-Reality Stroop Task based on user test performance; and (2) investigate the extent to which it is possible to accurately classify a user's arousal state into three levels, based on the user's physiological responses. Findings from the study suggested promise for the construction of the input signal and the affect recognition indices. The classifier can be used to indicate whether or not the user is near his/her optimal level of arousal. If not, one may also know whether it is excessively high or low. Results offer a platform for implementing the closed-loop adaptive computing system.

The VRST involves the subject being immersed into a virtual Humvee as it travels down the center of a road, during which Stroop stimuli appear on the windshield. The VRST stimuli are presented within both "safe" (low-threat) and "ambush" (high-threat) settings: start section, palm ambush, safe zone, city ambush, safe zone, and bridge ambush. Low-threat zones consist of little activity aside from driving down a desert road, while the more stressful high-threat zones include gunfire, explosions, and shouting, among other stressors.

The VRST assesses simple attention, gross reading speed, divided attentional abilities, and executive functioning. The task requires the subject to inhibit an overlearned response in favor of an unusual one. It takes advantage of the subject's ability to read words more quickly and automatically than s/he can name colors. If a word is displayed in a color different from the color it actually names (e.g., the word "red" is displayed with a blue colored font), the user would press the button corresponding with the word "red" more readily than s/he can respond with the color in which it is displayed, which in this case is "blue." The user must correctly respond to each Stroop stimulus immediately after it appears. In the "Color Naming" condition, the user must respond with the name of the color that appears on the screen. In the "Word Reading" condition, the user must respond with the word that appears on the screen. In the "Interference" condition, the user must press the button corresponding with the color of the word that appears on the screen, ignoring what the word says. Psychophysiological measures of skin conductance level (SCL), respiration (RSP), vertical electrooculography (VEOG), electrocardiographic activity (ECG), and electroencephalographic activity (EEG) are recorded continuously throughout exposure to the virtual environment.

While it is possible to train a generic model with group or normative data, in practice this tends to result in significantly lower performance than calibrating with individual data (Kerick et al., 2011). For the VRST, Parsons and colleagues initially used a support vector machine (SVM) to classify three task difficulty levels from neural and physiological signals while a user was immersed in a virtual reality–based Stroop task, which has been shown to have high individual differences in neural and physiological response as the task difficulty varies (Wu et al., 2010). Results revealed that when each user was considered separately, an average classification rate of 96.5 percent can be obtained by SVM; however, the average classification rate was much lower (36.9 percent, close to chance) when a user's perception of task difficulty level was predicted using only data from other subjects.

In a later study in Parsons's CNS lab (Wu, Lance, & Parsons, 2013) they used a collaborative filtering approach that combines training data from the individual user with additional training data from other, similar users. This approach is based on transfer learning (TL; Wu & Parsons, 2011a), active class selection (ACS; Wu & Parsons, 2011a), and a mean squared difference user-similarity heuristic (Wu & Parsons, 2012; Wu, Lance, & Parsons, 2013). The resulting adaptive system uses neural and physiological signals for automatic task difficulty recognition. Transfer learning improves the learning performance by combining a small number of user-specific training samples with a large number of auxiliary training samples from other similar users (Wu & Parsons, 2011a). Active class selection optimally selects the classes to generate user-specific training samples (Wu & Parsons, 2011b). Experimental results using both k-nearest neighbors and support vector machine classifiers demonstrate that the collaborative filtering approach can significantly reduce the number of user-specific training data samples. This collaborative filtering approach will also be generalizable to handling individual differences in many other applications that involve human neural or physiological data, such as affective computing.

Parsons and colleagues have taken the results from the virtual reality–based neuropsychological battery and the signal analysis results to develop adaptive virtual environments that can be explored by users under the supervision of a cyberpsychologist. These virtual adaptive assessment and training systems aim to place the user into a state of optimal experience defined as "flow" to trigger a broad recovery process (see Riva et al., 2004). According to Csikszentmihalyi (1990, 1994, 1997), "flow" is best understood as an optimal state of consciousness that is characterized by a state of concentration so focused that it results in complete immersion and absorption within an activity. Following the work of Fairclough (2009), Parsons partitions the "flow" state of the user into four quadrants or "zones" (see Figure 12.2).

Parsons's approach to cognitive assessment and training uses the assessment capabilities of the virtual reality–based cognitive assessments to place

Flow – Frustration vs. Boredom

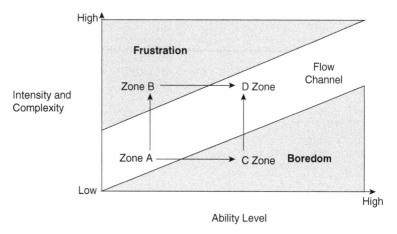

Figure 12.2 Flow model for understanding optimal states of consciousness (T.D. Parsons and C.G. Courtney, *Human Centered Design of E-Health Technologies*, 2011. Reprinted by permission of the publisher).

the user into the adaptive virtual environments at Zone A, which represents the optimal starting point (based upon individual differences assessments described above) for that user. It is important to note that they do not conceptualize the flow of training to be a static experience. A user's skill level tends to be low the first time s/he is immersed in the adaptive virtual environment.

As the user's experience of the adaptive virtual environment increases, his or her skills increase and he or she may become bored if the challenge remains constant (Zone C). Within the adaptive virtual environment, the challenge should increase, but usually at a different rate than the user's ability level. Hence, the user is constantly in a state of flux between the four points shown in Figure 12.2. At times, the user may begin to disengage (start to experience boredom and move toward Zone C) when the challenge does not increase in pace with his or her skills.

At other times, the user may move toward frustration (Zone B) when he or she is slow to learn the necessary skills. Particularly relevant to Csikszentimihalyi's concept of flow states is Zone B because it represents a "stretch" zone, in which the soldier is engaged and his or her ability levels are being increased as they are pushed toward frustration. Fairclough (2009) has explained that this state may be tolerated for short periods (e.g., a learning phase and/or a demanding but rewarding period of performance).

Overall, the goal of adaptive virtual environments is to keep the user in Zone D – continually adapting the intensity and difficulty of the environment to have the user in a flow state with improved skills and being able to function at a higher level of challenge. For the adaptive virtual environments in the CNS lab this conceptualization allows the adaptive virtual environment to make a distinction between two states of low performance, both of which require different categories of adaptive response. For example, when using the virtual-reality Stroop task, in Zone B, the intensity and complexity of the stimuli should be reduced until the user's ability level has been optimized. Further, if the user's results indicate that he or she is heading to Zone C, the virtual environment should adapt so that task demands be increased. This complex representation of the user provides the adaptive controller with greater specificity in order to target the adaptive response.

In summary, psychophysiological computing offers adaptive virtual environments that use the principles of flow, presence, neuropsychology, and psychophysiology to develop a novel application for training applications. This offers the potential for a broad empowerment process (see Riva et al., 2004) within the flow experience induced by a high sense of presence coupled with improved ecological validity.

12.6   Conclusion

A real-time adaptive virtual environment that is sensitive to cognitive and emotional aspects of user experience, as delineated in this chapter, is considered to be the future alternative for devising cognitive assessment and training measures that will have better ecological/predictive validity for real-world performance. In addition, the flexibility of stimulus delivery and response capture that are fundamental characteristics of such digital environments are viewed as a way for cyberpsychological researchers to more efficiently fashion protocols. Such flexibility would allow for this system to be viewed as an open platform on which a wide range of research questions could be addressed that would have significance to the cyberpsychology.

The development of adaptive virtual environment with neurocognitive and psychophysiological interfaces make possible psychophysiological computing systems that may facilitate substantive advances. First, there is need for the identification of the hierarchical or aggregational structure. Next, there is need for the establishment of the unidimensional facets (neurocognitive and psychophysiological domains of interest) and the determination of the content homogeneity of each of the interface's unidimensional facets. The establishment of psychometric properties (related to neurocognitive and psychophysiologial domains) removes the possibility that results reflect correlates of the target construct but are not prototypic of it. It is also important to assess the level to which all aspects of the target construct are under- or overrepresented in the psychophysiological interface's composition, and assess whether the experience of some aspects of the virtual environment introduce variance unrelated to the target construct. Following the development and validation of the psychophysiological interface, adaptive virtual environments can be used to investigate the impact of stimulus intensity, complexity, and stimulus modality (e.g., music tempo, audio presentation, olfaction) upon users within the adaptive virtual environment.

CHAPTER 13

Cyberpsychology of Videogames

13.1 Introduction

13.1.1 What Are Videogames?

Videogames are immersive activities that are rapidly increasing in popularity. Recent reporting from the Entertainment Software Association (2010) has revealed that 72 percent of the general population and 97 percent of teenagers (between the ages of 12 and 17) endorsed consistent playing of videogames. Further, video games have been found to be played more frequently and in more locations. Moreover, videogame play represents one of the most popular free-time activities, with 42 percent of Americans endorsing that they play at least three hours per week (Ipsos MediaCT, 2015). While reports reflect increases, it is important to note that the umbrella term of "videogame" encompasses a vast array of digital interactions. Research on "videogames" can refer to studies of activities ranging from basic matching of colored blocks on a smartphone to navigating with a group of players in a highly complex virtual environment (Apperley, 2006). As a result, cyberpsychology research tends to focus on exploration of particular game genres. For example, games may be grouped in terms of format, content, activities, and mechanics. One common distinction is between nonaction and action videogames.

13.1.2 Nonaction Videogames and Cognitive Processing

Early studies looked at the cognitive processing of gamers using first-generation arcade-type videogames and nonaction videogames (Clark, Lanphear, & Riddick, 1987; Dustman et al., 1992; Goldstein et al., 1997; Oei & Patterson, 2013; Okagaki & Frensch, 1994). For example, in an early study of gameplay and cognition, Goldstein and colleagues (1997) investigated the impact of repeated use of Super Tetris on the cognitive processing in older adults. They compared older adults who played Super Tetris for 25 hours to nongamers. They found that the older adults who played Super Tetris had improved (compared to nongamers) performance of the Sternberg reaction time task. However, these results were limited in that there was no difference on the Stroop Color Word Test (a measure of inhibition of overlearned responses). Typically, results from these studies with nonaction videogames reveal enhanced performance on reaction time tests, but not on tests of executive-control (e.g., Stroop, Trails-B).

13.1.3   *Action Videogames and Cognitive Processing*

In contrast to early studies, the vast majority of studies in the literature now focus upon action videogames. Green and Bavelier (2006a) have defined action videogames as "those that have fast motion, require vigilant monitoring of the visual periphery, and often require the simultaneous tracking of multiple targets." Action videogames include multifaceted three dimensional settings, rapidly moving and/or highly transitory targets, robust peripheral processing demands, and the requirement that the user make decisions while regularly switching between highly focused and highly distributed attention (Green & Bavelier, 2015). Furthermore, a number of studies tend to define videogame players as those players who spend a minimum of five to seven hours per week playing videogames (Green & Bavelier, 2003, 2007). It is important to note that these somewhat arbitrary criteria have recently been critiqued. Sobczyk and colleagues (2015) have argued that while arbitrary criteria may have been acceptable in early research, progress in videogame research will require enhanced research designs for increasing understanding of the mechanisms of cognitive performance improvements.

13.2   Videogame Play and Cognitive Abilities

A growing body of literature has emerged that focuses upon assessment of action videogame player cognition (Cain, Landau, & Shimamura, 2012; Colzato et al., 2010; Irons, Remington, & McLean, 2011; Karle, Watter, & Shedden, 2010). The relationship between playing action videogames and enhanced cognitive and visual-perceptual abilities is well documented. Visuospatial and perceptual enhancements have been reported in multiple areas: peripheral vision (Feng & Spence, 2007; Green & Bavelier, 2003, 2006a), contrast sensitivity (Li, Polat, Makous, & Bavelier, 2009), resistance to crowding effect (Green & Bavelier, 2007), and shorter periods of backward masking (Li, Polat, Scalzo, & Bavelier, 2010). These action videogames have in fact been found to enhance vision. A recent study from Daphne Bavelier's Lab at the University of Rochester used the contrast sensitivity function (CSF) to assess the impact of action video-game playing on vision. The CSF is routinely assessed in clinical settings with the goal of evaluating vision. Furthermore, it is an index of improvement following correction of the optics of the eye with surgery, contact lenses, or eyeglasses. Daphne and colleagues found that the very act of playing action videogames enhanced contrast sensitivity and provided a complementary route to eyesight improvement. The following improvements were noted:

(1) **Contrast sensitivity**: how well a participant can distinguish among different levels of gray;
(2) **Crowding acuity**: capacity for resolving small details in the context of clutter (e.g., participant reads text of a diminutive font and all the letters appear as being jumbled together);
(3) **Visual masking**: capacity for recognizing briefly presented visual stimuli.

In addition to visuospatial processing, regular play of action videogames has been shown to be related to enhanced cognitive abilities such as increased ability to attend simultaneously to multiple stimuli (Cohen, Green, & Bavelier, 2008; Green & Bavelier, 2003, 2004, 2006b) and reduced attentional blink effects (Green & Bavelier, 2003). It is apparent that ever since the seminal work by Green and Bavelier (2003) there has been converging evidence suggesting that playing action videogames (e.g., first-person shooter games like Call of Duty and Halo; and third-person shooter games like Gears of War and Grand Theft Auto) is associated with better performance in a wide range of areas (see Table 13.1).

Moreover, notable enhancements have been observed in performance on measures of executive-control such as working memory, inhibition, task switching, and reduced attentional capture (Boot et al., 2008; Cain, Landau, & Shimamura, 2012; Chisholm, Hickey, Theeuwes, & Kingstone, 2010; Chisholm & Kingstone, 2012; Colzato et al., 2010; Green et al., 2012). Given the important role of executive-control activities of daily living, there is abundant interest in developing proficient methods for improving executive functioning. Action videogame training appears to have promise for enhancing executive processing (Green & Bavelier, 2015). Recent studies have supported the notion of beneficial effects in action videogame players and generalizations to executive-control. For example,

Table 13.1 *Superior neurocognitive processing in action videogamers: Examples*

Domain	Cognitive Process	Studies
Visual processing	Perception	Boot et al., 2011; Donohue et al., 2010; Green, Pouget, & Bavelier, 2010; Green, Li, & Bavelier, 2010
	Visual sensitivity	Appelbaum et al., 2013; Li, Polat, Makous, & Bavelier, 2009
	Basic perimetry	Buckley, Codina, Bhardwaj, & Pascalis, 2010
	Visuospatial	Green & Bavelier, 2003, 2006a, 2007; Spence et al., 2009; Spence & Feng, 2010
	Perceptual-motor	Chen, Chen, & Li, 2015; Feng & Spence, 2007; Hubert-Wallander, Green, Sugarman, & Bavelier, 2011
Attention	Attentional skills	Chisholm et al., 2010, 2012; Dye, Green, & Bavelier, 2009; Green & Bavelier, 2003; Hubert-Wallander, Green, Sugarman, & Bavelier, 2011; West, Stevens, Pun, & Pratt, 2008
	Visuospatial attention	Green & Bavelier, 2003, 2006a; Greenfield et al., 1994
	Central and peripheral visuospatial attention	Green & Bavelier, 2007
	Number of objects that can be attended	Green & Bavelier, 2006b
	Temporal order processing	Donohue, Woldorff, & Mitroff, 2010
Executive functioning	Task switching	Andrews & Murphy, 2006; Boot et al., 2008; Cain, Landau, & Shimamura, 2012; Colzato et al., 2010, 2014; Green et al., 2012; Karle,

	Cognitive flexibility	Watter, & Shedden, 2010; Nelson & Strachan, 2009; Strobach, Frensch, & Schubert, 2012; Colzato et al., 2010
	Working memory representations	Baniqued et al., 2013; Colzato et al., 2013; Nouchi et al., 2012, 2013;
	Overcome attention capture	Chisholm et al., 2010; Chisholm & Kingstone, 2012
	Cognitive control	Colzato et al., 2013
	Track multiple moving objects	Dye & Bavelier, 2010; Green & Bavelier, 2006b; Trick et al., 2005; Sungur & Boduroglu, 2012
	Mental rotation of complex shapes	Feng, Spence, & Pratt, 2007
	Concurrent performance of multiple tasks	Chiappe et al., 2013; Strobach, Frensch, & Schubert, 2012
	Task selection	Castel, Pratt, & Drummond, 2005; Dye & Bavelier, 2010; Green & Bavelier, 2003, 2006a, 2007; Hutchinson & Stocks, 2013; Li et al., 2010; Pohl et al., 2014; Spence & Pratt, 2007; Wu & Spence, 2013, 75:673–686
Learning and memory	Sensorimotor learning	Gozli, Bavelier, & Pratt, 2014
	Recall of visually presented information	Blacker & Curby, 2013; Sungur & Boduroglu, 2012
Reaction time	Perceptual reaction time	de Kloet et al., 2012; Dye, Green, & Bavelier, 2009; Maillot, Perrot, & Hartley, 2012; Nouchi et al., 2012, 2013; Rivero et al., 2013

research comparing action videogame players to non-players have shown that action videogame players are better at switching between tasks (Green et al., 2012) and have increased cognitive flexibility (Colzato et al., 2010). Furthermore, action videogame players outperform nongamers on tasks that involve monitoring and updating of working memory (WM) representations (Colzato et al., 2013). It is interesting to note, however, that inhibitory control (i.e., an index of impulsivity) does not appear to be related to action videogame play. In fact, while Colzato and colleagues (2013) found enhanced working memory, the same was not true for their ability to stop an ongoing response, as indexed by stop-signal reaction times.

13.3 Neuroanatomy of the Videogamer

13.3.1 Structural Neuroimaging of Gamers' Brains

Several structural neuroimaging studies have found that videogame play can alter gray matter volume. The neural correlates underpinning the enhanced cognitive processing favoring videogamers are not well-understood. Results from cross-sectional studies have revealed that videogame players who play large amounts of videogames and professional gamers exhibit increased frontocortical thickness and regional gray matter volume in the dorsolateral prefrontal cortex and frontal eye field (Han, Lyoo, & Renshaw, 2012; Hyun et al., 2013; Kühn et al., 2014). Studies of expert action videogame players reveal heightened functional connectivity and grey matter volume in insular subregions compared to novices (Gong, 2015). Experts in action videogames have also been found to have greater ability for early filtering of extraneous information and selective attention than amateurs, as assessed by neural activities in frontoparietal areas (Bavelier et al., 2012). Moreover, action videogame experience has been found to be related to gray matter volume in brain areas responsible for attention and working memory: dorsal striatum (Erickson et al., 2010); right posterior parietal area (Tanaka et al., 2013); entorhinal area; hippocampal gyrus; occipital lobe (Kühn & Gallinat, 2014); and dorsolateral prefrontal cortex (Kühn et al., 2014).

Findings from structural neuroimaging studies have revealed that regional differences in brain volume are related to learning in tasks that require the use of perceptual, neurocognitive, and motor processes. In a study using voxel-based morphometry, Basak and colleagues (2011) found brain volume differences that were related to skill acquisition in complex tasks, such as the strategy-based videogame Rise of Nations. The study included 20 participants who took part in 15 one-and-a-half-hour sessions over four to five weeks, resulting in a total training time of 23.5 hours. Results revealed that variance in gray matter volume of numerous brain areas (medial prefrontal cortex, cerebellum, somatosensory area, right ventral anterior cingulate cortex, and the dorsolateral prefrontal cortex) predicted variability in learning of the game.

13.3.2 *Functional Neuroimaging of Gamers' Brains*

In addition to structural assessment of videogame players' brains, there is a growing body of literature assessing functional imaging of video-game play. In a pioneering neuroimaging study, Haier and colleagues (1992) placed eight participants in a positron emission tomography scanner and assessed functional processes as participants played the nonaction videogame Tetris. Participants were assessed both pre- and post-daily practice of Tetris (for 4–8 weeks). Furthermore, 16 participants from a control group were scanned while passively viewing visual stimuli. For the participants who underwent the videogame training, findings revealed a significant decrease in whole brain glucose metabolism. The level of improvement shown by participants in Tetris revealed inverse correlation with glucose metabolism levels. According to Haier and colleagues, the decrease in glucose metabolism may reflect increased efficiency in neural circuitry utilization resulting from learning and task mastery.

To compare the impact of nonviolent and violent videogame playing on the human brain, Chou and colleagues (2013) used single photon emission computed tomography (SPECT) to measure cerebral blood flow changes caused by videogame play in 30 healthy young adult volunteers. Each participant underwent three sessions of SPECT with a bolus injection of 20 mCi 99mTc ECD IV to measure their cerebral blood flow. The first measurement was performed at baseline, and the second and third mea-surements were performed after playing two different videogames for 30 minutes. The two different videogames were a nonviolent game (i.e., Super Mario 64) and a violent videogame (i.e., Dynasty Warriors 5). Results revealed that cerebral blood flow was significantly decreased in the pre-frontal cortex and significantly increased in the temporal and occipital cortices after playing each videogame. Findings also revealed decreased cerebral blood flow in the anterior cingulate cortex that was significantly correlated with the number of killed characters after playing the violent game (i.e., Dynasty Warriors 5). The finding of hypo-perfusion in pre-frontal regions following videogame play is consistent with a previous study by Matsuda and Hiraki (2006) that detected significant and sustained decreases in oxygenated hemoglobin in the dorsal prefrontal cortex with videogame play. The finding of decreased cerebral blood flow in the anterior cingulate cortex after playing a violent videogame (i.e., Dynasty Warriors 5) affords support for the role of the anterior cingulate cortex in regulating violent behavior.

In a comparison of videogame players and non-players, Granek et al. (2010) employed event-related fMRI to explore the effects of videogame expertise on cortical activations during the preparation of visually guided movements. While in the scanner, participants were required to complete visuomotor tasks, in which participants used a joystick to navigate a cursor control toward, or away from, a fixated target. The comparison of avid videogame players and non-players revealed a dissociation in activation weightings in a network of prefrontal, premotor, sensorimotor, and parietal regions. Videogame players displayed greater prefrontal activation. For the non-players, results revealed greater parietal activation. According to the authors, these differences may be due to the familiarity of videogame players and nongamers with novel visuomotor tasks. Further, it may not be as necessary for videogamers to attend as closely to the outcomes of their motor acts because they are able to generalize visuomotor response patterns that were developed through prolonged videogame play experiences. Contrariwise, it may be the case that nongamers find it necessary to attend more closely to the outcomes of their actions because they did not develop the appropriate response patterns.

The frontal and parietal lobes form a network that is involved in the selection of sensory contents by attention. This frontoparietal cortex has long been implicated as a source of attentional control. In a neuroimaging study of the frontoparietal attentional network and the middle temporal sulcus (a motion-sensitive area) Bavelier and colleagues (2012) compared skilled videogame players' performances with those of non-players on a visual search task with distractors. In the experiment, the participants were instructed to indicate whether a diamond or square was present in a ring of shapes surrounding the central fixation cross. This task was performed under either a low or high stimulus load and was accompanied by distractors. For the distractor component, a static or moving patch of dots was presented centrally or peripherally to either side of fixation. Results from the non-players' performance revealed a significant increase in activation of the frontoparietal attentional network in response to increased visual search load. This was not the case for the skilled videogame players.

While moving distracters (i.e., irrelevant moving dots) resulted in less activation in the middle temporal sulcus of skilled videogame players, this activation was not apparent for responses to attended motion stimuli. According to Bavelier and colleagues, the reduced utilization of frontoparietal attentional network in skilled videogame players may reflect lower use of attentional resources with higher task burdens.

The findings of Bavelier and colleagues (2012) are consistent with previous research by Mishra and colleagues (2011) that suggests skilled videogame players are better at suppressing, or disregarding, irrelevant stimuli. In the study by Mishra and colleagues (2011) there was a comparison of skilled videogame players and non-players on a selective attention task. The study used 62-channel EEG to evaluate cognitive processing as participants responded to instances of a numeral presentation in one cued letter set, while ignoring those presented in distractor sets. Specifically, they aimed to investigate a frequency-tagged neural response to periodic stimuli called the steady state visual evoked potential. Larger steady state visual evoked potentials are evoked when attention is directed at the periodic stimuli. Although results did not reveal significant group differences in the steady state visual evoked potential amplitude for attended stimuli, expert videogame players did show significantly reduced steady state visual evoked potential amplitudes for unattended stimuli. These results may suggest that enhanced attentional performance in skilled videogame players may be due to their greater capacity for filtering (i.e., ignoring) irrelevant stimuli.

13.3.3   *Large-Scale Brain Networks and Action Videogame Experience*

Research of resting-state functional connectivity reveals a salience network (anterior cingulate cortex; and anterior insula) that supports the detection of salient events; and an executive-control network (dorsolateral prefrontal cortex; and posterior parietal cortex) that supports attentional control and working memory. The salience network receives and delivers selective amplification of salient information to generate a top-down control signal that prompts the executive-control network to respond to salient information, attentional shift, and control processing (Menon & Uddin, 2010). Some have suggested that cognitive training may result in functional plasticity in the salience system and integration of the executive-control and salience networks (Lou et al., 2014). Furthermore, this integration between brain networks may reflect the neural correlates of cognitive control (Cocchi et al., 2013). Given these findings and those outlined above, action videogame experience may offer a venue to explore the interaction of the salience and executive-control networks.

In one study, Parsons and colleagues (2013) used graphic assets from Virtual Battlespace 2 (graphics assets are also found in the action videogame Arma 2) to develop a virtual-reality Stroop task, wherein Stroop stimuli are presented on the windshield of a virtual high-mobility multipurpose wheeled vehicle (HMMWV) in safe and ambush scenarios. The virtual-reality Stroop task assesses automatic processing and exogenous attention by presenting stimuli consistently in a fixed central location in the simple interference condition. The task also assesses controlled processing and endogenous attention during the complex interference condition by presenting stimuli at random positions throughout the computer screen. Hence, the adjustments to stimulus complexity on the VRST can be used to assess attention at both exogenous (automatic processing) and endogenous (controlled processing) levels. The VRST was designed to be a measure of supervisory attentional processing (executive-control) in a simulation environment with military-relevant stimuli (salience) in high- and low-threat settings. Psychophysiological responses were recorded throughout each participant's period of immersion within the virtual-reality Stroop task. Electrocardiogram (ECG), electrodermal activity (EDA), and respiration were recorded as participants rode in the simulated HMMWV through alternating zones of low threat and high threat. ECG, EDA, and respiration were recorded simultaneously throughout exposure to the VRST task.

Parsons and colleagues were interested in assessing both automatic and controlled processing, as well as salience processing. Whilst the executive network is frequently coactivated with the salience network in tasks of attention, working memory, and response selection (Kerns et al., 2004; Ridderinkhof, Ullsperger, Crone, & Nieuwenhuis, 2004), the salience network also activates in response to threats (Craig, 2002). Increased arousal may impact the processing of salient information and enhance the contrast between stimuli with different levels of salience (Critchley, 2005). This issue of intensity and attentional effort may be described as a top-down supervisory attentional network, in which threats to attention result in recruitment and integration of performance monitoring (prefrontal–anterior cingulate) and motivational (mesolimbic) systems (Sarter, Gehring, & Kozak, 2006). Further, the involvement of the anterior cingulate cortex in the Stroop color interference task has been delineated (Liotti, Woldorff, Perez, & Mayberg, 2000; Pardo, Pardo, Janer, & Raichle, 1990).

Analyses of the effect of threat level on the automatic (e.g., congruent color–word Stroop) and controlled (e.g., incongruent interference Stroop) scores for both simple and complex interference resulted in a main effect of threat level and condition. A significant interaction resulted from a significant difference in performance only during the complex interference condition, such that the high-threat zones resulted in poorer performance than the low-threat zones. These findings reflect the perspective that high-information-load tasks may be relatively automatic in controlled circumstances – for example, in low-threat zones with little activity. However, the total available processing capacities may be decreased by other factors such as arousal (e.g., threat zones with a great deal of activity). Maintenance of attention can be under voluntary control but not attentional intensity (Kahneman & Treisman, 1984). Further, these findings appear to reflect Seeley et al.'s (2007) differentiation of "executive-control" and "salience" networks. For the virtual-reality Stroop task, the executive network may be activated during low-threat conditions (Kerns et al., 2004; Ridderinkhof et al., 2004), and the salience network may activate in response to threats found in the high-threat zones (Craig, 2002).

In a neuroimaging study, Gong and colleagues (2016) used functional magnetic resonance imaging to examine the relation between action videogame experience and the integration of salience and executive-control networks. They compared action videogame experts (had at least four years of action videogame experience) to amateurs (had less than one year of action videogame experience). They set out to perform a systematic investigation of the proposition that action videogame experience is related to the integration between the salience network and the executive-control network. They analyzed the resting-state brain functions of action videogame experts and amateurs using graph theoretical analyses and assessment of functional connectivity. In general, the results revealed enhanced intra- and inter-network functional integrations in action videogame experts compared to the amateurs. Specific results from graph-theoretical analyses examining the combined salience and executive-control networks revealed significantly enhanced global characteristics in action videogame experts compared to amateurs, including global efficiency, mean clustering coefficient, and connections cost. Results from nodal (local) characteristics (clustering coefficient, degree, and efficiency) revealed increased nodal characteristics in the action videogame experts, suggesting that they have an enhanced information processing ability in local regions of executive-control and salience networks. Taken together, these findings offer preliminary support for a possible relation between action videogame experience and neural network plasticity.

13.3.4   Videogaming and the Reward System

Videogame play has been found to result in substantial dopamine release in the dopaminergic system (Koepp et al., 1998) as well as addiction (Weinstein, 2010). Results from neuroimaging studies have revealed that videogame play activates the brain's motivational systems. In an early positron emission tomography study, Koepp and colleagues (1998) found large releases of striatal dopamine in participants playing an action videogame (note that Egerton et al., 2009, point to the need for further replication). Furthermore, Hoeft and colleagues (2008) used functional magnetic resonance imaging of participants as they performed a simple computer game. Results revealed brain activation in regions typically associated with reward and addiction: nucleus accumbens and orbitofrontal cortex. The orbitofrontal cortex is involved in the coding of stimulus reward value, and along with the ventral striatum (i.e., nucleus accumbens), is implicated in representing predicted future reward (see Chapter 2 of this book). Ventral striatal reward-related activation in videogames has been found when the player's rewards (winning) were coupled to the observed rewards of another player (Kätsyri et al., 2013a).

Kätsyri and colleagues (2013b) investigated brain correlates of defeating an opponent in a competitive videogame. In the study, participants' brain activity was measured using functional magnetic resonance imaging while they played a competitive tank shooter game against alleged computer and human opponents. Brain responses to wins and losses were contrasted by fitting an event-related model to the hemodynamic data. They found that winning activated the brain's reward circuit and the ventromedial prefrontal cortex differently depending on the type of opponent. More robust activations occurred during wins in dorsal and ventral striatum areas as well as in the ventromedial prefrontal cortex. For the dorsal aspect of the striatum and the ventromedial prefrontal cortex more robust responses for winning were found when the participant was playing against a human rather than a computer. For the ventral striatum activations were associated with the participant's self-ratings of pleasure. While winning and the ventral striatum had significant functional coupling with right insula, coupling was weaker with dorsal striatum, sensorimotor pre- and postcentral gyri, and visual association cortices.

13.4 Dark Side of Videogaming

A host of warnings and concerns can be found in popular media about the potential negative impacts of videogame play. While the concerns circulating in the popular media offer interesting headlines, not all stand up to research scrutiny. As can be seen earlier in this chapter, a number of studies have found enhanced cognitive processing in videogamers. There has also been interest in the therapeutic and rehabilitative potential of videogames for a variety of nervous system disorders (Charlier et al., 2016; Horne-Moyer et al., 2014). That said, a number of cyberpsychology researchers have investigated the negative impact of videogames. Findings have revealed negative impacts for addiction (Kuss, 2013); the influence of violent content (Brockmyer, 2015; Gentile & Stone, 2005); and the impact of sexist content (Fox & Tang, 2014). Part of the inconsistency in the research literature is due to the type of videogame used in the studies. Violent videogames have been implicated in sleep disruption (Lam, 2014) and decreased response to negative stimuli (Montag et al., 2012). Furthermore, the violent content found in some videogame narratives has prompted concern that videogamers may imitate videogame scenarios in real life. These concerns have found support in the literature. Findings have revealed a relation between videogame play by adolescents and an increased proclivity toward carrying weapons to school (Ybarra et al., 2014). Research has also shown that videogamers are more likely to engage in risky driving behaviors after playing street-racing games (Vingilis et al., 2013).

Functional neuroimaging studies have been used to investigate the ways in which exposure to violent videogames may affect the functioning of specific neural structures. In one functional magnetic resonance imaging study, Weber and colleagues (2006) assessed the brain activity of 13 adult males as they played a violent videogame called Tactical Ops: Assault on Terror. They found reduced neural activity in the anterior cingulate cortex and the amygdala when participants performed aggressive acts in the game. Involvement in videogame-based violent activities also resulted in decreased activity in the rostral anterior cingulate cortex and increased activity in the dorsal anterior cingulate cortex. These findings suggest suppression of affective information processing. It is important to note this was a study only of acute effects. That said, repeated suppression of affective information processing could ultimately lead to desensitization to violence.

In a study aimed at investigating the possible link between long-term violent videogaming and altered emotional processing, Montag and colleagues (2012) used functional magnetic resonance imaging to measure the responses of adult males who played first-person shooters regularly to pictures from four categories: pleasant, unpleasant, neutral content, and pictures from the first-person-shooter videogame Counterstrike. The study included a control group who had never played such games. Results from image viewing revealed significantly higher activations of the left lateral frontal cortex in the control group than in the gamers. According to Montag and colleagues, this suggests that the videogamers had habituated to such stimuli as a result of frequent exposure to violent images during violent videogame play. Moreover, it was suggested that the lowered activity in the lateral prefrontal cortex may be interpreted as a decrease in empathy. However, these results have not been replicated. In fact, an earlier study using a similar design by Regenbogen and colleagues (2010) did not identify a difference in neural response related to violent videogame exposure. In the study, they used functional magnetic resonance imaging to evaluate a group of young males with (videogamers) and without (nongamers; controls) a history of long-term violent videogame experience. The stimuli included presentation of computer game and realistic video sequences. In videogamers the processing of violent content (in contrast to nonviolent) activated clusters in right inferior frontal, left lingual, and superior temporal brain regions. Virtual violent content activated a network comprising bilateral inferior frontal, occipital, postcentral, right middle temporal, and left fusiform regions. Results from the nongamers (i.e., control participants) revealed extended left frontal, insula, and superior frontal activations during the processing of real, and posterior activations during the processing of virtual, violent scenarios. The authors suggest that the ability to differentiate automatically between real and virtual violence has not been diminished by a long-term history of violent videogame play. Furthermore, the results suggest that the neural responses of videogamers to real violence have not resulted in desensitization processes.

Functional neuroimaging studies have also compared and contrasted pathological videogame playing with substance-related addiction. Lorenz and colleagues (2013) conducted a functional magnetic resonance imaging study using a dot probe paradigm with attentional bias (i.e., short-presentation) and cue reactivity (i.e., long-presentation) trials in eight males identified as pathological computer game players and nine healthy controls.

Results revealed that pathological computer game players had greater brain responses than healthy controls in the medial prefrontal cortex and anterior cingulate gyrus in attentional bias trials, and in the lingual gyrus in cue reactivity trials in comparison. These attentional bias and cue reactivity findings are consistent with the hypothesis that pathological computer game playing and substance-related addiction share some common mechanisms.

13.5 Serious Games

Videogames have been found to enhance a variety of cognitive skills and they appear to have promise for training abilities (Achtman et al., 2008; Anguera et al., 2013; Basak et al., 2008; Franceschini et al., 2013). There is emerging empirical support for serious games in health (Primack et al., 2012). Some of the most popular examples of serious games are exergames that encourage exercise by turning physical activity into a game (O'Loughlin et al., 2012). A relatively recent applications area for videogames is for interventional and rehabilitation purposes. Rehabilitation approaches have been evaluated in various cohorts, including traumatic and acquired brain injury (Llorens, Noé, Ferri, & Alcañiz, 2015), degenerative ataxia (Synofzik, 2013), dyslexia (Franceschini et al., 2013), stroke (Cho, Lee, & Song, 2012), autism (Crowder & Merritte, 2013), aging (Anguera et al., 2013; Basak et al., 2008; Marston & Smith, 2012). Serious games have also successfully been applied to counter depression in teenagers (Fleming et al., 2012) and social isolation in an older-age cohort (Harley, 2010).

Given the positive results from studies using serious games, a number of quantitative and qualitative reviews have been conducted (Ke, 2009; Sitzmann, 2011; Vogel et al., 2006). For example, the meta-analysis by Ke (2009) explored the field of game-based learning. A limitation of this meta-analysis was that it did not statistically summarize effect sizes. A meta-analysis by Vogel and colleagues (2006) investigated cognitive and attitudinal effects. Results from the meta-analysis revealed that videogames and interactive simulations yielded higher cognitive outcomes than did conventional learning methods. The meta-analysis by Sitzmann (2011) focused on simulation games. In another meta-analysis, Wouters and colleagues (2013) investigated whether serious games are more effective in terms of learning and more motivating than conventional instruction methods. Findings revealed that although serious games were more effective in terms of learning and retention, they were not more motivating than conventional instruction methods.

While there is growing support for the development and validation of serious games, there is a great deal of concern in the scientific community about claims from some commercial products. As such, it is important to note that some recent studies of commercially available brain training games have revealed that skills acquired during training have limited transferability (McDougall & House, 2012; Zickefoose et al., 2013). Furthermore, a recent consensus statement was signed by 74 scholars that expressed marked skepticism regarding commercial brain training programs (Allaire, 2014).

13.6 Neurogaming

Given the growing popularity of videogaming, there is a growing need for novel approaches to measuring player experiences that thoroughly keep persons immersed in videogames. One area that is gaining popularity rapidly in the gaming community is affective computing because it has great potential in the next generation of human–computer interfaces (Picard, 1997; Tao & Tan, 2005). One goal of affective computing is to design a computer system that responds in a rational and strategic fashion to real-time changes in user engagement (Wu, Lance, & Parsons, 2013), neurocognitive performance (Parsons, Courtney, & Dawson, 2013), and arousal (Wu et al., 2010). Recent approaches to psychophysiological computing have applied psychophysiological modeling to interactive videogames (Parsons & Reinebold, 2012). Electroencephalography (EEG) provides a means of accessing and recording neural activity, allowing a computer to retrieve and analyze information from the brainwave patterns produced by thought. EEG has been shown to have the capability to measure player experience (Wu et al., 2010; Wu, Lance, & Parsons, 2013). Beta rhythm has been shown to increase with attention and vigilance in general (Murthy & Fetz, 1992; Steriade, 1993) and during videogame play specifically (Salmin & Ravajja, 2007). In a study by Salmin and Ravajja (2007) EEG was used to measure and isolate specific game events from the EEG data. Using Super Monkey Ball 2 as their test platform they were able to detect changes in the brain wave bands as different events occurred during game play. Nacke and colleagues (2011) also showed that EEG data could be used to determine player experience across entire level designs. Using a Half Life 2 mod they measured EEG across three different levels designed to induce boredom, immersion, and flow. The data showed that there were increased levels of brain wave activity as the player moved across the levels. Further, gamma has been found to be involved in a host of other cognitive processes:

attention, arousal, object recognition, and top-down modulation of sensory processes (Engel, Fries, & Singer, 2001). Beta activity, gamma activity, and perceived action possibilities have been found in studies of virtual gaming environments (Nacke, 2010; Wirth et al., 2007).

13.7 Neurogaming and Brain–Computer Interfaces

Whilst there are many beneficial EEG applications, much of this technology has yet to leave the research lab. One large factor of this is the EEG devices. The majority of research and medical EEG devices are expensive, bulky, and require a number of skilled technicians. As technology progresses, the cost and size will continue to decrease. Recently, some inexpensive consumer-grade devices have become available. An example of this is the Emotiv EPOC, a compact, wireless headset that requires comparatively little effort to set up and allows much greater flexibility and mobility than traditional EEG. The EPOC was aimed at the gaming market, and is not classified as a medical device, though a few researchers have since adopted it for a variety of applications (Cinar & Sahin, 2013; Rosas-Cholula et al., 2010; Vi & Subramanian, 2012). Using the EPOC, researchers can detect facial movements, emotional states, and imagined motor movement.

A number of researchers have used the Emotiv EEG recordings for assessment of cognitive processes. Researchers have investigated different EEG processing algorithms to assess classification of shapes being thought about (Esfahani & Sundararajan, 2012), detection of hand movement intentions on the same side of the brain as the hand (Fok et al., 2011), classification of positive and negative emotion elicited by pictures (Jatupaiboon et al., 2013a, 2013b; Pham et al., 2012), and evaluation of cognitive workload (Andeson, 2011).

It is important to note that some have questioned "what" the Emotiv EEG is actually measuring (Heingartner, 2009), and it is known that the Emotiv sensors detect EMG along with EEG data. Nevertheless, the system has been found to work well for detecting events when the participant is told to picture various stimuli (Esfahani & Sundararajan, 2012; Knoll et al., 2011). Although the Emotiv EEG does not have the fidelity of a laboratory EEG it still offers the ability to provide a gamer's brain wave signature. Duvinage et al. (2013) compared the Emotiv headset to the Advance Neuro Technology (ANT) acquisition system during a run with the P300 speller system. Although the Emotiv headset was not found to be as accurate as the ANT system (a medical-grade device), it was able to capture EEG signal at a successful level that was deemed adequate for games. With the benefit of being noninvasive to the wearer, it is a tool that is practical for use by game developers (McMahan, Parberry, & Parsons, 2015a).

13.8   Conclusions

In this chapter there has been a review of the impact of videogame play on the user's brain. Research on "videogames" can refer to studies of activities ranging from basic matching of colored blocks on a smartphone to navigating with a group of players in a highly complex virtual environment. As a result, cyberpsychology research tends to focus on exploration of particular game genres. For example, games may be grouped in terms of format, content, activities, and mechanics. One common distinction is between nonaction and action videogames. Early studies looked at the cognitive processing of gamers using first-generation arcade-type videogames and nonaction videogames. Typically, results from these studies with nonaction videogames reveal enhanced performance on reaction time tests, but not on tests of executive-control.

In contrast to early studies, the vast majority of studies in the literature now focus upon action videogames. Action videogames include multifaceted three-dimensional settings, rapidly moving and/or highly transitory targets, robust peripheral processing demands, and the requirement that the user make decisions while regularly switching between highly focused and highly distributed attention. A growing body of literature has emerged that focuses upon assessment of action videogame player cognition. Notable enhancements have been observed in performance on measures of executive-control such as working memory, inhibition, task switching, and reduced attentional capture.

The chapter next turned to the neural correlates of videogaming. Several structural neuroimaging studies have found that videogame play can alter gray matter volume. The neural correlates underpinning the enhanced cognitive processing favoring videogamers are not well understood. Results from cross-sectional studies have revealed that videogame players who play large amounts of videogames and professional gamers exhibit increased frontocortical thickness and regional gray matter volume in the dorsolateral prefrontal cortex and frontal eye field. Studies of expert action videogame players reveal heightened functional connectivity and grey matter volume in insular subregions compared to novices. Experts in action videogames have also been found to have greater ability for early filtering of extraneous information and selective attention than amateurs, as assessed by neural activities in frontoparietal areas.

In addition to structural assessment of videogame players' brains, there is a growing body of literature assessing functional imaging of videogame play. The frontal and parietal lobes form a network that is involved in the selection of sensory contents by attention. This frontoparietal cortex has long been implicated as a source of attentional control. In a neuroimaging study of the frontoparietal attentional network and the middle temporal sulcus (a motion sensitive area), Bavelier and colleagues compared the performances of skilled videogame players and non-players on a visual search task with distractors. Results from the non-players' performance revealed a significant increase in activation of the frontoparietal attentional network in response to increased visual search load. This was not the case for the skilled videogame players. While moving distracters (i.e., irrelevant moving dots) resulted in less activation in the middle temporal sulcus of skilled videogame players, this activation was not apparent for responses to attended motion stimuli. The reduced utilization of frontoparietal attentional network in skilled videogame players may reflect lower use of attentional resources with higher task burdens.

Research of resting-state functional connectivity reveals a salience network (anterior cingulate cortex and anterior insula) that supports the detection of salient events, and an executive-control network (dorsolateral prefrontal cortex and posterior parietal cortex) that supports attentional control and working memory. The salience network receives and delivers selective amplification of salient information to generate a top-down control signal that prompts the executive-control network to respond to salient information, attentional shift, and control processing. Some have suggested that cognitive training may result in functional plasticity in the salience system and integration of the executive-control and salience networks. Furthermore, this integration between brain networks may reflect the neural correlates of cognitive control. Given these findings and those outlined above, action videogame experience may offer a venue to explore the interaction of the salience and executive-control networks.

Videogame play has been found to result in substantial dopamine release in the dopaminergic system as well as addiction. Results from neuroimaging studies have revealed that videogame play activates the brain's motivational systems. A host of warnings and concerns can be found in popular media about the potential negative impacts of videogame play. While the concerns circulating in the popular media offer interesting headlines, not all stand up to research scrutiny. As can be seen earlier in this chapter, a number of studies have found enhanced cognitive processing in videogamers. There has also been interest in the therapeutic and rehabilitative potential of videogames for a variety of nervous system disorders. That said, a number of cyberpsychology researchers have investigated the negative impact of videogames. Findings have revealed negative impacts for addiction; the influence of violent content; and the impact of sexist content.

This chapter also looked at the potential of serious games. Videogames have been found to enhance a variety of cognitive skills and they appear to have promise for training abilities. There is emerging empirical support for serious games in health. Some of the most popular examples of serious games are exergames that encourage exercise by turning physical activity into a game. A relatively recent application area for videogames is for interventional and rehabilitation purposes. Given the positive results from studies using serious games, a number of quantitative and qualitative reviews have been conducted. Results from meta-analyses have revealed that videogames and interactive simulations yielded higher cognitive outcomes than did conventional learning methods. While there is growing support for the development and validation of serious games, there is a great deal of concern in the scientific community about claims from some commercial products. As such, it is important to note that some recent studies of commercially available brain training games have revealed that skills acquired during training have limited transferability.

CHAPTER 14

NeuroIS
Cybersecurity and the Brain

14.1 Introduction

Information systems research is a recent area to incorporate the behavioral neuroscience literature. In the same way that other areas of cyberpsychology are drawing from recent advances in the brain and behavioral neurosciences, information systems researchers are looking at the complex interplay between information technology and neuroeconomics, information processing, and social neuroscience. Information systems researchers have started to investigate the potential of the human neurosciences (e.g., social, cognitive, and affective neurosciences) for information sciences research (Dimoka, 2010; Pavlou, Davis, & Dimoka, 2007; Riedl & Léger, 2016).

This chapter will review the development of NeuroIS and its relation to cybersecurity. First, in Section 14.2, "NeuroIS: Development and Refinement of a Definition," there will be a review of NeuroIS in general. Specifically, there will be a summary of its beginnings and discussions of potential areas of intersections with cognitive neuroscience, design science, and human–computer interaction. This is followed in Section 14.3, "Cyberpsychology and Cybersecurity," by a discussion of cybersecurity and NeuroIS. Next, in Section 14.4, "Cybersecurity and NeuroIS Research," there is a discussion of the ways in which findings from social, affective, and human neurosciences can play crucial roles in moving beyond subjective questionnaires to objective metrics that can guide future advances.

14.2 NeuroIS: Development and Refinement of a Definition

An interdisciplinary field of research called Neuro-Information-Systems (NeuroIS) has emerged that integrates findings from the neurosciences into information and communication technologies. The actual start of

NeuroIS can be traced back to the 2007 International Conference on Information Systems, and at two pre-ICIS meetings (Sixth Annual Workshop on Human-Computer Interaction Research in Management Information Systems and OASIS Workshop 2007). Hence, this is a new discipline and has little research published prior to 2007.

René Riedl and colleagues (2010) at the University of Applied Sciences Upper Austria defined NeuroIS in terms of its interdisciplinarity and emphasis upon incorporating knowledge from disciplines related to neurobiology, behavior, and engineering. They go on to describe two complementary goals:

(1) NeuroIS has the potential to enhance our understandings of the design, development, usage, and influence of information and communication technologies.
(2) NeuroIS can add to the design and development of information and communication technologies that positively impact pertinent outcome variables (e.g., health, quality of life, fulfilment, acceptance, and production).

Recently, Angelika Dimoka and colleagues (2011) at Temple University's Fox School of Business have extended the theoretical and applied aspects of NeuroIS via seven areas in which neuroscience and information systems research can be integrated:

(1) **Localization of neural correlates of IS constructs**: This involves linking of various neural correlates of IS constructs to theories and studies found in human neuroscience literature. Emphasis is given to mapping IS constructs into specific brain areas, and associating the functionality of these brain areas to IS constructs.
(2) **Measurement of automatic neurocognitive processes**: For this area, emphasis is placed upon measuring automatic cognitive (e.g., heuristics, biases) and affective (e.g., psychophysiological arousal) processes that are difficult to assess with measurement methods and tools that are currently used in IS research.
(3) **Supplementing existing IS data with brain-based data**: The objective responses from neuroimaging data are not subject to measurement biases and can complement findings from IS research.
(4) **Identification of IS construct antecedents**: Examination of the ways in which the brain areas are activated in response to antecedent IT stimuli (e.g., the Internet). The aim would be to enhance specific behavioral outcomes and productivity.

(5) **Assessing the IS construct consequences:** Demonstrating the ways in which brain activations occur as a consequence of particular IS constructs. The goal would be to use this neuroimaging information for the prediction of certain cyber behaviors (e.g., online purchasing).

(6) **Inferences of temporal ordering among IS constructs:** Examination of the temporal order of brain activations following a typical IT stimulus (that activates two or more IS constructs) to infer causal relations among IS constructs.

(7) **Exploring assumptions and enhancing IS theories:** Identification of differences between existing IS relationships and the brain's underlying functionality can be used to challenge IS assumptions. As a result, IS researchers may have enhanced abilities for developing and modifying IS theories that correspond to the brain's functionality.

The most recent formulation of NeuroIS can be found in Riedl and Léger's (2016) book, in which these seven areas are supported and further developed. In addition to these seven areas emphasized by Riedl and Léger (2016) an emphasis upon adaptive interfaces and human–computer interaction for NeuroIS is added. For example, neurocognitive processes can be used in real–time to develop adaptive systems that may impact outcome variables (e.g., health, quality of life, fulfilment, acceptance, and production). The real time information from a user's psychophysiological state (e.g., stress, arousal) constitutes a significant basis for a user to consciously control (via biofeedback systems) arousal. Finally, they emphasize the role electrophysiological measures of brain functioning can play in supplanting traditional input devices (e.g., keyboard, mouse) in human–computer interaction for entertainment (e.g., videogames) and productivity (e.g., enterprise systems).

An example of a virtual-reality study using NeuroIS can be found in the work of Minas and colleagues (2014) at Indiana University. Specifically, they used NeuroIS to understand information processing biases in virtual teams. For the study, Minas and colleagues emphasized decision-making in virtual teams using collaboration technology, which makes demands on the user's cognitive resources and may change how individual team members process information in virtual settings compared to face-to-face settings. While virtual teams are increasingly common in organizations, they have been found to often make poor decisions. They used EEG to assess cognition, as well as psychophysiological measures of electrodermal activity (EDA; skin conductance and electromyography; EMG; activation of the facial corrugator muscle) to assess affective responding. Results from the study suggest that information that challenged an individual's prediscussion decision is processed in a shallow manner similar to processing of irrelevant information. Contrariwise, information that supported an individual's prediscussion decision was processed more deeply. Findings from the EEG data revealed that different information activated different patterns of cognition. Results from the skin conductance data revealed that different information activated different emotional responses. A notable aspect of this study is that it uses psychophysiological metrics as part of its methodology for confirming the role of confirmation bias during online team decision-making. Furthermore, it enhances understanding of the cognitive processes underlying confirmation bias.

14.3 Cyberpsychology and Cybersecurity

With the abundant availability of over 3.1 billion people now having access to the Internet, there is great potential for cybersecurity risks. In fact, human users of the digital assets in an organization have been described as the weakest links in the information security defensive chain (Bulgurcu, Cavusoglu, & Benbasat, 2010; Hu et al., 2012). Cyberpsychologists are more and more cognizant of the crucial role of individual users in the safekeeping of information systems (Furnell & Clarke, 2012; Willison & Warkentin, 2013). For example, the coaxing of a single user into acting in an insecure manner can compromise the security of an entire system (Ursu, 2012). The vulnerability of a system due to individual users is known by cybercriminals and hackers, who regularly use social engineering schemes to convince users to install malicious software and/or allow access past their technical security controls (Abraham & Chengalur-Smith, 2010; Anderson, 2008).

Barbara Wiederhold (2014) has argued that cyberpsychologists are uniquely qualified for working with information systems security. Given their understanding of human behavior in cyberspace, cyberpsychologists can familiarize information security researchers with the cultural and behavioral content relevant to security at both the individual and collective levels. Specifically, she describes five areas that cyberpsychologists may contribute:

(1) **Behavioral economics:** Cyberpsychologists have an understanding of the behavioral economics guiding users' perceptions of risk and

reward. Moreover, cyberpsychologists are well-versed in the identification of social situations and the ways in which users reveal increased tendencies to reduce vigilance related to risks inherent in sharing private information. Support for Wiederhold's emphasis on behavioral economics can be found in a study by John, Acquisti, and Loewenstein (2011), in which findings revealed that there is increased likelihood that persons will reveal personal (even confidential) information in less formal settings (e.g., on social media networks).

(2) **Pattern recognition of malicious behavior**: Cyberpsychologists can aid the identification of malicious activity patterns via observational assessment of user deviations from normative behavior. Cyberpsychologists also have a good deal of knowledge that they can offer to technology providers for the development of security systems that have the capabilities necessary for detection of malicious activities.

(3) **Policymaking**: Cyberpsychologists can also advise legislators, steering groups, and policymakers on the psychological and the social impact of cybercrime. Such collaborative efforts would help to enhance legislation and awareness of virtual crimes.

(4) **Dissemination of research results**: Cyberpsychologists produce a great deal of research on cybersecurity and information science–related issues. The dissemination of lab results to the public via social media can help to raise awareness in the general public of cybersecurity risks. As a result, there may be some change in users' perception and behavior toward privacy.

(5) **Cybersecurity outcomes and impacts**: Given the broad training in psychology by cyberpsychologists, there is an enhanced capacity for understanding the impact of cybercrime on victims.

These emphases are actively being pursued in the labs of cyberpsychologists across the globe. As Wiederhold points out, cyberpsychologists are uniquely suited for research into risk perception because it involves a multipart amalgamation of psychological, economic, financial, social, cultural, and political factors (see also Chen, 2009; Grewal, Gotlieb, & Marmorstein, 1994; Slovic, 1987). Studies have investigated risk perceptions relative to information security, privacy, and social media (Anderson & Agarwal, 2010; Go et al., 2011; Malhotra et al., 2004). Research has also been done to investigate perceived risk and Internet users' willingness to share information about themselves online. Privacy researchers have also used the construct of perceived risk. These studies use perceived risk to explain Internet users' openness to share personal information online (Bélanger & Crossler, 2011; Hong & Thong, 2013; Xu, Luo, Carroll, & Rosson, 2011).

Traditionally, cyberpsychology research on information systems security has primarily employed self-report measures to assess users' perceptions of information security risks (Guo et al., 2011; Malhotra, Kim, & Agarwal, 2004). These measures are not difficult to develop or allocate. Moreover, they allow for a straightforward format for collection of users' endorsements. While much of this work has historically focused upon survey-based methods, there is a growing interest in the use of more objective approaches (e.g., psychophysiological logging, motion capture, and eye-tracking). Further, there is growing interest in the incorporations of neuroimaging technologies for enhanced understanding of both the rule breakers and the victims.

14.4 Cybersecurity and NeuroIS Research

14.4.1 Cybersecurity and Self-Reports: Biases and Limitations

Assessment of the impact of a cyberpsychology application on the user is often difficult. When used in isolation, self-report data are very vulnerable to influences outside the user's own targeted attitudes (Schwarz, 1999). For example, the item's wording, context, and format are all factors that may influence self-report responses. Moreover, users will invariably have different reactions to a given application/environment, and without an assessment tool that can be employed online, the cyberpsychology researcher will experience difficulties in identifying the causes of these differences, which may lead to a loss of experimental control of the research paradigm. A user may become increasingly frustrated with some aspect of the environment, but without proper measurement techniques to detect this frustration while it occurs, the user's sense of presence, or feeling of "being there" (Waterworth & Riva, 2014; see Chapter 8 in this book), may be diminished. In the NeuroIS and cybersecurity literature, there is a growing acceptance that although self-report measures have been found to be useful in some studies, these subjective questionnaires are susceptible to certain biases that can undercut the validity of study findings (Dimoka, Pavlou, & Davis, 2011; Dimoka et al., 2012; Vance et al., 2014).

When one turns to brain processing in NeuroIS and cybersecurity, one finds another important limitation that is apparent for survey measures – certain affective responses are automatic neurocognitive processes.

Unfortunately, self-reports miss this automatic processing because they are administered as questions and tap into controlled decision-making. According to dual-process models of automatic and controlled cognitive processing, controlled processes (e.g., performing a difficult calculus problem) are slow and accurate, and automatic processes (e.g., automatic response to a negative picture) reflect heuristics and biases that are fast and lower in accuracy (see Lieberman, 2007). The issue of automatic (i.e., unconscious) processing reflects one of the items from Dimoka and colleagues' (2011) list (see item number (2) above). Additionally, self-reported measures require controlled (i.e., conscious) decision-making. This is a limitation because studies have revealed that self-report measures are uncertainly related to measures in which participants may or may not be unaware (in control) of the impact of their attitude and cognition (Fazio & Olson, 2003; Skowronski & Lawrence, 2001). Such automatic responses are inherently difficult to self-report.

Another limitation of self-report measures is the temporal ordering of the questioning related to behaviors that were performed in the past. If a researcher wants to know risk perceptions as they occur (automatically and "in the moment"), then it is important to ask while the behavior is occurring instead of after the fact. Hence, a limitation of questionnaires is that they are given after the actual processing of the information occurred and represent post hoc appraisals of information that may have been processed automatically and unconsciously.

A further concern is that these questionnaires and related theoretical formulations have focused more on assessment of users' perceptions of intentions to act instead of the actual committing of the act (Crossler et al., 2013). This is a cause for concern because participant responses to surveys have revealed that while the responders tend to endorse security concerns, they subsequently fail to act in a secure manner online (Acquisti & Grossklags, 2004). Many of the studies in the literature on perceived risk have assessed intentions, instead of the actual behaviors. The concern is that research has revealed that people act in a manner that is not consistent with their self-reported apprehension for their security and privacy (Acquisti & Grossklags, 2004).

In addition to limitations, there are a number of biases that can result from survey methods. For example, "common methods bias" describes the variance that is attributable to artifacts of the survey instrumentation instead of the true variance between different constructs (Podsakoff, MacKenzie, Lee, & Podsakoff, 2003). Another example is "social desirability bias," which reflects the propensity of survey respondents to present themselves and their behaviors in a more socially acceptable manner (Paulhus, 1991). Subjectivity bias is another potential threat to the veracity of self-report study results. By subjectivity bias, psychometrists mean the difficulty of assessing the actual reality when asking participants for their subjective perceptions of reality (Theorell & Hasselhorn, 2005). Finally, there is the issue of demand bias, which relates to demand-induced behaviors when participants attempt to discern and intentionally confirm or disconfirm an experimenter's hypotheses (Orne & Whitehouse, 2000).

14.4.2 Quantitative Assessment Measures

As may be obvious from this list of biases and limitations, self-report measures may offer a rather incomplete story of risk perceptions and cybersecurity behaviors. Given these concerns, there is growing interest in adding more quantitative assessment measures to security-related protocols (Crossler et al., 2013). Recent advances in the social cognitive and affective neurosciences offer distinctive prospects for the study of human behavior without many of the biases common in the traditional cyberpsychology research literature. Increasingly, cybersecurity researchers are drawing upon findings from social, affective, and human neurosciences for mitigating the concerns found in survey research (Baddeley, 2011; Kirwan & Power, 2011; Krawczyk et al., 2013). The belief is that perspectives from neuroscience offer an important contribution to the understanding of human behavior and decision-making in the context of information security. Psychophysiological metrics (e.g., ECG, respiration, EMG, EDA; see Chapter 3), eye-tracking, EEG, and neuroimaging (e.g., fMRI) enable cyberpsychology (and cybersecurity) researchers to measure neural activity in the human brain, as research participants consider various options for decision-making, and as a result to investigate the neural correlates of decision-making processes. Moreover, these neurocognitive and psychophysiological approaches may considerably decrease social desirability biases in participant responses because neural processes are relatively free from conscious biases of the participants. These metrics allow for direct measurement of autonomic and brain processes. As a result, they offer more objective, quantitative, and unbiased assessment of the social, cognitive, and affective processes involved in decision-making. These advantages have not gone unnoticed by the cybersecurity community and the neuroscience perspective is beginning to attract significant attention (Crossler et al., 2013; vom Brocke & Liang, 2014). Furthermore, cybersecurity researchers have applied methods from the social, cognitive, and affective neurosciences to a wide range of information systems research issues including:

- Information security (Hu, West, & Smarandescu, 2015; Vance et al., 2014)
- Information processing biases (Koller & Walla, 2012; Minas et al., 2014)
- Online commerce (Hubert, Hubert, Riedl, & Kenning, 2014; Kuan, Zhong, & Chau, 2014; Senecal, Léger, Fredette, & Riedl, 2012)
- Trust (Boudreau, McCubbins, & Coulson, 2009; Dimoka, 2010; Riedl et al., 2014)
- Emotions in information systems research (Gregor et al., 2014; Lin & Vasilyeva, 2011)
- User beliefs in information systems (de Guinea, Titah, & Léger, 2014)
- Cognitive workload (Buettner, 2015; Buettner, Sauer, Maier, & Eckhardt, 2015).

14.4.3   NeuroIS and Cybersecurity Studies Using Electroencephalography

The application of findings and methods from the human neurosciences offers a promising approach to investigate the effectiveness of security warnings. In fact, cybersecurity researchers D'Arcy and Herath (2011) have called for research that applies NeuroIS to human–computer interaction. Specifically, they argue that increased understanding of the design of IT artifacts will be aided by studies in the timing of brain activations while users are completing decision tasks. Likewise, Crossler and colleagues (2013) have argued that NeuroIS approaches are notable for their promise of methods that can measure information security–related behaviors and attitudes.

Among these NeuroIS measures is electroencephalography and event-related potentials. Specifically, the P300 is used as a positive-going component that peaks between 250 and 500 milliseconds after stimulus onset. The P300 has been observed in tasks that require stimulus discrimination. Smaller P300 amplitudes result from passive stimulus processing (e.g., when task conditions are low in demand). Historically, EEG has been used in the human neuroscience literature to investigate risk-taking tendencies. For example, some EEG studies on risk-taking have had participants perform a gambling task while measuring the EEG either before or during the task. Other studies have compared self-report responses on risk-taking propensities to different EEG measurements (including ERP amplitudes and latencies; Massar, Rossi, Schutter, & Kenemans, 2012; Massar, Kenemans, & Schutter, 2013).

14.4.3.1   Self-Control in Information Security Violations

In a study into the role of self-control in information security violations, Hu and colleagues (2015) found that self-control plays an important role in information security policy compliance. Given that self-control has been identified as a significant factor influencing user behavior in the social neurosciences, criminology, and information security, they developed and validated a paradigm that used event-related potentials in scenario-based laboratory experiments of decision-making in the context of information security. Next, they incorporated this paradigm to investigate the relation between individual user differences in self-control and event-related potentials elicited while users deliberated over violations of information security policies. Using EEG, they examined event-related potentials to evaluate differences in brain region activations between users with high and low self-reported self-control. The EEG measurements were gathered as users considered hypothetical information security policy violations. Findings from the study revealed that the left and right brain hemispheres were involved in decision-making. Further, the users with lower self-control had lower levels of neural recruitment in both hemispheres relative to those with higher self-control. It is notable that this was especially the case for regions in (or near) the dorsal lateral prefrontal cortex and inferior frontal cortex. It can be argued that these findings extend results found in the neuroscience literature on the role of self-control in decision-making. Furthermore, these findings help to validate the use of the electroencephalography and event-related potentials for investigating theoretical questions in information security research.

In another study, Vance and colleagues (2014) investigated risk perceptions using both EEG and self-reported methods. In this NeuroIS study Anthony Vance and colleagues (2014) of Brigham Young University aimed to compare traditional subjective measures with quantitative psychophysiological assessment. They assessed whether risk perceptions could be efficiently measured using electroencephalography (EEG, see Chapter 3). Specifically, they used event-related potentials (ERPs), which measure neural events that have been activated by specific stimuli or actions. For Vance and colleagues, these ERPs were measured in response to gains and losses on the Iowa Gambling Task (IGT), a commonly used measure of somatic markers and decision-making (Bechara & Damasio, 2005; see also Chapter 8 for research using this task). Moreover, they investigated the differences in these measures of the neural responses to gains and losses using an additional laboratory-based computing task.

The IGT is a computerized assessment of reward-related decision-making that measures temporal foresight and risky decision-making (Bechara & Damasio, 2005). During IGT assessment, the patient is instructed to choose cards from four decks (A–D). Selection of each card results in on-screen feedback regarding either a "gain" or "loss" of currency. In the four decks there are two advantageous (C and D) decks that result in money gained ($250 every 10 cards) and low monetary loss during the trial. The other two decks (A and B) are disadvantageous and involve greater wins (around $100 each card) than C and D (around $50) but also incur greater losses, meaning that one loses $250 every 10 cards in Decks A and B. The primary dependent variables derived from the IGT are total score and net score ([C + D] – [A + B]) and block score ([C + D] – [A + B]) for each segment or block of 20 cards, frequency of deck choices, and spared or impaired performance according to a cut-off point of –10 (Bechara, Damasio, & Damasio, 2000), especially in brain-damaged subjects.

Findings revealed that EEG measurements were better at predicting users' disregard of security messages than self-reported measurements during an ecologically valid laboratory task. The EEG P300 difference score, which was derived from users' P300 amplitudes in response to losses in the IGT, was the most robust predictor of security warning disregard. Moreover, it was also the most significant measure because it predicted security warning disregard consistently before and after a security incident. In this study, objective neuroscience methods were incorporated to confirm the relation between risk perception and security behaviors. It is important to note that self-report measures of risk perception failed to indicate as robust a relation. This is likely due to biases that typically impact negatively most self-report methods (Dimoka, Pavlou, & Davis, 2011).

14.5 NeuroIS Studies Using Functional Magnetic Resonance Imaging

Functional magnetic resonance imaging (fMRI) is a rapidly growing technique for relating brain activity to behavior in NeuroIS. Using fMRI, cyberpsychologists can measure changes in the levels of the brain's blood oxygen that are indicative of neuronal activity (see Chapter 2 in this book). A number of NeuroIS studies using fMRI have emerged that demonstrate the ways in which brain activation patterns can be used to explain variations in behavior relative to information technology artifacts (Benbasat et al., 2010; Dimoka, 2010; Riedl, Hubert, & Kenning, 2010).

14.5.1   Mentalizing Network for Trust Assessments of Humans and Virtual Humans

Two important areas of research identified for NeuroIS are trust and mentalizing. One question for a brain-based cyberpsychology interested in cyber security has to do with what brain areas are involved in trust and mentalizing. The default-mode network is a large-scale brain network involved in thinking about one's self and others. When not engaged in some other activity, the brain tends to ruminate about others. Recent evidence suggests considerable overlap between the default-mode network and regions involved in social, affective, and introspective processes (Forbes & Grafman, 2010; Mars et al., 2012). Amft and colleagues (2015) identified overlapping brain regions thought to be involved in mentalizing, self-reference, and autobiographic information: the posterior cingulum/precuneus and dorsomedial prefrontal cortex.

Riedl and colleagues (2014) conducted a functional magnetic resonance imaging experiment based on a multiround trust game to gain insight into the differences and similarities of interactions between humans and virtual human interaction. Their results indicated that decision-making about whether or not to trust another actor activates the medial frontal cortex significantly more during interaction with humans. It is important to note that this brain area is significant for the prediction of the thoughts and intentions (mentalizing) of others. Specifically, they found higher activation in a brain network associated with mentalizing, namely the medial prefrontal cortex, the rostral anterior cingulate cortex, and the ventromedial prefrontal cortex.

14.5.2   Neural Correlates of Trust on eBay

While traditional approaches to assessing human-to-human interactions have focused on face-to-face interactions, interactions among humans are taking place increasingly online. While, traditional studies into trust and security incorporating face-to-face interactions are declining, computer-mediated interactions are increasing. Given this development, fMRI studies have emerged to investigate the neural correlates of trust while the users viewed eBay Websites (Dimoka, 2010; Riedl et al., 2010). The fMRI study by Dimoka (2010) used Internet sites of eBay feedback profiles with variable levels of trustworthiness (i.e., manipulation relative to ratios among positive, negative, and neutral feedback) as stimuli to activate brain areas. Feedback profiles from buyers were used to evaluate the quality of a transaction that they conducted with a seller. As a result, there is a belief that the sellers have an incentive to act in a trustworthy manner to develop a respectable reputation. Results from the study revealed trust is related to the caudate nucleus, a brain region associated with reward anticipation. Further, trust was related to the anterior paracingulate cortex (predicting the behavior of others), and the orbito-frontal cortex for calculating uncertainty. In contrast to trust, distrust was found to be linked with the amygdala (intense negative emotions) and the insular cortex for fear of loss.

In another study that used neuroimaging and Internet offers of eBay sellers as stimulus material, Riedl and colleagues (2010) developed product description texts with varying degrees of trustworthiness. In an effort to demonstrate empirically that online trust is related to activity changes in particular brain areas, they used fMRI. For the study, they captured the brain activity of 10 female and 10 male participants simultaneous to decisions on trustworthiness of eBay offers. Findings from the study revealed that the processing of trustworthy eBay offers activated reward processing areas of the striatum and thalamus. Furthermore, activations were found in the prefrontal regions and cingulate cortex for mentalizing. These findings are contrasted with the other findings related to the processing of untrustworthy eBay offers, which activated the insular cortex for perception of uncertainty. An interesting finding was that women also exhibit different brain activation patterns in the trustworthiness evaluation task. In fact, most of the brain areas that are linked to the encoding of trustworthiness were found to differ between women and men. Results revealed that women activated more brain areas than did men. The authors argued that these results confirm the empathizing–systemizing theory, which predicts gender differences in neural information processing modes.

14.5.3 Dual Task Interference

In a study by researchers at Brigham Young University, Anderson and colleagues (2015) used fMRI to explain the effect of dual task interference on security behavior. Specifically, they examined the ways in which security behavior is impacted by a cognitive limitation in which even simple tasks cannot be simultaneously performed without significant performance loss (i.e., dual task interference). They found that security messages that interrupt users result in increased vulnerability by increasing the disregarding of a recommended course of action of a security message. The researchers aimed to investigate the previously unexamined effect of dual task interference on a security message that acted as a secondary, interrupting task. They used fMRI to explore (1) the ways in which dual task interference occurs in the brain in response to interruptive security messages; and (2) the ways in which dual task interference impacts security message disregard. For the study, they used a repeated-measure, within-subject experimental design that required participants to respond to security warnings that either interrupted or did not interrupt a primary task. The security messages were operationalized as permission warnings that are like those displayed as users install a Google Chrome browser extension. Before starting the conditions, participants received training regarding acceptable and risky permissions. To measure security message disregard they used whether or not the user performed an inappropriate installation of a risky extension. Participants completed the experiment in both conditions presented in a random order. For the divided attention paradigm of dual task interference, users had to switch attention when a security message interrupted a primary task. Dual task interference occurred because the cognitive functions of users remain engaged in the primary task while they are responding to the security message. Findings revealed that neural activation in the medial temporal lobe (linked to declarative memory) is significantly reduced under a condition of high dual task interference, which in turn significantly predicts security message disregard.

14.6 Conclusions

In this chapter, there was a discussion of the potential of current findings from neuroscience research to enhance our understandings of the ways in which people make decisions in cybersecurity situations. The abundant availability of people now having access to the Internet offers increased potential for cybersecurity risks. The vulnerability of a system due to individual users is known by cybercriminals and hackers, who regularly use social engineering schemes to convince users to install malicious software and/or allow access past their technical security controls. Cyberpsychologists are increasingly aware of the crucial role individual users play in the safekeeping of information systems, and research is actively being pursued in the labs of cyberpsychologists across the globe. Cyberpsychologists are uniquely suited for research into risk perception because their work already involves an integration of psychological, economic, financial, social, cultural, and political factors.

In this chapter, there has been an emphasis upon the need to move from self-report measures alone to assess users' perceptions of information security risks. While these measures allow for a straightforward format for collection of users' endorsements, there is a growing interest in adding psychophysiological logging, motion capture, and eye-tracking. Further, there is growing interest in the incorporations of neuroimaging technologies for enhanced understanding of both the rule breakers and the victims.

Following the brain-based cyberpsychology advocated in this book, there is an increasing desire to have measures that better assess affective responses and automatic neurocognitive processes. Unfortunately, self-reports miss this automatic processing because they are administered as questions and tap into controlled decision-making. Self-report measures require controlled (i.e., conscious) decision-making. This is a limitation because studies have revealed that self-report measures are uncertainly related to measures in which participants may or may not be unaware (in control) of the impact of their attitude and cognition (Fazio & Olson, 2003; Skowronski & Lawrence, 2001). Such automatic responses are inherently difficult to self-report.

Another limitation of self-report measures is the temporal ordering of the questioning related to behaviors that were performed in the past. If a researcher wants to know risk perceptions as they occur (automatically and "in the moment"), then it is important to ask while the behavior is occurring instead of after the fact. Hence, a limitation of questionnaires is that they are given after the actual processing of the information occurred and represent post hoc appraisals of information that may have been processed automatically and unconsciously.

Given this book's emphasis on a brain-based cyberpsychology, it adopts the growing emphasis upon adding more quantitative assessment measures to security-related protocols. Recent advances in the social cognitive and affective neurosciences offer distinctive prospects for the study of human behavior without many of the biases common in the traditional cybersecurity research literature. Increasingly, cybersecurity researchers are drawing upon findings from social, affective, and human neurosciences for mitigating the concerns found in survey research. The belief is that perspectives from neuroscience offer an important contribution to the understanding of human behavior and decision-making in the context of information security. Psychophysiological metrics (e.g., ECG, respiration, EMG, EDA), eye-tracking, EEG, and neuroimaging (e.g., fMRI) enable cyberpsychology (and cybersecurity) researchers to measure neural activity in the human brain as research participants consider various options for decision-making, and as a result to investigate the neural correlates of decision-making processes. Moreover, these neurocognitive and psycho-physiological approaches may considerably decrease social desirability biases in participant responses because neural processes are relatively free from conscious biases of the participants. These metrics allow for direct measurement of autonomic and brain processes. As a result, they offer more objective, quantitative, and unbiased assessment of the social, cognitive, and affective processes involved in decision-making.

In summary, a brain-based cyberpsychology can enhance cybersecurity research via the addition of psychophysiological and neuroimaging techniques to current survey and behavior-based approaches. It is important to note that these psychophysiological and neuroimaging techniques do not need to replace current survey and behavior observation methods. Instead, they can be seen as a supplement to existing approaches. The emerging knowledgebase related to brain functionality and objective brain data offers a significant resource for cybersecurity research. This chapter's basic premise is that the human neurosciences can open up new research directions that may accelerate progress toward understanding the complex issues that exist for assessing automatic and controlled processing of cybersecurity information. The neurosciences also offer a rigorous scientific foundation for integrating objective psychophysiological and neuroimaging data on human decision-making in cybersecurity situations.

PART V

Conclusions

CHAPTER 15

Prospects for a Brain-Based Cyberpsychology

15.1 Introduction

Cyberpsychology and human neuroscience are two disciplines that are seeing extraordinary increases in their theory and praxis (Parsons, 2015). While cyberpsychology is a relatively new discipline, it is one that is growing at an alarming rate. Perhaps this is due to the fact that humans are witnessing a time of rapid progress in an increasingly connected world. Needless to say technology is seemingly ubiquitous in the everyday lives of most readers of this text. Users may connect or disconnect from others via multiple telecommunication options: Internet, smartphones, tablets, gaming consoles, and wearables (e.g., glass and watches). Interestingly, academic journals and books on cyberpsychology have offered very limited direct coverage of the rapid progress in brain sciences. This is surprising given the advances in the human neurosciences over the past couple of decades. Specifically, clinical, social, and affective neurosciences have seen extraordinary increases in their theory and praxis (Parsons, 2015). Recent growth in the human neurosciences has been spurred in part by the US government's designation of the 1990s as "The Decade of the Brain," the National Institute of Mental Health's Research Domain Criteria framework for studying mental disorders, and the White House's BRAIN (Brain Research through Advancing Innovative Neurotechnologies) Initiative. First, the Decade of the Brain (1990 to the end of 1999) was an interagency initiative that sponsored various activities (e.g., publications and programs) aimed at introducing cutting-edge research on the brain and encouraging public dialogue on the ethical, philosophical, and humanistic implications of these emerging discoveries.

15.1.1   National Institute of Mental Health's Research Domain Criteria

The National Institute of Mental Health's Research Domain Criteria (RDoC) is a research framework for developing and implementing novel approaches to the study of mental disorders. The RDoC integrates multiple levels of information to enhance understanding of basic dimensions of functioning underlying the full range of human behavior from normal to abnormal. The RDoC framework consists of a matrix with rows that represent particular functional constructs (i.e., concepts that represent a specified functional behavior dimension) categorized in aggregate by the genes, molecules, circuits, etc. used to measure it. In turn, the constructs are grouped into higher-level domains of functioning that reflect current knowledge of the major systems of cognition, affect, motivation, and social behavior.

15.1.2   National Institute of Health's BRAIN Initiative

The BRAIN Initiative represents an ambitious but achievable set of goals for advances in science and technology. Since the announcement of the BRAIN Initiative, dozens of leading academic institutions, scientists, technology firms, and other important contributors to neuroscience have responded to this call. A group of prominent neuroscientists have developed a 12-year research strategy for the National Institutes of Health to achieve the goals of the initiative. The BRAIN Initiative may do for neuroscience what the Human Genome Project did for genomics. It supports the development and application of innovative technologies to enhance our understanding of brain function. Moreover, the BRAIN initiative endeavors to aid researchers in uncovering the mysteries of brain disorders (e.g., Alzheimer's, Parkinson's, depression, and traumatic brain injury). It is believed that the initiative will accelerate the development and application of new technologies for producing dynamic imaging of the brain that express the ways in which individual brain cells and complex neural circuits interact at the speed of thought. Cyberpsychologists have a unique role to play in developing technologies that will open new doors to explore how the brain records, processes, uses, stores, and retrieves vast quantities of information. Furthermore, cyberpsychologists can help shed light on neuroscience findings to aid our understanding of the complex links between brain function and behavior.

There are now dozens of laboratories around the world that have converged to investigate neurocognitive, affective, and social questions. While there is a great deal of work in cyberpsychology that deals with neural correlates of persons interacting with technology and neuroscientific investigations of cyberpsychology issues, there is no text that pulls together this material for cyberpsychologists. This book has been a first attempt at bringing together this information for researchers and students in cyberpsychology.

15.2 Brain-Based Cyberpsychology

To encourage the inclusion of brain science research in the cyberpsychology domain, this book accentuates the potential of neuroscience for the study of cognitive, affective, and social processes found in cyberpsychological research and the neural systems that support them. Given these emphases, a brain-based cyberpsychology will be understood as a branch of psychology that studies (1) the neurocognitive, affective, and social aspects of humans interacting with technology; and (2) affective computing aspects of humans interacting with devices/systems that incorporate computation. As such, the cyberpsychologist studies both the ways in which persons make use of devices and the neurocognitive processes, motivations, intentions, behavioral outcomes, and effects of online and offline use of technology.

15.2.1 Systems Neuroscience: Large-Scale Brain Networks

This expanded definition and framework emphasizes a network approach to brain function that provides a principled approach to predicting cyberpsychological processes associated with specific brain systems. In this framework, a systems neuroscience view is adopted that considers cyberpsychological processes (cognitive and affective functions during media use) to arise from the interactions of brain areas in large-scale distributed networks (Bressler & Menon, 2010; Mesulam, 2000). Findings from systems neuroscience have characterized specific large-scale brain networks that are identifiable in the brain both while it is active and when it is at rest (Seeley et al., 2007). The three most prominent networks are the executive-control network, the default-mode network, and the saliency network. The first two networks can be recognized straightforwardly by observing the profile of activation and deactivation typically found during cognitive tasks. The executive-control network typically shows increases in activation during cognitively demanding tasks, whereas the default-mode network has decreased activation. The third network is a salience network that processes affective stimuli and allows for switching between the competitive interactions of two other major networks.

15.2.2   Neuroscience of Social Media

With the advent and rapid development of functional neuroimaging, cyberpsychologists have unparalleled contact with the neural correlates of media experiences and interactions. Cyberpsychologists are beginning to use these advanced technologies to garner a wave of new insights into neurocognitive, affective, motivational, learning, and social processes of persons as they interact with media. For example, Meshi, Tamir, and Heekeren (2015) recently reviewed the emerging neuroscience of social media. They discuss the growing global phenomenon of online social media (almost two billion users worldwide regularly using these social networking sites) and the potential for neuroscientists to make use of these pervasive social media sites to gain new understanding of social cognitive processes and the neural systems that support them. They also outline social motives that drive people to use social media and propose neural systems supporting social media use. Social media behaviors rely primarily on three domains: mentalizing (i.e., social cognition), self-referential cognition, and processing of social rewards. Meshi and colleagues suggest that the large-scale brain networks supporting these social cognitive processes include: mentalizing network (i.e., default-mode network); a self-referential cognition network; and a reward network.

15.2.3   Reconsideration of Existing Paradigms

As these insights from neuroscience suffuse the cyberpsychology literature, they may inspire reconsideration of existing paradigms. For example, the social brain hypothesis, which is the leading elucidation of the enlargement of the human brain during the course of evolution, was proffered by Oxford University's Robin Dunbar. According to the social brain hypothesis, human intelligence did not evolve mainly as a way to resolve ecological difficulties. Instead, human intelligence is argued to have evolved as a means of surviving and reproducing in complex social groups. The typical size of social groups in primates correlates closely with neocortex size in general (Dunbar, 1992), and with the more frontal units of the neocortex in particular (Dunbar, 2011; Joffe & Dunbar, 1997).

In the 1990s Dunbar proposed a neurocognitive limit to the number of people a person can have in their social network. For Dunbar, these relationships are ones in which a person knows who each person is in their social network and the ways in which each person in the network relates to every other person in the network (Dunbar, 1992, 1993). Dunbar's number was developed to explain the correlation between primate brain size and average social group size. Dunbar argues that natural social networks are regulated into a distinct succession of hierarchically inclusive layers that reflect both interaction frequencies and emotional closeness. In humans, these layers have values that approximate 5, 15, 50, and 150 (Dunbar, 2014). The resulting number of a 150 stable relationship limit was extrapolated from studies of primates and the average human brain size. It is important to emphasize that Dunbar's number is meant to reflect the number of stable relations a person knows and maintains social contact with. As such, it does not include people just generally known. According to Dunbar, this limit is relative to neocortical size, which in turn limits group size. Neocortical processing capacity limits the number of people that a person can have in their social network.

Recent studies of humans afford evidence of quantitative relations between social group size and brain regions that perform an important part in social cognition (Kanai et al., 2012; Lewis et al., 2011; Powell et al., 2012). Research has revealed that individual differences in human amygdala volume predicted variations in social network size and complexity (Bickart et al., 2011; Kanai et al., 2011; Sallet et al., 2011; Von Der Heide, Vyas, & Olson, 2014). From these studies it is apparent that the amygdala works in aggregate with an array of other brain regions that make up the "social brain." The amygdala is strongly connected with the vmPFC and superior temporal sulcus and has a broadly distributed topography of anatomical connections, which allows it to be considered a hub within the social brain. The connectional organization of the amygdala places it in an essential locus to influence a range of brain networks that are significant for social cognition (Bickart, Dickerson, & Barrett, 2014).

Dunbar's number comes primarily from work done before the advent of online social networks like Facebook. Does the seemingly ubiquitous and perpetual use of social media challenge the continued relevance of Dunbar's number? Perhaps it is possible to maintain more stable relations using Facebook, Twitter, and Instagram. Studies of offline social networking have found that the size and complexity of social networks correlated significantly with amygdala volume (Bickart et al., 2011). Recently, Kanai and colleagues (2012) investigated the relation between users' involvement in online social networks and the anatomical structure of human brain regions implicated in socio-cognitive behaviors. For the study, they made use of voxel-based morphometry in a large sample of adult humans. Specifically, they aimed to explore the relations between sociability indices (number of Facebook friends, and sociability) and amygdala volume as well as volume of several cortical regions. Specific brain regions were chosen (left middle temporal gyrus, right superior temporal sulcus, right entorhinal cortex) because they have been previously identified as being associated with theory of mind competences. Results revealed that the number of social contacts on a major online social networking site was strongly associated with the structure of focal brain regions. Specifically, they found that variation in the number of Facebook friends significantly predicted grey matter volume in left middle temporal gyrus, right superior temporal sulcus, and right entorhinal cortex. Furthermore, they found that the grey matter density of the amygdala that was earlier shown to be linked with offline social network size was also significantly related to online social network size.

While Kanai and colleagues' (2012) findings that the density of gray matter in the amygdala, right superior temporal sulcus, left middle temporal gyrus, and entorhinal cortex correlated with differences in social network size, other studies have also found that portions of the frontal lobe (including orbitofrontal cortex) have significant correlation with social network measures (Lewis et al., 2011). An issue that may be responsible for the discrepancies is the different social network measures used by different research groups. In a study by Von der Heide and colleagues (2014), efforts were taken to examine the importance of one online measure of social network size (e.g., number of Facebook friends) and two real-world measures (Dunbar's number and Norbeck Social Support Group). They found that volumetric differences predict social network size across a range of measures. Furthermore, findings provide support for left and right amygdal involvement. Support was also provided for the orbital frontal cortex and entorhinal/ventromedial anterior temporal lobe in processes required for the maintenance of robust social networks. While these results are preliminary, they offer interesting results that may lead to reconsideration of existing paradigms.

15.3   Addressing Concerns about Connecting Neuroscience to Cyberpsychology

Why has it taken so long for cyberpsychology to embrace neuroscientific approaches to studying human neurocognitive and affective processes? Researchers have only just started scratching the surface of exploring social media for insights into human social cognitive and affective processes. According to Mechi and colleagues (2015), the involvement of neuroscience in social media research appears to be particularly behind the times. In 2015, they were only able to find seven articles published on this topic. This reported dearth of studies is particularly astonishing given the uniquely suited nature of social media to support existing social neuroscience undertakings, and to facilitate new ones. In the following, there will be a discussion of potential concerns cyberpsychologists may have about adding neuroscience to their cyberpsychology research. These concerns are legitimate, but do not seem to negate the potential benefits of adding neuroscience to research in cyberpsychology. The chapter includes both articulations of some potential concerns and potential responses in favor of a brain-based cyberpsychology.

15.3.1   Theoretical and Language Issues

Each scientific discipline develops its own theoretical language with a specific vocabulary that both supports meaningful generalizations within the domain of study and helps to avoid irrelevant distinctions. As a subdiscipline of psychology, cyberpsychology is theoretically predisposed to a language that supports the description of supervenient (upon subvenient brain events) cognitive processes and behaviors as they occur during interactions with social media and simulation technologies. Neuroscience focuses upon subvenient neural events, and its vocabulary therefore may not support useful generalizations to supervenient mental processes found in cyberpsychology. The differences in the vocabularies of cyberpsychology and neuroscience may be so different that multidisciplinary theorizing is not possible. The vocabulary of cyberpsychology belongs to the social sciences and includes mental terms such as understanding and identity. It is fashioned for describing behavioral phenomena. By contrast, the vocabulary of neuroscience belongs to the biological sciences, in which material terms such as hemodynamic response and white matter tract are common parlance. The vocabulary of neuroscience is tailored for the description of physical phenomena. Why would we replace cyberpsychology language that has produced terms that are useful at the level of cognitive processing and behavior with reductionistic neuroscience terms (e.g., neurotransmitters, cell types, brain areas, genetics)? Even if the vocabulary of cyberpsychology could be comfortably reduced to that of neuroscience, the result may be of little practical significance to cyberpsychologists. What is the value of substituting a neuroscience description of a phenomenon for its cyberpsychological equivalent?

This is an interesting argument and one that is probably not that unfamiliar to cyberpsychologists. In fact, cyberpsychology itself is already the amalgamation of two languages: computer science and psychology. As Norman (2008) has pointed out, cyberpsychology can be broken down into prefix "cyber" and "psychology." The prefix "cyber" is from the term "cybernetics," which represents a study of the operation of control and communication systems. The "psychology" part of cyberpsychology refers to the study of behavior and cognitive processing. For Norman, cyberpsychology is best understood as research into the impact of computers, technology, and virtual environments on the psychology of individuals and groups. Instead of thinking of neuroscience and cyberpsychology as competing languages, it may be helpful to think of a brain-based cyberpsychology that incorporates theoretical findings and methods from neuroscience into the developing language of cyberpsychology. Given that cyberpsychology is already a blending of two languages, it may be well suited for incorporating an additional language.

15.3.2   Does Neuroscience Inform Cyberpsychology Research?

Neuroscience aims to identify the neural correlates of cognitive functions. To do this, neuroscientists collect data on brain areas that are selectively activated during various cognitive activities. A concern for the cyberpsychologist may be that knowledge of the location of a cognitive function tells us nothing about how to design a human–computer interface for affective computing. Furthermore, does the cyberpsychologist really need to know how Facebook likes are processed in the brain? In response to these questions, it is important to consider an aim of human neuroscience, which is to understand the neural bases of cognition and emotion. Historically, this has involved starting first with psychological constructs (e.g., working memory) and then identifying the neural correlates of that construct. Increasingly, however, neuroscience studies seek novel approaches to understanding the automatic and controlled cognitive (and affective) processes that are not readily apparent at the behavioral level.

The Internet offers cyberpsychologists a fertile area for investigating social networks. Online social networking and the increasing use of digital media might allow cyberpsychologists opportunities to assess the social brain and related hypotheses about relations among social networks and various brain areas. With the rise of social networking sites, cyberpsychologists have the opportunity to study the results of broadcasting one's information to many members of one's network at once. What happens when an individual receives a "like" to their posted content on a Facebook page? Typically, this represents a rewarding experience for the person and promotes further social networking.

The cyberpsychologist can take a cognitive behavioral perspective to explain what is happening when a person is liked on Facebook. For example, Facebook's strong impact on users can be discussed in terms of variable reinforcement schedules. Affirmations from social media (e.g., likes, text chimes, ringtones) from other users occur only sporadically. For a cyberpsychologist working within a behavioral perspective, this rate of online reinforcement represents a variable-ratio schedule that produces the sort of high steady rate of responding found in gambling and lottery games. How does this reward system become activated for Facebook users? The answer is that Facebook has multiple variable-ratio reinforcement schedules built into it – a user could receive a "like," friend request, comment on the user's status update, or be tagged in a photo. Any of these situations (among the many other possible) might place the user in a state of anticipation. This variable-ratio pattern of reinforcement can be more addicting than receiving affirmation every time because (at least in part) the user's brain endeavors to predict rewards. In variable-ratio reward schedules the brain cannot find the pattern and it will promote a behavior until it finds one. In situations where the rewards (e.g., affirmations, chimes) are random, the brain's attempt at pattern recognition may continue compulsively.

While this approach does give us an adequate explanation for behaviors within social media exchanges, it leaves out much of the story. What happens in the person's brain when he or she sees someone "like" their Facebook post? The answer may involve a part of the ventral striatum that lies in a region in the basal forebrain rostral to the preoptic area of the hypothalamus. Specifically, the reinforcing effect that occurs when a person experiences a "like" on Facebook reflects activity in the nucleus accumbens. There are a number of major inputs to the nucleus accumbens from specific brain areas (prefrontal cortex, amygdala (basolateral), and the ventral tegmental area (VTA)), and the nucleus accumbens is often described as being part of a cortico-striato-thalamo-cortical loop. The nucleus accumbens has an important role in the neurocognitive processing of reward, pleasure, reinforcement learning, aversion, and motivation. *Dopamine acts in the nucleus accumbens to attach motivational significance to stimuli associated with reward.* Dopaminergic neurons found in the VTA connect via the mesolimbic pathway and modulate the activity of neurons within the nucleus accumbens that are activated directly or indirectly by drugs like opiates and amphetamines. Dopamine offers a powerfully rewarding experience and has been linked to romantic love. In fact, the VTA and dopamine were important aspects of Helen Fisher (2006) of Match.com's model of the brain systems involved in mating and reproduction. She aimed to distinguish between romantic love and attachment. The brain activations associated with romantic love scores (e.g., VTA) have been found to be distinct from brain area activations associated with attachment (e.g., GP, SN).

This leads to the issue at hand. If cyberpsychologists want to explore social media and online dating sites they get an additional perspective if their theoretical formulations tap into literature on the reward areas of the brain and the ways in which these impact the user's ability to focus on other things. What does the nucleus accumbens and being liked have to do with Facebook? The answer is in the experience of being liked itself. This is a significant social event and essential to motivating human behavior.

We also discussed the impact of our default-mode network on cyberpsychology research. This large-scale brain network is inclined toward social processes and it takes the overriding control process of the executive-control network to inhibit automatic impulses, especially impulses to which we are strongly drawn. In the same way that the brain resists doing complex calculations in our heads, it requires extra effort to control impulses. Likewise, inhibiting impulses from the reward network requires a greater level of cognitive control. The realization that cognitive, affective, motivation, and social components are involved in something as simple as being liked on Facebook opens the door for enhanced understandings of cyberpsychology findings.

15.3.3 Are Neuroscience Methods Too Expensive to Apply to Education Research Questions?

The cost–benefit ratio may be a limiting factor for applying neuroscience methods to cyberpsychology studies. It costs approximately $1200 per participant hour to conduct a functional magnetic resonance imaging study. Most neuroimaging studies are performed at academic medical centers or with an affiliated hospital's scanner. Participants are often scanned later in the evening when the scanner is not being used for clinical purposes. When these requirements are compared to the infrastructure cost with the $25–$50 paid to a participant for an hour in a conventional laboratory experiment, or the $0 paid to students in a SONA study, the cost–benefit analysis does not support the much higher spending required for each neuroscience data point.

While it is the case that there are large differences between costs for a classroom study and neuroimaging, grant funding initiatives are in place that will support the extra costs. In fact, given the sorts of federal initiatives mentioned above and those in other countries, it is apparent that there is a great deal of interest in moving from small-scale studies to larger-budget studies that have potential to move science forward. Hence, neuroscience-relevant studies might attract additional research funding to cyberpsychology. For example, the National Institute of Mental Health's Research Domain Criteria (RDoC) is a heavily funded research framework for developing and implementing novel approaches to the study of mental disorders. Furthermore, there is a great deal of funding available from the BRAIN Initiative's ambitious but achievable set of goals for advances in science and technology. Since the announcement of the BRAIN Initiative, dozens of leading academic institutions, scientists, technology firms, and other important contributors to neuroscience have responded to this call. A group of prominent neuroscientists have developed a 12-year research strategy for the National Institutes of Health to achieve the goals of the initiative. The BRAIN Initiative may do for neuroscience what the Human Genome Project did for genomics. Funding is available to support the development and application of innovative technologies to enhance our understanding of brain function.

13.4   Neuroscience as Rapprochement of Theory-Driven and Data-Driven Differences

As a discipline, the psychology side of cyberpsychology tends to be theory-driven and the computer science side is data-driven. Reasoning about data can be understood by looking at how the data and hypotheses are related to each other. The theory-driven approach found in psychology reflects an integrated approach to understanding cognitive structures that are characterized by complex, descriptive categories with which the data are associated. In data-driven reasoning one reasons from the data to a hypothesis, whereas theory-driven reasoning involves using a hypothesis to explain the data. In practice, this means that the psychologist starts with a theoretical perspective that is constrained by prior findings found in the literature. From these prior findings, the psychologist develops a hypothesis and then analyzes the data to see whether the hypothesis is supported. This theory-driven approach is quite different from a data-driven approach found in computer science, wherein the researcher takes a dataset and runs analyses looking for patterns and associations that will inform the researcher of what questions to ask. For the cyberpsychologist, choosing between data-driven and theory-driven approaches can be a daunting task.

15.4.1 *General Linear Model versus Machine Learning*

In addition to differences in approaches to hypothesis generation between the cyber and psychology components of cyberpsychology, there are differences in data analytic techniques. Psychology research is largely focused upon theory-driven approaches that use the general linear model (GLM). Computer science research is often more interested in data-driven approaches that use a machine learning approach. A limitation of theory-driven regression analyses found in psychology is that they often lack the ability to contend effectively with non-linearity. A further limitation of regression analysis is that it is a theory-driven model, in which the significant assumptions concerning the underlying distribution of data must be specified in advance. Contrariwise, computer science approaches often neglect prior research and rely excessively upon the data to constrain theory development.

The GLM underlies most of the statistical analyses used in psychological research. It is a conceptualization of variance between groups (effect) and within groups (error). It is composed of three components: the grand mean, the predicted effect, and random error. In the GLM's regression analysis, relationships among variables are expressed in a linear equation that conveys a criterion as a function of a weighted sum of predictor variables. Psychological researchers use regression to assess both (1) the degree of accuracy of prediction, and (2) the relative importance of different predictors' contributions to variation in the criterion. Although the GLM is well known in data analysis, is reliable, and can provide robust particulars, the user must have the time and resources to perform an evaluation of the entire database. Further, managing the error independence problems found in psychological research necessitates even more sophisticated proficiencies.

The GLM tends to ascertain the more concrete significant trends while negating individual particularities. In cases where linear approximation is not possible due to noise (noise is not an inherent randomness or absence of causality in the world; rather, it is the effect of missing, or inaccurate, information about the world. In psychology, noise may include things such as confounding variables, nonparametric data, nonlinear associations, measurement error), or when nonlinear approximations may prove more efficacious, the models suffer accordingly. An example of a situation in which psychologists confront conditions where noise could confound a linear association is the testing of individuals with physical conditions that preclude standardized administration of tests or when testing environments face external interruptions. Nonlinear associations, not necessarily clearly understood but likely present, include age-related changes in cognition and differences in the qualitative characteristics of memories.

15.4.2   From Biological Neural Networks to Computationally Derived Artificial Neural Networks

There may be insights from neuroscience that aid the integration of psychology and computer science into cyberpsychology. Neuroscience has given us an understanding of biological neural networks that includes biological neurons that are networked together to form a complex, nonlinear, and parallel information processing system. The history of neuroscience reflects the history of its methods (Yuste, 2015). For over a century, neuroscience has embraced the neuron doctrine, in which the neuron is understood to be the structural and functional unit of the nervous system. The neuron has six basic functional properties: (1) input signals from the environment or other neurons; (2) integration and manipulation of the input; (3) conduction of the integrated information over distances; (4) output of information to other neurons or cells; (5) computational mapping of one type of information into another; and (6) representation subserving the formation of internal representations. While the neuron doctrine has provided a conceptual foundation for neuroscience, today newer multineuronal recording methods have revealed that ensembles of neurons, rather than individual cells, can form physiological units and generate emergent functional properties and states. Rafael Yuste (2015) recently reviewed the ways in which today neuroscientists are interested in a new paradigm for neuroscience, in which neural network models are used to describe emergent functional states that generate behavior and cognition.

From the biological neural networks found in neuroscience, computational approaches have been developed that mathematically simulate the function of a biological neuron. These artificial neural networks (especially back-propagated neural networks) have the following functional approximations of the biological neuron: (1) a processing unit set that is similar to the biological neuron itself; (2) an activation state that is similar to part of the input and integrative device of the biological neuron; (3) a unit-by-unit output function that is similar to the output of the biological neuron; (4) a connectivity pattern among units that is similar to the mapping of the biological neuron onto the conductive function of the biological neuron; (5) a propagation rule that propagates activity patterns through the artificial neural network that is also similar to the mapping of the biological neuron onto the conductive function of the biological neuron; (6) an activation rule that combines the signals of inputs stimulating a unit with the current condition of that unit to produce a new activation level for the unit. This is similar to the part of the input and integrative device of the biological neuron; (7) a learning rule that modifies the connectivity patterns relative to a given experience. This is part of the computational and representational functions of the biological neuron; and (8) the environment in which the artificial neural network is operating. This is also part of the computational and representational functions of the biological neuron.

An artificial neural network has the capacity to develop an information processing function from examples of that function for modeling curvilinear relations. The functional properties of artificial neural networks resemble biological neural networks in two respects: (a) knowledge is acquired by the network through a learning process; and (b) interneuron connection strengths (known as synaptic weights) are used to store that knowledge. Artificial neural networks offer a potential alternative information-processing paradigm that involves large interconnected networks of processing elements that are relatively simple non-linear units interconnected by communication channels. Connections transmit statistical (as opposed to symbolic) data, encoded by any of a variety of methods. Finally, the units operate only on their local data and on the inputs they receive via the connections.

Traditional data analytic strategies in psychology (i.e., theory-driven regression) and computational approaches (i.e., data-driven) may complement each other in solving previously intractable problems found in cyberpsychology. Although much of cyberpsychology research makes use of the general linear model's regression analysis and its derivatives for assessing relationships, computational approaches using artificial neural networks may be considered as additional statistical tools that researchers may use to overcome some of the disadvantages of conventional regression analysis. The addition of artificial neural networks to a cyberpsychology researcher's repertoire of data analytic tools can provide several advantages over the use of conventional regression models alone. Artificial neural networks are able to learn from a set of data without the need for a full specification of the decision model. Moreover, they automatically provide data transformations.

In a study using data from a virtual environment in a gertoological cohort, Parsons and colleagues (2004) compared the efficacy of GLM to a back-propagated artificial neural network. A simple multiple-layered, fully connected back-propagated artificial neural network typology (5-3-1 with systematically selected network parameters, a learning rate of 0.35, and about 500 epochs) outperformed the GLM's regression in both prediction and generalization. Although their reported regression analysis provided them with an adequate understanding of their data, the regression model's normality and independence of error variance restrictions limited its ability to predict and generalize under nonlinear conditions. Contrariwise, their back-propagated artificial neural network possessed the property to learn from a set of data without the need for a full specification of the decision model. When compared to the GLM's multiple regression analysis, the back-propagated artificial neural network was found to proffer an 18 percent increase in prediction of a common neuropsychological problem. A possible reason for this increase in predictability may be found in the back-propagated artificial neural network's ability to learn from new examples and generalize. Their ability to adjust the interconnectivity of weight coefficients between neurons results in error (between the computed output-dependent vector and the known dependent vector of the trained patterns) to be minimized. The training process of the back-propagated artificial neural network transmits backward the error to the network and adjusts the weights between the units connecting the output layer and the hidden layer and the hidden layer and the input layer. These findings suggest that cyberpsychologists can use insights from neurobiology to better model their data.

15.5 Ask Not What Neuroscience Can Do for Cyberpsychology, But What Cyberpsychology Can Do for the Neurosciences

It is important to note that the relation between cyberpsychologists and neuroscientists need not be viewed as asymmetrical. Just as neuroscience can inform cyberpsychology, there are methods and theoretical formulations from cyberpsychology that can enhance neuroscience. Cyberpsychology research is producing unique insights into the nature of complex cognition in simulated and online environments.

*15.5.1   Cyberpsychology and Simulated Environments for Affective
Neuroscience*

Cyberpsychology work in affective computing is an obvious area in which
neuroscience has played a role and an area of neuroscience that can be aided
by cyberpsychology. Affective computing aims to design machines that can
recognize, interpret, process, and simulate human affects. Support for what
is now called affective computing came from findings that persons interact
with computers and machines in a manner that is similar to the ways in
which humans interact socially with other humans. An obviously important aspect of affective computing is the participant's affective processing of
emotional content. Recent work in affective neuroscience suggests that
sophisticated cognitive–emotional behaviors have their base in the brain's
dynamic neural networks. It is important to note that none of these
dynamic coalitions of networks of brain areas should be understood as
explicitly cognitive or affective. Pessoa (2008) describes the brain areas
involved in these cognitive–emotional interactions as highly connected by
hubs that are significant for regulating the flow and integration of information among regions. Today, there are increasing efforts to move beyond
topographical localization to conceptualizations that emphasize a brain
network approach to emotions (Barrett & Satpute, 2013). In particular,
there is interest in conceptualizing emotional processing in terms of a large-
scale brain network for salience processing. The salience network is a large-
scale intrinsic network that has strong temporally organized coupling of
activity across distributed brain regions. Future cyberpsychology studies
can draw from work in dual process theories, findings related to the
salience network, and advances in affective computing to develop next-
generation studies of persons interacting with computers.

For affective neuroscience to move beyond static stimulus presentations
and/or paragraph-length descriptions of moral dilemmas, it needs to adopt
the simulation technologies found in cyberpsychology (Parsons, 2015;
Parsons, 2016; Parsons, Carlew, Magtoto, & Stonecipher, 2015; Parsons
& Phillips, 2016). For example, virtual-reality has recently become an
increasingly popular medium for assessment of various aspects of affective
arousal and emotional dysregulation (Parsons and Rizzo, 2008a). It has
been found to be an especially useful modality for assessing a participant
when real-world exposure would be too costly, time-consuming, or hazardous. For affective neuroscience, such simulation technologies offer
a chance to move beyond sterile stimulus paradigms to dynamic simulations of real-world activities.

One application of interest for affective neuroscience is the use of virtual environments for studies of fear conditioning. Virtual environments offer an ecologically valid platform for examinations of context-dependent fear reactions in simulations of real-life activities. Neuroimaging studies utilizing virtual environments have been used to delineate brain circuits involved in sustained anxiety to unpredictable stressors in humans. Virtual environments have also been used to elicit affective responses in everyday contexts. Perhaps most interesting is the ability to move beyond paragraph-based vignettes that require the participant to read and imagine an affectively arousing situation. Virtual environments are being applied to the affective neuroscience of moral decision-making. Recently, studies have emerged that take the classic Trolley Dilemma and modify the text-based approach via a Virtual Trolley Dilemma. Furthermore, while text-based hypothetical moral dilemmas led to gaps in our understanding of how results translate into real-world behaviors, virtual environments allow for observations of morally relevant decision-making behaviors in realistic three-dimensional simulations. With virtual environments, researchers can perform real-time assessment of the cognitive and affective factors inherent in explicit moral behaviors.

In summary, mere judgments about moral dilemmas result in a limited understanding. Hypothetical and text-based vignettes attempt to stimulate the imagination of participants and then use questionnaires or experiments involving low-level manipulations of harm to enhance understanding. The addition of virtual environments allows researchers to assess the expression of decision-making processes via real-time logging of behaviors. Given that virtual environments are more dynamic than text-based scenarios and that they do not involve the potential for harmful outcomes, they may bridge the gap between judgment and behavior via explorations of the underlying mechanisms. While the virtual environment approach does not offer a definitive solution to the long-standing trade-off between laboratory control and real-world behaviors, it does allow researchers a methodology for presenting participants with auditory and visual representations of real-world activities.

15.5.2 *Cyberpsychology and Simulated Environments for Social Neuroscience*

For social cognitive neuroscience there has been an increasing emphasis upon answering central questions about the nature of human neurocognition by adding neuroscience techniques to methods used by social scientists. A potential limitation to progress in social neuroscience is that many of the pioneering paradigms in social neuroscience reflect an emphasis upon laboratory control and experiments that fail to reflect social cognitive processing in everyday life. Zaki and Ochsner (2009) have argued that there are three critical ways that real-life social information differs from the sorts of laboratory stimuli found in many social neuroscience experiments. Specifically, they discuss the ways in which cues about target states in the real world are (1) multimodal (including visual, semantic, and prosodic information); (2) dynamic in that stimuli are presented serially or concurrently to participants over time; and (3) contextually embedded so that participants are presented with stimuli and environmental information that can frame their interpretation of another's internal states.

In addition to contextual embedding of dynamic and multimodal stimuli into social neuroscience research scenarios, there are limits to studies that do not involve social interactions. Our brains and behaviors are shaped by and typically take part in interaction with other humans. An unfortunate limitation of social neuroscience assessments is that it is difficult to generate study findings that can generalize beyond the narrow laboratory context. Many of the pioneering paradigms in social neuroscience involve observing static stimuli (e.g., simple, static representations of socially relevant stimuli; static photographs of emotionally valenced facial expressions) that are devoid of interactions. While there are a number of innovative paradigms to investigate the neural bases of various aspects of social interactions, they are missing essential everyday mechanisms.

While many of the pioneering paradigms in social neuroscience have used static stimuli to study social cognition in everyday activities, a number of researchers are beginning to question this approach (Chakrabarti, 2013; Risko et al., 2012; Schilbach et al., 2006). While video recordings, movies, and imagery techniques have been used by social neuroscientists to elicit emotions (Zaki & Ochsner, 2009), enhanced ecological approaches increase the capacity to manipulate the content of interactive media to induce specific emotional responses. As Neisser (1980) argued, participants observing video-recordings of others and then making judgments of what they saw miss an important interactive component that occurs in a social exchange. Recently, social neuroscientists have started incorporating the sorts of platforms and approaches that were historically used by cyberpsychologists into their experiments. Furthermore, they are increasingly using virtual-reality stimuli in social neuroscience research (Adolphs, 2003; Schilbach et al., 2013; Wilms et al., 2010).

Virtual environments offer the social neuroscientist the ability to induce a feeling of presence in participants as they experience emotionally engaging background narratives to enhance affective experience and social interactions (Diemer et al., 2015; Gorini et al., 2011). Recently, social neuroscientists have started incorporating virtual-reality into their experiments and are increasingly using virtual-reality stimuli in social neuroscience research (Adolphs, 2003; Schilbach et al., 2013; Wilms et al., 2010). In addition to advanced presentation of dynamic stimuli, virtual environments allow for moment-by-moment logging of interactive scenarios that comport well with the constraints of neuroimaging settings. As such, virtual environments offer promise for advancing the investigation of the neural underpinnings of joint actions (Kokal et al., 2009; Newman-Norlund et al., 2008; Pfeiffer et al., 2013; Schilbach et al., 2006, 2010). With advances in simulation technologies, the trade-off between the experimental control found in the laboratory and the ecological validity of naturalistic observation may be alleviated, as virtual technology can be modified and adapted without compromising measurement control (Bohil, Alicea, & Biocca, 2011).

15.5.3   *Cyberpsychology and Simulated Environments for Clinical Neuroscience*

Psychological assessment and intervention have become important components of cyberpsychology research and practice. During an intervention, patients may perform systematically presented and functionally oriented activities that are based upon an assessment and understanding of the patient's functioning (Harley, 1992). Methodical interventions are intended to increase the patient's ability to perform activities of daily living (Wilson, 2000). Interventions often aim at functional enhancements through reestablishing previously learned behavior patterns or establishing new patterns of activity or compensatory mechanisms.

Some approaches found in the clinical neurosciences focus upon increasing activities of daily living by systematic evaluation of current performance and reducing deficits by furnishing the patient with success strategies from a range of settings (Ylvisaker et al., 2001). These approaches to treatment of the cognitive, affective, and motor sequelae of central nervous system dysfunction often rely upon assessment measures to inform diagnosis and track changes in clinical status. The cyberpsychologist has much to offer to clinical neuroscience. Specifically, cyberpsychologists are aware of and practiced in the application of advanced technologies. This is important given the fact that many clinicians employ outmoded technologies in their research and praxes. For example, they employ assessments and interventions that involve standardized paper-and-pencil technologies that are limited in their stimulus presentation and logging of patient responses, and lack ecological validity (Parsons, 2015).

Within cyberpsychology there is a long history of using virtual-reality environments for clinical assessments and interventions. Early virtual environments attempted to build upon the construct-driven neuropsychological assessments found in traditional paper-and-pencil assessments. While early virtual environments had a number of limitations in their iterative development over the years, virtual-reality has now emerged as a promising tool in many domains of assessment (Jovanovski et al., 2012a; Parsons, 2015), therapy (Opris et al., 2012; Parsons et al., 2008a; Powers & Emmelkamp, 2008), training (Coyle, Traynor, & Solowij, 2015; Ke & Im, 2013), and rehabilitation (Parsons et al., 2009; Penn, Rose, & Johnson, 2009; Shin & Kim, 2015). Within this context VR technology represents a simulation of real-world training environments based on computer graphics. These can be useful as they allow instructors, therapists, and service providers to offer a safe, repeatable, and diversifiable environmental platform during treatment, which can benefit the learning of individuals, especially disabled users. Research has also pointed to VR's capacity to reduce patients' experience of aversive stimuli (Maskey et al., 2014) and reduce anxiety levels. The unique match between VR technology assets and the needs of various clinical application areas has been recognized by a number of authors (Cobb, 2007; Gorini & Riva, 2008; Trost & Parsons, 2014) and an encouraging body of research has emerged (Ke & Im, 2013; Parsons & Carlew, 2015; Riva, 2011, 2014).

Continuing advances in VR technology along with concomitant system cost reductions have supported the development of more usable, useful, and accessible VR systems that can uniquely be applied to a wide range of physical, psychological, and cognitive clinical targets and research questions (Bohil, Alicea, & Biocca, 2011). Virtual-reality makes use of virtual environments to present digitally recreated real-world activities to participants via immersive head-mounted displays (HMDs) and non-immersive (2D computer screens) media. Recent advances in VR technology allow for enhanced computational capacities for administration efficiency, stimulus presentation, automated logging of responses, and data analytic processing. Since virtual environments provide experimental control and dynamic presentation of stimuli in ecologically valid scenarios, they allow for controlled presentations of emotionally engaging background narratives to enhance affective experience and social interactions (Parsons, 2015). Moreover, the introduction of accessible and affordable HMDs has readied cyberpsychology to make the most of immersive and ecologically valid systems.

15.6   Need for Collaborative Cyberpsychological Knowledgebases

A further component needed for a brain-based cyberpsychology is that it be psychometrically validated and formalized for large-sample implementation and the development of collaborative cyberpsychological knowledgebases (Parsons, 2016). This will involve the development of repositories for linking cyberpsychological study results with data from neuroimaging, psychophysiology, and genetics. To develop this aspect of cyberpsychology, researchers should incorporate findings from the human genome project, advances in psychometric theory, information technologies, and neuroimaging. Enhanced evidence-based science and praxis is possible if cyberpsychologists do the following: (1) develop formal definitions of cyberpsychological concepts and tasks in cognitive ontologies; (2) create collaborative cyberpsychological knowledgebases; and (3) design novel assessment methods.

15.6.1   Formal Definitions of Cyberpsychological Concepts and Tasks in Cognitive Ontologies

An important growth area for cyberpsychology is the capacity for sharing knowledge gained from cyberpsychology studies with related disciplines. Obstacles to this shared knowledge approach include covariance among measures and the lack of operational definitions for key concepts and their interrelations. The covariance that exists among cyberpsychological measures designed to assess overlapping cognitive domains limits categorical specification into well-delineated domains. As such, cyberpsychological assessment batteries may be composed of multiple tests that measure essentially the same performance attributes. Poor test specificity may be revealed in the median correlations for common cyberpsychological tests. Future studies should look at multivariate approaches found in neuroinformatics that will allow for elucidation of the covariance information latent in cyberpsychological data.

15.6.2   Cyberpsychology's Need for Cognitive Ontologies

In addition to novel stochastic approaches to limiting covariance among measures, there is a need for formalizing cyberpsychological concepts into ontologies that offer formal descriptions of content domains. While ontologies abound in other biomedical disciplines, cyberpsychology lags in its development of formal ontologies. The idea of "ontologies" in neuroinformatics reflects the formal specification of entities that exist in a domain and the relations among them (Lenartowicz et al., 2010). A given ontology contains designations of separate entities along with a specification of ontological relations among entities that can include hierarchical relations (e.g., "is-a" or "part-of") or spatiotemporal relations (e.g., "preceded-by" or "contained-within"). These knowledge structures allow for consistent representations across models, which can facilitate communication among domains by providing an objective, concise, common, and controlled vocabulary. This consistency also allows for enhanced interoperability and provision of links among levels of analysis. Such ontologies have become central within many areas of neuroscience. In the realm of neuropsychology, several projects have been initiated to develop cognitive ontologies at the Consortium for Neuropsychiatric Phenomics (www.phenomics.ucla.edu). This consortium aims to enable more effective collaboration, and facilitation of knowledge sharing about cognitive phenotypes to other levels of biological knowledge (Bilder et al., 2011).

15.6.3   Web 2.0 and Collaborative Cyberpsychological Knowledgebases

In addition to shared definitions of cyberpsychological constructs, the development of ontologies enables systematic aggregation of cyberpsychological knowledge into shared databases. Technological developments in the use of the Internet for collective knowledge building are apparent in Web 2.0 practices that involve specialized Web tools. Web 2.0 represents a trend in open-platform Internet use that incorporates user-driven online networks and knowledgebases. A collaborative cyberpsychology knowledgebase would describe the "parts" and processes of cognitive functioning in a manner similar to descriptions of the cell's component parts and functions in gene ontology. Of course, such a project would require development if it is to provide a solid basis for annotation of brain-based cyberpsychological (e.g., neuroimaging of cognitive processes) data. Further, like other collaborative knowledgebases (e.g., Wikipedia), its realization will depend on the involvement of a large number of interested cyberpsychologists.

15.6   Conclusion

This book has consolidated a number of thoughts about the prospects for a brain-based cyberpsychology and solidified them with examples of how neuroscience and cyberpsychology can help each other. The addition of neuroscientific theories and praxes to cyberpsychology provides a new approach to historically studied phenomena. A brain-based cyberpsychology has the potential to revisit earlier findings, proffer considerable explanations of their mechanisms, and refocus theoretical debates when neuroscientific findings are in conflict with previous theorizing in cyberpsychology. That said, a brain-based cyberpsychology also enhances neuroscience research programs via the use of more dynamic and complex stimuli reflecting real-world functioning. Moreover, the computational sophistication of simulation technologies will allow for refined understanding and measurement of those stimuli. Crossing the bridges outlined in this book requires that cyberpsychologists formalize concepts for cyberpsychology ontologies. This will allow for the development of collaborative cyberpsychology knowledgebases that can connect cyberpsychology data with neuroscience databases. This will also enhance the attractiveness of cyberpsychology data for use by researchers involved in social, cognitive, and affective neuroscience. Given the current developments in cyberpsychology and the neurosciences outlined in this book, cyberpsychologists are encouraged to investigate the potential of a brain-based cyberpsychology.

References

Aardema, F., O'Connor, K., Côté, S., & Taillon, A. (2010). Virtual reality induces dissociation and lowers sense of presence in objective reality. *Cyberpsychology, Behavior, and Social Networking*, 13(4), 429–435.

Abascal, J., & Nicolle, C. (2005). Moving towards inclusive design guidelines for socially and ethically aware HCI. *Interacting with Computers*, 17(5), 484–505.

Abbate, J. (1999). *Inventing the Internet*. Cambridge, MA: MIT Press.

Abraham, S., & Chengalur-Smith, I. (2010). An overview of social engineering malware: Trends, tactics, and implications. *Technology in Society*, 32(3), 183–196.

Achtman, R. L., Green, C. S., & Bavelier, D. (2008). Video games as a tool to train visual skills. *Restorative Neurology and Neuroscience*, 26, 435–446.

Ackerman, P. L., Kanfer, R., & Goff, M. (1995). Cognitive and noncognitive determinants and consequences of complex skill acquisition. *Journal of Experimental Psychology: Applied*, 1, 270–304.

Acquisti, A., & Grossklags, J. (2004). Privacy attitudes and privacy behavior. In L. J. Camp & S. Lewis (Eds.), *Economics of information security* (Vol. 12, pp. 165–178). Boston, MA: Springer.

Adams, R., Finn, P., Moes, E., Flannery, K., & Rizzo, A. S. (2009). Distractibility in attention/deficit/hyperactivity disorder (ADHD): The virtual reality classroom. *Child Neuropsychology*, 15, 120–135.

Adler, R. F., & Benbunan-Fich, R. (2013). Self-interruptions in discretionary multitasking. *Computers in Human Behavior*, 29(4), 1441–1449.

Adolphs, R. (2003). Cognitive neuroscience of human social behaviour. *Nature Reviews Neuroscience*, 4(3), 165–178.

Adolphs, R. (2009). The social brain: Neural basis of social knowledge. *Annual Review of Psychology*, 60, 693.

Alcañiz, M., Rey, B., Tembl, J., & Parkhutik, V. (2009). A neuroscience approach to virtual reality experience using transcranial Doppler monitoring. *Presence*, 18(2), 97–111.

Alcaro, A., & Panksepp, J. (2011). The SEEKING mind: Primal neuro-affective substrates for appetitive incentive states and their pathological dynamics in addictions and depression. *Neuroscience & Biobehavioral Reviews*, 35(9), 1805–1820.

Alderman, N., Burgess, P. W., Knight, C., & Henman, C. (2003). Ecological validity of a simplified version of the multiple errands shopping test. *Journal of the International Neuropsychological Society*, 9(1), 31–44.

Alexander, G. E., DeLong, M. R., & Strick, P. L. (1986). Parallel organization of functionally segregated circuits linking basal ganglia and cortex. *Annual Review of Neuroscience*, 9, 357–381.

Allaire, J. C., Bäckman, L., Balota, D. A., Bavelier, D., Bjork, R. A., & Bower, G. H. (2014). A Consensus on the Brain Training Industry from the Scientific Community. *Max Planck Institute for Human Development and Stanford Center on Longevity*. Retrieved January 15, 2015 from *http://longev ity3.stanford.edu/blog/2014/10/15/the-consensuson-the-brain-training-industry from-the-scientific-community/*.

Allanson, J. (2002). Electrophysiologically-interactive computer systems. *IEEE Computers*, 35, 60–65.

Allanson, J., & Fairclough, S. H. (2004). A research agenda for physiological computing. *Interacting with Computers*, 16(5), 857–878.

Allison, B. Z., Brunner, C., Kaiser, V., Müller-Putz, G. R., Neuper, C., & Pfurtscheller, G. (2010). Toward a hybrid brain–computer interface based on imagined movement and visual attention. *Journal of Neural Engineering*, 7(2), 399–408.

Allison, B. Z., Dunne, S., Leeb, R., Millán, J. D. R., & Nijholt, A. (Eds.) (2012). *Towards practical brain-computer interfaces: Bridging the gap from research to real-world applications*. Berlin, Heidelberg: Springer Science & Business Media, Verlag.

Allison, B. Z., McFarland, D. J., Schalk, G., Zheng, S. D., Jackson, M. M., & Wolpaw, J. R. (2008). Towards an independent brain–computer interface using steady state visual evoked potentials. *Clinical Neurophysiology*, 119(2), 399–408.

Alsina-Jurnet, I., & Gutiérrez-Maldonado, J. (2010). Influence of personality and individual abilities on the sense of presence experienced in anxiety triggering virtual environments. *International Journal of Human-Computer Studies*, 68(10), 788–80.

Alvarez, R. P., Biggs, A., Chen, G., Pine, D. S., & Grillon, C. (2008). Contextual fear conditioning in humans: Cortical-hippocampal and amygdala contributions. *Journal of Neuroscience*, 28, 6211–6219.

Alvarez, R. P., Johnson, L., & Grillon, C. (2007). Contextual-specificity of short-delay extinction in humans: Renewal of fear-potentiated startle in a virtual environment. *Learning & Memory*, 14, 247–253.

Alzahabi, R., & Becker, M. W. (2013). The association between media multi-tasking, task-switching, and dual-task performance. *Journal of Experimental Psychology: Human Perception and Performance*, 39(5), 1485.

Amaoka, T., Laga, H., Yoshie, M., & Nakajima, M. (2011). Personal space-based simulation of non-verbal communications. *Entertainment Computing*, 2(4), 245–261.

Amaral, D. G., Price, J. L., Pitkaenen, A., & Carmichael, S. T. (1992). Anatomical organization of the primate amygdaloid complex. In J. P. Aggleton (Ed.), *The amygdala: Neurobiological aspects of emotion, memory, and mental dysfunction* (pp. 1–66). New York: Wiley.

American Psychiatric Association (2013). *Diagnostic and statistical manual of mental disorders* (5th edn.). Washington, DC: American Psychiatric Association.

Amft, M., Bzdok, D., Laird, A. R., Fox, P. T., Schilbach, L., & Eickhoff, S. B. (2015). Definition and characterization of an extended social-affective default network. *Brain Structure and Function*, 220(2), 1031–1049.

Amodio, D. M., & Frith, C. D. (2006). Meeting of minds: The medial frontal cortex and social cognition. *Nature Reviews Neuroscience*, 7(4), 268–277.

Amodio, D. M. (2014). The neuroscience of prejudice and stereotyping. *Nature Reviews Neuroscience*, 15, 670–682.

Anderson, B. B., Vance, A., Kirwan, B., Jenkins, J., & Eargle, D. (2015). Using fMRI to explain the effect of dual-task interference on security behavior. In *Information systems and neuroscience* (pp. 145–150). Switzerland: Springer International Publishing.

Anderson, B., Fagan, P., Woodnutt, T., & Chamorro-Premuzic, T. (2012). Facebook psychology: Popular questions answered by research. *Psychology of Popular Media Culture*, 1(1), 23.

Anderson, C. L., & Agarwal, R. (2010). Practicing safe computing: A multimedia empirical examination of home computer user security behavioral intentions. *MIS Quarterly*, 34(3), 613–643.

Anderson, E. W., Potter, K. C., Matzen, L. E., Shepherd, J. F., Preston, G. A., & Silva, C. T. (2011). A user study of visualization effectiveness using EEG and cognitive load. *Computer Graphics Forum*, 30(3), 791–800.

Anderson, J. R., & Schooler, L. J. (1991). Reflections of the environment in memory. *Psychological Science*, 2, 396–408.

Anderson, R. (2008). *Security engineering: A guide to building dependable distributed systems* (2nd edn.). Indianapolis, IN: Wiley.

Andrews, G., & Murphy, K. (2006). Does video-game playing improve executive function? *Frontiers in Cognitive Science*, 145–161.

Andrews-Hanna, J. R. (2012). The brain's default network and its adaptive role in internal mentation. *The Neuroscientist*, 18(3), 251–270.

Andrews-Hanna, J. R., Reidler, J. S., Sepulcre, J., Poulin, R., & Buckner, R. L. (2010). Functional-anatomic fractionation of the brain's default network. *Neuron* 65(4), 550–562.

Andrews-Hanna, J. R., Smallwood, J., & Spreng, R. N. (2014). The default network and self-generated thought: Component processes, dynamic control, and clinical relevance. *Annals of the New York Academy of Sciences*, 1316(1), 29–52.

Anguera, J. A., Boccanfuso, J., Rintoul, J. L., Al-Hashimi, O., Faraji, F., Janowich, J. et al. (2013). Video game training enhances cognitive control in older adults. *Nature*, 501, 97–101.

Appelbaum, L. G., Cain, M. S., Darling, E. F., & Mitroff, S. R. (2013). Action video game playing is associated with improved visual sensitivity, but not alterations in visual sensory memory. *Attention, Perception, and Psychophysics*, 75, 1161–1167.

Apperley, T. H. (2006). Genre and game studies: Toward a critical approach to video game genres. *Simulation & Gaming*, 37(1), 6–23.

Arbesman, S. (2012). *The half-life of facts: Why everything we know has an expiration date*. New York: Current.

Ariely, D., & Berns, G. S. (2010). Neuromarketing: The hope and hype of neuroimaging in business. *Nature Reviews Neuroscience*, 11(4), 284–292.

Armstrong, C., Reger, G., Edwards, J., Rizzo, A., Courtney, C., & Parsons, T.D. (2013). Validity of the Virtual Reality Stroop Task (VRST) in active duty military. *Journal of Clinical and Experimental Neuropsychology*, 35, 113–123.

Armstrong, G. B., Boiarsky, G. A., & Mares, M. (1991). Background television and reading performance. *Communications Monographs*, 58(3), 235–253.

Ashburner, J., & Friston, K. J. (2000). Voxel-based morphometry – the methods. *Neuroimage*, 11(6), 805–821.

Ashby, F. G., Maddox, W. T., & Lee, W. W. (1994). On the dangers of averaging across subjects when using multidimensional scaling or the similarity-choice model. *Psychological Science*, 5, 144–151.

Asimakopulos, J., Boychuck, Z., Sondergaard, D., Poulin, V., Ménard, I., & Korner-Bitensky, N. (2012). Assessing executive function in relation to fitness to drive: A review of tools and their ability to predict safe driving. *Australian Occupational Therapy Journal*, 59, 402–427.

Attrill, A., & Fullwood, C. (Eds.). (2016). *Applied cyberpsychology: Practical applications of cyberpsychological theory and research*. Palgrave Macmillan, UK.

Attrill, A. (Ed.). (2015). *Cyberpsychology*. Oxford University Press.

Aylett, R., Dias, J., & Paiva, A. (2006, June). An affectively driven planner for synthetic characters. In *Proceedings of the Sixteenth International Conference on Automated Planning and Scheduling ICAPS* (pp. 2–10).

Baas, J. M. P., van Ooijen, L., Goudriaan, A., & Kenemans, J. L. (2008). Failure to condition to a cue is associated with sustained contextual fear. *Acta Psychologica (Amsterdam)*, 127, 581–592.

Backs, R. W., & Seljos, K. A. (1994). Metabolic and cardiorespiratory measures of mental effort: The effects of level of difficulty in a working memory task. *International Journal of Psychophysiology*, 16, 57–68.

Baddeley, A. (1981). The cognitive psychology of everyday life. *British Journal of Psychology*, 72(2), 257–269.

Baddeley, M. (2011). *Information security: Lessons from behavioural economics*. Cambridge: Cambridge University.

Bainbridge, W. S. (2007). The scientific research potential of virtual worlds. *Science*, 317, 472–476. doi:10.1126/science.1146930.

Banaji, M., & Crowder, R. G. (1989). The bankruptcy of everyday memory. *American Psychologist*, 44, 1185–1193.

Banakou, D., Groten, R., and Slater, M. (2013). Illusory ownership of a virtual child body causes overestimation of object sizes and implicit attitude changes. *Proceedings of the National Academy of Sciences USA*, 110, 12846–12851.

Baniqued, P. L., Lee, H., Voss, M. W., Basak, C., Cosman, J. D., Desouza, S., et al. (2013). Selling points: What cognitive abilities are tapped by casual video games? *Acta Psychologica (Amsterdam)*, 142(1), 74–86.

Baños, R. M., Botella, C., Alcañiz, M., Liaño, V., Guerrero, B., & Rey, B. (2004). Immersion and emotion: Their impact on the sense of presence. *CyberPsychology & Behavior*, 7(6), 734–741.

Bar, M. (2007). The proactive brain: Using analogies and associations to generate predictions. *Trends in Cognitive Sciences*, 11(7), 280–289.

Bard, P., (1929). Emotion. I. The neuro-humoral basis of emotional reactions. In C. Murchsion (Ed.), *The foundations of experimental psychology* (pp. 449–487). Worcester, MA: Clark University Press.

Barnes, S. J., & Pressey, A. D. (2011). Who needs cyberspace? Examining drivers of needs in Second Life. *Internet Research*, 21(3), 236–254.

Baron, R. M., & Kenny, D. A. (1986). The moderator–mediator variable distinction in social psychological research: Conceptual, strategic, and statistical considerations. *Journal of Personality and Social Psychology*, 51(6), 1173.

Barr, N., Pennycook, G., Stolz, J. A., & Fugelsang, J. A. (2015). The brain in your pocket: Evidence that smartphones are used to supplant thinking. *Computers in Human Behavior*, 48, 473–480.

Barrett, L. F., & Satpute, A. B. (2013). Large-scale brain networks in affective and social neuroscience: Towards an integrative functional architecture of the brain. *Current Opinion in Neurobiology*, 23(3), 361–372.

Barsalou, L. W. (2008). Grounded cognition. *The Annual Review of Psychology*, 59, 617–645.

Bart, O., Raz, S., & Dan, O. (2014). Reliability and validity of the Online Continuous Performance Test among children. *Assessment*, 21(5), 637–643.

Bartolomeo, P. (2011). The quest for the "critical lesion site" in cognitive deficits: Problems and perspectives. *Cortex*, 47(8), 1010–1012.

Basak, C., Boot, W. R., Voss, M. W., and Kramer, A. F. (2008). Can training in a real-time strategy video game attenuate cognitive decline in older adults? *Psychology and Aging*, 23, 765–777.

Basak, C., Voss, M. W., Erickson, K. I., Boot, W. R., & Kramer, A. F. (2011). Regional differences in brain volume predict the acquisition of skill in a complex real-time strategy videogame. *Brain and Cognition*, 76(3), 407–414.

Bauer, R. M., Iverson, G. L., Cernich, A. N., Binder, L. M., Ruff, R. M., & Naugle, R. I. (2012). Computerized neuropsychological assessment devices: Joint position paper of the American Academy of Clinical Neuropsychology and the National Academy of Neuropsychology. *Clinical Neuropsychology*, 26, 177–196.

Baumann, S., Neff, C., Fetzick, S., Stangl, G., Basler, L., Vereneck, R., et al. (2003). A virtual reality system for neurobehavioral and functional MRI studies. *Cyberpsychology and Behavior*, 6, 259–266. doi:10.1089/109493103322011542.

Baumgartner, S. E., Weeda, W. D., van der Heijden, L. L., & Huizinga, M. (2014). The relationship between media multitasking and executive function in early adolescents. *The Journal of Early Adolescence*, 34(8), 1120–1144.

Baumgartner, T., Speck, D., Wettstein, D., Masnari, O., Beeli, G., & Jäncke, L. (2008). Feeling present in arousing virtual reality worlds: Prefrontal brain regions differentially orchestrate presence experience in adults and children. *Frontiers in Human Neuroscience*, 2, 1–12.

Baumgartner, T., Valko, L., Esslen, M., & Jäncke, L. (2006). Neural correlate of spatial presence in an arousing and noninteractive virtual reality: An EEG and psychophysiology study. *CyberPsychology & Behavior*, 9(1), 30–45.

Bavelier, D., Achtman, R. L., Mani, M., & Föcker, J. (2012). Neural bases of selective attention in action video game players. *Vision Research*, 61, 132–143.

Bavelier, D., Green, C. S., & Dye, M. W. (2010). Children, wired: For better and for worse. *Neuron*, 67(5), 692–701.

Bayless, J., Varney, N.R., & Roberts, R. (1989). Tinker Toy Test performance and vocational outcome in patients with closed head injuries. *Journal of Clinical and Experimental Neuropsychology*, 11, 913–917.

Beardon, L., Parsons, S., & Neale, H. (2001). An inter-disciplinary approach to investigating the use of virtual reality environments for people with Asperger syndrome. *Educational and Child Psychology*, 18(2), 53–62.

Beatty, J., & Wagoner, B. L. (1978). Pupillometric signs of brain activation vary with level of cognitive processing. *Science*, 199, 1216–1218.

Becchio, C., Sartori, L., & Castiello, U. (2010). Toward you the social side of actions. *Current Directions in Psychological Science*, 19(3), 183–188.

Bechara, A. (2007). *Iowa gambling task professional manual*. Lutz, FL: Psychological Assessment Resources, Inc.

Bechara, A., & Damasio, A. R. (2005). The somatic marker hypothesis: A neural theory of economic decision. *Games and Economic Behavior*, 52(2), 336–372.

Bechara, A., Damasio, A. R., Damasio, H., & Anderson, S. W. (1994). Insensitivity to future consequences following damage to human prefrontal cortex. *Cognition*, 50(1), 7–15.

Bechara, A., Damasio, H., Damasio, A. R., and Lee, G. P. (1999). Different contributions of the human amygdala and ventromedial prefrontal cortex to decision-making. *The Journal of Neuroscience*, 19, 5473–5481.

Bechara, A., Damasio, H., Tranel, D., & Anderson, S. W. (1998). Dissociation of working memory from decision making within the human prefrontal cortex. *The Journal of Neuroscience*, 18(1), 428–437.

Bechara, A., Damasio, H., Tranel, D., & Damasio, A. R. (1997). Deciding advantageously before knowing the advantageous strategy. *Science*, 275(5304), 1293–1295.

Bechara, A., Tranel, D., & Damasio, H. (2000). Characterization of the decision-making deficit of patients with ventromedial prefrontal cortex lesions. *Brain*, 123(11), 2189–2202.

Bechara, A., Damasio, H., & Damasio, A. R. (2000). Emotion, decision making and the orbitofrontal cortex. *Cerebral Cortex*, 10(3), 295–307.

Bechara, A., Tranel, D., Damasio, H., & Damasio, A. R. (1996). Failure to respond autonomically to anticipated future outcomes following damage to prefrontal cortex. *Cerebral Cortex*, 6, 215–225.

Bechara, A., & Van der Kooy, D. (1989). The tegmental pedunculopontine nucleus: A brainstem output of the limbic system critical for the conditioned place references produced by morphine and amphetamine. *Journal of Neuroscience*, 9, 3440–3449.

Becker, M. W., Alzahabi, R., & Hopwood, C. J. (2013). Media multitasking is associated with symptoms of depression and social anxiety. *Cyberpsychology, Behavior, and Social Networking*, 16(2), 132–135.

Beer, J. S. (2014). Exaggerated positivity in self-evaluation: A social neuroscience approach to reconciling the role of self-esteem protection and cognitive bias. *Social and Personality Psychology Compass*, 8(10), 583–594.

Behm-Morawitz, E. (2013). Mirrored selves: The influence of self-presence in a virtual world on health, appearance, and well-being. *Computers in Human Behavior*, 29(1), 119–128.

Bélanger, F., & Crossler, R. E. (2011). Privacy in the digital age: A review of information privacy research in information systems. *MIS Quarterly*, 35(4), 1017–1042.

Bell, M., & Fox, N. (2003). Cognition and affective style: individual differences in brain electrical activity during spatial and verbal tasks. *Brain and Cognition*, 53, 441–451.

Benbasat, I., Dimoka, A., Pavlou, P. A., & Qiu, L. (2010). Incorporating social presence in the design of the anthropomorphic interface of recommendation agents: Insights from an fMRI study. In *Proceedings of the 31st International Conference on Information Systems* (December, pp. 1–22). Atlanta: Association for Information Systems.

Bennett, K. B., Cress, J. D., Hettinger, L. J., Stautberg, D., & Haas, M.W. (2001). A theoretical analysis and preliminary investigation of dynamically adaptive interfaces. *International Journal of Aviation Psychology*, 11, 169–196.

Ben-Shakhar, G. (1985). Standardization within individuals: A simple method to neutralize individual differences in skin conductance. *Psychophysiology* 22, 292–299.

Berka, C., Levendowski, D. J., Lumicao, M. N., Yau, A., Davis, G., Zivkovic, V. T., Olmstead, R. E., Tremoulet, P. D., & Craven, P. L. (2007). EEG correlates of task engagement and mental workload in vigilance, learning, and memory tasks. *Aviation, Space, and Environmental Medicine*, 78, B231–B244.

Berntson, G. G., Boyson, S. T., & Cacioppo, J. T. (1992). Cardiac orienting and defensive responses: Potential origins in autonomic space. In B.A. Campbell,

H. Hayne, & R. Richardson (Eds.), *Attention and information processing in infants and adults: Perspectives from human and animal research* (pp. 163–200). Hillsdale, NJ: Erlbaum.

Berretty, P. M., Todd, P. M., & Martignon, L. (1999). Categorization by elimination: Using few clues to choose. In G. Gigerenzer, P. M. Todd, & the ABC Research Group (Eds.), *Simple heuristics that make us smart* (pp. 235–254). New York: Oxford University Press.

Berthoz, S., Armony, J. L., Blair, R. J. R., & Dolan, R. J. (2002). An fMRI study of intentional and unintentional (embarrassing) violations of social norms. *Brain*, 125(8), 1696–1708.

Bessiere, K., Fleming, A., & Kiesler, S. (2007). The Ideal Elf: Identity exploration in world of warcraft. *CyberPsychology & Behaviour*, 10(4), 530–535.

Bickart, K. C., Dickerson, B. C., & Barrett, L. F. (2014). The amygdala as a hub in brain networks that support social life. *Neuropsychologia*, 63, 235–248.

Bickart, K. C., Hollenbeck, M. C., Barrett, L. F., & Dickerson, B. C. (2012). Intrinsic amygdala–cortical functional connectivity predicts social network size in humans. *The Journal of Neuroscience*, 32(42), 14729–14741.

Bickart, K. C., Wright, C. I., Dautoff, R. J., Dickerson, B. C., & Barrett, L. F. (2011). Amygdala volume and social network size in humans. *Nature Neuroscience*, 14(2), 163–164.

Bilder, R. M. (2011). Neuropsychology 3.0: Evidence-based science and practice. *Journal of the International Neuropsychological Society*, 17(01), 7–13.

Billieux, J., Schimmenti, A., Khazaal, Y., Maurage, P., & Heeren, A. (2015). Are we overpathologizing everyday life? A tenable blueprint for behavioral addiction research. *Journal of Behavioral Addictions*, 4, 142–144.

Billieux, J., & Van der Linden, M. (2012). Problematic use of the Internet and self-regulation: A review of the initial studies. *The Open Addiction Journal*, 5, 24–29.

Biocca, F. (1992a). Communication within virtual reality: Creating a space for research. *Journal of Communication*, 42(4), 5–22.

Biocca, F. (1992b). Virtual reality technology: A tutorial. *Journal of Communication*, 42(4), 23–72.

Biocca, F., & Delaney, B. (1995). Immersive virtual reality technology. In F. Biocca & M. R. Levy (Eds.), *Communication in the age of virtual reality* (pp. 57–124). Hillsdale, NJ: Erlbaum.

Biocca, F., Harms, C., & Burgoon, J. K. (2003). Toward a more robust theory and measure of social presence: Review and suggested criteria. *PRESENCE: Teleoperators and Virtual Environments*, 12, 456–480.

Biocca, F., & Levy, M. R. (1995). Communication applications of virtual reality. In F. Biocca & M. R. Levy (Eds.) (Eds.), *Communication in the age of virtual reality* (pp. 127–157). Hillsdale, NJ: Erlbaum.

Bioulac, S., Lallemand, S., Rizzo, A., Philip, P., Fabrigoule, C., & Bouvard, M. P. (2012). Impact of time on task on ADHD patient's performances in a virtual classroom. *European Journal of Paediatric Neurology*, 16(5), 514–521.

Błachnio, A., & Przepiorka, A. (2015). Dysfunction of self-regulation and self-control in Facebook addiction. *Psychiatric Quarterly*, 1–8.

Blacker, K. J., & Curby, K. M. (2013). Enhanced visual short-term memory in action video game players. *Attention, Perception, and Psychophysics*, 75, 1128–1136.

Blair, R. J. R., Morris, J. S., Frith, C. D., Perrett, D. I., & Dolan, R. J. (1999). Dissociable neural responses to facial expressions of sadness and anger. *Brain*, 122(5), 883–893.

Blascovich, J. (2001). Immersive virtual environments and social behavior. *Science Briefs: Psychological Science Agenda*, 14, 8–9.

Blascovich, J., Loomis, J., Beall, A. C., Swinth, K. R., Hoyt, C. L., & Bailenson, J. N. (2002). Immersive virtual environment technology as a methodological tool for social psychology. *Psychological Inquiry*, 13, 103–124.

Boehm-Davis, D. A., Gray, W. D., Adelman, L., Marshall, S., & Pozos, R. (2003). Understanding and measuring cognitive workload: A coordinated multi-disciplinary approach. *Defense Technical Information Center OAI-PMH Repository*, 1–46.

Bohil, C. J., Alicea, B., & Biocca, F. A. (2011). Virtual reality in neuroscience research and therapy. *Nature Reviews Neuroscience*, 12(12), 752–762.

Boiten, F. A., Frijda, N. H., & Wientjes, C. J. E. (1994). Emotions and respiratory patterns: Review and critical analysis. *International Journal of Psychophysiology*, 17, 103–128.

Boot, W. R., Blakely, D. P., & Simons, D. J. (2011). Do action video games improve perception and cognition? *Frontiers in Psychology*, 2, 226. doi: 10.3389/fpsyg.2011.00226.

Boot, W. R., Kramer, A. F., Simons, D. J., Fabiani, M., & Gratton, G. (2008). The effects of video game playing on attention, memory, and executive control. *Acta Psychologica*, 129, 387–398.

Bos, D. P. O., Reuderink, B., van de Laar, B., Gürkök, H., Mühl, C., Poel, M., . . . & Heylen, D. (2010). Brain-computer interfacing and games. In *Brain-computer interfaces* (pp. 149–178). London: Springer.

Bottari, C., Dassa, C., Rainville, C., & Dutil, E. (2009). The criterion-related validity of the IADL Profile with measures of executive functions, indices of trauma severity and sociodemographic characteristics. *Brain Injury*, 23, 322–335.

Bouchard, S., St-Jacques, J., Robillard, G., & Renaud, P. (2008). Anxiety increases the feeling of presence in virtual reality. *Presence* 17, 376–391.

Boudreau, C., McCubbins, M. D., & Coulson, S. (2009). Knowing when to trust others: An ERP study of decision making after receiving information from unknown people. *Social Cognitive and Affective Neuroscience*, 4(1), 23–34.

Boulos, M. N., & Wheeler, S. (2007). The emerging Web 2.0 social software: An enabling suite of sociable technologies in health and healthcare education. *Health Information and Libraries Journal*, 24, 2–23. doi:10.1111/j.1471-1842.2007.00701.x.

Boulous, M. N., Hetherington, L., & Wheeler, S. (2007). Second Life: An overview of the potential of 3-D virtual worlds in medical and health education. *Health Information and Libraries Journal*, 24, 233–245. doi:10.1111/j.1471-1842.2007.00733.x.

Bowman, L. L., Levine, L. E., Waite, B. M., & Gendron, M. (2010). Can students really multitask? An experimental study of instant messaging while reading. *Computers & Education*, 54(4), 927–931.

Boyd, D. M., & Ellison, N. B. (2007). Social network sites: Definition, history and scholarship. *Journal of Computer-Mediated Communications*, 13, 210–230.

Boyle, E., Terras, M. M., Ramsay, J., & Boyle, J. M. (2013). Executive functions in digital games. *Psychology, Pedagogy, and Assessment in Serious Games*, 19–46.

Bradley, M. M., & Lang, P. J. (2000). Affective reactions to acoustic stimuli. *Psychophysiology*, 37, 204–215.

Branco, P., & Encarnacao, L. M. (2004). Affective Computing for Behavior-based UI Adaptation, *Procedures of Intelligent User Interface 2004 Conference*, Ukita.

Brand, M., Young, K. S., & Laier, C. (2014). Prefrontal control and Internet addiction: A theoretical model and review of neuropsychological and neuroimaging findings. *Frontiers in Human Neuroscience*, 8, 375–390.

Brandt, J., Sullivan, C., Burrell II, L. E., Rogerson, M., & Anderson, A. (2013). Internet-based screening for dementia risk. *PloS one*, 8(2), e57476.

Brave, S., Nass, C., & Hutchinson, K. (2005). Computers that care: Investigating the effects of orientation of emotion exhibited by an embodied computer agent. *International Journal of Human-Computer Studies*, 62(2), 161–178.

Brennan, D. M., Mawson, S., & Brownsell, S. (2009). Telerehabilitation: Enabling the remote delivery of healthcare, rehabilitation, and self-management. *Studies in Health Technology and Informatics*, 145, 231–248.

Bressler, S. L. (1995) Large-scale cortical networks and cognition. *Brain Research Reviews*, 20, 288–304.

Bressler, S. L., & Menon, V. (2010). Large-scale brain networks in cognition: emerging methods and principles. *Trends in Cognitive Sciences*, 14(6), 277–290.

Bressler, S. L., Tang, W., Sylvester, C. M., Shulman, G. L., & Corbetta, M. (2008). Top-down control of human visual cortex by frontal and parietal cortex in anticipatory visual spatial attention. *The Journal of Neuroscience*, 28(40), 10056–10061.

Brevers, D., & Noël, X. (2013). Pathological gambling and the loss of willpower: a neurocognitive perspective. *Socioaffective Neuroscience & Psychology*, 3.

Brock, L.L., Rimm-Kaufman, S.E., Nathanson, L., & Grimm, K.J. (2009). The contributions of "hot" and "cool" executive function to children's academic achievement, learning-related behaviors, and engagement in kindergarten. *Early Childhood Research Quarterly*, 24, 337–349.

Brockmyer, J. F. (2015). Playing violent video games and desensitization to violence. *Child and Adolescent Psychiatric Clinics of North America*, 24(1), 65–77.

Brookings, J. B., Wilson, G. F., & Swain, C. R. (1996). Psychophysiological responses to changes in workload during simulated air traffic control. *Biological Psychology*, 42, 361–377.

Buckley, D., Codina, C., Bhardwaj, P., & Pascalis, O. (2010). Action video game players and deaf observers have larger Goldmann visual fields. *Vision Research*, 50, 548–556.

Buckner, R. L., Andrews-Hanna, J. R., & Schacter, D. L. (2008). The brain's default network. *Annals of the New York Academy of Sciences*, 1124(1), 1–38.

Buelow, M. T., & Suhr, J. A. (2009). Construct validity of the Iowa gambling task. *Neuropsychology Review*, 19(1), 102–114.

Buettner, R. (2015). Investigation of the relationship between visual website complexity and users' mental workload: A NeuroIS perspective. In *Information systems and neuroscience* (pp. 123–128). Switzerland: Springer International Publishing.

Buettner, R., Sauer, S., Maier, C., & Eckhardt, A. (2015, January). Towards ex ante prediction of user performance: A novel NeuroIS methodology based on real-time measurement of mental effort. In *System Sciences (HICSS), 2015 48th Hawaii International Conference on* (pp. 533–542). IEEE.

Bulgurcu, B., Cavusoglu, H., & Benbasat, I. (2010). Information security policy compliance: An empirical study of rationality-based beliefs and information security awareness. *MIS Quarterly*, 34(3), 523–548.

Burak, L. (2012). Multitasking in the university classroom. *International Journal for the Scholarship of Teaching and Learning*, 6(2), 8.

Burgess, P. W. (1997). Theory and methodology in executive function and research. In P. Rabbitt (Ed.), *Methodology of frontal and executive function* (pp. 81–116). Hove, UK: Psychology Press.

Burgess, P. W. (2000). Strategy application disorder: The role of the frontal lobes in human multitasking. *Psychological Research*, 63, 279–288.

Burgess, P. W., Alderman, N., Evans, J., Emslie, H., & Wilson, B. A. (1998). The ecological validity of tests of executive function. *Journal of the International Neuropsychological Society*, 4(06), 547–558.

Burgess, P. W., Alderman, N., Forbes, C., Costello, A., Coates, L., Dawson, D. R., Anderson, N. D., Gilbert, S. J., Dumontheil, I., and Channon, S. (2006). The case for the development and use of "ecologically valid" measures of executive function in experimental and clinical neuropsychology. *Journal of the International Neuropsychological Society*, 12(02), 194–209.

Burgess, P. W., & Simons, J. S., (2005). Theories of frontal lobe executive function: Clinical applications. In P. W. Halligan & D. T. Wade (Eds.), *Effectiveness of rehabilitation for cognitive deficits* (pp. 211–231). Oxford: Oxford University Press.

Burgess, P. W., Veitch, E., de Lacy Costello, A., & Shallice, T. (2000). The cognitive and neuroanatomical correlates of multitasking. *Neuropsychologia*, 38, 848–863.

Bush, G., Luu, P., & Posner, M. I. (2000). Cognitive and emotional influences in anterior cingulate cortex. *Trends in Cognitive Sciences*, 4(6), 215–222.

Bush, G. (2010). Attention-deficit/hyperactivity disorder and attention networks. *Neuropsychopharmacology* 35, 278–300.

Buxbaum, L., Dawson, A., & Linsley, D. (2012). Reliability and validity of the virtual reality lateralized attention test in assessing hemispatial neglect in right hemisphere stroke. *Neuropsychology*, 26, 430–441.

Byrne, E. A., & Parasuraman, R. (1996). Psychophysiology and adaptive automation. *Biological Psychology*, 42, 249–268.

Bzdok, D., Schilbach, L., Vogeley, K., Schneider, K., Laird, A. R., Langner, R., & Eickhoff, S. B. (2012). Parsing the neural correlates of moral cognition: ALE meta-analysis on morality, theory of mind, and empathy. *Brain Structure and Function*, 217(4), 783–796.

Cacioppo, J. T. (1994). Social neuroscience: Autonomic, neuroendocrine, and immune responses to stress. *Psychophysiology*, 31(2), 113–128.

Cacioppo, J. & Berntson, G. (1992). Social psychological contributions to the decade of the brain. Doctrine of multilevel analysis. *American Psychologist*, 47(8), 1019–1028.

Cacioppo, J. T., Berntson, G. G., & Crites, S. L. (1996). Social neuroscience: Principles of psychophysiological arousal and response. In E. T. Higgins & A. W. Kruglanski (Eds.), *Social psychology: Handbook of basic principles*, pp. 72–101. New York: Guilford.

Cacioppo, J. T., Berntson, G. G., & Decety, J. (2010). Social neuroscience and its relationship to social psychology. *Social Cognition*, 28(6), 675.

Cacioppo, J. T., & Decety, J. (2011). Social neuroscience: Challenges and opportunities in the study of complex behavior. *Annals of the New York Academy of Sciences*, 1224(1), 162–173.

Cacioppo, S., Frum, C., Asp, E., Weiss, R. M., Lewis, J. W., & Cacioppo, J. T. (2013). A quantitative meta-analysis of functional imaging studies of social rejection. *Scientific Reports*, 3.

Cacioppo, J. T., & Tassinary, L. G. (1990). Inferring psychological significance from physiological signals. *American Psychologist*, 45(1), 16.

Cacioppo, J. T., Tassinary, L. G., & Berntson, G. (Eds.), (2007). *Handbook of psychophysiology*. Cambridge: Cambridge University Press.

Cain, M. S., Landau, A. N., & Shimamura, A. P. (2012) Action video game experience reduces the cost of switching tasks. *Attention, Perception, & Psychophysics*, 1–7.

Cain, M. S., & Mitroff, S. R. (2011). Distractor filtering in media multitaskers. *Perception-London*, 40(10), 1183.

Calhoun, V. D., & Pearlson, G. D. (2012). A selective review of simulated driving studies: Combining naturalistic and hybrid paradigms, analysis approaches and future directions. *NeuroImage*, 59, 25–35.

Calvo, R., & D'Mello, S. (2010). Affect detection: An interdisciplinary review of models, methods, and their applications. *Affective Computing, IEEE Transactions on*, 1(1), 18–37.

Calvo, R. A., D'Mello, S., Gratch, J., & Kappas, A. (Eds.), (2014). *The Oxford handbook of affective computing*. Oxford University Press, USA.

Campbell, C. M., et al. (2010). Catastrophizing delays the analgesic effect of distraction. *Pain*, 149(2), 202–207.

Campbell, Z., Zakzanis, K. K., Jovanovski, D., Joordens, S., Mraz, R., & Graham, S. J. (2009). Utilizing virtual reality to improve the ecological validity of clinical neuropsychology: An FMRI case study elucidating the neural basis of planning by comparing the Tower of London with a three-dimensional navigation task. *Applied Neuropsychology*, 16(4), 295–306.

Cao, X., Douguet, A. S., Fuchs, P., & Klinger, E. (2010). Designing an ecological virtual task in the context of executive functions: a preliminary study. *Proceedings of the 8th International Conference on Disability, Virtual Reality and Associated Technologies*, 31, 71–78.

Carberry, S., & de Rosis, F. (2008). Introduction to special Issue on "Affective modeling and adaptation." *User Modeling and User-Adapted Interaction*, 18(1–2), 1–9.

Carlin, A. S., Hoffman, H. G., & Weghorst, S. (1997). Virtual reality and tactile augmentation in the treatment of spider phobia: A case report. *Behaviour Research and Therapy*, 35, 153–158.

Carr, N. (2010). *The shallows: How the Internet is changing the way we think, read and remember*. Atlantic Books Ltd.

Carrier, L. M., Rosen, L. D., Cheever, N. A., & Lim, A. F. (2015). Causes, effects, and practicalities of everyday multitasking. *Developmental Review*, 35, 64–78.

Carroll, D., Turner, J. R., & Hellawell, J. C. (1986). Heart rate and oxygen consumption during active psychological challenge: The effects of level of difficulty. *Psychophysiology*, 23, 174–181.

Carter, E. J., & Pelphrey, K. A. (2008). Friend or foe? Brain systems involved in the perception of dynamic signals of menacing and friendly social approaches. *Social Neuroscience*, 3(2), 151–163.

Carter, Sid & Smith Pasqualini, Marcia (2004). Stronger autonomic response accompanies better learning: A test of Damasio's somatic marker hypothesis. *Cognition and Emotion*, 18(7), 901–911.

Castel, A. D., Pratt, J., & Drummond, E. (2005). The effects of action video game experience on the time course of inhibition of return and the efficiency of visual search. *Acta Psychologica (Amsterdam)*, 119, 217–230.

Castellanos, F. X., Margulies, D. S., Kelly, C., Uddin, L. Q., Ghaffari, M., Kirsch, A., ... & Sonuga-Barke, E. J. (2008). Cingulate-precuneus interactions: A new locus of dysfunction in adult attention-deficit/hyperactivity disorder. *Biological Psychiatry*, 63(3), 332–337.

Castellanos, F. X., & Proal, E. (2012). Large-scale brain systems in ADHD: Beyond the prefrontal–striatal model. *Trends in Cognitive Sciences*, 16(1), 17–26.

Castellanos, F. X., Sonuga-Barke, E. J., Milham, M. P., & Tannock, R. (2006). Characterizing cognition in ADHD: Beyond executive dysfunction. *Trends in Cognitive Sciences*, 10(3), 117–123.

Catani, M., & Mesulam, M. (2008). What is a disconnection syndrome? *Cortex*, 44(8), 911–913.

Chakrabarti, B. (2013). Parameterising ecological validity and integrating individual differences within second-person neuroscience. *Behavioral and Brain Sciences*, 36(04), 414–415.

Chaminade, T., Hodgins, J., & Kawato, M. (2007). Anthropomorphism influences perception of computer-animated characters' actions. *Social Cognitive and Affective Neuroscience*, 3, 206–216.

Chan, R. C. K., Shum, D., Toulopoulou, T., & Chen, E. Y. H. (2008). Assessment of executive functions: Review of instruments and identification of critical issues. *Archives of Clinical Neuropsychology*, 23(2), 201–216.

Chandler J, Mueller P, & Paolacci G. 2014. Nonnaïveté among AmazonMechanical Turk workers: Consequences and solutions for behavioral researchers. *Behavior Research Methods*, 46, 112–130.

Chang, L. J., Yarkoni, T., Khaw, M. W., & Sanfey, A. G. (2012). Decoding the role of the insula in human cognition: Functional parcellation and large-scale reverse inference. *Cerebral Cortex*, 23, 739–749.doi:10.1093/cercor/bhs065.

Charlier, N., Zupancic, N., Fieuws, S., Denhaerynck, K., Zaman, B., & Moons, P. (2016). Serious games for improving knowledge and self-management in young people with chronic conditions: A systematic review and meta-analysis. *Journal of the American Medical Informatics Association*, 23(1), 230–239.

Chaytor, N., & Schmitter-Edgecombe, M. (2003). The ecological validity of neuropsychological tests: A review of the literature on everyday cognitive skills. *Neuropsychology Review*, 13(4), 181–197.

Chaytor, N., Schmitter-Edgecombe, M., & Burr, R. (2006). Improving the ecological validity of executive functioning assessment. *Archives of Clinical Neuropsychology*, 21(3), 217–227.

Chelune, G. J., & Moehle, K. A. (1986). Neuropsychological assessment and everyday functioning. In D. Wedding, A. M. Horton, & J. Webster (Eds.), *The neuropsychology handbook* (pp. 489–525). New York: Springer.

Chen, H. L. (2009). Consumer risk perception and addictive consumption behavior. *Social Behavior and Personality: An International Journal*, 37(6), 767–780.

Chen, R., Chen, J., & Li, L. (2015). Action videogame play improves visual motor control. *Journal of Vision*, 15, 42. doi: 10.1167/15.12.42.pmid:26325730.

Chiappe, D., Conger, M., Liao, J., Caldwell, J. L., & Vu, K. L. (2013). Improving multi-tasking ability through action videogames. *Applied Ergonomics*, 44, 278–284.

Chisholm, J. D., Hickey, C., Theeuwes, J., & Kingstone, A. (2010). Reduced attentional capture in action video game players. *Attention, Perception & Psychophysics*, 72, 667–671.

Chisholm, J. D., & Kingstone, A. (2012). Improved top-down control reduces oculomotor capture: The case of action video game players. *Attention, Perception & Psychophysics*, 74, 257–262.

Cho, K. H., Lee, K. J., & Song, C. H. (2012). Virtual-reality balance training with a video-game system improves dynamic balance in chronic stroke patients. *The Tohoku Journal of Experimental Medicine*, 228(1), 69–74.

Chou, Y. H., Yang, B. H., Hsu, J. W., Wang, S. J., Lin, C. L., Huang, K. L., . . . & Lee, S. M. (2013). Effects of video game playing on cerebral blood flow in young adults: A SPECT study. *Psychiatry Research: Neuroimaging*, 212(1), 65–72.

Choudhury, S., & McKinney, K. A. (2013). Digital media, the developing brain and the interpretive plasticity of neuroplasticity. *Transcultural Psychiatry*, 1363461512474623.

Christensen, A. L. (1996). Alexandr Romanovich Luria (1902–1977): Contributions to neuropsychological rehabilitation. *Neuropsychological Rehabilitation*, 6(4), 279–304.

Ciaramelli, E., Muccioli, M., Ladavas, E., & di Pellegrino, G. (2007). Selective deficit in personal moral judgment following damage to ventromedial prefrontal cortex. *Social Cognitive and Affective Neuroscience*, 2(2), 84–92.

Cinar, E., & Sahin, F. (2013). New classification techniques for electroencephalogram (EEG) signals and a real-time EEG control of a robot. *Neural Computing and Applications*, 22(1), 29–39.

Cincotti, F., Mattia, D., Aloise, F., Bufalari, S., Schalk, G., Oriolo, . . . Babiloni, F. (2008). Non-invasive brain-computer interface system: Towards its application as assistive technology. *Brain Research Bulletin*, 75(6), 796–803.

Citi, L., Poli, R., Cinel, C., & Sepulveda, F. (2008). P300-based BCI mouse with genetically-optimized analogue control. *Neural Systems and Rehabilitation Engineering*, 16(1), 51–61.

Clark, A. (1997). *Being there: Putting brain body and world together again.* Cambridge, MA: MIT Press.

Clark, A. (1999). Embodied, situated, and distributed cognition. In W. Betchel and G. Graham (Eds.), *A Companion to Cognitive Science.* Malden, MA: Blackwell Publishing.

Clark, A. (2008). *Supersizing the mind: Embodiment, action, and cognitive extension.* Oxford University Press.

Clark, A., & Chalmers, D. (1998). The extended mind. *Analysis*, 58(1), 7–19.

Clark, J. E., Lanphear, A. K., & Riddick, C. C. (1987). The effects of videogame playing on the response selection processing of elderly adults. *Journal of Gerontology*, 42(1), 82–85.

Clark, L., & Manes, F. (2004). Social and emotional decision-making following frontal lobe injury. *Neurocase*, 10(5), 398–403.

Climent, G., and Bánterla, F. (2011). *Nesplora classroom, ecological assessment of attentional processes.* Theoretical Manual. Donostia, Spain: Nesplora.

Clowes, R. W. (2013). The cognitive integration of e-memory. *Review of Philosophy and Psychology*, 4(1), 107–133.

Cobb, S.V. (2007). Virtual environments supporting learning and communication in special needs education. *Topics in Language Disorders*, 27(3), 211–225.

Cocchi, L., Zalesky, A., Fornito, A., & Mattingley, J. B. (2013). Dynamic cooperation and competition between brain systems during cognitive control. *Trends in Cognitive Sciences*, 17(10), 493–501.

Cohen, J. E., Green, C. S., & Bavelier, D. (2008). Training visual attention with video games: Not all games are created equal. In H. F. O'Neil & R. S. Perez (Eds.), *Computer games and team and individual learning*. Oxford, UK: Elsevier Ltd.

Cole, D. M., Beckmann, C. F., Long, C. J., Matthews, P. M., Durcan, M. J., & Beaver, J. D. (2010). Nicotine replacement in abstinent smokers improves cognitive withdrawal symptoms with modulation of resting brain network dynamics. *Neuroimage*, 52(2), 590–599.

Collinger, J. L., Boninger, M. L., Bruns, T. M., Curley, K., Wang, W., & Weber, D. J. (2013). Functional priorities, assistive technology, and brain-computer interfaces after spinal cord injury. *Journal of Rehabilitation Research & Development*, 50(2), 145–159.

Colzato, L. S., van den Wildenberg, W. P., Zmigrod, S., & Hommel, B. (2013). Action video gaming and cognitive control: Playing first person shooter games is associated with improvement in working memory but not action inhibition. *Psychological Research*, 77, 234–239.

Colzato, L. S., van den Wildenberg, W., & Hommel, B. (2014). Cognitive control and the COMT Val158Met polymorphism: Genetic modulation of videogame training and transfer to task-switching efficiency. *Psychological Research*, 78, 670–678. doi: 10.1007/s00426-013-0514-8. pmid:24030137.

Colzato, L. S., Van Leeuwen, P. J., Van Den Wildenberg, W. P., & Hommel, B. (2010). DOOM'd to switch: Superior cognitive flexibility in players of first person shooter games. *Frontiers in Psychology*, 1.

Connolly, I., Palmer, M., Barton, H., and Kirwan, G. (Eds.), (2016). *An introduction to cyberpsychology*. New York: Routledge.

Conway, M. A. (1991). In defense of everyday memory. *American Psychologist*, 46, 19–26.

Cook, L., Hanten, G., Orsten, K., Chapman, S., Li, X., Wilde, E., et al. (2013). Effects of moderate to severe traumatic brain injury on anticipating consequences of actions in adults: A preliminary study. *Journal of the International Neuropsychological Society*. 19, 508–517.

Corbetta, M., & Shulman, G. L. (2002). Control of goal-directed and stimulus-driven attention in the brain. *Nature Reviews Neuroscience*, 3(3), 201–215.

Costa, L. (1983). Clinical neuropsychology: A discipline in evolution. *Journal of Clinical Neuropsychology*, 5, 1–11.

Costanzo, M. E., Leaman, S., Jovanovic, T., Norrholm, S. D., Rizzo, A. A., Taylor, P., & Roy, M. J. (2014). Psychophysiological response to virtual reality and subthreshold posttraumatic stress disorder symptoms in recently deployed military. *Psychosomatic Medicine*, 76(9), 670–677.

Côté, S., & Bouchard, S. (2005). Documenting the Efficacy of Virtual RealityExposure with Psychophysiological and Information Processing Measures. *Applied Psychophysiology and Biofeedback*, 30(3), 217–232.

Courtney, C., Dawson, M., Rizzo, A., Arizmendi, B., & Parsons, T. D. (2013). Predicting navigation performance with psychophysiological responses to threat in a virtual environment. *Lecture Notes in Computer Science*, 8021, 129–138.

Courtney, C. G., Dawson, M. E., Schell, A. M., Iyer, A., & Parsons, T. D. (2010). Better than the real thing: Eliciting fear with moving and static computer-generated stimuli. *International Journal of Psychophysiology*, 78, 107–114.

Coyle, H., Traynor, V., & Solowij, N. (2015). Computerized and virtual reality cognitive training for individuals at high risk of cognitive decline: Systematic review of the literature. *The American Journal of Geriatric Psychiatry*, 23(4), 335–359.

Coyne, J. T., Baldwin, C., Cole, A., Sibley, C., & Roberts, D. M. (2009). Applying real time physiological measures of cognitive load to improve training. *Lecture Notes in Artificial Intelligence*, 5638, 469–478.

Cozolino, L. (2014). The neuroscience of human relationships: Attachment and the developing social brain *(Norton Series on Interpersonal Neurobiology)*. New York: WW Norton & Company.

Craig, A. D. (2002). How do you feel? Interoception: The sense of the physiological condition of the body. *Nature Reviews Neuroscience*, 3, 655–666.

Craig, A. D. (2003). Interoception: The sense of the physiological condition of the body. *Current Opinion in Neurobiology*, 13(4), 500–505.

Craig, A. D. (2009a). Emotional moments across time: A possible neural basis for time perception in the anterior insula. *Philosophical Transactions Of the Royal Society of London B: Biological Sciences*, 364, 1933–1942. doi:10.1098/rstb.2009.0008.

Craig, A. D. (2009b). How do you feel – now? The anterior insula and human awareness. *Nature Reviews Neuroscience*, 10, 59–70.doi:10.1038/nrn2555.

Craig, A. D. (2010a). Once an island, now the focus of attention. *Brain Structure and Function*, 214, 395–396.doi:10.1007/s00429-010-0270-0.

Craig, A. D. (2010b). The sentient self. *Brain Structure and Function*, 214, 563–577. doi:10.1007/s00429-010-0248-y.

Critchley, H. D. (2005). Neural mechanisms of autonomic, affective, and cognitive integration. *Journal of Comparative Neurology*, 493, 154–166.

Critchley, H. D., Elliott, R., Mathias, C. J., & Dolan, R. J. (2000). Neural activity relating to generation and representation of galvanic skin conductance responses: A functional magnetic resonance imaging study. *Neuroscience*, 20(8), 3033–3040.

Critchley, H. D., Wiens, S., Rotshtein, P., Öhman, A., & Dolan, R. J. (2004). Neural systems supporting interoceptive awareness. *Nature Neuroscience*, 7(2), 189–195.

Cromwell, H. C., & Panksepp, J. (2011). Rethinking the cognitive revolution from a neural perspective: How overuse/misuse of the term "cognition" and the neglect of affective controls in behavioral neuroscience could be delaying progress in understanding the BrainMind. *Neuroscience & Biobehavioral Reviews*, 35(9), 2026–2035.

Crone, E. A., Somsen, R. J., Beek, B. V., & Van Der Molen, M. W. (2004). Heart rate and skin conductance analysis of antecendents and consequences of decision making. *Psychophysiology*, 41(4), 531–540.

Crossler, R. E., Johnston, A. C., Lowry, P. B., Hu, Q., Warkentin, M., & Baskerville, R. (2013). Future directions for behavioral information security research. *Computers & Security*, 32, 90–101.

Crowder, S. A., & Merritte. K. (2013). The possible therapeutic benefits of utilizing motion gaming systems on pediatric patients presenting autism. *Journal of the Tennessee Medical Association*, 106(8), 41–43.

Csikszentmihalyi, M. (1990). *Flow: The psychology of optimal experience*. New York, HarperCollins.

Csikszentmihalyi, M. (1994). *The evolving self.* New York, Harper Perennial.

Csikszentmihalyi, M. (1997). *Finding flow.* New York, Basic Books.

Cuthbert, B. N. (2014). The RDoC framework: Facilitating transition from ICD/DSM to dimensional approaches that integrate neuroscience and psychopathology. *World Psychiatry*, 13(1), 28–35.

Cuthbert, B. N., Bradley, M. M., & Lang, P. J. (1996). Probing picture perception: Activation and emotion. *Psychophysiology*, 33, 103–111.

Cuthbert, B. N., & Insel, T. R. (2013). Toward the future of psychiatric diagnosis: The seven pillars of RDoC. *BMC Medicine*, 11(1), 126.

Cuthbert, B. N., Schupp, H. T., Bradley, M. M., Birbaumer, N., & Lang, P. J. (2000). Brain potentials in affective picture processing: Covariation with autonomic arousal and affective report. *Biological Psychology*, 52, 95–111.

Dai, W., Han, D., Dai, Y., & Xu, D. (2015). Emotion recognition and affective computing on vocal social media. *Information & Management*, 52(7), 777–788.

Damasio, A. R. (1994). *Descartes' error: Emotion, rationality and the human brain.* New York: GP Putnam.

Damasio, A. R. (2000). A second chance for emotion. In R. D. Lane & L. Nadel (Eds.), *Cognitive neuroscience of emotion* (pp. 12–23). New York: Oxford University Press.

Damasio, A., & Carvalho, G. B. (2013). The nature of feelings: evolutionary and neurobiological origins. *Nature Reviews Neuroscience*, 14(2), 143–152.

Damasio, H., & Damasio, A. R. (1989). *Lesion analysis in neuropsychology.* New York: Oxford University Press.

Danziger, Z. (2014). A reductionist approach to the analysis of learning in brain-computer interfaces. *Biological Cybernetics*, 108(2), 183–201.

D'Arcy, J., & Herath, T. (2011). A review and analysis of deterrence theory in the IS security literature: Making sense of the disparate findings. *European Journal of Information Systems*, 20(6), 643–658.

Das, D. A., et al. (2005). The efficacy of playing a virtual reality game in modulating pain for children with acute burn injuries: A randomized controlled trial [ISRCTN87413556]. *BMC Pediatr.*, 5(1), 1.

Davey, C. G., Allen, N. B., Harrison, B. J., Dwyer, D. B., & Yücel, M. (2010). Being liked activates primary reward and midline self-related brain regions. *Human Brain Mapping*, 31(4), 660–668.

Davidson, R. J. (1995). Cerebral asymmetry, emotion, and affective style. In R. J. Davidson & K. Hugdahl (Eds.), *Brain asymmetry* (pp. 361–387). Cambridge: MIT Press.

Davidson, R. J. (1998). Affective style and affective disorders: Perspectives from affective neuroscience. *Cognition and Emotion*, 12, 307–320.

Davidson, R. J. (2000). Affective style, psychopathology, and resilience: Brain mechanisms and plasticity. *American Psychologist*, 55, 1196–1214.

Davidson, R. J. (2003). Affective neuroscience and psychophysiology: Toward a synthesis. *Psychophysiology*, 40, 655–665.

Davidson, R. J., Jackson, D. C., & Kalin, N. H. (2000). Emotion, plasticity, context, and regulation: Perspectives from affective neuroscience. *Psychological Bulletin*, 126(6), 890.

Davis, R. C. (1957). Section of psychology: Response patterns. *Transactions of the New York Academy of Sciences*, 19 (8 Series II), 731–739.

Dawson, D. R., Anderson, N. D., Burgess, P., Cooper, E., Krpan, K. M., and Stuss, D. T. (2009). Further development of the Multiple Errands Test: Standardized scoring, reliability and ecological validity for the Baycrest version. *Archives of Physical Medicine and Rehabilitation*, 90, S41–S51.

Dawson, M. E., Filion, D. L., & Schell, A. M. (1989). Is elicitation of the autonomic orienting response associated with allocation of processing resources? *Psychophysiology*, 26(5), 560–572.

Dawson, M. E., Schell, A. M., Beers, J. R., & Kelly, A. (1982). Allocation of cognitive processing capacity during human autonomic classical conditioning. *Journal of Experimental Psychology: General*, 111(3), 273.

de Borst, A. W., & de Gelder, B. (2015). Is it the real deal? Perception of virtual characters versus humans: An affective cognitive neuroscience perspective. *Frontiers in Psychology*, 6.

de Gelder, B., & Hortensius, R. (2014). The many faces of the emotional body. In *New Frontiers in Social Neuroscience* (pp. 153–164). Switzerland: Springer International Publishing.

de Guinea, A. O., Titah, R., & Léger, P. M. (2014). Explicit and implicit antecedents of users' behavioral beliefs in information systems: A neuropsychological investigation. *Journal of Management Information Systems*, 30(4), 179–210.

de Kloet, A. J., Berger, M. A., Verhoeven, I. M., van Stein, C. K., Vlieland, T. P. (2012). Gaming supports youth with acquired brain injury? A pilot study. *Brain Injury*, 26(7–8), 1021–1029.

Decety, J., & Yoder, K. J. (2015). Empathy and motivation for justice: Cognitive empathy and concern, but not emotional empathy, predict sensitivity to injustice for others. *Social Neuroscience*, (ahead-of-print), 1–14.

Decker, S. A., & Gay, J. N. (2011). Cognitive-bias toward gaming-related words and disinhibition in World of Warcraft gamers. *Computers in Human Behavior*, 27(2), 798–810.

Dehaene S, Cohen L. (2007). Cultural recycling of cortical maps. *Neuron*, 56, 384–98.

Deng, L. Y., Hsu, C. L., Lin, T. C., Tuan, J. S., & Chang, S. M. (2010). EOG-based human–computer interface system development. *Expert Systems with Applications*, 37(4), 3337–3343.

Denny, B. T., Kober, H., Wager, T. D., & Ochsner, K. N. (2012). A meta-analysis of functional neuroimaging studies of self-and other judgments reveals a spatial gradient for mentalizing in medial prefrontal cortex. *Journal of Cognitive Neuroscience*, 24(8), 1742–1752.

De Raedt, R. (2006). Does neuroscience hold promise for the further development of behavior therapy? The case of emotional change after exposure in anxiety and depression. *Scandinavian Journal of Psychology*, 47, 225–236.

deWall, C., Wilson, B. A., & Baddeley, A. D. (1994). The Extended Rivermead Behavioral Memory Test: A measure of everyday memory performance in normal adults. *Memory*, 2, 149–166.

Diamond, A. (2013). Executive functions. *Annual Review of Psychology*, 64, 135–168.

Díaz-Orueta, U., Garcia-López, C., Crespo-Eguílaz, N., Sánchez-Carpintero, R., Climent, G., and Narbona, J. (2014). AULA virtual reality test as an attention measure: Convergent validity with Conners' continuous performance test. *Child Neuropsychol.*, 20, 328–342.

Diemer, J. E., Alpers, G. W., Peperkorn, H. M., Shiban, Y., and Mühlberger, A. (2015). The impact of perception and presence on emotional reactions: A review of research in virtual reality. *Frontiers in Psychology*, 6, 26. doi: 10.3389/fpsyg.2015.00026.

Diemer, J., Mühlberger, A., Pauli, P., & Zwanzger, P. (2014). Virtual reality exposure in anxiety disorders: Impact on psychophysiological reactivity. *The World Journal of Biological Psychiatry*, 15(6), 427–442.

Dimoka, A. (2010). What does the brain tell us about trust and distrust? Evidence from a functional neuroimaging study. *Mis Quarterly*, 34(2), 373–396.

Dimoka, A., Banker, R. D., Benbasat, I., Davis, F. D., Dennis, A. R., Gefen, D., Gupta, A., Ischebeck, A., Kenning, P., Müller-Putz, G., Pavlou, P. A., Riedl, R., vom Brocke, J., & Weber, B. (2012). On the use of neurophysiological tools in IS research: Developing a research agenda for NeuroIS. *MIS Quarterly*, 36(3), 679–702.

Dimoka, A., Pavlou, P. A., & Davis, F. D. (2011). Research commentary-NeuroIS: The potential of cognitive neuroscience for information systems research. *Information Systems Research*, 22(4), 687–702.

Ding, W. N., Sun, J. H., Sun, Y. W., Zhou, Y., Li, L., Xu, J. R., & Du, Y. S. (2013). Altered default network resting-state functional connectivity in adolescents with Internet gaming addiction. *PloS one*, 8(3), e59902.

Ding, W. N., Sun, J. H., Sun, Y. W., Chen, X., Zhou, Y., Zhuang, Z. G., . . . & Du, Y. S. (2014). Trait impulsivity and impaired prefrontal impulse inhibition function in adolescents with internet gaming addiction revealed by a Go/No-Go fMRI study. *Behavioral and Brain Functions*, 10(20), 1–9.

Domínguez D. J. F. (2015). Toward a neuroanthropology of ethics. In J., Clausen & N. Levy (Eds.), *Handbook of neuroethics* (pp. 289–298). Berlin: Springer.

Donchin, E., Spencer, K. M., & Wijesinghe, R. (2000). The mental prosthesis: Assessing the speed of a P300-based brain–computer interface. *IEEE Transactions on Rehabilitation Engineering*, 8, 174–179.

Dong, G., DeVito, E. E., Du, X., & Cui, Z. (2012). Impaired inhibitory control in "internet addiction disorder": a functional magnetic resonance imaging study. *Psychiatry Research: Neuroimaging*, 203(2), 153–158.

Dong, G., Hu, Y., Lin, X., & Lu, Q. (2013). What makes Internet addicts continue playing online even when faced by severe negative consequences? Possible explanations from an fMRI study. *Biological Psychology*, 94(2), 282–289.

Dong, G., Lin, X., & Potenza, M. N. (2015). Decreased functional connectivity in an executive control network is related to impaired executive function in Internet gaming disorder. *Progress in Neuro-Psychopharmacology and Biological Psychiatry*, 57, 76–85.

Dong, G., Lin, X., Zhou, H., & Lu, Q. (2014). Cognitive flexibility in Internet addicts: fMRI evidence from difficult-to-easy and easy-to-difficult switching situations. *Addictive Behaviors*, 39(3), 677–683.

Dong, G., Lu, Q., Zhou, H., & Zhao, X. (2010). Impulse inhibition in people with Internet addiction disorder: Electrophysiological evidence from a Go/NoGo study. *Neuroscience Letters*, 485(2), 138–142.

Dong, G., Shen, Y., Huang, J., & Du, X. (2013). Impaired error-monitoring function in people with Internet addiction disorder: An event-related FMRI study. *European Addiction Research*, 19(5), 269–275.

Dong, G., Zhou, H., & Zhao, X. (2011). Male Internet addicts show impaired executive control ability: Evidence from a color-word Stroop task. *Neuroscience Letters*, 499(2), 114–118.

Donohue, S. E., Woldorff, M. G., & Mitroff, S. R. (2010). Video game players show more precise multisensory temporal processing abilities. *Attention, Perception and Psychophysics*, 72, 1120–1129.

Doricchi, F., de Schotten, M. T., Tomaiuolo, F., & Bartolomeo, P. (2008). White matter (dis) connections and gray matter (dys) functions in visual neglect: Gaining insights into the brain networks of spatial awareness. *Cortex*, 44(8), 983–995.

Dotsch, R., and Wigboldus, D. H. J. (2008). Virtual prejudice. *Journal of Experimental Social Psychology*, 44, 1194–1198.

Draper, J. V., Kaber, D. B. & Usher, J. M. (1998). Telepresence. *Human Factors*, 40, 354–375.

Dreher, J. C., Koechlin, E., Tierney, M., & Grafman, J. (2008). Damage to the fronto-polar cortex is associated with impaired multitasking. *PLoS One*, 3(9), e3227–e3227.

Droutman, V., Bechara, A., & Read, S. J. (2015). Roles of the different sub-regions of the insular cortex in various phases of the decision-making process. *Frontiers in Behavioral Neuroscience*, 9.

Duddu, V., Isaac, M. K., & Chaturvedi, S. K. (2006). Somatization, somatosensory amplification, attribution styles and illness behaviour: A review. *International Review of Psychiatry*, 18(1), 25–33.

Dunbar, R. (1992). Neocortex size as a constraint on group size in primates. *Journal of Human Evolution*, 22(6), 469–493.

Dunbar, R. (1993). Coevolution of neocortical size, group size and language in humans. *Behavioral and Brain Sciences*, 16(4), 681–93.

Dunbar, R. (1998). The social brain hypothesis. *Brain*, 9, 10.

Dunbar, R. & Shultz, S. (2007). Understanding primate brain evolution. *Philosophical Transactions of the Royal Society B*, 362, 649–658.

Dunbar, R. I. M. (2011). Evolutionary basis of the social brain. In J. Decety & J. Cacioppo (Eds.), *Oxford handbook of social neuroscience* (pp. 28–38). Oxford: Oxford University Press.

Dunbar, R. I. M. (2012). Bridging the bonding gap: The transition from primates to humans. *Philosophical Transactions of the Royal Society of London B: Biological Sciences*, 367(1597), 1837–1846.

Dunbar, R. I. (2014). The social brain psychological underpinnings and implications for the structure of organizations. *Current Directions in Psychological Science*, 23(2), 109–114.

Dunbar, R. I. M. (2016). Do online social media cut through the constraints that limit the size of offline social networks? *Royal Society Open Science*, 3(1), 150292.

Duncan, J., & Owen, A. M. (2000). Common regions of the human frontal lobe recruited by diverse cognitive demands. *Trends in Neuroscience*, 23, 475–483. doi:10. 1016/s0166-2236(00)01633-7.

Dunn, E. J., Searight, H. R., Grisso, T., Margolis, R. B., & Gibbons, J. L. (1990). The relation of the Halstead-Reitan Neuropsychological Battery to functional daily living skills in geriatric patients. *Archives of Clinical Neuropsychology*, 5, 103–117.

Durlach, N. I., & Mavor, A. S. (1994). Committee on virtual reality research, commission on behavioral development, social science, mathematics education, commission on physical sciences, and applications, national research council, virtual reality: Scientific and technological challenges, *National Academy Press*, p. 189.

Dustman, R. E., Emmerson, R. Y., Steinhaus, L. A., Shearer, D. E., & Dustman, T. J. (1992). The effects of videogame playing on neuropsychological performance of elderly individuals. *Journal of Gerontology*, 47(3), 168–171.

Dutta, A., Kumar, R., Malhotra, S., Chugh, S., Banerjee, A., & Dutta, A. (2013). A low-cost point-of-care testing system for psychomotor symptoms of depression affecting standing balance: A preliminary study in India. *Depression Research and Treatment*.

Duvinage, M., et al. (2013). A P300-based quantitative comparison between the Emotiv Epoc headset and a medical EEG device. *Biomedical Engineering*, 765.

Dux, P. E., Tombu, M. N., Harrison, S., Rogers, B. P., Tong, F., & Marois, R. (2009). Training improves multitasking performance by increasing the speed of information processing in human prefrontal cortex. *Neuron*, 63(1), 127–138.

Dye, M. W. G., & Bavelier, D. (2010). Differential development of visual attention skills in school-age children. *Vision Research*, 50, 452–459.

Dye, M. W. G., Green, C. S., & Bavelier, D. (2009). The development of attention skills in action video game players. *Neuropsychologia*, 47, 1780–1789.

Earls, H. A., Englander, Z. A., & Morris, J. P. (2013). Perception of race-related features modulates neural activity associated with action observation and imitation. *Neuroreport*, 24(8), 410–413.

Egerton, A., Mehta, M. A., Montgomery, A. J., Lappin, J. M., Howes, O. D., Reeves, S. J., . . . & Grasby, P. M. (2009). The dopaminergic basis of human behaviors: A review of molecular imaging studies. *Neuroscience & Biobehavioral Reviews*, 33(7), 1109–1132.

Eisenberger, N. I. (2012). The neural bases of social pain: Evidence for shared representations with physical pain. *Psychosomatic Medicine*, 74, 126–135.

Eisenberger, N. I. (2013). An empirical review of the neural underpinnings of receiving and giving social support: Implications for health. *Psychosomatic Medicine*, 75(6), 545.

Eisenberger, N. I. (2015). Social pain and the brain: Controversies, questions, and where to go from here. *Annual Review of Psychology*, 66, 601–629.

Eisenberger, N. I., Lieberman, M. D., & Williams, K. D. (2003). Does rejection hurt? An fMRI study of social exclusion. *Science*, 302(5643), 290–292.

Elkind, J. S., Rubin, E., Rosenthal, S., Skoff, B., and Prather, P. (2001). A simulated reality scenario compared with the computerized Wisconsin card sorting test: An analysis of preliminary results. *Cyberpsychology & Behavior*, 4, 489–496.

Ellison, N. B., Steinfield, C., & Lampe, C. (2011). Connection strategies: Social capital implications of Facebook-enabled communication practices. *New Media & Society*, 1461444810385389.

Emonds, G., Declerck, C. H., Boone, C., Vandervliet, E. J., & Parizel, P. M. (2012). The cognitive demands on cooperation in social dilemmas: An fMRI study. *Social Neuroscience*, 7(5), 494–509.

Engel, A. K., Fries, P., & Singer, W. (2001). Dynamic predictions: Oscillations and synchrony in top-down processing. *Nature Reviews Neuroscience*, 2, 704–716.

Entertainment Software Association (2010). Essential facts about the computer and video game industry: Sales, demographic, and usage data.

Enzinger, C., Ropele, S., Fazekas, F., Loitfelder, M., Gorani, F., Seifert, T., ... & Müller-Putz, G. (2008). Brain motor system function in a patient with complete spinal cord injury following extensive brain-computer interface training. *Experimental Brain Research*, 190(2), 215–223.

Erickson, K. I., Boot, W. R., Basak, C., Neider, M. B., Prakash, R. S., Voss, M. W., ... & Kramer, A. F. (2010). Striatal volume predicts level of video game skill acquisition. *Cerebral Cortex*, 293.

Ernst, M., Bolla, K., Mouratidis, M., Contoreggi, C., Matochik, J. A., Kurian, V., et al. (2002). Decision-making in a risk-taking task: A PET study. *Neuropsychopharmacology*, 26, 682–691.

Esfahani, E. T., & Sundararajan, V. (2012). Classification of primitive shapes using brain–computer interfaces. *Computer-Aided Design*, 44(10), 1011–1019.

Etzel, J. A., Johnsen, E. L., Dickerson, J., Tranel, D., & Adolphs, R. (2006). Cardiovascular and respiratory responses during musical mood induction. *International Journal of Psychophysiology*, 61, 57–69.

Fairclough, S. H. (2009). Fundamentals of physiological computing. *Interacting with Computers*, 21(1), 133–145.

Fairclough, S. H. (2014). *Advances in physiological computing*. K. Gilleade (Ed.). London: Springer-Verlag.

Fairclough, S.H., & Venables, L. (2006). Prediction of subjective states from psychophysiology: A multivariate approach. *Biological Psychology*, 71, 100–110.

Farmer, H., Tajadura-Jiménez, A., & Tsakiris, M. (2012). Beyond the colour of my skin: How skin colour affects the sense of body-ownership. *Consciousness and Cognition*, 21(3), 1242–1256.

Farwell, L. A., & Donchin, E. (1988). Talking off the top of your head: Toward a mental prosthesis utilizing event related brain potentials. *Electroencephalographic Clinical Neurophysiology*, 70, 510–523.

Fassbender, C., Zhang, H., Buzy, W. M., Cortes, C. R., Mizuiri, D., Beckett, L., & Schweitzer, J. B. (2009). A lack of default network suppression is linked to increased distractibility in ADHD. *Brain Research*, 1273, 114–128.

Faur, C., Clavel, C., Pesty, S., and Martin, J. C. (2013). PERSEED: A self-based model of personality for virtual agents inspired by socio-cognitive theories. In *Human Association conference on affective computing and intelligent interaction* (pp. 467–472). Geneva: IEEE.

Fazio, R. H., & Olson, M. A. (2003). Implicit measures in social cognition research: Their meaning and use. *Annual Review of Psychology*, 54(1), 297–327.

Fehr, F. S., & Stern, J. A. (1970). Peripheral physiological variables and emotion: The James-Lange theory revisited. *Psychological Bulletin*, 74(6), 411.

Fellows, L. K., & Farah, M. J. (2005). Different underlying impairments in decision making following ventromedial and dorsolateral frontal lobe damage in humans. *Cerebral Cortex*, 15(1), 58–63.

Feng, J., Spence, I., & Pratt (2007). Playing an action video game reduces gender differences in spatial cognition. *Psychological Science*, 18, 850–855.

Ferguson, A. M., McLean, D., & Risko, E. F. (2015). Answers at your fingertips: Access to the Internet influences willingness to answer questions. *Consciousness and Cognition*, 37, 91–102.

Finlay, B.L., & Darlington, R.B. (1995). Linked regularities in the development and evolution of mammalian brains. *Science*, 268(5217), 1578–1584.

Fisher, H. E., Aron, A., & Brown, L. L. (2006). Romantic love: A mammalian brain system for mate choice. *Philosophical Transactions of the Royal Society of London B: Biological Sciences*, 361(1476), 2173–2186.

Fisher, M., Goddu, M. K., & Keil, F. C. (2015). Searching for explanations: How the Internet inflates estimates of internal knowledge. *Journal of Experimental Psychology: General*, 144(3), 674.

Fitzsimons, G. M., Finkel, E. J., & vanDellen, M. R. (2015). Transactive goal dynamics. *Psychological Review*, 122(4), 648–673.

Flach, J.M., & Holden, J.G. (1998). The reality of experience: Gibson's way. *Presence-Teleoperators and Virtual Environments*, 7, 90–95.

Flavián-Blanco, C., Gurrea-Sarasa, R., & Orús-Sanclemente, C. (2011). Analyzing the emotional outcomes of the online search behavior with search engines. *Computers in Human Behavior*, 27(1), 540–551.

Fleming, T., Dixon, R., Frampton, C., & Merry, S. (2012). A pragmatic randomized controlled trial of computerized CBT (SPARX) for symptoms of depression among adolescents excluded from mainstream education. *Behavioural and Cognitive Psychotherapy*, 40(05), 529–541.

Foerde, K., Knowlton, B. J., & Poldrank, R. A. (2006). Modulation of competing memory systems by distraction. *Proceedings of the National Association of Sciences*, 103, 11778–11783.

Fok, S., Schwartz, R., Wronkiewicz, M., Holmes, C., Zhang, J., Somers, T., ... & Leuthardt, E. (2011). An EEG-based brain computer interface for rehabilitation and restoration of hand control following stroke using ipsilateral cortical physiology. In *Engineering in Medicine and Biology Society, EMBC, 2011 Annual International Conference of the IEEE* (pp. 6277–6280).

Forbes, C. E., & Grafman, J. (2010). The role of the human prefrontal cortex in social cognition and moral judgment. *Annual Review of Neuroscience*, 33, 299–324.

Forman, S. D., Dougherty, G. G., Casey, B. J., Siegle, G. J., Braver, T. S., Barch, D. M., ... & Lorensen, E. (2004). Opiate addicts lack error-dependent activation of rostral anterior cingulate. *Biological Psychiatry*, 55(5), 531–537.

Fox, C. J., Iaria, G., & Barton, J. J. (2008). Disconnection in prosopagnosia and face processing. *Cortex*, 44(8), 996–1009.

Fox, J., Arena, D., & Bailenson, J. N. (2009). Virtual reality: A survival guide for the social scientist. *Journal of Media Psychology*, 21(3), 95–113.

Fox, J., & Tang, W. Y. (2014). Sexism in online video games: The role of conformity to masculine norms and social dominance orientation. *Computers in Human Behavior*, 33, 314–320.

Fraga, T., Pichiliani, M., & Louro, D. (2013). Experimental art with brain controlled interface. *Lecture Notes in Computer Science*, 8009, 642–651.

Franceschini, S., Gori, S., Ruffino, M., Viola, S., Molteni, M., and Facoetti, A. (2013). Action video games make dyslexic children read better. *Current Biology*, 23, 462–466.

Franklin, T. R., Acton, P. D., Maldjian, J. A., Gray, J. D., Croft, J. R., Dackis, C. A., . . . & Childress, A. R. (2002). Decreased gray matter concentration in the insular, orbitofrontal, cingulate, and temporal cortices of cocaine patients. *Biological Psychiatry*, 51(2), 134–142.

Franzen, M. D., & Wilhelm, K. L. (1996). Conceptual foundations of ecological validity in neuropsychological assessment. In R. J. Sbordone & C. J. Long (Eds.), *Ecological validity of neuropsychological testing* (pp. 91–112). Boca Raton, FL: St. Lucie Press.

Fredrickson, M. (1981). Orienting and defensive reactions to phobic and conditioned fear stimuli in phobics and normals. *Psychophysiology*, 18, 456–465.

Freeman, D., Pugh, K., Antley, A., Slater, M., Bebbington, P., Gittins, M., et al. (2008). Virtual reality study of paranoid thinking in the general population. *British Journal of Psychiatry*, 192, 258–263.

Freeman, J., Avons, S. E., Pearson, D. E., & IJsselsteijn, W. A. (1999). Effects of sensory information and prior experience on direct subjective ratings of presence. *Presence*, 8(1), 1–13.

Freese, J. L. & Amaral, D. G. (2009). Neuroanatomy of the primate amygdala. In P. J. Whalen & E. A. Phelps (Eds.), *The human amygdala*. New York, NY: The Guilford Press.

Friedman, D., Steed, A., & Slater, M. (2007, September). Spatial social behavior in second life. In *Intelligent virtual agents* (pp. 252–263). Berlin, Heidelberg: Springer.

Frith, C. D., & Frith, U. (2008). Implicit and explicit processes in social cognition. *Neuron*, 60(3), 503–510.

Frith, U., & Frith, C.D. (2003). Development and neurophysiology of mentalizing. *Philosophical Transactions of the Royal Society London B: Biological Sciences*, 358(1431), 459–473.

Funkenstein, D. H. (1956). Nor-epinephrine-like and epinephrine-like substances in relation to human behavior. *The Journal of Nervous and Mental Disease*, 124(1), 58–68.

Funkenstein, D. H., King, S. H., & Drolette, M. (1954). The direction of anger during a laboratory stress-inducing situation. *Psychosomatic Medicine*, 16(5), 404–413.

Furnell, S., & Clarke, N. (2012). Power to the people? The evolving recognition of human aspects of security. *Computers & Security*, 31(8), 983–988.

Fuster, J. M. (2000). The module: Crisis of a paradigm. *Neuron*, 1(26), 51–53.

Gadanho, S. C. (2003). Learning behavior-selection by emotions and cognition in a multi-goal robot task. *The Journal of Machine Learning Research*, 4, 385–412.

Gallagher, S. (2011). The overextended mind. *Versus: Quaderni di studi semiotici*, 113–115.

Gallagher, S., & Crisafi, A. (2009). Mental institutions. *Topoi*, 28(1), 45–51.

Gandhi, T., Trikha, M., Santhosh, J., & Anand, S. (2010). Development of an expert multitask gadget controlled by voluntary eye movements. *Expert Systems with Applications*, 37(6), 4204–4211.

Garavan, H. (2010). Insula and drug cravings. *Brain Structure and Function*, 214, 593–601. doi: 10.1007/s00429-010-0259-8.

Gazzaniga, M. S. (2008). *Human: The science behind what makes your brain unique*. New York, NY: Harper Perennial.

Geniole, S. N., Carré, J. M., & McCormick, C. M. (2011). State, not trait, neuroendocrine function predicts costly reactive aggression in men after social exclusion and inclusion. *Biological Psychology*, 87(1), 137–145.

Gentile, D. A., Choo, H., Liau, A., Sim, T., Li, D., Fung, D., & Khoo, A. (2011). Pathological video game use among youths: A two-year longitudinal study. *Pediatrics*, 127(2), e319–e329.

Gentile, D. A., & Stone, W. (2005). Violent video game effects on children and adolescents. A review of the literature. *Minerva Pediatrica*, 57(6), 337–358.

Georgescu, A. L., Kuzmanovic, B., Roth, D., Bente, G., & Vogeley, K. (2014). The use of virtual characters to assess and train non-verbal communication in high-functioning autism. *Frontiers in Human Neuroscience*, 8.

Gilbert, R. L., Murphy, N. A., & Ávalos, M. C. (2011). Realism, idealization, and potential negative impact of 3D virtual relationships. *Computers in Human Behavior*, 27(5), 2039–2046.

Glenberg, A. (1999). Why mental models must be embodied. In G. Rickheit and C. Habel (Eds.). *Mental models in discourse processing and reasoning*. New York: Elsevier.

Globisch, J., Hamm, A. O., Esteves, F., & Öhman, A. (1999). Fear appears fast: Temporal course of startle reflex potentiation in animal fearful subjects. *Psychophysiology*, 36(1), 66–75.

Glotzbach, E., Ewald, H., Andreatta, M., Pauli, P., and Mühlberger, A. (2012). Contextual fear conditioning predicts subsequent avoidance behavior in a virtual reality environment. *Cognition and Emotion*, 26, 1256–1272.

Glotzbach-Schoon, E., Andreatta, M., Reif, A., Ewald, H., Tröger, C., Baumann, C., et al. (2013). Contextual fear conditioning in virtual reality is affected by 5HTTLPR and NPSR1 polymorphisms: Effects on fear-potentiated startle. *Frontiers in Behavioral Neuroscience*, 7, 31.

Go, Y. H., Chua, B. H., Chai, B. B. H., Lee, C. Y., & Ning-Jia, E. (2011, July). The effect of risk perception on the usage of social network sites: A conceptual model and research propositions. In *The 2nd international research symposium in service management* (pp. 554–558).

Goel, V., & Dolan, R. J. (2003). Reciprocal neural response within lateral and ventral medial prefrontal cortex during hot and cold reasoning. *Neuroimage*, 20(4), 2314–2321.

Goldstein, G. (1996). Functional considerations in neuropsychology. In R. J. Sbordone & C. J. Long (Eds.), *Ecological validity of neuropsychological testing* (pp. 75–89). Delray Beach, FL: GR Press/St. Lucie Press.

Goldstein, J., Cajko, L., Oosterbroek, M., Michielsen, M., Van Houten, O., & Salverda, F. (1997). Video games and the elderly. *Social Behavior and Personality: An International Journal*, 25(4), 345–352.

Gong, D., He, H., Liu, D., Ma, W., Dong, L., Luo, C., & Yao, D. (2015). Enhanced functional connectivity and increased gray matter volume of insula related to action video game playing. *Scientific Reports*, 5.

Gong, D., He, H., Ma, W., Liu, D., Huang, M., Dong, L., . . . & Yao, D. (2016). Functional integration between salience and central executive networks: A role for action video game experience. *Neural Plasticity*, 1, 1–9.

Goodale, M. A., & Milner, A. D. (1992). Separate visual pathways for perception and action. *Trends in Neurosciences*, 15(1), 20–25.

Goodkind, M., Eickhoff, S. B., Oathes, D. J., Jiang, Y., Chang, A., Jones-Hagata, L. B., . . . & Grieve, S. M. (2015). Identification of a common neurobiological substrate for mental illness. *JAMA psychiatry*, 72(4), 305–315.

Gordon, M., Barkley, R.A., & Lovett, B.J. (2006). Tests and observational measures. In: R. A. Barkley (Ed.), *Attention-deficit hyperactivity disorder: A handbook for diagnosis and treatment* (3rd edition, pp. 369–388). New York: Guilford,.

Gorini, A., Capideville, C. S., DeLeo, G., Mantovani, F., & Riva, G. (2011). The role of immersion and narrative in mediated presence: The virtual hospital experience. *Cyberpsychology, Behavior and Social Networking*, 14, 99–105.

Gorini, A., Gaggioli, A., Vigna, C., & Riva, G. (2008). A Second Life for e-health: Prospects for the use of 3-D virtual worlds in clinical psychology. *Journal of Medical Internet Research*, 10, e21. doi:10.2196/jmir.1029.

Gorini, A., & Riva, G. (2008). The potential of virtual reality as anxiety management tool: A randomized controlled study in a sample of patients affected by generalized anxiety disorder. *Trials*, 9(25), 1745–6215.

Gosling, S. D., & Mason, W. (2015). Internet research in psychology. *Annual Review of Psychology*, 66, 877–902.

Gosling, S. D., Vazire, S., Srivastava, S., & John, O. P. (2004). Should we trust Web-based studies? A comparative analysis of six preconceptions about Internet questionnaires. *The American Psychologist*, 59, 93–104. doi:10.1037/0003-066X.59.2.93.

Gouveia, P. A. R., Brucki, S. M. D., Malheiros, S. M. F., & Bueno, O. F. A. (2007). Disorders in planning and strategy application in frontal lobe lesion patients. *Brain and Cognition*, 63(3), 240–246.

Gozli, D. G., Bavelier, D., & Pratt, J. (2014). The effect of action video game playing on sensorimotor learning: evidence from a movement tracking task. *Human Movement Science*, 38, 152–162. doi: 10.1016/j.humov.2014.09.004.

Granek, J. A., Gorbet, D. J., & Sergio, L. E. (2010). Extensive video-game experience alters cortical networks for complex visuomotor transformations. *Cortex*, 46(9), 1165–1177.

Grant, S., Bonson, K. R., Contoreggi, C., & London, E. D. (1999). Activation of the ventromedial prefrontal cortex correlates with gambling task performance: A FDG-PET study. *Society for Neuroscience Abstracts*, 25, 1551.

Graybiel, A. M. (2000). The basal ganglia. *Current Biology*, 10(14), R509–R511.

Green, C. S., & Bavelier, D. (2003). Action video game modifies visual selective attention. *Nature*, 423, 534–537.

Green, C. S., & Bavelier, D. (2004). Does action video game play really enhance the number of items that can be simultaneously attended? *Journal of Vision*, 4, 632.

Green, C. S., & Bavelier, D. (2006a). Effect of action video games on the spatial distribution of visuospatial attention. *Journal of Experimental Psychology: Human Perception and Performance*, 32(6), 1465.

Green, C. S., & Bavelier, D. (2006b). Enumeration versus multiple object tracking: The case of action video game players. *Cognition*, 101, 217–245.

Green, C. S., & Bavelier, D. (2007). Action-video-game experience alters the spatial resolution of vision. *Psychological Science*, 18, 88–94.

Green, C. S., & Bavelier, D. (2015). Action video game training for cognitive enhancement. *Current Opinion in Behavioral Sciences*, 4, 103–108.

Green, C. S., Li, R., & Bavelier, D. (2010). Perceptual learning during action video game playing. *Topics in Cognitive Science*, 2, 202–216.

Green, C. S., Pouget, A., & Bavelier, D. (2010). Improved probabilistic inference as a general learning mechanism with action video games. *Current Biology*, 20, 1573–1579.

Green, C. S., Sugarman, M. A., Medford, K., Klobusicky, E., & Bavelier, D. (2012). The effect of action video game experience on task-switching. *Computers in Human Behavior*, 28, 984–994.

Greene, J. D. (2008). The secret joke of Kant's soul. In W.S. Armstrong (Ed.), *Moral psychology: The neuroscience of morality – emotion, brain disorders and development* (Vol.3) (pp. 35–80). Cambridge: MIT Press.

Greene, J. D., Nystrom, L. E., Engell, A. D., Darley, J. M., & Cohen, J. D. (2004). The neural bases of cognitive conflict and control in moral judgment. *Neuron*, 44(2), 389–400.

Greenfield, D. (2011). The addictive properties of Internet usage. *Internet addiction: A handbook and guide to evaluation and treatment* (pp. 135–153). Hoboken, NJ: Wiley.

Greenfield, P. M., de Winstanley, P., Kilpatrick, H., & Kaye, D. (1994). Action videogames and informal education: Effects on strategies for dividing visual attention. *Journal of Applied Developmental Psychology*, 15, 105–123. doi:10.1016/0193-3973 (94)90008-6.

Gregor, S., Lin, A. C., Gedeon, T., Riaz, A., & Zhu, D. (2014). Neuroscience and a nomological network for the understanding and assessment of emotions in information systems research. *Journal of Management Information Systems*, 30(4), 13–48.

Grewal, D., Gotlieb, J., & Marmorstein, H. (1994). The moderating effects of message framing and source credibility on the price-perceived risk relationship. *Journal of Consumer Research*, 145–153.

Griffiths, M. (2000). Does Internet and computer "addiction" exist? Some case study evidence. *CyberPsychology and Behavior*, 3(2), 211–218.

Griffiths, M. D. (1995). Technological addictions. *Clinical Psychology Forum*, 76, 14–19.

Griffiths, M. D. (1999a). Internet addiction: Fact or fiction? *The Psychologist*.

Griffiths, M. D. (1999b). Internet addiction: Internet fuels other addictions. *Student British Medical Journal*, 7, 428–429.

Grossberg, S., & Schmajuk, N. A. (1987). Neural dynamics of attentionally modulated Pavlovian conditioning: Conditioned reinforcement, inhibition, and opponent processing. *Psychobiology*, 15(3), 195–240.

Guilmette, T. J., & Kastner, M. P. (Eds.) (1996). *The prediction of vocational functioning from neuropsychological data*. Delray Beach, FL: GR Press/St. Lucie Press.

Guo, K. H., Yuan, Y., Archer, N. P., & Connelly, C. E. (2011). Understanding nonmalicious security violations in the workplace: A composite behavior model. *Journal of Management Information Systems*, 28(2), 203–236.

Gutierrez-Martinez, O., Gutierrez-Maldonado, J., and Loreto-Quijada, D. (2011). Control over the virtual environment influences the presence and efficacy of a virtual reality intervention on pain. *Studies in Health Technology and Informatics*, 167, 111–115.

Haarmann, A., Boucsein, W., & Schaefer, F. (2009). Combining electrodermal responses and cardiovascular measures for probing adaptive automation during simulated flight. *Applied Ergonomics*, 40, 1026–1040.

Haber, S. N., & Knutson, B. (2010). The reward circuit: linking primate anatomy and human imaging. *Neuropsychopharmacology*, 35(1), 4–26.

Haier, R. J., Siegel, B. V., MacLachlan, A., Soderling, E., Lottenberg, S., & Buchsbaum, M. S. (1992). Regional glucose metabolic changes after learning a complex visuospatial/motor task: A positron emission tomographic study. *Brain Research*, 570(1), 134–143.

Hall, J. A., Tickle-Degnen, L., Rosenthal, R., & Mosteller, F. (1994). Hypotheses and problems in research synthesis. In H. Cooper & L. V. Hedges (Eds.), *Handbook of research synthesis* (pp. 17–28). New York: Russell Sage Foundation

Halliday, A. M., Butler, S. R. & Paul, R. (1987). *A textbook of clinical neurophysiology*. Chichester: Wiley.

Hammer, R., Ronen, M., Sharon, A., Lankry, T., Huberman, Y., & Zamtsov, V. (2010). Mobile culture in college lectures: Instructors' and students' perspectives. *Interdisciplinary Journal of E-Learning and Learning Objects*, 6(1), 293–304.

Hampton, K. N., Goulet, L. S., Rainie, L., & Purcell, K. (2011). Social networking sites and our lives: How people's trust, personal relationships, and civic and political involvement are connected to their use of social networking sites and other technologies. Pew Internet & American Life Project. www.pewinternet .org/~/media/Files/Reports/2011/PIP%20-%20Social%20networking%20sit es%20and%20our%20lives.pdf.

Han, D. H., Bolo, N., Daniels, M. A., Arenella, L., Lyoo, I. K., & Renshaw, P. F. (2011). Brain activity and desire for Internet video game play. *Comprehensive Psychiatry*, 52(1), 88–95.

Han, D. H., Hwang, J. W., & Renshaw, P. F. (2010). Bupropion sustained release treatment decreases craving for video games and cue-induced brain activity in patients with Internet video game addiction. *Experimental and Clinical Psychopharmacology*, 18(4), 297.

Han, D. H., Lee, Y. S., Yang, K. C., Kim, E. Y., Lyoo, I. K., & Renshaw, P. F. (2007). Dopamine genes and reward dependence in adolescents with excessive internet video game play. *Journal of Addiction Medicine*, 1(3), 133–138.

Han, D. H., Lyoo, I. K., & Renshaw, P. F. (2012). Differential regional gray matter volumes in patients with on-line game addiction and professional gamers. *Journal of Psychiatric Research*, 46(4), 507–515.

Hancock, P. A., & Szalma, J. L. (2003). The future of neuroergonomics. *Theoretical Issues in Ergonomic Science*, 44, 238–249.

Hare, R. M. (1984). Supervenience. *Aristotelian Society*, 58, 1–16.

Hari, R., & Kujala, M. V. (2009). Brain basis of human social interaction: From concepts to brain imaging. *Physiological Reviews*, 89, 453–479. doi: 10.1152/ physrev.00041.2007.

Hariri, A. R., Bookheimer, S. Y., & Mazziotta, J. C. (2000). Modulating emotional responses: Effects of a neocortical network on the limbic system. *Neuroreport*, 11, 43–48.

Harley, D., Fitzpatrick, G., Axelrod, L., White, G., & McAllister, G. (2010). *Making the Wii at home: Game play by older people in sheltered housing* (pp. 156–176). Berlin Heidelberg: Springer.

Harley, J. P., Allen, C., Braciszewski, T. L., Cicerone, K. D., Dahlberg, C., Evans, S., . . . & Malec, J. F. (1992). Guidelines for cognitive rehabilitation. *NeuroRehabilitation*, 2(3), 62–67.

Harris, L. T., & Fiske, S. T. (2010). Neural regions that underlie reinforcement learning are also active for social expectancy violations. *Social Neuroscience*, 5(1), 76–91.

Healey, J. A., & Picard, R. W. (2005). Detecting stress during real-world driving tasks using physiological sensors. *Intelligent Transportation Systems, IEEE Transactions on*, 6(2), 156–166.

Heaton, R. K. (1993). *Wisconsin card sorting test: Computer version 2*. Odessa: Psychological Assessment Resources.

Heim, C., & Nemeroff, C. B. (1999). The impact of early adverse experiences on brain systems involved in the pathophysiology of anxiety and affective disorders. *Biological Psychiatry, 46*(11), 1509–1522.

Heingartner, D. (2009). Mental block. *Spectrum, IEEE, 46*(1), 42–43.

Henninger, D. E. (2006). Ecological validity of neuropsychological assessment: The roles of vocational assessment and employment in aging HIV+ adults. Fordham University, New York.

Henrich, J., Heine, S. J., & Norenzayan, A. (2010). The weirdest people in the world? *Behavioral and Brain Sciences, 33*(2–3), 61–83.

Henry, M., Joyal, C. C., & Nolin, P. (2012). Development and initial assessment of a new paradigm for assessing cognitive and motor inhibition: The bimodal virtual-reality Stroop. *Journal of Neuroscience Methods,* 210(2), 125–131.

Hermans, E. J., Henckens, M. J., Joëls, M., & Fernández, G. (2014). Dynamic adaptation of large-scale brain networks in response to acute stressors. *Trends in Neurosciences,* 37(6), 304–314.

Hinson, J. M., Jameson, T. L., & Whitney, P. (2002). Somatic markers, working memory, and decision making. *Cognitive, Affective, & Behavioral Neuroscience,* 2(4), 341–353.

Hinson, J. M., Jameson, T. L., & Whitney, P. (2003). Impulsive decision making and working memory. *Journal of Experimental Psychology: Learning, Memory, and Cognition,* 29(2), 298.

Hodges, L. F., Watson, B. A., Kessler, G. D., Rothbaum, B. O., & Opdyke, D. (1996). Virtually conquering fear of flying. *Computer Graphics and Applications,* 16, 42–49.

Hoeft, F., Watson, C. L., Kesler, S. R., Bettinger, K. E., and Reiss, A. L. (2008). Gender differences in the mesocorticolimbic system during computer game-play. *Journal of Psychiatric Research,* 42, 253–258.

Hoffman, H. G., et al. (2000). Virtual reality as an adjunctive pain control during burn wound care in adolescent patients. *Pain,* 85(1–2), 305–309.

Hoffman, H. G., Prothero, J., Wells, M., et al. (1998). Virtual chess: The role of meaning in the sensation of presence. *Int. Journal of Human-Computer Interaction,* 10, 251–263.

Hong, S. B., Kim, J. W., Choi, E. J., Kim, H. H., Suh, J. E., Kim, C. D., ... & Yi, S. H. (2013). Reduced orbitofrontal cortical thickness in male adolescents with internet addiction. *Behavioral and Brain Functions,* 9(11), 9081–9089.

Hong, W., & Thong, J. Y. (2013). Internet privacy concerns: An integrated conceptualization and four empirical studies. *MIS Quarterly,* 37(1), 275–298.

Höök, K. (2009). Affective loop experiences: Designing for interactional embodiment. *Philosophical Transactions of the Royal Society B: Biological Sciences,* 364(1535), 3585–3595.

Horne-Moyer, H. L., Moyer, B. H., Messer, D. C., & Messer, E. S. (2014). The use of electronic games in therapy: A review with clinical implications. *Current Psychiatry Reports,* 16(12), 1–9.

Hoshi, E. (2013). Cortico-basal ganglia networks subserving goal-directed behavior mediated by conditional visuo-goal association. *Frontiers in Neural Circuits*, 7.

Hoshikawa, Y., & Yamamoto, Y. U. (1997). Effects of Stroop color-word conflict test on the autonomic nervous system responses. *American Journal of Physiology-Heart and Circulatory Physiology*, 272(3), H1113–H1121.

Hou, H., Jia, S., Hu, S., Fan, R., Sun, W., Sun, T., & Zhang, H. (2012). Reduced striatal dopamine transporters in people with Internet addiction disorder. *BioMed Research International.*

Hu, Q., Dinev, T., Hart, P., & Cooke, D. (2012). Managing employee compliance with information security policies: The critical role of top management and organizational culture*. *Decision Sciences*, 43(4), 615–660.

Hu, Q., West, R., & Smarandescu, L. (2015). The role of self-control in information security violations: Insights from a cognitive neuroscience perspective. *Journal of Management Information Systems*, 31(4), 6–48.

Hubert, M., Hubert, M., Riedl, R., & Kenning, P. (2014). How consumer impulsiveness moderates online trustworthiness evaluations: Neurophysiological insights. In: Proceedings of the 35th International Conference on Information Systems, Auckland.

Hubert-Wallander, B., Green, C. S., Sugarman, M., Bavelier, D. (2011). Changes in search rate but not in the dynamics of exogenous attention in action videogame players. *Attention, Perception and Psychophysics*, 73, 2399–2412.

Huettel, S. A., Song, A. W., & McCarthy, G. (2004). *Functional magnetic resonance imaging* (Vol. 1). Sunderland: Sinauer Associates.

Hugues, S. K., Lewis, R. F. (2015). Frequent use of social networking sites is associated with poor psychological functioning among children and adolescents. *Cyberpsychol Behavior and Social Networks*, 18(7): 380–385.

Hung, Y., Vetivelu, A., Hird, M. A., Yan, M., Tam, F., Graham, S. J., ... & Schweizer, T. A. (2014). Using fMRI virtual-reality technology to predict driving ability after brain damage: A preliminary report. *Neuroscience Letters*, 558, 41–46.

Hunter, J. E., Schmidt, F. L., & Judiesch, M. K. (1990). Individual differences in output variability as a function of job complexity. *Journal of Applied Psychology*, 75(1), 28.

Hunter, J. E., & Schmidt, F. L. (1997). Cumulative research knowledge and social policy formation: The critical role of meta-analysis. *Psychology, Public Policy, and Law*, 2, 324–347. doi:10.1037/1076-8971.2.2.324.

Hussain, Z., & Griffiths, M. D. (2008). Gender swapping and socializing in cyberspace: An exploratory study. *CyberPsychology & Behavior*, 11(1), 47–53.

Hutchinson, C. V., & Stocks, R. (2013). Selectively enhanced motion perception in core video gamers. *Perception*, 42, 675–677.

Hyun, G. J., Shin, Y. W., Kim, B. N., Cheong, J. H., Jin, S. N., & Han, D. H. (2013). Increased cortical thickness in professional on-line gamers. *Psychiatry Investigation*, 10(4), 388–392.

Iacoboni, M. (2009). Neurobiology of imitation. *Current Opinion in Neurobiology*, 19(6), 661–665.

Iacoboni, M., Lieberman, M. D., Knowlton, B. J., Molnar-Szakacs, I., Moritz, M., Throop, C. J., & Fiske, A. P. (2004). Watching social interactions produces dorsomedial prefrontal and medial parietal BOLD fMRI signal increases compared to a resting baseline. *Neuroimage*, 21(3), 1167–1173.

Iengo, S., Origlia, A., Staffa, M., & Finzi, A. (2012, September). Attentional and emotional regulation in human-robot interaction. In *RO-MAN, 2012 IEEE* (pp. 1135–1140). IEEE.

Imam, B., & Jarus, T. (2014). Virtual reality rehabilitation from social cognitive and motor learning theoretical perspectives in stroke population. *Rehabilitation Research and Practice*, 1, 1–11.

Immordino-Yang, M. H., & Damasio, A. (2007). We feel, therefore we learn: The relevance of affective and social neuroscience to education. *Mind, Brain, and Education*, 1(1), 3–10.

Insel, T., Cuthbert, B., Garvey, M., Heinssen, R., Pine, D. S., Quinn, K., ... & Wang, P. (2010). Research domain criteria (RDoC): Toward a new classification framework for research on mental disorders. *American Journal of Psychiatry*, 167(7), 748–751.

Internet Live Stats. (2015). Internet users. Retrieved from Internet Live Stats: www.internetlivestats.com/internet-users-by-country/.

Inventado, P., Legaspi, R., Suarez, M., & Numao, M. (2011). Predicting student emotions resulting from appraisal of its feedback. *Research and Practice in Technology Enhanced Learning*, 6(2), 107–133.

Inzlicht, M., Bartholow, B. D., & Hirsh, J. B. (2015). Emotional foundations of cognitive control. *Trends in Cognitive Sciences*, 19(3), 126–132.

Ipsos MediaCT. (2015). The 2015 essential facts about the computer and video game industry. Entertainment Software Association. Available online at: www.theesa.com/wp-content/uploads/2015/04/ESA-Essential-Facts-2015 .pdf.

Iriarte, Y., Diaz-Orueta, U., Cueto, E., Irazustabarrena, P., Banterla, F., and Climent, G. (2012). AULA-advanced virtual reality tool for the assessment of attention: normative study in Spain. *Journal of Attention Disorders* doi: 10.1177/1087054712465335 [Epub ahead of print].

Irons, J. L., Remington, R. W., & McLean, J. P. (2011). Not so fast: Rethinking the effects of action video games on attentional capacity. *Australian Journal of Psychology*, 63, 224–231.

Iyer, A., Cosand, L., Courtney, C., Rizzo, A. A., & Parsons, T. D. (2009). Considerations for designing response quantification procedures in non-traditional psychophysiological applications. *Lecture Notes in Artificial Intelligence*, 5638, 479–487.

Jacobsen, W. C., & Forste, R. (2011). The wired generation: Academic and social outcomes of electronic media use among university students. *Cyberpsychology, Behavior, and Social Networking*, 14(5), 275–280.

Jaeggi, S. M., Buschkuehl, M., Jonides, J., & Perrig, W. J. (2008). Improving fluid intelligence with training on working memory. *Proceedings of the National Academy of Sciences*, 105(19), 6829–6833.

Jagaroo, V. (2009). *Neuroinformatics for Neuropsychology* (pp. 25–84). New York: Springer-Verlag.

James, W. (1884). What is an emotion? *Mind*, 9(34), 188–205.

James, W. (1890). *The principles of psychology* (Vol. 1). New York: Holt.

James, W. (1894). The physical basis of emotion. *Psychological Review*, 1, 516–529.

Jansari, A. S., Froggatt, D., Edginton, T., and Dawkins, L. (2013). Investigating the impact of nicotine on executive functions using a novel virtual reality assessment. *Addiction*, 108, 977–984.

Jatupaiboon, N., Pan-ngum, S., & Israsena, P. (2013a). Emotion classification using minimal EEG channels and frequency bands. In *Computer Science and Software Engineering (JCSSE), 2013 10th International Joint Conference on* (pp. 21–24). IEEE.

Jatupaiboon, N., Pan-ngum, S., & Israsena, P. (2013b). Real-time EEG-based happiness detection system. *The Scientific World Journal*, 618649, 1–12.

Jennings, J. & Coles, M. G. (Eds.) (1991). *Handbook of cognitive psychophysiology: Central and autonomic nervous system approaches*. Chichester: Wiley.

Jerome, L. W., & Jordan, P. J. (2007). Psychophysiological perspective on presence. *Psychological Services*, 4(2), 75–84.

Joffe, T. H., & Dunbar, R. I. M. (1997). Visual and socio–cognitive information processing in primate brain evolution. *Proceedings Of the Royal Society, London*, 264(1386), 1303–1307.

John, L. K., Acquisti, A., & Loewenstein, G. (2011). Strangers on a plane: Context-dependent willingness to divulge sensitive information. *Journal of Consumer Research*, 37(5), 858–873.

Jovanovski, D., Zakzanis, K., Campbell, Z., Erb, S., & Nussbaum, D. (2012a). Development of a novel, ecologically oriented virtual reality measure of executive function: The Multitasking in the City Test. *Applied Neuropsychology: Adult*, 19, 171–182.

Jovanovski, D., Zakzanis, K., Ruttan, L., Campbell, Z., Erb, S., & Nussbaum, D. (2012b). Ecologically valid assessment of executive dysfunction using a novel virtual reality task in patients with acquired brain injury. *Applied Neuropsychology*, 19, 207–220.

Junco, R., & Cotten, S. R. (2011). Perceived academic effects of instant messaging use. *Computers & Education*, 56(2), 370–378.

Junco, R., & Cotten, S. R. (2012). No A 4 U: The relationship between multitasking and academic performance. *Computers & Education*, 59(2), 505–514.

Kahneman, D. (1973). *Attention and effort*. Englewood Cliffs, NJ: Prentice Hall.

Kahneman, D., & Treisman, A. (1984). Changing views of attention and automaticity. In R. Parasuraman, D. R. Davies, & J. Beatty (Eds.), *Varieties of attention* (pp. 29–61). New York, NY: Academic Press.

Kalechstein, A. D., Newton, T. F., & Van Gorp, W. G. (2003). Neurocognitive functioning is associated with employment status: A quantitative review. *Journal of Clinical and Experimental Neuropsychology*, 25(8), 1186–1191.

Kallinen, K., Salminen, M., Ravaja, N., Kedzior, R., & Sääksjärvi, M. (2007). Presence and emotion in computer game players during 1st person vs. 3rd person playing view: Evidence from self-report, eye-tracking, and facial muscle activity data. *Proceedings of the PRESENCE*, 187–190.

Kanai, R., Bahrami, B., Roylance, R., & Rees, G. (2012). Online social network size is reflected in human brain structure. *Proceedings of the Royal Society of London B: Biological Sciences*, 279(1732), 1327–1334.

Kandel, E. R., Schwartz, J. H. Jessell, T. M., & Siegelbaum, S. A. (2012). *Principles of neural science*, (5th Edition). Elsevier.

Karle, J.W., Watter, S., & Shedden, J.M. (2010). Task switching in video game players: Benefits of selective attention but not resistance to proactive interference. *Acta Psychologica*, 134, 70.

Kassner, M. P., Wesselmann, E. D., Law, A. T., & Williams, K. D. (2012). Virtually ostracized: Studying ostracism in immersive virtual environments. *Cyberpsychology, Behavior, and Social Networking*, 15(8), 399–403.

Kätsyri, J., Hari, R., Ravaja, N., & Nummenmaa, L. (2013a). Just watching the game ain't enough: Striatal fMRI reward responses to successes and failures in a video game during active and vicarious playing. *Frontiers in Human Neuroscience*, 7.

Kätsyri, J., Hari, R., Ravaja, N., & Nummenmaa, L. (2013b). The opponent matters: Elevated fMRI reward responses to winning against a human versus a computer opponent during interactive video game playing. *Cerebral Cortex*, 23(12), 2829–2839.

Kaufmann, T., HOlz, E., Kubler, A. (2013). Comparison of tactile, auditory, and visual modality for brain-computer interface use: A case study with a patient in the locked-in state. *Frontiers in Neuroscience*, 7, 129.

Ke, F. (2009). A qualitative meta-analysis of computer games as learning tools. In R. E. Ferdig (Eds.), *Handbook of research on effective electronic gaming in education* (Vol. 1, pp. 1–32). Hershey, PA: Information Science Reference.

Ke, F., & Im, T. (2013). Virtual-reality-based social interaction training for children with high-functioning autism. *The Journal of Educational Research*, 106(6), 441–461.

Keefe, F. J., Huling, D. A., Coggins, M. J., Keefe, D. F., Rosenthal, M. Z., Herr, N. R., & Hoffman, H. G. (2012). Virtual reality for persistent pain: A new direction for behavioral pain management. *PAIN*, 153(11), 2163–2166.

Kelley, W.M., Macrae, C.N., Wyland, C.L., Caglar, S., Inati, S., & Heatherton, T.F. (2002). Finding the self? An event-related fMRI study. *Journal of Cognitive Neuroscience*, 14, 785–794.

Kelly, A. C., Uddin, L. Q., Biswal, B. B., Castellanos, F. X., & Milham, M. P. (2008). Competition between functional brain networks mediates behavioral variability. *Neuroimage*, 39(1), 527–537.

Kennedy, D.O., & Scholey, A.B. (2000). Glucose administration, heart rate and cognitive performance: Effects of increasing mental effort. *Psychopharmacology*, 149, 63–71.

Kerns, J. G., Cohen, J. D., MacDonald, A. W., III., Cho, R. Y., Stenger, V. A., & Carter, C. S. (2004). Anterior cingulate conflict monitoring and adjustments in control. *Science*, 303, 1023–1026.

Kerr, A., & Zelazo, P.D. (2004). Development of hot executive function: The children's gambling task. *Brain and Cognition*, 55, 148–157.

Keysers, C., & Gazzola, V. (2007). Integrating simulation and theory of mind: From self to social cognition. *Trends in Cognitive Science*, 11(5), 194–196.

Kibby, M. Y., Schmitter-Edgecombe, M., & Long, C. J. (1998). Ecological validity of neuropsychological tests: Focus on the California Verbal Learning Test and the Wisconsin Card Sorting Test. *Archives of Clinical Neuropsychology*, 13(6), 523-534.

Kim, M. K., Kim, M., Oh, E., & Kim, S. P. (2013). A review on the computational methods for emotional state estimation from the human EEG. *Computational and Mathematical Methods in Medicine*, 2013.

Kim, S. H., Baik, S. H., Park, C. S., Kim, S. J., Choi, S. W., & Kim, S. E. (2011). Reduced striatal dopamine D2 receptors in people with Internet addiction. *Neuroreport*, 22(8), 407–411.

Kinzie, M. B., Whitaker, S. D., & Hofer, M. J. (2005). Instructional uses of instant messaging (IM) during classroom lectures. *Journal of Educational Technology & Society*, 8(2), 150–160.

Kiper, P., Piron, L., Turolla, A., Stozek, J., & Tonin, P. (2011). The effectiveness of reinforced feedback in virtual environment in the first 12 months after stroke. *Neurologia i Neurochirurgia Polska*, 45(5), 436–444.

Kirwan G, & Power A. (2011). *The psychology of cyber crime*. Pennsylvania: IGI Global Press.

Klinger, E., Bouchard, S., Légeron, P., Roy, S., Lauer, F., Chemin, I., & Nugues, P. (2005). Virtual reality therapy versus cognitive behavior therapy for social phobia: A preliminary controlled study. *Cyberpsychology & Behavior*, 8(1), 76–88.

Klinger, E., & Weiss, P. L. (2009). Shifting towards remote located virtual environments for rehabilitation. *Proceedings of the Chais Conference on Instructional Technologies Research*. Haifa, Israel.

Knight, C., Alderman, N., & Burgess, P. W. (2002). Development of a simplified version of the multiple errands test for use in hospital settings. *Neuropsychological Rehabilitation*, 12(3), 231–255.

Knoll, A., Wang, Y., Chen, F., Xu, J., Ruiz, N., Epps, J., & Zarjam, P. (2011). Measuring cognitive workload with low-cost electroencephalograph. In *Human-computer interaction–INTERACT 2011* (pp. 568–571). Berlin Heidelberg: Springer.

Ko, C. H., Liu, G. C., Hsiao, S., Yen, J. Y., Yang, M. J., Lin, W. C., ... & Chen, C. S. (2009). Brain activities associated with gaming urge of online gaming addiction. *Journal of Psychiatric Research*, 43(7), 739–747.

Ko, C. H., Liu, G. C., Yen, J. Y., Chen, C. Y., Yen, C. F., & Chen, C. S. (2013). Brain correlates of craving for online gaming under cue exposure in subjects with Internet gaming addiction and in remitted subjects. *Addiction Biology*, 18(3), 559–569.

Ko, C. H., Yen, J. Y., Yen, C. F., Chen, C. S., & Chen, C. C. (2012). The association between Internet addiction and psychiatric disorder: A review of the literature. *European Psychiatry*, 27(1), 1–8.

Kobayashi, N., Yoshino, A., Takahashi, Y., & Nomura, S. (2007). Autonomic arousal in cognitive conflict resolution. *Autonomic Neuroscience: Basic and Clinical*, 132, 70–75.

Koenig, S.T., Crucian, G.P., Dalrymple-Alford, J.C., Dünser, A. (2009). Virtual reality rehabilitation of spatial abilities after brain damage. *Studies in Health Technology and Informatics*, 144, 105–107.

Koenigs, M., & Tranel, D. (2007). Irrational economic decision-making after ventromedial prefrontal damage: Evidence from the Ultimatum Game. *The Journal of Neuroscience*, 27(4), 951–956.

Koepp, M. J., Gunn, R. N., Lawrence, A. D., Cunningham, V. J., Dagher, A., Jones, T., . . . & Grasby, P. M. (1998). Evidence for striatal dopamine release during a video game. *Nature*, 393(6682), 266–268.

Kohler, C. G., Walker, J. B., Martin, E. A., Healey, K. M., & Moberg, P. J. (2010). Facial emotion perception in schizophrenia: A meta-analytic review. *Schizophrenia Bulletin*, 36, 1009–1019.

Kokal, I., Gazzola, V., and Keysers, C. (2009). Acting together in and beyond the mirror neuron system. *Neuroimage*, 47, 2046–2056.

Kolb, B., & Whishaw, I. Q. (2015). *Fundamentals of human neuropsychology*. New York: Macmillan.

Kolek, E. A., & Saunders, D. (2008). Online disclosure: An empirical examination of undergraduate Facebook profiles. *Journal of Student Affairs Research and Practice*, 45(1), 1–25.

Koller, M., & Walla, P. (2012). Measuring affective information processing in information systems and consumer research–introducing startle reflex modulation. ICIS 2012 Proceedings, AIS.

Kononova, A. G. (2013). Effects of distracting ads and cognitive control on the processing of online news stories with stereotype-related information. *Cyberpsychology, Behavior, and Social Networking*, 16(5), 321–328.

Konvalinka, I., & Roepstorff, A. (2012). The two-brain approach: How can mutually interacting brains teach us something about social interaction? *Frontiers in Human Neuroscience*, 6, 215. doi: 10.3389/fnhum.2012.00215.

Kosinski, M., Matz, S. C., Gosling, S. D., Popov, V., & Stillwell, D. (2015). Facebook as a research tool for the social sciences: Opportunities, challenges, ethical considerations, and practical guidelines. *American Psychologist*, 70(6), 543.

Kovács, Á. M., Kühn, S., Gergely, G., Csibra, G., & Brass, M. (2014). Are all beliefs equal? Implicit belief attributions recruiting core brain regions of theory of mind. *PloS one*, 9(9), e106558.

Koziol, L. F., & Budding, D. E. (2009). *Subcortical structures and cognition: Implications for neuropsychological assessment.* New York: Springer Science & Business Media.

Krawczyk, D., Bartlett, J., Kantarcioglu, M., Hamlen, K., & Thuraisingham, B. (2013, June). Measuring expertise and bias in cyber security using cognitive and neuroscience approaches. In *Intelligence and Security Informatics (ISI), 2013 IEEE International Conference on* (pp. 364–367). IEEE.

Kreibig, S. D., Wilhelm, F. H., Roth, W. T., & Gross, J. J. (2007). Cardiovascular, electrodermal, and respiratory response patterns to fear- and sadness-inducing films. *Psychophysiology, 44,* 787–806.

Kuan, K. K., Zhong, Y., & Chau, P. Y. (2014). Informational and normative social influence in group-buying: Evidence from self-reported and EEG data. *Journal of Management Information Systems, 30*(4), 151–178.

Kuhl, J. (1981). Motivational and functional helplessness: The moderating effect of state versus action orientation. *Journal of Personality and Social Psychology, 40*(1), 155.

Kühn, S., & Gallinat, J. (2014). Amount of lifetime video gaming is positively associated with entorhinal, hippocampal and occipital volume. *Molecular Psychiatry, 19*(7), 842–847.

Kühn, S., Gleich, T., Lorenz, R. C., Lindenberger, U., & Gallinat, J. (2014). Playing Super Mario induces structural brain plasticity: Gray matter changes resulting from training with a commercial video game. *Molecular Psychiatry, 19*(2), 265–271.

Kurzban, R., Tooby, J., & Cosmides, L. (2001). Can race be erased? Coalitional computation and social categorization. *Proceedings of the National Academy of Sciences, 98*(26), 15387–15392.

Kurzweil, R. (2005). *The singularity is near: When humans transcend biology.* New York: Viking.

Kurzweil, R. (2012). *How to create a mind: The secret of human thought revealed.* New York: Viking.

Kuss, D. J. (2013). Internet gaming addiction: Current perspectives. *Psychology Research and Behavior Management, 6,* 125.

Kuss, D. J., & Griffiths, M. D. (2012). Internet and gaming addiction: A systematic literature review of neuroimaging studies. *Brain Sciences, 2*(3), 347–374.

Lacey, J. I., (1959). Psychophysiological approaches to the evaluation of psychotherapeutic process and outcome. In E.A. Rubenstein & M.B. Parloff (Eds.), *Research in psychotherapy* (pp. 160–208). Washington, DC: American Psychological Association.

Lallart, E., Lallart, X., & Jouvent, R. (2009). Agency, the sense of presence, and schizophrenia. *Cyberpsychology & Behavior, 12*(2), 139–145.

Lalonde, G., Henry, M., Drouin-Germain, A., Nolin, P., & Beauchamp, M. H. (2013). Assessment of executive function in adolescence: A comparison of traditional and virtual reality tools. *Journal of Neuroscience Methods, 219,* 76–82. doi: 10.1016/j.jneumeth.2013.07.005.

Lam, L. T. (2014). Internet gaming addiction, problematic use of the Internet, and sleep problems: A systematic review. *Current Psychiatry Reports*, 16(4), 1–9.

Laming, D. (1992). Analysis of short-term retention: Models for Brown–Peterson experiments. *Journal of Experimental Psychology: Learning, Memory, & Cognition*, 18, 1342–1365.

Lang, P. J., Bradley, M. M., & Cuthbert, B. N. (1997). International affective picture system (IAPS): Technical manual and affective ratings. *NIMH Center for the Study of Emotion and Attention*, 39–58.

Lange, C. G. (1885). The mechanism of the emotions. *The Classical Psychologist*, 672–685.

Langhan, T. S. (2008). Simulation training for emergency medicine residents: Time to move forward. *CJEM*, 10(05), 467–469.

Lanier, J., & Biocca, F. (1992). An insider's view of the future of virtual reality. *Journal of Communication*, 42, 150–172.

Lanius, R. A., Frewen, P. A., Tursich, M., Jetly, R., & McKinnon, M. C. (2015). Restoring large-scale brain networks in PTSD and related disorders: a proposal for neuroscientifically-informed treatment interventions. *European Journal of Psychotraumatology*, 6.

Larson, E. B., Feigon, M., Gagliardo, P., & Dvorkin, A. Y. (2014). Virtual reality and cognitive rehabilitation: A review of current outcome research. *NeuroRehabilitation*, 34(4), 759–772.

Lazer, D., Pentland, A. S., Adamic, L., Aral, S., Barabasi, A. L., Brewer, D., . . . & Jebara, T. (2009). Life in the network: The coming age of computational social science. *Science (New York, NY)*, 323(5915), 721.

Le Bihan, D., Mangin, J. F., Poupon, C., Clark, C. A., Pappata, S., Molko, N., & Chabriat, H. (2001). Diffusion tensor imaging: Concepts and applications. *Journal of Magnetic Resonance Imaging*, 13(4), 534–546.

LeDoux, J., (2003). *Synaptic self*. New York: Penguin Books.

LeDoux, J. (2012). Rethinking the emotional brain. *Neuron*, 73(4), 653–676.

Lee, J. (2012). A mixed-methods study investigating the relationship between media multitasking orientation and grade point average. Doctoral dissertation, University of North Texas. Denton, Texas. Available at http://digital .library.unt.edu/ark:/67531/metadc177221/m1/1/.

Lenartowicz, A., Kalar, D. J., Congdon, E., & Poldrack, R. A. (2010). Towards an ontology of cognitive control. *Topics in Cognitive Science*, 2(4), 678–692.

Lessiter, J., Freeman, J., Keogh, E., & Davidoff, J. (2001). A cross-media presence questionnaire: The ITC-Sense of Presence Inventory. *Presence*, 10(3), 282–297.

Lewis, P., Rezaie, R., Brown, R., Roberts, N., Dunbar, R.I.M. (2011). Ventromedial prefrontal volume predicts understanding of others and social network size. *NeuroImage*, 57(4), 1624–1629.

Lezak, M.D. (2004). *Neuropsychological assessment* (4th edn.), New York: Oxford University Press.

Lezak, M. D., Howieson, D. B., & Loring, D. W. (1983). *Neuropsychology assessment*. New York: Oxford University Press.

Li, B., Friston, K. J., Liu, J., Liu, Y., Zhang, G., Cao, F., ... & Hu, D. (2014). Impaired frontal-basal ganglia connectivity in adolescents with Internet addiction. *Scientific Reports*, 4.

Li, W., Mai, X., & Liu, C. (2014). The default mode network and social understanding of others: What do brain connectivity studies tell us. *Frontiers in Human Neuroscience*, 8, 74.

Li, R., Polat, U., Makous, W., & Bavelier, D. (2009). Enhancing the contrast sensitivity function through action video game training. *Nature Neuroscience*, 12, 549–551.

Li, R., Polat, U., Scalzo, F., Bavelier, D. (2010). Reducing backward masking through action game training. *Journal of Vision*, 10, 1–13.

Li, W., Li, Y., Yang, W., Zhang, Q., Wei, D., Li, W., ... & Qiu, J. (2015). Brain structures and functional connectivity associated with individual differences in Internet tendency in healthy young adults. *Neuropsychologia*, 70, 134–144.

Lieberman M. (2013). *Social: Why our brains are wired to connect*. New York, NY: Crown.

Lieberman, M. D. (2007). The X-and C-systems. In E. Harmon-Jones & P. Winkielman (Eds.), *Social neuroscience: Integrating biological and psychological explanations of social behavior* (pp. 290–315). New York: Guilford Press.

Lieberman, M. D., & Eisenberger, N. I. (2009). Neuroscience. Pains and pleasures of social life. *Science*, 323, 890–891.

Lim, M. Y. (2012). Memory models for intelligent social companions. In *Human-computer interaction: The agency perspective* (pp. 241–262). Berlin Heidelberg: Springer.

Lim, M. Y., Aylett, R., Ho, W. C., Enz, S., & Vargas, P. (2009, January). A socially-aware memory for companion agents. In *Intelligent virtual agents* (pp. 20–26). Berlin Heidelberg: Springer.

Lin, A., & Vasilyeva, O. (2011). Envisioning the concept of emotions for theory development and testing in information systems research: A study of one positive emotion – enjoyment. In Proceedings of JAIS theory development workshop. *Sprouts: Working Papers on Information Systems*, 11(155), 11–155.

Lin, L. (2009). Breadth-biased versus focused cognitive control in media multitasking behaviors. *Proceedings of the National Academy of Sciences*, 106(37), 15521–15522.

Lin, L., Robertson, T., & Lee, J. (2009). Reading performances between novices and experts in different media multitasking environments. *Computers in the Schools*, 26(3), 169–186.

Lindquist, K. A., Wager, T. D., Kober, H., Bliss-Moreau, E., & Barrett, L. F. (2012). The brain basis of emotion: A meta-analytic review. *Behavioral and Brain Sciences*, 35(03), 121–143.

Liotti, M., Woldorff, M. G., Perez, R., & Mayberg, H. S. (2000). An ERP study of the temporal course of the Stroop color-word interference effect. *Neuropsychologia*, 38(5), 701–711.

Littel, M., Berg, I., Luijten, M., Rooij, A. J., Keemink, L., & Franken, I. H. (2012). Error processing and response inhibition in excessive computer game players: An event-related potential study. *Addiction Biology*, 17(5), 934–947.

Liu, T., & Pelowski, M. (2014). Clarifying the interaction types in two-person neuroscience research. *Frontiers in Human Neuroscience*, 8.

Llorens, R., Noé, E., Ferri, J., & Alcañiz, M. (2015). Videogame-based group therapy to improve self-awareness and social skills after traumatic brain injury. *Journal of Neuroengineering and Rehabilitation*, 12(1), 37.

Logie, R. H., Law, A., Trawley, S., Nissan, J. (2010). Multitasking, working memory and remembering intentions. *Psychologica Belgica*, 50(3–4), 309–326.

Logie, R. H., Trawley, S., & Law, A. (2011). Multitasking: Multiple, domain-specific cognitive functions in a virtual environment. *Memory & Cognition*, 39(8), 1561–1574.

Loh, K. K., & Kanai, R. (2014). Higher media multi-tasking activity is associated with smaller gray-matter density in the anterior cingulate cortex. *PLoS One*. 9, e106698.

Lomanowska, A. M., & Guitton, M. J. (2012). Spatial proximity to others determines how humans inhabit virtual worlds. *Computers in Human Behavior*, 28(2), 318–323.

Long, C. J. (1996). Neuropsychological tests: A look at our past and the impact that ecological issues may have on our future. In R. J. Sbordone & C. J. Long (Eds.), *Ecological validity of neuropsychological testing* (pp. 1–14). Delray Beach, FL: GR Press/St. Lucie Press.

Loomis, J. M. (1992). Distal attribution and presence. *Presence: Teleoperators & Virtual Environments*, 1(1), 113–119.

Lorenz, R. C., Krüger, J. K., Neumann, B., Schott, B. H., Kaufmann, C., Heinz, A., & Wüstenberg, T. (2013). Cue reactivity and its inhibition in pathological computer game players. *Addiction Biology*, 18(1), 134–146.

Luck, S. J., & Kappenman, E. S. (Eds.). (2011). *The Oxford handbook of event-related potential components*. Oxford University Press.

Lui, K. F., & Wong, A. C. N. (2012). Does media multitasking always hurt? A positive correlation between multitasking and multisensory integration. *Psychonomic Bulletin & Review*, 19(4), 647–653.

Lysaker, P., Bell, M., & Bean-Goulet, J. (1995). Wisconsin Card Sorting Test and work performance in schizophrenia. *Psychiatry Research*, 56, 45–51.

MacDorman, K. F., Green, R. D., Ho, C. C., & Koch, C. T. (2009). Too real for comfort? Uncanny responses to computer generated faces. *Computers in Human Behavior*, 25(3), 695–710.

Macedonio, M. F., Parsons, T. D., Digiuseppe, R. A., Weiderhold, B. A., & Rizzo, A. A. (2007). Immersiveness and physiological arousal within panoramic video-based virtual reality. *Cyberpsychology & Behavior*, 10(4), 508–515.

Maclean, N., et al. (2002). The concept of patient motivation: A qualitative analysis of stroke professionals' attitudes. *Stroke*, 33(2), 444–448.

Magina, C. A. (1997). Some recent applications of clinical psychophysiology. *International Journal of Psychophysiology*, 25(1), 1–6.

Maillot, P., Perrot, A., & Hartley, A. (2012). Effects of interactive physicalactivity video-game training on physical and cognitive function in older adults. *Psychology and Aging*, 27(3), 589–600.

Maister, L., Sebanz, N., Knoblich, G., and Tsakiris, M. (2013). Experiencing ownership over a dark-skinned body reduces implicit racial bias. *Cognition*, 128, 170–178.

Maister, L., Slater, M., Sanchez-Vives, M. V., and Tsakiris, M. (2015). Changing bodies changes minds: Owning another body affects social cognition. *Trends in Cognitive Sciences*, 19, 6–12.

Mak, J. N., & Wolpaw, J. R. (2009). Clinical applications of brain-computer interfaces: Current state and future prospects. *IEEE Reviews in Biomedical Engineering*, 2, 187–199.

Makatura, T. J., Lam, C. S., Leahy, B. J., Castillo, M. T., & Kalpakjian, C. Z. (1999). Standardized memory tests and the appraisal of everyday memory. *Brain Injury*, 13(5), 355–367.

Malhotra, N. K., Kim, S. S., & Agarwal, J. (2004). Internet users' information privacy concerns (IUIPC): The construct, the scale, and a causal model. *Information Systems Research*, 15(4), 336–355.

Malinen, S., Vartiainen, N., Hlushchuk, Y., Koskinen, M., Ramkumar, P., Forss, N., . . . & Hari, R. (2010). Aberrant temporal and spatial brain activity during rest in patients with chronic pain. *Proceedings of the National Academy of Sciences*, 107(14), 6493–6497.

Malloy, K.M., & Milling, L.S. (2010). The effectiveness of virtual reality distraction for pain reduction: A systematic review. *Clinical Psychology Review*, 30 (8), 1011–1018.

Manchester, D., Priestley, N., and Howard, J. (2004). The assessment of executive functions: Coming out of the office. *Brain Injury*, 18, 1067–1081.

Manes, F., Sahakian, B., Clark, L., Rogers, R., Antoun, N., Aitken, M., & Robbins, T. (2002). Decision-making processes following damage to the prefrontal cortex. *Brain*, 125(3), 624–639.

Mannino, M., & Bressler, S. L. (2015). Foundational perspectives on causality in large-scale brain networks. *Physics of Life Reviews*, 15, 107–123.

Mantovani, G., & Riva, G. (1999). "Real" presence: How different ontologies generate different criteria for presence, telepresence, and virtual presence. *Presence: Teleoperators and Virtual Environments*, 8(5), 540–550.

Mapou, R. L., (1988). Testing to detect brain damage: An alternative to what may no longer be useful. *Journal of Clinical and Experimental Neuropsychology*, 10 (2), 1988.

Marcotte, T. D., & Grant, I. (Eds.). (2009). *Neuropsychology of everyday functioning*. New York: Guilford Press.

Maria, K. A., & Zitar, R. A. (2007). Emotional agents: A modeling and an application. *Information and Software Technology*, 49(7), 695–716.

Mars, R. B., Neubert, F. X., Noonan, M. P., Sallet, J., Toni, I., & Rushworth, M. F. (2012). On the relationship between the "default mode network" and the "social brain." *Frontiers in Human Neuroscience*, 6.

Marsella, S., Gratch, J., & Petta, P. (2010). Computational models of emotion. In *A blueprint for affective computing – A sourcebook and manual* (pp. 21–46), Oxford University Press.

Marston, H. R., & Smith, S. T. (2012). Interactive videogame technologies to support independence in the elderly: A narrative review. *GAMES FOR HEALTH: Research, Development, and Clinical Applications*, 1(2), 139–152.

Marusan, M., Kulistak, P., & Zara, J. (2006). Virtual reality in neurorehabilitation: Mental rotation. *Proceedings of the third Central European Multimedia and Virtual Reality Conference* (pp. 77–83). Veszprém: Pannonian University Press.

Maskey, M., Lowry, J., Rodgers, J., McConachie, H., & Parr, J. R. (2014). Reducing specific phobia/fear in young people with autism spectrum disorders (ASDs) through a virtual reality environment intervention. *PLoS ONE*, 9(7), e100374. doi: 10.1371/journal.pone.0100374.

Masmoudi, S., Dai, D. Y., & Naceur, A. (Eds.). (2012). *Attention, representation, and human performance: Integration of cognition, emotion, and motivation.* New York: Psychology Press.

Massar, S. A. A., Kenemans, J. L., & Schutter, D. J. L. G. (2013). Resting-state EEG theta activity and risk learning: Sensitivity to reward or punishment? *International Journal of Psychophysiology*.

Massar, S. A. A., Rossi, V., Schutter, D. J. L. G., & Kenemans, J. L. (2012). Baseline EEG theta/beta ratio and punishment sensitivity as biomarkers for feedback-related negativity (FRN) and risk-taking. *Clinical Neurophysiology*, 123(10), 1958–1965.

Masur, E. F., & Flynn, V. (2008). Infant and mother-infant play and the presence of television. *Journal of Applied Developmental Psychology*, 29, 76–83.

Matheis, R. J., Schultheis, M. T., Tiersky, L. A., DeLuca, J., Millis, S. R., & Rizzo, A. (2007). Is learning and memory different in a virtual environment? *Clinical Neuropsychology*, 21, 146–161.

Matsuda, G., & Hiraki, K. (2006). Sustained decrease in oxygenated hemoglobin during video games in the dorsal prefrontal cortex: A NIRS study of children. *Neuroimage*, 29(3), 706–711.

McCaul, K.D., Malott, J.M. (1984). Distraction and coping with pain. *Psychological Bulletin*, 95(3), 516–533.

McCracken, L.A., & Eccleston, C. (2003). Coping or acceptance: What to do about chronic pain? *Pain*, 105(1–2), 197–204.

McDougall, S., & House, B. (2012). Brain training in older adults: Evidence of transfer to memory span performance and pseudo-Matthew effects. *Neuropsychology, Development, and Cognition. Section B, Aging, Neuropsychology and Cognition*, 19(1–2), 195–221.

McDuff, D., Kaliouby, R., Senechal, T., Amr, M., Cohn, J., & Picard, R. (2013). Affectiva-mit facial expression dataset (am-fed): Naturalistic and spontaneous facial expressions collected. In *Proceedings of the IEEE Conference on Computer Vision and Pattern Recognition Workshops* (pp. 881–888).

McEneaney, J. E. (2013). Agency effects in human–computer interaction. *International Journal of Human-Computer Interaction*, 29(12), 798–813.

McGeorge, P., Phillips, L. H., Crawford, J. R., Garden, S. E., Sala, S. D., and Milne, A. B. (2001). Using virtual environments in the assessment of executive dysfunction. *Presence Teleoperators Virtual Environ.*, 10, 375–383.

McGurk, S. R., & Mueser, K. T. (2006). Cognitive and clinical predictors of work outcomes in clients with schizophrenia receiving supported employment services: 4-year follow-up. *Administration and Policy in Mental Health and Mental Health Services Research*, 33(5), 598–606.

McLuhan, M. (1964). *Understanding media: The extensions of man*. New York: McGraw Hill.

Mcmahan, T., Parberry, I., & Parsons, T. D. (2015a). Modality specific assessment of video game player's experience using the emotiv. *Entertainment Computing*, 7, 1–6.

Mcmahan, T., Parberry, I., & Parsons, T.D. (2015b). Evaluating player task engagement and arousal using electroencephalography. *Procedia Manufacturing*, 3, 2303–2310.

Mcmahan, T., Parberry, I., & Parsons, T.D. (2015c). Evaluating electroencephalography engagement indices during video game play. *Proceedings of the Foundations of Digital Games Conference*, June 22 – June 25, 2015.

Meacham, J. A. (1982). A note on remembering to execute planned actions. *Journal of Applied Developmental Psychology*, 3, 121–133.

Meehan, M., Insko, B., Whitton, M. & Brooks, F.P. (2002). Physiological measures of presence in stressful virtual environments. *Acm Transactions on Graphics*, 21, 645–652.

Meehan, M., Razzaque, S., Insko, B., Whitton, M., & Brooks Jr, F. P. (2005). Review of four studies on the use of physiological reaction as a measure of presence in stressful virtual environments. *Applied Psychophysiology and Biofeedback*, 30(3), 239–258.

Mega, M. S., & Cummings, J. L. (1994). Frontal–subcortical circuits and neuropsychiatric disorders. *Journal of Neuropsychiatry and Clinical Neurosciences*, 6(4), 358–370.

Mehler, B., Reimer, B., Coughlin, J.F., & Dusek, J.A. (2009). Impact of incremental increases in cognitive workload on physiological arousal and performance in young adult drivers. *Journal of the Transportation Research Board*, 2138, 6–12.

Meikle, S. R., Beekman, F. J., & Rose, S. E. (2006). Complementary molecular imaging technologies: High resolution SPECT, PET and MRI. *Drug Discovery Today: Technologies*, 3(2), 187–194.

Menon, V. (2011). Large-scale brain networks and psychopathology: A unifying triple network model. *Trends in Cognitive Sciences*, 15(10), 483–506.

Menon, V., & Uddin, L. Q. (2010). Saliency, switching, attention and control: A network model of insula function. *Brain Structure & Function*, 214, 655–667.

Meshi, D., Morawetz, C., & Heekeren, H. R. (2013). Nucleus accumbens response to gains in reputation for the self relative to gains for others predicts social media use. *Frontiers in Human Neuroscience*, 7.

Meshi, D., Tamir, D. I., & Heekeren, H. R. (2015). The emerging neuroscience of social media. *Trends in Cognitive Sciences*, 19(12), 771–782.

Mesulam, M. M. (1985). Patterns in behavioral neuroanatomy: Association areas, the limbic system, and hemispheric specialization. In *Behavioral neurology* (pp. 1–70). Philadelphia: Davis.

Mesulam, M. M. (1990). Large-scale neurocognitive networks and distributed processing for attention, language, and memory. *Annals of Neurology*, 28, 597–613.

Mesulam, M. M. (2000). Behavioral neuroanatomy: Large-scale networks, association cortex, frontal syndromes, the limbic system, and hemispheric specializations. In M. M. Mesulam (Ed.), *Principles of behavioral and cognitive neurology* (2nd Edition) (pp. 1–120). New York: Oxford University Press.

Meyer, D. E., & Kieras, D. E. (1997). A computational theory of executive cognitive processes and multiple-task performance: Part 1. Basic mechanisms. *Psychological Review*, 104, 3–65.

Meyerbröker, K., & Emmelkamp, P. M. (2011). Virtual reality exposure therapy for anxiety disorders: The state of the art. In *Advanced computational intelligence paradigms in healthcare 6. Virtual reality in psychotherapy, rehabilitation, and assessment* (pp. 47–62). Berlin, Heidelberg; Springer.

Middendorf, M., McMillan, G., Calhoun, G., & Jones, K. S. (2000). Brain-computer interfaces based on the steady-state visual-evoked response. *IEEE Transactions on Rehabilitation Engineering*, 8, 211–214.

Millan, J. D., Rupp, R., Muller-Putz, G. R., Murray-Smith, R., Giugliemma, C., Tangermann, M., ... & Mattia, D. (2010). Combining brain-computer interfaces and assistive technologies: State-of-the-art and challenges. *Frontiers in Neuroscience*, 4, 10.

Miller, D. C., & Thorpe, J. A. (1995). SIMNET: The advent of simulator networking. *Proceedings of the IEEE*, 83(8), 1114–1123.

Miller, E., Seppa, C., Kittur, A., Sabb, F., & Poldrack, R. A. (2010). The cognitive atlas: Employing interaction design processes to facilitate collaborative ontology creation. *Nature Proceedings*. http://dx.doi.org/10.1038/npre.2010.4532.1.

Miller, G. A. (2003). The cognitive revolution: A historical perspective. *Trends in Cognitive Sciences*, 7(3), 141–144.

Mills, K. L. (2014). Effects of Internet use on the adolescent brain: Despite popular claims, experimental evidence remains scarce. *Trends in Cognitive Sciences*, 18(8), 385–387.

Milner, B. (1963). Effects of different brain lesions on card sorting: The role of the frontal lobes. *Archives of Neurology*, 9(1), 90–100.

Minas, R. K., Potter, R. F., Dennis, A. R., Bartelt, V., & Bae, S. (2014). Putting on the thinking cap: Using neuroIS to understand information processing biases in virtual teams. *Journal of Management Information Systems*, 30(4), 49–82.

Minear, M., Brasher, F., McCurdy, M., Lewis, J., & Younggren, A. (2013). Working memory, fluid intelligence, and impulsiveness in heavy media multitaskers. *Psychonomic Bulletin & Review*, 20(6), 1274–1281.

Mishra, J., Zinni, M., Bavelier, D., & Hillyard, S. A. (2011). Neural basis of superior performance of action videogame players in an attention-demanding task. *The Journal of Neuroscience*, 31(3), 992–998.

Mitrushina, M., Boone, K. B., Razani, J., & D'Elia, L. F. (2005). *Handbook of normative data for neuropsychological assessment.*, 2nd edition. New York: Oxford University Press.

Montag, C., & Reuter, M. (Eds.). (2015). *Internet addiction: Neuroscientific approaches and therapeutical interventions*. Springer.

Montag, C., Weber, B., Trautner, P., Newport, B., Markett, S., Walter, N. T., . . . & Reuter, M. (2012). Does excessive play of violent first-person-shooter-video-games dampen brain activity in response to emotional stimuli? *Biological Psychology*, 89(1), 107–111.

Montague, P. R., Berns, G. S., Cohen, J. D., McClure, S. M., Pagnoni, G., Dhamala, M., et al. (2002). Hyperscanning: Simultaneous fMRI during linked social interactions. *Neuroimage*, 16, 1159–1164.

Montgomery, C., Ashmore, K., & Jansari, A. (2011). The effects of a modest dose of alcohol on executive functioning and prospective memory. *Human Psychopharmacology*, 26, 208–215.

Moor, B. G., Crone, E. A., & van der Molen, M. W. (2010). The heartbreak of social rejection heart rate deceleration in response to unexpected peer rejection. *Psychological Science*, 21, 1326–1333.

Mori, M. (1970). The valley of eeriness (Japanese). *Energy*, 7(4), 33–35.

Mori, M., MacDorman, K. F., & Kageki, N. (2012). The uncanny valley [from the field]. Robotics & Automation Magazine, *IEEE*, 19(2), 98–100.

Morris, J. S., Frith, C. D., Perrett, D. I., Rowland, D., Young, A. W., Calder, A. J., et al. (1996). A differential neural response in the human amygdala to fearful and happy facial expressions. *Nature*, 383, 812–815.

Morris, R. G., Kotitsa, M., Bramham, J., Brooks, B. M., & Rose, F. D. (2002). Virtual reality investigation of strategy formation, rule breaking and prospective memory in patients with focal prefrontal neurosurgical lesions. In *Proceedings of the 4th International Conference on Disability, Virtual Reality and Associated Technologies*.

Mühlberger, A., Bülthoff, H., Wiedemann, G., & Pauli, P. (2007). Virtual reality for the psychophysiological assessment of phobic fear: Responses during virtual tunnel driving. *Psychological Assessment*, 19, 340–346. doi: 10.1037/1040-3590.19.3.340.

Mühlberger, A., Wieser, M. J., & Pauli, P. (2008). Darkness-enhanced startle responses in ecologically valid environments: A virtual tunnel driving experiment. *Biological Psychology*, 77, 47–52.

Muir, B.M. (1988). Trust between humans and machines, and the design of decision aids. In E. Hollnagel, G. Mancini, & D. D. Woods (Eds.), *Cognitive engineering in complex dynamic worlds* (pp. 71–83). London. UK: Academic.

Murphy, R. R., Lisetti, C. L., Tardif, R., Irish, L., & Gage, A. (2002). Emotion-based control of cooperating heterogeneous mobile robots. *Robotics and Automation, IEEE Transactions on*, 18(5), 744–757.

Murthy, V. N., & Fetz, E. E. (1992). Coherent 25- to 35-Hz oscillations in the sensorimotor cortex of awake behaving monkeys. *Proceedings of the National Academy of Sciences, USA*, 89, 5670–5674.

Muusses, L. D., Finkenauer, C., Kerkhof, P., & Righetti, F. (2013). Partner effects of compulsive Internet use: A self-control account. *Communication Research*, 0093650212469545.

Nacke, L. E. (2013). An introduction to physiological player metrics for evaluating games. In *Game analytics* (pp. 585–619). London: Springer.

Nacke, L. E., Grimshaw, M. N., & Lindley, C. A. (2010). More than a feeling: Measurement of sonic user experience and psychophysiology in a first-person shooter game. *Interacting with Computers*, 22 (5), 336–343. doi: 10.1016/j. intcom.2010.04.005.

Nacke, L. E., Stellmach, S., & Lindley, C. A. (2011). Electroencephalographic assessment of player experience a pilot study in affective ludology. *Simulation & Gaming*, 42(5), 632–655.

Nacke, L., & Lindley, C. A. (2008a). Flow and immersion in first-person shooters: Measuring the player's gameplay experience. In *Proceedings of the 2008 conference on future play: Research, Play, Share (Future Play '08)* (pp. 81–88). Toronto: ACM. doi: 10.1145/1496984.1496998.

Nacke, L., Lindley, C., & Stellmach, S. (2008b). Log who's playing: Psychophysiological game analysis made easy through event logging. In P. Markopoulos, B. D. Ruyter, W. Ijsselsteijn, & D. Rowland (Eds.), *Proceedings of Fun and Games, Second International Conference* (Lecture Notes in Computer Science) (pp. 150–157). Dordrecht: Springer. doi: 10.1007/978-3-540-88322-7_15.

Naglieri, J. A., & Das, J. P. (1987). Construct and criterion-related validity of planning, simultaneous, and successive cognitive processing tasks. *Journal of Psychoeducational Assessment*, 4, 353–363.

Nahab, F. B., Kundu, P., Gallea, C., Kakareka, J., Pursley, R., Pohida, T., ... & Hallett, M. (2011). The neural processes underlying self-agency. *Cerebral Cortex*, 21(1), 48–55.

Navarrete, C. D., McDonald, M. M., Mott, M. L., & Asher, B. (2012). Virtual morality: Emotion and action in a simulated three-dimensional "trolley problem." *Emotion*, 12(2), 364.

Neisser, U. (1978). Memory: What are the important questions? In M. M. Gruneberg, P. E. Morris, & R. N. Sykes (Eds.), *Practical aspects of memory* (pp. 3–24). San Diego, CA: Academic Press.

Neisser, U. (1980). On "social knowing." *Personality and Social Psychology Bulletin*, 6, 601–605.

Neisser, U. (1982). Memory: What are the important questions? In U. Neisser (Ed.), *Memory observed: Remembering in natural contexts* (pp. 3–19). San Francisco, CA: Freeman.

Neisser, U. (1985). Toward an ecologically oriented cognitive science. In T. M. Shlechter & M. P. Toglia (Eds.), *New directions in cognitive science* (pp. 17–32). Norwood, New Jersey: Ablex.

Nelson, R. A., & Strachan, I. (2009). Action and puzzle video games prime different speed/accuracy tradeoffs. *Perception* 38, 1678–1687. doi: 10.1068/p6324.

Nelson, S. M., Dosenbach, N. U. F., Cohen, A. L., Wheeler, M. E., Schlaggar, B. L., & Petersen, S. E. (2010). Role of the anterior insula in task-level control and focal attention. *Brain Structure and Function*, 214, 669–680.doi:10.1007/s00429-010-0260-2.

Newman-Norlund, R. D., Bosga, J., Meulenbroek, R. G., & Bekkering, H. (2008). Anatomical substrates of cooperative joint-action in a continuous motor task: Virtual lifting and balancing. *Neuroimage*, 41, 169–177.

Nicholas, C. (2008). Is Google making us stupid? *The Atlantic Monthly*, July-August.

Nicholas, D., Huntington, P., & Jamali, H. (2008). In D. Nicholas & I. Rowlands (Eds.), *The virtual scholar in digital consumers* (pp. 113–158), London: Facet Publishing.

Nigg, J. T. (2003). Response inhibition and disruptive behaviors. *Annals Of the New York Academy Of Sciences*, 1008, 170–182.

Nigg, J. T. (2006). Temperament and developmental psychopathology. *Journal of Child Psychology & Psychiatry*, 47, 395–422.

Nigg, J.T. (2000). On inhibition/disinhibition in developmental psychopathology: Views from cognitive and personality psychology and a working inhibition taxonomy. *Psychological Bulletin*, 126, 220–246.

Noonan, M. P., Kolling, N., Walton, M. E., & Rushworth, M. F. S. (2012). Re-evaluating the role of the orbitofrontal cortex in reward and reinforcement. *European Journal of Neuroscience*, 35(7), 997–1010.

Norman, K. L. (2008). *Cyberpsychology: An introduction to human-computer interaction* (Vol. 1). New York, NY: Cambridge University Press.

Normand, J. M., Giannopoulos, E., Spanlang, B., & Slater, M. (2011). Multisensory stimulation can induce an illusion of larger belly size in immersive virtual reality. *PLoS One*, 6:e16128. doi: 10.1371/journal.pone.0016128.

Northoff G, Grimm S, Boeker H, Schmidt C, Bermpohl F, Heinzel A, et al. (2006). Affective judgment and beneficial decision making: Ventromedial prefrontal activity correlates with performance in the Iowa Gambling Task. *Human Brain Mapping*, 27, 572–587.

Nouchi, R., Taki, Y., Takeuchi, H., Hashizume, H., Akitsuki, Y., Shigemune, Y., et al. (2012). Brain training game improves executive functions and processing speed in the elderly: A randomized controlled trial. *PLoS One*, 7(1), e29676.

Nouchi, R., Taki, Y., Takeuchi, H., Hashizume, H., Nozawa, T., Kambara, T., et al. (2013). Brain training game boosts executive functions, working memory and processing speed in the young adults: A randomized controlled trial. *PLoS One*, 8(2), e55518.

Novak, D., Mihelj, M., & Munih, M. (2012). A survey of methods for data fusion and system adaptation using autonomic nervous system responses in physiological computing. *Interacting with Computers*, 24(3), 154–172.

Nyhus, E., & Barceló, F. (2009). The Wisconsin Card Sorting Test and the cognitive assessment of prefrontal executive functions: A critical update. *Brain and Cognition*, 71(3), 437–451.

Obdržálek, Š., Kurillo, G., Ofli, F., Bajcsy, R., Seto, E., Jimison, H., & Pavel, M. (2012). Accuracy and robustness of Kinect pose estimation in the context of coaching of elderly population. In *Proceedings of the 34th Annual International Conference of the IEEE Engineering in Medicine and Biology Society* (pp. 1188–1193).

Ochsner, K. N. (2004). Current directions in social cognitive neuroscience. *Current Opinion in Neurobiology*, 14(2), 254–258.

Ochsner, K. N., & Lieberman, M. D. (2001). The emergence of social cognitive neuroscience. *American Psychologist*, 56, 717–734.

Oei, A. C., & Patterson, M. D. (2013). Enhancing cognition with video games: A multiple game training study. *PLoS One*, 8(3), e58546.

Ohman, A. (1992). Orienting and attention: Preferred preattentive processing of potentially phobic stimuli. In B. A. Campbell, H. Hayne, & R. Richardson (Eds.), *Attention and information processing in infants and adults: Perspectives from human and animal research*, pp. 263–95. Hillsdale, NJ: Erlbaum.

Öhman, A., & Soares, J. J. (1994). "Unconscious anxiety": phobic responses to masked stimuli. *Journal of Abnormal Psychology*, 103(2), 231.

Okagaki, L., & Frensch, P. A. (1994). Effects of video game playing on measures of spatial performance: Gender effects in late adolescence. *Journal of Applied Developmental Psychology*, 15, 33–58.

O'Loughlin, E. K., Dugas, E. N., Sabiston, C. M., & O'Loughlin, J. L. (2012). Prevalence and correlates of exergaming in youth. *Pediatrics*, 130, 806–814.

Ophir, E., Nass, C., & Wagner, A. D. (2009). Cognitive control in media multitaskers. *Proceedings of the National Academy of Sciences of the United States of America*, 106(37), 15583–15587. doi:10.1073/pnas.0903620106.

Opris, D., Pintea, S., García-Palacios, A., Botella, C., Szamosközi, S., & David, D. (2012). Virtual reality exposure therapy in anxiety disorders: A quantitative meta-analysis. *Depression and Anxiety*, 29, 85–93. doi:10.1002/da.20910 PMID:22065564.

Ord, J. S., Greve, K. W., Bianchini, K. J., & Aguerrevere, L. E. (2010). Executive dysfunction in traumatic brain injury: The effects of injury severity and effort of the Wisconsin card sorting test. *J. Clin. Exp. Neuropsychol.*, 32, 132–140.

O'Reilly, T. (2007). What is Web 2.0: Design patterns and business models for the next generation of software. *Communications & Strategies*, (1), 17.

Orne, M. T., & Whitehouse, W. G. (2000). Relaxation techniques. *Encyclopedia of Stress*, 3, 341–348.

Otto, T., Zijlstra, F. R., & Goebel, R. (2014). Neural correlates of mental effort evaluation – involvement of structures related to self-awareness. *Social Cognitive and Affective Neuroscience*, 9(3), 307–315.

Owens, M. E., & Beidel, D. C. (2014). Can virtual reality effectively elicit distress associated with social anxiety disorder?. *Journal of Psychopathology and Behavioral Assessment*, 37(2), 296–305.

Pan, X., & Slater, M. (2011). Confronting a moral dilemma in virtual reality: A pilot study. In *Proceedings of the 25th BCS Conference on Human-Computer Interaction* (pp. 46–51). Swinton: British Computer Society.

Panksepp, J. (1998). *Affective neuroscience*. Oxford: Oxford University Press.

Panksepp, J. (2005). On the embodied neural nature of core emotional affects. *Journal of Consciousness Studies*, 12, 158–184.

Panksepp, J. (2006). The core emotional systems of the mammalian brain: The fundamental substrates of human emotions. In J. Corrigall, H. Payne, & H. Wilkinson, (Eds.), *About a body: Working with the embodied mind in psychotherapy*, (pp. 14–32). London: Routledge.

Panksepp, J. (2007). Affective consciousness. In M. Velmans & S. Schneider (Eds.), *The Blackwell companion to consciousness* (pp. 114–129). Malden, MA: Wiley-Blackwell.

Panksepp, J. (2009b). Brain emotional systems and qualities of mental life: From animal models of affect to implications for psychotherapeutics. In D. Fosha, D. J. Siegel, & M. F. Solomon (Eds.), *The healing power of emotion: Affective neuroscience, development, and clinical practice*. New York: W. W. Norton.

Panksepp, J. (2009). Primary process affects and brain oxytocin. *Biological Psychiatry*, 65, 725–727. doi: 10.1016/j.biopsych.2009.02.004.

Panksepp, J. (2010). Affective neuroscience of the emotional brainmind: Evolutionary perspectives and implications for understanding depression. *Dialogues in Clinical Neuroscience*, 12, 533–545.

Parasuraman, R., & Rizzo, M. (Eds.) (2006). *Neuroergonomics: The brain at work*. Oxford University Press.

Parasuraman, R., & Wilson, G. F. (2008). Putting the brain to work: Neuroergonomics past, present, and future. *Human Factors: The Journal of the Human Factors and Ergonomics Society*, 50(3), 468–474.

Pardo, J. V., Pardo, P. J., Janer, K. W., & Raichle, M. E. (1990). The anterior cingulate cortex mediates processing selection in the Stroop attentional conflict paradigm. *Proceedings of the National Academy of Sciences*, 87(1), 256–259.

Park H. S., Kim S. H., Bang S. A., Yoon E. J., Cho S. S., & Kim S. E. (2010). Altered regional cerebral glucose metabolism in Internet game overusers: A 18F-fluorodeoxyglucose positron emission tomography study. *CNS Spectrums*, 15(3), 159–166.

Parkinson, B. (2014). Emotions in interpersonal life: Computer mediation, modeling, and simulation. *The Oxford handbook of affective computing* (pp. 68).

Parsey, C. M., & Schmitter-Edgecombe, M. (2013). Applications of technology in neuropsychological assessment. *The Clinical Neuropsychologist*, 27(8), 1328–1361.

Parsons, S., & Cobb, S. (2014). Reflections on the role of the "users": challenges in a multi-disciplinary context of learner-centred design for children on the autism spectrum. *International Journal of Research & Method in Education*, 37(4), 421–441.

Parsons, T. D. (2012). Virtual simulations and the Second Life metaverse: Paradigm shift in neuropsychological assessment. In V. Zagalo, T. Morgado, & A. Boa-Ventura (Eds.), *Virtual worlds, Second Life and metaverse platforms: New communication and identity paradigms* (pp. 234–250). Hershey: IGI Global.

Parsons, T. D. (2015). Virtual reality for enhanced ecological validity and experimental control in the clinical, affective and social neurosciences. *Frontiers in Human Neuroscience*, 9, 660.

Parsons, T. D. (2016). *Clinical neuropsychology and technology: What's new and how we can use it*. New York: Springer Press.

Parsons, T. D., Bowerly, T., Buckwalter, J. G., & Rizzo, A. A. (2007). A controlled clinical comparison of attention performance in children with ADHD in a virtual reality classroom compared to standard neuropsychological methods. *Child Neuropsychology*, 13, 363–381.

Parsons, T. D., & Carlew, A.R. (2016). Bimodal virtual reality Stroop for assessing distractor inhibition in autism spectrum disorders. *Journal of Autism and Developmental Disorders*, 46(4), 1255–1267.

Parsons, T. D., Carlew, A. R., Magtoto, J., & Stonecipher, K. (2015). The potential of function-led virtual environments for ecologically valid measures of executive function in experimental and clinical neuropsychology. *Neuropsychological Rehabilitation*, 1–31.

Parsons, T. D., & Courtney, C. (2011). Neurocognitive and psychophysiological interfaces for adaptive virtual environments. In C. Röcker & M. Ziefle (Eds.), *Human centered design of e-health technologies* (pp. 208–233). Hershey: IGI Global.

Parsons, T. D., & Courtney, C. (2014). An initial validation of the Virtual Reality Paced Auditory Serial Addition Test in a college sample. *Journal of Neuroscience Methods*, 222, 15–23.

Parsons, T. D., & Courtney, C. (in press). Interactions between threat and executive control in a virtual reality Stroop task. *IEEE Transactions on Affective Computing*.

Parsons, T. D., Courtney, C., Arizmendi, B., & Dawson, M. (2011). Virtual Reality Stroop Task for neurocognitive assessment. *Studies in Health Technology and Informatics*, 143, 433–439.

Parsons, T. D., Courtney, C., Cosand, L., Iyer, A., Rizzo, A. A., & Oie, K. (2009b). Assessment of psychophysiological differences of West Point cadets and civilian controls immersed within a virtual environment. *Lecture Notes in Artificial Intelligence*, 5638, 514–523.

Parsons, T. D., Courtney, C., & Dawson, M. (2013). Virtual Reality Stroop Task for assessment of supervisory attentional processing. *Journal of Clinical and Experimental Neuropsychology*, 35, 812–826.

Parsons, T. D., Courtney, C., Dawson, M., Rizzo, A., & Arizmendi, B. (2013). Visuospatial processing and learning effects in virtual reality based mental rotation and navigational tasks. *Lecture Notes in Artificial Intelligence*, 8019, 75–83.

Parsons, T. D., Courtney, C., Rizzo, A. A., Edwards, J., & Reger, G. (2012). Virtual reality paced serial assessment tests for neuropsychological assessment of a military cohort. *Studies in Health Technology and Informatics*, 173, 331–337.

Parsons, T. D., Iyer, A., Cosand, L., Courtney, C., & Rizzo, A. A. (2009a). Neurocognitive and psychophysiological analysis of human performance within virtual reality environments. *Studies in Health Technology and Informatics*, 142, 247–252.

Parsons, T. D., McPherson, S., & Interrante, V. (2013). Enhancing neurocognitive assessment using immersive virtual reality. *Proceedings of the 17th IEEE Virtual Reality Conference: Workshop on Virtual and Augmented Assistive Technology (VAAT)* (pp. 1–7).

Parsons, T. D., & Phillips, A. (2016). Virtual reality for psychological assessment in clinical practice. *Practice Innovations*, 1, 197–217.

Parsons, T. D., & Reinebold, J. (2012). Adaptive virtual environments for neuropsychological assessment in serious games. *IEEE Transactions on Consumer Electronics*, 58, 197–204.

Parsons, T. D., & Rizzo, A. A. (2008a). Affective outcomes of virtual reality exposure therapy for anxiety and specific phobias: A meta-analysis. *Journal of Behavior Therapy and Experimental Psychiatry*, 39, 250–261.

Parsons, T. D., & Rizzo, A. A. (2008b). Initial validation of a virtual environment for assessment of memory functioning: Virtual reality cognitive performance assessment test. *Cyberpsychology and Behavior*, 11, 17–25.

Parsons, T. D., & Rizzo, A. A. (2008c). Neuropsychological assessment of attentional processing using virtual reality. *Annual Review of CyberTherapy and Telemedicine*, 6, 23–28.

Parsons, T. D., Rizzo, A. A., & Buckwalter, J. G. (2004). Backpropagation and regression: comparative utility for neuropsychologists. *Journal of Clinical and Experimental Neuropsychology*, 26, 95–104.

Parsons, T. D., Rizzo, A. A., Courtney, C., & Dawson, M. (2012). Psychophysiology to assess impact of varying levels of simulation fidelity in a threat environment. *Advances in Human-Computer Interaction*, 5, 1–9.

Parsons, T. D., Rizzo, A. A., Rogers, S. A., & York, P. (2009a). Virtual reality in pediatric rehabilitation: A review. *Developmental Neurorehabilitation*, 12, 224–238.

Parsons, T. D., & Trost, Z. (2014). Virtual reality graded exposure therapy as treatment for pain-related fear and disability in chronic pain. In M. Ma,

(Ed.), *Virtual and augmented reality in healthcare* (pp. 523–546). Germany: Springer-Verlag.

Partala, T., & Surakka, V. (2003). Pupil size variation as an indication of affective processing. *International Journal of Human-Computer Studies*, 59, 185–198.

Partala, T. (2011). Psychological needs and virtual worlds: Case Second Life. *International Journal of Human-Computer Studies*, 69, 787–800.

Parvizi, J. (2009). Corticocentric myopia: Old bias in new cognitive sciences. *Trends in Cognitive Sciences*, 13(8), 354–359.

Pasek, J., More, E., & Hargittai, E. (2009). Facebook and academic performance: Reconciling a media sensation with data. *First Monday*, 14, 5.

Patil, I., Cogoni, C., Zangrando, N., Chittaro, L., & Silani, G. (2014). Affective basis of judgment-behavior discrepancy in virtual experiences of moral dilemmas. *Social Neuroscience*, 9(1), 94–107.

Paulhus, D. L. (1991). Measurement and control of response bias. In J. P. Robinson, P. R. Shaver, & L. S. Wrightsman (Eds.), *Measures of personality and social psychological attitudes*. San Diego: Academic Press.

Paulhus, D. L., & Vazire, S. (2007). The self-report method. In R. W. Robins, R. C. Fraley, & R. Krueger (Eds.), *Handbook of research methods in personality psychology* (pp. 224–239). New York, NY: Guilford Press.

Pavlou, P., Davis, F., & Dimoka, A. (2007). Neuro IS: The potential of cognitive neuroscience for information systems research. *ICIS 2007 Proceedings*, 122.

Pea, R., Nass, C., Meheula, L., Rance, M., Kumar, A., Bamford, H., Nass, M., Simha, A., Stillerman, B., Yang, S., & Zhou, M. (2012). Media use, face-to-face communication, media multitasking, and social well-being among 8- to 12-year-old girls. *Developmental Psychology*, 48(2), 327.

Peck, T. C., Seinfeld, S., Aglioti, S. M., & Slater, M. (2013). Putting yourself in the skin of a black avatar reduces implicit racial bias. *Consciousness and Cognition*, 22, 779–787.

Pellicano, E., & Stears, M. (2011). Bridging autism, science and society: Moving toward an ethically informed approach to autism research. *Autism Research*, 4(4), 271–282.

Pelphrey, K. A., Singerman, J. D., Allison, T., & McCarthy, G. (2003). Brain activation evoked by perception of gaze shifts: The influence of context. *Neuropsychologia*, 41, 156–170. doi: 10.1016/s0028-3932(03)00111-8.

Pelphrey, K. A., Viola, R. J., & McCarthy, G. (2004). When strangers pass: Processing of mutual and averted social gaze in the superior temporal sulcus. *Psychological Science*, 15, 598–603. doi: 10.1111/j.0956-7976.2004.00726.x.

Penn, P. R., Rose, F. D., & Johnson, D. A. (2009). Virtual enriched environments in paediatric neuropsychological rehabilitation following traumatic brain injury: Feasibility, benefits and challenges. *Developmental Neurorehabilitation*, 12(1), 32–43.

Pennington, B. F., Bennetto, L., McAleer, O. K., & Roberts, R. J. (1996). Executive functions and working memory: Theoretical and measurement issues. In G.R. Lyon & N. A. Krasnegor (Eds.), *Attention, memory and executive function*. Baltimore: Brookes.

Pessoa, L. (2008). On the relationship between emotion and cognition. *Nature Reviews Neuroscience*, 9(2), 148–158.

Pessoa, L. (2013). *The cognitive-emotional brain: From interactions to integration*. Cambridge: MIT Press.

Pfeifer, J. H., Dapretto, M., & Lieberman, M. D. (2010). The neural foundations of evaluative self-knowledge in middle childhood, early adolescence and adulthood. *Developmental Social Cognitive Neuroscience*, 141–163.

Pfeifer, R. (1988). Artificial intelligence models of emotion. In *Cognitive Perspectives on Emotion and Motivation* (pp. 287–320). Netherlands: Springer.

Pfeiffer, U. J., Timmermans, B., Vogeley, K., Frith, C. D., & Schilbach, L. (2013). Towards a neuroscience of social interaction. *Frontiers in Human Neuroscience*, 7.

Pham, T., & Tran, D. (2012). Emotional recognition using the Emotiv EPOC device. *Neural Information Processing*, 7667, 394–399.

Phelps, E. A., Lempert, K. M., & Sokol-Hessner, P. (2014). Emotion and decision making: Multiple modulatory neural circuits. *Annual Review of Neuroscience*, 37, 263–287.

Picard, R. W. (1997). *Affective computing* (Vol. 252). Cambridge: MIT Press.

Picard, R. W. (2003). Affective computing: challenges. *International Journal of Human-Computer Studies*, 59(1), 55–64.

Picard, R. W. (2014). The promise of affective computing. *The Oxford handbook of affective computing*, 11.

Picard, R. W., Vyzas, E., & Healey, J. (2001). Toward machine emotional intelligence: Analysis of affective physiological state. *Pattern analysis and machine intelligence, IEEE Transactionson*, 23(10), 1175–1191.

Plutchik, R., & Ax, A. F. (1967). A critique of determinants of emotional state by Schachter and Singer (1962). *Psychophysiology*, 4(1), 79–82.

Podsakoff, P. M., MacKenzie, S. B., Lee, J. Y., & Podsakoff, N. P. (2003). Common method biases in behavioral research: A critical review of the literature and recommended remedies. *Journal of Applied Psychology*, 88(5), 879.

Podzebenko, K., Egan, G. F., & Watson, J. D. G. (2005). Real and imaginary rotary motion processing: Functional parcellation of the human parietal lobe revealed by fMRI. *Journal of Cognitive Neuroscience*, 17(1), 24–36.

Pohl, C., Kunde, W., Ganz, T., Conzelmann, A., Pauli, P., & Kiesel, A. (2014). Gaming to see: Action video gaming is associated with enhanced processing of masked stimuli. *Frontiers in Psychology*, 5, 70.

Poldrack, R. A. (2010). Mapping mental function to brain structure: How can cognitive neuroimaging succeed?. *Perspectives on Psychological Science*, 5(6), 753–761.

Poldrack R. A., & Foerde K (2007) Category learning and the memory systems debate. *Neuroscience and Biobehavioral Reviews*, 32, 197–205.

Pollak, Y., Shomaly, H. B., Weiss, P. L., Rizzo, A. A., & Gross-Tsur, V. (2010). Methylphenidate effect in children with ADHD can be measured by an ecologically valid continuous performance test embedded in virtual reality. *CNS Spectrums*, 15(2), 125–130.

Pomplun, M., & Sunkara, S. (2003). Pupil dilation as an indicator of cognitive workload in human-computer interaction. In V.D.D. Harris, M. Smith, & C. Stephanidis (Eds.), *Proceedings of the 10th International Conference on Human-Computer Interaction*.

Pontius, A. A., & Yudowitz, B. S. (1980). Frontal lobe system dysfunction in some criminal actions as shown in the narratives test. *Journal of Nervous and Mental Disease*, 168, 111–117.

Pool, M. M., Koolstra, C. M., & Van der Voort, Tom H. A. (2003a). Distraction effects of background soap operas on homework performance: An experimental study enriched with observational data. *Educational Psychology*, 23(4), 361–380.

Pool, M. M., Koolstra, C. M., & Voort, T. H. (2003b). The impact of background radio and television on high school students' homework performance. *Journal of Communication*, 53(1), 74–87.

Pool, M. M., Van der Voort, Tom HA, Beentjes, J. W., & Koolstra, C. M. (2000). Background television as an inhibitor of performance on easy and difficult homework assignments. *Communication Research*, 27(3), 293–326.

Pope, A. T., Bogart, E. H., & Bartolome, D. S. (1995). Biocybernetic system evaluates indices of operator engagement in automated task. *Biological Psychology*, 40, 187–195.

Porter, G., Troscianko, T., & Gilchrist, D. (2002). Pupil size as a measure of task difficulty in vision. *Perception*, 31, 170–171.

Potenza, M., & De Wit, H. (2010). Control yourself: Alcohol and impulsivity. *Alcoholism: Clinical and Experimental Research*, 34, 1303–1305.

Powell, J., Lewis, P., Roberts, N., García-Fiˉnana, M., & Dunbar, R. (2012). Orbital prefrontal cortex volume predicts social network size: An imaging study of individual differences in humans. *Proceedings Of the Royal Society, London*, 279B, 2157–2162.

Power, A., & Kirwan, G. (2013). *Cyberpsychology and new media: A thematic reader*. New York: Psychology Press.

Powers, M. B., & Emmelkamp, P. M. (2008). Virtual reality exposure therapy for anxiety disorders: A meta-analysis. *Journal of Anxiety Disorders*, 22(3), 561–569.

Prado, J., & Weissman, D. H. (2011). Heightened interactions between a key default-mode region and a key task-positive region are linked to suboptimal current performance but to enhanced future performance. *Neuroimage*, 56(4), 2276–2282.

Prensky M. (2001). Digital natives, digital immigrants part 1. *On the Horizon*, 9, 1–6.

Preston, C., & Ehrsson, H. H. (2014). Illusory changes in body size modulate body satisfaction in a way that is related to non-clinical eating disorder psychopathology. *PLoS One*, 9:e85773. doi: 10.1371/journal.pone.0085773.

Price, M., & Anderson, P. (2007). The role of presence in virtual reality exposure therapy. *Journal of Anxiety Disorders*, 21(5), 742–751.

Price, M., Mehta, N., Tone, E. B., & Anderson, P. L. (2011). Does engagement with exposure yield better outcomes? Components of presence as a predictor of treatment response for virtual reality exposure therapy for social phobia. *Journal of anxiety disorders*, 25(6), 763–770.

Primack, B. A., Carroll, M. V., McNamara, M., et al. (2012). Role of video games in improving health-related outcomes: A systematic review. *American Journal of Preventative Medicine*, 42, 630–638.

Probosz, K., Wcislo, R., Otfinoski, J. Slota, R., Kitowski, J., Pisula, M., & Sobczyk, A. (2009). A multimedia holistic rehabilitation method for patients after stroke. *Annual Review of Cybertherapy and Telemedicine*, 7, 261–263.

Pugnetti, L., Meehan, M., & Mendozzi, L. (2001). Psychophysiological correlates of virtual reality: A review. *Presence*, 10, 384–400.

Pugnetti, L., Mendozzi, L., Attree, E. A., Barbieri, E., Brooks, B. M., Cazzullo, C. L., et al. (1998). Probing memory and executive functions with virtual reality: Past and present studies. *Cyberpsychology and Behavior*, 1, 151–161.

Pugnetti, L., Mendozzi, L., Motta, A., Cattaneo, A., Barbieri, E., & Brancotti, S. (1995). Evaluation and retraining of adults' cognitive impairments: Which role for virtual reality technology? *Computers in Biology and Medicine*, 25, 213–227.

Qin, P., & Northoff, G. (2011). How is our self related to midline regions and the default-mode network?. *Neuroimage*, 57(3), 1221–1233.

Rabbitt, P. (1997). Introduction: Methodologies and models in the study of executive function. In P. Rabbitt (Ed.), *Methodology of frontal executive function* (pp. 1–38). East Sussex, UK: Psychology.

Rabin, L. A., Burton, L. A., & Barr, W. B. (2007). Utilization rates of ecologically oriented instruments among clinical neuropsychologists. *The Clinical Neuropsychologist*, 5, 727–743.

Raichle, M. E. (2015). The brain's default mode network. *Annual Review of Neuroscience*, 38, 433–447.

Raichle, M. E., & Snyder, A.Z. (2007). A default mode of brain function: A brief history of an evolving idea. *Neuroimage*, 37, 1083–1099.

Rainville, P., Bechara, A., Naqvi, N., & Damasio, A. R. (2006). Basic emotions are associated with distinct patterns of cardiorespiratory activity. *International Journal of Psychophysiology*, 61, 5–18.

Ralph, B. C., Thomson, D. R., Seli, P., Carriere, J. S., & Smilek, D. (2015). Media multitasking and behavioral measures of sustained attention. *Attention, Perception, & Psychophysics*, 77(2), 390–401.

Rand, D., Rukan, S. B. A., Weiss, P. L., & Katz, N. (2009). Validation of the Virtual MET as an assessment tool for executive functions. *Neuropsychological Rehabilitation*, 19(4), 583–602.

Rand, D. G., Arbesman, S., & Christakis, N. A. (2011). Dynamic social networks promote cooperation in experiments with humans. *Proceedings of the National Academy of Sciences*, 108(48), 19193–19198.

Ravaja, N., Turpeinen, M., Saari, T., Puttonen, S., & Keltikangas-Järvinen, L. (2008). The psychophysiology of James Bond: Phasic emotional responses to violent video game events. *Emotion*, 8(1), 114.

Raz, S., Bar-Haim, Y., Sadeh, A., & Dan, O. (2014). Reliability and validity of the online continuous performance test among young adults. *Assessment*, 21(1), 108–118.

Reeves, B., & Nass, C. (1996). *How people treat computers, television, and new media like real people and places* (p. 119). CSLI Publications and Cambridge University Press.

Regenbogen, C., Herrmann, M., & Fehr, T. (2010). The neural processing of voluntary completed, real and virtual violent and nonviolent computer game scenarios displaying predefined actions in gamers and nongamers. *Social Neuroscience*, 5(2), 221–240.

Renaud, P., Bouchard, S., & Proulx, R. (2002). Behavioral avoidance dynamics in the presence of a virtual spider. *IEEE Transactions on Information Technology in Biomedicine*, 6, 235–243.

Renison, B., Ponsford, J., Testa, R., Richardson, B., & Brownfield, K. (2012). The ecological and construct validity of a newly developed measure of executive function: The virtual library task. *Journal of the International Neuropsychological Society*, 18, 440–450.

Ridderinkhof, K. R., Ullsperger, M., Crone, E. A., & Nieuwenhuis, S. (2004). The role of the medial frontal cortex in cognitive control. *Science*, 306, 443–447.

Rideout, V. (2011). *Zero to eight: Children's media use in America*. Retrieved from www.commonsensemedia.org.

Rideout, V. J. (2015). *The Common Sense census: Media use by tweens and teens*. Retrieved from www.commonsensemedia.org.

Rideout, V. J., Foehr, U. G., & Roberts, D. F. (2010). Generation M^2 Media in the lives of 8- to 18-year-olds. *Henry J. Kaiser Family Foundation*.

Riedl, R., Banker, R. D., Benbasat, I., Davis, F. D., Dennis, A. R., & Dimoka, A., et al. (2010). On the foundations of NeuroIS: Reflections on the Gmunden Retreat 2009. *Communications of the Association for Information Systems*, 27, 243–264.

Riedl, R., Hubert, M., & Kenning, P. (2010). Are there neural gender differences in online trust? An fMRI study on the perceived trustworthiness of eBay offers. *MIS Quarterly*, 34, 397–428.

Riedl, R., & Léger, P. M. (2016). *Fundamentals of NeuroIS: Information systems and the brain*. Springer Berlin.

Riedl, R., Mohr, P. N., Kenning, P. H., Davis, F. D., & Heekeren, H. R. (2014). Trusting humans and avatars: A brain imaging study based on evolution theory. *Journal of Management Information Systems*, 30(4), 83–114.

Ring, C., Carroll, D., Willemsen, G., Cooke, J., Ferraro, A., & Drayson, M. (1999). Secretory immunoglobulin A and cardiovascular activity during mental arithmetic and paced breathing. *Psychophysiology*, 36, 602–609.

Risko, E. F., Laidlaw, K. E., Freeth, M., Foulsham, T., & Kingstone, A. (2012). Social attention with real versus reel stimuli: Toward an empirical approach to concerns about ecological validity. *Frontiers in Human Neuroscience*, 6, 143.

Riva, G. (1999). Virtual reality as communication tool: A sociocognitive analysis. *Presence: Teleoperators and Virtual Environments*, 8(4), 462–468.

Riva, G. (2011). The key to unlocking the virtual body: Virtual reality in the treatment of obesity and eating disorders. *Journal of Diabetes Science and Technology*, 5(2), 283–292.

Riva, G. (2014). Out of my real body: Cognitive neuroscience meets eating disorders. *Frontiers in Human Neuroscience*, 8. doi: 10.3389/fnhum.2014.00236.

Riva, G., Botella, C., Baños, R., Mantovani, F., García-Palacios, A., Quero, S., et al. (2015). Presence-inducing media for mental health applications. In M. Lombard, F. Biocca, J. Freeman, W. Ijsselsteijn, & R. J. Schaevitz (Eds.), *Immersed in media* (pp. 283–332). New York: Springer International Publishing.

Riva, G., & Galimberti, C. (2001). *Towards cyberpsychology: Mind, cognition, and society in the internet age*. IOS Press.

Riva, G., Mantovani, F., & Gaggioli, A. (2004). Presence and rehabilitation: Toward second-generation virtual reality applications in neuropsychology. *Journal of NeuroEngineering and Rehabilitation*, 1, 9.

Riva, G., Mantovani, F., Capideville, C. S., Preziosa, A., Morganti, F., Villani, D., . . . & Alcañiz, M. (2007). Affective interactions using virtual reality: The link between presence and emotions. *CyberPsychology & Behavior*, 10(1), 45–56.

Rivero, T. S., Covre, P., Reyes, M. B., & Bueno, O. F. (2013). Effects of chronic video game use on time perception: Differences between sub- and multi-second intervals. *Cyberpsychology Behavior and Social Networking*, 16(2), 140–144.

Rizzolatti, G., & Sinigaglia, C. (2010). The functional role of the parieto-frontal mirror circuit: Interpretations and misinterpretations. *Nature Reviews Neuroscience*, 11, 264–274. doi: 10.1038/nrn2805.

Robertson, I. H., Ward, T., Ridgeway, V., & Nimmo-Smith, I. (1994). *The test of everyday attention*. Bury St. Edmunds, England: Thames Valley Test Company.

Robillard, G., Bouchard, S., Fournier, T., & Renaud, P. (2003). Anxiety and presence during VR immersion: A comparative study of the reactions of phobic and non-phobic participants in therapeutic virtual environments derived from computer games. *CyberPsychology & Behavior*, 6(5), 467–476.

Robison, A. J., & Nestler, E. J. (2011). Transcriptional and epigenetic mechanisms of addiction. *Nature Reviews Neuroscience*, 12(11), 623–637.

Roelofs, J., et al. (2004). Does fear of pain moderate the effects of sensory focusing and distraction on cold pressor pain in pain-free individuals? *Journal of Pain*, 5(5), 250–256.

Rogoff, B. E., & Lave, J. E. (1984). *Everyday cognition: Its development in social context*. Harvard University Press.

Rosas-Cholula, G., Ramírez-Cortes, J. M., Alarcón-Aquino, V., Martinez-Carballido, J., & Gomez-Gil, P. (2010). On signal P-300 detection for BCI applications based on wavelet analysis and ICA preprocessing. In *Electronics, Robotics and Automotive Mechanics Conference (CERMA), 2010* (pp. 360–365). IEEE.

Rosen, L. D., Carrier, L. M., & Cheever, N. A. (2013). Facebook and texting made me do it: Media-induced task-switching while studying. *Computers in Human Behavior*, 29(3), 948–958.

Ross, E. D. (2010). Cerebral localization of functions and the neurology of language: Fact versus fiction or is it something else? *The Neuroscientist*, 16(3), 222–243.

Rotge, J. Y., Lemogne, C., Hinfray, S., Huguet, P., Grynszpan, O., Tartour, E., et al. (2014). A meta-analysis of the anterior cingulate contribution to social pain. *Social Cognitive and Affective Neuroscience*, 10, 19–27.

Rothbaum, B. O., & Schwartz, A. C. (2002). Exposure therapy for posttraumatic stress disorder. *American Journal of Psychotherapy*, 56(1), 59.

Rourke, B. P. (1982). Central processing deficiencies in children: Toward a developmental neuropsychological model. *Journal of Clinical and Experimental Neuropsychology*, 4(1), 1–18.

Roy, S., Klinger, E., Légeron, P., Lauer, F., Chemin, I., & Nugues, P. (2003). Definition of a VR-based protocol to treat social phobia. *Cyberpsychology & Behavior.*, 6, 411–420.

Rubia, K. (2011). "Cool" inferior frontostriatal dysfunction in attention-deficit /hyperactivity disorder versus "hot" ventromedial orbitofrontal-limbic dysfunction in conduct disorder: A review. *Biological Psychiatry*, 69, e69–e87.

Rubia, K., Smith, A. B., Taylor, E., & Brammer, M. (2007). Linear age-correlated functional development of right inferior fronto-striato-cerebellar networks during response inhibition and anterior cingulate during error related processes. *Human Brain Mapping*, 28, 1163–1177.

Rubia, K., Smith, A. B., Woolley, J., Nosarti, C., Heyman, I., Taylor, E., & Brammer, M. (2006). Progressive increase of frontostriatal brain activation from childhood to adulthood during event-related tasks of cognitive control. *Human Brain Mapping*, 27, 973–993.

Rupp, R. (2014). Challenges in clinical applications of brain computer interfaces in individuals with spinal cord injury. *Frontiers in Neuroengineering*, 7.

Russell, J. A. (2003). Core affect and the psychological construction of emotion. *Psychological Review*, 110(1), 145.

Ruthruff, E., Van Selst, M., Johnston, J. C., & Remington, R. (2006). How does practice reduce dual-task interference: Integration, automatization, or just stage-shortening?. *Psychological Research*, 70(2), 125–142.

Sacheli, L. M., Christensen, A., Giese, M. A., Taubert, N., Pavone, E. F., Aglioti, S. M., & Candidi, M. (2015). Prejudiced interactions: Implicit racial bias reduces predictive simulation during joint action with an out-group avatar. *Scientific Reports*, 5. doi:10.1038/srep08507

Salisbury, D., Driver, S., & Parsons, T. D. (2015). Brain-computer interface targeting non-motor functions after spinal cord injury. *Spinal Cord*, 53, S25–S26.

Sallet, J., Mars, R. B., Noonan, M. P., Andersson, J. L., O'Reilly, J. X., Jbabdi, S., et al. (2011). Social network size affects neural circuits in macaques. *Science*, 334, 697–700.

Salminen, M., & Ravaja, N. (2007). Oscillatory brain responses evoked by video game events: The case of supermonkey ball 2. *CyberPsychology & Behavior*, 10(3), 330–338.

Sampasa-Kanyinga, H., & Lewis, R. F. (2015). Frequent use of social networking sites is associated with poor psychological functioning among children and adolescents. *Cyberpsychology, Behavior, and Social Networking*, 18(7), 380–385.

Sanbonmatsu, D. M., Strayer, D. L., Medeiros-Ward, N., & Watson, J. M. (2013). Who multi-tasks and why? Multi-tasking ability, perceived multi-tasking ability, impulsivity, and sensation seeking. *PLoS One*, January 23. Available at http://journals.plos.org/plosone/article?id=10.1371/journal.pone.0054402.

Sanchez, J. (2009). A social history of virtual worlds. *Library Technology Reports*, 45(2), 9–13.

Sanchez-Vives, M. V., & Slater, M. (2005). From presence to consciousness through virtual reality. *Nature Reviews Neuroscience*, 6(4), 332–339.

Sarter, M., Gehring, W. J., & Kozak, R. (2006). More attention must be paid: The neurobiology of attentional effort. *Brain Research Reviews*, 51(2), 145–160.

Saur, D., Kreher, B. W., Schnell, S., Kümmerer, D., Kellmeyer, P., Vry, M. S., . . . & Huber, W. (2008). Ventral and dorsal pathways for language. *Proceedings of the National Academy of Sciences*, 105(46), 18035–18040.

Saxe, R., & Kanwisher, N. (2003). People thinking about thinking people: The role of the temporo-parietal junction in "theory of mind." *Neuroimage*, 19(4), 1835–1842.

Sbordone, R. J. (1996). Ecological validity: Some critical issues for neuropsychologist. In R. J. Sbordone & C. J. Long (Eds.), *Ecological validity of neuropsychological testing* (pp. 15–41). Delray Beach, FL: GR Press/St. Lucie Press.

Sbordone, R.J. (2008). Ecological validity of neuropsychological testing: Critical issues. *The Neuropsychology Handbook*, 367, 394.

Scallen, S. F., & Hancock, P. A. (2001). Implementing adaptive function allocation. *International Journal of Aviation Psychology*, 11, 197–221.

Scerbo, M. W., Freeman, F. G., Mikulka, P. J., Parasuraman, R., Di Nocero, F., & Prinzel, L. J. (2001). *The efficacy of psychophysiological measures for implementing adaptive technology (NASA TP-2001–211018)*. Hampton, VA: NASA Langley Research Center.

Schacter, D. L. (1983). Amnesia observed: Remembering and forgetting in a natural environment. *Journal of Abnormal Psychology*, 92, 236–242.

Schachter, S., & Singer, J. (1962). Cognitive, social, and physiological determinants of emotional state. *Psychological Review*, 69(5), 379.

Schaefer, T., Ferguson, J. B., Klein, J. A., & Rawson, E. B. (1968). Pupillary responses during mental activities. *Psychonomic Science*, 12, 137–138.

Schaie, K. W., Dutta, R., & Willis, S. L. (1991). Relationship between rigidity-flexibility and cognitive abilities in adulthood. *Psychology and Aging*, 6, 371–378.

Scherer, K. R. (2005). What are emotions? And how can they be measured? *Social Science Information*, 44(4), 695–729.

Scheutz, M. (2004, July). Useful roles of emotions in artificial agents: A case study from artificial life. *AAAI*, 4, 42–48.

Scheutz, M., & Schermerhorn, P. (2004). The role of signaling action tendencies in conflict resolution. *Journal of Artificial Societies and Social Simulation*, 7, 1.

Schilbach, L. (2010). A second-person approach to other minds. *Nature Reviews Neuroscience*, 11, 449. doi: 10.1038/nrn2805-c1.

Schilbach, L. (2014). On the relationship of online and offline social cognition. *Frontiers In Human Neuroscience*, 8(278), 1–8.

Schilbach, L. (2015). Eye to eye, face to face and brain to brain: Novel approaches to study the behavioral dynamics and neural mechanisms of social interactions. *Current Opinion in Behavioral Sciences*, 3, 130–135.

Schilbach, L., Bzdok, D., Timmermans, B., Fox, P. T., Laird, A. R., Vogeley, K., & Eickhoff, S. B. (2012). Introspective minds: Using ALE meta-analyses to study commonalities in the neural correlates of emotional processing, social & unconstrained cognition. *PloS One*, 7(2), e30920.

Schilbach, L., Eickhoff, S. B., Rotarska-Jagiela, A., Fink, G. R., & Vogeley, K. (2008). Minds at rest? Social cognition as the default mode of cognizing and its putative relationship to the "default system" of the brain. *Consciousness and Cognition*, 17(2), 457–467.

Schilbach, L., Eickhoff, S. B., Schultze, T., Mojzisch, A., & Vogeley, K. (2013). To you I am listening: Perceived competence of advisors influences judgment and decision-making via recruitment of the amygdala. *Social Neuroscience*, 8(3), 189–202.

Schilbach, L., Wohlschläger, A. M., Newen, A., Krämer, N., Shah, N. J., Fink, G. R., et al. (2006). Being with others: Neural correlates of social interaction. *Neuropsychologia*, 44, 718–730.

Schneider, W., & Shiffrin, R. M. (1977). Controlled and automatic human information processing: I. Detection, search, and attention. *Psychological Review*, 84(1), 1–66.

Schoenbaum, G., Takahashi, Y., Liu, T., & McDannald, M. (2011). Does the orbitofrontal cortex signal value? *Annals of the New York Academy of Sciences*, 1239, 87–99.

Schomer, D. L., & Da Silva, F. L. (2012). *Niedermeyer's electroencephalography: Basic principles, clinical applications, and related fields*. Philadelphia, PA: Lippincott Williams & Wilkins.

Schreiber, D., Fonzo, G., Simmons, A. N., Dawes, C. T., Flagan, T., Fowler, J. H., & Paulus, M. P. (2013). Red brain, blue brain: Evaluative processes differ in Democrats and Republicans. *PLoS ONE*, 8:e52970. 10.1371/journal.pone.0052970.

Schreuder, M., Riccio, A., Risetti, M., Dähne, S., Ramsay, A., Williamson, J., . . . & Tangermann, M. (2013). User-centered design in brain–computer interfaces – A case study. *Artificial Intelligence in Medicine*, 59(2), 71–80.

Schultheis, M. T., Rebimbas, J., Mourant, R., & Millis, S. R. (2007). Examining the usability of a virtual reality driving simulator. *Assistive Technology*, 19.

Schwark, J. D. (2015). Toward a taxonomy of affective computing. *International Journal of Human-Computer Interaction*, 31(11), 761–768.

Schwartz, J. M. (1998). Neuroanatomical aspects of cognitive-behavioural therapy response in obsessive–compulsive disorder. An evolving perspective on brain and behaviour. *The British Journal of Psychiatry* (Suppl.), 38–44.

Schwartz, M. F. (2006). The cognitive neuropsychology of everyday action and planning. *Cognitive Neuropsychology*, 23, 202–221.

Schwartz, M. S. & Andrasik, F. (2003). *Biofeedback: A practitioner's guide*. New York: Guilford Press.

Schwarz, N. (1999). Self-reports: How the questions shape the answers. *American Psychologist*, 54(2), 93.

Scott, J. C., Woods, S. P., Vigil, O., Heaton, R. K., Schweinsburg, B. C., Ellis, R. J., . . . & Marcotte, T. D. (2011). A neuropsychological investigation of multitasking in HIV infection: Implications for everyday functioning. *Neuropsychology*, 25(4), 511.

Sebanz, N., Bekkering, H., & Knoblich, G. (2006). Joint action: bodies and minds moving together. *Trends in Cognitive Sciences*, 10, 70–76.

Sebastian, C. L., Fontaine, N. M., Bird, G., Blakemore, S. J., De Brito, S. A., McCrory, E. J., & Viding, E. (2012). Neural processing associated with cognitive and affective theory of mind in adolescents and adults. *Social Cognitive and Affective Neuroscience*, 7(1), 53–63.

Seeley, W. W., Menon, V., Schatzberg, A. F., Keller, J., Glover, G. H., Kenna, H., et al. (2007). Dissociable intrinsic connectivity networks for salience processing and executive control. *The Journal of Neuroscience*, 27, 2349–2356.

Seery, M. D., Weisbuch, M., & Blascovich, J. (2009). Something to gain, something to lose: The cardiovascular consequences of outcome framing. *International Journal of Psychophysiology*, 73, 308–312.

Seguin, J. R., Arseneault, L., & Tremblay, R. E. (2007). The contribution of "cool" and "hot" components of decision-making in adolescence: Implications for developmental psychopathology. *Cognitive Development*, 22, 530–543.

Senecal, S., Léger, P. M., Fredette, M., & Riedl, R. (2012). Consumers' online cognitive scripts: A neurophysiological approach. *Proceedings of the International Conference on Information Systems, Orlando, Florida*.

Seraglia, B., Gamberini, L., Priftis, K., Scatturin, P., Martinelli, M., & Cutini, S. (2011). An exploratory fNIRS study with immersive virtual reality: A new method for technical implementation. *Frontiers in Human Neuroscience*, 5(176), 1–9.

Seth, A. K., Suzuki, K., & Critchley, H. D. (2011). An interoceptive predictive coding model of conscious presence. *Frontiers in Psychology*, 2.

Sexton, J. A., Deshpande, G., Li, Z., Glielmi, C. B., & Hu, X. P. (2013). *Functional magnetic resonance imaging. In neural engineering* (pp. 473–497). New York: Springer US.

Shafir, R., Schwartz, N., Blechert, J., & Sheppes, G. (2015). Emotional intensity influences pre-implementation and implementation of distraction and reappraisal. *Social Cognitive and Affective Neuroscience*, nsv022.

Shallice, T., & Burgess, P. W. (1991). Deficits in strategy application following frontal lobe damage in man. *Brain*, 114, 727–741.

Shallice, T., & Burgess, P. (1996). The domain of supervisory processes and temporal organization of behaviour. *Philosophical Transactions of the Royal Society, London. B: Biological Sciences*, 351, 1405–1412.

Shepard, R. N. (1980). Multidimensional scaling, tree-fitting, and clustering. *Science*, 210, 390–398.

Shiffrin, R. M., & Schneider, W. (1977). Controlled and automatic human information processing: II. Perceptual learning, automatic attending and a general theory. *Psychological Review*, 84(2), 127–190.

Shih, J. J., Krusienski, D. J., & Wolpaw, J. R. (2012). Brain-computer interfaces in medicine. *Mayo Clinic Proceedings*, 87(3), 268–279.

Shin, H., & Kim, K. (2015). Virtual reality for cognitive rehabilitation after brain injury: A systematic review. *Journal of Physical Therapy Science*, 27(9), 2999.

Short, J., Williams, E., & Christie, B. (1976). *The social psychology of telecommunications*. London: John Wiley & Sons.

Sijtsema, J. J., Shoulberg, E. K., & Murray-Close, D. (2011). Physiological reactivity and different forms of aggression in girls: Moderating roles of rejection sensitivity and peer rejection. *Biological Psychology*, 86(3), 181–192.

Singhal, S., & Zyda, M. (1999). *Networked virtual environments: Design and implementation*. New York: ACM Press/Addison-Wesley Publishing Co.

Sinnott, J. D. (Ed.). (1989). *Everyday problem solving: Theory mid applications*. New York: Praeger.

Sitzmann, T. (2011). A meta-analytic examination of the instructional effectiveness of computer-based simulation games. *Personnel Psychology*, 64, 489–528.

Skowronski, J. J., & Lawrence, M. A. (2001). A comparative study of the implicit and explicit gender attitudes of children and college students. *Psychology of Women Quarterly*, 25(2), 155–165.

Skulmowski, A., Bunge, A., Kaspar, K., & Pipa, G. (2014). Forced-choice decision-making in modified trolley dilemma situations: A virtual reality and eye tracking study. *Frontiers in Behavioral Neuroscience*, 8, 426.

Slagter van Tryon, P. J., & Bishop, M. J. (2012). Evaluating social connectedness online: The design and development of the Social Perceptions in Learning Contexts Instrument. *Distance Education*, 33(3), 347–364.

Slater, M. (1999). Measuring presence: A response to the Witmer and Singer presence questionnaire. *Presence-Teleoperators and Virtual Environments*, 8, 560–565.

Slater, M. (Ed.) (2005). *Presence 2005: The 8th international workshop on presence*. London. University College London: Department of Computer Science.

Slater, M., Brogni, A., & Steed, A. (2003). Physiological responses to breaks in presence: A pilot study. *The 6th Annual International Workshop on Presence* Vol. 2003 (Aalborg, Denmark, 2003).

Slater, M., Khanna, P., Mortensen, J., & Yu, I. (2009). Visual realism enhances realistic response in an immersive virtual environment. *IEEE Computer Graphics and Applications*, 29, 76–84.

Slater, M., & Sanchez-Vives, M. V. (2014). Transcending the self in immersive virtual reality. *Computer*, 47, 24–30.

Slater, M., Spanlang, B., Sanchez-Vives, M. V., & Blanke, O. (2010). First person experience of body transfer in virtual reality. *PloS One*, 5:e10564. doi: 10.1371/journal.pone.0010564.

Slater, M., & Wilbur, S. (1997). A framework for immersive virtual environments (FIVE): Speculations on the role of presence in virtual environments. *Presence-Teleoperators and Virtual Environments*, 6, 603–616.

Slater, M., Rovira, A., Southern, R., Swapp, D., Zhang, J. J., Campbell, C., & Levine, M. (2013). Bystander responses to a violent incident in an immersive virtual environment. *PloS one*, 8(1), e52766.

Sloan, R. P., Korten, J. B., & Myers, M. M. (1991). Components of heart rate reactivity during mental arithmetic with and without speaking. *Physiology & Behavior*, 50, 1039–1045.

Sloman, A., Chrisley, R., & Scheutz, M. (2005). The architectural basis of affective states and processes. In *Who needs emotions*. New York: Oxford University Press.

Sloman, A., & Croucher, M. (1981). Why robots will have emotions. In T. Dean (Ed.), *Proceedings of the Seventh International Joint Conference on Artificial Intelligence* (Vol. I). San Francisco, CA: Morgan Kaufman.

Slovic, P. (1987). Perception of risk. *Science*, 236(4799), 280–285.

Small G, & Vorgan G. (2008). Meet your iBrain. *Sci Am Mind*, 19, 42–9.

Small, G. W., Moody, T. D., Siddarth, P., & Bookheimer, S. Y. (2009). Your brain on Google: Patterns of cerebral activation during Internet searching. *American Journal of Geriatric Psychiatry*, 17, 116–126.

Smart, P. R. (2012). The web-extended mind. *Metaphilosophy*, 43(4), 446–463.

Smith, L., & Gasser, M. (2005). The development of embodied cognition: Six lessons from babies. *Artificial Life*, 11(1–2), 13–29.

Sobczyk, B., Dobrowolski, P., Skorko, M., Michalak, J., & Brzezicka, A. (2015). Issues and advances in research methods on video games and cognitive abilities. *Frontiers in Psychology*, 6.

Sonuga-Barke, E.J., & Castellanos, F.X. (2007). Spontaneous attentional fluctuations in impaired states and pathological conditions: A neurobiological hypothesis. *Neuroscience and Biobehavioral Reviews*, 31, 977–986.

Sparrow, B., & Chatman, L. (2013). Social cognition in the Internet age: Same as it ever was?. *Psychological Inquiry*, 24(4), 273–292.

Sparrow, B., Liu, J., & Wegner, D. M. (2011). Google effects on memory: Cognitive consequences of having information at our fingertips. *Science*, 333(6043), 776–778.

Spence I., & Feng J. (2010). Video games and spatial cognition. *Review of General Psychology*, 14, 92. doi: 10.1037/a0019491.

Spence I., & Pratt J. (2007). Playing an action video game reduces gender differences in spatial cognition. *Psychological Science*, 18(37), 850–855.

Spence I., Yu J. J., Feng J., & Marshman J. (2009). Women match men when learning a spatial skill. *Journal of Experimental Psychology: Learning, Memory, and Cognition*, 35, 1097.

Spooner, D. M., & Pachana, N. A. (2006). Ecological validity in neuropsychological assessment: A case for greater consideration in research with neurologically intact populations. *Archives of Clinical Neuropsychology*, 21 (4), 327–337.

Sporns, O. (2011). The human connectome: A complex network. *Annals of the New York Academy of Sciences*, 1224(1), 109–125.

Sporns, O., Chialvo, D. R., Kaiser, M., & Hilgetag, C. C. (2004). Organization, development and function of complex brain networks. *Trends in Cognitive Sciences*, 8(9), 418–425.

Spreij, L. A., Visser-Meily, J. M., van Heugten, C. M., & Nijboer, T. C. (2014). Novel insights into the rehabilitation of memory post acquired brain injury: A systematic review. *Frontiers in Human Neuroscience*, 8.

Spreng, R. N., Mar, R. A., & Kim, A. S. (2009). The common neural basis of autobiographical memory, prospection, navigation, theory of mind, and the default mode: A quantitative meta-analysis. *Journal of Cognitive Neuroscience*, 21(3), 489–510.

Spunt, R. P., Satpute, A. B., & Lieberman, M. D. (2011). Identifying the what, why, and how of an observed action: An fMRI study of mentalizing and mechanizing during action observation. *Journal of Cognitive Neuroscience*, 23(1), 63–74.

Sridharan, D., Levitin, D. J., & Menon, V. (2008). A critical role for the right fronto-insular cortex in switching between central-executive and default-mode networks. *Proceedings of the National Academy of Sciences*, 105(34), 12569–12574.

Stanley, D. A., & Adolphs, R. (2013). Toward a neural basis for social behavior. *Neuron*, 80(3), 816–826.

Stanney, K. M. (Ed.). (2002). *Handbook of virtual environment: Design, implementation, and applications*. Mahwah, NJ: Lawrence Erlbaum Associates.

Starcevic, V. (2013). Is Internet addiction a useful concept? *Australian and New Zealand Journal of Psychiatry*, 47, 16–19.

Steers, M. L. N., Wickham, R. E., & Acitelli, L. K. (2014). Seeing everyone else's highlight reels: How Facebook usage is linked to depressive symptoms. *Journal of Social and Clinical Psychology*, (33), 701–731.

Steriade, M. (1993). Cellular substrates of brain rhythms. In E. Niedermeyer & F. Lopes da Silva (Eds.), *Electroencephalography: Basic principles, clinical applications, and related fields* (3rd edn., pp. 27–62). Baltimore: Williams & Wilkins.

Sternberg, R. J., & Wagner, R. K. (Eds.). (1986). *Practical intelligence: Nature and origins of competence in the everyday world.* Cambridge University Press Archive.

Stichter, J. P., Laffey, J., Galyen, K., & Herzog, M. (2014). iSocial: Delivering the social competence intervention for adolescents (SCI-A) in a 3D virtual learning environment for youth with high functioning autism. *Journal of Autism and Developmental Disorders, 44*(2), 417–430.

Strauss, E., Sherman, E., & Spreen O. (Eds.). (2006). *A compendium of neuropsychological tests. Administration, norms and commentary,* 3rd edn. New York: Oxford University Press.

Strobach, T., Frensch, P. A., &Schubert, T. (2012). Video game practice optimizes executive control skills in dual-task and task switching situations. *Acta Psychologica, 140,* 13–24. doi: 10.1016/j.actpsy.2012.02.001. pmid:22426427.

Stuss, D. T. (2007). New approaches to prefrontal lobe testing. *The Human Frontal Lobes: Functions and Disorders, 2,* 292–305.

Stuss, D. T., Benson, D. F., Weir, W. S., Naeser, M. A., Lieberman, I., & Ferrill, D. (1983). The involvement of orbitofrontal cerebrum in cognitive tasks. *Neuropsychologia, 21*(3), 235–248.

Stuss, D. T., Binns, M. A., Murphy, K. J., & Alexander, M. P. (2002). Dissociations within the anterior attentional system: Effects of task complexity and irrelevant information on reaction time speed and accuracy. *Neuropsychologia, 16,* 500–513.

Stuss, D. T., Floden, D., Alexander, M. P., Levine, B., & Katz, D. (2001). Stroop performance in focal lesion patients: Dissociation of processes and frontal lobe lesion location. *Neuropsychologia, 39,* 771–786.

Stuss, D. T., & Levine, B. (2002). Adult clinical neuropsychology: Lessons from studies of the frontal lobes. *Annual Review of Psychology, 53*(1), 401–433.

Suchy, Y. (2011). *Clinical neuropsychology of emotion.* New York: Guilford Press.

Sun, D. L., Chen, Z. J., Ma, N., Zhang, X. C., Fu, X. M., & Zhang, D. R. (2009). Decision-making and prepotent response inhibition functions in excessive Internet users. *CNS spectrums, 14*(2), 75–81.

Sun, Y., Ying, H., Seetohul, R. M., Xuemei, W., Ya, Z., Qian, L., . . . & Ye, S. (2012). Brain fMRI study of crave induced by cue pictures in online game addicts (male adolescents). *Behavioural Brain Research, 233*(2), 563–576.

Sungur, H., & Boduroglu, A. (2012). Action video game players form more detailed representation of objects. *Acta Psychologica, 139,* 327–334. doi:10.1016/j.actpsy.2011.12.002.

Sutton, S. K., & Davidson, R. J. (1997). Prefrontal brain asymmetry: A biological substrate of the behavioral approach and inhibition systems. *Psychological Science, 8,* 204–210.

Suzuki, A., Hirota, A., Takasawa, N., & Shigemasu, K. (2003). Application of the somatic marker hypothesis to individual differences in decision making. *Biological Psychology*, 65(1), 81–88.

Sweeney, S., Kersel, D., Morris, R. G., Manly, T., & Evans, J. J. (2010). The sensitivity of a virtual reality task to planning and prospective memory impairments: Group differences and the efficacy of periodic alerts on performance. *Neuropsychological Rehabilitation*, 20, 239–263.

Synofzik, M., Schatton, C., Giese, M., Wolf, J., Schöls, L., & Ilg, W. (2013). Videogame-based coordinative training can improve advanced, multisystemic early-onset ataxia. *Journal of Neurology*, 260(10), 2656–2658.

Tamietto, M., & De Gelder, B. (2010). Neural bases of the non-conscious perception of emotional signals. *Nature Reviews Neuroscience*, 11(10), 697–709.

Tamir, D. I., & Mitchell, J. P. (2012). Disclosing information about the self is intrinsically rewarding. *Proceedings of the National Academy of Sciences*, 109 (21), 8038–8043.

Tan, D., & Nijholt, A. (2010). Brain-computer interfaces and human-computer interaction. In *Brain-computer interfaces* (pp. 3–19). London: Springer.

Tanabek, H. C., Kosaka, H., Saito, D. N., Koike, T., Hayashi, M. J., Izuma, K., et al. (2012). Hard to "tune in": neural mechanisms of live face-to-face interaction with high-functioning autistic spectrum disorder. *Frontiers In Human Neuroscience*, 6, 268. doi: 10.3389/fnhum.2012.00268.

Tanaka, S., Ikeda, H., Kasahara, K., Kato, R., Tsubomi, H., Sugawara, S. K., . . . & Watanabe, K. (2013). Larger right posterior parietal volume in action video game experts: A behavioral and voxel-based morphometry (VBM) study. PLoS One, 8(6), e66998.

Tangney, J. P., Baumeister, R. F., & Boone, A. L. (2004). High self-control predicts good adjustment, less pathology, better grades, and interpersonal success. *Journal of Personality*, 72(2), 271–324.

Tao, J., & Tan, T. (2005). Affective computing: A review. In *Affective computing and intelligent interaction* (pp. 981–995). Berlin, Heidelberg: Springer.

Tate, D. G., Kalpakjian, C. Z., & Forchheimer, M. B. (2002). Quality of life issues in individuals with spinal cord injury. *Archives of Physical Medicine and Rehabilitation*, 83(12), S18–S25.

Tate, D. G., Boninger, M. L., & Jackson, A. B. (2011). Future directions for spinal cord injury research: Recent developments and model systems contributions. *Archives of Physical Medicine and Rehabilitation*, 92(3), 509–515.

Taylor, S. F., Kornblum, S., Lauber, E. J., Minoshima, S., & Koeppe, R. A. (1997). Isolation of specific interference processing in the Stroop task: PET activation studies. *Neuroimage*, 6(2), 81–92.

Tenenbaum, J. B. (1999). Bayesian modeling of human concept learning. In M. S. Kearns, S. A. Solla, & D. A. Cohn (Eds.), *Advances in neural information processing systems* (pp. 59–65). Cambridge, MA: MIT Press.

Theorell, T., & Hasselhorn, H. M. (2005). On cross-sectional questionnaire studies of relationships between psychosocial conditions at work and health – are they reliable?. *International Archives of Occupational and Environmental Health*, 78(7), 517–522.

Thomson, J. J. (1985). Double effect, triple effect and the trolley problem: Squaring the circle in looping cases. *Yale Law Journal*, 94(6), 1395–1415.

Tian, M., Chen, Q., Zhang, Y., Du, F., Hou, H., Chao, F., & Zhang, H. (2014). PET imaging reveals brain functional changes in internet gaming disorder. *European Journal of Nuclear Medicine and Molecular Imaging*, 41(7), 1388–1397.

Tikka P., Väljamäe A., de Borst A. W., Pugliese R., Ravaja N., Kaipainen M., et al. (2012). Enactive cinema paves way for understanding complex real-time social interaction in neuroimaging experiments. *Frontiers in Human Neuroscience*, 6, 298. 10.3389/fnhum.2012.00298.

Tindell, D. R., & Bohlander, R. W. (2012). The use and abuse of cell phones and text messaging in the classroom: A survey of college students. *College Teaching*, 60(1), 1–9.

Tomb, I., Hauser, M., Deldin, P., & Caramazza, A. (2004). Do Somatic markers mediate decisions on the gambling task? *Nature Neuroscience*, 5, 1103–1104.

Townsend, D. W., Valk, P. E., & Maisey, M. N. (2005). *Positron emission tomography*. Springer-Verlag London Limited.

Treder, M. S., & Blankertz, B. (2010). Research covert attention and visual speller design in an ERP-based brain-computer interface. *Behavioral & Brain Functions*, 6.

Trick, L. M., Jaspers-Fayer, F., & Sethi, N. (2005). Multiple-object tracking in children: The "Catch the Spies" task. *Cognitive Development*, 20, 373–387.

Trost, Z., & Parsons, T. D. (2014). Beyond distraction: Virtual reality graded exposure therapy as treatment for pain-related fear and disability in chronic pain. *Journal of Applied Biobehavioral Research*, 19, 106–126.

Troyer, A. K., Rowe, G., Murphy, K. J., Levine, B., Leach, L., & Hasher, L. (2014). Development and evaluation of a self-administered on-line test of memory and attention for middle-aged and older adults. *Frontiers in Aging Neuroscience*, 6.

Tupper, D. E., & Cicerone, K. D. (Eds.) (1990). *The neuropsychology of everyday life: Assessment and basic competencies* (Vol. 2). Boston, MA: Kluwer Academic.

Tupper, D. E., & Cicerone, K. D. (1991). *The neuropsychology of everyday life: Issues in development and rehabilitation* (Vol. 3). Boston, MA: Kluwer Academic.

Turel, O., & Serenko, A. (2012). The benefits and dangers of enjoyment with social networking websites. *European Journal of Information Systems*, 21(5), 512–528.

Turel, O., He, Q., Xue, G., Xiao, L., & Bechara, A. (2014). Examination of neural systems sub-serving Facebook "addiction." *Psychological Reports*, 115(3), 675–695.

Tversky, A. (1977). Features of similarity. *Psychological Review*, 84, 327–352.

Uddin, L. Q., & Menon, V. (2009). The anterior insula in autism: Under-connected and under-examined. *Neuroscience & Biobehavioral Reviews*, 33(8), 1198–1203.

Uncapher, M. R., Thieu, M. K., & Wagner, A. D. (2015). Media multitasking and memory: Differences in working memory and long-term memory. *Psychonomic Bulletin & Review*, 1–8.

Ursu, C. (2012). Techniques for securing web content. *Journal of Mobile, Embedded and Distributed Systems*, 4(2), 63–79.

Usakli, A. B., & Gurkan, S. (2010). Design of a novel efficient human–computer interface: An electrooculagram based virtual keyboard. *Instrumentation and Measurement, IEEE Transactions on*, 59(8), 2099–2108.

Usoh, M., Catena, E., Arman, S., & Slater, M. (2000). Using presence questionnaires in reality. *Presence*, 9(5), 497–503.

Van Damme, S., Crombez, G., & Eccleston, C. (2004). Disengagement from pain: The role of catastrophic thinking about pain. *Pain*, 107(1–2), 70–76.

Van Damme, S., et al.: Keeping pain in mind (2010). A motivational account of attention to pain. *Neuroscience and Biobehavioral Reviews*, 34(2), 204–213.

van der Hoort, B., Guterstam, A., & Ehrsson, H. H. (2011). Being Barbie: The size of one's own body determines the perceived size of the world. *PLoS One*, 6, e20195. doi: 10.1371/journal.pone.0020195.

Van Gorp, W. G., Rabkin, J. G., Ferrando, S. J., Mintz, J., Ryan, E., Borkowski, T., & Mcelhiney, M. (2007). Neuropsychiatric predictors of return to work in HIV/AIDS. *Journal of the International Neuropsychological Society*, 13(01), 80–89.

van Holst, R. J., Lemmens, J. S., Valkenburg, P. M., Peter, J., Veltman, D. J., & Goudriaan, A. E. (2012). Attentional bias and disinhibition toward gaming cues are related to problem gaming in male adolescents. *Journal of Adolescent Health*, 50(6), 541–546.

Van Overwalle, F., & Baetens, K. (2009). Understanding others' actions and goals by mirror and mentalizing systems: A meta-analysis. *Neuroimage*, 48(3), 564–584.

Van Oyen Witvliet, C., & Vrana, S.R. (1995). Psychophysiological responses as indices of affective dimensions. *Psychophysiology*, 32, 436–443.

Van Rooij, A. J., Schoenmakers, T. M., Vermulst, A. A., Van Den Eijnden, R. J., & Van De Mheen, D. (2011). Online video game addiction: Identification of addicted adolescent gamers. *Addiction*, 106(1), 205–212.

Vance, A., Anderson, B. B., Kirwan, C. B., & Eargle, D. (2014). Using measures of risk perception to predict information security behavior: Insights from electroencephalography (EEG). *J. Assoc. Inf. Syst*, 15(10), 679–722.

Verdejo-García, A., & Bechara, A. (2009). A somatic marker theory of addiction. *Neuropharmacology*, 56, 48–62.

Vi, C., & Subramanian, S. (2012, May). Detecting error-related negativity for interaction design. In *Proceedings of the SIGCHI Conference on Human Factors in Computing Systems* (pp. 493–502). ACM.

Vingilis, E., Seeley, J., Wiesenthal, D. L., Wickens, C. M., Fischer, P., & Mann, R. E. (2013). Street racing video games and risk-taking driving: An Internet survey of automobile enthusiasts. *Accident Analysis & Prevention, 50,* 1–7.

Vlaeyen, J., et al. (2012). *Pain-related fear: Exposure-based treatment for chronic pain.* Seattle: IASP Press.

Vogel, J. J., Vogel, D. S., Cannon-Bowers, J., Bowers, C. A., Muse, K., & Wright, M. (2006). Computer gaming and interactive simulations for learning: A meta-analysis. *Journal of Educational Computing Research, 34,* 229–243.

vom Brocke, J., & Liang, T. P. (2014). Guidelines for neuroscience studies in information systems research. *Journal of Management Information Systems,* 30(4), 211–234.

Von Der Heide, R., Vyas, G., & Olson, I. R. (2014). The social network-network: Size is predicted by brain structure and function in the amygdala and paralimbic regions. *Social Cognitive and Affective Neuroscience,* 9(12), 1962–1972.

Vossel, S., Geng, J. J., & Fink, G. R. (2014). Dorsal and ventral attention systems distinct neural circuits but collaborative roles. *The Neuroscientist,* 20(2), 150–159.

Vowles, K. E., & Thomson, M. (2011). Acceptance and commitment therapy for chronic pain. In L. McCracken (Ed.), *Mindfulness and acceptance in behavioral medicine* (pp. 31–60). Oakland: Context Press.

Vytal, K., & Hamann, S. (2010). Neuroimaging support for discrete neural correlates of basic emotions: A voxel-based meta-analysis. *Journal of Cognitive Neuroscience,* 22(12), 2864–2885.

Waggett, J. L., & Lane, D. M. (1990). Sex differences in the personality and cognitive correlates of spatial ability. *Journal of Personality and Social Psychology, 58,* 1037–1039.

Wagner, B., & Maercker, A. (2010). Internet-based intervention for posttraumatic stress disorder. In *Internet use in the aftermath of trauma* (255–269). Amsterdam: IOS Press.

Wagner, D. D., Haxby, J. V., & Heatherton, T. F. (2012). The representation of self and person knowledge in the medial prefrontal cortex. *Wiley Interdisciplinary Reviews: Cognitive Science,* 3(4), 451–470.

Waldzus, S., Schubert, T. W., & Paladino, M. P. (2012). Are attitudes the problem, and do psychologists have the answer? Relational cognition underlies intergroup relations. *Behavioral and Brain Sciences,* 35(06), 449–450.

Walter, H., Adenzato, M., Ciaramidaro, A., Enrici, I., Pia, L., & Bara, B. G. (2004). Understanding intentions in social interaction: The role of the anterior paracingulate cortex. *Journal of Cognitive Neuroscience, 16,* 1854–1863.

Wang, H., Jin, C., Yuan, K., Shakir, T. M., Mao, C., Niu, X., ... & Zhang, M. (2015). The alteration of gray matter volume and cognitive control in adolescents with Internet gaming disorder. *Frontiers in Behavioral Neuroscience, 9.*

Wang, L., Zhu, C., He, Y., Zang, Y., Cao, Q., Zhang, H., . . . & Wang, Y. (2009). Altered small-world brain functional networks in children with attention-deficit/hyperactivity disorder. *Human Brain Mapping*, 30(2), 638–649.

Wang, Z., & Tchernev, J. M. (2012). The "myth" of media multitasking: Reciprocal dynamics of media multitasking, personal needs, and gratifications. *Journal of Communication*, 62(3), 493–513.

Ward, A. F. (2013). Supernormal: How the Internet is changing our memories and our minds. *Psychological Inquiry*, 24(4), 341–348.

Ware, M. P., McCullagh, P. J., McRoberts, A., Lightbody, G., Nugent, C., McAllister, G., . . . & Martin, S. (2010, December). Contrasting levels of accuracy in command interaction sequences for a domestic brain-computer interface using SSVEP. In *Biomedical Engineering Conference (CIBEC), 2010 5th Cairo International* (pp. 150–153). IEEE.

Watt, D. (1999). Consciousness and emotion: Review of Jaak Panksepp's "Affective Neuroscience." *Journal of Consciousness Studies* 6, 191–200.

Weber, R., Ritterfeld, U., & Mathiak, K. (2006). Does playing violent video games induce aggression? Empirical evidence of a functional magnetic resonance imaging study. *Media Psychology*, 8(1), 39–60.

Wegner, D. M., Giuliano, T., & Hertel, P. T. (1985). Cognitive interdependence in close relationships. In *Compatible and incompatible relationships* (pp. 253–276). New York: Springer.

Weinstein, A. M. (2010). Computer and video game addiction – A comparison between game users and non-game users. *The American Journal of Drug and Alcohol Abuse*, 36(5), 268–276.

Welsh, M. C., & Pennington, B. F. (1988). Assessing frontal lobe functioning in children: Views from developmental psychology. *Developmental Neuropsychology*, 4(3), 199–230.

Welsh, M. C., Pennington, B. F., & Groisser, D. B. (1991). A normative-developmental study of executive function: A window on prefrontal function in children. *Developmental Neuropsychology*, 7(2), 131–149.

Weng, C. B., Qian, R. B., Fu, X. M., Lin, B., Han, X. P., Niu, C. S., & Wang, Y. H. (2013). Gray matter and white matter abnormalities in online game addiction. *European Journal of Radiology*, 82(8), 1308–1312.

Wesselmann, E. D., Wirth, J. H., Mroczek, D. K., & Williams, K. D. (2012). Dial a feeling: Detecting moderation of affect decline during ostracism. *Personality and Individual Differences*, 53, 580–586.

West, G. L., Stevens, S. A., Pun, C., & Pratt, J. (2008). Visuospatial experience modulates attentional capture: Evidence from action video game players. *Journal of Vision*, 8, 13. doi: 10.1167/8.16.13.

Widyanto, L., & McMurran, M. (2004). The psychometric properties of the Internet addiction test. *CyberPsychology & Behavior*, 7(4), 443–450.

Wiederhold, B. K. (2014). The role of psychology in enhancing cybersecurity. *Cyberpsychology, Behavior, and Social Networking*, 17(3), 131–132.

Wiederhold, B. K., & Rizzo, A. S. (2005). Virtual reality and applied psychophysiology. *Applied Psychophysiology and Biofeedback*, 30(3), 183–185.

Wilhelm, F. H., Pfaltz, M. C., Gross, J. J., Mauss, I. B., Kim, S. I., & Wiederhold, B. K. (2005). Mechanisms of virtual reality exposure therapy: The role of the behavioral activation and behavioral inhibition systems. *Applied Psychophysiology and Biofeedback*, 30(3), 271–284.

Wilhelm, F. H., & Roth, W. T. (1998). Taking the laboratory to the skies: Ambulatory assessment of self-report, autonomic, and respiratory responses in flying phobia. *Psychophysiology*, 5, 596–606.

Willcutt, E. G., Doyle, A. E., Nigg, J. T., Faraone, S. V., & Pennington, B. F. (2005). Validity of the executive function theory of attention-deficit/hyperactivity disorder: A meta-analytic review. *Biological Psychiatry*, 57(11), 1336–1346.

Williams, J. M. (1988). Everyday cognition and the ecological validity of intellectual and neuropsychological tests. In J. M. Williams & C. J. Long (Eds.), *Cognitive approaches to neuropsychology* (pp. 123–141). New York: Plenum.

Williams, K. D. (2007). Ostracism. *Annual Review of Psychology*, 58, 425–452.

Williams, L. M., Phillips, M. L., Brammer, M. J., Skerrett, D., Lagopoulos, J., Rennie, C., ... & Gordon, E. (2001). Arousal dissociates amygdala and hippocampal fear responses: Evidence from simultaneous fMRI and skin conductance recording. *Neuroimage*, 14(5), 1070–1079.

Willison, R., & Warkentin, M. (2013). Beyond deterrence: An expanded view of employee computer abuse. *MIS Quarterly*, 37(1), 1–20.

Wilms, M., Schilbach, L., Pfeiffer, U., Bente, G., Fink, G. R., & Vogeley, K. (2010). It's in your eyes – Using gaze-contingent stimuli to create truly interactive paradigms for social cognitive and affective neuroscience. *Social Cognitive and Affective Neuroscience*, 5, 98–107.

Wilson, B., Cockburn, J., & Baddeley, A. (1985). *The Rivermead Behavioral Memory Test*. Thames Valley Test Co. Reading and National Rehabilitation Services, Gaylord.

Wilson, B. A. (1993). Ecological validity of neuropsychological assessment: Do neuropsychological indexes predict performance in everyday activities? *Applied & Preventive Psychology*, 2, 209–215.

Wilson, B. A. (2000). Compensating for cognitive deficits following brain injury. *Neuropsychology Review*, 10(4), 233–243.

Wilson, B. A. (2011). Cutting edge developments in neuropsychological rehabilitation and possible future directions. *Brain Impairment*, 12, 33–42.

Wilson, B. A. (2013). Neuropsychological rehabilitation: State of the science. *South African Journal of Psychology*, 43(3), 267–277.

Wilson, B. A., Alderman, N., Burgess, P. W., Emslie, H., & Evans, J. J. (1996). *Behavioral Assessment of the Dysexecutive Syndrome*. Bury St. Edmunds: Thames Valley Test Company.

Wilson, B. A., Shiel, A., Foley, J., Emslie, H., Groot, Y., Hawkins, K., et al. (2004). *Cambridge Test of Prospective Memory*. Bury St. Edmunds, England: Thames Valley Test Company.

Wilson, B., Cockburn, J., Baddeley, A., & Hiorns, R. (1989). The development and validation of a test battery for detecting and monitoring everyday memory problems. *Journal of Clinical and Experimental Neuropsychology*, 11(6), 855–870.

Wilson, R. E., Gosling, S. D., & Graham, L. T. (2012). A review of Facebook research in the social sciences. *Perspectives on Psychological Science*, 7, 203–220.

Wilson-Mendenhall, C. D., Barrett, L. F., & Barsalou, L. W. (2013). Neural evidence that human emotions share core affective properties. *Psychological Science*, 24(6), 947–956.

Windmann, S., Kirsch, P., Mier, D., Stark, R., Walter, B., Gunturkun, O., et al. (2006). On framing effects in decision making: Linking lateral versus medial orbitofrontal cortex activation to choice outcome processing. *Journal of Cognitive Neuroscience*, 18(7), 1198–1211.

Wirth, J. H., Sacco, D. F., Hugenberg, K., & Williams, K. D. (2010). Eye gaze as relational evaluation: Averted eye gaze leads to feelings of ostracism and relational devaluation. *Personality and Social Psychology Bulletin*, 36, 869–882.

Wirth, W., Hartmann, T., et al. (2007). Process model of the formation of spatial presence experiences. *Media Psychology*, 9(3), 493–493.

Wise, K., Alhabash, S., & Park, H. (2010). Emotional responses during social information seeking on Facebook. *Cyberpsychology, Behavior, and Social Networking*, 13(5), 555–562.

Wise, R. A. (2008). Dopamine and reward: The anhedonia hypothesis 30 years on. *Neurotoxicity Research*, 14(2–3), 169–183.

Witmer, B. G., & Singer, M. J. (1998). Measuring presence in virtual environments: A presence questionnaire. *Presence: Teleoperators and Virtual Environments*, 7(3), 225–240.

Wixted, J. T., & Ebbesen, E. B. (1997). Genuine power curves in forgetting: A quantitative analysis of individual subject forgetting functions. *Memory & Cognition*, 25, 731–739.

Wood, E., Zivcakova, L., Gentile, P., Archer, K., De Pasquale, D., & Nosko, A. (2012). Examining the impact of off-task multi-tasking with technology on real-time classroom learning. *Computers & Education*, 58(1), 365–374.

Wood, J. N., Romero, S. G., Knutson, K. M., & Grafman, J. (2005). Representation of attitudinal knowledge: Role of prefrontal cortex, amygdala and parahippocampal gyrus. *Neuropsychologia*, 43(2), 249–259.

Woodward, A. L., Sommerville, J. A., Gerson, S., Henderson, A. M., & Buresh, J. (2009). The emergence of intention attribution in infancy. *Psychology of Learning and Motivation*, 51, 187–222.

Wouters, P., Van Nimwegen, C., Van Oostendorp, H., & Van Der Spek, E. D. (2013). A meta-analysis of the cognitive and motivational effects of serious games. *Journal of Educational Psychology*, 105(2), 249.

Wu, D., Lance, B., & Parsons, T. D. (2013). Collaborative filtering for brain-computer interaction using transfer learning and active class selection. *PloS One*, 1–18.

Wu, D., & Parsons, T. D. (2011a). Inductive transfer learning for handling individual differences in affective computing. *Lecture Notes in Computer Science*, 6975, 142–151.

Wu, D., & Parsons, T. D. (2011b). Active class selection for arousal classification. *Lecture Notes in Computer Science*, 6975, 132–141.

Wu, D., Parsons, T. D., & Narayanan, S. S. (2010). Acoustic feature analysis in speech emotion primitives estimation. In *INTERSPEECH* (pp. 785–788).

Wu, S., & Spence, I. (2013). Playing shooter and driving videogames improves top-down guidance in visual search. *Attention, Perception and Psychophysics*, 75, 673–686.

Xing, L., Yuan, K., Bi, Y., Yin, J., Cai, C., Feng, D., . . . & Xue, T. (2014). Reduced fiber integrity and cognitive control in adolescents with Internet gaming disorder. *Brain Research*, 1586, 109–117.

Xu, H., Luo, X. R., Carroll, J. M., & Rosson, M. B. (2011). The personalization privacy paradox: An exploratory study of decision making process for location-aware marketing. *Decision Support Systems*, 51(1), 42–52.

Xu, S. (2012). Internet addicts' behavior impulsivity: Evidence from the Iowa Gambling Task. *Acta Psychologica Sinica*, 44, 1523–1534.

Xu, S., Wang, Z. J., & David, P. (2016). Media multitasking and well-being of university students. *Computers in Human Behavior*, 55, 242–250.

Yang, H., Yang, S., & Isen, A. M. (2013). Positive affect improves working memory: Implications for controlled cognitive processing. *Cognition & Emotion*, 27(3), 474–482.

Yap, J. Y., & Lim, S. W. H. (2013). Media multitasking predicts unitary versus splitting visual focal attention. *Journal of Cognitive Psychology*, 25(7), 889–902.

Yarkoni, T., Poldrack, R. A., Nichols, T. E., Van Essen, D. C., & Wager, T. D. (2011). Large-scale automated synthesis of human functional neuroimaging data. *Nat. Methods*, 8, 665–670.doi:10.1038/nmeth.1635.

Ybarra, M. L., Huesmann, L. R., Korchmaros, J. D., & Reisner, S. L. (2014). Cross-sectional associations between violent video and computer game playing and weapon carrying in a national cohort of children. *Aggressive Behavior*, 40(4), 345–358.

Ybarra, O., Burnstein, E., Winkielman, P., Keller, M. C., Manis, M., Chan, E., & Rodriguez, J. (2008). Mental exercising through simple socializing: Social interaction promotes general cognitive functioning. *Personality and Social Psychology Bulletin*, 34(2), 248–259.

Ybarra, O., & Winkielman, P. (2012). On-line social interactions and executive functions. *Frontiers in Human Neuroscience*, 6.

Yee, N., Bailenson, J. N., Urbanek, M., Chang, F., & Merget, D. (2007). The unbearable likeness of being digital: The persistence of nonverbal social norms in online virtual environments. *The Journal of CyberPsychology and Behavior*, 10, 115–121. doi:10.1089/cpb.2006.9984.

Yen, J. Y., Ko, C. H., Yen, C. F., Wu, H. Y., & Yang, M. J. (2007). The comorbid psychiatric symptoms of Internet addiction: Attention deficit and hyperactivity disorder (ADHD), depression, social phobia, and hostility. *Journal of Adolescent Health*, 41(1), 93–98.

Yerkes, R.M., & Dodson, J.D. (1908). The relation of strength of stimulus to rapidity of habit-formation. *Journal of Comparative Neurology and Psychology*, 18, 459–482.

Ylvisaker, M., Szekeres, S. F., & Feeney, T. (2001). Communication disorders associated with traumatic brain injury. In R. Chapey (Ed.), *Language intervention strategies in aphasia and related neurogenic communication disorders* (pp. 745–800). Philadelphia: Lippincott, Williams & Wilkins.

Young, K. S. (1998a). *Caught in the net*. New York: John Wiley.

Young, K. S. (1998b). Internet addiction: The emergence of a new clinical disorder. *CyberPsychology & Behavior*, 1(1), 237–244.

Young, K. S. (1999). The research and controversy surrounding internet addiction. *CyberPsychology & Behavior*, 2, 381–383.

Young, K. (2015). The evolution of Internet addiction. *Addictive Behaviors*. Advance online publication. Retrieved from www.sciencedirect.com/science/article/pii/ S0306460315001884.

Young, K. S. (2016). The evolution of Internet addiction disorder. In *Internet addiction* (pp. 3–17). Switzerland: Springer International Publishing.

Yuan, K., Cheng, P., Dong, T., Bi, Y., Xing, L., Yu, D., ... & Qin, W. (2013). Cortical thickness abnormalities in late adolescence with online gaming addiction. *PloS One*, 8(1), e53055.

Yuan, K., Qin, W., Wang, G., Zeng, F., Zhao, L., Yang, X., ... & Gong, Q. (2011). Microstructure abnormalities in adolescents with Internet addiction disorder. *PloS One*, 6(6), e20708.

Yuan, K., Qin, W., Yu, D., Bi, Y., Xing, L., Jin, C., & Tian, J. (2015). Core brain networks interactions and cognitive control in Internet gaming disorder individuals in late adolescence/early adulthood. *Brain Structure and Function*, 1–16.

Yuste, R. (2015). From the neuron doctrine to neural networks. *Nature Reviews Neuroscience*, 16(8), 487–497.

Zadro, L., Williams, K. D., & Richardson, R. (2004). How low can you go? Ostracism by a computer lowers belonging, control, self-esteem and meaningful existence. *Journal of Experimental Social Psychology*, 40, 560–567.

Zaki, J., & Ochsner, K. (2009). The need for a cognitive neuroscience of naturalistic social cognition. *Annals of the New York Academy of Sciences*, 1167(1), 16–30.

Zakzanis, K. K., & Azarbehi, R. (2014). Introducing BRAIN screen: Web-based real-time examination and interpretation of cognitive function. *Applied Neuropsychology: Adult*, 21(2), 77–86.

Zald, D. H., & Kim, S. W. (1996). Anatomy and function of the orbital frontal cortex: II. Function and relevance to obsessive–compulsive disorder. *Journal of Neuropsychiatry and Clinical Neurosciences*, 8(3), 249–261.

Zanon, M., Novembre, G., Zangrando, N., Chittaro, L., & Silani, G. (2014). Brain activity and prosocial behavior in a simulated life-threatening situation. *Neuroimage*, 98, 134–146.

Zappala, G., Thiebaut de Schotten, M., & Eslinger, P. J. (2012). What can we gain with diffusion tensor imaging? *Cortex*, 48(2): 156–165.

Zelazo, P. D., Müller, U., Frye, D., Marcovitch, S., Argitis, G., Boseovski, J., . . . & Carlson, S. M. (2003). The development of executive function in early childhood. *Monographs of the Society for Research in Child Development*, 68, i–151.

Zhou, Y., Lin, F. C., Du, Y. S., Zhao, Z. M., Xu, J. R., & Lei, H. (2011). Gray matter abnormalities in Internet addiction: A voxel-based morphometry study. *European Journal of Radiology*, 79(1), 92–95.

Zhou, Z., Yuan, G., & Yao, J. (2012). Cognitive biases toward Internet game-related pictures and executive deficits in individuals with an Internet game addiction. *PloS One*, 7(11), e48961.

Zickefoose, S., Hux, K., Brown, J., & Wulf, K. (2013). Let the games begin: A preliminary study using attention process training-3 and Lumosity brain games to remediate attention deficits following traumatic brain injury. *Brain Injury* 27(6), 707–716.

Zwolinski, J. (2012). Psychological and neuroendocrine reactivity to ostracism. *Aggressive Behavior*, 38, 108–125

Index

Aardema, F., 175–176
academic achievement, in children, 182–183
ACC. *See* anterior cingulate cortex
acetylcholine, 29
action selection, 190
action videogames, 14, 310
  cognitive processing and, 294
  large-scale brain networks and, 301–304
adaptation, 190
adaptive feedback, 273
adaptive system, 274–275
adaptive training, virtual reality and, 284–291
adaptive virtual environments, 278, 291–292
addiction. *See also* cyber addiction disorder;
  Internet addiction
  computer, 145
  Facebook, 115–116
  Internet gaming, 162–163
  reflective systems and, 115–116
  reflexive systems and, 115–116
ADHD, 149, 254–256, 259
  social media and, 52
adolescents. *See also* children
  learning in, 126–127
  MMT of, 126–127
Adolphs, R., 103
AER. *See* average evoked response
affect
  dysfunctions, 235–236
  frontal-subcortical circuits and, 50–51
  generation, 193
  virtual environments for assessments of, 207
affective arousal, Riva on, 208
affective computing, 17–18, 188–189
  affective generation and, 193
  affective understanding and, 193
  areas of development in, 192–195
  human emotions recognized by, 18
  integration and, 193
  platform and, 193
  real-time changes and, 18–19

system purpose, 193
  virtual environments and, 271–272
affective loops, 224–225
affective neuroscience
  cognitive revolution and, 7
  cyberpsychology and, 14–15, 346–347
  ecological validity and, 176–177
  large-scale brain networks and, 201–202
  Panksepp on, 198–201
  psychophysiology and, 55–56
affective processes, 195
  Cannon-Bard theory, 196
  evolution and, 15
  James-Lange theory, 195–196
  Schachter and Singer's theory, 196
affective responses
  in threatening contexts, 208–210
  virtual environments eliciting, 208–210
affective states
  in artificial agents, 189–192
  roles for, 190
Affective Systems Model, 275–277
affective understanding, affective computing
  and, 193
affectively hot cognitions, 16–17
AI. *See* anterior insula
alarm mechanisms, 190
Alexander, G. E., 47–50
Alpha-World, 36–37
Alzheimer's disease, 92–93
American Psychiatric Association (APA), 163–164
Amft, M., 20, 109–111, 324
amygdala, 16–17, 41, 104, 108, 113–114, 118–119
  activation, 59–61
  damage to, 204
  emotions and, 38–39
  gray matter in, 108–109
Anderson, B. B., 325–326
Annual Conference on CyberPsychology,
  CyberTherapy and Social Networking, 4
ANS. *See* autonomic nervous system

Index